C0-AJZ-904

Culture and the Changing Environment

Culture and the Changing Environment

Uncertainty, Cognition and Risk Management in Cross-Cultural Perspective

Edited by

Michael J. Casimir

Berghahn Books
New York • Oxford

First published in 2008 by
Berghahn Books
www.berghahnbooks.com

Library of Congress Cataloging-in-Publication Data

A C.I.P. catalog record for this book is available from the Library of Congress

British Library Cataloguing in Publication Data

A catalogue record for this book is available from the British Library

Printed in the United States on acid-free paper

ISBN 978-1-57181-478-4 (hardback)

Dedicated to the memory
of my dear wife and colleague
Aparna Rao (1950–2005)

Contents

Part II: Knowledge, Meaning and Discourse

List of Maps, Figures and Tables

Maps

Figures

Photos

Tables

PREFACE

This book is about the interdependence between human culture(s) and their environment(s) and focuses on the effects which the changes in the one have on the other. All the chapters in this volume are original papers based on recent (and partly on-going) longitudinal research carried out in different parts of the world by anthropologists, geographers, psychologists and sociologists. Coming from a variety of theoretical and methodological backgrounds they all discuss a range of different, but interrelated environmental problems.

The chapters also represent a major cross section of contemporary environment-related social science research in Germany – all funded by the German Research Council (DFG) – and all but one was carried out under the aegis of either the multidisciplinary *Schwerpunktprogram (SPP) Mensch und Globale Umweltveränderungen – Sozial- und Verhaltenswissenschaftliche Dimensionen* (Special Research Program: 'Humans and Global Environmental Change, the Social and Behavioural Dimensions'), or the project *IMPETUS* ('Integrated Approach to the Efficient Management of Scarce Water Resources in West Africa') sponsored by the German Ministry of Education and Research (BMBF). Both these programs aimed at deepening our understanding of environmental problems from the perspective of the social sciences. Natural sciences can detect and analyse the causes of environmental problems but since most of them are related to culture-specific human behaviour, values, norms, needs and wants, the social sciences can and must play a much greater role in understanding and solving them. The result of such research could and should provide politicians and other policy makers with information and analyses which can help solve the pressing problems that we are all facing. It is hoped that this volume will go some way in doing this.

As the anthropology coordinator of both the research programs, I wish to thank the DFG and the BMBF for their support and funding. I also thank Ute Stahl for her help in editing the earliest versions of these chapters and last but not least Marion Berghahn and Mark Stanton for their help and patience.

Michael J. Casimir
Cologne

The Mutual Dynamics of Cultural and Environmental Change: An Introductory Essay

Michael J. Casimir

> What surrounds humans does not affect only them, they too react upon it. By allowing themselves to be modified, they again modify what surrounds them. (Johann Wolfgang von Goethe 1775–6, translation mine)[1]

The Many Meanings of Environment and Nature

The picture that won the first award at the annual international competition for photo journalism in Amsterdam on 11 February 2005 shows a grieving Indian woman who had lost her family in the recent tsunami. For days the Western media in particular devoted much space and time to the 'Century's Catastrophe', the 'Killer Waves' of 26 December 2004 which left in its wake well over 200,000 dead or missing. Was the devastation wrought by these 'cruel forces of nature' inevitable, or was it itself partly a result of the interplay of environmental and cultural agency and change? This introductory essay considers the various aspects of this basic issue of mutuality. The chapters that follow examine from different disciplinary perspectives the nature of such interplay over time in a variety of cultural and environmental contexts.

Some Conceptual and Terminological Considerations

Influenced primarily by concepts that evolved within the Judeo-Christian traditions and then through Cartesian thinking, the unique positioning ascribed in Western thought to humans led early to a cognitive distinction into the categories of 'humanity' and 'nature', 'humans' and 'animals'. These categories were, perhaps, not 'consistent dichotomi[es]', but were rather part of what Strathern (1980: 177) refers to as a 'matrix of contrasts'. Yet, under the influence of Cartesian thinking which separates body and soul/mind, only humans were increasingly believed to be endowed with capacities and qualities such as mind/spirit, reason and free will (e.g., Damasio 1994), and considered capable of attributing meaning to all phenomena. Not realising that these phenomena themselves are products of human cognition, these attributed meanings were then related to different values attached to specific types and clusters of phenomena. Accordingly, the environment and environmental phenomena were also imbued with value-meanings, and classified in clusters, such as those of 'animate' and 'in-animate'. Whereas the so-called 'inanimate' category was subdivided into a multitude of sub-categories, such as soil, water, rocks, climate, etc. (each of these being broken down into yet more sub-categories), the so-called 'animate' category was broken up into fauna and flora, comprising animals (including hominids) and plants respectively, and these two sub-categories were, in their turn, divided into various 'families', 'genera', 'species' and 'sub-species'. Another set of constructed categories was that of 'wilderness', and 'nature' – thought to be opposite to human 'culture'[2] – with its 'natural resources' (for an overview see for example Delaney 2001).

It is only more recently that such classifications have been questioned,[3] partly because of our knowledge of the way in which all organisms depend on one another, tied together as they are, directly or indirectly, into food webs of varying dimensions. Modern science has shown how all animals, including humans, as part of such food webs, depend on the intake of other organisms, either plant or animal, or both (with the omnivorous human positioned at the top of the trophic levels), and how only green plants can use the sun's energy to transform the soil's nutrients into their species-specific tissue with the help of the biocatalyst chlorophyll. Notably, however, Cartesian thinking in this realm has also been challenged by a growing awareness and knowledge of a variety of non-Western systems of classification that do not make such distinctions.

One of the very first and most influential studies that brought together these issues of categorisation, cognition and practice is the volume edited by Ellen and Fukui (1996). In his comprehensive introduction to this volume Roy Ellen rightly observes that dichotomies such as nature-nurture may be useful or misleading, but not true or false, and that 'opposition of nature and culture is … a pseudo-problem arising out of reflexive symbolic constructs … within culture itself (Ellen 1996: 31). Ingold (2000: 40ff.) also convincingly deduced that if 'nature' is a category constructed by humans, then the category 'culture' must also and equally be a construct. Quoting MacCormack (1980: 6) Ingold argued that 'Neither the concept of nature nor that of culture are "given"…'. The same is true of many other 'scientific' bio-concepts and categories, such as 'genus', 'species', etc. The constructed category 'nature', however, must be based, he argued, on what he calls the 'really natural' – which, to paraphrase Heidegger, can only be experienced through our bodily 'being in the world'. We thus face the dilemma of dealing with two different categories of nature – the 'really natural' and the 'culturally perceived nature' (Ingold 2000: 40–43).

Keeping these issues and perspectives in mind, in the following I shall use the term 'environment' to denote the contemporary Western scientific concept of what Ingold refers to as the 'really natural'; the term 'nature' will be restricted to mean the culturally constructed category of the animated or unanimated world, or parts thereof, and are imbued with meanings that are more or less culture-specific. However, as the following pages and the individual chapters show there are few clear boundaries between these concepts, only broad frontiers.

A Short History of Human Environment Interaction

> Historical Ecology may be defined as the undertaking of a diachronic analysis of living ecological systems, with the view to accounting more fully to the structural and functional properties. Historical ecology, more an approach or a research strategy than a paradigm, addresses a central question: 'How does environmental change relate to the historical development of human societies?' (Rival 2006: 79)

Since the days of the first hominids our species, like every other, has been a part of food webs, and has hence directly or indirectly influenced every other species in its habitat and has in turn been differentially influenced by them all. The dynamic interaction between all members of a habitat (understood as interactions in a predator-prey system) has always led to changes of varying pace and degree in the environment as a whole, either in terms of demography or of the composition of species.

Due to their omnivorous and cognitive capacities, early hunting and gathering peoples adapted rapidly to different environments by niche-learning, and

> the first population consequence from [this] niche-learning of which we have clear evidence was the occupation of virtually all geographic regions of the earth by hunter-gatherer peoples. Ways of life suited to places as different as .African rain forest and Siberian tundra were found for this species by niche-learning before 20,000 years ago … (Colinvaux 1982: 394; cf. also Bellwood 2001; Bennett 1976)

Early foraging societies left traces of their influence on the environment, and in some regions even transformed environmental conditions. In parts of the high Arctic ecosystem the quality of certain lake water changed. When, for example, about eight centuries ago incoming Thule Inuit whalers from Alaska built their winter settlements on Somerset Island in northern Canada, the nutrition-rich bowhead whale bones used for construction reached the lakes, drastically changing the composition and amount of micro-organisms, specially diatoms. This also led to the expansion of a moss substrate (Douglas et al. 2004).

In more favourable environments where early hunter-gatherers settled and built more complex societies, they gradually domesticated plants and animals (for an overview see Levin and Foley 2004: 500–10). A more sedentary lifestyle and the concomitant social change were a driving force towards domestication and the beginning of agriculture and animal husbandry. This shift from an incipient economy to a food-producing one led to changed dietary patterns, as described recently for a case in Britain (e.g., Richards et al. 2003), and this once again led to rapid population growth. Some 12,000 years ago, when cooler and drier conditions returned after the last glacial period, with its warm, wet winters and hot, dry summers, Nutufian foraging communities in southwest Asia replaced their incipient economy with new labour-intensive subsistence strategies of plant cultivation and animal husbandry. This led to population growth, craft specialisation and even class formation (Weiss and Bradley 2001: 610; see also Bökönyi 1976). However, coping with the climatic deterioration of the younger Dryas they returned to a more mobile way of life (Grosman 2003). But the search for a single unifying model explaining the beginning of all plant and animal domestication throughout the world appears futile. Rather it seems that various mechanisms in different combinations operated more or less simultaneously in different parts of the world, leading to Neolithic transformations, accelerating population growth, spurring human cultural development and with it, growing impact on the environment.

With the onset of the Neolithic, human populations grew and great stretches of land were transformed into agricultural areas (Redman 1999). Impacted by the grazing and browsing of domesticated ungulates, meadows and shrublands changed into various pasture-plant communities (Dasgupta 2001: 127–31; May et al. 1992). Until recently it was believed that humans had only a local or regional influence on the environment, but there is good evidence now for a global influence on the world's climate ever since the onset of the Neolithic. As Ruddiman (2003) showed, the anthropogenic greenhouse effect developed as early as about 8000 B.C., when, with the beginning of forest clearance and extensive agriculture, CO_2 concentrations rose. With the introduction of rice irrigation roughly 5,000 years ago, the concentration of CH_4 in the atmosphere also rose. Since then increasing climate change has taken place and the temperature has risen by about 0.3°C to 0.8°C. There is no doubt now that in

> less than 200 years, human activity has increased the atmospheric concentration of greenhouse gasses by some 50% relative to pre-industrial levels ... At about 372 ppm, today's atmospheric carbon dioxide level is higher than at any time in at least the past 420,000 years. (King 2004: 176)

But in these early times humans were not alone in influencing the environment. Recent investigations show that the extinction of the Beringian Steppe Bison (Shapiro et al. 2004) took place long before large human populations were present on the continent. Changing environmental conditions themselves often had a dramatic influence on the development of human culture. Not just short term events like floods, earthquakes and volcanic eruptions, but also drastic long-term climatic changes – for example the ice-age(s) and the subsequent warm periods – forced humans to change their cultures, especially their economies, in order to cope with changing environmental constraints. Indeed, relatively sudden and drastic climatic changes effecting large regions over a long period of time have been the driving force for cultural change in the Old World (cf. Fagan 2005). For example, after a short but severe drought, a wetter phase around 3200–3000 B.C. enabled

> politically centralized and class-based urban societies [to] emerge and expand across the riverine and dry-farming landscapes of the Mediterranean, Egypt, and West Asia. The Akkadian empire of Mesopotamia, the pyramid-constructing Old Kingdom civilization of Egypt, the Harappan C3 civilization of the Indus valley, and the Early Bronze III civilization of Palestine, Greece, and Crete all reached their economic peak at about 2300 B.C. This period was abruptly terminated before 2200 B.C. by catastrophic drought and cooling that generated regional abandonment, collapse, and habitat-tracking. (Weiss and Bradley 2001: 610)

In fact, wherever vast empires arose, anthropogenic environmental changes took place on a large scale for military and economic reasons. The Romans decimated the cedar forests of Lebanon in order to build their enormous fleets, and in Imperial China forest cover slowly disappeared from about 1500/1000 B.C. onwards, and again during the Song dynasty after about 1000 A.D. With more and more land being brought under agriculture, relentless deforestation continued, and by the eighteenth to nineteenth centuries most parts of China were transformed into an anthropogenic landscape with widespread shortage of wood (Elvin 2004).

For long periods of time most human environments may have remained close to an equilibrium – or, in terms of resilience (Holling 1973), influenced by internal or external disturbances, they may have shifted to a new state, oscillating around a new equilibrium. Some disturbances may have been caused by climatic changes to which certain species could not adapt rapidly enough, or by the invasion of a new predator species whose extent of predation some species could not survive. Both situations would, within a given region, have led to a change in the entirety of a habitat's species – in short, to the formation of a new, relatively different biotope. From the subjective, anthropocentric perspective of humans, such situations are catastrophes or disasters, terms which can, following Oliver-Smith (1996: 303), be defined broadly as

> a process/event involving the combination of a potentially destructive agent(s) from the natural and/or technological environment and a population in a socially and technologically produced condition of vulnerability. (cf. also Hoffmann and Oliver-Smith 2002)

Such dangerous situations are not recent, they have always occurred wherever humans have lived. But a diachronic review of the negative effects of human-induced local environmental changes and catastrophes shows that with increasing and widespread industrialisation, exponential demographic human growth and finally globalisation, many local disasters have begun to impact the entire world. Today the magnitude of human-made catastrophes is infinitely greater and is threatening vast populations and eventually all humankind.

Towards Modernity

It was only around the sixteenth century, with emerging Western colonialism that human influences on the environment began to effect large stretches of land and even entire continents. In many regions biodiversity was drastically reduced. The arrival of European colonists with their exotic predatory mammals led to the extinction of hundreds if not thousands of avian species in Oceania (Blackburn at al. 2004).This general trend was exacerbated with the onset of the Industrial Revolution. With the exploitation of 'natural resources' across different world regions by Western colonial powers, with intensive coal mining in the West and than the emergence of the post-Second World War oil industry, human impact began to be felt at global levels. Today with growing industrialisation and globalising markets, many of the still fairly localised human-induced ecological changes and creeping disasters are assuming global proportions.

With extreme overpopulation in the world as a whole, the overexploitation of all natural resources and the impact of chemical agents in intensive agriculture, the resilient capacity of ecosystems in several parts of the world has come to an end and climatologists, political economists and geographers are warning of the growing probability of global catastrophes. Their warnings are based on the scientific analyses of the proximate causes of local or regional environmental degradation; alternatively, they deal with the causes of global climate change and its repercussions on the world's ecosystem at large or on its various ecological sub-systems. However, the human factor, the different and complex motivations behind individual and group actions in different cultural settings that lead to ecological transformations and disasters are rarely analysed and understood. The variety of world-views that impel the different attitudes that people have towards their environments, the varying and changing culture- and habitus-specific needs and wants that regulate the gamut of behaviours towards the habitat, have been largely ignored while examining the complex causal interconnections that lead to often irreversible local and even global environmental change.

Western environmentalism has a long history (Grove 1992; Little 1999). But it was only with Rachel Carson's (1962) study, *Silent Spring*, that social, political and scientific consciousness about the impact of human over-exploitative behaviour and environmental pollution at the local (cf. Kasperson et al. 1995) and global levels really developed. Public discourse about the effects of ecological mismanagement or industrial pollution which transcends locality and endanger the global commons (cf. WBR 2002: 87–105) is a relatively recent phenomenon. It seems that only with catastrophes such as that of Chernobyl which threatened the well-being and lives of peoples far and near, we at last 'woke up' and started seriously pondering over the causes that led to such disasters and how to prevent them in future.

Disasters which had a global impact are brought about primarily by the 'late modern' industrialised Western societies which Beck (1992) describes as 'risk societies' where, 'the proliferation of risks as a consequence of technological innovation has got out of control' (Lupton 1999b: 13). Although 'environmental disasters' seem to have increased greatly over the last decades, it is not their frequency that has risen but rather the number of people affected, mostly the poorest. Hence also the classification of these events as 'disasters'.[4] Once again the blurring of distinction between 'purely environmental' and human-made disasters becomes obvious. Whereas in Cuba an efficient disaster response system enabled the evacuation in the 2004 cyclone of two million people with no deaths, the lack of policy in Haiti left 5,000 dead and 300,000 affected. The recent tsunami not only highlighted the ineptitude of the Indian government to deal with recurring disasters, but also the extent to which environmental laws are violated along the costal regions where habitation is banned within a 500m broad strip. Similar violations of building laws caused innumerable deaths in Turkey's earthquake in August 1999. In other words the impact of major and sudden environmental events is intimately linked to political systems, structures and their efficiency. Undoubtedly, the problems 'relating particular rates of [environmental] change and management methods to political dispensations are … considerable' (Grove et al. 1998: 14). In their papers in this volume Casciarri and Schlehe also discuss such issues. But any change in restructuring of power and the enforcement of new laws must lead to insecurity that environment related transactions which had thus far been successful, may now fail; in her paper here Göbel analyses this problem.

The blurring of distinctions between 'purely environmental' and 'human-made' disasters often translates at the local community level of perception into cause and effect explanations. While in many industrial societies this blurring may lead, as Nerb et al. discuss in their paper here, to environmental damage being attributed to human agency, in more 'traditional' societies perceptions of cause and effect often draw on cosmological theories in which no basic distinction is made between 'environmental', 'natural' and 'social'. This evidenced by the fact that many Western survivors of the recent tsunami have gone to court against a variety of organisations, charging them with negligence leading to loss of life. In their experimental studies in Germany and Tonga Nerb et al. analysed how people react to similar environmental damages. Their theoretical assumption is that a causal analysis of a negative event is often a necessary first step in implementing a coping strategy. They found that in Germany people have a strong tendency to attribute the cause of environmental damage to human agency, even though it was explicitly mentioned to them that the event was caused by purely natural forces. In coping with negative events it is essential, their study suggests, to identify the agent responsible for the damage because this enables one to prevent the agent from repeating further transgressions. In contrast, their respondents from Tonga see the negative event as more inevitable and beyond their control. It is interpreted as an 'act of God', who has caused the problem, but will also solve it. Sadness, rather than anger, is the main emotional reaction here.

In different societies and cultures the 'environment' is indeed attributed with different 'values' and connotations. Innumerable religious beliefs and descriptions across cultures refer to specific actions with regard to the environment. 'Sacred groves' everywhere embodied both religious and political power (Ramakrishnan et al. 1998), and Minangkabau scholars stress the closeness of local custom (*adat*) and nature: 'adat is sacred because it is a primordial aspect of nature' (Sanday 2002: 24). Yet such beliefs, prescriptions and theories are not even implicitly concerned with environmentalism, which is everywhere a fairly recent episteme.[5] They are concerned rather with the trespassing of social and/or religious norms that structure the social fabric (see the paper by Schlehe, this volume). Every extraordinary environmental event – earthquakes, volcanic eruptions, floods, eclipses, comets, etc. – are perceived as omens or warnings, and a variety of cultural practices are set in motion to mitigate their impact and ask for pardon. The biblical Deluge, the Egyptian Plagues, the destruction of Sodom and Gomorra and Haley's Comet were all seen as divine punishments. Today for some Islamists in Aceh, the recent tsunami was 'a warning from Allah' (Aglionby 2005), just as it symbolised 'the birth pangs of the Apocalypse' for some American Evangelists (www.rapture-ready.com). Judith Schlehe's chapter here discusses examples of the ways Indonesian people have explained volcanic eruptions (of Tambora and Krakatau) in former times. Schlehe then explores the reactions to the recent eruptions of Mount Merapi. The perceptions, interpretations and rituals of the villagers living on the slopes of Merapi and of the inhabitants of the nearby city of Yogyakarta are at odds with the government's interests. Mythical and mystical traditions are revitalised by eruptions, imbued with new meanings and directed against transmigration programmes and, more generally, against those in power. Her analysis shows how the cultural appropriation of volcanoes can be seen as a field of discourse, important for dealing with the unpredictability of the environment and significant for political struggle; that it can serve either to legitimise political power in a conservative manner, or provide inspiration for rebellious behaviour.

It is from such partly culture-specific but dynamic baseline that the synchronically and diachronically varying perceptions, attitudes and value-related motivations and actions impinging on the environment must be understood, if behavioural changes towards it are to be encouraged in order to reduce the growing danger of a global ecological crisis. If we wish to apply the 'act local, think global' perspective, we must first understand this variety and diversity of specific behaviours, meanings and related cognitions and attitudes towards specific environments, together with the dynamic culture-specific needs and wants. In his study of the modalities of knowledge change among fisher-communities of southern India, Götz Hoeppe examines how the fisher folks' knowledge, embedded in decades of environmental and socio-economic change is dealing with external 'global' knowledges. Such often mutually contradicting epistemological and ontological knowledges are often today at the heart of much conflict about 'development' and environmental change.

The recognition of local ecological knowledge and experience, sometimes reflected in ancient land and sea-tenure systems and in negotiations between community-based interest groups and local and state institutions, or sometimes even global interest groups, can prevent major conflicts. This recognition can help lead to compromises, which preserve the 'self-regulation' of the human-environment interplay, while also allowing room for subtle and carefully planned rural and urban development schemes (for an excellent example see Hviding and Baines 1994). As Skewes and Guerra (2004) have shown, political movements which resist the threats and dangers of environmental pollution can successfully integrate scientific ecological knowledge with local transcendental meaning. In his paper in this volume, his comparative study of northern Australia and central Namibia, Thomas Widlok analyses problems in this process of incorporating social institutions of local cultures with reference to external experts. In northern Australia government experts for arid land management and agriculture attempt to revive Aboriginal patterns of controlled burning of the Bush as a strategy to avoid the risk of large-scale, destructive bush fires. In central Namibia non-governmental organisations encourage indigenous people to maintain their long-established seasonal patterns of harvesting wild fruits as a strategy to maintain a fragile ecosystem, namely the !Khuiseb area, a linear oasis in the Namib desert. But reviving cultural patterns of behaviour which have been previously suppressed, or maintaining such patterns in a rapidly changing world, is not unproblematic. One recurring dilemma arises from the fact that the external ecologists and development workers seek to establish 'expert systems' or 'coping strategies' from a host of different indigenous practices. But indigenous cultural practices may provide sustainable uses of resources through general routines of creating well-being, which are sometimes more akin to gambling or diffusing the effects of individual action than to strategic planning. Such unresolved dilemmas, Widlok argues, account for much of the standstill and insufficient impact of ecological programmes in Third World countries.

The 'Values' of Environment

Human habitats, or parts thereof, are usually considered to be natural resources and values are attributed to them. Dasgupta (2001: 124) differentiates between those that are natural resources which are of direct use in consumption (e.g., fisheries), those of indirect use as inputs in production (e.g., oil and natural gas) and those of use in both (air and water). With their biodiversity, many of these habitats possess, he suggests (p. 137), three types of mutually related values: 1. *utilitarian* (e.g., as a source of food) known among economists as 'use-value'; 2. *aesthetic* (e.g., places of scenic beauty), and 3. *intrinsic* (i.e. non-human species, like the great apes, which are 'intrinsically valuable … because they should have no other value [and] … are an end in themselves, not a means to anything' (Dasgupta 2001: 137; Krutilla 1967; cf. also Hayward 1994).

The Utilitarian Value: Interdependence and Exploitation

As Baviskar (2003: 5053) observes in a recent paper, the very expression 'natural resources' indicates how 'something that is not an artefact of human making … invoke[s] utility, culturally produced use and exchange values, something to be efficiently managed. Linking these antinomies are notions of property and possession, stewardship … the right to use and appropriate'. A second expression underlining this basic attitude and now much in vogue in the realm of participatory eco-management is that of 'stakeholder'. Whether then as sources of subsistence or pleasure, habitats are spaces that are culturally inscribed in terms of power and profit. And at the core of every environmental legislation is the notion of transaction costs conceived of both in political (e.g., 'public' or 'national' interest) and economic (e.g., efficiency) terms. Not surprisingly, also, this utilitarian thinking leads to conceiving of natural resources in terms of increasing competition.

The Myth of the 'gentle savage'

Yet, at no times it seems have humans consciously renounced the use-values of their habitat. Undoubtedly, prior to modern industrialisation human influence on the habitat remained largely localised, on the whole affecting relatively small areas, few populations and species. But the 'noble and gentle savage' who willingly and consciously employed strategies in order to live in equilibrium and harmony with other species is a figment of our imagination, with little basis in reality. Archaeological records have identified various 'overkills' (Kay 1994; Krech 1999; Liebersohn 1994), though, as the case of the Beringian Steppe Bison shows (Shapiro et al. 2004), not all animal populations have been decimated by the human hand (see also Barnosky et al. 2004; Broughton 2003). Yet, early in human history landscapes were changed and biodiversity reduced by human activities in many parts of the world (Bird 1995; Butzer 1992; Denevan 1992; Levy 1999; Lewis 1989). Many, mainly animal species, became extinct as they were hunted for meat and for producing goods for subsistence or exchange (Saul 1992). Many early burgeoning populations often mismanaged their habitats to such an extent that their civilisations declined drastically. Sometimes overexploitation, mainly massive deforestation, even led to their own extinction (cf. Flenley and Bahn 2002; Malone et al. 1994; Pain 1994; Runnels 1995; Zizka 1989: 21–38, but see Hunt 2006). As Rolett and Diamond (2004) recently showed, certain Pacific Island societies collapsed due to both environmental and cultural factors that led to massive deforestation, while others who retained their forest due to different environmental and attitudinal reasons survived.

Often, even when a 'harmonious' togetherness exists between a human population and other species within a habitat (this is mainly thought to be the case for foraging societies), it is not the result of conscious conservation efforts or an ethical thinking reinforcing conservation mechanisms (Alvard 1993; Casimir 1994; Ellen 1993; Stearman 1994; but see also Gottesfeld 1994; for a comprehensive discussion see Hunn et al. 2003). If conservational effects are observed, they appear to be mainly due to one or both of two reasons. First, given their 'inefficient' extraction technology, these small, mainly foraging populations simply did not have the means to overexploit their habitat (Low 1996). Second, as optimal foraging theory (e.g. Smith 1983; Smith 1991) suggests, foragers cease to hunt/collect different animals or plants when they are reduced in quantity to such an extent that the energy spent in foraging exceeds the energy gained. The forager now mainly looks for other food items, but the depleted populations are still large enough to recover and, after a while, again approach the carrying capacity of their habitat. Also, if a foraged produce can not be transferred into symbolic or other forms of capital, it makes no sense to collect excessive amounts. Why, for example, would a hunter take the trouble to trap two hundred polar foxes if only twenty are needed to keep him and his family warm, provided, of course, that owning two hundred furs increases neither his prestige nor enables him to exchange the excess for other goods or services – as happened when, with the onset of the fur trade, the sea-otter of the northwestern coastal areas of North America became nearly extinct in a relatively short period (for an other example see Nietschmann 1987). Here, as everywhere, with innovations and new inducements older norms and values lost their power and clashed with actual attitudes and behaviour (cf. also Gottesfeld 1994).

All this does not in principle, however, contradict the attitude found in many 'traditional' northern hunting societies where the hunted animal is perceived by the hunter not as the prey in a predator–prey relationship, but as part of a relationship of sharing in which it gives itself to the hunter as a gift (Ingold 1986: 243–76; Ingold 2000; see also Harrod 2000; Nadasdy 2007). Thus among the Huna Tlingit of southeastern Alaska, their '"Respect for everything provided by the Holy Spirit" is understood as to require that one not harvest fish or deer, for example, in excess of one's needs' (Hunn et al. 2003: 80; cf. also Moss 2003: 97).

Romantic images of people living in harmony with their natural environment are, however, not restricted to hunter-gatherer societies alone. Such images are conjured up for most pre- and non-industrial societies which have been seen by many as entirely different, if not opposed to, highly industrialised contemporary Western societies, and whose members often appear to urban Westerners as living in fond intimacy with their 'natural' environment. This has been the image of pastoral nomads (for a discussion see Ruttan and Borgerhoff Mulder 1999) and many peasant societies as well (e.g., Norberg-Hodge 1991; for a critique see Wiley 1997). As so often, the truth seems to lie somewhere in between. In many cases 'conservation' can be an epiphenomenon of an optimal foraging strategy (sometimes also including an emic moral epistemology); in others overexploitation, followed by species extinction and/or environmental degradation may take place. In yet other contexts a 'real' conservationist ideology, based on the recognition of an intrinsic value of species and environment, may lead to a long-term sustainable situation. Each case has to be analysed carefully and judged independently to avoid sweeping statements, meaningless watertight categories and ideologically grounded generalisations and orthodoxies (cf. Broughton 2003; Hunn et al. 2003).

Water as a Natural Resource: From a Free Good to an Economic Commodity

Water has always been perceived as a natural resource, but it has not always been an economic commodity. Indeed, certain religious traditions such as Islam make access to water mandatory for all, and in many other traditions water symbolises a variety of social relationships. For instance, in the Thar Desert in western India historical documents and oral traditions show that there water was transformed in the villages from a mythical source to a communal property and then to a public resource. There water is remembered and constructed and access reflects the continuities in perception and behaviour between seasonal, temporary, sporadic and long-term environmental changes. Whereas earlier access to water was a continuous problem only for people in arid regions, today it is much more restricted. Water has become scarce the world over. The annual withdrawal of water from the world's lakes, rivers and underground aquifers has doubled over the latter half of the last century to an estimated annual 3,800 km^3. It has been predicted that by the year 2025 some 3.5 billion people will be living in water-stressed countries (WCD 2001: 2f.), and that future armed conflicts in many parts of the world will revolve around water scarcity (cf. Gleick 1993; Haftendorn 2000; Scheumann and Schiffer 1998; Townsend 2002; for useful websites see W1–W6).

Water, which was always perceived of as a free good and resource is now valued as a limited commodity and an economic good. The final ministerial declaration issued at the conclusion of the 3rd World Water Forum in Kyoto in March 2003 made this clear: 'Water has to be treated primarily as an economic good, not only as a social good.' The follow-up Camdessus Report (2003) concluded that the solution to water financing, notably in poorer countries, was to privatise it. Such conclusions contravene a UN declaration of 2002 which declares that 'Water should be treated as a social and cultural good, and not primarily as an economic good'. Yet, poor countries like Bolivia, Ghana, Mexico and India which signed the GATS agreement under the aegis of the WTO have been obliged to begin putting this conclusion into practice and treat water as a 'service'. In the poorest parts of central India, for example, fishermen and peasants have lost access to long stretches of the River Mahanadi, sole rights of access to which have been sold by the provincial government to private companies (Krishnakumar 2003). The river which for centuries was common property has overnight become private property, access to which is too heavily priced for most of the local population. Today a large percentage of global water is in the hands of a few multinational corporations, but these firms are not always interested in investing in poor countries, as the dividends are low and people's resistance high.

Resistance to another ubiquitous aspect of water management is also increasing: dams. For thousands of years dams have been a major means of supplying people with water for drinking and irrigation, thereby reducing the impact of unpredictable and erratic rainfall. Drawing on this logic in modern times, it was thought that large dams would solve both water and electricity shortages. Thus, between the 1930s and the 1970s big dams became synonymous with development activities, progress and modernity (WCD 2001: 2), and since the 1950s 45,000 large dams have been constructed in different parts of the world. Many of these huge projects date back to plans drafted much earlier: the Epupa in northern Namibia for example, planned by the South African government in the 1960s, followed concepts formulated during the German colonial period. Similarly, the construction of the Sudanese dam at the Fourth Cataract of the Nile goes back to planning by the Anglo-Egyptian administration in the 1940s. After decades during which much else has changed, these freshwater resources are being tapped in the hope of stabilising and increasing national economic growth in these arid lands.

In the past decade southern Africa has seen a massive extension of large scale dam-construction for hydro-electric purposes (see also Turton and Henwood 2002). Existing structures like the Kariba Dam in Zimbabwe/Zambia and the Cabora Bassa Dam in Mozambique have been refurbished with World Bank money, while many new dams have also been built. The huge Katse Dam in Lesotho is only one of ten dams of the Lesotho highland scheme which produces electricity for internal consumption and the needs of the wider Johannesburg area. Together with Angola, Namibia has planned a dam on the Kunene river (Heyns 1995). This would have a major impact on the local ecosystem and on northwestern Namibia's pastoral population, and resistance against it has gained international publicity. Indeed, while nearly half the world's rivers now house at least one big dam, many of these projects have increasingly led to disastrous side-effects for the environment and ruin for major sections of local and regional populations. Chinese dams across the Mekong, for example, are causing devastating droughts in the downstream riparian regions of Laos and Kampuchea (see also Berkoff 2003).

Increasing humanitarian problems are attached to the construction of mega-dams (McCully 1996; Thukral 1992; see also Loker 2003). In many countries various organisations have warned against such projects, and in some instances, such as that of the Arun River in Nepal or the Narmada in India, the World Bank finally withdrew its financial support (Gyawali 2003). Typical for such conflict situations are the three current largest projects – the Kemal Attatürk Dam in Turkey, the Sardar Sarovar Dam in India (Bavadam 2004; Baviskar 1995; Baviskar 2003), and the Three Gorges Dam in China (Heming et al. 2001). The highest priority for these states lies apparently in the production of hydro-electric energy, flood control and navigation requirements coming next. In all these cases hope has been held out that thousands of square kilometres of fertile rain-fed or pasture land could be made irrigable for the benefit of poor peasants who could then be settled there. However, as in India, tens of thousands of the poorest are often evicted from their lands, with no compensation worth the name to add to the millions of homeless in the name of 'national interest' and 'development' (cf. Sharma 2003). The various organisations warning and protesting against the construction of such big dams put forward numerous arguments that range from the extreme risk of uncalculated negative environmental effects on the entire region, through the irretrievable loss of ancient archaeological sites, of scenic beauty, to the often catastrophic fate of tens of thousands of families who will be displaced from their deluged homes and lands and either not compensated at all, or only very inadequately so.

During the last decade large-scale inter-basin transfer schemes have also been implemented, in order to transfer water from one river basin with an apparent abundance of water to another river basin less endowed with water, or to urban areas where water consumption levels are high (Heyns 1995). As the director of Water Affairs in Namibia Heyns regards the development of large regional water transfer schemes as the major infrastructural development in SADC countries over the next twenty years. South Africa already has numerous water-transfer schemes and Namibia currently depends on the working of two of these schemes: a major part of the population of former Ovamboland lives off the waters of southern Angola's Calueque Dam on the Kunene (with a capacity of 3.2 m^3/second) and the Okavango-Swakop carrier (with a capacity of 2 m^3/second). Further major transfer schemes are now being planned: a giant project is to connect the Kasai/Congo, the Kavango and the Lualubala/Congo with the Zambesi, with a total capacity of up to 150 m^3/second. In northeastern Africa only a few projects are of similar magnitude, but the supply of artesian water to coastal towns through a water carrier from the Lybian oasis Kufra and from several dams on the Nile are of importance.

In Asia major projects are also being developed. China plans to divert the Brahmaputra northwards from Tibet (e.g. Tso 2004), thus leading to the devastation of the ecosystem of the world's longest and deepest canyon and furthermore to the desiccation of the Ganga- Brahmaputra riverine network and great parts of northern India. While India protests against this plan, it is itself trying to dam several rivers that are part of the Indus system, thus depriving Pakistan of essential irrigation facilities. It is also planning to link its major rivers (Bandyopadhyay and Perveen 2004; Divan 2005; see also the websites W7–W9). These plans are grounded on the concept of 'surplus' river basins from which water can be transferred to 'deficit' water basins, and on that of water being 'wasted' when a river flows out to sea. In other words they are based on purely utilitarian notions of both 'surplus' and 'waste'.

Aesthetic and Numinous Value: From Wilderness to Nature

'Wilderness', 'nature' and 'landscape' are terms whose connotations have varied across cultures and over history. An opposition between the 'pure', 'unspoiled' beauty of the 'wilderness/nature' and the 'civilised', refined town, especially the royal court, is the central theme of Kālidāsa's classical Sanskrit drama '*Śakuntalā and the Ring of Recollection*' dating back to the fourth century A.D. – a piece of Indian literature that had an enormous influence on European, and specially German, Romantic literature (for a detailed analysis see Thapar 2000, see also Inden 2007). Paraphrasing Sherry Ortner (1974), the equation 'woman to nature – man to culture' is central to this story about the love of a cultivated king, Dusyanta, for the 'naturkind' (child of nature) Śakuntalā, who grew up in the forests as the daughter of a sage and a celestial nymph. From the Classical period of Greece and Rome onwards into the Italian, Spanish and English traditions (Gregg 1906) 'wilderness/nature' also had romantic connotations, as is obvious from the whole genre of pastoral poetry and drama. These pastoral themes, however, had little or nothing to do with the real life of shepherds; as Gregg (1906: 4f., 7) observed:

> At no stage in its development does literature, or at any rate poetry, concern itself with the obvious, with the bare scaffolding of life: whenever we find an author interested in the circle of prime necessity we may be sure that he himself stands outside it … It was left to a later, perhaps a wiser and a sadder, generation to gaze with fruitless and often only half sincere longing at the shepherd-boy asleep under the shadow of the thorn, lulled by the low monotonous rustle of the grazing flock … Only when the shepherd-songs ceased to be the outcome of unalloyed pastoral conditions did they become distinctively pastoral … As a result of this contrast there arises an idea which comes perhaps as near being universal in pastoral as any – the idea, namely of the 'golden age'… I have said that a sense of the contrast between town and country was essential to the development of a distinctively pastoral literature.

Indeed, at least since Henry David Thoreau (1817–1862), the father of environmentalism, we know that the various meanings of environment and parts thereof are, following the specific Zeitgeist, culturally semantisised aspects of what Ingold (2000) termed 'the really natural'. Thus, even within Europe connotations have varied over time and across regions (for a comprehensive historical analysis see Schama 1996). In the centuries prior to the Enlightenment and even thereafter, 'wilderness' was opposed to 'culture' and uncultivated environments were usually perceived as more or less dangerous spheres (cf. Düwel 1994). In European painting, for instance, the landscape merely served as a backdrop for religious themes or secular activities. It was only with the onset of the Romantic period that in the West 'wilderness' and the 'landscape' became a theme in itself, and now came to be understood as 'nature' – the paintings of J.M.W. Turner and Caspar David Friedrich are good examples of this development. In the twentieth century numerous illustrated books and magazines, as well as poetry, continued to project romantic and often nostalgic images in which the countryside is a metaphor for the 'beloved homeland' (e.g., Conyngham Green 1932). This romantic attitude towards the countryside and the 'simple life' projected on to the space outside the larger towns and cities has remained a theme in prose and poetry right down to our days, albeit in modified forms, suited to the political and economic Zeitgeist of the particular epoch.

'Nature' served as a metaphor for the 'pure', the 'uncorrupted' and as a projection in Christian Europe of the longing for a Paradisical state. The use of Edenic terminology in the cognitive and official construction of botanical gardens and botany classes in Renaissance and Post-Renaissance Europe mirrors this development (Prest 1981). This was reflected also in Jean-Jacques Rousseau's philosophy and his theory of education as expressed in *Emile*, which opens with: 'God makes all things good; man meddles with them and they become evil. He forces one soil to yield the products of another, one tree to bear another fruit. He confuses and confounds time, place, and natural conditions.' (Rousseau 1933: 5). And Friedrich Schiller (1830: 1277), in his *Über naive und sentimentalische Dichtung* of 1795/6, noted that 'In the same way that nature slowly began to vanish from human life as an experience and as an (acting and feeling) subject, we see it emerging in the world of poetry as ideal and as tope' (translation mine). Thus nature was glorified in a romantic, sometimes even mystified, pantheistic manner, as in the Shaftesbury hymn: 'O glorious Nature! Supremely Fair, and sovereignly Good! All-Loving and All-Lovely, All-divine!' and in Alexander Pope's *An Essay on Man* (1733) – 'All are but parts of a stupendous whole, whose body Nature is, and God the soul' (Epistle i, l. 267; cf. also Binde 2000: 18–21) – where he expressed his view of the oneness of the hand of God and the natural: 'Nor think in NATURE'S STATE the blindly trod. The state of Nature was the reign of God' (Epistle iii, l. 147f.; quoted after Warnock 2003: 447). A similar attitude towards nature can be observed in sixteenth-century German vernacular literature where numerous prints indicate a widespread curiosity about the natural world. They too 'reveal a pervasive sense of nature as divinely created and deep conviction that contemplation of the natural world would lead to greater piety' (Crowther-Heyck 2003). In England such contemplation was provided from the middle of the eighteenth century onwards by the institution of gardens and parks.[6] The ideal in laying these out changed from the formal Perso-French to the imitation of the 'natural landscape' (cf. Hennebo and Hoffmann 1963: 15ff.), whereby a somewhat modified, 'improved natural environment' could mirror the perfect and harmonious creation of God's world.

But the contemplation of 'untouched nature', and even an exhilarating and secret, individual bond with it, came to full bloom in the Romantics: 'There is a pleasure in the pathless woods / There is a rapture on the lonely shore / There is society where none intrudes' (Lord Byron). In Germany, in the Romantic period, the 'Deutsche Wald' became a metaphor for beauty and nobility, a symbol of sublimity and reverence (cf. Schriewer 2000), and especially since Riehl's works, for a romantic love for the 'Heimat' (cf. Schama 1996: 113ff.). This enthusiastic, romantic and even numinous attitude continued to be an important theme for the next two hundred years, so much so that at the beginning of the twentieth century, love for an 'unspoiled nature', especially for forests, could be so perverted and misused for political propaganda. In Nazi Germany under the 'SS-Lehr und Forschungsgemeinschaft "Das Ahnenerbe"' organised by Dr Walther Wüst, researchers of the project 'Wald und Baum' further mystified the 'Deutsche Wald' and tried to link it with their ideology of a Germanic and Nordic 'Aryan' race and religion (for an excellent analysis see Rusinek 2000).

In his *Ambivalence and Modernity* Zygmunt Bauman (1993: 7) discussed how 'nature' has been imagined in modern times – as something free of intervention, as unordered existence, as something singularly unfit for human habitation, not to be trusted and not to be left to its own devices. 'Nature' is something to be mastered, subordinated and remade, so as to be readjusted to human needs. This imagination is, however, not that new: it goes back at least to the New Testament. As late as in December 2001 this biblical idea of stewardship was echoed in a pronouncement by the Vatican: 'Man has the right and a duty to act within and on the created order, making use of other creatures to create the final goal of all creation: the glory of God through the promotion of Man' (in Warnock 2003: 446). Baumann is however right in observing that today there is 'nothing ... more artificial than naturalness'. This is amply evident in tourism brochures that sell the attractions of 'remote', 'idyllic' beaches and 'magic islands'. Tourist resorts in Bali, Goa the South Pacific Islands, parts of Thailand and Sri Lanka all serve as seasonal 'second homes' for Westerners in search of the last, temporary paradises. That the visual sense largely dominates environmental perception is by now well established. In their paper here, Vorlaufer et al. use this approach to elicit interesting responses regarding environmental pollution on Thai beaches. Their discussion of the problems created by increasing amounts of garbage in these paradises opens up new questions concerning the multiple environmental impact of tourism and perceptions thereof.

The transition in modernity from 'wilderness' to 'nature' 'readjusted to human needs', as a landscape with supposedly intrinsic value, can be best demonstrated by the history of National Parks, Sanctuaries and Protected Areas. It is also a history of the Western, especially male thrill for discovery and adventure through centuries of pre-colonial, colonial, imperial and post-colonial dominance.

From Utilitarian to Intrinsic Value? Peoples and Parks

Towards the beginning of the nineteenth century governments in Europe gradually came to realise that in many parts of the world the overexploitation of natural resources had caused dramatic environmental changes. This resulted in the formulation of the first protection laws. These legislations were, however, not passed to protect nature for its intrinsic value, 'for ... [its] own sake', as 'we would love it [nature] as we love another human being whom we know is not our slave' (Warnock 2003: 450). These laws were passed only out of fear that the economic exploitation of specific regions would soon no longer be possible. When in the beginning of the nineteenth century the first forest laws were enacted in Prussia to allow the felling of trees only on condition that an equal number of trees were planted, the goal was to attain the sustainability of state forests, in order to ensure the continuous exploitation of lumber – not to secure scenic beauty, biodiversity or even the intrinsic value of biotopes. This was also the case when the British in their colonies in Africa and India finally noticed an overkill of game by their countrymen (cf. Anglás Grande 1999; Casimir 2001; Dovers et al. 2002; Grove 1987; Kjekshus 1977; Lenhart and Casimir 2001; Rao 2002). But instead of curbing this, thousands of local inhabitants were driven out of their ancient homes and lands, and wildlife sanctuaries were established in order to ensure further 'sporting' and 'manly' hunting leisure-time for the British imperial class. The net 'effect of game regulations was to restrict hunting to the gentleman, sportsman, administrator and soldier' (MacKenzie 1989: 58).

Hunting in Europe had long been the privilege of the nobility and the upper classes, and thus a symbol of dominance; it was also an ideology that became part and parcel of imperial colonial attitudes (Bennett 1984; MacKenzie 1989; Pandian 1998). This was of course often combined with commercial interests, and between 1850 and 1890, hunting and the extraction of ivory, for example, led to a dramatic decrease in the enormous elephant herds of southern Africa. It was this drastic depletion of big game that caused mainly rich and politically important hunters to stand up for the protection of wild animals (a similar decrease in smaller game was also of concern to the British in the Himalayas; cf. Rao 2002). Indeed, game- and natural reserves, as well as national parks and other categories of protected areas (for a typology and their objectives see Wells and Brandon 1995: 2), were not established for their intrinsic value, but in order to control deforestation and preserve wildlife for white hunters. The 'traditional' users, the Africans and Asians, were usually blamed for the decrease in game, but it was only much later, at the close of the nineteenth century and the start of the twentieth that 'the link between conservation and the hunt [lay] in the demarcation of the privilege and power of the new rulers of Africa' (MacKenzie 1989: 58), and hunting was restricted for white hunters too.

In the seventeenth and early eighteenth centuries, Europeans by and large perceived most non-Europeans as 'primitive natives', close to beasts, and often conceptualised them as part of 'nature'. When they finally came to be accepted as 'real human beings', it was suggested that 'real' nature had to be a landscape without human inhabitants, where 'natural forces' alone would govern the interaction between plant and animal species, a process, it was thought, that would keep them in a 'natural state of equilibrium'. This ideology led to policies which forbade habitation and the exploitation of natural produce in the 'protected' zones, and often entire communities were violently forced off their native lands. In some countries even in the second half of the twentieth century, with the intrinsic value of plants and animals being recognised and the extinction of certain species feared, herding and foraging communities were expelled from their lands and a ban imposed on their use of the natural resources of their own areas. 'Almost by definition … conservational protected areas have been at odds with "indigenous people's" rights to self-determination and territorial control' (Colchester 1997: 109),[7] for this notion of conservation 'operates by sealing off portions of wilderness and their animal inhabitants, and by restricting or banning human intervention' (Ingold 1994: 10).

However, de facto, no park was ever an 'empty wilderness' (Lye Tuck-Po 1997: 8); indeed, parks are often located within the existing territories of sedentary or nomadic communities. Once such a park is created, however, the authorities normally restrict access to the area and prohibit all activities within it, because they regard them as obstacles to effective natural resource management. Thus, for example, in 1926, with the creation of the Kruger National Park, one of the first protected areas in Africa, 3,000 individuals, mainly sedentary Thonga, were driven out of the demarcated area and those who remained were forbidden to use the 'public' routes of the park; special paths were built for them, so that they remained invisible to visitors who would get the impression of really being in 'pure nature' (Carruthers 1995; see Rao 2002 for a similar situation in the Kashmir Himalayas). Later, when across all the semi-arid savannahs of eastern and southern Africa protected areas and National Parks were created, pastoral peoples and foragers were seen as a threat to the environment (Århem 1985; Brockington and Homewood 2001; Bunn and Auslander 1999; Casimir 2001, 2002; Dieckmann 2001; Job 1999; Johnsen 2000; Myers 1972; McCabe 1997; for an overview also see Lenhart and Casimir 2001).

In many post-colonial states tourism has become a major source of revenue, and the dominant classes which benefit from these revenues tend to feel that local communities, their settlements and access to livelihood spoil the romantic and idyllic view for Western visitors, who wish to experience 'wilderness' and 'pure nature'. This is true of both African and Asian states. In the late 1970s, for example, all Mursi who lived in the border area between south Ethiopia and the Sudan were forced out of their riverine agricultural lands and choicest pastures (Turton 1994). Similarly, sheer persecution has been the fate of the Wanniyala-Aetto of Sri Lanka (Stegeborn 2001; Stegeborn 2004). When, however, it was felt that 'the natives' fitted into the image of the 'real Africa' that was in the minds of Western tourists, their settlement in such areas was sometimes allowed – again, due to the same 'romantic', Western fantasies. Thus, for instance, in 1958 George Silberbauer was appointed as 'Bushman Survey Officer' by the British Colonial Administration in Botswana; he classified those Bushmen who still hunted and gathered as 'wild' Bushmen, and when the Central Kalahari Game Reserve was finally established in 1961 the government followed his recommendations and allowed some 3,000 of these 'wild' Bushmen to hunt in the reserve (see Kuper 2003: 393).

So more often than not we have the preposterous situation in which communities who live and use vast areas are shunted out of their homes and habitats, while state agencies, conservationists (and sometimes scientists) gain access to these and invite tourists to come and visit for a fee. Occasionally, nominal monetary compensation or resettlement outside the park may be offered in return for such expulsion. But usually, park planning does not include access to viable resources, let alone employment opportunities for the evicted – not even as forest rangers or guides. Thus, for example, the 592 Maldhari families who were evicted between 1972 and 1986 from the Gir Sanctuary in western India were 'resettled' in twenty-eight scattered areas; a little arid, unirrigated land was given to these pastoralists, but even in 1999 neither seeds nor loans nor any cash to even start off with (cf. Casimir 2001). Finally, despite lip-service being paid to the crucial importance of local environmental knowledge regarding flora and fauna – which could be very fruitfully incorporated into conservation measures – few steps are taken to tap this specialised knowledge through these communities. Instead, 'specialists' are brought in to study the problems and make recommendations (see Widlok in this volume for a detailed discussion of this aspect) that often end up in the complete negation, if not criminalisation, of local communities.

Beyond Purism and Green Primitivism: Community Based Management Schemes

> It is sad that we now have to have a term – community-oriented conservation – for something that used to come to all of us naturally. Man has many unfair advantages now over his environment. We see ourselves as separate from the environment and in our arrogance we impose on other living beings. We are changing at such a phenomenal rate that we have forgotten that other living creatures still accept the pace of nature ... We believe it to our right that we are first in the order of things ...When this sacred trust is violated, we have to create what we call protected areas. (Mike Leach, Chief of the Tit'qet St'at'imc Nation, Canada 2003 at the 5th World Parks Congress in Durban)

The developments of the last decades have shown clearly that both extreme points of view – the myth of 'true nature' and the romantic and misconceived construct of 'noble savages living in harmony with their environment' – have failed as concepts for human-environment negotiation in order to secure biodiversity and save rare fauna and flora from extinction. New approaches are urgently required to solve the problems of how, and following which principles, institutions can and should organise the various, often competing, claims of different interest groups to their 'Rights to Nature' (Hanna et al. 1996). Most recently, a few programmes have been initiated to integrate communities who live or have lived in reserved areas into the management of natural reserves and national parks, so that they can earn a decent livelihood (for an overview see, for example, Furze et al. 1996; Hulme and Murphree 2001; Igoe and Brockington 1999; Kothari et al. 1996; Nelson 2004; Saberwal et al. 2001). Some, though not all initiatives to place the management of game reserves entirely into local hands, appear fairly promising (but see Weber 1991 for problems in Nepal's Sagarmatha Park). Such management practice provides for a certain amount of culling by hunting (for example, of large ungulate herds), of the sale of this meat and of selling licences to hunters. The long-term success of such strategies assumes a substantial animal growth rate, specially of rare 'big game', which would require regular and strictly supervised culling that could simultaneously satisfy the controlled demand for hunting trophies. Jonsen (2000: 170) has convincingly shown for the impoverished Maasai, specially in the Ngorongoro, that

> a new approach to conservation based on community cooperation and local empowerment is probably the best way … Maasai communities do … have a strong potential as cost effective allies in conservation, once it is realized that their pastoral mode of production is not antagonistic to conservation objectives, but to a large extent the very means by which this landscape was culturally constructed in the first place.

In many cases, community control and involvement in forest management schemes have enabled a more detailed assessment of forest resources and management needs than centralised forest management did or could, thus 'challeng[ing] the notion that forest communities are problems, while state bodies deliver solutions' (Wolvekamp 1999: xviii). An analysis of twenty-three recently launched integrated conservation-development projects (ICDPs) in different parts of the world indicates an optimistic trend (Wells and Brandon 1995; see also Horowitz 1998). Although these projects accepted the World Bank's 1986 definition of wildlands as 'natural areas relatively untouched by human activities', they also 'recognized the importance of wildland management to development projects and require[d] that wildland management be considered in economic and sectorial planning' (Dedec and Goodard 1988 in Wells and Brandon 1995: 3). Wells and Brandon (1995: x) point out that 'ICDPs need to challenge the widespread but unsupported assumption that people who are made better off as a result of a development project will refrain from illegal exploitation of a nearby protected area even in the absence of the negative incentive provided by more effective penalties'.

To establish ICDP's, many factors must be taken into account (Horowitz 1998). Of utmost importance are traditional legislative infrastructures and management practices, and the already functioning institutions and systems of customary law. On the basis of these new conservation strategies should be implemented in collaboration and cooperation with the people, their political leaders or other persons of influence. Of crucial importance is the willingness of politicians and administrators to justly share the profits garnered through tourism and other sources of revenue with local communities, who will then and only then actively protect their environment. This will, hopefully, be one step towards helping them to participate in the overall equitable development of their respective regions.

Today in many regions conflicts between the local population and conservationists arise mainly from the different aims and interests between them and these 'outsiders', who warn of the deterioration of a 'natural equilibrium'. For example, many inhabitants of Europe's Alpine zones attribute a 'use value' to their mountain slopes and advocate the construction of yet more ski resorts and lifts which would lead to growth in incomes. Environmentalists on the other hand, caution against the deteriorating biodiversity and loss of scenic beauty. Especially in Germany, nature conservationists and the local land-users thus often find themselves in opposite camps. As Stoll-Kleemann (2001) has shown, strong emotional and cultural drives lead to negative perceptions and experiences regarding nature conservation. Here conservationists are stereotyped as 'out-groups' and their activities perceived as authoritarian and threatening. Again, as in other parts of the world, a lack of inclusive and meaningful participation in conservation management by the local land-owning population plays a crucial role in the problems of managing the sustainability of certain habitats and their biodiversity.

Major conservation groups are now beginning to realise that their old, hard-line protectionist approach simply does not work (Pearce 2003). If local communities do not perceive relatively short-term benefits from efforts to protect their habitat and from the 'soft exploitation' of their environment, biodiversity will not be sustained. 'Bioprospecting' (Moran et al. 2001) is one type of environmental 'soft exploitation' (for a successful implementation of such a pragmatic strategy see Sturm 2002). That may also help both to produce new medicines and preserve traditional healing systems, thus demonstrating the therapeutic, economic and social values of these habitats. It can bring biotechnology and other benefits to biodiversity-rich but technology-poor countries. Only by respecting the intellectual property rights of the people, giving them a fair share of the profits of such undertakings, can a burgeoning form of colonialism, 'bioimperialism', be avoided (cf. Greene 2004).

The Rights of Indigenous Peoples – Between Romanticism and 'Progress'

Respecting people's rights generally must also mean that indigenous peoples have as much right to use their habitat for foraging as agriculturists to plough their lands and urban dwellers to construct buildings. This was recently pointed out for India (Rao and Sankaran 2003), where even today many *adivasi* peoples are forced out of their forests and lands to make way for National Parks or Reserves, commercial plantations, agro-industries, dams, military testing sites or even construction projects (Rao and Casimir 2003: 23ff.).

Indeed, community rights to pastureland, and in particular the institution of commons in areas with low annual rainfall averages, high annual variance and hence unpredictability of grazing, has been proved to be the optimal way of keeping the ecosystem more or less sustainable (Casimir 1992a,b; Casimir 2002; Casimir 2003; Casimir and Rao 1998; Burke 2001; McCabe 1990; Sandford 1983; cf. also Acheson 2003; Brockington and Homewood 2002; Feeny et al. 1990; McCay and Acheson 1987). Yet, local power-brokers use the much-trumpeted argument of Hardin's (1968) 'Tragedy of the Commons' to often forcefully privatise customary communal lands to their own advantage, arguing that such old 'traditional' land use systems are anyway doomed to fail. The struggle is often between 'traditionalists' and 'modernists' within the community itself. A recent example is that of the pastoral Samburu of Siambu (Lesorogol 2003), among whom the increasingly capitalist land policies of the postcolonial

Kenyan government have led to institutional changes and different power-groups emerging, some of whom fight the age-old culturally shared values of common pasture use and now claim private land ownership (cf. Mazonde n.d., see also, Fratkin 2002).

In poor countries intergenerational conflicts exacerbated by globalising influences are indeed an increasingly important factor in human-environment dynamics. An interesting example is that of the pre-Hispanic Andean cult of Pacha Mama. As Göbel discusses in her chapter here, this cult regulates and mediates all relations between humans and their environment. The transition to Catholicism did not much effect this. However, the conversions since about the 1950s to a variety of mostly U.S. -based evangelical sects has destroyed the Pacha Mama cult among the young. The destruction is both physical and cognitive, with the 'earth and animals ceas[ing] to be manifestations of a living spirit and [being] converted into things, exploitable and quantifiable resources' (Segato 2003: 186). An interesting comparison is provided by the Saora of southeastern India, who became Baptists (Vitebsky 1998).

But it is here equally that many NGOs supporting the rights of local and indigenous peoples themselves fall prey to the dangers of lurking ecological romanticism (Prasad 2003). Their attitude implies, partly at least, that in spite of a rapidly industrialising and capitalist socio-political environment, such communities should or will choose to continue with their foraging, mobile pastoralism or slash and burn cultivation, provided that their rights to their lands are finally recognised. They forget that in almost all such communities today the interplay of internal and external socio-economic and political forces is leading to the meaningful future of such supposedly 'traditional' lifestyles being questioned, and thus also to conflicts between different local power groups – often between the young, who have experienced a few of the so-called advantages of modernity, and the older generation who recall the advantages of their 'traditional lifestyle'. Seitz's chapter here provides an example of just such change as a response to a variety of environmental factors among the former foraging Aeta of the western Philippines. Even before the eruption of the volcano on Mount Pinatubo, Aeta families had been impacted by numerous NGO development projects. With the volcanic eruption further and sudden changes were required, and the Aeta managed to find new resources and means of subsistence, partly using their flexibility as foragers, even to go in for wet-rice cultivation.

From Local Problems to Global Concerns

Local Concerns and Human Behaviour

Most of us use our habitats for survival and seem to take care of them only if and when our well-being is directly affected by local and immediate circumstances. The pollution that is 'out of sight' was and often still is nobody's business, and huge spaces on the outskirts of most cities are used to get rid of massive amounts of garbage and scrap metal. Here the individual often sacrifices the 'higher environmental goal' for personal advantage. A good example of such behaviour was the municipal policy in the Swiss capital, Bern, where the fees for garbage bins were calculated according to their size. Many people ordered the smallest, but because many households produced more litter than could be stored in these small bins for domestic use, there was a sudden overflow of household litter into the bins in parks and other public places (Dieckmann and Preisendörfer 1994: 26). These public spaces are often interpreted and understood by the individual as a no-man's land, as a space of concern to none. In order to save money or time, free riding is often observed here, and people use such common spaces to get rid of their private waste. The problem is then passed on to be taken care of by the anonymous institutions of the city or state (cf. Chakrabarty 1991). The closely related, somewhat fuzzy areas of 'common' and 'no-man's land' are open to everyone's interpretation on the basis of his or her moral convictions.

In their paper in this volume Vorlaufer et al. use the example of beaches in Thailand to analyse the contexts in which beaches and tourist resorts are littered with plastic bags, cans and other waste. Curbing pollution and managing an effective disposal of litter was found to be successful only when the pressure to keep the area clean came from tourists who avoided the places which were polluted, thus leading to economic loss for their owners. In their comparative study in this volume of conventional and organic farming in Germany, Döring et al. also consider the issue of morality, and apply what they refer to as a theory of the development of moral judgements. In these two agricultural orientations they identify two different systems of thought and risk management. These systems, they suggest, constitute the framework for reconstructing the opportunities for action and the perception of risk with regard to ecological, economic and social challenges.

All these observations seem to lead to what we may consider a general 'law': cultural rules which help preserve the environment usually develop only if and when the individual does not perceive him/herself as sacrificing what he or she considers to be excessive time, money or energy; and further, if he or she feels that there is more to 'gain' than to 'lose' or 'spend' by environment-conscious behaviour. However, it is not only such 'material' or 'materialistic' goals that count – as with charity and other moral commitments, the knowledge and feeling of being 'a good human being', often a culturally high-ranking goal, also counts and may, together with the aforementioned 'material' benefits, lead to the successful implementation of environmentally friendly measures. What happens, however, when a community maintains cultural institutions that influence only resource distribution, while access to the resource is not restricted? Andrea Bender examines this issue in her paper here and presents data from an island community in the Ha'apai-group of Tonga, where everyone has free access to all marine resources and cooperation and food-sharing remain highly cherished values. With the gradual transition from subsistent to commercial fishing, non-cooperative strategies of resource use are arising, as opportunities to sell fish are increasing and maximising profits is becoming a goal. Obviously the danger of overexploitation, if not depletion, is high. Bender compares two villages whose responses to this changing situation are very different.

Motivations, Strategies and the 'Master Value', Well-Being

All human actions are the direct or indirect outcome of motivations of individuals acting singly or in groups. Rational actor theory assumes that individual behaviour is strategically directed at optimising well-being, and other theories also presume that well-being is a 'master value' (Wolf 2003). All this does not imply, however, that individuals always

> deliberately act in order to advance their well-being, but rather insofar as they act rationally they do in fact advance their well-being, even if this is not the occurrent motivation from which they acted ... [and] although there are various ways of advancing one's well-being, and often people's action will have this effect, or be directed towards it in some sense, this just does not give any clear guidance as to what is to count as rational and irrational action. (Wolf 2003: 342f.)

If we assume the broad influence of the 'master value' well-being, the motives inducing specific behaviours can be related to aiming generally at fulfilling the basic needs that are more or less common to all species and, in humans, in addition, at fulfilling culture-specific derived needs, the 'wants' (Diligensky 1981). From a proximate perspective, the motivation for action lies in most cases in the wish to enhance physical and/or psychological well-being. Many physically felt morphological/physiological and psychological needs – those of curbing hunger, fulfilling sexual desires, etc. – while fundamentally related to innate structures, are transformed and refined by cultural values and norms. The actual enhancement of an individual's proximate desires or her/his well-being is of course an optimising process, and consists of maximising the desired effects under given environmental and/or socio-cultural constraints. The results of such actions are either in accordance with the values and norms of a society, or they are in conflict with these; in the latter case, if such actions violate laws, they might be labelled as anti-social or even criminal.

Concern, Anxiety, Fear and the Future

Every thing that happens in this world is the result of the fear of pain.
(Franz Werfel 1941/90; translation mine)

An essential component of well-being is feeling (relatively) secure. This is born out by the variety and importance of measures and methods employed by both generalists and specialists in all societies to 'foretell' the immediate or long-term future – the future being understood in terms of both individual and group, both society and environment. Reducing uncertainty,'that source and archetype of all fear' (Bauman 1993: 7), has always been the driving force behind the desire to learn about the future and develop strategies that reduce concern and anxiety. Rosen (1987: 155) asked why this desire 'is one of the most ancient human cravings', and went on to suggest that

> perhaps the most obvious [answer] is: so that we shall be able to decide what to do *now*. Perhaps the preponderance of conscious human behavior is the execution of *plans*; and the making of plans always requires some information pertaining to the future. For this reason, forecasting has always been a central human activity. (cf. also Sjöberg 1998: 91)

We try to predict the future on the basis of more or less incomplete information and experience regarding the past and present, which are largely embedded in our traditional knowledge. On the basis of such facts, thoughts, feelings and ideas, we have constructed a model of the world whose purpose it is to make predictions (Rosen 1978: 158). On the basis of our judgement 'about what is or will be the state of some aspects of the world' (Yates and Stone 1992: 68), we then extrapolate from the present into the future and predict possible events and how these may affect us. Such considerations concern probabilistic 'if-assumptions' which can be expressed as 'if this goes on like this, then ...'; 'if x happens, then ...'; or 'if I act in this or that way, rather than in these other ways, then ...'. From this baseline, possible future scenarios are deduced, but since information is always incomplete, every decision carries in itself a risk which is not completely calculable (for a discussion see, for example, Luhmann 1991: 84 ff.; Luhmann 1996). A decision is thus basically the selection 'of an action with the aim of producing outcomes at least as satisfactory as would result from any other available action (Yates and Stone 1992: 68).

On the one hand, worrying, which is always about the future, is a bodily experience in so far as in the Heideggerian sense of 'being in the world', the world can only be experienced through the body (Csordas 1994). Reducing uncertainty also means reducing the pain of worrying which we experience if unfavourable circumstances are expected and the situation is thought to deteriorate. On the other hand, worrying is an unpleasant psychological experience, since it involves 'preoccupation with thoughts about uncertain and unpleasant events', as a response to a 'perceived level of risk [that] calls for a more intellectual judgement and worry tends to refer to emotional reactions' (Sjöberg 1998: 85). Worry may be related to bodily pain and/or psychological stress in the near future, or to punishment in the long term, even in the 'next' or 'afterlife'. Fear, that basic physical, mental/psychological or spiritual needs or wants may not be fulfilled if some action is not taken, are the prime movers behind actions that involve taking risk, and in principle, the greater the danger the more the willingness to take high risk (also because one feels one may have little to lose).

The releasers of worry and fear related to probable risk and the danger of 'loss' must be understood in relation to the different hierarchical structures of culture-specific values, and also in relation to individual circumstances (Rohrmann 1994). As Yates and Stone (1992: 69ff.) observed, in risk-taking situations and in risk evaluation we tend to synthesise the various risks involved into an 'overall risk appraisal' on the basis of our current situation, past experiences and specific emotions (cf. Böhm and Pfister 2000), but also according to our present culture-specific values, norms, needs and wants. All of these then dictate the risk-taker's choice of the appropriate coping strategy and behaviour vis-à-vis risk. In their chapter here, Böhm and Pfister analyse individual risk perception and define five antinomies that are typical for environmental risks: proximal vs. distal effects, short-term vs. long-term consequences, individual vs. collective perspectives, biospheric vs. anthropocentric orientation, and ethical vs. consequentialistic evaluation. They suggest that the mental representation of environmental problems implies these antinomies, and prevent straightforward solutions for both individual and societal decision-makers. They further argue that these antinomies are reflected in individual cognitive representations of environmental risks and thus affect risk evaluation, as well as individual environmental behaviour. They also outline a model that explains how these antinomies are processed in individual judgements and sketch some applications in risk communication and mediation, arguing that one means of conflict resolution is to identify and integrate such antinomies.

Even in situations that are objectively extremely life-threatening, some individuals may experience excitement and even happiness (e.g. during extreme rock-climbing); this is also true of contexts in which the 'loss' of life is considered minimal or negligible because the highest possible reward is expected in return for the life 'lost'. This, may occur, for instance, when people 'happily give their life for a greater cause' – seeing themselves and being seen by others as heroes or martyrs, as in early Christian martyrdom, among some contemporary Islamists, and generally in war propaganda. In such cases the individual is supposed to more or less voluntarily decide to suffer, in order to attain a socially high-ranking emotional, cognitive or spiritual reward.

Of Causes and Explanations

Being in the world inherently implies being endangered and hence all events and actions contain, under given circumstances and with a certain probability, one or more negative or undesirable effects for individuals and groups. In all societies people ask themselves implicitly or explicitly about the causes that lead to desired and undesired events. As discussed briefly above, especially in contemporary Western societies 'rational' and materialist models based on axioms of modern science are used to explain such events. To deal with a precarious situation this hypothetical 'rational actor' will consider various strategies, but also the differential risks that these may involve. But in many societies, including those in the West, such 'rational' explanations are either not sought, or even when they are, ultimate 'irrational'[8] or immaterial causes are found behind such 'rational' explanations. Not fulfilling duties – for example, the failure to perform the prescribed rituals for the ancestors, or the violation of religious prescriptions, such as drinking alcohol among Muslims or leading a 'sinful' life among Christians – and/or flouting social and moral norms (murder, adultery, theft, etc.) are often interpreted as sins for which due punishment is sent down by the relevant supernatural authority. Thus, for example, when AIDS broke out, the Pope eagerly explained that this was a punishment for the sin of homosexual behaviour and corrected himself only after protests, by saying it was 'a warning' from God. The idea that misfortune is a result of the violation of culture-specific taboos is at the heart of this cognitive process (cf. Casimir 1987; Casimir 2004). As mentioned above, the misfortune that befalls an individual, a family, or even an entire community, for example in the form of an environmental disaster, can then be interpreted as the expression of just such a punishment or warning.

Among the Kanak of New Caledonia who imbue their natural surroundings with sacredness, as the realm of the spiritual and human ancestors, and where landscape features are an essential part of mythology and cultural heritage, some youth now blame Western economic activities for the degradation and destruction of their environment and hence also for the painfully felt loss of their tradition and culture (Horowitz 2001). In their papers in this volume Goebel, Schlehe and Seitz refer to such immaterialist, cognitive linkages in Argentina, Indonesia and the Philippines respectively. However, as some of the other articles in this volume show, in most societies even before disaster strikes or while in the midst of deciding how to deal with it, people cogitate about their possible causes. The pastoral Hima of southwestern Uganda are thus convinced that any contact between women and cows will certainly lead to disaster (Elam 1973 in Boholm 2003). Often in search of guilt, people detect 'causes' which they relate to the violation of religious duties or social norms (cf. Casimir 2004; Douglas 1985: 53). An expected disaster is then linked and understood as punishment and preventive measures are taken. Repentance and purification rituals and other religious acts are then performed to placate the punishing supernatural forces.

A combination of strategies based on both materialist and immaterialist causal links – what Boholm (2003: 165) refers to as an 'amalgamation of objectivity and subjectivity' – seems to be what most people in all societies actually do to cope with danger and risk. It seems that the more life-threatening the perception of a situation, the higher the likelihood of 'irrational' strategies being applied simultaneously with 'rational' ones, sometimes leading to dilemmas concerning their mutual compatibility; failing the effectiveness of the latter, only the former may be resorted to. As Barbara Goebel shows in her chapter here, there is often a cultural logic to economic practices. Discussing data on the cultural handling of uncertainty in a pastoral community of the Puna de Atacama, in northwestern Argentina, she shows how success in handling these uncertainties depends, from the local perspective, largely on two factors: the technical knowledge of each herder and his/her emotional commitment towards the flocks. The former, which rests on long experience, is transmitted within each household from one generation to the other, and is further added to through daily practice. However, it is felt that in order to cope with these risks it is not sufficient to become a skilful herder; households must also minimise uncertainties by the effective management of luck potentials. Luck (*suerte*) is the innate capacity a person has (or does not have) to positively influence the procreation of herd animals. This individual luck potential can be exploited adequately only if it is known socially and if its use is embedded in a reciprocal relationship with Mother Earth (*Pachamama*). Goebel discusses how herders try to accumulate and stabilise their luck through social networks, rituals and the respect of norms concerning the modes of interaction with their environment. This analytical perspective, she suggests, also provides tools to explain why conflicts arise when local perceptions of risk are confronted with development propositions of 'experts', such as agronomists and politicians.

Uncertainty, Risk and Vulnerability

In recent decades the concepts of 'uncertainty and risk' have often been successfully discussed and used by anthropologists under different aspects (e.g., Boholm 2003; Caplan 2000; Cashdan 1990; Douglas 1985; Douglas 1992; Giordano and Boscoboinik 2002; Rao 2000; Scoons 1995; Salter 2002), in cultural studies (Lupton 1999a,b), by geographers (e.g., Adams 1995; Kasperson et al. 1995), and sociologists (Adam et al. 2000; Beck 1992; Luhmann 1990; Luhmann 1991), to better understand how humans make decisions in order to solve social, political, economic, environmental and health problems that threaten their well-being. The basic assumption has been that with declining information about threatening situations, uncertainty, together with feelings of insecurity, grows. This uncertainty refers to the probability with which future events can be foreseen correctly. The higher this uncertainty, the lower the probability of finding the best (or an optimal) strategy as a countermeasure. How individuals cope with their problems under the constraints imposed by various socio-political and environmental factors are the topics of these different studies.

However, there still remains a certain confusion about the connotation and application of the term 'risk'. 'Risk(y)' and 'danger(ous)' are usually used interchangeably to describe specific situations, actions or decisions: for environmental phenomena synonymously with 'hazardous', to denote events such as floods, earthquakes and environmental pollution; for lifestyles with regard to specific foods or drugs; and even for interpersonal emotions and situations as for love, friendship and parenting (see for instance Lupton [1999a: 13f.], who identifies six such major categories of 'risk'). If everything can be more or less 'risky', then we need to know under which circumstances events can be classified or are interpreted as 'threatening' or 'dangerous'.

In principle as Luhmann (1990; 1991: 117; Luhmann 1996) pointed out, it is possible to differentiate between 'risk' and 'danger', because 'risks are decision related, while dangers arise externally'. However, the involvement of the decision-maker in the actual process of decision-making contradicts this hypothesis, since the risks the decision-maker takes in themselves constitute a danger for him. We are thus confronted with a classic social paradox: 'risks are dangers and dangers are risks because here we are dealing with the same factuality that is observed differentially, requiring the differentiation of both sides. The same is different' (Luhmann 1991: 117, translation mine).

To define or describe the phenomenon 'risk',[9] two very different approaches are usually used. One, the standardised and rigid 'scientific' Western definition based on contemporary insurance mathematics, which relates the term 'risk' to the probability of the amount of loss that results from a given event, or when a specific strategy has been decided upon (e.g. Farny 1995: 17ff.). The other, what Lupton (1999a: 35) referred to as a 'strong constructivist' epistemological position which holds, that 'Nothing is a risk in itself – what we understand to be a "risk" (or a hazard, threat or danger) is a product of historically, socially and politically contingent "ways of seeing"'. Labelling specific situations as 'threatening', 'risky' or 'dangerous' depends not only on the attributing individual's socio-cultural context, but also on his/her past experiences that were eventually embedded in situations comparable to the current one. As so often, a middle path seems to be the most useful; one that acknowledges that there are objective risks/dangers (related, for example, to basic human needs or life-threatening situations), but that these are often mediated differentially through individual, cultural and historical processes (cf. Lupton 1999a: 35; for the interrelationship of risk, culture and health see Harthorn and Oaks 2003).

Lupton's approach seems to be the most useful when attempting to understand decision-making and related behaviour in different cultures. This is not only because of the culturally different connotations of and attributions to 'risk' and 'danger', but also because of different value and norm relatedness. Thus, if we aspire to cross-cultural comparison, we must first enquire how situations that we would classify under the ambiguous term 'risky' are interpreted by different individuals in different cultural settings, and which terminology they apply to denote and connote the possible negative effects of different events (cf. Rohrmann 1994). The universal application of only contemporary politically and economically dominant Western concepts of risk and uncertainty in understanding the behaviour of peoples in all cultures and at all times in history is doomed to fail, since these concepts are closely related to current Western values and norms. What under comparable economic circumstances is considered a minor threat or loss by an individual in one group may be understood as a major one by someone elsewhere (see e.g., Spittler 1989a,b; cf. also Hill 1985). Therefore different risk perceptions in which 'reference is made to a judgement that there is a risk of a certain size at hand' (Sjöberg 1998: 85) have to be analysed, taking into account varying cultural, class- and gender-specific perceptions and attitudes. Fieldwork experience in the non-Western world also shows that many languages do not differentiate between a threatening situation per se (e.g., a hailstorm or a lion, which in English we may describe as 'dangerous') and a situation in which a decision has to be taken between alternative strategies, all of which we may consider more or less risky. In all these situations only one term may be used which can be glossed as 'danger' or 'dangerous'; many of the papers in this volume exemplify this pattern.

Every human behaviour has a differential effect: first, on some or all the other members of the group; second, on other human groups in this habitat; third, on the non-human animals and vegetation; and last but not least, on the inanimate factors, such as climate and soil quality. Some behaviour is explicitly directed towards changing an environment (e.g., deforestation, use of fertilisers, pesticides, etc.), other environmental changes are the result or outcome of enterprises designed/planned to fulfil primarily socio-political purposes (e.g., infrastructural developments like building roads, dams, etc.). In both cases, negative side-effects which change the environment usually take place, but are often nonetheless accepted as inevitable. Often such changes have an unexpectedly direct and negative influence on the actor's present or future well-being, leading to spirals of new actions and counteractions. The effects of an action taken by an individual to optimise his/her situation may also lead to more or less pronounced environmental changes which could be judged by him/her as negligible or unbearable. If such environmental side-effects are in great conflict with his/her environment-related moral sentiments, he/she may decide not to act in this manner again.

In recent years geographers (Kasperson et al. 1995) and psychologists have begun to empirically analyse human–environment interactions and the resulting problems. In psychology, socially mediated risk perceptions and evaluations (e.g., Böhm et al. 1998; Jungermann and Slovic 1993a,b; Pawlik 1991; Stern 1992; Yates and Stone 1992) often based on implicit causal hypotheses (e.g. Böhm and Mader 1998), social learning and institutional change in the environmental context (e.g., Breit et al. 2003) have been the focus of much research. 'Hazard', 'catastrophe' and 'disaster' are overwhelmingly anthropocentric categories which are largely culturally constructed (Hoffman and Oliver-Smith 2002; Jungermann and Slovic 1993a). However, the culture-specific appraisal of environmental degradation or environmental dangers like floods or droughts have received very little attention. The hazardous situation of the agropastoral communities in the Indian Thar Desert, for instance, which in many societies would be appraised as extremely dangerous, is understood there as fairly normal. Because of the high frequency of droughts; only extreme forms of deprivation are classified there as dangerous (Rao, pers. comm.). Indeed, the manner in which objectively precarious conditions are perceived by those who live in them as 'dangerous', and the degree to which an individual considers these as threatening often varies greatly from culture to culture, and within cultures, depending, for example, on what Amartya Sen (1990) referred to as the issue of 'human capabilities'.

The dangers people are exposed to and the risk they face in a given environment are indeed twofold. On the one hand they face more or less recurrent and hence relatively predictable hazards – recurring droughts, floods, earthquakes, etc. On the other hand they are more or less exposed to such events, depending on the political, social and economic circumstances under which they live. Such circumstances structure the safe or unsafe conditions which make people more or less vulnerable to these hazards and dangers (Hilhorst and Bankoff 2004). Therefore, to understand why disasters occur, Blaikie et al (1994: 2) explained that 'it is not only the natural events that cause them. They are also products of social, political, and economic environments (as distinct from the natural environments) because of the way they structure the lives of different groups of people.'

No wonder that usually it is the poorer and often suppressed part of society which suffers most when natural catastrophes occur. Another major and largely neglected aspect of risk, danger and disaster is the political use of their apparent inevitability, especially given the impact of globalisation on vulnerable populations (see Oliver-Smith 2004 for an interesting discussion; also Robbins 2004; Zimmerer and Bassett 2003). Barbara Casciarri's chapter here focuses on this issue in the changing environmental conditions in six oases of southeastern Morocco. She shows how variously the all-pervasive disaster of drought is perceived here, and talked about by farmers, pastoralists, religious specialists and ex-slaves in this region that lies on the old caravan route from Timbuktu. Her analysis brings out the multi-levelled perception and discourse regarding the assumed inevitability of the lack of water – a lack largely exacerbated by the Moroccan state's water policies.

Information and Transaction Costs in a Changing World

Today, with the individual everywhere hedged in by the increasing pressures of the forces of globalisation, local concepts and perceptions, however meaningful, are becoming more and more marginalised. Regional and global policies affecting local decision-making have also multiplied, and with this, the transaction costs involved in developing optimal strategies to solve long-term problems. But more often than not, individuals lack considerable information and are hence not in a position to understand the functioning of the various new systems and subsystems with which they have to cope. The complex yet largely familiar systemic intermeshing of factors with which they dealt under more 'traditional' conditions have now mutated into hyper-complex probabilistic systems, which they have great difficulty in managing. Under such circumstances much 'indigenous knowledge', and many of the 'traditional culture-specific' strategies with low transaction costs, can no longer be used singly to solve the problems that arise with relatively sudden economic, socio-political and environmental change. New coping strategies are either not yet devised or, if they are available, there is not enough information on their functioning and application.

This lack of information also leads to a high degree of uncertainty[10]. People may be afraid of taking the wrong decision because they are reluctant to run the risk of applying a new strategy whose effects and outcomes they cannot yet estimate. Such situations can be witnessed in a variety of contemporary contexts undergoing drastic processes of transformation in the Southern Hemisphere and in the societies of the ex-Soviet Republics (Hann 2002; Finke 2004).

But such uncertainty is equally evident in many highly industrialised and capitalist Western contexts where, for example, there has been growing insecurity among farmers in recent years. The public in many Western countries has become increasingly concerned with issues concerning the safety of foodstuffs (Gewin 2004; Stokstad 2002; Woodward 2002). Soil conservation, which 'remains firmly ... at the foundations of human life' (McNeill and Winiwarter 2004), the conservation of microfauna and the prevention of erosion can be better attained by organic farming or by combining organic and traditional methods (Macilwain 2004; Mäder et al. 2002). However, better quality can be attained only with a higher labour input and this usually leads to higher pricing, therefore organic foods usually cost much more than those produced by conventional methods using artificial fertilisers, pesticides and even genetically manipulated seeds. As Döring et al. show in this volume, German farmers who decide to use organic methods are more insecure about the success of their undertaking and about the development of market prices, especially because the distribution networks for the sale of their produce are not yet well organised.

Global Concerns and Human Behaviour

With increasing environment-related problems over the last few decades, the overall interest in a 'Human Ecology' has grown and, together with the rise of environmental consciousness, the environmental sciences are now focusing not only on local problems, but are also trying to link these to the global situation. The best known and constantly discussed example is the interrelation between the depletion of the ozone layer (cf. Anderson and Sarma 2002) through FCKW (FH) and related compounds, the increasing production of CO_2 leading to the greenhouse effect and global warming, and the threat of the rising seas (for an overview see Walther et al. 2002). It was primarily with the 1987 'Montreal Protocol on Substances that Deplete the Ozone Layer' (and the 'Club of Rome' 1992) that global ecological consciousness rose. 'Think global and act local' now became one of the slogans created to make people aware of the pressing ecological problems and disasters we are all facing.

The possibility of solving pressing global problems is, however, more often than not blocked by a variety of economic and political interests. A well-known example is the problem of reaching an international agreement on the reduction of CO_2 emissions. The excessive emission of harmful substances that cross national boundaries and the disasters caused by tanker accidents in offshore waters are examples related to the well known 'Tragedy of the Commons' and the problem of 'free riding'. Many governments, even when they are aware of their pressing environmental problems, are so preoccupied with economic, defence and political problems that the environment comes as a late or no topic at all on the political and fiscal agenda. Thus, for example, in December 1997 the U.S.A. refused for economic reasons to sign the Kyoto Protocol (International Climate Policy for the Twenty-first Century), although it emits almost one-fourth of the world's greenhouse gases (Harris 1997: 269). Similarly, in the recent 'United Nations Water Development Report' (*Water for People, Water for Life*), India figures third-worst in a list of 122 countries regarding the pollution of its rivers, the availability and quality of drinking water, and its ability and commitment to improve the situation. The environment simply does not figure as a topic in the annual budget for 2003, which allocates US$ 100 billion over the next ten years for the purchase of weapon systems (Kumar 2003: 13). Economics and politics have always played a role in environmental management at the global level. The recent international competition for selling tsunami warning systems well illustrates this. Even 'aid' given for disaster relief is taken from the funds routinely set apart for 'development assistance' by rich countries.

Even when international environmental agreements are reached, the question remains of how these agreements match local perceptions of environmental crises and preferred local coping strategies. This crucial question is considered by Anita Engels in her chapter here. Examining the case of a coastal zone in Senegal, she argues that there is a large gap between global resource management schemes stemming from international environmental agreements and the heterogeneous perceptions and coping strategies of the local population. Using the example of the Framework Convention on Climate Change (FCCC), she shows how a variety of different coping strategies is narrowed down to one dominant coping model. Also, the way in which the use of resources is linked to gender is made invisible by this dominant model, which provides a technical and cost-benefit-oriented approach. Even more importantly, she argues that different international environmental agreements develop diverging and sometimes contradictory schemes of global resource management.

Political Ecology and the Quest for Sustainable Development

The human-environment interface and the problems of environmental degradation were of little concern to sociologists of the mid-nineteenth and early twentieth centuries. As Goldblatt (1996: 2–6) notes, their references to the 'natural world' were too unspecific, and factors such as population density were seen only as a driving force of human history and a motor for social stratification. Their knowledge of biological and ecological facts was rather limited. While Durkheim, for example, rejected all forms of biological explanation and branded these as deterministic, Weber denied the importance of psychological and physiological explanations. Culture-specific cognitions, which we now know are of major importance for the way we understand the environment and react to environmental problems, were simply ignored (see in this volume Böhm and Pfister; Döring et al; Hoeppe). Even Marx, who saw 'labour' as the key variable that mediated between the natural world and human societies, never discussed the interdependence between the various factors. Hawley (1984: 914) was right in observing that 'a greater sensitivity to environmental effects could have enriched Marxian theory, just as a further development of the political-economic implications of its theory can raise the explanatory power of human ecology'. Modern sociologists such as Giddens (1990), Luhmann (1985) and notably Beck (1992; Beck 2000) have now dealt intensely, but mainly theoretically (cf. Grundmann 1999) with the relationship between modern technology, science, environmental degradation, social institutions and political power; for a critical evaluation of Beck's 'Risk Society' see Adams (1995: 179ff.) and Adam et al. (2000). These different approaches try to find an answer to why both socialist and capitalist political institutions failed to solve the environmental problems which they partly created, and most of them discuss different social theories and their approaches to environmental degradation. As Goldblatt concludes (1996: 202f.):

> We know that environmental degradation is dangerous. We know that we cannot go on as before. But how to go on, how to live individually and collectively, how to make the transition soon and how to persuade the intransigent, the selfish, the powerful and the uninterested? These are the questions that neither classical

socialism nor contemporary social theory have provided sufficient intellectual or moral resources to answer.

In the late 1970s and 1980s many geographers, and notably researchers working in the field of Development Studies (e.g. Blaikie 1985; Blaikie and Brookfield 1987; Kent 1987; Robbins 2004) analysed the interdependence between political structures, economy, ecological catastrophes, disasters and human suffering (for an excellent case study see Upham 1987). They argued that a better understanding of human and cultural ecology can be obtained only on a broad interdisciplinary basis that considers political power relations in a wider theoretical framework (e.g. Bryant 1998; Bryant and Bailey 1997; Drèze and Sen 1990; Escobar 1996; Escobar 1998). This political ecology approach argued that only by analysing the various complex regional interdependencies between political institutions, economic systems and ecological conditions, and by applying measures to counter degradation, can pressing global environmental problems eventually also be tackled in the quest for sustainable global development in which both the economy and the environment are in a state of resilient equilibrium (Engels and Moss 2003; Mitchell 2003).

But critics have argued that here, again, this is only one side of the medal and that political ecology tends to neglect the 'natural' side in the analysis of disasters (e.g. Vayda and Walters 1999; see also McCabe 2005: 240). Only with the increasing influence on state policy of local and international environmental institutions representing the broadest possible constituencies can the local and regional antagonisms between political, economic and environmental goals on the one hand and global ecological concerns on the other be bridged. To this end changes are necessary in the many formal and informal institutions, in rules and social practices (see also Little 1999). This is perhaps especially true in the rapidly urbanising context of many societies. In their paper Krüger and Grotzke focus on this issue in the context of the changing characteristics of risk perception and coping in rapidly transforming rural Botswana. Their data show that households tend to rely increasingly on national relief, and expect the government to intervene in times of drought. Traditionally successful coping and adaptive measures, which included rural-urban linkages, are being forgotten. Government concepts of relief also tend to ignore the importance of such linkages as a safety-net for vulnerable urban groups. With the state attempting to stabilise endangered livelihood systems by introducing national welfare schemes, local perceptions and concepts of risk, drought, livelihood insecurity and destitution, as well as coping strategies and certain adaptive measures, are now being either complemented or even partly replaced by new mechanisms of risk management, which are, however, not unproblematic.

Approaching Equilibrium – Sustainability Again

As discussed earlier, individuals of all species try continuously – consciously or unconsciously and in accordance with their capacities – to accommodate and adapt to their ever-changing social and environmental situations in order to enhance well-being. Thus understood as systems, environments and the habitats of all species and communities are in constant flux. These systems may theoretically approach a state of equilibrium swinging to and fro over short spans for briefer or longer periods of time, and for moments even reach a steady state (cf. Foin and Davis 1987). If some environmental variables, understood as disturbances, reach a certain level, some 'players' (species or groups) may leave their habitat, become drastically reduced in numbers and/or some invaders may occupy the now empty or new niches. The system may then exceed its resilient capacity and transform to a state with a different structure and some new interdependent functions, and move around a new equilibrium. In extreme cases, events which change the system affect a human population in such a way that they are experienced as a disaster, and the well-being of the majority declines drastically.

Continuing with the 'ecosystem approach' (e.g., Moran 1990), what is now termed the 'new ecological thinking' 'has become the study of "disturbance, disharmony, and chaos" (Worster 1990: 3). According to geographer Karl Zimmerer the "new ecology" accents disequilibria, instability, and even chaotic fluctuations in biophysical environments, both "natural" and "human impacted" (1994: 108)' (McCabe 2005: 4–5). However, here again the question of the observational time-scale arises. It is only in times of drastic environmental changes, when whole populations (human and non-human) are suddenly threatened, that we can speak of a 'non-equilibrium ecosystem', of 'disturbance' and even call it chaotic. Long term changes of the 'natural' environment are only detectable in retrospect. If, for instance, a biotope slowly, say in some hundred years, changes its species composition due to an invader, we would find a 'harmonious' intermeshing of species tied together in a more or less complex food-web.

The notion of equilibrium brings us to a second notion, that of 'sustainability'. This was one of the keywords used at the 'United Nations Conference on Environment and Development' (UNCED), or 'Earth Summit', held in Rio in June 1992. Chapter 13 of Agenda 21 as approved in Rio deals with the management of fragile ecosystems, especially highly endangered mountain systems of the world. The text for this chapter was drafted by the International Centre for Integrated Mountain Development (ICIMOD 1992: 1, cf. also Ives 1993); Programme B states that its objectives are: 'to promote income-generating activities; such as sustainable tourism, fisheries, and environmentally-sound mining, and to improve infrastructure and social services; to protect the livelihood of local communities and indigenous peoples'.

The term 'sustainability' was, however, not defined either at Rio, or on any other occasion by any institution. Indeed, the term has been used at various times with varied connotations, and as Lélé (1991: 613, see also Lélé 1996) comments, it has become 'a "metafix" that will unite everybody'. It often carries with it the vague implication of an even vaguer state of being 'in harmony with nature' (Murdoch and Clark 1994).

In the fields of economics, ecology and resource management, expressions such as 'sustainable development', 'sustained yields', 'optimum sustainable yield' or 'maximum sustained yield' are commonly used, but as Kalinin and Boykov (1972: 361) remarked, 'The general goal of management of a biological resource is maximum sustained yield, a nebulous term at the very best'. They went on to explain:

> Maximum sustained yield implies the removal of production from a stock over and above that needed to replace the amount removed. Theoretically, for maximum yield the standing crop at harvest time should be the maximum biomass the ecosystem will support. Harvest or removal takes the population down to a level at which the amount removed can be replaced by the remaining stock by the next harvest period. But in practice the maximum sustained yield is quite variable depending upon the size of breeding stock, or principal, the exploiter is willing to allow to remain. The maximum sustained yield then depends upon the size of the principal. The lower the principal, the lower the sustained yield, generally. What constitutes a low principal is, of course, highly dependent upon the biology of the ... species involved. (Kalinin and Bykov 1972: 361)

In the case of coastal fish populations for example, the new laws and regulatory devices which aim at solving the problems of over-exploitation 'require that fisheries be managed for attainment of what is called Optimum Sustainable Yield (OSY); that is, the most you can take and still maintain the fish stock'. But Bennett (1990: 446f.) pointed out that however benign the goals,

> the law itself made no attempt to define Optimum Sustainable Yield for the simple reason that no one knew how to define it or what types of data to include in the definition. Nor was there any systematic attempt to define the human institutions and activity patterns which modify the physical circumstances.

Even a 'simple' relationship between a single predator and a single prey is complex. No wonder, then, that the idea inherent in the term 'sustainability' – that of maintaining, if possible infinitely, an equilibrium between all populations in a biotope or habitat (cf. Gurung 1993) – is so highly problematic. It implies that the various populations at the different trophic levels, which interact with one another in an ecosystem forming a highly complex food-web, must remain more or less stable in a climax situation. It is of course impossible to reach a state in which all the species involved remain for long in such equilibrium that mortality does not exceed natality, or vice versa. Such an hypothetical state would consolidate a system in which no change would – and from a human point of view should – take place, once the homeostatic goal had been reached. Alternatively, if one 'player' in the game changed, all the other 'players' involved would as rapidly as possible have to change their strategies in such a way, that they would 'co-evolve' (Norgaard 1992), and thus with the least effort homeostasis would once again be attained. This would imply either that the human populations concerned would remain stable and no cultural change would take place, or that every cultural change and innovation would be accompanied by management strategies which counterbalanced all the possible negative effects on all the other populations involved. Hence a definition of sustainability such as that advanced by Viederman (1993: 179) must remain a completely unrealistic concept:

> A sustainable society ensures the health and vitality of human life and culture and of nature, for present and future generations, by *ending* activities that destroy human life and culture and nature, by *conserving* what exists, *restoring* what has been damaged, and *preventing* future harm.' (italics in original)

Even this all embracing definition distinguishes between human life and 'nature', and indeed all existing discourse on 'sustainability' and 'sustainable development' has basically only the well-being of human populations in mind, all other species being protected not for their own sake, but only in so far as they are important factors in supporting human life and well-being. The Brundlandt report, for example, states that 'Sustainable development is development that meets the needs of the present without compromising the ability of future generations to meet their own needs.' (WECD 1987: 43). There is, however, no attempt here to differentiate between the terms 'needs' and 'basic needs', and furthermore no effort has been made to distinguish either of these from 'wants', which are often culture-specific. In an even shorter version, the report of the World Bank (WBR 1992: 8) offers the following definitions:

1. Development is about improving the well-being of people,
2. Sustainable development is development that lasts.

The general problem with all such highly generalising definitions is that they are based on fairly static concepts (for dynamic approaches Lance et al. 2002). The well-being aimed at must of course be directly linked to 'needs' and 'wants', but both are related to changing norms and values which vary not only over time, but also between societies, ethnic and religious communities, class, gender and age groups. Reducing 'needs' to 'basic needs' would a priori deny many populations their culture-specific wants, and these have indeed been neglected and disregarded far too often as irrelevant, if not outright irrational in the eurocentric development concepts inaugurated by Western aid organisations and faithfully followed by national policies in the countries of both the North and the South (Sen 1990). Furthermore, the well-being of an individual or group can not be conceived of as a final state that can be reached, but as a goal which must be constantly redefined under the constraints of ever-changing local and global circumstances. Each developmental step which leads to attaining a desired goal opens up the prospect of new goals, with the promise of even higher levels of conceivable well-being.

Until now, humans seem rarely to have been able to disregard possible changes which promise them improvement, even if these are at the cost of other humans, let alone non-human populations. However, if we start at the local level and try to reach the possible, any discussion of sustainability must begin, as Haripriya Rangan (2000: 191) suggests in her history of the Chipko movement of the Garhwal Himalayas,

> by addressing the regional question of improved access to resources and social well-being in the *present continuous*, and not as a state that might be restored by return to an idyllic past or miraculously created in the distant future. Sustainability needs to be redefined in terms of social practices that enable the continuation of the lived dimensions of social life through diverse pathways that are open-ended and changeable.

Such open-endedness could question the generalised goal wherein a socio-political system strives for the 'maximum happiness of the maximum number of people'; it could imply a constant search for a steady state between the changing 'lived dimension of the social life' and the changing environment. Until now, however, humans as hedonists (Phillips 2003) seem to have striven more often towards a maximum, and tended to overexploit the environment's use-value. We have a long way to go before we understand that, as Hardin's aphorism goes: 'the maximum is not the optimum' (quoted after Easterbrook 2003). This would lead to a new paradigm by which we would strive for 'optimal happiness for the optimal number of people'. This optimal number must be understood in relation to the possible sustainability of as many individuals in human and non-human populations as possible. We cannot hope that the means for such an end will develop 'automatically' by an evolutionary process. Sustainability, with its different dimensions (cf. Stirling 1999) can only be approached by the formulation of a set of open-ended laws, based on a non-anthropocentric moral. These general laws have to comprise rules by which they can be adapted to solve specific local environmental problems which emerge from the constant interplay of the culture-specific 'lived dimension of the social life' and the 'non-human environment'.

Conclusion: Sustaining Biodiversity and Human Well-Being

As mentioned earlier, the promoters of nature conservation and 'sustainability', who have written the intrinsic value of (rare) plants and animals on their banner, often find themselves in opposition to local communities of land users. Also, many of them, especially biologists, who fight for the sustainability of biodiversity, do not integrate or consult local communities in the planning process of their projects and thus at least appear implicitly opposed to all those who are concerned with the well-being of present and future human generations. Yet it is clear that 'Conservation is about people as much as it is about species or ecosystems' (Bawla et al. 2004; Mascia et al. 2003: 1; in Berkes 2003: 94; for an overview see O'Riordan et al. 2002).

There is, of course, a logical link between the terms 'development', 'sustainability' and 'conservation'. Most descriptions and definitions of these terms, however, take into account only the anthropocentric human use-value (Dasgupta 2001: 124). Thus, for instance, 'development' was defined by the IUCN (1980) as:

> the modification of the biosphere and the application of human, financial, living and non living resources *to satisfy human needs and improve the quality of human life.* For development to be sustainable it must take account of social and ecological factors, as well as economic ones; of the living and non-living resource base; and of long term as well as the short term advantages and disadvantages of alternative actions [italics mine].

Similarly, for Kasperson et al. (1995: 25) 'sustainability', specially 'ecological sustainability'

> refers to situations in which nature-society relations are so structured that the environment can *support the continuation of human use-systems, the level of human well-being,* and the preservation of options for future generations over long time-periods [italics mine].

Along much the same lines, 'conservation' was defined by the IUCN (1980) as

> *the management of human use of the biosphere so that it may yield the greatest sustainable benefit* to present generations while maintaining its potential to meet the needs and aspirations of future generations. Thus conservation is positive, embracing preservation, maintenance, sustainable utilisation, restoration, and enhancement of the natural environment … [italics mine].

The term 'environmental degradation' is equally or primarily related to its negative effects on human well-being. Other populations are explicitly or implicitly taken into account only for their utilitarian and sometimes aesthetic value (cf. Goldblatt 1996: 28). But from a non-anthropocentric and perhaps ethical point of view we must enlarge our perspective and include in our ideal of 'sustainable development' also the demand for the intrinsic value and well-being of all (other) species. We would then be obliged to reformulate our anthropocentric ethics towards an universal one somewhat along the lines of Albert Schweitzer who, as early as in 1931, observed that

The great mistake of all past ethics is, that they felt that they had to deal only with the behaviour of humans towards other humans ... Ethical is only he for whom life as such, that of plants and animals as of humans, is holy ... Only the universal ethic of an experience of responsibility which is enlarged into the indefinite responsibility for everything alive can be grounded in thought [translation mine].[11]

Sadly, however, such an universal ethic alone, even if it could be applied, will not be sufficient to preserve biodiversity. We as humans often prefer smaller, immediate returns over larger ones that are deferred (Fehr 2002), and therefore tend to avoid behaviours without any noticeable (and possibly altruistic) benefits. If we wish to preserve ourselves and as many of the millions of other species living on our planet as possible, we must take into account 'human nature' and the necessary fulfilment of our basic needs, as well as our culture-specific wants. But we must, especially in the West, develop cultures, in which changed norms and values counterbalance the expectations of ever-growing 'progress'. The political and economic strategies of present Western systems, leading to further North–South iniquities and the continuing exploitation and deprivation of the nations of the Southern Hemisphere, are one of the main reasons for the ongoing overexploitation of natural resources and the deterioration of many environments (e.g., Ehrenfeld 2003; Kothari and Ahmad 2003; Thaler 2004). Terms of fair trade are one of the major factors which can lead to the growth of well-being in these countries, finally also curbing the extremely high demographic growth-rates, which are among the key variables that cause many local ecological crises that further exacerbate the global ecological situation. We must above all consider the nature and degree to which formal, institutional definitions of human development, environmental change, sustainability and well-being (seek to) legitimise the interests of the politically and economically powerful and then try and redefine these based on the broadest possible consensus. Then, and only then do we also have a chance of ending the current continuous increase in human poverty and conflict that is accompanied by loss of biodiversity and of entire biotopes.

Notes

1. 'Was den Menschen umgibt, wirkt nicht allein auf ihn, er wirkt auch wieder zurück auf selbiges, und indem er sich modifizieren lässt, modifiziert er wieder rings um sich her.'
2. We may distinguish between cultural traits which are based on cognitive and behavioural innovations that are passed on over the generations and traits and capacities that are based solely on mutations, selection and adaptation. We should, however, remember that the ability to develop cultural capacities found in humans and in some higher non-human primates is also a product of the process of 'natural' evolution.
3. Much earlier attempts to question this, for example by the eighteenth century French mathematician Dupuis, did not go far (cf. Schama 1996: 250ff.).
4. Dramatic environmental events, long viewed from an exclusively anthropocentric perspective, are gradually being classified as 'disasters' and perceived more biocentrically. The *Exxon Valdes* and other oil spills and the mass destruction of avian species in the Persian Gulf during the first Gulf War are two examples.
5. This is true also of religions and philosophies which are said to be concerned with non-violence in general (see e.g., Cort 2002).
6. The comparison of royal gardens, parks and specific landscapes with 'Paradise' is ancient. Aelian (Claudius Aelianus) refers to such domains in India and Iran (Hughes 1998: 82ff.) and Inden (forthcoming) discusses similar traditions within South Asia.
7. See, for example, Kuper 2003 for a critical discussion of the term 'indigenous peoples'.
8. I am aware of the problems involved in using the terms 'rational' and 'irrational'. If logical thinking is defined as based on a search for cause-effect relations, then the connotation 'irrational' makes little sense. For the believer, an 'act of God', or of demons, is as causal and logical as the law of gravitation is for a physicist. The distinction here should connote both kinds of logic.
9. The origin of the English term 'risk' and its French and German equivalents is not clear. They could stem from the Arabic '*rizq*' or the Persian '*ruzi*', which denote those gifts from God which sustain life and daily food respectively (cf. Ashbaghi 1988: 135). Alternatively, they may derive from the Greek word '*risikón*' denoting a rock or a cliff which threatens the sailor and his ship. Meaning 'danger' and 'daring', *risico, risco* emerged in middle-Italian and *arsisco, risgo* in Spanish (cf. Lokotsch 1927; Schulz/Basler 1977: 452–53). It seems that the ambivalence of the term – intrinsic or decision-related danger – arose only with the onset of modernity (cf. Bauman 1993: 1ff.) when it came to be used, from the sixteenth century, among merchants to also denote the dangers inherent in decision-making.
10. For a detailed discussion of the different types of uncertainty (known, unknown and unknowable) and their influence on decisions see Chua Chow and Sarin 2002.
11. 'Der große Fehler aller bisherigen Ethik ist, daß sie es nur mit dem Verhalten des Menschen zum Menschen zu tun zu haben glaubt … Ethisch ist er nur, wenn ihm das Leben als solches, das der Pflanzen und der Tiere wie das des Menschen heilig ist … Nur die universelle Ethik des Erlebens der ins Grenzenlose erweiterten Verantwortung gegen alles, was lebt, läßt sich im Denken begründen …' (Albert Schweitzer 1931).

References

Acheson, James M. 2003. *Capturing the Commons. Devising Institutions to Manage the Maine Lobster Industry.* London: University Press of New England.

Adam, Barbara, Ulrich Beck and Joost van Loon, eds. 2000. *The Risk Society and Beyond.* London: Sage.

Adams, John 1995. *Risk.* London: Routledge.

Aglionby, John 2005. '"Good Muslims" Survived Tsunami Claim the Fundamentalists', *The Guardian*, 8 January 2005.

Alvard, Michael S. 1993. 'Testing the "Ecologically Noble Savage" Hypothesis: Interspecific Prey Choice by Piro Hunters of Amazonian Peru', *Human Ecology* 21(4): 355ff.

Anderson, Stephen O. and K. Madhava Sarma 2002. *Protecting the Ozone Layer – The United Nations History.* London: Earthscan, U.K. United Nations Environment Programme (UNEP).

Anglás Grande, S.M. 1999. 'Beyond the Ecologically Noble Savage: Deconstructing the White Man's Indian', *Environmental Ethics* 2(3): 307–20.

Århem, Kay 1984. 'Another Side of Development: Maasai Pastoralism and Wildlife Conservation in Ngorongoro, Tanzania', *Ethnos* 49: iii–iv.

——— 1985. *Pastoral Man in the Garden of Eden: The Maasai of Ngorongoro Conservation Area, Tanzania.* Uppsala: Scandinavian Institute of African Studies.

Asbaghi, Asya 1988. *Persische Lehnwörter im Arabischen.* Wiesbaden: Otto Harrassowitz.

Azarya, V. 1996. 'Pastoralism and the State in Africa: Marginality or Incorporation?', *Nomadic Peoples* 38: 11–36.

Bandyopadhyay, Jayanta and Shama Perveen. 2004. 'Interlinking of Rivers in India. Assessing the Justifications', *Economic and Political Weekly* XXXIX(50): 5307–16.

Barnosky, Anthony D. et al. 2004. 'Assessing the Cause of Late Pleistocene Extinction on the Continents', *Science* 306: 70–75.

Bauman, Zygmunt 1993 (repr. 1998). *Modernity and Ambivalence.* Cambridge: Polity Press.

Bavadam, Lyla 2004. 'Water and Votes', *Frontline*, 21 May: 102–3.

Baviskar, Amita 1995. *In the Belly of the River: Tribal Conflicts over Development in the Narmada Valley.* Delhi: Oxford University Press.

——— 2003. 'For a Cultural Politics of Natural Resources', *Economic and Political Weekly* XXXVIII(48): 5051–55.

Bawla, Kamaljit S. et al. 2004. 'Tropical Ecosystems into the 21st Century', *Science* 306: 227–8.

Beck, Ullrich 1992. *Risk Society: Towards a New Modernity.* London: Sage.

——— 2000. 'Risk Society Revisited: Theory, Politics and Research Programmes', in *The Risk Society and Beyond*, eds. Barbara Adam, Ulrich Beck, Ulrich and Joost van Ioon, 210–29. London: Sage Publications.

Bellwood, Peter 2001. 'Early Agriculturalist Population Diasporas? Farming, Language, and Genes', *Annual Review of Anthropology* 30: 181–207.

Bennett, J.W. 1976. *The Ecological Transition. Cultural Anthropology and Human Adaptation.* New York: Pergamon Press.

——— 1990. 'Ecosystems, Environmentalism, Resource Conservation, and Anthropological Research', in *The Ecosystem Approach in Anthropology*, ed. E.F. Moran, 435–57. Ann Arbor: The University of Michigan Press.

Bennett, S. 1984. 'Shikar and the Raj', *South Asia*, n.s. VII(2): 72–88.

Berkes, Fikret 2003. Comment on: Hunn et al. 2003, 'Huna Tlingit Traditional Knowledge, Conservation, and the Management of a "Wilderness" Park`, *Current Anthropology* 44 (Supplement): 94–5.

Berkoff, J. 2003. 'China: The South-North Water Transfer Project – Is it Justified?' *Water Policy* 5(1): 1–28.

Binde, Per 2000. 'Nature in Roman Catholic Tradition', *Anthropological Quarterly* 74(1): 15–27.

Bird, Michael I. 1995. 'Fire, Prehistoric Humanity, and the Environment', *Interdisciplinary Science Reviews* 20(2): 141–54.

Blackburn, Tim M. et al. 2004. 'Avian Extinction and Mammalian Introductions on Oceanic Islands', *Science* 305: 1955–60.

Blaikie, Piers M. 1985. *The Political Economy of Soil Erosion in Developing Countries.* London: Longman.

——— and Harold C. Brookfield 1987. *Land Degradation and Society.* London: Methuen.

———, Terry Cannon, Ian Davis and Ben Wisner 1994. *A Risk. Natural Hazards, Peoples' Vulnerability, and Disaster.* London: Routledge.

Böhm, Gisela, Jürgen Rost and Hans Spada 1998. 'Psychologische Aspekte von Umweltrisiken', *Zeitschrift für Experimentelle Psychologie* 45(4): 243–50.

——— and Sabine Mader 1998. 'Subjektive kausale Szenarien globaler Umweltveränderungen', *Zeitschrift für Experimentelle Psychologie* 45(4): 270–85.

——— and Hans-Rüdiger Pfister 2000. 'Action Tendencies and Characteristics of Environmental Risks', *Acta Psychologica* 104: 317–37.

Boholm, Åsa 2003. 'The Cultural Nature of Risk: Can there be an Anthropology of Uncertainty?' *Ethos* 68: 159–78.

Bökönyi, S. 1976. 'Development of Early Stock Rearing in the Near East', *Nature* 264: 19–23.

Breit, Heiko et al. eds. 2003. *How Institutions Change. Perspectives on Social Learning in Global and Local Environmental Contexts.* Opladen: Leske & Budrich.

Brockington, Dan and Katherine Homewood 2001. 'Degradation Debates and Data Deficiencies: The Mkomazi Game Reserve, Tanzania', *Africa* 71(3): 449–80.

Broughton, Jack M. 2003. Comment on: Hunn et al. 2003; 'Huna Tlingit Traditional Knowledge, Conservation, and the Management of a "Wilderness" Park', *Current Anthropology* 44 (Supplement): 95.

Bryant, Raymond L. 1998. 'Power, Knowledge and Political Ecology in the Third World: A Review', *Progress in Physical Geography* 22(1): 79–94.

——— and Sinéad Bailey 1997. *Third World Political Ecology.* London: Routledge.

Bunn, D. and M. Auslander 1999. 'Owning the Kruger Park. The Arts, Culture and Heritage Guide to South Africa', *Arts* 1999: 60–3.

Burke, Bryan E. 2001. 'Hardin Revisited: A Critical Look at Perception and the Logic of the Commons', *Human Ecology* 29(4): 449–76.

Butzer, K.W. 1992. 'The Americas Before and After 1492: An Introduction to Current Geographical Research', *Annals of the Association of American Geographers* 82(3): 345–68.

Caplan, Pat, ed. 2000. *Risk Revisited.* London: Pluto Press.

Carruthers, J. 1995. *The Kruger National Park. A Social and Political History.* Pietermartitzburg: University of Natal Press.

Carson, Rachel 1962. *Silent Spring.* Boston: Houghton Mifflin.

Cashdan, Elizabeth, ed. 1990. *Risk and Uncertainty in Tribal and Peasant Economies.* Boulder: Westview Press.

Casimir, Michael J. 1987. 'In Search of Guilt: Legends on the Origin of the Peripatetic Niche', in *The Other Nomads. Peripatetic Minorities in Cross-Cultural Context*, ed. A. Rao, 373–90. Cologne: Böhlau Verlag.

——— 1992a. 'The Dimensions of Territoriality: An Introduction', in *Mobility and Territoriality. Social and Spatial Boundaries among Foragers, Fishers, Pastoralists and Peripatetics*, eds. M.J. Casmir and A. Rao, 1–26. Oxford: Berg.

——— 1992b. 'The Determinants of Rights to Pasture: Territorial Organisation and Ecological Constraints', in *Mobility and Territoriality. Social and Spatial Boundaries among Foragers, Fishers, Pastoralists and Peripatetics*, eds. M.J. Casmir and A. Rao, 153–203. Oxford: Berg.

——— 1994. 'Mitwelt oder Umwelt. Kulturökologie im Spannungsfeld zwischen Romantik und Wissenschaft', in *Zusammenhänge. Ureinwohner und Industrienationen, Infoestudien* (Special Issue), eds. M. Jarnuszak and F. Kressing, 9: 17–28.

——— 2001. 'Of Lions, Herders and Conservationists: Brief Notes on the Gir Forest National Park in Gujarat (Western-India)', in *Environment, Property Resources and the State, Nomadic Peoples* (Special Issue), eds. L. Lenhart and M.J. Casmir, 5(2): 154–62.

——— 2002. 'Pastoral Nomadism in a West Himalayan Valley: Sustainability and Herd Management', in *Nomadism in South Asia*, eds. A. Rao and M.J. Casimir, 81–103. Oxford in India, Readings in Sociology and Social and Cultural Anthropology. Delhi: Oxford University Press.

——— 2003 'Pastoral Nomadism in a West Himalayan Valley: Sustainability and Herd Management', in *Nomadism in South Asia*, eds. A. Rao and M.J. Casmir, 81–103. Delhi: Oxford University Press.

——— 2004 '"Once upon a Time ...": Reconciling the Stranger', in *Customary Strangers: New Perspectives on Peripatetic Peoples in the Middle East, Africa and Asia*, eds. J.C. Berland and A. Rao, 31–54. Westport, CT.: Praeger.

——— and Aparna Rao 1998. 'Sustainable Herd Management and the Tragedy of No Man's Land: An Analysis of West Himalayan Pastures Using Remote Sensing Techniques', *Human Ecology* 26(1): 113–34.

Chakrabarty, Dipesh 1991. 'Open Space/Public Place: Garbage, Modernity and India', *South Asia* XIV(1): 15–31.

Chua Chow, Clare and Rakesh Sarin 2002. 'Known, Unknown, and Unknowable Uncertainties', *Theory and Decision* 52(2): 127–38.

Colchester, M. 1997. 'Salvaging Nature: Indigenous Peoples and Protected Areas', in *Social Change and Conservation: Environmental Politics and Impacts of National Parks and Protected Areas*, eds. K.B. Ghimire and M.P. Pimbert, 97–130. London: Earthscan Publications Limited and UNRISD.

Colinvaux, P.A. 1982. 'Towards a Theory of History: Fitness, Niche and Clutch of Homo sapiens', *Journal of Ecology* 70: 393–412.

Conyngham Green, Kathleen 1932. *The English Landscape in Pictures, Prose and Poetry.* London: Ivor Nicholson & Watson, Ltd.

Cort, John E. 2002. 'Green Jainism? Notes and Queries toward a Possible Jain Environmental Ethic', in *Jainism and Ecology: Nonviolence in the Web of Life*, ed. C.K. Chapple, 63–94. Cambridge (Mass.): Harvard University Press.

Crowther-Heyck, Kathleen 2003. 'Wonderful Secrets of Nature. Natural Knowledge and Religious Piety in Reformation Germany', *Isis* 94(2): 253–73.

Csordas, T., ed. 1994. *Embodiment and Experience. The Existential Ground of Culture and Self.* Cambridge: Cambridge University Press.

Damasio, A.R. 1994. *Descartes' Error: Emotion, Reason, and the Human Brain.* New York: Grosset/Putnam.

Dasgupta, Partha 2001. *Human Well-Being and the Natural Environment.* New Delhi: Oxford University Press.

Delaney, David 2001. 'Making Nature/Marking Humans: Law as a Site of (Cultural) Production', *Annals of the Association of American Geographers* 91(3): 487–503.

Denevan, W.M. 1992. 'The Pristine Myth: The Landscape of the Americas in 1492', *Annals of the Association of American Geographers* 82(3): 369–85.

Dieckmann, Andreas and Peter Preisendörfer 1994. 'Wasser Predigen, Wein trinken. Warum unser Engagement für die Umwelt oft nur ein Lippenbekenntnis ist', *Psychologie Heute* (May 1994): 22–7.

Dieckmann, Ute 2001. '"The Vast White Place": A History of the Etosha National Park in Namibia and the Hai//om', in *Environment, Property and the State, Nomadic Peoples* (Special Issue), eds. L. Lenhart and M.J. Casimir, 5(2): 125–53.

Diligensky, G. 1981. 'Problems of the Theory of Human Needs', *Social Science Information* 20(1): 169–85.

Divan, Vijay 2005. 'Maharashtra Inter-Basin Water Transfer Proposal'. *Economic and Political Weekly* XL(1): 22–4

Dörner, C.D. 1975. 'Wie Menschen eine Welt verändern wollten', *Bild der Wissenschaft* 2: 48–53.

Douglas, Marianne S.V. et al. 2004. 'Prehistoric Inuit Whalers Affected Arctic Freshwater Ecosystems', *Proceedings of the National Academy of Science* (*PNAS*) 101(6): 1613–17.

Douglas, Mary 1985. *Risk. Acceptability According to the Social Sciences.* London: Routledge.

——— 1992. *Risk and Blame. Essays in Cultural Theory.* London: Routledge.

Dovers, Stephen, Ruth Edgecombe and Bill Guest, eds. 2002. *South Africans Environmental History. Cases & Comparisons.* Athens: Ohio University Press.

Drèze, J. and A. Sen 1990. *The Political Economy of Hunger*, vols. 1–3. Oxford: Clarendon Press.

Düwel, Klaus 1994. 'Wilde Natur-Höfische Kultur', in *Von der Angst zur Ausbeutung. Umwelterfahrung zwischen Mittelalter und Neuzeit*, eds. Ernst Schubert und Bernd Herrmann, 137–156. Frankfurt am Main: Fischer Taschenbuch Verlag.

Easterbrook, Gregg 2003. 'How a Man can be Wise ? and Awfully Wrong, Too', *Wall Street Journal Europe*, 22 October 2003.

Ehrenfeld, David 2003. 'Globalisation: Effects on Biodiversity, Environment and Society', *Conservation and Society* 1(1): 99–111.

Ekins, P. 1993. '"Limits of Growth" and "Sustainable Development": Grappling With Ecological Realities', *Ecological Economics* 8: 269–88.

Elam, Yitzchak 1973. *The Social and Sexual Roles of Hima Women.* Manchester: Manchester University Press.

Ellen, Roy 1993. 'Rhetoric, Practice and Incentive in the Face of the Changing Times. A Case Study in Nuaulu Attitudes in Conservation and Deforestation', in *Environmentalism. The View from Anthropology*, ed. K. Milton, 126–43. London: Routledge.

——— 1996. 'Introduction', in *Redefining Nature. Ecology, Culture and Domestication*, eds. Roy Ellen and K. Fukui, 1–36. Oxford: Berg.

——— and Katsuyoshi Fukui 1996. *Redefining Nature. Ecology, Culture and Domestication.* Oxford: Berg.

Elvin, Mark 2004. *The Retreat of the Elephants. An Environmental History of China.* New Haven: Yale University Press.

Engels, Anita and Timothy Moss 2003. 'Institutional Change in Environmental Contexts', in *How Institutions Change. Perspectives on Social Learning in Global and Local Environmental Contexts*, eds. Heiko Breit et al., 355–75. Opladen: Leske + Budrich.

Escobar, Arturo 1996. 'Constructing Nature. Elements for a Poststructural Political Ecology', in *Liberation Ecologies Environment, Development, Social Movements*, eds. R. Peet and M. Watts, 46–68. London: Routledge.

——— 1998. 'Whose Knowledge, Whose Nature? Biodiversity, Conservation, and the Political Ecology of Social Movements', *Journal of Political Ecology* 5: 53–82.

Fagan, Brian 2005. *The Long Summer. How Climate Changed Civilization.* London: Granta Books.

Farny, Dieter 1995. *Versicherungsbetriebslehre* (2nd, ed). Karlsruhe: Verlag Versicherungswirtschaft e.V.

Feeny, D. et al. 1990. 'The Tragedy of the Commons: Twenty-Two Years Later', *Human Ecology* 18(1): 1–19.

Fehr, Ernst 2002. 'The Economy of Impatience', *Nature* 415: 269–72.

Finke, Peter 2004. *Nomaden im Transformationsprozess. Kasachen in der post-sozialistischen Mongolei.* Münster: LIT-Verlag.

Flenley, John and Paul Bahn 2002. *The Enigmas of Easter Island.* Oxford: Oxford University Press.

Foin, Theodore C. and William G. Davis 1987. 'Equilibrium and Nonequilibrium Models in Ecological Anthropology: An Evaluation of "Stability" in Maring Ecosystems in New Guinea,' *American Anthropologist* 89: 9–31.

Fratkin, Elliot 2002. 'East African Pastoralism in Transition: Maasai, Boran, and Rendille Cases'. *African Studies Review* 44(3): 1–25.

Furze, Brian, Terry De Lacy and Jim Birckhead 1996. *Culture, Conservation and Biodiversity. The Social Dimension of Linking Local Level Development and Conservation through Protected Areas.* New York: John Wiley & Sons.

Gewin, Virginia 2004. 'Can Organic Farming Replace Conventional Agriculture?' *Nature* 428: 798.

Giddens, Anthony 1990. *The Consequences of Modernity.* Stanford: Stanford University Press.

Giordano, Christian and Andrea Boscoboinik 2002. *Constructing Risk, Threat, Catastrophe. Anthropological Perspectives.* Fribourg: Fribourg University Press.

Glantz, Michael H. 1988. *Societal Responses to Regional Climate Change. Forecasting by Analogy.* Boulder: Westview Press.

Gleick, Peter H. 1993. 'Water Conflicts: Fresh Water Resources and International Security', *International Security* 18(1): 79–112.

Goldblatt, David 1996. *Social Theory and the Environment.* Cambridge: Polity Press.

Gottesfeld, Leslie M. Johnson 1994. 'Conservation, Territory, and Traditional Beliefs: An Analysis of Gitksan and Wet'suwet'en Subsistence, Northwest British Columbia, Canada', *Human Ecology* 22(4): 443–65.

Greene, Shane 2004. 'Indigenous People Incorporated', *Current Anthropology* 45(2): 211–37.

Gregg, Walter W. 1906. *Pastoral Poetry and Pastoral Dama. A Literary Inquiry, with Special Reference to the Pre-Restoration Stage in England.* London: A.H. Bullen.

Grosman, Leore 2003. 'Preserving Cultural Traditions in a Period of Instability: The Late Nutufian of the Hilly Mediterranean Zone', *Current Anthropology* 44(4): 571–80.

Grove, R.H. 1987. 'Early Themes in African Conservation: The Cape in the Nineteenth Century.', in *Conservation in Africa. People, Policies and Practice*, eds. D. Anderson and R. Grove, 21–39. Cambridge: Cambridge University Press.

——— 1992. 'Origins of Western Environmentalism', *Scientific American* 27 (July): 42–47.

——— 1995. *Green Imperialism. Colonial Expansion, Tropical Island Edens and the Origins of Environmentalism, 1600–1860.* Cambridge: Cambridge University Press.

——— Vinita Damodaran and Satpal Sangwan 1998. 'Introduction', in *Nature and the Orient*, eds. R.H. Grove, Vinita Damodaran and Satpal Sangwan, 1–26. Delhi: Oxford University Press.

Grundmann, Reiner 1999. 'Wo steht die Risikosoziologie', *Zeitschrift für Soziologie* 28(1): 44–59

Gurung, C. 1993. 'Conservation for Sustainable Development: Myth or Reality?' *Himalayan Research Bulletin* XIII(1–2): 31–8.

Gyawali, Dipak 2003. *Rivers, Technology and Society: Learning the Lessons of Water Management in Nepal.* London: Zed Books.

Haftendorn, Helga 2000. 'Water and International Conflict'. *Third World Quarterly* 21(1): 51–68.

Hann, Christopher, ed. 2002. *Postsocialism. Ideals, Ideologies and Practices in Eurasia.* London: Routledge.

Hanna, Susan, Carl Folke and Karl-Göran Mäler, eds. 1996. *Rights to Nature. Ecological, Economic, Cultural, and Political Principles of Institutions for the Environment.* Washington: Island Press.

Hardin, G. 1968. 'The Tragedy of the Commons', *Science* 162: 1243–48.

Harris, Jack 1997. 'Global Warming and the Kyoto Conference', *Interdisciplinary Science Reviews* 22(4): 265–71.

Harrod, Howard L. 2000. *The Animals Came Dancing. Native American Sacred Ecology and Animal Kinship.* Tucson: The University of Arizona Press.

Harthorn, Barbara and Laury Oaks 2003. *Risk, Culture, and Health Inequalities. Shifting Perceprtions of Danger and Blame.* London: Praeger.

Hawley, Amos H. 1984. 'Human Ecological and Marxian Theories', *American Journal of Sociology* 89(4): 904–17.

Hayward, Tim 1994. *Ecological Thought. An Introduction.* Cambridge: Polity Press.

Heming, Li, Paul Waley and Phil Rees 2001. 'Reservoir Resettlement in China: Past experience and the Three Gorges Dam', *The Geographical Journal* 167: 195–212.

Hennebo, Dieter and Alfred Hoffmann 1963. *Geschichte der deutschen Gartenkunst* Vol. III. *Der Landschaftsgarten* . Hamburg: Broschek Verlag.

Heyns, P.S. v H. 1995. 'The Namibian Perspective on Regional Collaboration in the Joint Development of International Water Resources', *International Journal of Water Resources Development* 14(6).

Hilhorst, Dorothea and Greg Bankoff 2004. 'Introduction: Mapping Vulnerability' in *Mapping Vulnerability. Disasters, Development and People*, eds. Greg Bankoff, Georg Ferks and Dorothea Hilhorst, 1–9. London: Earthscan.

Hill, Allan G. 1985. *Population, Health and Nutrition in the Sahel. Issues in the Welfare of Selected West African Communities.* London: KPI.

Hoffman, Susanna M. and Anthony Oliver-Smith, eds. 2002. *Catastrophe & Culture: The Anthropology of Disaster.* Santa Fe: School of American Research Press.

Holling, C.S. 1973. 'Resilience and Stability of Ecological Systems', *Annual Review of Ecology and Systematics.* 4: 1–23.

Horowitz, Lea Sophie. 1998. 'Integrating Indigenous Resource Management with Wildlife Conservation: A Case Study of Batang Ai National Park, Sarawak, Malaysia', *Human Ecology* 26: 371–403.

——— 2001. 'Perception of Nature and Responses to Environmental Degradation in New Caledonia', *Ethnology* 40(3): 237–50.

Hughes, J. Donald 1998. 'Early Ecological Knowledge of India from Alexander and Aristotle to Aelian', in *Nature and the Orient,* eds. R.H. Grove, Vinita Damodaran and Satpal Sangwan, 70–86. Delhi: Oxford University Press.

Hulme, David and Marshall Murphree, eds. 2001. *African Wildlife & Livelihoods. The Promise and Performance of Community Conservation.* Oxford: James Currey.

Hunn, Eugene S., Daryll R. Johnson, Priscilla N. Russell and Thomas F. Thornton 2003. 'Huna Tlingit Traditional Knowledge, Conservation, and the Management of a "Wilderness" Park', *Current Anthropology* 44 (Supplement): 79–103.

Hunt, Terry 2006. 'Rethinking the Fall of the Easter Island'. *American Scientist* 94(5): 412–19.

Hviding, Evard and Graham B.K. Baines 1994. 'Community-based Fisheries Management, Tradition and Challenges of Development in Moravo, Solomon Islands', in *Development and Environment. Sustaining People and Nature,* ed. Dharam Gheri. Oxford: Blackwell.

ICIMOD 1992. The International Centre for Integrated Mountain Development.

Igoe, J. and D. Brockington 1999. *Pastoral Land Tenure and Community Conservation: A Case Study from North-East Tanzania.* Pastoral Land Tenure Series no. 11. Drylands Programme. London: International Institute for Environment and Development.

Inden, Ronald 2007 (in press). 'Kashmir as Paradise on Earth', in, A. Rao (ed.) *The Valley of Kashmir: The Making and Unmaking of a Composite Culture?* New Delhi: Manohar Publishers.

Ingold, Tim 1986. *The Appropriation of Nature: Essays on Human Ecology and Social Relations.* Manchester: Manchester University Press.

——— 1994 'From Trust to Domination: An Alternative View of Human-Animal Relation', in *Animals and Human Society: Changing Perspectives,* eds. A. Manning and J. Serpell, 1–22. London: Routledge.

——— 2000. *The Perception of the Environment. Essays on Livelihood, Dwelling and Skill.* London: Routledge.

IUCN 1980. World Conservation Strategy. Living Resource Conservation for Sustainable Development. Gland: IUCN-UNEP-WWF-FAO-UNESCO.

Ives, J. 1993. 'Beyond UNCED: A Strategic Plan of Action', *Himalayan Research Bulletin* XIII(1–2): 27–30.

Job, H. 1999. 'Probleme afrikanischer Großschutzgebiete – die Situation Kenias und das Fallbeispiel Samburu National Reserve', *Petermanns Geographische Mitteilungen* 143: 3–15.

Johnsen, Nina 2000. 'Place-Making, Pastoralism, and Poverty in the Ngorongoro Conservation Area, Tanzania', in *Producing Nature and Poverty in Africa,* eds. V. Broch-Due and R.A. Schroeder, 148–72. Stockholm: Nordiska Afrikansinstitutet.

Jungermann, Helmut. and Paul Slovic 1993a. 'Characteristics of Individual Risk Perception', in *Risiko ist ein Konstrukt. Wahrnehmungen zur Risikowahrnehmung*, ed. Bayerische Rückversicherung, 89–197. München: Knesebeck.

——— 1993b. 'Die Psychologie der Kognition und Evaluation von Risiko', in *Risiko und Gesellschaft. Grundlagen und Ereignisse interdisziplinärer Risikoforschung*, ed. G. Bechmann. Opladen: Westdeutscher Verlag.

Kalinin, G.P. and V.D. Bykov 1972. 'The World's Water Resources, Present and Future', in *The Ecology of Man: An Ecosystem Approach*, ed. R.L. Smith, 349–63. New York: Harper & Row.

Kasperson, Jeanne X., Roger E. Kasperson and B.L. Turner II 1995. *Regions at Risk. Comparisons of Threatened Environments.* New York: United Nations University Press.

Kay, Charles E. 1994. 'Aboriginal Overkill: The Role of Native Americans in Structuring Western Ecosystems', *Human Nature* 5: 359–98.

Kent, G. 1987. *Fish, Food, and Hunger.* Boulder: Westview Press

King, David A. 2004. 'Climate Change Science: Adapt, Mitigate, or Ignore?' *Science* 303:176–77

Kjekshus, Helge 1977. *Ecology Control and Economic Development in East African History. The Case of Tanganyika 1850–1950.* London/Nairobi: James Currey/EAEP.

Kothari, A., N. Singh and S. Suri, eds. 1996. *People and Protected Areas. Towards Participatory Conservation in India.* Delhi: Sage Publications.

Kothari, Smitu and Imtiaz Ahmad 2003. 'Nature as Value: Ecological Politics in India', in *The Value of Nature. Ecological Politics in India*, eds. Simitu Kothari, Imtiaz Ahmad and Helmut Reifeld. Delhi: Rainbow Publishers.

Krech III, Shepard 1999. *The Ecological Indian: Myth and History.* New York: W.W. Norton.

Krishnakumar, Asha 2003. 'Peoples Battle for a River', *Frontline* 7.

Krutilla, J.V. 1967. 'Conservation Reconsidered', *American Economic Review* 57: 777–86.

Kumar, Krishna 2003. 'We all Fall Down. A Hole in Humanity's Conscience', *The Times of India*, 6 March 2003.

Kuper, Adam 2003. 'The Return of the Native', *Current Anthropology* 44(3): 389–402.

Lance, H., H. Gunderson and C.S. Holling ed.2002. *Panarchy. Understanding Transformations in Human and Natural Systems.* Washington: Island Press.

Lélé S. 1991. 'Sustainable Development: A Critical Review', *World Development* 19(6): 607–21.

——— 1996. 'Resilience, Sustainability, and Environmentalism', *Environmental and Development Economics* 3(2): 251–5.

Lenhart, Lioba and Michael J. Casimir 2001. 'Environment, Property Resources and the State: An Introduction', in *Environment, Property Resources and the State. Nomadic Peoples* (Special Issue), eds. L. Lioba, and M.J. Casimir, 5(2): 6–20.

Lesorogol, Caroline K. 2003. 'Transforming Institutions among Pastoralists: Inequality and Land Privatisation', *American Anthropologist* 105(3): 531–42.

Levin, Roger and Robert A. Foley 2004. *Principles of Human Evolution.* Oxford: Blackwell Publishing.

Levy, S. 1999. 'Death by Fire', *New Scientist* 162 (2184): 38–43

Lewis, H.T. 1989. 'Ecological and Technological Knowledge of Fire: Aborigines Versus Park Rangers in North Australia', *American Anthropologist* 91(4): 940–61.

Liebersohn, H. 1994. 'Discovering Indigenous Nobility: Tocqueville, Chamisso, and Romantic Traval Writing', *The American Historical Review* 99(3): 746–66.

Little, P.E. 1999. 'Environments and Environmentalism in Anthropological Research: Facing a New Millennium', *Annual Review of Anthropology* 28: 253–84.

Loker, William M. 2003. 'Dam Impacts in a Time of Globalization: Using Multiple Methods to Document Social and Environmental Change in Rural Honduras', *Current Anthropology* 44 (Supplement): 118–21.

Lokotsch, Karl 1927. *Etymologisches Wörterbuch der Europäischen germanischen, romanischen und slavischen) Wörter orientalischen Ursprungs.* Heidelberg: Carl Winter's Universitätsbuchhandlung.

Low, Bobbi S. 1996. 'Behavioral Ecology of Conservation in Traditional Societies',. *Human Nature* 7(4): 353–79.

Luhmann, Niklas 1985. *Social Systems.* Stanford: Stanford University Press.

——— 1990. 'Risiko und Gefahr', *Soziologie der Aufklärung 5. Konstruktivistische Perspektiven.* Opladen: Westdeutscher Verlag.

——— 1991. *Soziologie des Risikos.* Berlin: Walter de Gruyter.

——— 1996. 'Das Risiko der Versicherung gegen Gefahr', *Soziale Welt* 47: 273–83.

Lupton, Deborah 1999a. *Risk.* London: Routledge.

— (ed.) 1999b. *Risk and Sociocultural Theory. New Directions and Perspectives.* Cambridge: Cambridge University Press.

Lye Tuck-Po 1995. 'Boundary/Quandry: Colliding Modernities, Forest Peoples, and Conservation in Malaysia', unpublished paper, Presented at the Conference on Tribal Communities in the Malay World, Singapore: Institute of Southeast Asian Studies.

McCabe, Terrence 1990. 'Turkana Pastoralism: A Case Against the Tragedy of the Commons', *Human Ecology* 18(1): 81–103.

——— 1997. 'Risk and Uncertainty among the Maasai of the Ngorongoro Conservation Area in Tanzania', *Nomadic Peoples* (n.s.) 1(1): 54–65.

——— *Cattle Bring Us to Our Enemies. Turkana Ecology, Politics, and Raiding in a Disequilibrium System.* Ann Arbor: University of Michigan Press.

McCay Bonnie M. and James M. Acheson, eds. 1987. *The Question of the Commons. The Culture and Ecology of Communal Resources.* Tucson: The University of Arizona Press.

MacCormack, C. 1980. 'Nature, Culture and Gender: A Critique', in *Nature, Culture and Gender*, eds. C. MacCormack and M. Strathern,, 1–24. Cambridge: Cambridge University Press.

McCully, Patrick 1996. *Silenced Rivers. The Ecology and Politics of Large Dams.* London: Zed Books.

Macilwain, Collin 2004. 'Organic: Is it the Future of Farming?' *Nature* 428: 792–93.

MacKenzie, J.M. 1989. 'Chivalry, Social Darwinism and Ritualized Killing: The Hunting Ethos in Central Africa up to 1914', in *Conservation in Africa. People, Policies and Practice*, eds. D. Anderson and R. Grove, 41–61. Cambridge: Cambridge University Press.

McNeill, J.R. and Verena Winiwarter 2004. 'Breaking the Sod: Humankind, History and Soil', *Science* 304: 1627–9.

Mäder, Paul et al. 2002. 'Soil Fertility and Biodiversity in Organic Farming', *Science* 296 (5573): 1694–7.

Malone, C. et al. 1994. 'The Death Cults of Prehistoric Malta', *Scientific American* 269(6): 76–83.

Mascia, M.B., Brosius, J.P., Dobson, T.A., Forbes, B.C., Horowitz, L., Mc Kean, M.A., and N.J. Turner 2003. 'Conservation and the Social Sciences', *Conservation Biology* 17: 649–50.

May, Thomas, Thomas Schumacher and Johannes Müller 1992. 'Zur Frage anthropogener Einwirkungen auf die Vegetation im Rahmen der Neolithisierung des Mittelmeerraumes. Beispiele aus Ost-Spanien und Dalmatien', *Die Erde* 123: 29–47.

Mazonde, I. n.d. 'From Communal Water Points to Private Wells and Boreholes in Botswana's Communal Areas', in *Property, Poverty and People: Changing Rights in Property and Problems of Pastoral Development*, eds. P.T.W. Baxter and R. Hogg, 182–90. Manchester: Dept. of Social Anthropology and International Development Centre, University of Manchester.

Mitchell, Ronald B. 2003. 'Of Course International Institutions Matter: But When and How?', in *How Institutions Change. Perspectives on Social Learning in Global and Local Contexts*, eds. H. Breit et al., 35–52. Opladen: Leske + Budrich.

Moran, Emilio, ed. 1990. *The Ecosystem Approach in Anthropology: From Concept to Practice.* Ann Arbor: University of Michigan Press.

Moran, Katy, Steven R. King and Thomas J. Carlson 2001. 'Biodiversity Prospecting: Lessons and Prospects', *Annual Review of Anthropology* 30: 505–26.

Moss, Madonna, L. 2003. 'Comment on Hunn et al. 2003, 'Huna Tlingit Traditional Knowledge, Conservation, and the Management of a "Wilderness" Park', *Current Anthropology* 44 (Supplement): 96–7.

Murdoch, J. and J. Clark 1994. 'Sustainable Knowledge', *Geoforum* 25(2): 115–32.

Myers, N. 1972. 'National Parks in Savannah Africa', *Science* 178: 1255–63.

Nadasdy, Paul 2007. 'The Gift in the Animal: The Ontology of Hunting and Human-Animal Sociality'. *American Ethnologist* 34(1): 25–43.

Nair, Madhavan R. 2003. 'Displaced by Deceit', *The Hindu*, 9 March 2004: 16–7.

Nelson, Fred 2004. *The Evolution and Impacts of Community-Based Ecotourism in Northern Tanzania.* International Institute for Environment and Development, no. 131.

Nietschmann, Bernhard 1987. 'Subsistence and Market: When the Turtle Collapses', in *Conformity and Conflict: Readings in Cultural Anthropology*, eds. J.P. Spradley and D.W McCurdy, 265–74. Boston: Little Brown.

Norberg-Hodge, Helena 1991. *Ancient Futures: Learning from Ladakh.* San Francisco: Sierra Club Books.

Norgaard, R. 1992. 'Coevolution of Economy, Society and Environment', in *Real-Life Economics*, eds. P. Ekin and Max-Neef, 76–86. London: Routlege.

Oliver-Smith, Anthony 1996. 'Anthropological Research on Hazards and Disasters', *Current Anthropology* 25: 303–328.

——— 2004. 'Theorizing Vulnerability in a Globalized World: A Political Ecological Perspective', in *Mapping Vulnerability. Disasters, Development and People*, eds. Greg Bankoff, Georg Ferks and Dorothea Hilhorst, 10–24. London: Earthscan.

O'Riordan, Tim and Susanne Stoll-Kleeberg, eds. 2002. *Biodiversity, Sustainability and Human Communities.* Cambridge: Cambridge University Press.

Ortner, Sherry, B. 1974. 'Is Female to Male as Nature is to Culture?' in *Woman, Culture, and Society*, eds. M.Z. Rosaldo and L. Lamphere, 67–87. Stanford: Stanford University Press.

Pain, Stephanie 1994. '"Rigid" Cultures Caught out by Climate Change', *New Scientist* 1915: 13.

Pandian, M.S.S. 1998. 'Hunting and Colonialism in the Nineteenth-Century Nilgiri Hills of South India', in *Nature and the Orient. The Environmental History of South and Southeast Asia*, eds. R.H. Grove, V. Damodaran and S. Sangwan, 273–97. Delhi: Oxford University Press.

Pawlik, K. 1991. 'The Psychology of Global Environmental Change: Some Basic Data and an Agenda for Cooperative International Research', *International Journal of Psychology* 26(5): 547–563.

Pearce, Fred 2003. 'A Greyer Shade of Green', *New Scientist* 178(2400): 41–3.

Phillips, Helen 2003. 'The Pleasure Seekers', *New Scientist* 180(2416): 36–43.

Prasad, Archana 2003. *Against Ecological Romanticism. Verrier Elwin and the Making of an Anti-Modern Tribal Identity.* New Delhi: Three Essays Collective.

Prest, John 1981. *The Garden of Eden: The Botanic Garden and the Re-Creation of Paradise.* New Haven: University of Connecticut.

Ramakrishnan, K.S., K.G. Saxena and U.M. Chandrashekara 1998. *Conserving the Sacred: For Biodiversity Management.* Delhi: Oxford and IBH Publishing Co.

Rangan, Haripriya 2000. *Of Myths and Movements. Rewriting Chipko into Himalayan History.* Delhi: Oxford University Press

Rao, Aparna 2000. Blood, Milk, and Mountains: Marriage Practice and the Concept of Predictability among the Bakkarwal of Jammu and Kashmir, in *Culture, Creation and Procreation. Concepts of Kinship in South Asian Practice*, eds. Monika Böck and Aparna Rao,101–34. Oxford: Berhahn Books.

——— 2002. 'Pastoral Nomads, the State and a National Park: The Case of Dachigam, Kashmir'; *Nomadic Peoples* 6(2): 72–98.

——— and Michael J. Casmir 2003. 'Nomadism in South Asia: An Introduction', in *Nomadism in South Asia*, eds. Aparna Rao and Michael J. Casimir. New Delhi: Oxford University Press.

Rao, R.K. and S.R. Sankaran 2003. 'Forest Myths, Jungle Laws and Social Justice', *Economic and Political Weekly* Vol. XXXVIII (No. 46): 4819–24.

Redman, Charles L. 1999. *Human Impact on Ancient Environments.* Tucson: University of Arizona Press.

Richards, Michael P., Rick J. Schulting and Robert E.M. Hedges 2003. 'Sharp Shift in Diet at Onset of Neolithic', *Nature* 425: 366.

Rival, Laura 2006. 'Amazonian Historical Ecologies', *Journal of the Royal Anthropological Institute* (n.s.) 12: 79–94.

Robbins, Paul 2004. *Political Ecology. A Critical Introduction.* London: Blackwell Publishing.

Rohrman, Bernd 1994. 'Risk Perception of Different Societal Groups. Australian Findings and Crossnational Comparisons', *Australian Journal of Psychology* 46(3): 150–63.

Rolett, Barry and Jared Diamond 2004. 'Environmental Predictors of Pre-European Deforestation on Pacific Islands', *Nature* 43: 443–6.

Rosen, Robert 1978. 'On Anticipatory Systems: When Can a System Contain a Predictive Model of Another?' *Journal of Social and Biological Structures* 1: 155–62

Rousseau, Jean-Jaques 1762–1933. *Emile or Education*, trans. Barbara Foxley. London: J.M. Dent & Sons Ltd.

Ruddiman, William F. 2003. 'The Anthropogenic Greenhouse Era Began Thousands of Years Ago', *Climatic Change* 61(3): 261–93.

Runnels, C.N. 1995. 'Umweltzerstörung im griechischen Altertum', *Spektrum der Wissenschaften* May 1995: 84ff.

Rusinek, Bernd-A. 2000. '"Wald und Baum in der arisch-germanischen Geistes- und Kulturgeschichte" ? Ein Forschungsprojekt des "Ahnenerbe" der SS 1937–1945', in *Der Wald? Ein deutscher Mythos?*, eds. Albrecht Lehmann and Klaus Schriewer, 267–353. Berlin: Dietrich Reimer Verlag.

Ruttan, L.M. and M. Borgerhoff Mulder 1999. 'Are East African Pastoralists Truly Conservationists?' *Current Anthropology* 40(5): 621–52.

Saberwal, V.K., M. Rangarajan, and A. Kothari 2001. *People, Parks and Wildlife. Towards Coexistence.* Delhi: Orient Longmans.

Salter, Frank, K. 2002. *Risky Transaktions. Trust, Kinship, and Ethnicity.* New York: Berghahn Books.

Sanday, Peggy Reeves 2002. *Women at the Center.* Ithaca: Cornell University Press.

Sandford, S. 1983. *Management of Pastoral Development in the Third World.* Chichester: John Wiley and Sons.

Saul, H. 1992. 'How Humans Massacred the Mammoth', *New Scientist* 1819: 14.

Schama, Simon 1996. *Landscape and Memory.* New York: Vintage Books.

Scheumann, Waltina and Manuel Schiffer 1998. *Water in the Middle East: Potential for Conflicts and Prospects for Cooperation.* Berlin: Springer Verlag.

Schiller, Friedrich 1795/96 (1830). 'Über naïve und sentimentalische Dichtung', in *Friedrich's von Schiller. Sämtliche Werke.* Haag: Verlagsbuchhandlung der Gebrüder Hartmann.

Schriewer, Klaus 2000. 'Aspekte des Naturbewußtseins. Zur Differenzierung des "Syndroms Deutscher Wald"'; in *Der Wald? Ein deutscher Mythos?*, eds. Albrecht Lehmann and Klaus Schriewer, 67–82. Berlin: Dietrich Reimer Verlag.

Schulz/Basler 1977. *Deutsches Fremdwörterbuch* Vol 3(1) begonnen von Hans Schulz, fortgeführt von Otto Basler. Berlin: Walter de Gruyter.

Schweitzer, Albert 1931/1959. *Aus meinem Leben und Denken.* Leipzig.

Scoons, Ian, ed. 1995. *Living with Uncertainty: New Directions for Pastoral Development in Africa.* London: IT Publications.

Segato, Rita Laura 2003. 'Religious Change and De-Ethnification: The Evangelical Expansion in Central Andes of Argentina', in *Religions in Transition. Mobility, Merging and Globalization in Contemporary Religious Adhesions*, eds. Jan-Åke Alvarsson and Rita Laura Segato, 160–95. Uppsala: Acta Universitatis Upsaliensis 37.

Sen, Armathia. 1990. *On Ethics and Economics.* Delhi: Oxford University Press.

Shapiro, Beth et al. 2004. 'Rise and Fall of the Beringian Steppe Bison', *Science* 306: 1561–65.

Sharma, Kalpana 2003. 'Adivasis – The Forgotten India', *The Hindu*, 9 March 2003: 16–7.

Sjöberg, Lennart 1998. 'Worry and Risk Perception', *Risk Analysis* 18(1): 85–93.

Skewes, Juan Carlos and Debbie Guerra 2004. 'The Defense of Maiquillahue Bay: Knowledge, Faith and Identity in an Environmental Conflict', *Ethnology* 43(3): 217–31.

Smith, Eric Alden 1983. 'Anthropological Applications of Optimal Foraging Theory: A Critical Review', *Current Anthropology* 24: 625–51.

——— 1991 *Inujjuamiut Foraging Strategies. Evolutionary Ecology of an Arctic Hunting Economy.* New York: Aldine de Gruyter.

Spittler, Gerd 1989a. *Dürren, Kriege und Hungerkrisen bei den Kel Ewey (1900–1985).* Stuttgart: Steiner Verlag.

——— 1989b. *Handeln in der Hungerkriese. Tuaregnomagen und die große Dürre von 1984.* Opladen: Westdeutscher Verlag.

Stearman, A.M. 1994. '"Only Slaves Climb Trees". Revisiting the Myth of the Ecologically Noble Savage in Amazonia'; *Human Nature* 5(4): 339–57.

Stegeborn, A. Wiveca 2001. 'Endangered Wanniyala-Aetto Women as Sex Slaves in the Middle East', *Nomadic Peoples* (n.s.) 5(1): 175–8.

——— 2004. 'The Disappearing Wanniyala-Aeto ('Veddahs') of Sri Lanka: A case study', *Nomadic Peoples* (n.s.) 8(1): 43–63.

Sterling, Andrew 1999. 'The Appraisal of Sustainability: Some Problems and Possible Responses', *Local Environment* 4(2): 111–35.

Stern, P.C. 1992. 'Psychological Dimensions of Global Environmental Change', *Review of Psychology* 43: 269–302.

Stokstad, Erik 2002. 'Organic Farms Reap Many Benefits', *Science* 296 (5573): 1.

Stoll-Kleemann, Susanne 2001. 'Barriers to Nature Conservation in Germany: A Model Explaining Opposition to Protected Areas', *Journal of Environmental Psychology* 21: 369–85.

Strathern, Marilyn 1980. 'No Nature no Culture: The Hagen Case', in *Nature, Culture and Gender*, eds. C. MacCormack and M. Strathern. Albany: State University of New York Press.

Sturm, Michael 2002. 'The Mixed Experience of Private Sector Involvement in Biodiversity Management in Costs Rica', in *Biodiversity, Sustainability and Human Communities*, eds. O'Riordan, Tim and Susanne Stoll-Kleeberg, 243–59. Cambridge: Cambridge University Press.

Thaler, Barbara 2004. *Biopiraterie und Indigener Widerstand. Mit Beispielen aus Mexiko.* Frankfurt am Main: Peter Lang.

Thapar, Romilar 2000. *Śakuntalā. Texts, Readings, Histories.* Delhi: Kali for Women.

Thukral, Enakshi Ganguly, ed. 1992. *Big Dams, Displaced People: Rivers of Sorrow, Rivers of Change.* New Delhi: Sage Publications.

Townsend, Mark 2002. 'Water fight is looming', *Environment* 74(4): 10–1.

Tso, T.C. 2004. 'Agriculture of the Future', *Nature* 428: 215.

Turton, David 1994. 'Mursi Survival Identity & Warfare: The Survival of an Idea', in *Ethnicity & Conflict in the Horn of Africa*, eds. K. Fukui and J. Marsalis, 15–31. London: James Currey.

Turton, Anthony and Roland Henwood eds. 2002. *Hydropolitics in the Developing World. A Southern African Perspective.* Pretoria: African Water Issues Research Unit (AWIRU).

Upham, Frank K. 1987. 'Environmental Tragedy and Response', in *Law and Social Change in Postwar Japan*, ed. F.K. Upham, 28–77. Cambridge: Harvard University Press.

Vayda, Andrew P. and Bradley B. Walters 1999. 'Against Political Ecology', *Human Ecology* 27(1): 167–79.

Viederman S. 191993. 'A Dream of Sustainability', *Ecological Economics* 8: 177–80.

Vitebsky, Piers 1998. 'A Farewell to Ancestors? Deforestation and the Changing Spiritual Environment of the Sora', in *Nature and the Orient*, eds. R.H. Grove, V. Damodaran and S. Sangwan, 969-82-26. Delhi: Oxford University Press.

W1. http://www.cesr.org/PROGRAMS/water.htm

W2. http://www.wateryear2003.org/

W3. http://www.thewatwerpage.com/

W4. http://www.wateraid.org/

W5. http://www.worldwatercouncil.org/

W6. http://www.worldwaterforumOS PLAN.org/

W7. http://www.environmentnepal.com.np/riverlink.asp

W8. http://www.environmentnepal.com.np/news_d.asp?id=622

W9. http://www. http://www.environmentnepal.com.np/articles_d.asp?id=190

Walther, Gian-Reto et al 2002. Ecological Responses to Recent Climate Change. *Nature* 416: 389–395.

Warnock, Mary 2003. 'What is Natural? And Should We Care?', *Philosophy* 78(306): 445–59.

WBR 2002. *World Bank Report 1999/2000. Entering the 21st Century.* Oxford: Oxford University Press.

WCD 2001. *Final Report of the World Commission on Dams.* Forum Report, Responses, Discussions and Outcomes.[http://www.dams.org./]

Weber, W. 1991. 'Enduring Peaks and Changing Cultures: The Sherpas and Sagarmatha (Mount Everest) National Park', in *Resident Peoples and National Parks: Social Dilemmas and Strategies in International Conservation*, eds. P. West and S. Brechin, 206–14. Tuscon: University of Arizona Press.

WECD 1987. *Our Common Future (The Brundtland Report) World Commission on Environment and Development.* Oxford.

Weiss, Harvey and Raymond S. Bradley 2001. 'What Drives Societal Collaps?', *Science* 291: 609–610.

Wells, M. and K. Brandon with L. Hannah 1995. *Peoples and Parks: Linking Protected Area Management with Local Communities.* Washington DC: The World Bank / The World Wildlife Fund / U.S. Agency for International Development.

Werfel, Franz 1941/1990. *Eine blassblaue Frauenschrift.* Frankfurt am Main: Fischer Taschenbuch Verlag.

Wiley, Andrea S. 1997. 'A Role for Biology in the Cultural Ecology of Ladakh', *Human Ecology* 25(2): 273–95.

Wolf, Jonathan 2003. Scanlon on Well-Being. *Ratio* (New Series) XVI(4): 332–45.

Wolvekamp, P., ed. in collaboration with A.D. Usher, V. Paranjpe, and M. Ramanath 1999. *Forests for the Future. Social Strategies for Forest Protection, Economic Welfare and Social Justice.* London: Zed Books.

Woodward, Lawrence 2002. 'The Scientific Basis of Organic Farming', *Interdisciplinary Science Reviews* 27(2): 114–9.

Worster, D. 1990. 'The Ecology of Order and Chaos'. *Environmental History Review* 14(1–2): 1–18.

Yaeger, R. and N.N. Miller 1986. *Wildlife, Wild Death: Land Use and Survival in Eastern Africa.* Albany: State University of New York Press.

Yates, J. Frank and Eric R. Stone 1992. 'Risk Appraisal', in *Risk-taking Behavior*, ed. J. Frak Yates, 49–85. New York: John Wiley & Sons.

Zimmerer, Karl S. 1994. 'Human Geography and the "New Ecology": The Prospect and Promise of Integration'. *Annals of the Association of American Geographers* 84(1): 108–25.

Zimmerer, Karl S. and Thomas J. Bassett 2003. *Political Ecology. An Integrative Approach to Geography and Environment-Development Studies.* New York: The Guilford Press.

Zizka, Georg 1989. 'Naturgeschichte der Osterinsel', in *1500 Jahre Kultur der Osterinsel*, 21–38. Mainz: Verlag P. von Zabern.

Part I

Evaluating, Attributing and Deciding

1

Antinomies of Environmental Risk Perception: Cognitive Structure and Evaluation

Gisela Böhm and Hans-Rüdiger Pfister

Introduction

The field of environmental risk perception is, compared to the perception of more mundane risks such as smoking or mountain climbing, special in several respects. First of all, environmental problems are among the most urgent problems in today's world, especially if we are concerned with global risks, which will be the focus of this paper; the greenhouse effect and ozone layer depletion, for example, are among the most serious hazards for the whole globe. Second, almost everybody is part of the problem, either as a causal agent – most people contribute, for instance, to increasing air pollution by using a car and are responsible for its detrimental effects on the environment – or as a victim suffering the consequences of a polluted environment. The essential question for the social sciences as well as for political decision-makers has been how to change people's attitudes and behaviours towards more pro-environmental behaviour, e.g., towards using public transport instead of private cars or avoiding unnecessary use of toxic chemicals.

The notion of 'risk' comes in various meanings. The economic tradition defines risk as the product of probability and amount of losses, e.g., number of casualties (Bernstein 1996). Psychologically, this definition is too narrow; humans use the term risk more broadly referring to any event, entity or action that is associated with danger, fear or harm, and which is socially constructed via norms, media and other factors (Renn 1998). The formal definition of probability and amount of loss is only weakly correlated with the social usage of the term risk, or with individual judgments of riskiness; e.g., instead of probability, it is the (un)familiarity of an action or event which is connected with its judged degree of riskiness (Slovic 1987). It is in this latter informal sense that we use the term 'risk'.

Environmental behaviour is more complex than most other behaviours, and environmental decisions are more difficult than many other political and societal decisions. To change environmentally harmful behaviour into pro-environmental behaviour is as important as it is difficult. This is due, we suggest, to the intricate way humans perceive and cognitively represent and process environmental phenomena. We argue that the mental representation of environmental problems implies several antinomies which prevent straightforward solutions for individual and for societal decision-makers. In order to provide convincing arguments and recommendations for pro-environmental policies we need to know the antinomies involved in the cognitive processing of environmental risks.

Antinomies (the concept goes back to Kant 1956) are commonly defined as two or more logically contradicting propositions within a theoretical system; however, each single proposition is valid or 'true' in its own right. Hence, antinomies cannot be resolved within the confines of the system. Antinomies are well-known in modern logic, e.g., the paradox of the liar (Poundstone 1988): assuming that exactly two classes of people exist, the one class is always lying, the other class always saying the truth – to which class does a person belong who says 'I am a liar'?

We will use the term 'antinomy' not in its strict formal sense, but as a psychological concept that plays a role in evaluation and decision-making processes. A psychological antinomy occurs if a person evaluates two disjunctive alternatives (i.e., two decision options only one of which can actually be carried out) which are entirely reasonable and rational if evaluated in isolation. However, comparing both alternatives makes it obvious that they oppose each other, because performing one option will achieve objectives directly contradicting the objectives achieved by the omitted option, and no shared dimension of comparison is available.

Evaluations are based on the mental representation of a problem, i.e., the way a person subjectively perceives and construes the situation under consideration, including salient relations among relevant objects, events and actions. Antinomies indicate that two evaluatively opposing alternatives follow in a reasonable way from the same mental representation but cannot be resolved without substantially modifying the representation. With respect to environmental risks, the opposing alternatives commonly are two actions, one pro-environmental, the other environmentally harmful (e.g., going to work by car or by public transportation). Good arguments exist in favour of each action alternative – based on the mental representation of the environmental problem – but a clear trade-off is not possible; the two alternatives are not rationally commensurable within the person's mental representation. Which alternative is eventually enacted depends on psychological operations such as shifting one's attentional focus, or on metacognitive processes. The individual often feels trapped in the antinomy, since whatever option he or she actually implements, there are always good reasons why he or she should have done otherwise, and why he or she will regret his or her decision.

In the next section we describe five key antinomies that arise in the domain of environmental risks. Of course, psychological antinomies are not only found in environmental problems, but the perception and mental representation of environmental risks is, we argue, especially prone to producing antinomical evaluations. The antinomies we identify are described along five dimensions with opposing poles, each pole supporting either the pro-environmental or the environmentally harmful action alternative, but not both. The five dimensions are not orthogonal, i.e., ecologically relevant behaviours are correlated across the five antinomical dimensions. Following a phenomenological description of the antinomies in the next section, in the third section we propose a cognitive model that attempts to explain why antinomies arise and how they are dealt with individually. In the fourth section, we discuss some applications for risk communication.

Antinomies of Environmental Risks

We identify five salient antinomies in the area of environmental risks. The antinomies are explicated along five evaluative dimensions of environmental decisions, labelled shortly as (i) individual versus collective perspective, (ii) proximal versus distal effects, (iii) short-term versus long-term consequences, (iv) anthropocentric versus biospheric orientation, and (v) consequentialistic versus ethical evaluations.

Individual versus Collective Perspective

In contrast to commonplace personal risks such as smoking or overeating, environmental risks such as the greenhouse effect concern the individual who performs an environmentally relevant action as well as the general public who suffers the potential effects of these actions (Vlek 1996a). The individual and the collective perspective, as we call it, are usually not compatible (there is also, arguably, a collective perspective of personal risks such as smoking). The antinomy that results from the contradiction between an evaluative focus on either the individual or on the collective perspective is possibly the most serious antinomy as far as environmental behaviour is concerned. It is at the core of most or even all environmental problems, and other antinomies may complement, but do not substitute the individual–collective antinomy. The essential contradiction here is that an individual's contribution to an environmental problem is infinitely small, but the sum of all individual contributions will most likely have disastrous effects for the collective. Take, as an example, the well-known problem of overfishing. The number of fish in a lake is a finite but replenishable resource, but only if the number of fish does not decline below a specific threshold. Hence, if all fishermen fish as much as they can, the lake will soon be void of fish. Only a moderate rate of fishing of the majority of fishermen will ensure that the number of fish will remain sufficiently high. How much then should an individual fisherman fish? From an individual point of view, keeping all other things constant, the rational decision would be to fish as much as possible, because this decision will yield personal benefit, irrespective of the behaviour of others: if all others stick to a moderate amount of fishing, the effect of one individual fishing the maximum is negligible though highly profitable for the individual; if most others fish the maximum too, there is no reason why the individual should receive less until the resource is depleted.

Situations such as this have been studied extensively in the context of social dilemma theory (Liebrand et al. 1992), going back to what Hardin (1968) called the 'tragedy of the commons'. In decision theory, decisions are considered as rational, if they are in accordance with certain reasonable axioms of preference and probability theory (Yates 1990), such as transitivity (if you prefer A to B and B to C then you should necessarily prefer A to C) or conjunctive probability (the joint probability of two events can never exceed the probability of either single event). There are, however, limits to this individualistic perspective, which become evident in social dilemma situations. Here, as can be seen in the overfishing example, for the individual the rational decision is to fish as much as possible. However, as a consequence, everybody will be worse off if all or most of them behave 'rationally' than if they collectively do not follow the individual perspective. Hence, the collectively rational decision would be not to fish a maximum, but to agree on a moderate amount. However, given this agreement, the temptation is high to have a 'free ride', i.e., to fish more than permitted without serious consequences, since everybody else sticks to the rule. Environmental risks have been successfully conceptualised as special cases of social dilemmas (Pfister and Böhm 2001a; Vlek 1996b; Vlek and Keren 1992).

This antinomy is clear and profound. If an individual decision-maker focuses on the individual perspective, reasonable arguments can be found to support this view: whatever all others do, she will be best off if she maximally exploits the resource. What all others do is highly uncertain, and even if a collective agreement can be reached, the danger of free riding is ever lurking. If the decision-maker focuses on the collective perspective, convincing arguments that support this view can be found as well: only a moderate amount of exploitation keeps the resource alive in the long run, and, in case of a contract, it is a moral obligation to keep agreements. The antinomy is not resolvable, as long as the problem is mentally represented in this way. A decision-maker may well oscillate between the individual and collective perspective, and feel more inclined to act as individualistic today and collective tomorrow. Only a new and different representation can resolve the dilemma, e.g., if a severe fine with strict control is enforced on overfishing, everybody will prefer the collectively rational option; but then the situation is qualitatively different.

Proximal versus Distal Effects

The second antinomy deals with the geographical distance of the effects of environmentally harmful behaviour, especially if global risks are concerned. For many major environmental phenomena, proximal as well as distal effects occur. Also, cause (e.g., increasing private traffic in Europe) and effect (e.g., temperature rise in Antarctica) are often separated geographically. However, the proximal effects that occur in one's near neighbourhood are quite different from the distal effects thousands of miles away. For example, if someone lives in Europe, depletion of the ozone layer in the Antarctic region caused by CFCs is proximally irrelevant. The proximal negative effects are infinitesimally small, whereas the positive effects are obvious for the individual person. Only if one considers seriously what will happen somewhere far away when using an environmentally dangerous substance, one might decide not to use it and give up the benefits one could enjoy by its use. If a person focuses on proximal effects, he or she will usually prefer the environmentally harmful alternative, i.e., the use of CFC. Arguments for this preference are rather plausible: its use is convenient, and no negative effects will be felt personally in one's immediate surroundings (CFC is not toxic); furthermore, the effects of the ozone layer depletion in a distant region seem irrelevant for the person's life (now and most likely in the long run). However, a focus on distant effects draws one's attention to the changes in the ozone layer and good arguments for this perspective come into view: decline of the ozone layer will cause severe health damage to other people, though far away, and these effects might weigh heavily compared to the negligible convenience of using hairspray in an aerosal can. Fortunately, an international agreement to prohibit the use of CFC has solved this antinomy by legal intervention.

Short-Term versus Long-Term Consequences

The third antinomy refers to the temporal delay of environmental effects that result from environmentally harmful behaviour. Short-term consequences, i.e., effects on humans which are immediate or only shortly delayed, are usually different and less severe than long-term consequences, but psychologically much more salient. Long-term consequences, on the other hand, are more severe but psychologically less salient; in the extreme, their emotional impact is highly elusive, since only future generations are affected. As an example, take the effects of heating by burning fossil fuels. The positive short-term effects, on the one hand, are of course warmth and pleasure in one's home, and the negative short-term effects such as increased air pollution are usually hardly noticeable. Long-term effects, however, are fairly negative – they include, in the long run, significant increases in CO_2 concentration in the atmosphere and, via the greenhouse effect, significant increases in the global temperature which in turn might cause a dramatic climate change. Note that the objective mechanisms of climate change are far from clear from a scientific point of view, but this is irrelevant for the manifestation of psychological antinomies; here, we are concerned only with the subjective perception and representation of environmental risks, irrespective of their scientific validity.

Again, good arguments can be found for each side of the short- versus long-term dimension. People who focus on the long-term consequences will argue that the expected global warming of the climate will most likely be very harmful for the majority of people affected, including one's own children, and that we are responsible for the well-being of future generations. People who focus on the short-term consequences have good arguments too: heating is a basic need and each individual has the right to enjoy warmth if possible at all, and future generations will most likely be able to solve their problems by new technologies.

Anthropocentric versus Biospheric Orientation

When evaluating environmental risks, one of three types of value orientations is commonly involved: an egoistic, a social-altruistic, or a biospheric value orientation (Stern et al. 1993). More generally, there is a contrast between a biospheric value orientation, taking the well-being of nature and living organisms as a value in itself, irrespective of the role humans play, and an anthropocentric value orientation (including egoistic and altruistic orientations), taking nature and biological resources primarily as means to increase the well-being of the self and other humans.

The antinomy arises if anthropocentric and biospheric orientations are confronted during an individual's decision process, i.e., if an individual partly accepts both attitudes. For example, from a biospheric point of view, the worldwide dramatic increase in individual traffic is clearly rejectable. The biosphere will most certainly not be able to cope with the output of carbon monoxide and other toxic substances from millions of cars and the construction of streets and highways further destroys the natural environment. However, how can one justify that, e.g., millions of Chinese people should not in the near future drive their own cars, just as Americans and Europeans do with pleasure and have felt justified to do for decades? It is certainly true that every human on earth has the same right to benefit from the blessings of modern technology as do Europeans or Americans, but it is as true that this will in its extreme lead to an environmental collapse. Since more and more Europeans are willing to refrain from driving, one could speculate that this problem could be settled if every nation were to reduce the relative amount of private traffic compared to public transport. But take another example: the vast majority of Europeans and Americans aspire to have their own home with some land around, preferably somewhere away from the city; and nobody seems willing, as is to a certain extent the case with car driving, to give up this claim. Now think of the environmental effects if each single individual on this planet would try and fulfil this aspiration. Even if this could be managed at all without an ecological disaster, it would imply fundamental changes to the natural environment.

Again, the antinomy is not resolvable within the mental representation of the risk as commonly adopted by most individuals. From a biospheric point of view, every measure should be taken to prevent the increase of private traffic and private residences in order to preserve the proportion of 'untouched' nature. From an anthropocentric point of view, however, the modification of natural habitats into artificial habitats is completely justifiable, if it increases human welfare in general.

Consequentialistic versus Ethical Evaluation

The consequentialistic–ethical antinomy is related to the first antinomy of individual versus collective perspectives. Ethical evaluations are based on moral principles about classes of actions, i.e., what one should or should not do, irrespective of its consequences. Not to lie, even if the lie pays off, is one such frequently violated principle. Consequentialistic evaluations, on the other hand, are based on the utility of the consequences of one's actions, irrespective of the type of action itself. Actions are considered only as means, as causes of consequences, and as evaluatively neutral.

This consequentialistic-ethical antinomy becomes salient if collective agreements and responsibilities are involved, as is the case with the overfishing discussed above. From a consequentialistic perspective, a fisherman might well break a contract that restricts the amount of fishing if the probability of getting caught is low; the extra profit might be substantial and no negative consequences are expected. However, from an ethical perspective, the same fisherman will refrain from breaking the treaty because he does not wish to violate a moral principle that says 'one should not break a social contract'. He might even anticipate that he will feel guilty, and he does not want to be that type of despicable person. Hence, again for both decision alternatives, to keep or break the contract, reasonable arguments are found, depending on whether the focus is on ethical or consequentialistic considerations. We shall return to this distinction in the next section.

The Cognitive Representation of Risk

We conceptualise risk perception within a general information processing framework and thus assume that the process of risk perception involves several stages (Böhm, Rost and Spada 1998). During the first stage a person perceives and encodes information about an environmental risk. For instance, we may hear or read something about an environmental risk in the media or a friend tells us something about it. At that point, relevant cognitions about the environmental risk are activated, recollected or constructed. The essential aspect of this process is the construction of a mental representation about the causes and potential consequences of the risk, i.e., a *causal mental model* is constructed (Böhm and Mader 1998; Craik 1943; Gentner and Stevens 1983; Thüring and Jungermann 1986; Pfister and Böhm 2001a; Thüring 1991). A causal mental model is a coherent though partial representation of the domain under consideration, and it permits the mental simulation of dynamic events. The mental model an individual construes when thinking about a risk is the fundamental cognitive representation from which other evaluations and judgements follow; i.e., the judged seriousness or controllability of consequences are based upon this mental model (Böhm and Mader 1998; Böhm and Pfister 2001). Most important for the arguments in this chapter is that behavioural preferences are formed on the basis of available actions implied by the mental model. The structure and the components of the individual's current mental model determine which alternatives are preferred and which arguments are available to support the preferred alternatives. Thus, the mental model enhances or attenuates the antinomies outlined in the previous section. Two judgmental aspects of the mental model are particularly relevant for both the evaluation of environmental risks in general (Böhm and Pfister 2000) and for the strength of antinomies in particular: potential consequences and ethical values. Next, we elaborate on the relevant characteristics of mental models and explicate the two judgmental aspects in more detail.

Causal Mental Models

Faced with an environmental risk, be it via some media report or because an environmentally relevant decision needs to be made, a mental model is construed or recollected. The most relevant components of this mental model are causal relationships among the represented elements of the environmental domain, i.e., the model represents causes and potential consequences referring to the environmental risk under consideration. Once the model is constructed, the meaning of a risk is represented by the totality of the model's components and relations. For instance, the following mental model was found to correspond to lay conceptions of ozone depletion (Böhm and Mader 1998): air pollution and emission of CFC cause the ozone hole, which in turn, causes damage to health, in particular affecting the skin. The mental model is constructed from the person's basic knowledge of the world as well as from recent information; hence, it both remains partly stable and is continuously updated. The content and structure of the mental model determine how the environmental risk is evaluated in relevant judgmental dimensions and which behavioural preferences are formed. For instance, with respect to the judged seriousness of a risk's consequences, a person whose model includes skin cancer as a potential consequence of the ozone hole will evaluate it as more serious and dangerous than a person who is not aware that it may result in skin cancer. Similarly, judged personal relevance will depend on whether the mental model includes consequences that may affect the person himself, for instance, whether the consequences included in the model are proximal rather than distal. Also, in order for a person to consider environmental actions, the model must include behavioural options that the person considers feasible and efficient, e.g., the purchase of CFC-free consumer products.

A mental model can increase or decrease the subjective salience of any antinomy the person is currently aware of, depending upon a) which causal factors are represented in the model and b) structural aspects of the model, such as the length and strength of causal relations.

Consequentialistic versus Ethical Evaluation

We distinguish two types of evaluation that have been found to be essential in the domain of environmental risks (Böhm 2003; Böhm and Pfister 2000) and that we assume to play a crucial role in affecting antinomies: consequentialistic and ethical evaluations. Both types of evaluation are based upon the mental model; i.e., the mental model provides the necessary information required to commence the evaluative process.

Consequentialistic evaluation refers to an evaluation of the potential consequences of actions or events. This type of evaluation corresponds to risk perception in the narrow sense; i.e., to an assessment of the risk involved in an event or action in terms of its probability and amount of harm or loss. This assessment is based upon the anticipation of potential consequences, judgements of likelihoods, and the estimation of how serious the losses associated with the consequences would be if they occurred (Yates and Stone 1992). Consequentialistic evaluation refers to natural events such as volcano eruptions, as well as to societal (building of nuclear power plants) and individual (smoking) human actions.

Ethical evaluation refers to whether an environmental risk is believed to violate ethical values and is particularly relevant for environmental risks because of their social dilemma structure. Since the natural environment is a shared resource, environmentally relevant behaviour always affects other people. Whenever an action affects other people's well-being, an ethical judgement needs to be made

(Baron 1994). Thus, environmental behaviour touches upon ethical issues such as social justice, equity and fairness of outcomes. In contrast to consequentialistic evaluation, ethical evaluation focuses on actions per se, irrespective of their consequences; i.e., ethical evaluations are non-consequentialistic (Baron 1994)[1] and are related to what Baron and Spranca (1997) call 'protected values'. According to these authors, protected values arise from deontological rules pertaining to classes of actions. The involvement in some type of action is what matters to the evaluator, not the consequences that result from it. Protected values are absolute, i.e., they are not traded off against other values; people strongly resist such trade-offs. For instance, most people are not willing to trade off destruction of natural resources or loss of human lifes against monetary gains. Such trade-offs are considered taboo (Fiske and Tetlock 1997) and trigger intense anger (Baron and Spranca 1997). In sum, ethical evaluation focuses on an action rather than on its consequences. An action is considered morally blameworthy if it violates some deontological rule according to which we should, in principle, not perform such type of action, no matter what the benefits may be.

Both consequentialistic and ethical evaluation operate on the individual's mental model. The consequentialistic evaluation results from the consequences that are represented in the model. The ethical evaluation results from inferences about (a) who the causal agents are and who is responsible for the environmental risk, (b) who suffers the potential consequences, and (c) whether the distribution of risks and benefits is fair. To a large degree the two types of evaluation use the same information, but consider it from different evaluative perspectives. Consequentialistic evaluation weighs the positive and negative consequences and forms an aggregated judgement about the overall risk or seriousness of the consequences. Ethical evaluation, on the other hand, may also look at the consequences, but will primarily ask if it is morally blameworthy to perform actions which imply such a risk. Ethical evaluation may use information about consequences, but is largely insensitive to their quantity and probability (Baron and Spranca 1997). For instance, if a person finds the destruction of natural resources morally prohibited, he or she will object to it if the extent of the destruction is limited or the probability of harmful consequences is low.

Exploring Cognitive and Evaluative Implications of Antinomies

We shall now explore the character of environmental antinomies in more detail, based upon the assumptions about mental models and types of evaluation outlined in the previous section. We shall argue that antinomies become more or less salient depending on the person's current focus, i.e., which components of the mental model are considered and elaborated, and which type of evaluation is more available. All antinomies hinge on the potential antagonism of consequentialistic and ethical evaluations, which in turn are both based on the individual's mental model about the risk. The content and structure of the mental model are particularly relevant for the two antinomies that refer to proximal versus distant effects and to short- versus long-term consequences, as these two antinomies require that the model includes both proximal and distant effects in one case, or short-term as well as long-term consequences in the other case. The disparity between consequentialistic and ethical evaluations becomes particularly prominent in the anthropocentric/biospheric realm and is, not surprisingly at the core of the ethical/consequentialistic antinomy.

The Individual/Collective Antinomy

The individual versus collective is the most prevalent antinomy in the context of environmental risks. It is also the most prominent example for the opposition of consequentialistic and ethical evaluation. This antinomy arises most easily in the case of environmental behaviour that contributes to an environmental risk caused by the aggregated actions of many individuals, e.g., the emission of carbon dioxide by cars. From a consequentialistic point of view, travelling by car rather than by public transport provides greater personal benefits in terms of comfort, independence from train schedules, etc., and the damage to the environment is infinitesimally small: the contribution of a single car ride will not affect the greenhouse effect. Thus, taking the car would be the preferred option if the decision were evaluated consequentialistically. On the other hand, while the contribution of each individual to CO_2 increase may be small: the contributions of many individuals accumulate, resulting in collective damage that may lead to climate change and adverse effects for people in distant regions or for future generations. Thus, if we assume responsibility for other people and future generations, public transport would be the preferred option from this ethical evaluative perspective.

The Proximal/Distal Antinomy

The proximal versus distal antinomy results if the causal mental model includes both types of effect and at least two behavioural options, one in favour of the proximal and the other favouring the distant effects. The available components of the model, as well as mentally 'running' the model (Jungermann 1985; Thüring and Jungermann 1986), i.e., generating or simulating new effects, influence the number and salience of available proximal and distal outcomes. Obviously this antinomy is strongly correlated with both short-term and long-term effects, since the proliferation of natural effects across long distances implies temporal delays, sometimes over several decades or more.

The Short-Term/Long-Term Antinomy

This antinomy requires that the mental model include the following conditions: (a) short-term and long-term consequences; (b) two behavioural alternatives, one of which improves the short-term consequences and worsens the long-term consequences, the reverse holding for the other alternative; and (c) short-term and long-term consequences are of approximately equal importance to the person. Thus, when a person focuses on the short-term consequences, he or she will prefer one alternative, but preference will change to the other alternative when the focus shifts to the long-term consequences. In the heating example, a strong antinomy would result from a model such as the following: the two behavioural options are to turn on the heating or not to turn it on. Turning it on increases personal comfort in the short run, but may increase the greenhouse effect and thus contribute to climate change in the long run; not turning it on, on the other hand, results in personal discomfort in the short run, but saves energy and thus helps to prevent climate change in the long run. The antinomy would be reduced if other consequences or other behavioural options were represented in the model so that the consequences generally favoured one of the options; e.g., if financial costs rather than personal comfort were represented as short-term consequences. In that case, not turning on the heating would both save money and prevent climate change, and thus improve both short-term as well as long-term consequences. No preferential antinomy would result from such a model and the person would clearly prefer not to turn on the heating. Similarly, the antinomy may vanish if the represented behavioural options were different, e.g., to turn on the heating or to put on a sweater. In this case, both options would improve personal comfort, but the sweater would additionally save money and prevent climate change. Again, one of the behavioural options is preferentially dominant across all consequences and no antinomy arises.

The Anthropocentric/Biospheric Antinomy

The biospheric versus anthropocentric antinomy is above all a conflict between two ethical positions. Again, the information needed for the evaluation is derived from the mental model – e.g., the amount of environmental damage, the reversibility of changes in the environment and the amount and distribution of benefits for humans from the various behavioural options. This information is then compared to two competing moral principles, one that states that we should value nature per se, as a value independent of human aspirations and desires, and not destroy it, and an opposing principle that emphasises that we should foster human rights and well-being, and that nature serves first and foremost as a resource to improve the quality of human life.

The Consequentialistic/Ethical Antinomy

The consequentialistic versus ethical antinomy arises whenever the two types of evaluation yield directly opposing behavioural preferences. It has been elaborated above for the conflict between individual and collective interests, which is the most prevalent constellation that produces a consequentialistic versus ethical antinomy.

Applications

In this last section we discuss selected applications of the antinomy perspective we have presented and of the proposition that antinomies arise from the content and structure of the subjective mental representation of environmental risks. We consider two areas of application: risk communication, particularly between conflicting social groups, and individual environmental risk behaviour.

Risk Communication

Environmental issues often give rise to conflict between social groups, e.g., between different political parties or between industry and environmentalists. We think that many of these conflicts exist because each of the opponents adopts one of the two contrary positions of an antinomy, often without being aware that the issue is an antinomy. By definition, as long as the representation of the problem is not changed by either party, the conflict is not resolvable by pure argument. Presumably, the most prevalent case is that between consequentialistic and ethical evaluation. One group, the consequentialists, considers the natural environmental as a resource that can and should be used for human benefit and weighs expected benefits against costs, whereas the other group, the moralists, argues that we should not harm the environment, either because it is an asset in itself or because we are responsible for future generations. A first step to conflict resolution in such a situation is to identify the two opposing evaluative modes that are employed by the opponents and try and create a mutually shared evaluative base. We propose two strategies as means to this end: informed meta-communication and two-sided communication.

Informed Meta-Communication

Meta-communication means communication about the process and content of communication itself. If an impasse has occurred in a discourse, either due to the arguments or due to the social dynamics of the discussants, it is necessary to take a more distant stance in order to clarify the reasons for the impasse. In the context of an environmental antinomy, this implies communicating explicitly about the antinomy itself, and not trying to resolve or justify the opposed poles of that antinomy. Three steps should be followed here, if the discussants are willing in principle to reach some agreement: First, the type of the antinomy should be identified, i.e., which one of the five dimensions discussed above is involved; more than one dimension could be relevant. Second, it should be explicitly stated and accepted that the source of the conflict is an antinomy, i.e., that there is no principled way even for a 'rational neutral' mediator to determine which side is 'right' and which is 'wrong'. Third, the discourse should shift to the content of the antinomy, and the discussants should ponder the meaning of the antinomical dimension and try to make a reflected effort to clarify their own attitude towards the poles of the antinomy. Frequently, people have not been consciously aware that they are 'consequentialists' or 'moralists'. Only if a shared understanding about these three points is reached can the discourse shift back onto the level of the original contentious issue. Of course, there is no guarantee that this strategy is successful, but at least it leads to a better understanding of each other's position, and at best to a modification of one's own position.

Two-Sided Communication

Two-sided messages are communications on a controversial issue that provide both pro- and contra-arguments with respect to that issue. For example, if a salesperson wants to sell a specific product, he or she will accentuate the advantages but might call attention to some disadvantages to increase his or her integrity. Two-sided messages have been shown in attitude research to enhance the credibility of the communicator and of the message (McGuire 1985). Political decision-makers who want to convey their position on an environmental risk should be aware of the existence of the various antinomies in this area. Especially if the goal is to convince and persuade people to adopt a certain position, a one-sided communication is mostly futile and the persuasion will probably fail. Of course, those who already adhere to one side of the antinomy dimension will agree without reflecting on it, but then no communication is needed. But those whose position is at exactly the opposite pole of this antinomy will not even engage in a rational discussion, since from the very beginning they will resist any argumentative efforts. Hence, some kind of informed meta-communication as outlined above might serve as a good starting point for a productive two-sided communication process. Again, there is no guarantee for success, but there is some probability that the discourse provides the chance of learning and mutual understanding for all parties involved – and this is an essential ingredient of a democratic society.

Informed meta-communication and two-sided communication are strategies that can be applied by all types of societal decision-makers, opinion leaders and political protagonists. The mad cow disease (BSE) crisis is an instructive lesson on the failure of risk communication. Instead of providing sufficient information on all aspects of BSE, politicians refrained from an explicit discourse about its highly ambiguous implications and insisted for much too long on no-risk messages (Leiss and Powell 2004; for more details see Pfister and Böhm 2001b).

Risk Behaviour

Communication about environmental risks is not an end in itself: the main goal is to change behaviour towards pro-environmental options. Pro-environmental behaviour is not as widespread as one might expect from the generally positive attitude towards the environment and environment protection (Finger 1994). This discrepancy between attitude and behaviour (Eagly and Kulesa 1997; Spada 1991) is often explained with the inherent conflict between individual and collective interests that is typical for most environmental risks (Bazerman et al. 1996) and that corresponds to the individual versus collective antinomy outlined in this chapter. As we mentioned in our introductory section, the antinomical dimensions are not independent. Every so often it is the environmentally harmful behavioural option that provides immediate personal benefits, whereas the resulting damage is minimal, collective, delayed and distant. The pro-environmental behaviour option, on the other hand, is characterised by immediate personal costs and delayed collective benefits. Thus, the environmentally destructive option should be preferred on consequentialistic grounds, whereas the pro-environmental behaviour option should be favoured when focusing on ethical considerations.

We have argued throughout this chapter that the dimensions are antinomical, i.e., that both poles of an antinomy are considered valid and both behavioural options are preferred. This implies that egoistic and altruistic motives are equally strong. If one of these two orientations is dominant, the individual will lean towards the corresponding behavioural alternative. It seems, then, that an important vantage point for risk communication that aims at fostering pro-environmental behaviour is to emphasise ethical issues and to promote personal responsibility (Pfister and Böhm 2001a).

Notes

1. In philosophy there are two types of moral theory, deontological and teleological. Deontological theories assume that moral thinking is based upon action categories, whereas teleological theories (utilitarianism) argue that moral thinking is based upon the consequences of actions. Thus, the term 'moral' is more comprehensive in philosophy than our usage of it. We restrict the term to its deontological meaning, assuming that psychologically deontological moral thinking is the prevalent way of moral thinking in everyday lay evaluation. We use the terms moral and ethical interchangeably.

References

Baron, Jonathan 1994. 'Nonconsequentialist decisions', *Behavioral and Brain Sciences* 17: 1–42.

——— and Mark Spranca 1997. 'Protected Values', *Organizational Behavior and Human Decision Processes* 70: 1–16.

Bazerman, Max H., Kimberley A. Wade-Benzoni and Francisco J. Benzoni 1996. 'Environmental Degradation: Exploring the Rift between Environmentally Benign Attitudes and Environmentally Destructive Behaviors', in *Codes of Conduct*, eds. David M. Messick and Ann E. Tenbrundel, 256–74.New York: Russell Sage Foundation.

Bernstein, Peter L. 1996. *Against the Gods. The Remarkable Story of Risk.* New York: Wiley.

Böhm, Gisela 2003. 'Emotional Reactions to Environmental Risks: Consequentialist versus Ethical Evaluation', *Journal of Environmental Psychology* 23: 199–212.

——— and Sabine Mader 1998. 'Subjektive kausale Szenarien globaler Umweltveränderungen', *Zeitschrift für Experimentelle Psychologie* 45: 270–85.

——— and Hans-Rüdiger Pfister 2000. 'Action Tendencies and Characteristics of Environmental Risks', *Acta Psychologica* 104: 317–37.

——— and Hans-Rüdiger Pfister 2001. 'Mental Representation of Environmental Risks', *Research in Social Problems and Public Policy* 9: 1–30.

———, Jürgen Rost and Hans Spada 1998. 'Editorial: Psychologische Aspekte von Umweltrisiken', *Zeitschrift für Experimentelle Psychologie* 45: 243–50.

Craik, K. 1943. *The Nature of Explanation.* Cambridge MA: Cambridge University Press.

Eagly, Alice H. and Patrick Kulesa 1997. 'Attitudes, Attitude Structure, and Resistance to Change: Implications for Persuasion on Environmental Issues', in *Environment, Ethics, and Behavior*, eds. David M. Messik, Ann E. Tenbrunsel, X. Kimberley and A. Wade-Benzoni. San Francisco: Lexington Press.

Finger, Matthias 1994. 'From Knowledge to Action? Exploring the Relationship between Environmental Experiences, Learning, and Behavior', *Journal of Social Issues* 50: 141–60.

Fiske, Alan Page and Philip E. Tetlock 1997. 'Taboo Trade-offs: Reactions to Transactions that Transgress the Spheres of Justice', *Political Psychology* 18: 255–97.

Gentner, D. and A.L. Stevens 1983. *Mental Models.* Hillsdale NJ: Erlbaum.

Hardin, Garrett R. 1968. 'The Tragedy of the Commons', *Science* 162: 1243–48.

Jungermann, Helmut 1985. 'Inferential Processes in the Construction of Scenarios', *Journal of Forecasting* 4: 321–27.

Kant, Immanuel 1956. *Kritik der reinen Vernunft.* Darmstadt: Wissenschaftliche Buchgesellschaft, cited according to 2nd ed, 1787.

Leiss, William and Douglas Powell. 2004. *Mad Cows and Mother's Milk*, (2nd ed.). Montreal: McGill-Queens's University Press.

Liebrand, Wim B.G., David M. Messick and Henk A.M. Wilke, eds. 1992. *Social Dilemmas: Theoretical Issues and Research Findings.* Oxford: Pergamon Press.

McGuire, William J. 1985. 'The Nature of Attitudes and Attitude Change', in *Handbook of Social Psychology*, eds. Gardner Lindzey and E. Aronson. New York: Random House.

Pfister, Hans-Rüdiger and Gisela Böhm 2001a. 'Decision Making in the Context of Environmental Risks', in *Decision Making: Social and Creative Dimensions*, eds. Carl Allwood, and Marcus Selart, 89–111. Dordrecht: Kluwer.

——— and Gisela Böhm 2001b. 'BSE – Sozialpsychologische Aspekte eines umstrittenen Risikos', *Zeitschrift für Sozialpsychologie* 4: 213–22.

Poundstone, William 1988. *Labyrinths of Reason.* New York: Anchor Press.

Renn, Ortwin 1998. 'Three Decades of Risk Research: Accomplishments and New Challenges,' *Journal of Risk Research* 1: 49–71.

Slovic, Paul 1987. Perception of Risk. *Science* 236: 280–85.

Spada, Hans 1991. 'Umweltbewußtsein: Einstellung und Verhalten', in *Umweltpsychologie: Ein Handbuch in Schlüsselbegriffen*, eds. Lenelis Kruse, Carl F. Graumann and Ernst Lantermann. Munich: Urban and Schwarzenberg.

Stern, Paul C., Thomas Dietz and Linda Kalof 1993. 'Value Orientations, Gender, and Environmental Concern', *Environment and Behavior* 25: 322–48.

Thüring, Manfred 1991. *Probabilistisches Denken in kausalen Modellen.* Weinheim: Psychologie Verlags Union.

——— and Helmut Jungermann 1986. 'Constructing and Running Mental Models for Inferences about the Future', in *New Directions in Research on Decision Making*, eds. B. Brehmer, H. Jungermann, P. Lourens and G. Sevon. North-Holland: Elsevier Science Publishers B.V.

Vlek, Charles 1996a. 'A Multi-Level, Multi-Stage and Multi-Attribute Perspective on Risk Assessment, Decision-Making and Risk Control', *Risk Decision and Policy* 1: 9–31.

——— 1996b. 'Collective Risk Generation and Risk Management: The Unexploited Potential of the Social Dilemmas Paradigm', in *Frontiers in Social Dilemmas Research*, eds. W.B.G. Liebrand and D.M. Messick. Berlin: Springer Verlag.

——— and Gideon Keren 1992. 'Behavioral Decision Theory and Environmental Risk Management: Assessment and Resolution of Four "Survival" Dilemmas', *Acta Psychologica* 80: 249–78.

Yates, John F. 1990. *Judgment and Decision Making.* Englewood Cliffs, NJ: Prentice Hall.

——— and Eric R. Stone 1992. 'Risk Appraisal' in *Risk-Taking Behavior*, ed. J. Frank Yates, 49–85. New York: Wiley.

2

Risk Management and Morality in Agriculture: Conventional and Organic Farming in a German Region

Thomas Döring, Lutz H. Eckensberger, Annette Huppert and Heiko Breit[1]

Introduction

Moral dimensions in risk perception and risk-taking in agriculture, a cultural domain, which is in various respects particularly conflict-ridden, determine ideas of responsibility for remedial ecological action. Moral judgements constitute a fundamental cultural rule system for initiating processes of change in environmental contexts. In Western cultures there are basically two different risk management strategies in this field, involving different risks and uncertainties with respect to marketing, income and environment. One is called 'conventional', the other 'organic' farming. When differences and similarities between these are outlined on the basis of recent literature, it turns out that in the conventional strategy economic conditions are more relevant than ecological ones. This orientation can be characterised as being more instrumental and profit-maximising than organic farming where the importance of ecology and sustainable development are primarily referred to. Some aspects of the organic perspective also appear to be more 'moral' in the sense that interests of others as well as natural ecological resources are largely taken into account. To substantiate this conjecture, the 'moral dimension' will be analysed in more detail by applying a theory of the development of moral judgements. The two strategic orientations will be presented as polarised stereotypes in order to highlight their differences. However, the real issue is whether this polarisation can also be identified empirically in the answers of interviewed farmers, experts and decision-makers. Are the stereotypes useful and fruitful when describing risk management in everyday agricultural life? What role does moral judgement play in the opinions expressed by interviewees? Is there empirical support for the assumed relationship between conventional orientation and heteronomous judgements, between moral judgements and orientations in farming? The theory on the development of moral judgements allows one (a) to distinguish between the decision for or against one style of farming (content of the decision) and its structure (reasons given for the decision), and (b) to evaluate the reasons given for choosing one of the alternatives in terms of complexity understood as 'moral maturity'. In the present context moral judgements refer to (a) evaluations of the alternative orientations, and (b) the role consumers and their rights play in agricultural contexts.

Risks in Agriculture

In the West agriculture is situated in a complex field of tension characterised by a variety of discrete conflict domains and risks (Agrarbericht 1995). These relate to

- *economics,* because agriculture in general is under pressure and at least for smaller farms the income and market situations are highly unsatisfactory (Wellhausen 1985);
- *ecology,* because nowadays farming is considered one of the greatest sources of environmental pollution;
- *social factors,* because rural traditions no longer appear to fit into the modern world (Wellhausen 1985). This has the economic consequence that often no successors are found in the farmers' families to take over the farm.

Similarly, Linnartz (1994) pointed out that agriculture is criticised because of environmental pollution, food-scandals, over-production and unjustified subventions. All these accusations damage the public reputation of farmers, compelling them and their associations to justify and publicly comment on these reproaches. From a psychological perspective this means that people who earn their living by farming have to cope with tremendous demands; in other words, they have to take economic, social and ecological risks into account.

Strategies of Agricultural 'Risk Management': Organic and Conventional Orientations

In debates and discussions of current scandals (such as the mad cow disease, swine fever, foot-and-mouth disease) two distinct, if not mutually exclusive orientations to agriculture, the 'conventional' and the 'organic' orientation, can be differentiated (e.g., Barth 1995; Mayer 1994; Quirbach 1989; Wolf 1996). Generally speaking, the designations 'conventional' vs. 'organic' refer to competing 'ideologies' prevalent in agricultural activities in Western cultures. They denote 'philosophies' about techniques of farming and marketing strategies, and can be considered two different ways of coping with the above mentioned domains of conflict and risk management. As modern myths, they are not only restricted to farmers, but are also frameworks guiding actions of politicians, decision-makers and experts. In the following paragraphs, issues are outlined that allow for a better understanding of what these myths or philosophies imply about how to pursue farming properly. The perspectives are intentionally polarised and contrasted to highlight differences. In organic and conventional agriculture the following characteristics differ clearly.

Methods of Farming

In contrast to conventional farming, which allows the use of chemical-synthetic herbicides and/or pesticides, their use is forbidden in organically oriented farming. These restrictions are seen as a necessary condition for minimising ecological risks in agriculture.

Ecological and Health Risks

In general, one can maintain that the organic orientation in farming developed in reaction to ecological dangers and health hazards caused by conventional agricultural production. The conventionally oriented group does not share this view, because it does not see an *essential* contradiction between the agricultural utilisation of nature and its protection or conservation; nor does it share the view that health risks increase, for instance, by fertilising intensively.

Marketing Strategies

Both orientations also differ with respect to their marketing strategies and related expectations about consumer behaviour. From the conventional perspective, the basic aim is mass production. Thus marketing focuses on wholesalers, bulk purchasers and big supermarkets, and targets groups of buyers who predominantly prefer low-priced products. In contrast, the focus of the organic orientation is on direct marketing and on small regional farmers' markets, targeting groups of buyers willing to pay above average prices for 'natural' products. Organically oriented farmers want to specify the criteria and standards their products need to fulfil to be labelled 'organic' or 'bio' because they want to emphasise differences with 'conventional' products.

Genetic Engineering

There are also huge discrepancies in the assessments of the risks involved and changes caused by using new technologies such as genetic engineering among members and spokespersons of the respective farmers' associations and organisations. Whereas the conventional perspective emphasises the chances and positive opportunities of biotechnology for providing possible solutions to food problems caused by the increasing world population, from the organic perspective hunger in the world is interpreted rather as an organisational and thus political problem of food distribution. Therefore farmers ought to do without green biotechnology, as the risks involved are not acceptable, despite economic pressures.

Relations to Nature

From the conventional perspective the relationship with nature is purely *instrumental.* Nature is regarded as a means of economic output, which leaves no room for alternatives; it is considered the one and only way of treating nature in order to succeed in ensuring human existence. In contrast to this instrumental orientation, the organic perspective entails a relationship to nature which can be called *interactionistic or interactive.* This view postulates that there is an intrinsic contradiction between the (economic) utilisation of nature and its protection. They claim that every agricultural activity seriously interferes with nature, disturbing the equilibrium and the natural cycles. Thus the formulation of restrictions – e.g., banning chemical fertilisers – is demanded in order to guarantee organically oriented farming. The specific restrictions called for do not primarily aim at maintaining the purity of products or the production of 'health food', but rather focus on the protection of nature and guaranteeing sustainable development.

Treatment of Farm Animals

The two orientations also seem to imply different ideas about the relations between humans and animals. In the conventional view the well-being of livestock seems to be determined primarily in terms of maximising *output.* Conventional farmers obviously also take 'good care' of animals, as they are interested in achieving economic welfare in the long run. Yet this economic attitude leads to forms of stock management that often involve keeping the animals in anything but their natural environment and are based on extensive use of medicine. In contrast, the organic perspective argues that all economic use of animals is structurally in conflict with their 'natural behaviour' – and thus with their *well-being*. Consequently, attending to the well-being of animals constitutes the frame for utilisation and economic action.

But there is also some *common ground between the two orientations,* because both emphasise the independence of farmers and champion self-employment. In this context, critical voices comment on the lack of agricultural lobbies in politics and deplore the many bureaucratic regulations which often impede free enterprise (Mayer 1994; Wolf 1996). Additionally, both orientations complain about the fact that only big farms receive subsidies. Despite this criticism they do not completely reject legal regulations, although these are often not designed to meet the concrete requirements and hardly leave any room for adjustment – for example, when distributions of subsidies and marketing in the European Union are considered unequal and unjust. Thus, they are seen as constraining. Although this view is in principle shared by the proponents of the organic perspective, organically oriented persons feel that many of these regulations would be unnecessary if farming were generally subject to the guidelines customary in organic cultivation. Thus, for instance, limiting the use of dangerous substances would not be necessary if these substances were not used at all. On the whole, it seems that the conventional orientation does not see as many opportunities and possibilities of changing the actual situation as the organic orientation.

The Relationship between the Risk Management and 'Morality'

As already mentioned, the two orientations differ in the way they perceive risks. From an action-theoretical perspective, risk can be characterised in terms of three aspects: it implies (a) the *intention* of the decision to act, (b) a component of *uncertainty* with respect to the occurrence of intended and unintended consequences, and (c) an *evaluative dimension* concerning the moral intuitions and consequences of action (Eckensberger et al. 2001). Because all three aspects are central concepts of cultural action theory, this theory is considered most suitable for analysing risks and risk taking (see e.g., Boesch 1991; Cole 1996; Eckensberger 1990, 2001).

What, however, is the relationship between risk management and morality? In fact, the close interrelationship between risk-taking and morality becomes evident from the very same action-theory perspective. This is so because in most decisions the evaluations of consequences refer not only to the actor and his/her agency, but also to others. For example, benefits that accrue to the actor can imply costs for others, or for classical 'free riders', who benefit from others' actions, even if they themselves have not contributed to them (Ostrom 1990). Therefore, evaluations of risk-taking activities almost inevitably have moral implications with regard to whether a decision is socially justified, and to what extent certain consequences have to be tolerated.

In fact, there is often disagreement about the acceptability of decisions, i.e., whether the risks should be taken and whether individuals or a social group should be expected to tolerate disadvantages for the benefit of all. This implies that decisions – particularly those which affect the entire society, as in the case of environmental risks – are closely connected to questions of 'justice', 'responsibility', goodwill or care and 'solidarity' (Eckensberger et al. 2001). But what exactly is meant by 'morality' in this context?

Moral Judgements

First, when speaking of morality in the present context we do not mean 'behaving' morally; rather, the term 'morality' refers to moral judgements or justifications. Second, moral judgements refer to what people *should do* (i.e., they are counterfactual, prescriptive) rather than to what people *would do* (according to expectations, norms or experiences). Third, moral judgements refer to judgements about justice, judgements about whose interests are to be considered and respected when making a decision, and ideally this should embrace all 'moral patients' (people) potentially affected by a decision. The normatively formulated 'moral point of view' integrates the interests of all persons involved in conflicting decisions within an idealised, impartial process of communication (Kohlberg 1986). The theory of moral judgements represents an *empirical reconstruction* of a *normative* concept of morality, and does not focus on the *direction* of a decision taken, or on values, vices or virtues, but rather on the structure of the arguments given to justify a decision (Kohlberg 1976). It is used for empirical research in developmental psychology, in which the question of how these 'ideal types' of justice arguments develop ontogenetically is investigated. Besides moral norms, other social rule or normative systems, such as laws and conventions, can be distinguished (e.g., Eckensberger 1993).

Eckensberger and his co-workers based their analysis of the ontogenetic structures of moral arguments upon Piaget's (1973/1932) early work, but primarily on Kohlberg's (e.g., 1976) tremendous empirical and theoretical contributions to the field (Eckensberger and Burgard 1986; Eckensberger and Reinshagen 1980). Deviating conceptually and methodically from these authors, however, they use the action elements taken into account in a specific argument to define the structure of a judgement. Subjects had to propose solutions to hypothetical, conflicting actions and argue about them. These arguments were analysed in action terms, that is, whether the goals of others are taken into account, whether the means they apply and the consequences they produce are considered. These differentiations not only enabled a more exact formulation of the developmental logic of arguments, but also led to modifications of the stage structure. Following Piaget's terminology, the developmental trend of moral judgements can be reconstructed as a movement from heteronomy to autonomy.

Heteronomy in this context means that while actions are interpreted as given, rules are interpreted as an existing fact. The individual thus takes a rule as being in force, and considers it valid. So reasoning refers to the *factual acceptance* of rules, which are also, however, considered as being *obligatory* (and therefore prescriptive) for everyone. Conflict-solving for example, is regarded as an authoritarian intervention or as unchallengeable judicial decision. Autonomy, in contrast, implies mutual respect for intentions and the detailed reconstruction of an entire conflict. As a consequence, joint processes of conflict-solving are proposed which integrate the opinions, interests and decisions of others. Norms are understood as shared rules, oriented toward searching for superordinate common goals. To continue upholding the norms in spite of their being disappointed, an autonomous moral orientation needs *counterfactual* thinking.

In contrast to Piaget and Kohlberg, it is claimed that the movement from heteronomy to autonomy takes place in two spheres of interpreting social reality: first it is specified in the 'interpersonal sphere' of concrete relations, then it is repeated on a second, more abstract level, referred to as the 'transpersonal social sphere'. This sphere is constructed or understood in terms of laws, procedures and principles. These are regarded as objective on the transpersonal-heteronomous level and as related to participation and communication processes on the transpersonal-autonomous level (Breit et al. 2003). The two social spheres are compatible with Tönnies' (1887/1963) distinction between *Gemeinschaft* and

Table 2.1. Morality, spheres of interpretation and social relations: summary of moral levels

Sphere of interpretation	**Interpersonal**		**Transpersonal**	
Moral orientation	Heteronomous (IH)	Autonomous (IA)	Heteronomous (TH)	Autonomous (TA)
Respect	One-sided respect	Mutual respect	Respecting social and legal systems	Universalised respect (respecting humankind per se)
Conflict-solving	Authority and power	Communication	Laws, procedures and principles	Communication on the basis of laws, procedures and principles
Appreciation of rules	Intuitive and unchallenged acceptance of rules	Shared rules and norms (contrafactual)	'Objective' understanding of rules and norms	Rules and norms depending on justice and morality

Gesellschaft (community and society) as well as with recent discussions on *communitarianism* and *liberalism* (Strike 2000). Combining the movement from heteronomy to autonomy with the two spheres of interpretation of social reality results in four 'levels' of moral judgement: level one is called 'interpersonal-heteronomous', level two 'interpersonal-autonomous', level three 'transpersonal-heteronomous' and level four 'transpersonal-autonomous'. Table 1 summarises the structures of these four levels of moral judgement.[2]

Enrichment of the Structural Levels by Additional Psychological Concepts – Ideal Types of Everyday Morality

Research in developmental psychology dealing with the structure of moral judgements has primarily been conducted on the basis of *hypothetical dilemmas*, which deliberately intend that interviewees are not personally involved in the conflict at hand. Applying the theory of moral judgements to the analysis of real life conflicts – as, for example, in the field of agriculture – requires a theoretical and methodical extension. This broader framework was developed in a more general discussion of context as culture (Boesch 1991; Eckensberger 1979, 1995, 1996). The hypothetical dilemma method was not applied; instead, biographical interviews were used. In addition to the structure of moral judgements, other normative concepts have to be considered, such as responsibility and solidarity. Apart from this, various other psychological constructs, such as the interpretation of facts (knowledge), control beliefs, identity structures and risk conceptions were the focus of attention. Again, these constructs are embedded in an action theory framework, which distinguishes *three levels* of action (for more details see Eckensberger 1979, 1990, 1996).

(a) *Primary actions* (first level) are what is usually meant by actions. They are 'oriented towards the world' and can be instrumental (effect-oriented), thus implying a 'physical' or 'natural' interpretation of the world. Consequently they are based on causal or functional processes. They can also be oriented towards interpreting the world as 'social', and are then based on understanding the intentional processes implied in (human) social interactions. With respect to the subject, these primary actions derive from personal concerns (goal structures and hierarchies). From a cognitive point of view they are based on and lead to figurative and simple operative schemata in the Piagetian sense, to scripts and descriptive social cognitions (understanding others', feelings, intentions and actions). With respect to culture they result in the so-called 'material culture' and in social habits/rituals. Primary actions are, for example, oriented towards the perception of facts about the environment and conservation of nature or perceived dangers for sustainable development and human health.

(b) *Secondary actions* (second level) are action-oriented, that is, they aim at the reflection and regulation of primary actions. However, they are also actions because these regulations are themselves goal-directed. They result primarily from experiencing barriers/impediments during primary actions. If they occur in instrumental actions they represent *problems* that have to be *removed.* In the context of social actions they are called *conflicts* that have to be solved. With respect to the subject they lead to representations of beliefs and normative or even prescriptive frameworks, like moral or ethical convictions and ideas about responsibility, or more specifically about conflict solutions. They represent ideals of how to solve conflicts. These normative schemata also become part of the 'ideational' aspects of culture – conventions, laws and ethics serving as frameworks (demands, affordances, prohibitions, taboos) for development and socialisation. But schemata of problem-solving also lead to the formation of ideals about technical knowledge by the subject, and to science and technology in the culture. Control beliefs and motivational resources derive from secondary actions as well. 'Situational control' is a central issue here. There are very different notions about what degree of freedom to allocate to members of a society in general as well as to oneself and others. From a moral perspective 'control' is closely linked to the question of *responsibility*, i.e., who can and should act. Who is *responsible* for ecological damage – for instance, oneself as an unreflective consumer, or politicians and experts?

(c) *Tertiary actions* (third level) are agency-oriented. There is an agency who acts, and to whom acts are related, and this agency reflects not only upon his or her actions (secondary actions), but also upon him/herself. Tertiary actions are additionally related to the agencies' very existence because of their relation to some ultimate entity, a process which is usually called contemplation. This theoretically implies religious thinking, representing the existential aspects of the self. Thus the process of *self-reflectivity* becomes a crucial feature in action theories. However, this agency is also oriented towards the social-cultural 'environment', which implies that actions can also have 'dramaturgical' aspects (cf. Eckensberger 1995, 1996; Habermas 1981). With respect to culture these tertiary actions relate to roles or role-systems and to concepts such as 'personhood' or 'cultural identity'. From the dynamic perspective coping and defence mechanisms have also to be mentioned (Haan 1977) and from the moral perspective, the central notion is 'solidarity' and its reach: is it up to us to take future generations into consideration?

Obstacles to primary and secondary actions and how they are handled are psychologically relevant: agency itself is 'created' or emerges as a result of experiencing and overcoming difficulties at the level of secondary actions. From this point of view, concepts of identity and especially of solidarity are considered relevant in contextualised moral judgements.

It is important to note that though all three action levels are differentiated analytically, empirically they are simultaneously present in a single act. It is also important to realise that in order to understand primary actions one has to know how they are embedded in rule systems and standards (secondary actions), and what these mean for the identity of the subject (tertiary actions).

Table 2.2. The three levels of action

Level of action	Questions of contextualisation	Action-perspectives	Contextualised moral dimensions
Third level of action	Who am I, who are the others, to whom do I belong?	**Agency oriented** Perspective of identity	Solidarity
Second level of action	Who possesses what possibilities of action, how to deal with barriers?	**Action oriented** Normative systems control beliefs	Responsibility
First level of action	What is the situation, what are the costs and benefits of actions?	**World oriented** Perception of facts	Risk

Since the main aim of all these research efforts has been to contextualise different moral orientations, the four moral levels and the three action levels were integrated. This results in four 'types of everyday morality' which differ in moral maturity. They comprise more information than the structurally determined moral levels shown in Table 2.1. These types are considered 'ideal types' in the Weberian sense, as they aim at explicating a phenomenon's structure of meaning (Saegesser 1975). Determining the validity of ideal types involves two aspects: one deals with the *analytical definition* of the interrelations among the constructs involved and this corresponds precisely to the integration of action levels and moral levels. The second deals with *empirically determining* the substantive reality of the types themselves.

Types of Everyday Morality: Risk, Responsibility and Solidarity

The entire empirical basis for constructing these *ideal types* comprises 180 semi-structured interviews conducted in the course of different projects. The types were constructed through a process in which theory, sampling, data collection and empirical analysis were closely interrelated. The strategy of 'theoretical sampling' (Glaser and Strauss 1967) was used, which starts off with the construction of a theoretical model (in our case the ideal types) based on a few subjects, and then adds contrasting cases, aimed at 'testing' the validity of the model (types). This process is brought to an end when new cases no longer add anything substantial to the model (types). Contrary to the original suggestion of Glaser and Strauss (1967), the ideal types were not primarily derived from the data, but, as explained above, achieved through analytical work (combining moral levels and action levels). Hence, the '*ideal types of everyday morality*' were in fact developed by alternating inductive and deductive steps as part of a large-scale research project. They were continually refined during this process. Table 2.3 summarises these types. A detailed description of the types has been presented elsewhere (Breit and Eckensberger 1998; Eckensberger et al. 1999, 2001), and are thus only presented here in a summarised form.

Table 2.3. Contextualised ideal types of moral judgements (everyday types)

	Interpersonal-heteronomous (IH)	Interpersonal-autonomous (IA)	Transpersonal-heteronomous (TH)	Transpersonal-autonomous (TA)
Identity	Similarity	Relationship, community	Functional role	Reflected (autonomous) self
Solidarity (Tertiary actions)	*Community of interests through similarities*	*Community through mutual recognition*	*Formally regulated relationships*	*All potentially affected persons*
Notions of control	Following rules, adjustment,	Inter-subjective recognition of norms	Technocratic feasibility	Reflection of goals
Responsibility (Secondary actions) conformity	*Delegated to authoritative power*	*Individual responsibility for the group/trust in others*	*Legal responsibility of the authoritative expert*	*Moral responsibility of all for all potentially affected persons by establishing democratic forms of actions*
Perception of facts	Concrete individual perception	Depends on interests	Objectivity	Reflection of limits of knowledge
Risk (Primary actions)	*Individual standard of living, existence*	*Social community, lifestyle, recognition*	*System-functionality*	*Global society, justice and alienation*

As mentioned, these types are not just understood as alternative normative interpretations of the social world differing in complexity; instead, it is claimed that they represent increases in 'moral maturity'. This is certainly speculative, but there are two justifications for this claim. First, the original definition of our 'moral stages' (Eckensberger and Burgard 1986) was based upon a cross-sectional sample of people who differed in age (ten to thirty years and older). To our astonishment we found that many adults also use rather simple arguments (structurally equivalent to twelve year-olds) regarding moral issues, when these are embedded in real-life contexts. The structure of moral judgements, therefore, can help to differentiate 'world-views' differing in complexity. The four types of everyday morality differ not only in scope, but also in the levels of abstraction in the normative interpretation of the social world. Secondly, arguments on higher levels also refer to those on lower levels, in the sense that these are discussed and reflected upon. This 'reflection' is exactly what Piaget (1985) had in mind when he devised the 'mechanism' of 'reflective abstraction' as a basic developmental principle.

Type I: Interpersonal-Heteronomous

For this type *conformity* and *similarity* are crucial prerequisites for *solidarity.* All persons whom the individual feels responsible for and who are part of the his/her group have to have the same interests and conform to the same values, because according to the interviewees life does not offer any other choice. Under these circumstances they see no other possibility than adaptation. Adaptation even becomes an ethical duty. Because *everybody* is confronted with existential threats, it is of general interest that nobody be allowed to withdraw from the existential and normative constraints of the natural and social environment. From this perspective, each person, as an individual, has to try to be as successful as possible. Yet *responsibility* is *delegated* to those who are in charge of a situation because of their position and their function, and to those who implement the rules that have to be followed. The rules themselves are not considered or mentioned at all. The interviewees of this type seem to have resigned and adapted to power structures, and mainly discuss practical constraints. They only take charge of something when they feel that their own interests are being threatened – then they might even take extensive action and blame those responsible. The *risks* mentioned are either exaggerated or played down, depending on how much they affect the interviewees, and above all risks are considered threats to *individual or collective interests.*

Type II: Interpersonal-Autonomous

For this type, conforming interests are not crucial to affiliating with the community (reflective abstraction), rather the crucial point is to belong to a group. Hence, *empathy* forms the basis for concepts of *solidarity* and the focus is on mutual relations. The interviewees see themselves as loyal to their own group, but they also sympathise with groups that are geographically distant (e.g., Native Americans, peoples of the Third World). This depends on whether for some reason sympathy has developed for these groups. Trusting that others follow inter-subjective norms is the key to changing from a heteronomous interest-orientation to an autonomous community-orientation. Every individual member bears *responsibility* for the cohesion of the group or community and for conserving environment and nature. Authorities and rulers are also obliged to protect the public weal, and they are judged according to their contribution to this goal. It is worth mentioning that trust in inter-subjective norms is also *counterfactual*. This means they are based on expectations which are maintained even when they are disappointed. Persons with this orientation rely largely on moral concepts about how humans ought to be, although their experiences repeatedly provoke scepticism about the assumed 'goodwill' of all persons. Nevertheless, they believe that *risks*, feared mainly because of their negative consequences for the social community and lifestyle, can only be managed through mutual processes of learning, based on enlightenment and on the acquisition of knowledge.

Type III: Transpersonal-Heteronomous

Type III does not believe that individuals themselves can uphold the functional integration of society and master risks by following inter-subjective norms (reflective abstraction). Instead, the most important issues for this type are efficient organisation, factual and objective knowledge as well as instrumental and strategic actions. *Solidarity* thus represents a fairly 'abstract' category that refers to competently filling functional roles in expert-systems or in communities of law. Other people's conceptions of solidarity are also viewed from a functional perspective, and their significance becomes evident in social conflict- or problem-solving. In type III's opinion the reconstruction of *responsibility* in terms of adherence to inter-subjectively acknowledged norms is no longer appropriate (as is the case for type II, reflective abstraction). Instead, a legal framework and expertise (science) are deemed necessary to define *responsibility*. Maintaining the system and functioning social forces can only be guaranteed by the legally binding responsibility of expert authority.

Therefore the reconstruction of *risk* does not take place within the interpersonal sphere that relates to individual interests in type I or to the rules of the community or a lifestyle in type II. Rather, risks are articulated with regard to their functionality and dysfunctionality for social or ecological systems, something for which economic, technical and juridical regulations are a prerequisite. Questions of technocratic feasibility thus attain central importance in the evaluation and reconstruction of risks.

Type IV: Transpersonal-Autonomous

This functional feasibility is precisely what the transpersonal-autonomous type distrusts (reflective abstraction). Type IV is more likely to question the meaning and the sense of human goals of action so that subjective moments (obligations, emotions) regain the relevance they no longer had for the previous type. Subjectively reflecting the goals of action as well as satisfying human needs and interests within the respective historical, cultural and social contexts are their main concerns. However, in contrast to type II, respecting the interests of a single fellow being is less important than generally respecting all human beings beyond of one's personal world. *Solidarity* with all other people (universalism) becomes a central principle for this type.

This universalistic (justice-) perspective actually requires impartial processes of judgement and, in so doing, transcends the world of type II as well as the objective cognition of type III in order to evaluate interests of others and to do justice to their lifestyles. A 'global' perspective is maintained in reconstructing *responsibility* and *risk*. Hence, risks are 'moralised' – because according to the interviewees risk-related decisions inherently lead to unjust solutions of conflicts when the principle of impartiality is violated and all potentially affected persons are not taken into consideration. Consequently, a sense of moral responsibility towards everyone potentially affected by the risk is a necessity. Although the morality of justice is based on obligation, the interviewees do not believe that a moral world is an ascetic world in which obligations dominate desires. More justice leads to increased humanity and hence to a better life. A really 'good life' eliminates the kind of thoughtlessness that a non-reflected lifestyle implies, and replaces it with a principle of justice that satisfies profound human needs through guaranteeing mutual respect.

Parallels between the Orientations in Agriculture and Heteronomy/Autonomy

In the following these types, which were constructed and validated on the basis of the total sample of one 180 interviews, will be used as the framework for the interpretation of arguments in the context of agriculture. The comparison of the two agricultural orientations and types of everyday morality suggests some parallels. In general, the *conventional* perspective of farming seems to correspond more closely to a heteronomous than to an autonomous judgement. This is mainly due to the fact that the central guiding principle of conventional thinking can be described as 'insight into necessity'. This means that reasonable acts relate to unchangeable conditions and restrictions; moreover, real freedom of action is restricted to reacting to the actual situation. To act responsibly also means having to gain direct insight into a 'tough' reality, otherwise one might have to bear the consequences. There seems to be a defensive tendency to reject all criticism of agriculture as generally unjustified or irrational, when negative economic consequences are expected.

Conversely, the organic perspective shows some similarities to autonomous judgements. The opportunities expected to arise by communicating and cooperating with groups that have different interests are more pronounced than in the conventional orientation. In spite of perceived constraints and restrictions, there are more counterfactual expectations which emphasise aspects of 'should' rather than of 'must'. Even though 'overreactions' to reports on food scandals by the general public are criticised, legitimate elements in criticisms are accepted and not dismissed as completely irrational.

Method

Sampling aimed at testing the applicability of the 'everyday types' of morality to the two agricultural orientations implies a qualitative comparison of the arguments in the samples. Beyond this, however, the distribution of types was expected to differ in the two agricultural orientations. This called for a 'classical' sampling strategy for selecting a minimum number of subjects in both orientations; this also allows for quantitative comparison and generalisation.

A total of forty persons who are professionally involved in agriculture in a variety of ways were interviewed, using a guideline of questions about risks in agriculture, their causes, and possible solutions. The interviewees were ten conventional farmers; ten organic farmers; ten conventionally and organically oriented 'experts' with academic training; and ten conventionally and organically oriented decision-makers (officials, politicians, entrepreneurs). All subjects were selected a priori so that the two orientations were represented equally. The farmers could be classified easily according to the type of agricultural production or cultivation methods used. The five persons comprising each of the two other groups (experts with academic training and decision-makers) categorised themselves as having either a conventional or an organic orientation.

The study was conducted in Saarland, a region in western Germany. The farms in this area use extensive cultivation rather than the intensive cultivation methods of the agricultural industry. This is a consequence of the fairly poor quality of soil. One third of the farms are cultivated on a full-time basis, two thirds are managed to provide additional income. Large scale livestock farming with more than 300 animals (e.g., pigs, chickens, cows) does not exist. Fodder and dairy farming are the most prevalent forms of full-time farming. Most farmers are conventionally oriented, with only 2.5 percent of the farming in Saarland being organically oriented. This percentage corresponds to the ratio in Germany as a whole. The average size of farms is approximately 80 ha, which is above the average calculated for all the federal states of Germany. According to a recent report on agriculture by the federal government, Saarland farming is in a relatively good state (Agrarbericht 1999).

Results

Qualitative Analysis of the Moral Dimension in Agricultural Risk Management Strategies

First of all, it was important that all arguments of the interviewees could be categorised as representing a conventional and/or organic orientation. No third orientation emerged. The qualitative and structural analysis of the conventional and organic orientation indicates, basically, that the conventionalists focus primarily on the economic consequences of risks. They express the opinion that 'Ecology is important, but it has to be paid for, and because of the economic situation farmers are struggling to survive'. In the organic orientation the importance of ecological risks is highlighted. They point out that: 'all agricultural production must lead to income and positive economic consequences, but profits have to be subordinated to ecology in the end'.

But this picture is not a homogenous one. On the one hand, there are conventional farmers who do not wish to enter the competitive world market and prefer selling high-quality products within the region, thereby following the example of their organically oriented colleagues. Some conventional farmers attempt to enter markets of regional farmers, for example, by marketing on their own, marking their products with domestic-quality seal labels and selling these in grocery chains. Similarly, some organic farmers aim at gaining access to supermarket chains to increase sales and achieve lower prices for organic products. Thus the empirical analysis demonstrates that the two perspectives cannot always be distinguished easily in the interviews because there are parallels in how both orientations weigh economic and ecological aspects. Here the distinction between the three action-levels as part of the type definition proves to be helpful.

However, weighing economic and ecological factors against each other in risk management (first level of action) does not say much about the moral reasoning or the structural basis of this process of rating. So it is important to analyse the moral structures at 'higher' action levels, where concepts of responsibility (second action level) and solidarity (third action level) are located. Both concepts are also theoretically linked to the perception and evaluation of risks, in that they serve as interpretational baselines in risk construction because other persons are always involved in this process in different ways, for example as victims and offenders or as responsible agencies. Risks are always constructed against the backdrop of 'solidarity' and 'responsibility' and this simultaneously constitutes the frame for answering the questions 'who counts as member of one's group' (solidarity) and 'who is blameless or who is to blame' (responsibility).

In our context of agriculture the aspect of solidarity in risk management (the tertiary action-level) impinges on the question of how to deal with the competing orientation. So the following issues arise: how do the 'two groups' of agricultural orientation evaluate one another? Do they disparage each other? How do the interviewees interact with persons who differ in orientation? The aspect of responsibility (secondary action level) deals with questions of third parties restricting other individuals' freedom of action. These can be consumers, politicians, governments or impersonal institutions, such as laws and markets. Responsibility for causing or avoiding agricultural risks can be ascribed to all of them. The focus in the present study is on reconstructing the consumer behaviour regarded as responsible for the present economic and ecological situation and ways of improving it through agriculture. How do the interviewees refer to potential customers? What kinds of relationship exist between individuals in the market arena, in particular between consumers and agricultural agents?

Moral Evaluations of Persons Who Differ in Orientation (Solidarity)

First of all, the four 'types of everyday morality' turned out to be applicable to this sample too, and neither a new type nor mixed types had to be formulated. Table 2.4 presents examples of arguments expressed by informants which refer to the evaluation of the 'other group'.

At the *interpersonal-heteronomous level* the interviewees of each orientation distinguish themselves strictly from those of the other orientation, often also by devaluing it. The *conventionally oriented interviewees* consider organic cultivation unnecessary, see no environmental or health risks in conventional farming, and consider risks as inevitable or as sufficiently controllable by existing standards. They think that only ideologists or 'cranks' practice organic farming, which they regard as nothing but profit-making without providing a true alternative. From the standpoint of *organic agriculture*, however organic farming is regarded as crucial to the survival of humankind because the risks involved in conventional farming are considered a great threat to health and environment. According to these farmers, individuals who do not realise this are being manipulated by the chemical or agricultural industry.

At the *interpersonal-autonomous* level people were found to have a more harmonious stance and primarily saw all the parties involved as members of the same regional community. Hence they are prepared to treat other points of view with benevolence and engage in discussions with persons having a different point of view. Here, contrasting views are toned down, the other person's position is understood, even though one is convinced of one's own opinion. At this level even the most convinced *advocates of organic farming* tend to reduce the differences between organic and conventional by referring to regional characteristics such as quality of products and damage to the environment, while the *conventionally oriented group* even expresses open sympathy for organic farming. However, the latter doubt that it can actually be realised and question their own economic capacity to change. For the near future though, they do foresee a balanced adjustment of production methods and are willing to contribute to bringing this about.

Table 2.4. Stance towards the competing orientation and (contextualised) moral levels

	Conventional orientation	Organic orientation
Interpersonal heteronomous	*'Many conventional farmers are under strong economic pressure and the organic farmers are receiving subventions. But there are enough scientific studies proving that organic products are no better than conventional ones. Right, organic farmers are convinced by their kind of production and it is good if you are sure of yourself. But there are no purely organic farms because they could not be managed successfully. It's all ideology.'* (farmer)	*Agriculture produces terrific risks. Take a look at the conventional farmers, they are not free, because the entire agricultural industry is breathing down their necks. They are paid, regulated and controlled. And they are fed with all information they need.'* (farmer)
Interpersonal autonomous	*'In my opinion organic products are a good thing. I also cultivate without using excessive fodder additives and try to avoid certain procedures. There are some farmers in the neighbourhood who took the risk of producing organically and take trouble to establish private marketing. I respect this.'* (farmer)	*'You must be discriminating in your evaluation of conventional agriculture. Here, in this region, the production is not as intensive as in the northern part of the Federal Republic. Because of this the difference between conventional and organic production is not that great. I have good contacts with a farmer in the neighbourhood, even though he only works conventionally. Maybe he will change his attitude at some point in time.'* (farmer)
Transpersonal heteronomous	*'Ultimately the market will decide the question of who will prevail and this is OK. There will always be a small percentage of consumers, who will buy "bio-products". Of course, the wishful thinking of organically oriented farmers aims at something else.'* (decision-maker)	*'In any case we need different rules and guidelines for the market and its regulation, as this is the key to our success. One has to demand: If you as producer of this product or as a user of this production method cannot exclude certain ecological risks or see health hazards, then these products must be kept away from the market.'* (farmer)
Transpersonal autonomous	*'The idea of organic production is good and changes are going in the right direction. One has to do more to enlighten consumers but has to rid them of their romantic misconceptions because farming is done at a high technical level. Will there be more than a market niche for organic farming? I don`t think so but this depends on complex developments in society.'* (decision-maker)	*It is correct that not everyone can afford organic products but one has to take a look at the development of prices in the last thirty years and to compare this with prices of other products. Consumer behaviour has also changed because more money is spent on other things. Especially for conventional farmers this tendency means economic pressure which they have to submit to unwillingly. These are socio-political problems in the context of discussing sustainability.'* (decision-maker)

At the *transpersonal-heteronomous level* the two positions can be characterised as involving strategically different forms of access to the market. Moreover, there is a moral preference for one's own perspective because it is considered superior to the other, based on specific rational criteria. The *organically oriented* take a more systemic approach by including a large range of aspects (economy, ecology, health) in their considerations of risks. *Conventionally oriented* persons attribute higher economic realism to themselves and frequently ascribe irrational motives to those with organic views because they are considered incapable of correctly assessing the conditions necessary for realising organic farming.

In contrast, there is no strict separation between the organic and conventional orientations at the *transpersonal-autonomous level.* The *organically oriented* group primarily takes into account the partially global economic pressures that determine actions in agriculture. They see the economic advantages of cheap mass production while aiming their organically grown products mainly at consumers with high purchasing power. The interviewees also react fairly in their appreciation of conventional agricultural produce and underline its high quality. This is possible because risks are not constructed primarily in terms of health, but rather in terms of the ecological risks of agricultural production to the environment and as a means of guaranteeing sustainable development. The *conventionally oriented* transpersonal-autonomous persons are openly sympathetic to organic agriculture, but more so than the interpersonal-autonomous interviewees. They even agree with the organic orientation, in that they strive for organic farming as a future model because of the smaller health and environmental risks involved. At the same time, however, they do not see it as a *realistic* alternative to conventional agriculture given the *present* economic and social circumstances. Conventionally orientated persons at this level believe that conventional agriculture can only unfold its potential to change in the direction of organic agriculture, if it is not used as a scapegoat in public discussions.

Moral Evaluations of Interactions with Consumers (Responsibility)

Depending on the level of moral judgements, the category 'consumer' is also constructed in completely different ways. In Table 2.5 statements recorded during interviews are again contrasted according to the moral level.

Those conventionally and organically oriented interviewees classified as either interpersonal or transpersonal *heteronomous type* regard consumers as acting in their own best interests. Consumers are looked upon as passive recipients, who only need the 'right' information to be able to make appropriate decisions when buying products. *Conventionally oriented* interviewees primarily emphasise consumers' hysterical reactions to exaggerated reports of agricultural scandals in the mass media. *Organically oriented* persons see the consumer as 'blinded' and 'misled' by publicity and information launched by the agricultural industry. In both orientations the *interpersonal-heteronomous* types regard the consumer as

Table 2.5. Attitudes towards consumers and (contextualised) moral levels

	Conventional orientation	**Organic orientation**
Interpersonal heteronomous	*'The media falsifies and distorts the truth. You can imagine the kind of attitude the consumer has towards agriculture. This is our biggest problem.'* (farmer)	*'Most of all people are indolent and lazy, they only consume. The consumer doesn`t know anything about nutrition. Much could already have been done in kindergarten but there are other dominating interests.'* (farmer)
Interpersonal autonomous	*'Why shouldn't consumers buy cheap products? In many cases they have high standards which they want to attain with little effort. This is their 'right'.* (farmer)	*'I think that in the long run we don't have a chance of getting consumers to trust us, if we don`t try minimising risks. Consciousness and awareness will become stronger and we have to take up this trend.'* (farmer)
Transpersonal heteronomous	*'How can we take measures to counteract the resentments against certain agricultural projects if we cannot reach the people by information campaigns? This is the real problem area. But beside consumers` reactions one always has to take legal conditions and regulations into account.'* (decision-maker)	*'Consumers simply have to be better informed about possible risks. Sometimes the hysteria is really exaggerated but without this mass reaction there would be no pressure on the politicians and the administration.' (expert)*
Transpersonal autonomous	*'The consumers' behaviour has to be interpreted as one aspect of a general lifestyle. In society there are different concepts and evaluations of what "quality of life" should be. They must be discussed in the context of economic conditions. Are the decisions of consumers deliberate and free? Surely not, but are there only habits and automatisms?'* (expert)	*After having indoctrinated generations of people that they should buy cheap products one cannot expect them to pay double the price when the situation changes. This is a societal process which needs time. This implies changes on the political and institutional level.'* (decision-maker)

being largely responsible for exerting pressure on price policies as well as for economic, ecological and social risks in agriculture. Therefore, from the point of view of the interviewees, the consumers are the true source of risks. Organic and conventional interviewees evaluate consumers as abstract self-interested super-persons and lay the blame on them. Changes in consumer behaviour are assumed to occur only, if at all, because of individual insights and experiences (e.g., illness). The *transpersonal-heteronomous* interviewees additionally consider functional processes that go beyond individual intentions. Depending on their orientation, they see a possibility of achieving positive changes with the help of consumer behaviour, if they could succeed in directing their behaviour towards the chosen goals through pricing and well-selected information. Conventional persons emphasise that information policy, in the sense of politicians' and experts' providing education, aims at immunising consumers against emotional overreaction to reports on disasters in the mass media. Organically oriented interviewees feel clearly disadvantaged, because organic agriculture is too weak to determine information politics. From their functionalist point of view they especially recognise the unintended effects of fear: irrational consumer behaviour can sometimes lead to risk reduction because it results in high standards of risk evaluation provoked by fear and overreactions. But even if consumers are regarded as necessary for processes of change, this is not taken as a sign of their understanding or/and scientific cooperation, but rather as the result of chance and behaviour controlled by technical and institutional precautions.

In contrast, the two *autonomous* types, regardless of their orientation, do not construct the 'consumer' as a homogeneous category, but rather as persons having different orientations and interests with whom interaction is considered possible. From this perspective the consumer is an independent agent with the right and ability to select products, and problems can be solved jointly by consumers and reasonable farmers or agricultural representatives. Trying to influence consumers to act in a specific way is considered irrelevant. Instead, farmers and their organisations should make concessions to consumers and develop an understanding of their problems. This could be achieved by measures of innovative and consumer-friendly marketing. Moreover, this should be an integral part of farmers' professional approach. Indeed, farmers bear the social responsibility for satisfying the basic food and health needs of the population; in turn they should be respected and receive adequate remuneration and be treated appropriately. Especially conventionally oriented interviewees emphasise the latter point: they feel that society does not respect conventional farmers enough. With regard to experiencing environmental risk, strictly speaking there is no difference between farmers and consumers. Ultimately both groups face the same problems, the chemical risks and the dominant food industry. They are both subjected to the anonymity of the market and unable to properly assess risks because of experts' contradictory opinions. The consumer, conceived of as a real, participating agent, is potentially able to make reasonable decisions as responsible citizen and is a partner in joint risk management. Moreover, critical and cautious consumers are desirable because they demand standards which have to be acknowledged by agriculture. These standards apply to risks that have become unacceptable even to farmers because of the increasing industrialisation of farming in recent years. Consumers are therefore not just the object of educational efforts by experts, farmers and politicians, but under certain circumstances are educators in their own right. In any case, the consumer is a partner in a mutual learning process. With regard to the mass media, a more differentiated view also dominates. Mass media do not just 'brainwash' immature consumers, but rather sensitise them to existing problems.

The difference between *interpersonal- and transpersonal-autonomous types* is that the transpersonals of both orientations focus less on individual intentions or the goodwill of persons, than on the institutional framework that enables the realisation of positive intentions. Thus, the transpersonal group does not blame individual persons or hold them responsible, but rather takes objective conditions of action (e.g., economy or politics) into consideration. However, they also point out that these conditions are primarily shaped by responsible actions or by individual or collective agents.

One could of course, regard the autonomy of both orientations as naïve, but this is not the case. In fact consumers do not meet their normative expectations. From the *interpersonal perspective* they do not show enough initiative in trying to become well-informed trading partners. They confess to preferring to invest money in status symbols rather than in good and healthy food. Additionally, from the *transpersonal perspective*, it is regarded as highly unlikely that the constraints of global marketing interests leave enough room for influencing institutions. In fact the two autonomous types do not differ that much from the two heteronomous types in their descriptions of reality, because reality is largely objectively determined by external pressures, markets and politics. The crucial difference between the autonomous and heteronomous constructions of societal processes is that the negative evaluations described fit the expectations of the heteronomous, but they disappoint the expectations of the autonomous group. However, this disappointment does not result in refraining from having normative expectations in general. These counterfactual convictions lead to a greater willingness to take risks, to supporting processes of change and to having the confidence that others will co-operate in the process.

Quantitative Distributions

Table 2.6 shows that the distribution of types differs across the various groups of interviewees (farmers, decision-makers). Since the sample size is small, the quantitative aspects have to be treated cautiously. There are some interesting trends, however.

Table 2.6. Moral judgement and different groups of interviewees

		Types of everyday morality			
Orientation	**Action-Group**	**I (IH)**	**II (IA)**	**III (TH)**	**IV (TA)**
Conventional	Farmers	5	4	1	0
Organic	Farmers	3	5	1	1
Conventional	Decision-makers	1	1	1	2
Organic	Dcision-makers	–	–	1	4
Conventional	Experts	1	1	3	–
Organic	xperts	–	3	2	–
	Total	10	14	9	7

Table 2.7. Moral judgement and different groups of interviewees

		Types of everyday morality			
Orientation	**Action-Group**	**Heteronomous**	**Autonomous**	**Interpersonal**	**Transpersonal**
Conventional	Farmers	6	4	**9**	1
Organic	Farmers	4	6	**8**	2
Conventional	Decision-makers	2	3	2	**3**
Organic	Decision-makers	1	4	–	**5**
Conventional	Experts	4	1	2	3
Organic	Experts	2	3	3	2
	Total	19	21	24	16

First of all, within each of the sub-groups (farmers, experts, decision-makers) no remarkable differences are evident in the number of organically and conventionally oriented persons pronouncing autonomous and heteronomous (or respectively interpersonal and transpersonal) judgements (Table 2.6). This becomes even clearer if we add together the heteronomous, the autonomous, the interpersonal and the transpersonal judgements (Table 2.7). However, as Fig. 2.1 shows, when only conventional or organic orientations are looked at the frequency of moral types within the conventional group decreases from type I to type IV, whereas in the organic orientation the autonomous types are slightly more frequent. This is in agreement with the hypothesis that the organic orientation is connected with an autonomous morality.

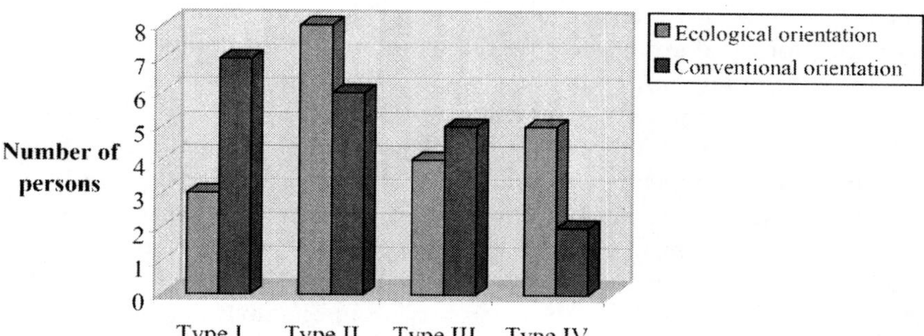

Figure 2.1. Association of risk management strategies and types of everyday morality

This trend becomes yet more evident when the autonomous and heteronomous sub-types – interpersonal and transpersonal – are lumped together. Then the relation of autonomy to heteronomy in the organic orientation is 13:7; in the conventional group this trend appears to be inverted, i.e. there are more heteronomous arguments (8:12). This distribution of agrarian orientations x moral judgements approaches a 5 percent significance level (Chi^2 one tailed, $p < .055$). So from this point of view there is some support for our expectation. Evidently, however, this trend is mainly due to an overrepresentation of decision-makers on the transpersonal level (see table 2.7): only three of the twenty farmers argued on the transpersonal level; on the other hand, eight of ten decision-makers argued transpersonally. This relationship is highly significant (Chi^2 two tailed, $p < .001$), but has to be treated cautiously because expected frequencies per cell are smaller than five.

Summary and Conclusions

Two different orientations characterising different systems of thought and risk management can be distinguished in the context of agricultural action. They constitute the frame for reconstructing the opportunities for action and the perception of risks with regard to ecological, economic and social challenges. Although at first glance both orientations also appear to differ with reference to central moral convictions (about the other group as well as the consumers of their products), a detailed analysis of their contextualised moral judgements demonstrates that this view is too simple.

First, the results demonstrate the general fruitfulness of distinguishing between content of decisions (the style of farming) and structure (reasons given for the decision). This distinction enables a much more detailed understanding of the normative convictions involved in risk management in agriculture than the stereotypical distinction between conventional and organic orientations alone. There is, indeed, a strong trend towards more autonomous arguments in the organically oriented group, because the more 'holistic' philosophy of organic agriculture regarding sustainable development entails an interactive view of the relationship both between humans and nature and among humans. This trend is in fact empirical; it is not merely a logical implication because distinguishing between agricultural orientations and moral judgements reveals that many of the conventionalists have moral convictions similar to those of organically oriented persons and vice versa (a considerable number of conventionalists also argue autonomously, and several of the organically oriented people also argue heteronomously). In addition, a preference for autonomous arguments in the organically oriented group is just not true for farmers. They are almost equally distributed across autonomous and heteronomous judgements. The same is true for the experts. But whereas the farmers argue primarily on the interpersonal level, the experts also argue on the transpersonal (heteronomous) level to a considerable degree, so they appear slightly more morally mature in their judgements in both orientations (conventional and organic).

By concentrating on the structure of moral judgements (reasons given for the decision) instead of on the content of decisions (the style of farming), discussions of learning procedures and communication processes become inevitable. Differentiating between autonomous and heteronomous moral judgements provides a better explanation of different 'world-views' than the label of organic and conventional orientations, and indicates possible ways of changing them, as well as the willingness to learn. In this connection the significance of 'open vs. closed' conceptions of the world is apparent (Horton 1967). This dimension differentiates between objective, social and subjective world-views. It also refers to the degree of reflection, corresponding to the capacity of self-criticism and the ability to change oneself. It is clearly evident from the interviews that in particular autonomous moral judgements entail this potential for reflection and learning. Autonomy implies taking others' criticism 'seriously', heeding different positions in one's own judgements, and maintaining the tension between facts and norms through stabilising counterfactual claims and expectations. As these expectations are relatively resistant to disappointments, they consolidate a willingness to act and provide opportunities for further cooperation.

Therefore one can say that *autonomous conventionally* and *autonomous organically* oriented types have more in common through their willingness to learn and cooperate than the heteronomous types of either conventional or organic orientation. Willingness to learn and cooperate also underlines that autonomy as a cultural orientation is more efficient than a heteronomous orientation when it comes to actions aimed at changing the environment in the direction of sustainable development and integrating different cultural world views. Attending to moral judgements helps identify where tendencies to 'lock' into positions exist, and where risk management takes on the character of ideology. Heteronomous moral judgements (especially interpersonal-heteronomous ones) indicate that conflicts and risks are reconstructed from the self-centred perspective of one's own conception of the world. Interpersonal-heteronomous conventionally and interpersonal-heteronomous organically oriented persons are 'furthest apart' in so far as they both persist in maintaining their position as the only 'correct' or 'reasonable' one.

In a world where no knowledge is absolutely certain, because it is always considered perspectival, the question of how to behave towards people with other views is pivotal. This also implies that rational risk-management takes place in joint social learning processes, in other words, in terms of changing perspectives and judgements through discourses that include different points of view. Public discourses are fundamental for institutional change and social learning in democratic societies (Breit and Troja 2003), because individual and institutional commitment to ecological remedial action are debated (Breit et al. 2003).

There are different cultural orientations having different impact on changing the environment in a particular local context. On the basis of a comparison of the two orientations from a moral point of view, we conclude that there appears to be a higher *potential* for obtaining autonomous judgements in the organic, rather than in the conventional orientation. This implies that on the whole the organic risk-management strategy might be more adequate for coping with a modern risk society, in that it is more open to the requisite learning processes that take different points of view into account. But our study also shows that one has to be cautious with hasty generalisations. Finally, the finding that decision-makers in particular dominate the transpersonal (especially the transpersonal autonomous) level supports the theory of moral judgements. This substantiates the assumption that participation in decision-making, particularly from a 'neutral' or personally uninvolved point of view, 'triggers' more mature moral arguments or allows them to emerge. This group in particular is forced to consider non-intended causal chains resulting from decisions, and it must also mediate between conflicting groups. It is worthwhile mentioning, once again, that half of the experts argued on the transpersonal level.

Notes

1. We thank Ingrid Plath for her critical remarks. Without her this contribution could not have been realised in this way.
2. For a detailed description of the theoretical background of the construction of these levels and the relation to Kohlberg's developmental theory of moral judgement see Eckensberger (1986); Eckensberger and Reinshagen (1980); Eckensberger and Burgard (1986).

References

Agrarbericht der Bundesregierung 1995. Bonn: Bundesministerium für Ernährung, Landwirtschaft und Forsten.

——— 1999. Bonn: Bundesministerium für Ernährung, Landwirtschaft und Forsten.

Barth, W.E. 1995. *Naturschutz – Das Machbare.* Hamburg: Paul Parley.

Boesch, E.E. 1991. *Symbolic Action Theory and Cultural Psychology.* Berlin: Springer.

Breit, H. and L.H. Eckensberger 1998. 'Moral, Alltag und Umwelt', in *Umweltbildung und Umweltbewußtsein. Forschungsperspektiven im Kontext nachhaltiger Entwicklung,* eds. G. De Haan and U. Kuckartz, 69–89. Opladen: Leske & Budrich.

Breit, H., T. Döring and L.H. Eckensberger 2003. 'Law, Politics and Citizens' Responsibility. Justice Judgements in the Every Day Reconstructions of Environmental Conflicts', in *How Institutions Change. Perspectives on Social Learning in Environmental Contexts,* eds. H. Breit, A. Engels, T. Moss and M. Troja, 179–203. Opladen: Leske & Budrich.

Breit, H. and M. Troja 2003. 'Institutional Change and Social Learning in Environmental Contexts: An Introduction', in *How Institutions Change. Perspectives on Social Learning in Environmental Contexts,* 13–30. Opladen: Leske & Budrich.

Cole, M. 1996. *Cultural Psychology. A Once and Future Discipline.* Cambridge, MA: The Belknap Press of Harvard University Press.

Eckensberger, L.H. 1979. 'A Metamethodological Evaluation of Psychological Theories from a Cross-Cultural Perspective', in *Cross-Cultural Contributions to Psychology,* eds. L.H. Eckensberger, W.J. Lonner and Y.H. Poortinga, 255–75. Amsterdam: Swets and Zeitlinger.

——— 1986. 'Handlung, Konflikt und Reflexion: Zur Dialektik von Struktur und Inhalt im moralischen Urteil', in *Zur Bestimmung der Moral: Philosophische und sozialwissenschaftliche Beiträge zur Moralforschung,* eds. W. Edelstein and G. Nunner-Winkler, 409–42. Frankfurt/M: Suhrkamp.

——— 1990. 'From Cross-Cultural Psychology to Cultural Psychology', *The Quarterly Newsletter of the Laboratory of Comparative Human Cognition* 12(1): 37–52.

——— 1993. 'Moralische Urteile als handlungsleitende normative Regelsysteme im Spiegel der kulturvergleichenden Psychologie', in *Einführung in die kulturvergleichende Psychologie*, ed. A. Thomas, 259–95. Göttingen: Hogreve.

——— 1995. 'Auf der Suche nach den (verlorenen?) Universalien hinter den Kulturstandards', in *Psychologie interkulturellen Handelns*, ed. A. Thomas, 165–97. Göttingen: Hogreve.

——— 1996. 'Agency, Action and Culture: Three Basic Concepts for Cross-Cultural Psychology', in *Asian Contributions to Psychology*, eds. J. Pandey, D. Sinha and D.P.S. Bhawuk, 72–102. Delhi: Sage.

——— 1998. 'Die Entwicklung des moralischen Urteils', in *Lehrbuch Entwicklungspsychologie*, ed. H. Keller, 475–516. Bern: Huber.

——— 2001. 'Psychology of Action Theory', in *International Encyclopedia of the Social and Behavioral Sciences*, eds. N. J. Smelser and P. B. Baltes, 45–9. Oxford: Elsevier Science Ltd.

——— and H. Reinshagen 1980. 'Kohlbergs Stufentheorie der Entwicklung des Moralischen Urteils: Ein Versuch ihrer Reinterpretation im Bezugsrahmen handlungstheoretischer Konzepte', in *Entwicklung sozialer Kognitionen: Modelle, Theorien, Methoden, Anwendung*, eds. L.H. Eckensberger and R.K. Silbereisen, 65–131. Stuttgart: Klett-Cotta.

——— and P. Burgard 1986. *Zur Beziehung zwischen Struktur und Inhalt in der Entwicklung des moralischen Urteils aus handlungstheoretischer Sicht.* Saarbrücken: Universität des Saarlandes, Arbeiten der Fachrichtung Psychologie 77.

———, H. Breit and T. Döring 1999. 'Ethik und Barriere in umweltbezogenen Entscheidungen: Eine entwicklungspsychologische Perspektive', in *Barrieren* 'umweltgerechter' *politischer und privater Entscheidungen*, eds. V. Linneweber and E. Kals,165–89. Bern: Huber.

———, T. Döring and H. Breit 2001. 'Moral Dimensions in Risk Evaluation', in *Environmental Risks: Perception, Evaluation and Management*, eds. G. Boehm, J. Nerb, T. McDaniels and H. Spada. Special issue of *Research in Social Problems and Public Policy* 9: 137–64.

Glaser, B.G. and A.L. Strauss 1967. *The Discovery of Grounded Theory. Strategies of Qualitative Research.* Chicago: Aldine.

Haan, N. 1977. *Coping and Defending. Processes of Self-Environment Organisation.* New York: Academic Press.

Habermas, J. 1981. *Theorie des kommunikativen Handelns*, vol. 1. Frankfurt/M: Suhrkamp.

Horton, R. 1967. 'African Traditional Thought and Western Science', *Africa* 37: 155–87.

Kohlberg, L. 1976. 'Moral Stages and Moralisation. The Cognitive Developmental Approach', in *Moral, Development and Behavior. Theory, Research, and Social Issues*, ed. T. Lickona, 31–53. New York: Holt, Rinehart Winston.

——— 1986. 'A Current Statement on Some Theoretical Issues', in *Lawrence Kohlberg. Consensus and Controversy*, eds. A. Modgil and D. Modgil, 485–546. Philadelphia: Farmer Press.

Linnartz, T. 1994. *Die Landwirtschaft und ihre Probleme im Meinungsbild der Bevölkerung. Eine Analyse hinsichtlich ausgewählter agrarpolitischer Themen und ihrer Bestimmungsgründe.* Ph.D. Thesis, Bonn: Schriftenreihe der Forschungsgesellschaft für Agrarpolitik und Agarsoziologie e.V.

Mayer, J. 1994. *Ökologische Landbau-Perspektive für die Zukunft.* Special issue no. 58. Bad Dürkheim: Stiftung ökologischer Landbau.

Ostrom, E. 1990. *Governing the Commons. The Evolution of Institution for Collective Action.* Cambridge: Cambridge University Press.

Piaget, J. 1970. 'Piaget's Theory', in *Carmichael's Manuel of Child Psychology*, ed. P.H. Museen, vol.1: 703–32. New York: Wiley.

——— 1985. *The Equilibration of Cognitive Structures. The Central Problem of Intellectual Development.* Chicago: University of Chicago Press.

——— 1973. *Das moralische Urteil beim Kinde.* Frankfurt: Suhrkamp (1st edn 1932, *Le jugement chez l'enfant.* Paris: Lacan).

Quirbach, K.-H. 1989. *Ökologische Landwirtschaft: Prinzipien, Fehler, Folgen, Ansatzpunkte.* Karlsruhe: Institut für Regionalwissenschaften der Universität Karlsruhe.

Saegesser, B. 1975. *Der Idealtypus Max Webers und der naturwissenschaftliche Modellbegriff.* Ph.D. Thesis, Basel: University of Basel.

Strike, K.A. 2000. 'Liberalism, Communitarianism and the Space Between: *Praise of* Kindness', *Journal of Moral Education 2000*: 133–47.

Tönnies, F. 1887. *Gemeinschaft und Gesellschaft: Grundbegriffe der reinen Soziologie* (rev. edn 1963). Darmstadt: Wissenschaftliche Buchgesellschaft.

Wellhausen, J. 1985. *Landwirtschaft als Thema ethnologischer Forschungen. Eine Analyse empirischer und theoretischer Studien.* Ph.D. Thesis, Cologne: Herodot.

Wolf, P. 1996. 'Nachhaltige Ressourcenschonung', *Der Tropenlandwirt. Journal of Agriculture in the Tropics and Subtropics* 56. Witzenzhausen: Selbstverlag des Verbandes der Tropenlandwirte.

3

Attributed Causes of Environmental Problems: A Cross-Cultural Study of Coping Strategies

Josef Nerb, Andrea Bender and Hans Spada

Introduction

In June 1991, after the largest eruption of the Philippine volcano Pinatubo in the twentieth century, the Aeta (Ayta) explained the catastrophe as having been caused by human misbehaviour that disturbed both the environment and the sacred places of the spirits and the Supreme Being. The Aeta belong to the oldest indigenous population of the Philippines and supplement their subsistence with hunting and gathering. Most Aeta held the drilling of the Philippine Oil Company responsible for the disaster, a claim that was confirmed by *manganitos*, the mediums of the spirits. Some *manganitos* suggested further causes for the catastrophe: they blamed the government for having cleared a forest in order to build a large road and the U.S. Air Force for holding military exercises near the site of the volcano, they were convinced that the Pinatubo was 'taking revenge' for this human interference and demanded. among other measures, that the government and the U.S. Air Force provide for animal sacrifices in order to stop the eruption.

In August 1998, a consultant of the World Bank visited Tongan villages to survey existing coastal resource management. His task was to derive efficient measures for the protection of local fish stocks, which were declining dramatically due to overfishing (e.g., *TSFR* 1998). However, contrary to the consultant's expectations, several fishermen claimed that there was no decline at all or that declines in certain fish stocks were not primarily caused by the exploitation itself. According to these Tongan fishermen, the fish were deliberately hiding in the deep sea because they were afraid of the fishermen. Several men stated that God is responsible for the well-being of human and fish populations and that praying might increase the catches. Most others concluded that leaving them undisturbed for a while would be sufficient to make them return and added that with better equipment, even such protective measures may not be necessary (Bender 2001a,b).

The Maltese-registered tanker *Erika* broke in two near the coast of Brittany, France, in December 1999. The twenty-six-member Indian crew was evacuated. According to some experts, the sinking of the *Erika* has constituted Europe's worst-ever oil disaster for wildlife: more than 300,000 birds were affected by the 12,000 tons of heavy oil that leaked when the tanker broke. The tanker was run by the world's fourth largest oil company, Total Fina, and Greenpeace and other environmental organisations blamed the company for its failure to take responsibility for cleaning up the environmental pollution. In Brest and elsewhere, thousands of people joined protests against Total Fina and accused the company of negligence in using this risky ship that did not have the security guarantees necessary for transport.

Although the reactions of the Aeta, the Tongan fishermen, and the people in Brittany were very different, there is nevertheless an important similarity in how people from such different cultures respond to environmental threats. For people in all these cultures it is crucial to know the cause of the catastrophe. In all cases, the causal attribution and the subsequent ascription of responsibility for the disaster are significant determinants of what people consider appropriate measures for coping with the situation.

This chapter is about how people from different cultures (Germany and Tonga/Polynesia) try to cope with environmental threats by causal attribution. In particular, an important first step of individual coping strategies is discussed, namely the cognitive appraisal of the threatening situation. From an applied standpoint, detecting cross-cultural differences in appraisal and coping processes is crucial to providing culturally tailored risk-communication and crisis-response strategies. In the first section of the chapter different coping strategies are outlined. The focus is on strategies such as wishful thinking and blaming, which are very common ways of reducing stress but mostly do not allow a solution to the environmental problems. Dispositionalist and situationalist attributions and coping are defined and discussed in the context of cross-cultural studies. The Tongan cultural background is outlined in the second section, before giving a description of experiments on the types of appraisal and coping under environmental threats in Germany and Tonga in the third. A discussion of the results of these experimental studies concludes this chapter.

Appraisal of Environmental Problems

The central tenet of so-called appraisal theories of emotions (Scherer et al. 2001; Ellsworth and Scherer 2003) is that emotions are not simply reactions to situational stimuli, but the result of the cognitive appraisal of a situation. Such appraisal reflects the personal implications of the situation by taking into account the person's individual beliefs and desires. Within this approach, appraisal of an environmental problem plays a central role in coping with the threatening situation.

Means for repairing environmental damages and for preventing further threats are usually beyond the scope of individuals or even community actions. This feeling of loss of control causes discomfort, even distress. People are eager to avoid this feeling, either by appraising the situation as less stressful and threatening, or by taking action to overcome the perceived loss of control. According to Lazarus and Folkman (1984), the former is a 'wishful-thinking' strategy and pertains to what they call *emotion-focused* coping. The latter belongs to the category of *problem-focused* coping strategies. Problem-focused coping includes efforts that are directed at the sources of the stress (e.g., by repairing or preventing the negative outcome or by controlling the sources of the stress). Emotion-focused coping strategies are attempts to manage emotional responses towards the threatening event (e.g., by wishful thinking or by seeking emotional support). These coping strategies are related and may be used simultaneously. In addition, people may change their coping strategies in response to changing demands. Which kinds of coping strategy individuals primarily employ is determined by whether they view the situation as alterable. A problem-focused strategy may only be effective if people feel they can change the situation; when people feel powerless to do so, an emotion-focused strategy may be the most effective.

Wishful Thinking

The Greek stoic philosopher Epictetus (*c.*55–*c.*135 CE) stated that humans are disturbed by their views of things rather than by the things themselves. This 'philosophy' is widely accepted in modern psychotherapy (e.g., in cognitive behaviour therapy), where it is acknowledged that emotions such as anger, sadness, guilt or anxiety are created by our perceptions and evaluations of events rather than by the events themselves (Ellis and Dryden 1987). More generally, this view implies that while many situations are potentially stressful, the degree of stress that we experience will depend on the way we appraise a situation. This relativistic notion of stress and adversity should also be applicable to environmental problems. First, impending negative outcomes may be appraised as less likely; second, already existing problems may be considered less threatening. Both classes of strategies are what Taylor (1989) has identified as *positive illusions.*

The first class of strategies corresponds with the so-called optimism bias in risk perception. Several investigations have demonstrated this kind of bias; people typically see themselves as less likely than others to experience negative life events. Generally, this optimism bias is a tendency to perceive positive events as more likely to happen to oneself than to others and negative events as more likely to happen to others than to oneself. Such an unrealistic optimism may help to protect self-esteem, to project a positive social image, or to reduce anxiety (Weinstein and Klein 1996). For instance, a positive illusion in the form of an unrealistic optimism exists when people believe they will be personally immune against a disaster such as an impending earthquake. Burger and Palmer (1992) found that people who had actually experienced the California earthquake of 1989 had had their unrealistic optimism shattered. However, over the course of three months the optimism returned.

The second class of strategies involves trying to underestimate or ignore the threats of a situation. This may be accomplished by avoiding disturbing thoughts about the stressor, by denying the problem, or by creating a new view of the situation that makes it less threatening and alarming. Evidence for such strategies was found in Tonga in the South Pacific. During field research conducted there by Bender (this volume), fishermen in the Island group of Ha'apai were asked whether they saw a need to regulate their activities in threatened fishing grounds. Up to twenty-eight species of fish and five other marine species were listed as declining by the eighty-one fishermen interviewed. Thirty-one fishermen (38 percent) stated that there was no decline at all and twenty (25 percent) expressed concern about declining stocks. However, a considerable number of fishermen (thirty, or 37 percent) recognised that there were declines in fish stocks, but did not consider regulations necessary. Instead, they evaluated this decline as part of natural fluctuation and opted for better equipment and fishing techniques in order to increase their yields (Bender 2001b). This downplaying and ignoring of the problem, however, does not seem to be a motivationally driven excuse to continue over-harvesting. Even the majority of the fishermen from the small village of Lofanga, who themselves still employ a traditional resource-adapted fishing strategy, did not consider their fishing grounds endangered and did not call for a regulation. This is astonishing, since regulations would deter people from neighbouring villages from depleting the openly accessible fishing grounds (Bender 2001a and this volume).

Of course these two wishful-thinking strategies may be used simultaneously. For instance, Lehman and Taylor (1987) explored reactions to an impending California earthquake whose occurrence was likely, but whose timing was unknown. They found that people denied the seriousness of the situation and doubted the experts' predictions. Consequently, they showed ignorance of basic earthquake safety information and had taken no measures to prepare for an earthquake. Even worse, these wishful-thinking strategies were most pronounced among people who lived in buildings that were rated as unsafe with regard to seismic disturbances. It should be noted here that unrealistic optimism and the downplaying of problems are adaptive only to the extent that they help to reduce anxiety and stress. The other result of these illusions may be that people fail to take adequate precautions and actions to avoid negative events in the future or to solve existing problems.

Blaming

Since preventing or repairing environmental damages is often beyond the scope of individuals or even community actions, problem-focused coping becomes difficult. One possible way to overcome this situation consists of assigning responsibility for the outcome to an agent who can be blamed and controlled. Incidental and situational effects can affect anyone, whereas effects of intentional human actions can be avoided if brought under control. Thus, blaming the responsible agents can prevent them from further transgressions. This explains why the feeling of lack of control after an event leads to increasing efforts in attributing causality (Hewstone 1999). If people experience a continuous lack of control and expect that negative outcomes are not only unpredictable but also independent of what they are doing, a feeling of helplessness (Abramson et al. 1978) and a general negative affective state may result (Burger 1992).

Walster (1966) found that as the effects of an accident become more serious, people become more eager to assign responsibility and blame. Assigning responsibility for a negative event could be seen as a control-oriented coping strategy. Collins et al. (1983) suggest that coping strategies that create or preserve actual or illusory control can be effective in reducing psychological distress resulting from technological disaster. Similarly, research on communities located near a hazardous waste landfill found that the more people blamed the operator of the landfill for the problems, the less psychological distress they experienced (Hallman 1989, cited in Hallman and Wandersman 1992). However, this positive influence of blaming on distress should not be generalised. For example, Bulman and Wortman (1977) reported that victims of accidents who blamed others for their accidents coped less well with spinal cord injuries than those victims who engaged in self-blame. Similar results are also reported for coping with some health problems (for an overview see Shaver and Drown 1986).

Assigning responsibility for a particular situation and blaming the responsible agent are important not only to understand what has happened, but also to develop a sense of control over what might happen in the future. This is in accordance with findings from the field of *counterfactual thinking*:

> After the fact, individuals continue to focus on the avoidance of unpleasant things, imagining steps that might have been taken that would have enabled the avoidance of that past unpleasant event. (Roese 1997: 135)

As people tend to overestimate the predictability of events in retrospect (Fischhoff 1975), the assignment of blame towards the responsible agent may even be increased.

Assigning responsibility not only involves attributing the cause of an event. Causal analysis is however a necessary step in the process of ascribing responsibility, because people infer different degrees of responsibility for a negative event from information about its causation. Appraising an event as naturally caused does not require an assignment of responsibility at all. If the event is attributable to human agency, the agent is judged as more responsible, the more controllable the cause. While controllability increases responsibility, mitigating circumstances alleviate, or even totally eliminate assigned responsibility. Mitigating circumstances are given if (a) an act serves a higher goal, or if (b) the agent is lacking insight or knowledge and thus is not able to comprehend the 'wrongfulness' of the action (Shaver 1985; Weiner 1995). Applied to environmental problems, a higher goal may be assigned if an action is intended to create an overall benefit for society, or to attain a highly valued societal objective. Knowledge or insight reflects, for example, whether agents knew in advance that there was a possible contingency between their action and threats to the environment. More generally, attributing an event to internal and dispositional forces of a person is a prerequisite for ascribing responsibility to that person, whereas attributions to external, situational forces decrease or even eliminate the ascription of responsibility.

Assigning different levels of responsibility for negative events subsequently elicits distinct emotional reactions and behavioural intentions (e.g., Weiner 1995; Smith and Ellsworth 1985). Recent findings about the evaluation of environmental accidents in Germany show that the ascription to others of responsibility for a negative event corresponds to strong feelings of anger and the intention to boycott the responsible agent As Nerb and colleagues suggest, boycotting the responsible agent which can be interpreted as trying to prevent the agent from further executing transgressions (Nerb 2000; Nerb and Spada 2001; Nerb et al. 1998, 2001).

Dispositionalist vs. Situationalist Attributions and Coping

According to attribution theory, people's behaviour is jointly determined by their dispositions and the situations in which they find themselves. Dispositional influences are internal and examples of such influences are personality characteristics, motives and abilities. In contrast, situational influences encompass everything that is external to the person. There is considerable evidence in psychological literature for a stable tendency towards internal, dispositional rather than external, situational attributions to explain the behaviour of other people. Since many studies have pointed to this consequential 'tendency to underestimate the impact of situational factors and to overestimate the role of dispositional factors in controlling behavior', Ross termed this attribution pattern the *fundamental attribution error* (Ross 1977: 183). The tendency towards dispositional attribution was called an error or even a stable bias because it leads people away from the actual situational causes of an event. To speak of an error or a bias is undoubtedly most justified in cases where participants attribute the cause of an event to individuals and their dispositions, even when informed that situational causes were present (Jones and Harris 1967). Initially, this bias was assumed to be domain-independent and culturally universal, perhaps even innate. Yet studies of lay people in non-Western cultures have found an opposite tendency towards external (situational) attributions for certain kinds of events. Evidence for this situationalist attribution style came for instance from studies with Chinese, Native American, or Hindu Indian participants (Morris et al. 1995 for an overview). These findings from anthropologists (e.g., Hsu 1953; Selby 1975) and cross-cultural psychologists (e.g., Miller 1984; Shweder and Bourne 1984) seriously challenge both the domain-generality and the cultural-generality of the dispositionalist tendency.

In the context of coping with threatening situations, dispositionalist and situationalist attributions correspond to different coping styles. The tendency to attribute situations to internal and dispositional forces may be seen as a problem-focused, control-oriented coping strategy, because the effects of human actions can be avoided if brought under control. Such a strategy is quite typical for our Western industrialised societies (Hallman and Wandersman 1992; Nerb 2000). As Morris et al. (1995) show, situationalist attributions are more common in non-Western cultures (cf. also Choi and Nisbett 1998). An inappropriate attribution to natural (situational) forces per se need not necessarily be considered a wishful-thinking strategy. If, however, this situationalist attribution is coupled with the belief that natural forces have not only caused but will also solve the problem, then a positive illusory coping strategy is at work. In this case, a situationalist attribution may be a first step in using a wishful-thinking strategy. The findings of Bender (2001b) suggest that many fishermen from Ha'apai in Tonga employ such a strategy; they consider the depletion of their fishing grounds as being naturally caused, despite the human cause for it. Appraising the negative development as inevitable and beyond their control, they hope and believe that God will solve the problem.

The Tongan Background

The Polynesian Kingdom of Tonga consists of 170 islands, situated in the subtropical southwest of the Pacific. A fifth of the islands are inhabited by descendants of the Austronesian speaking seafarers and planters who reached the island group some 3,500 years ago (Campbell 1992). Until today, most of them have based their subsistence on planting root crops, bananas and fruit trees as well as exploiting marine species such as fish, shellfish, lobster and octopus. While men do most of this work, women are engaged in household activities, reef gleaning and weaving mats for ceremonial purposes.

In most households, at least three generations are present, and the nuclear family is usually extended by adopted children, unmarried siblings or other relatives. Kinship is fostered in various ways and has a tremendous impact on each household's activities through both mutual help and the obligations toward higher-ranking relatives. According to the *fahu*-system, older siblings rank higher than younger ones and sisters higher than brothers (Bott 1981). The same system also sets up the social classes that constitute Tongan society. A nobility has evolved which still controls large parts of the land which was ruled for more than a thousand years by the *Tu'i-Tonga*-dynasty. During a civil war at the beginning of the nineteenth century, the present reigning house of *Tupou* established itself, while simultaneously the European influence grew considerably stronger (Campbell 1992). The greater changes in social life came with the missionaries, especially the Wesleyans who succeeded in converting the islanders into adherents. Most other Christian denominations and the Mormon Church are also present.

For the members of this Polynesian culture, abandoning their former religion, which was based on natural deities, on the power concept of *mana* and related taboos, primarily meant getting rid of a complicated system of restrictions (Rutherford 1977). Of course new rules and principles of conduct were introduced and adapted to the new religion, among them those concerning the management and control of emotions (*fakama'uma'u*). Combining traditional values with the new Christian ones, these standards particularly stress the importance of restraining negatively valued emotions such as anger (*'ita*) or envy (*meheka*) (Kavaliku 1977; Morton 1996). In addition, the notion of having influence and some sort of control on environmental events through offerings was also rejected after adopting the new religion that instead required faith in an almighty and unfathomable God.

Today, the churches are firmly embedded in Tongan society. Their demands for fund-raising are high and engaging in their activities is connected to a rise in social status (cf. Bender this volume). In addition, the churches provide education in their high schools, which are in many cases the only option after completing the compulsory primary schools usually run by the government. The four colleges in the central island-group of Ha'apai are under the jurisdiction of different denominations (i.e., the Wesleyan Church, the Church of Tonga, the Catholics, and the Mormons); the Catholic St Joseph's College, where our empirical investigation took place, is the second largest. Within the partly Western-oriented curriculum, ecology has meanwhile become one of the topics. Although its concepts and implications have not been internalised by most of the inhabitants – much to the regret of the members of the Ha'apai Conservation Area Project established in 1996 (S. Faka'osi, personal communication) – the younger generation seems to be developing a stronger awareness of anthropogenic environmental threats than the older fishermen.

The majority of these fishermen still make use of their basic resources according to traditional goals and do not regard environmental threats as anthropogenic. Instead, they hold the fish themselves responsible for apparent declines because they hide in the deep sea. Having faith in God as the provider of their needs, these fishermen do not consider regulations necessary. Most of them also object to restricting access to the fishing grounds since this would imply denying people access to resources given to all by God. Those fishermen who perceive a decline in yields favour either a reduction of pressure on certain species – consistent with the concept of fish as autonomous actors – in order 'to let them come back', or improved equipment in order to catch fish in even deeper waters (Bender 2001b).

Experimental Studies

Tongan adults seem to appraise environmental threats differently from people in industrialised Western society, such as the aforementioned fisheries consultant (Bender 2001b). To scrutinise whether young people from Tonga employ similar coping strategies to their parents' generation or whether they have meanwhile adopted appraisals that are common in Western societies, we conducted a cross-cultural experimental study. Students from Tonga and Germany were given a newspaper report about a threatening environmental problem and completed a questionnaire after they had read the report. The questionnaire aimed at assessing cognitive and emotional reactions and behavioural intentions of participants from both cultures towards the reported environmental problems. In the context of this paper, we will focus particularly on the causal attributions that were made by the participants.

In the experiments, the causation of a reported negative environmental event was varied at three levels, the damage being held constant. Varying the causation of an event should yield interesting insights about how participants from both cultures appraise a problem. In one condition (a) the damage was said to have been caused by human agency; in another condition (b) the damage was said to have been caused by natural circumstances; and in a third condition (c) nothing was mentioned about the cause of the damage. For the experiments, we chose separate problems that were deemed to be equally alarming for the participants in both cultures. For the German sample (Freiburg, southern Germany), the problem was about birds dying on the estuary of the river Elbe (northern Germany); in the Tongan sample (Pangai, Ha'apai), the problem was about dead fish in the well known but distant Fanga'uta-lagoon (Tongatapu).

Method

After a brief introduction from the experimenter, all participants read one newspaper report and then completed a questionnaire that requested ratings concerning the causal attributions (human-made vs. natural), the intensity of anger felt, and the intention to boycott the agent responsible. The newspaper report and the questionnaire were in Tongan and in German, respectively. In the Tongan version, all questions had a binary response format ('yes' vs. 'no'). In the German version, only the question concerning agency had a binary response format; the other two questions were assessed by nine-point rating scales. In both samples, the boycott questions had only to be answered if the cause was appraised as human-made.

Participants

The German sample consisted of 80 paid volunteers (35 female, 45 male), mainly students from the University of Freiburg. Psychology students were not allowed to participate. The median age was 23 (range 20 to 46). Participants were randomly assigned to the three experimental conditions in a between-subjects design. Data collection took place in groups of 10–15 participants. Participants completed the questionnaire as part of a larger series of judgement studies. The Tongan sample consisted of 45 older pupils from St Joseph's College/Pangai, Ha'apai (24 female, 21 male). The median age was 17 (range 16 to 23). Participants were randomly assigned to the three experimental conditions in a between-subjects design. Data collection took place in the classroom and pupils received a small gift for their voluntary participation.

Material

In the German experiment the material consisted of fictitious but realistic newspaper reports about an environmental problem: the dying of birds at the estuary of the river Elbe. The material was construed according to the principle that, besides reporting the damage and the cause of the accident, the circumstances of the cause (manipulation) were described. Three experimental conditions were created: (a) a human cause of the problem was given; (b) a natural cause of the problem was given; and (c) in a neutral condition no information about the causation was given (ambiguous cause). Table 3.1 shows all three versions of the newspaper report.

Table 3.1. Material used in the experiment in Germany

Dead birds at the estuary of the river Elbe

Hamburg – The dying of birds at the Elbe estuary is worrying bird conservationists. According to the latest findings, the birds – among them some highly endangered species – are falling victim to botulism bacteria. 'Due to the low water level, the animals come into contact with the shore mud where the bacterium lives. On metabolism, it produces a lethal toxin', says a spokesperson for the Nature Conservation Association Jordsand. | | Picking at the banks for food, aquatic birds and waders absorb the toxin produced by the bacteria. At the moment, a forecast of the epidemic's development is not possible.

(a) The bacteria, named Clostridium botulinum, breed especially in shallow waters, where in fair-weather periods anoxia occurs. This is due to overfertilization, e.g. with phosphates, by large agro-firms.	(b) The bacteria named Clostridium botulinum breed especially in shallow waters, where in fair-weather periods anoxia occurs. This is a matter of natural process with precarious consequences.

Note: The neutral or ambiguous version does not provide information about the causation. Substituting the marker | | with Part a (left column) yields the conditioning 'human cause given'; substituting the marker with Part b (right column) yields the condition 'natural cause given'.

In the Tongan experiment, the material also consisted of fictitious but realistic newspaper reports about an environmental problem: fish dying in the Fanga'uta-lagoon (Tongatapu). The material was created according to the same principle as in the German experiment. Table 3.2 shows all three versions of this newspaper report.

Results

Analysing the data aggregated across all experimental conditions produced no significant gender differences for any variable, either in the German or in the Tongan Experiment.

Table 3.2. Material used in the experiment inTonga

Dead fish in the Fanga'uta-lagoon

Nuku'alofa – In the Fanga'uta-lagoon a major part of the fish stock is threatened. According to initial findings of the fisheries department, the animals (among them some very rare and threatened species) are falling victim to bacteria which are spreading rapidly in this area.| |At the moment, a forecast of the epidemic development is not possible.

(a) The exceptional multiplication of these bacteria is due to a cargo-steamer which dumped large quantities of organic waste into the ocean	(b) The exceptional multiplication of these bacteria is due to this summer's very hot weather, combined with only gentle breezes. These two factors led to a low intermix of the highly warmed-up water surface and therefore constituted optimal conditions for the bacteria.

Note. The neutral or ambiguous version does not provide information about the causation. Substituting the marker| | with Part a (left column) yields the condition 'human cause given'; substituting the marker with Part b (right column) yields the condition 'natural cause given'.

Germany

In the condition where nothing about the causation was mentioned, 50 percent of the participants appraised the problem as human-made. Even more astonishing, 43 percent of the participants attributed it to anthropogenic reasons even when informed that situational causes were present (see fig. 3.1). The results of the studies show that participants from Germany have a strong tendency to attribute the causation of the environmental damage to human agency, even when it was explicitly mentioned that the event was caused by purely natural forces.

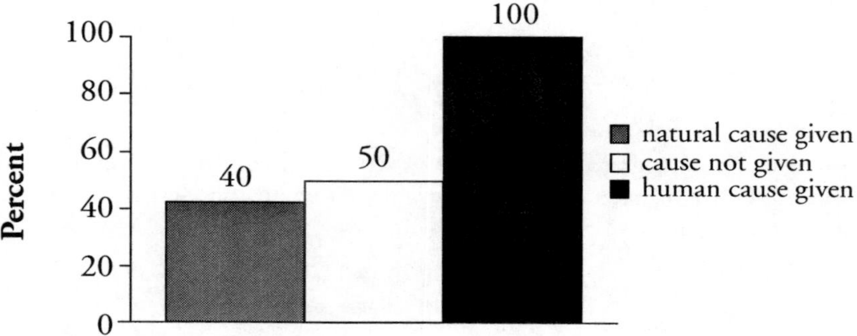

Figure 3.1. Human cause (Germany). Percentage of participants who rated the cause as anthropogenic for all three conditions of the experiment: a natural cause of the problem was given (left); no information about the causation was given (middle); and a human cause of the problem was given (right)

In accordance with prior findings about the relationship between agency and anger (Nerb and Spada 2001), participants showed higher anger ratings when they appraised the problem as anthropogenic (mean = 5.9; n = 52) than when they considered the problem as naturally caused (mean = 4.1; n = 28), $t(78) = 4.15$, $p < 0.001$. Participants also expressed intentions to boycott the responsible agent (mean = 5.4; n = 52).

Tonga

The results from the Tongan sample were quite similar to the pattern of results obtained from the German sample. Tongan participants also showed a strong tendency to attribute the causation of the environmental damage to human agency. This tendency was even more pronounced than in the German experiment. Here, in the condition where nothing about the causation was mentioned, 67 percent of the participants appraised the problem as human-made. When it was explicitly mentioned that the event was caused by purely natural forces, 53 percent of the participants attributed the cause as anthropogenic (see fig. 3.2).

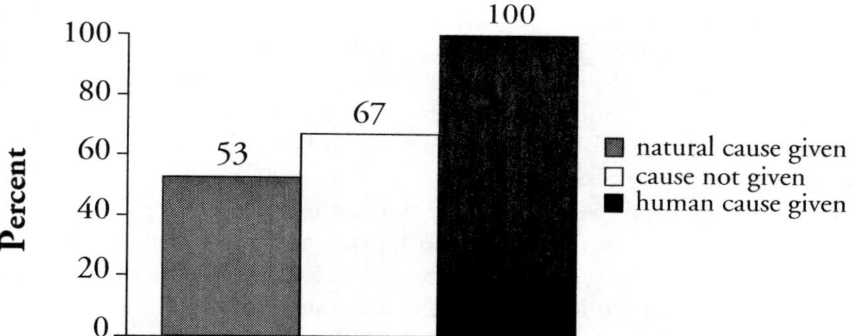

Figure 3.2. Human cause (Tonga). Percentage of participants who rated the cause as anthropogenic for all three conditions of the experiment: a natural cause of the problem was given (left); no information about the causation was given (middle); and a human cause of the problem was given (right).

As in the German experiment, results showed an association between human agency and anger ratings: 97 percent of the participants who rated the problem as anthropogenic also expressed anger about it (32 out of 33), whereas only 75 percent of the participants who rated it as natural expressed anger (9 out of 12). This association, however, only shows marginal significance, $c^2(1) = 2.88$, $p < .09$. Almost all participants who appraised the problem as human-made expressed their willingness to boycott the responsible agent (97 percent).

To sum up, participants from both cultures showed a similar pattern of results for causal analysis, emotional reactions, and behavioural intentions. Thus, the data of the experiments do not support the hypothesis that young people from Tonga employ different coping strategies from people from a Western industrialised society. However, the data suggest that young Tongan pupils make causal attributions that are different from older Tongan fishermen. Whereas most of the fishermen do not consider human action responsible for the decline in fish stocks, the pupils do show a bias towards appraising the problem as anthropogenic.

Discussion

Assigning responsibility for a threatening situation and blaming the responsible agent allows the development of a sense of control over what might happen in the future. In this sense, 'blaming' is a coping strategy. Another strategy to cope with a threatening event is wishful thinking. Here, the likelihood of an impending negative outcome is appraised as less probable, or an already existing problem is considered less threatening or alarming. The appraisal of a situation and in particular the causal analysis of the problem plays a key role in choosing and implementing a coping strategy. Attributing the causation to human agency is necessary for blaming the responsible agent. Conversely, appraising a problem as naturally caused and simultaneously hoping that natural forces will also solve the problem may be a wishful thinking strategy – at least when there actually is a human cause for the problem.

In a cross-cultural experiment, we found that young people from both Germany and Tonga show a tendency to appraise an environmental problem as anthropogenic. Such a tendency is quite typical for participants from Western industrialised societies (Nerb 2000). It is more surprising that young Tongan participants show this appraisal pattern, since earlier related results from members of the older generation had suggested that the opposite tendency prevails in Tonga, namely to appraise environmental problems as naturally caused (see Bender 2001b). The prevalence of anthropogenic attributions in the Tongan sample may be explained by the conjecture that the students felt that they were in a situation of achievement. At school, Tongan students are educated according to a Western curriculum. This curriculum tries to impart ecological knowledge and, in particular, emphasises the prominent role of humans in the destruction of environmental resources.

Participants from Germany and Tonga not only made similar attributions; they also showed a similar pattern in the ratings for anger and for the intentions to boycott. This is particularly noteworthy, given that in Tonga the expression of negative emotions such as anger is negatively sanctioned. Moreover, the intention to boycott someone is definitely at odds with the Polynesian value system that is based upon the idea of *'ofa*, which glosses as 'concern, kindness, care, help, generosity, sharing and love' and characterises the ideal emotional relationship between all people (Morton 1996: 80; see also Bender this volume; Kavaliku 1977). However, it would be unwarranted to conclude from our data that schoolchildren in Tonga have started abandoning their traditional value system and generally drifting towards Western norms. We are suggesting rather that the situation elicited in the experiment is not 'typical' for their daily life and that cultural patterns for dealing with this situation may not be available. The lack of cultural regulations for this novel situation may have allowed the expression of emotions and behavioural intentions that are otherwise negatively sanctioned.

Finally, methodological problems in cross-cultural research designs need to be addressed. First, a general problem exists in translating and employing materials and questionnaires across cultural borders. Second, the familiarity with data collection methods such as rating scales differs substantially between Tongan and German participants. This was a major problem in a pilot study we conducted in Tonga, the results of which could not be interpreted, because we found that Tongan participants were not experienced in dealing with nine-point rating scales. To circumvent this problem, we used a binary response format in the study presented in this chapter.

These methodological problems certainly restrict the conclusions that can be drawn from our investigation. Nevertheless, we consider such cross-cultural laboratory studies an important supplement to field research. Indeed, for a detailed theory-driven comparative analysis of coping behaviour such a research design is indispensable.

Acknowledgements

This research was supported by grant no. Sp 251/10-x from the Deutsche Forschungsgemeinschaft (DFG) to the third author and by a fellowship from the Alexander von Humboldt Foundation to the first author. We thank Moana and Sione Faka'osi for translating the material used in the experiment into Tongan. We are grateful to Susanne Frings, Fabian Hermann, Miriam Tonne, and Stefan Wahl for their assistance. We thank Stefan Seitz for his valuable comments on an earlier version of this chapter.

References

Abramson, Lyn Y., Martin E.P. Seligman and John D. Teasdale 1978. 'Learned Helplessness in Humans: Critique and Reformulation', *Journal of Abnormal Psychology* 87: 49–74.

Bender, Andrea 2001a. *Fischer im Netz: Strategien der Ressourcennutzung und Konfliktbewältigung in Ha'apai, Tonga (Fisher in the Net: Strategies of Resource Use and Conflict Management in Ha'apai, Tonga).* Herbolzheim: Centaurus.

——— 2001b. "'God Will Send Us the Fish" – Perception and Evaluation of an Environmental Risk in Ha'apai, Tonga', *Research in Social Problems and Public Policy* 9: 165–90.

Bott, Elizabeth 1981. 'Power and Rank in the Kingdom of Tonga', *Journal of the Polynesian Society* 90: 7–81.

Bulman, Ronnie J. and Camille B. Wortman 1977. 'Attribution of Blame and Coping in the "Real World": Severe Victims React to their Lot', *Journal of Personality and SocialPsychology* 35: 351–63.

Burger, Jerry M. 1992. *Desire for Control: Personality, Social and Clinical Perspectives.* New York: Plenum Press.

——— and Michele L. Palmer 1992. 'Changes in the Generalisation of Unrealistic Optimism Following Experiences with Stressful Events: Reactions to the 1989 California Earthquake', *Personality and Social Psychology Bulletin* 18: 39–43.

Campbell, Ian C. 1992. *Island Kingdom: Tonga Ancient and Modern.* Christchurch: Canterbury University Press.

Choi, Incheol and Richard E. Nisbett 1998. 'Situational Salience and Cultural Differences in the Correspondence Bias and in the Actor-Observer Bias', *Personality and Social Psychology Bulletin* 24: 949–60.

Collins, Daniel L., Andrew Baum and Jerome E. Singer 1983. 'Coping With Chronic Stress at Three Mile Island: Psychological and Biochemical Evidence', *Health Psychology* 2: 149–66.

Ellis, Albert and Windy Dryden 1987. *The Practice of Rational-Emotive Therapy.* New York: Springer.

Ellsworth, Phoebe C. and Klaus R. Scherer 2003. 'Appraisal Processes in Emotion', in *Handbook of the Affective Sciences,* eds. R.J. Davidson, H. Goldsmith, K.R. Scherer, 572–95. New York and Oxford: Oxford University Press.

Fischhoff, Baruch 1975. 'Hindsight is Not Equal to Foresight: The Effect of Outcome Knowledge on Judgment under Uncertainty', *Journal of Experimental Psychology: Human Perception and Performance* 1: 288–99.

Hallman, William K. and Abraham Wandersman 1992. 'Attribution of Responsibility and Individual and Collective Coping with Environmental Threats', *Journal of Social Issues,* 48(4): 101–18

Hewstone, Miles 1999. *Causal attribution.* Oxford: Blackwell Publishers.

Hsu, Francis L.K. 1953. *Americans and Chinese: Two Ways of Life.* New York: Schuman.

Jones, Edward E. and Victor A. Harris 1967. 'The Attribution of Attitudes', *Journal of Experimental Social Psychology* 3: 1–24.

Kavaliku, S. Langi 1977. 'Ofa! The treasure of Tonga', *Pacific Perspective,* 6: 47–67.

Lazarus, Richard S. and Susan Folkman 1984. *Stress, Appraisal and Coping.* New York: Springer.

Lehman, Darrin and Shelley E. Taylor 1987. 'Date With an Earthquake: Coping With a Probable, Unpredictable Disaster', *Personality and Social Psychology Bulletin,* 13: 546–55.

Miller, Joan G. 1984. 'Culture and the Development of Everyday Social Explanation', *Journal of Personality and Social Psychology* 46: 961–78.

Morris, Michael W., Richard E. Nisbett and Kaiping Peng 1995. 'Causal Attribution Across Domains and Cultures', in *Causal Cognition: A Multidisciplinary Debate,* eds. D. Sperber, D. Premack and A.J. Premack, 577–612. Oxford: Clarendon Press.

Morton, Helen 1996. *Becoming Tongan: An Ethnography of Childhood.* Honolulu: University of Hawaii Press.

Nerb, Josef 2000. *Die Bewertung von Umweltschäden: Kognitive und emotionale Folgen von Medienmeldungen (The Evaluation of Environmental Damages: Cognitive and Emotional Consequences of Media Reports).* Bern: Huber.

——— and Spada, Hans 2001. 'Evaluation of Environmental Problems: A Coherence Model of Cognition and Emotion', *Cognition and Emotion* 15: 521–51.

———, Hans Spada and Katja Lay 2001. 'Environmental Risk in the Media: Modeling the Reactions of the Audience', *Research in Social Problems and Public Policy* 9: 57–85.

———, Hans Spada and Stefan Wahl 1998. 'Kognitive Determinanten der emotionalen Bewertung von Umweltschäden: Modellierung und Empirie' ('Cognition and Emotion in the Evaluation of Environmental Accidents: Modeling and Empirical Studies'), *Zeitschrift für Experimentelle Psychologie* 45: 251–69.

Roese, Neal J. 1997. 'Counterfactual Thinking', *Psychological Bulletin* 121: 133–48.

Ross, Lee D. 1977. 'The Intuitive Psychologist and His Shortcomings: Distortions in the Attribution Process', in *Advances in Experimental Social Psychology*, ed. L. Berkowitz, 10: 173–220. New York: Random House.

Rutherford, Noel, ed. 1977. *Friendly Islands: A History of Tonga.* Melbourne: Oxford University Press.

Scherer, Klaus R., Angela Schorr and Tom Johnstone, eds. 2001. *Appraisal Processes in Emotion: Theory, Methods, Rresearch.* Oxford: Oxford University Press.

Seitz, Stefan 1998. *Die Aeta am Vulkan Pinatubo (The Aeta living at the Volcano Pinatubo).* Pfaffenweiler: Centaurus.

Selby, Henry A. 1975. 'Semantics and Causality in the Study of Deviance', in *Sociocultural Dimensions of Language and Causality*, eds. M. Sanches and B. Blount, 11–24. New York: Academic Press.

Shaver, Kelly G. 1985. *The Attribution of Blame: Causality, Responsibility and Blameworthiness.* Berlin: Springer Verlag.

Shaver, Kelly G. and Debra Drown 1986. 'On Causality, Responsibility, and Self-Blame. A Theoretical Note', *Journal of Personality and Social Psychology* 50: 697–702.

Shweder, Richard A. and Edmund J. Bourne 1984. 'Does the Concept of the Person Vary Cross-Culturally?', in *Culture Theory: Essays on Mind, Self, and Emotion*, eds. R. Shweder and R. Levine, 158–199. New York: Cambridge University Press.

Smith, Craig A. and Phoebe C. Ellsworth 1985. 'Patterns of Cognitive Appraisal in Emotion', *Journal of Personality and Social Psychology* 48: 813–38.

Taylor, Selley E. 1989. *Positive Illusions: Creative Self-Deception and the Healthy Mind.* New York: Basic Books.

TFSR [Tonga Fisheries Sector Review] 1998. *Tonga Fisheries Sector Review*, vol. 1: *Main Report of the Consultants.* Bangkok: Food and Agriculture Organization of the United Nations, and Australian Agency for International Development.

Walster, Elaine 1966. 'Assignment of Responsibility for an Accident', *Journal of Personality and Social Psychology* 3: 73–9.

Weiner, Bernard 1995. *Judgements of Responsibility: A Foundation for a Theory of Social Conduct.* New York, NY: Guilford Press.

Weinstein, Neil D. and William M. Klein 1996. 'Unrealistic Optimism: Present and Future', *Journal of Social and Clinical Psychology* 15: 1–8.

4

Decision-Making in Times of Disaster: The Acceptance of Wet-Rice Cultivation among the Aeta of Zambales, Philippines

Stefan Seitz

Introduction

The gradual transformation of the environment through human activities generally enables the populations affected by it to adapt to their changing surroundings step-by-step, mainly through a selective modification of common techniques of resource utilisation. Sudden environmental changes resulting from natural disasters, on the other hand, invariably necessitate a rapid adaptation to the new conditions. Short-term decision-making processes during stress situations like these caused by natural disasters are largely determined by the reaction of the whole group. This is so despite the urgency of quick reaction, which must be taken by some group members who, mostly keeping socio-economic traditions, by the action of some of the group, however, developing individual initiatives and, especially in the case of minorities, by the response of dominant population groups showing willingness to help the affected group is a key factor.

In this paper the example of the Aeta of Zambales (on the Mt Pinatubo in Western Luzon, Philippines) after the eruption of the volcano is used to illustrate the relevance of anthropological research for cultural responses to the effects of natural disaster in indigenous societies, a subject that has until now been dealt with only by a small number of studies (see Oliver-Smith and Hoffman1999).

The Aeta World before the Eruption of Mt Pinatubo

The Aeta, an ethnic minority of former foragers, had long adopted swidden cultivation, but hunting and gathering and the collection of non-timber forest products continued to be important to Aeta subsistence, notwithstanding their focus on swidden agriculture. Indeed, the Aeta continued to regard themselves as hunters rather than farmers – a view shared by many lowland residents. They continued to follow characteristic hunter-gatherer traditions, for example by living in more or less mobile and small, socio-economically flexible, family groupings. Until the eruption of the volcano they lived mostly on the slopes of the Pinatubo and adjacent mountains. For them, the Pinatubo was the centre of both their habitat and their spiritual world. Those Aeta residing along the volcano's western flanks in Zambales province were divided into two large groups, one in the hinterlands of Botolan, west of Mt Pinatubo, and the other in the hinterlands of San Marcelino, southwest of the volcano. For centuries these Aeta were in constant contact with their neighbours in the densely settled coastal zone, with the Sambal around Botolan and from the nineteenth century with the Ilocano immigrants around San Marcelino. Yet they always maintained a certain spatial distance from the lowland groups.

Due to the clear separation of lowland, the coastal plane, and highland habitats, the mountainous area and the tableland between the coast and the Mt Pinatubo, the Aeta in the highland had largely managed to remain economically independent and culturally autonomous in the years before the disaster (Shimizu 1989: 3,14; 1992: 5). Differences in elevation, ranging from the Pinatubo's slopes through the plateau region to the lowland-highland transition zone, have always been the main factors in shaping environmental conditions in the Aeta habitat. It is thus not surprising that these conditions – in addition to the different intensity of their contacts with lowland groups, which itself was determined largely by the spatial distance between highland and lowland communities – resulted in the development of diverse lifestyles among the group Aeta (Seitz 1984). Both Aeta and the lowland residents distinguished between those 'acculturated' Aeta living close to the lowlands and having adopted a largely agricultural lifestyle and 'non-acculturated' Aeta still following a more traditional way of life in the Pinatubo highlands (Fox 1952: 183; Shimizu 1989: 12, 1992: 5,8).

A later, though no less important cause of social differentiation among the Aeta was the launching of developmental projects a few years prior to the disaster. These projects quickly opened up the way for socio-economic differences and social disparities to emerge within the traditionally egalitarian structure of Aeta society. Primarily responsible for this was the selective support of individual Aeta communities by certain NGOs. This process began in the 1980s, when private and church groups, and to a certain extent the government also, established aid programmes simply because the Aeta were perceived as a culturally archaic, mostly not yet Christianised, people living in a remote environment, supposedly threatened by physical and cultural extinction.

Even before the disaster the Aeta have certainly not proved to be lacking in either willingness or ability to adapt to new living conditions. Their economic attitudes and practices were far from being static or unimaginative. This can be seen in their ready adoption of swidden agriculture. During this transition from foraging to farming, they displayed adaptive ability by focusing mostly on the planting of tubers brought from the Americas by the Spaniards and not on the cultivation of rice, the favourite cultigen of their neighbours (Fox 1952). Hence today, in addition to the native banana (*ha'a: Musa sapientum, Musa paradisiaca*), the sweet potato (*kamoti, camote: Ipomoea batata*) and manioc (*moros, modos: Manihot utilissima*) play an important role in Aeta agriculture; so also does corn (*ma-i: Zea Mays*), though of lesser importance. It remains unclear, however, whether the Aeta began farming only after the introduction of the foreign tubers or whether, as J. Brosius claims (1990: 23), they shifted from the cultivation of native Southeast Asian plants like taro (*talu, tau: Colocasia esculenta*) and yams (*ubi: Dioscorea alata*) to manioc and sweet potatoes. The Aeta probably decided to focus their agricultural efforts on the cultivation of these foreign plants and not on rice (*pali: Oryza sativa*), because the tubers required less attention, long-term planning and investment in storage facilities, which left them with enough spare time to engage in more traditional hunting and gathering activities. Another incentive may have been the yield-to-effort ratio of manioc and sweet potatoes.

To spend much time in planting, tending and harvesting crops like rice would also have tied the Aeta too rigidly to their fields, would have restricted their spatial mobility and in the end would thus have forced them to curb other economic activities, especially hunting and gathering. As a result, before the eruption almost none of the Aeta were interested in owning agricultural lands, and land ownership would have contributed in no way in their egalitarian society to increasing personal status. Rather, authority and prestige derived from an individual's accomplishments, connections, and ability to assert oneself, rather than from material possessions. In this attitude the Aeta clearly differed from their lowland neighbours, among whom land ownership was a much-coveted goal.

Whenever Aeta farmers did own land, they were often unaware of its real worth and willing to sell it far below value. Aeta who had accumulated debts or simply needed money to cover urgent expenses were particularly tempted to do just that, to get rid of their land at almost any price. As a result, Aeta often lost land to lowland residents even in areas where only they, as an ethnic-cultural minority, were entitled to hold it.

The cultivation of tubers had been the mainstay of Aeta agriculture, while at the same time hill-rice cultivation had remained economically a less important food source. By combining foraging and agricultural strategies the Aeta had achieved an optimum level of adaptation to their environment. Neither population pressures nor food shortages had forced them to switch to more intensive farming methods, such as wet-rice cultivation on rain-fed or irrigated fields. Just how well-balanced the Aeta subsistence-procurement system had been before the disaster can be seen from the fact that in times of need lowland farmers almost habitually viewed the situation of their Aeta neighbours as more secure than their own. This awareness found an even more overt expression in the not insubstantial number of impoverished lowland residents who married into Aeta families, which suggests that such marriages had become part of what might be called a traditional socio-economic safety-net.

Prior to the eruption the Aeta had shown barely any interest in taking up wet-rice cultivation. But even had they been willing to do so on a larger scale, they probably would have had a hard time finding suitable land in the lower regions of their habitat. And in the hinterland, what few adequate acres there may have been had often been taken away from the Aeta by large landowners or lowland settlers and squatters, who were attracted by the region's extensive stands of forest. This particular process of land disenfranchisement began in the 1960s and increased in intensity during the 1980s, as the opening of trails and roads for lumber transports made it ever more easy for outsiders to penetrate Aeta territory (see Brosius 1990: 133f.).

Any activities related to wet-rice cultivation among the Aeta before the eruption were rare exceptions and came about only as a result of initiatives from the outside. Yet is also true that a first attempt at introducing wet-rice cultivation into the spectrum of Aeta agriculture had been made at a very early date, in 1907. This initiative had its roots in the U.S. minority policies of the time and culminated in the establishment of a Farm Settlement School in Villar, an Aeta settlement founded in 1898. Part of the project was devoted to the establishment of wet-rice fields, an experiment without any lasting success over the century.

It was not until the 1980s when lowland families started to move into the highlands, partially introducing wet-rice cultivation in this area. Around the same time NGOs as well as church institutions gradually increased their activities among the Aeta. A few Aeta families began to make first tentative efforts to take up wet-rice cultivation. Such single wet-rice fields were located in creek-side wetlands and seasonally flooded river confluences. In addition, rice fields relying primarily on seasonal rainfall were cultivated along a few rivers. Most of the fields were owned by Filipinos from the lowlands and were worked under lease agreements by the Aeta. A similar situation existed in the San Marcelino highlands before the eruption. In contrast to the hinterlands of Botolan, however, there had been (except in Santa Fe on the Santo Tomas River) no influx of settlers from the lowlands. On the other hand, lowland farmers used the outer margins of Aeta territory agriculturally much more intensively than was the case further north in the hinterlands of Botolan. In San Marcelino Aeta and Ilocanos were noticeably separated from each other spatially as well as socially, quite unlike the Aeta and Sambal in the Botolan highlands who were then essentially living side by side.

Like their counterparts in the hinterlands of Botolan, the San Marcelino Aeta had shown no enthusiasm for wet-rice agriculture. Whatever activities there had been in this direction had been initiated by NGOs. In 1975, for instance, the PDO (Pinatubo Development Organisation) had launched a project (Kakilingan) that had as its objective the adoption of plough agriculture and, ultimately, the acceptance of sustained sedentism by the Aeta. This attempt had also ended in failure (Shimizu 1989: 20–44). During the late 1980s, shortly before the eruption, the ADA (Aeta Development Association) seems to have persuaded a few Aeta families to experiment with wet-rice cultivation on a number of seasonally flooded fields near Santa Fe, but likewise without any lasting success. Not even among the small number of Aeta families already living in the coastal lowlands before the eruption had there been any initiative to take up wet-rice cultivation. Here, as elsewhere, the impetus came from NGOs, e.g., the Aeta of Zambales Development Organisation Inc. working for the Aeta in Cadman/Reserva since 1986. This organisation, had attempted to put in an irrigation system for wet-rice fields (Nass 1988), although the project again had lasted only a few years. There are only a few cases where Aeta who had married into families of lowland farmers residing in communities along the lower Santo Tomas river had become wet-rice cultivators. Culturally, however, these Aeta had become integrated into the local Ilocano society.

That there had indeed been any attempts at all to induce the Aeta to adopt wet-rice cultivation was an oft-overlooked fact. Thus it is that among the lowland population, as well as even among the Aeta themselves, assertions about how the Aeta had always eschewed this form of agriculture were generally accepted as true. On the other hand, many Aeta families who were viewed as acculturated were familiar with the techniques of wet-rice cultivation. These families had been living between the highland and the lowland transition zone for quite some time and, using the opportunity to work as day-labourers on lowland farms, had become acquainted with wet-rice cultivation during the sowing and harvesting of the irrigated rice fields. Such jobs, whether they entailed working in rice fields, in coconut plantations, in sugar-cane fields, or in livestock-caretaking, were generally carried out on a temporary basis; sometimes without any long-term commitments to the landowner, sometimes in a partnership which, if it involved autochthonous Sambal farmers, often developed into a form of patron-client relationship. Any Aeta tied into such a relationship thus came under the care of the landowner.

Even prior to the disaster, rice cultivation in general and wet-rice cultivation in particular may have been economically unimportant to the Aeta, but the product, rice, was highly valued by them, even though it was essentially nothing more than a supplement to the typical Aeta diet. Rice was generally acquired through barter or, among those Aeta who were participating in the monetary economy, bought with the money they had made from the sale of non-timber forest products, wild tree fruits or tubers sold to the lowlanders, who like to eat tubers especially for *merienda* (snacks). Not infrequently, day-labourers working in the fields of lowland farmers also asked for and received rice as compensation for their efforts.

Interestingly enough, rice was also a preferred offering in rituals designed to appease the spirits, e.g., in the *atang*, a sacrifice made to avoid offending and irritating the spirits (Rice and Tima 1973: 29f.) or in the *patay*, the offering or sacrifice presented to *Apo Namalayari* or other spirits after the harvest, probably a ceremony originally practised by lowland farmers during the rice harvest. It is indeed remarkable that the Aeta, as decided non-cultivators of rice, had adopted a rice-harvest ritual of the lowland farmers, a case of cultural borrowing dating back to a time long before the ritual which had fallen victim to the Christianisation and Hispanisation process of the lowland population (Fox 1952: 195; Shimizu 1983: 134; 1989: 14).

The Aeta at the Time of the Disaster

For many years to come, a limited area of the Aeta habitat will suffer severely from immense deposits of pyroclastic materials (map 4.1). Deeply penetrating the traditional territory and emitting hot gases along the way, some of these surges even reached the settlement of Villar. A total of 8–10 km^3 of this material thus eventually buried some 166 km^2 – or approximately one-third of the Aeta homeland – under deposits between 30– 200 m thick. For a long time, however, extensive areas around Mt Pinatubo will have to deal with greater, more critical threat: the *lahar*. This is a collective term for a fluid jumble of volcanic debris, loose ash and pyroclastic material. *Lahar* wears down easily and, when mixed with rainwater, drains off quickly. While flowing slower than lava or pyroclastic slides, *lahar* deposits can cover much longer distances (Tayag 1991: 28f.).

During the eruption in June 1991 nearly all Aeta families in Zambales were evacuated to the coast. They passed through many different evacuation centres where they as well as parts of the lowland population were provided with temporary accommodation. Aeta from Botolan mostly stayed together as one group, however Aeta from the hinterland of San Marcelino was splinter into several groups in this process.

Life in the evacuation centres turned out to be exceedingly difficult for the Aeta. They were forced to stay in unfamiliar environments with thousands of other evacuees. Many Aeta had never before been in close contact with the lowland population, and were now confronted with a completely different world. Dwelling in tents, they were greatly exposed to extremes of temperature; sanitary installations were in short supply; and further problems arose from the daily rations of mostly canned food. In the light of all this, it is not surprising that today the Aeta still vividly recall the tough times of the evacuation centres, and it appears as if the unsavoury diet in the camps left a particularly strong and unpleasant mark on their collective memory of this period.

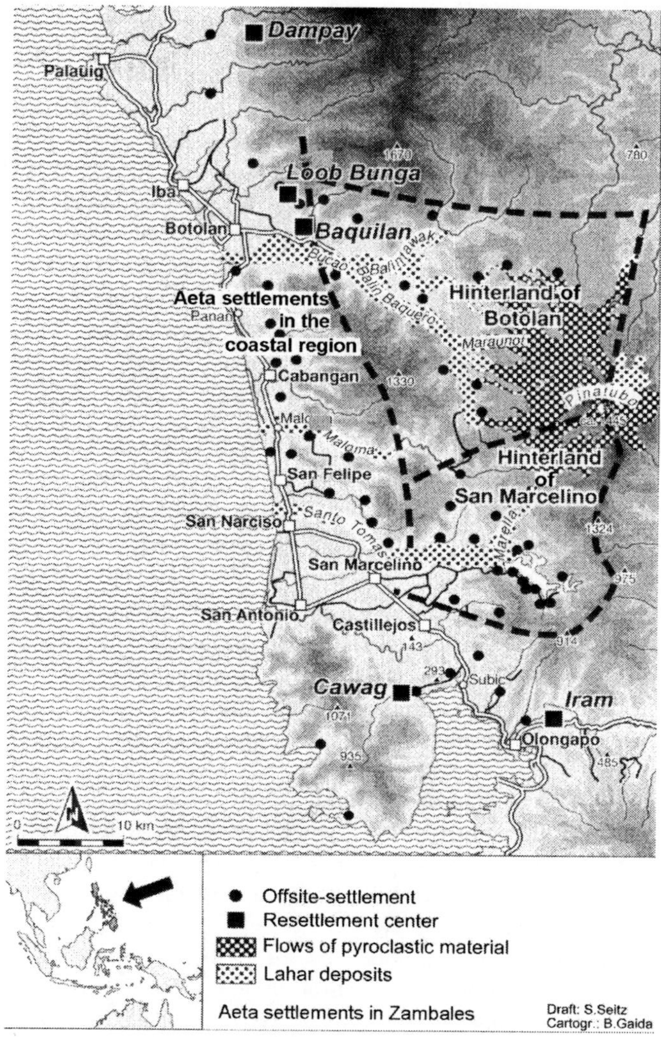

Map 4.1. Aeta settlements in Zambales

A few months later some 2,000 Aeta families (this is my own estimate; 3,000 according to the Mt Pinatubo Commission [MPC] were transferred from the evacuation centres to five resettlement sites established specifically for this minority group from the highlands, where they received support from both government and non-government organisations (Fondevilla 1991; Shimizu 1992; Banzon Bautista 1993). An almost equal number of families (about 1,800 in my own estimate; 2,500 according to the ONCC), however, were eligible for a place in the resettlement sites yet chose to live elsewhere instead. Through their own initiative or with the help of NGOs, most of these families preferred to start a new existence in so-called off-site settlements among the lowland population, particularly near the national highway that runs parallel to the coastal piedmont.

Aeta families returned to the mountain zone around the Pinatubo in the hinterlands of San Marcelino, or reoccupied those areas in the hinterland of Botolan not affected by *lahar* flows. Still, these zones can only be reached by passing over these extensive deposits of *lahar* and pyroclastic debris. All in all, about fifty off-site settlements were established in Zambales away from the five resettlement sites (Seitz 1998). All this sudden and inexorable relocation forced them to adapt to life in a new environment. Efforts by the Aeta to cope with the dramatic changes in living conditions were clearly facilitated by traditional patterns of foraging behaviour, namely a strong desire for self-determined spatial and temporal freedom and economic strategies characterised by immediacy of planning and execution.

Aeta Survival Strategies and Agricultural Activities after the Disaster

Established in the resettlement sites and lowland off-site settlements, the Aeta were forced to quickly find new resources. Retaining hunter-gatherer traditions in their life as swidden agriculturalists was the kind of behaviour that left the Aeta with enough leeway to address at least their short-term subsistence needs through a mixture of self-initiative and creativity. Living in their new surroundings, the majority of Aeta was able to secure their survival by combining very different activities as wage labourers or as independent farmers and entrepreneurs, such as swidden cultivation and horticulture, wage labour, small businesses, and the collection of non-timber forest products, a process which government and non-government organisations have from the beginning tried to support financially and logistically.

Non-agricultural activities pursued by the Aeta have come to include, for instance, the manufacture of baskets or brooms, as well as the processing of rattan and bamboo. Yet demand for these products has been largely lacking, thus enabling only a small number of Aeta families to make a living in this area. Moreover, the production of such items has generally not been market-orientated, nor have the items qualitatively measured up to market standards. Cogon-grass (*yabot: Imperata cyclindrica, Imperata exaltata;* Fox 1952: 183) is another source of income when cut and sold as thatching material. Some families have again also had the opportunity to use highland resources, thus adding to income just as they had done before the disaster. Particularly important in this resumption of more traditional patterns of resource use have been the making of charcoal, and the cutting and collecting of lumber, firewood and commercial non-timber forest products, especially rattan. All these activities, often carried out during one and the same trip to the highlands, have allowed the Aeta to retain some of their former spatial mobility and temporal flexibility.

Agricultural tasks are organised in a similar fashion with this traditional freedom in mind. Today many more Aeta men make part of their living by working as seasonal wage labourers in the rice fields of lowland farmers than had been the case before the disaster. A strong demand for agricultural labour has built up in the area around Botolan since the mid-to late 1990s, with the decrease of damaging effects on wet-rice fields during the first years after the disaster. Nonetheless, depending on the situation, individual Aeta nuclear families rather than groups of families (the traditional decision-making unit before the disaster), often have different options on how to use land. They have opportunities to engage in small-scale horticulture on garden plots surrounding their homes, or to practise swidden cultivation in the vicinity of the resettlement sites and off-site settlements, or even further away in portions of their old highland habitat. There are also opportunities to work wet-rice fields bought or leased by NGOs in the lowlands, or to establish seasonal wet-rice fields on *lahar*.

Inside the resettlement sites, for instance, the Aeta have space only sufficient for some limited gardening. With settlement plots of 150 or 200 m^2 per family, depending on the resettlement site, the space not occupied by the house is generally used for a vegetable garden and for the planting of tubers (chiefly sweet potatoes, called *camote*), bananas and fruit trees. On the other hand, every resettlement site has also been allotted farmland nearby, which is parcelled out to Aeta families for cultivation on a temporary basis. On average, such plots range in size from 0.3 to 0.5 ha.

In most cases, the land thus apportioned is government property and had not been cultivated previously. In areas already being used by lowland residents for grazing livestock, the Mt Pinatubo Commission (MPC), the organisation responsible for the coordination of rehabilitation measures after the disaster, was expected to buy land. Frequently, however, unclear legal precepts have delayed such transactions. And, even more importantly, the land in question is often too rough and pebble-strewn, sometimes even downright craggy, with soil qualities adequate only for the cultivation of fruit trees and not for swidden agriculture. In a number of instances Aeta were so appalled by the soil quality of allotted plots that they returned their land-use certificates (Abaya et al. 1993: 48). What few fields suitable for agriculture there are, the Aeta have been using to cultivate tubers, again mainly sweet potatoes and dry rice for their own consumption, as well as yams, taro, and manioc for sale at local farmers' markets.

For Aeta families living in the two resettlement sites in the vicinity of Botolan the problems associated with re-establishing an agricultural subsistence base have been less dramatic. Their new homes are relatively close to their old habitat in the hinterland, an arrangement that allows the families to work at least some of the old fields again. The fields are planted with manioc, taro, yams, sweet potatoes and dry rice. To access the hinterlands, however, one has to pass across extensive *lahar* deposits, a journey possible only during the dry season. For the most part these families travel back and forth between their resettlement sites and their old highland habitat. Only very few stay permanently in the hinterlands.

Aeta families have more opportunities to engage in cultivation when living in off-site settlements along the coast. Some families have relatively easy access to agricultural land with adequate soil to cultivate vegetables, tubers, bananas and various fruit trees. The spectrum of cultigens utilised by these families appears more varied than elsewhere, with a clear focus on commercial production in that tubers and tree crops offer substantially higher profits in the local markets than rice.

The coastal zone is, however, densely populated, a very problematic situation as far as access to land is concerned. In a few cases private landowners came to tolerate the existence of off-site settlements – of small villages, mostly inhabited by Aeta and at the same time by lowland residents – and, on their land, allowed the Aeta to work fields for a limited period free of charge. In addition, some off-site settlements received land from the Forestry Department. A small number of Aeta families also leased land privately, but under guidance from NGOs.

In the hinterlands of San Marcelino, Aeta families have established themselves in off-site settlements located on mountain slopes, away from the main channels of the seasonal *lahar* flows. These Aeta base their subsistence almost entirely on tubers, especially taro. The ash deposited by the eruption has enhanced soil qualities and created a new soil consistency, favouring the cultivation of tubers and vegetables (see also Mendoza and Cabangbang 1992: 125).

In the wake of the disaster, the attitude of the Aeta towards agriculture has undergone dramatic changes. Many Aeta families have visibly intensified their agricultural activities in general and the cultivation of tubers, which had already played an important role before the eruption, in particular. Often tubers were sold and the Aeta repeatedly stated that they wanted to expand production towards a monetary economy. The possession of agricultural land has concomitantly become an enormously important and desirable asset for the Aeta, many of whom are now eager to lease or buy plots suitable for cultivation. The increasing focus on the cultivation of tubers after the eruption has been partially matched by a simultaneous expansion of dry-rice cultivation. Yet overall, tubers are still predominant among Aeta food plants.

The Acceptance of Wet-Rice Cultivation among the Aeta after the Disaster

To attain long-term stability, however, those Aeta who have over time no longer maintained strong emotional ties with the home territory and chosen to remain in the lowlands have hardly any alternative but to adapt to the behaviour and culture of the dominant lowland population, constituted primarily by Sambal farmers. The willingness of the Sambal to accept the Aeta as immediate neighbours was to a certain degree driven by the expectation that the new settlers would at least partially adapt to the Sambal way of life. Such expectations were probably also fuelled by the fact that a few Aeta who were already more or less integrated into lowland society had assumed roles of leadership in the acculturation process.

Given the lowland population's economically, socially, and cognitively all-encompassing focus on wet-rice cultivation, the Aeta were also confronted with the complexities surrounding this particular form of agriculture practice.

The lowland population generally perceived the swidden agriculture commonly practised by the Aeta as a clearly antiquated way of making a living. Not surprisingly, therefore, lowland residents quickly came to judge the economic and social development of the Aeta and their state of integration into lowland society among other criteria by the degree to which they adopted wet-rice agriculture. But this was not a view restricted to the Sambal only. Some of the non-government organisations (NGOs) working for the Aeta repeatedly declared that the goal of their economic-technological support was not only to improve education and vocational training in general, but also to bring the Aeta to accept wet-rice cultivation on a wide scale, while government organisations attempted to pressure them into abandoning their traditional slash and burn cultivation to prevent deforestation and destruction of the land.

And yet, despite all the efforts by NGOs and others, and also notwithstanding the frequent mention of wet-rice cultivation, by 2000, nine years after the catastrophe, only very few Aeta had taken up wet-rice agriculture. It remains to be seen to what extent this pattern is the result not only of difficulties in gaining access to wet-rice fields in the densely populated lowlands, but also of a form of economic behaviour typical for hunter-gatherers, a behaviour which may have prompted the Aeta to react to population pressures and scarcity of land by means other than agricultural intensification (in the sense of Boserup 1965, 1981). At the same time, however, there is the question of why the few families that did adopt wet-rice cultivation decided to do so, instead of choosing one or more alternative strategies.

Without help from outside, the Aeta were unable to acquire agricultural plots in the lowlands and thus unable to take up wet-rice cultivation. Agricultural lands allotted to the resettlement sites by the government were, with the exception of one site, usually not in a condition that would allow wet-rice cultivation. A number of fields in the vicinity of the two sites near Botolan would have been suitable, but these were already in the possession of non-Aeta families.

Not only for the access to land but also to water buffaloes (*carabaos*), ploughs and seeds, help from outside was needed. As a result, Aeta who become active in wet-rice cultivation in general could do so only as lessees. Initiatives to promote the adoption of wet-rice cultivation were mostly started by NGOs. Almost as soon as the resettlement phase was concluded, self-help-NGOs and cooperatives had attempted to buy or lease fields, both of the seasonally rain-fed and permanently irrigated variety, as well as draught animals for Aeta families to use for wet-rice cultivation. In the Botolan area, for instance, the LAKAS organisation (*Lubos na Alyansa ng mga Katutubong Aeta sa Sambales*) had acquired a number of irrigated rice fields. This NGO had worked among the Aeta even before the eruption and during the mid-1990s was supporting about 140 families. A splinter group of LAKAS, the SMT (*Samahang ng Maghaharaman sa Tumangan* or Farmers' Association of Tumangan), a self-help-group consisting of approximately twenty Aeta families organised by an Aeta leader, likewise attempted to take up wet-rice agriculture (Koshida 1992: 51, 58–60). Members of yet another ex-LAKAS faction, organised under the name PINATUBO (*Pinagkaisang Aeta na Tutulong sa Botolan*), leased irrigated wet-rice fields which they intended to plant during the dry season, in addition to the fields of dry-rice (*kaingin*) they were cultivating in the mountains during the rainy season. Like the SMT, the PINATUBO comprised about twenty families.

In all these cases, however, success remained elusive. Those Aeta families in which one partner came from the lowland community, or families which were very near the lowland area or in which Aeta men had acted as leaders of their group during the disaster, were more or less successful. There were more families like that among those living in the hinterland of Botolan before the eruption than among those in the hinterland of San Marcelino. Near Botolan some families already had begun to cultivate wet-rice before the eruption in the swamps along the rivers. This means that especially such Aeta who had been already in intensive contact for a long time with the lowland society, or who had an outstanding position in their own group and therefore had become negotiators between the two groups after the disaster, were now relatively eager to participate in the lifestyle of the lowland people, and so also in wet-rice agriculture.

It is characteristic that often other members without such intentions left the organisations, did not attach themselves to a group on a long-term basis and invest in a project that would not yield immediate returns. In the eyes of at least some of these Aeta the necessary investment of labour also seemed to be out of proportion with any expected returns. Aeta who promoted such innovations were in one case a pastor, in several other cases leaders of Aeta-NGOs or Aeta who had experience of working with the Americans; all of these oriented themselves on the lifestyle of the lowland people. Only in cases such as these did an individual group member start an initiative. Otherwise, the decision of whether or not to adopt wet-rice cultivation was typically made by the NGOs. In other words, only those Aeta who had already demonstrated a talent for organisation while guiding a group or organising a job, even before the various attempts at introducing wet-rice cultivation on a group-wide scale, showed some initiative and willingness to take risks. These were Aeta who, in an otherwise egalitarian society, had acquired a special status and who had functioned as contacts for relief organisations during the disaster, who had been *barangay capitan*, or had played an active role in one of the self-help-groups. With their experience and motivation they usually managed to organise a small number of families, which then became pioneering groups, often forged together by kinship ties, similar to the traditional family groupings.

Due to constant fluctuations and vague lease conditions, the exact number of Aeta lessees at any given time is essentially a matter of speculation. Perhaps 5 percent of Aeta families living in resettlement sites may work wet-rice fields under lease agreements. During the study period from 1995 to 2000 this percentage remained largely constant, given that some families abandoned wet-rice cultivation while others took it up during that time. As a rule of thumb, not more than two or three families per *barangay* of a resettlement site inhabited by 20 – 150 families may then have been involved in wet-rice cultivation.

Only in the case of one resettlement site, Dampay-Salaza, had there also been a development of land suitable for wet-rice cultivation during the initial configuration of the site (Shimizu 1992: 15–17). Similarly, one group of such 'advanced' Aeta, coming from villages in which some families were already engaged in wet-rice cultivation and were before the eruption already in more intensive contact with the lowland population, under the leadership of an Aeta tribal chief near the resettlement centre of Dampay beside the river, started constructing an irrigation canal system to gain some hectares of land for wet-rice cultivation, and also to regain some rice fields abandoned by lowland farmers. The lack of buffaloes put an end to these activities (Shimizu 2001: 22,23).

In 1999 the resident Aeta were still practising swidden farming (*kaingin*). The proportion of Aeta families in Dampay-Salaza's overall population had dropped to 30 percent (from about 450 Aeta families to about 130 families), a decline largely reflecting the steady influx of lowland residents. These latecomers had quickly appropriated the riverine bottomlands, that is, the lands best suited for wet-rice agriculture.

Those families living in the resettlement sites near Botolan (Loob Bunga and Baquilan) would also have the opportunity, albeit on a limited scale, to cultivate wet-rice on swampland plots; only in the hinterlands had lowland families in most cases not beaten them to the land. For these, Aeta support from NGOs had initially not been forthcoming, mainly because the Botolan hinterlands had remained officially off-limits during the first years after the eruption. Those few Aeta who nonetheless did manage to engage in wet-rice cultivation in the hinterland area had married into lowland families. Even the more readily available opportunity to establish fields on the openly accessible, waterlogged *lahar* during the dry season was, for example in 1999, used only by two Aeta families. This is of course a somewhat provisional form of wet-rice cultivation; every year, shortly before the start of the rainy season and the resulting flows of *lahar*, the fields have to be abandoned.

As was the case in the hinterlands of Botolan, only a few attempts have been made to cultivate wet rice in the San Marcelino highlands. A handful of Aeta families are still working leased wet-rice fields located far away from their homes. The most suitable fields around Santa Fe, in the floodplain of the Santo Tomas river, are generally claimed by families from the lowlands. The fields can only be worked during the dry season, because during the rainy season they are flooded by *lahar*.

Wet-rice cultivation has also failed to become popular among those Aeta living in off-site settlements, in the small villages on the coastal plain in the densely populated coastal zone. Irrigated rice fields found in the immediate vicinity of Aeta settlements are almost invariably owned by lowland families. According to the official off-site list of the ONCC (the former Office for Northern Cultural Communities) for 1994, only six out of thirty-two communities had up to that point seen the establishment of rice fields. Not surprisingly, every one of these communities had then been a field of activity for NGOs. Five years later, in 1999, my own re-evaluation of the situation in over forty Aeta off-site settlements along the coast showed that the number of sites with Aeta families practising wet-rice cultivation had shrunk to five communities, three of which had not been listed in 1994. In one community, Cadman/Reserva and Bakuli, wet-rice cultivation had already been initiated by NGOs (in this case by the ADA) before the eruption, but had, contrary to public estimation and the official ONCC list, been abandoned by the Aeta in the wake of the disaster. Not even in coastal settlements where Aeta had been living since before the eruption was wet-rice cultivation practised. There may have been, at most, between two and five families working wet-rice fields as tenants in a few coastal off-site settlements.

New opportunities, on the other hand, presented themselves to the Aeta outside their original habitat and sphere of activities. In the thinly populated, partly unutilised hinterlands of Iba and Palauig, to the north of Botolan, Aeta evacuees either received land from large landowners or land for settlement, and agricultural use was bought by NGOs. In this area two new settlements occupied almost exclusively by Aeta were established, each with a population of about sixty families. In addition, there are two mixed settlements where Aeta make up less than 20 percent of the residents. All these Aeta had come from the resettlement sites around Botolan and from the former evacuation centre near Palauig. In the two Aeta villages every family has access to an agricultural plot about 1 ha. in size. Here wet-rice can be planted on rain-fed fields or seasonally flooded swamp plots, but not on modern irrigated fields. This at least leaves open the prospect of a gradual transition from rain-fed rice farms with their lower investments of time and resources and only one harvest in one year, depending on the rainfall, to a more intensive and demanding form of agriculture centred on irrigated rice fields with two or three harvests throughout the year, independent of precipitation (cf. Schneider 1995, for Indonesia).

Aside from the permanently resident Aeta, there are also families who come to the area on a temporary basis to work leased fields. It usually takes these families about a day of travel on foot to cover the distance from their homes in the resettlement sites and off-site settlements around Botolan. Such movements between resettlement sites and the newly opened activity area are quite frequent and resemble similar movements between the resettlement sites and the hinterlands of Botolan. For the Aeta, all this follows in the tradition of their old mobile lifestyle. Neither the permanently resident Aeta nor the tenants from the resettlement sites and off-site settlements, however, place any priority on wet-rice cultivation. Among them, it is but one of several forms of land use, as they cultivate many different plants on their fields, following a seasonal pattern.

That Aeta have seized the opportunity to engage in agriculture on land available in the area north of Botolan underscores just how pressing the central problem of insufficient agricultural space still is. Yet at the same time, the fact that for these Aeta wet-rice cultivation remains only an additional economic strategy, even under the adverse circumstances of the post-eruption period, clearly shows that the lack of agricultural land, even if it is frequently mentioned by the Aeta themselves, cannot be the only reason for the limited acceptance of wet-rice cultivation among them.

The Aeta in the resettlement sites, for their part, are demanding a legal solution of as yet unsettled questions regarding land-use rights, as well as the development of new land and its transformation into permanent property rather than temporary holdings. Land-use rights in the highlands have undergone fundamental changes. On 28 July 1997, the long-awaited law for the regulation of the so-called 'Ancestral Domain' was finally passed as Republic Act no. 8371, known as the 'Indigenous People Rights Act of 1997', and incorporated into Chapter III, 'Rights to the Ancestral Domain'. The Aeta expect this law to substantially improve their legal status as potential or actual landowners.

The Aeta are now able to claim as private property land settled and worked by them before the disaster. While earlier decrees (1974, 1987) aimed at protecting the claims of ethnic minorities regarding their ancestral lands were never put into practice (Griffin 1988: 12; Okamura 1988: 18), the new regulations are now indeed used as the legal foundation in cases of land litigation. With the establishment of the new legal foundation, the number of Aeta families interested in holding land has increased. However, titles of possession are only valid if the land in question is under cultivation, encouraging more families to return to the Botolan highlands in order to clear fields and thus be eligible to file for legal ownership of land. For the most part, however, agricultural plots throughout the highland region are unsuited for wet-rice cultivation. As a result, the new laws will most likely help the Aeta in establishing themselves in dry farming, but at the same time may not really facilitate their taking up wet-rice cultivation. Only in the few coastal communities where Aeta have been living since before the eruption may there be a chance for them to lay claim to lands that might be suitable for wet-rice cultivation. But given the dense lowland population, the size of any such plots will almost certainly be negligible.

Socio-Economic Factors Influencing the Adoption of Wet-Rice Cultivation by the Aeta

The multitude of activities pursued by the Aeta allows them to endure even in the unfamiliar situation of having to live among the lowland population. Wet-rice cultivation is not essential to their survival. The few Aeta families that have taken up this particular form of agriculture can be regarded as a kind of new elite, living between the lowland society and the Aeta community, with its originally egalitarian society. As such, however, their elevated social status is not rooted in economic advantages but is a result of NGO programmes that have intensified incipient socio-economic disparities, as well as of individual leadership qualities that became evident particularly at the height of the disaster. Thus, it seems as if these Aeta have adopted wet-rice cultivation primarily to approach an equal social level with the lowland farmers rather than to meet an economic necessity, mainly to adapt the lifestyle of the lowland community and to integrate themselves in this society.

The establishment, maintenance, and cultivation of irrigated fields requires a certain degree of organisational capacity and continuity, which is not demanded by swidden agriculture and is therefore alien to the average Aeta family. It is thus not surprising that among the Aeta such fields are worked primarily by those individuals who had assumed leadership roles during the disaster, and whose training and education at the hands of NGOs has made them familiar with the way of life of the lowland population. At the same time, they have acquired valuable experience in how to deal with government agencies and their representatives, and have become acquainted with their rights as tenants.

The Aeta themselves, as well as their lowland neighbours and the NGOs, claim that their best chance of economic development lies in the intensification of agricultural activities and the expansion of agricultural lands. When I spoke with the Aeta about their future, they repeatedly stated that they would be willing to cut back on their mobility and settle down permanently if they had access to sufficient land for cultivation (see also Shimizu 1992: 28). This may be true for agricultural activities in general, but as far as wet-rice cultivation is concerned most of the Aeta have hardly shown any enthusiasm to commit themselves to this particular technique, even in areas where they have access to land. Clearly, the decision of whether to independently take up wet-rice cultivation on rain-fed or irrigated fields is not solely determined by the availability or lack of land, but rather is influenced by a variety of factors, some of which make wet-rice cultivation appear as a superfluous technique from a conceptual perspective, while others in one way or another simply hamper its development in more tangible ways.

The cultivation of wet-rice generally has to be based on a long-term strategy of food production and storage, unlike the production of tubers or fruits. Such a strategy differs sharply from traditional Aeta economic practice, which involves short-term planning and activities and immediate food consumption, a pattern typical for hunter-gatherers (cf. Woodburn's classification 1980, and Testard 1982: 523). In addition, wet-rice cultivation requires a persistent, continuous labour investment in the fields and thus sharply curtails mobility. It also requires strict adherence to certain economic requirements, to be present for maintaining the fields, waiting for the harvest and calculating the amount of crops for storage. This basic condition is again largely incompatible with spatial as well as temporal mobility. All this runs counter to current social and economic behaviour among the Aeta, most of whom as their vertical migrations indicate, still seem to prefer a life characterised by spatial mobility.

With its high labour requirements, especially when irrigated fields are involved, and its demand for continuous maintenance, wet-rice cultivation leaves little space for other economic activities. The Aeta, however, prefer to utilise a wide range of different resources. This preference can be interpreted as part of a foraging survival strategy. Of course it is also a strategy used by many other Filipinos to survive in the economically desperate situation facing the country. In contrast, farmers like the lowland neighbours of the Aeta usually focus their economic efforts only on the cultivation of a few core resources, although many of them today are forced to take different opportunities.

The development of wet-rice cultivation, however slow and painstaking it may be, brings with it new ideas of capital and land ownership, especially with respect to intensive cultivation. Aeta attitudes towards land ownership have changed considerably since 1991. Prior to the eruption, agricultural land had held no specific value for the Aeta, rights of possession then being defined on the basis of the family group. Today, however, land held as private property is a highly coveted asset. Yet, interestingly enough, the same is not necessarily true for wet-rice fields. To own such fields does not automatically convey more prestige on their owners. The Aeta deem wet-rice fields no more valuable than those used for dry rice; a position quite unlike that of their lowland neighbours, among whom the size of a farmer's wet-rice fields, together with the number of *carabaos*, is considered a measuring stick for personal wealth. So far, the complex of wet-rice cultivation has thus hardly left any impression on the social life of the Aeta.

The problem of acquiring land and draught animals, as well as the dilemma of financing agricultural equipment, seeds and fertiliser, forces the Aeta into cooperation that reaches beyond the traditional family groupings. This need for cooperation to gain a foothold in wet-rice cultivation, though, can make the Aeta dependent on help from NGOs and other institutions. These complex organisations may set up cooperatives in order to use animals collectively or to improve labour assignments in the cultivation of fields. To operate in large groups, however, is something the traditionally individualistic and independent Aeta find hard to do. Their focus on the individual, and the individual family has always given them the flexibility they need for their culture and society to survive. It is thus not surprising that the few cooperatives initiated and guided by Aeta leaders often fell apart after only a short time; the same goes for wet-rice cultivation.

In the eyes of the Aeta, it is today much easier to acquire rice by trading it in exchange for the fruits of other activities than by going through the trouble of taking up wet-rice cultivation themselves. The decision to accept wet-rice cultivation as a means of integration into the lowland society, especially under the stress of living in an overpopulated environment and therefore under the requirement of intensification of labour, is for the Aeta as former hunters and gatherers less desirable in the sense of economic improvement, but more so in the sense of social improvement: it offers a chance to get on an equal basis with lowland society.

Summary

Before the eruption of Mt Pinatubo, the Aeta living in the hinterland on this volcano, a marginal group who were formerly hunter-gatherers and are today swidden farmers with a strong foraging orientation, managed to remain economically independent and culturally autonomous. Thanks to their mobile spatial strategy, their utilisation of the multifarious resources of their habitat, and their very flexible social organisation in small family groupings, they preserved their autonomy even though for centuries they remained in close contact with the lowland farmers. They continued themselves to regard as hunters and not as farmers, using economic strategies characterised by short-term planning and immediate food consumption, a pattern typical for hunter gatherers. Therefore they concentrated their agricultural activities not on rice, which was highly valued by them, but on tuber cultivation, which needed no storage, and ownership on agricultural land was neglected. Their work as day labourers also corresponded to this economic behaviour, as they helped on lowland farms at the time when the irrigated rice fields were planted and harvested. This led to some Aeta becoming familiar with the techniques of wet-rice cultivation.

After the disaster and the evacuation to the lowland, for few Aeta families an independent wet-rice cultivation on rain-fed or irrigated fields became one of the new economic possibilities, besides, wage labour, swidden cultivation and horticulture, small businesses or collection of forest products other than timber. The decision to take over such intensive field cultivation means that the Aeta must accept profound changes of their lifestyle. In the densely populated coastal area, the Aeta were unable to acquire agricultural plots without help from outside. Only in a few cases did NGOs or private landowners make access to fields for the Aetas possible as lessees, providing them with water buffalos, ploughs and seeds. So a scant number of families accepted the new agricultural methods, especially those who, already been living close to the lowlands or those who had been involved in developmental projects by some NGOs a few years before disaster.

Those Aeta families which were successful were mainly those in which one partner came from the lowland farmer society or in which Aeta men had assumed leadership roles during the disaster, and therefore had intensive contact with the lowland society. Only in such cases did an individual group member start an initiative. Otherwise, the decision as to whether they should adopt wet-rice cultivation was made mostly by the NGOs. But the Aetas appreciation of land ownership has changed considerably, and private property as land now is highly valued. Now, more than one decade after the disaster, only very few Aeta have taken up wet-rice agriculture.

Even if the main problem, the availability of agricultural land, is still pressing – the regulation of the so-called 'Ancestral Domain' through the 'Indigenous Peoples Rights Act of 1997' has consequences for the hinterland only – this cannot be the only reason for the limited acceptance of wet-rice cultivation among the Aeta.

Wet-rice cultivation requires continuous investment of labour and thus limits mobility: it requires a long-term strategy, waiting for the harvest or calculating the amount of crops for storage. This runs counter to the traditional economic and social behaviour among the Aeta. In the same way, the need for cooperation in large groups beyond traditional family groupings, for the acquisition of land and draught animals, runs against the traditionally individualistic and independent behaviour of the Aeta.

The wet-rice cultivation is not essential to their survival in the lowland. The multitude of activities carried out by the Aeta ensures a more or less adequate livelihood even among the lowland population.

The few Aeta families that have taken up wet-rice agriculture can be regarded as a new stratum between the lowland farmer society and the Aeta hinterland community. This effect is also a result of NGO programmes, that have intensified incipient socio-economic disparities among the Aeta as well as individual leadership qualities generated during the disaster. Thus, it seems that the few Aeta who made the decision to shift to this intensive form of agriculture were primarily seeking an equal to that of social-level lowland farmers, rather than meeting economic necessity. For them it is an attempt to adopt the lifestyle of the lowland society in order to integrate themselves in that community on an equal basis.

References

Abaya, E.C., P.M. Buenconsejo, M.L.L. Fernan, M.R.R. Lopez, and P.C. Salvador 1993. *Disaster Response: Lessons from Mt. Pinatubo.* Baguio City: Jaime V. Ongpin Foundation, Inc.

Banzon Bautista, M.C.R., ed. 1993. *In the Shadow of the Lingering Mt. Pinatubo Disaster.* Quezon City: College of Social Sciences and Philosophy, University of the Philippines.

Boserup, E. 1965. *The Conditions of Agricultural Growth: The Economics of Agrarian Change Under Population Pressure.* London: Allen and Unwin.

——— 1981. *Population and Technological Change. A Study of Long-Term Trends.* Chicago: University of Chicago Press.

Brosius, J.P. 1983. 'The Zambales Negritos: Swidden Agriculture and Environmental Change', *Philippine Quarterly of Culture and Society* 11: 123–48.

Brosius, J.P. 1990. *After Duwagan. Deforestation, Succession, and Adaption in Highland Luzon, Philippines.* Ann Arbor: The University of Michigan Press.

Fondevilla, E.F. 1991. *Eruption and Exodus: Mt. Pinatubo and the Aytas of Zambales.* Quezon City: LAKAS.

Fox, R. 1952. 'The Pinatubo Negritos: Their Useful Plants and Material Culture', *The Philippine Journal of Science* 81: 173–414.

Griffin, P.B. 1988. 'National Policy on Minority Cultural Communities: The Philippine Case', *Southeast Asian Journal of Social Science* 16: 5–16.

Koshida, K. 1992. 'Ayta Power for Survival', in *After the Eruption. Pinatubo Aetas at the Crisis of their Survival,* ed. H. Shimizu, 50–62. Tokyo: Foundation for Human Rights in Asia.

Mendoza, T.C. and R.P. Cabangang 1992. 'Effects of Mt. Pinatubo Eruption in Crop Production Systems', in *Proceedings International Scientific Conference on Mt. Pinatubo,* 27–30 May 1992, p.125. Department of Foreign Affairs. Pasay: Metro Manila.

Mercado, L.N., ed. 1994. *Working With Indigenous Peoples. A Philippine Source Book.* Manila: Mercado.

Nass, G. 1988. 'Aetas of Zambales – A People in Transition', Unpubl. Paper Presented at the 22nd International Council of Anthropology and Ethnology, Zagreb, Yugoslavia, 24–31 July.

Newhall, C.G., ed. 1996. *Fire and Mud: Eruptions and Lahars of Mount Pinatubo, Philippines.* Quezon City: Philippine Institute of Volcanology and Seismology.

Okamura, J.Y. 1988. 'The Politics of Neglect: Philippine Ethnic Minority Policy', *Southeast Asian Journal of Social Science* 16: 17–46.

Oliver-Smith, A. and S.M. Hoffman, eds. 1999. *The Angry Earth: Disaster in Anthropological Perspective.* New York: Routledge.

Rice, D. 1973. 'Pattern for Development', *Philippine Sociological Review* 21: 255–60.

——— and S. Tima 1973. 'A Pattern for Development', The Baseline Research Report San Marcelino Negrito Reservations Zambales, Philippines. Quezon City.

Schneider, J. 1995. *From Highland to Irrigated Rice – The Development of Wet Rice Agriculture in Rejang Musi, Southwest-Sumatra.* Berlin: Reimer.

Seitz, S. 1984. 'Von der wildbeuterischen zur agrarischen Lebensweise. Die Negrito im Westen von Luzon', *Paideuma* 30: 257–74.

——— 1998. *Die Aeta am Vulkan Pinatubo. Katastrophenbewältigung in einer marginalen Gesellschaft auf den Philippinen.* Pfaffenweiler: Centaurus Verlagsgesellschaft.

Shimizu, H. 1983. 'Communicating with Spirits: A Study of the Manganito Seance among the Southwestern Pinatubo Negritos', *East Asian Cultural Studies* 22: 129–67.

——— 1989. *Pinatubo Aytas. Continuity and Change.* Quezon City: Ateneo de Manila University Press.

———, ed. 1992. *After the Eruption. Pinatubo Aetas at the Crisis of their Survival.* Tokyo: Foundation for Human Rights in Asia.

——— 2001. *The Orphans of Pinatubo. The Ayta Struggle for Existence.* Manila: Solidardad Publishing House.

Tayag, J.C. 1991. *Pinatubo Volcano Wakes from 450 Years Slumber.* Quezon City: Philippine Institute of Volcanology and Seismology (PHILVOCS).

Testard, A. 1982. 'The Significance of Food Storage among Hunter-Gatherers: Residence Patterns, Populations Densities, and Social Inequalities', *Current Anthropology* 23: 523–37.

Woodburn, J. 1980. 'Hunters and Gatherers Today and Reconstruction of the Past', in *Soviet and Western Anthropology*, ed. E. Gellner, 95–117. New York: Columbia University Press.

5

Drought and 'Natural' Stress in the Southern Dra Valley: Varying Perceptions among Nomads and Farmers

Barbara Casciarri

The Dra Valley consists of six oases stretching from the southern fringes of the High Atlas mountains to the Sahara. The area has been inhabited since early times by several groups and communities – Arabs and Berbers; nomads, farmers and traders; religious and lay groups; 'freemen', clients and slaves – differentiated according to various parameters, but integrated in complex socio-economic formations. This part of south-eastern Morocco, known in the pre-colonial past as a rich region in the heart of the trans-Saharan route linking Timbuktu with northern Africa, was affected by radical change during colonial times, but most of all in the first decades of independence. Nonetheless, till the mid-1970s, the almost exclusively rural population of the Dra Valley still seemed able to adapt locally to global economic transformations: traditional agriculture and herding still ensure the subsistence of both nomad and sedentary communities. The progressive deterioration of ecological conditions during the last two decades reached a drastic level in the mid-1990s, with grave consequences for economic production. For the various actors involved in the region in different ways – state agencies, development organisations, research institutions – the diagnosis is clear: drought is the major problem in Wadi Dra. The local population often agreed with this assumption, while applying complex strategies to overcome the severe effects of drought in their daily life.

My research in southeastern Morocco (cf. Casciarri 2003) focused on the management of water as a rare resource in the Wadi Dra catchment.[1] I concentrated on the two southern oases of Ktaoua and Mhamid, where the situation is more critical than in the northern part of the valley, and did fieldwork among two mutually integrated communities: the nomadic Ait Unzâr and the oasis inhabitants of Tiraf village. Both groups share material and social spaces of daily life, despite their distinct identities. I was interested in the interaction between pastoralists and sedentists in the exploitation of natural resources, the strategies of domestic units to cope with crises and the role of local institutions in managing conflict regarding water and land.

In this chapter I shall formulate some hypotheses about the ways in which a rural society may face a grave crisis that threatens its material and social reproduction. The process will be analysed at two levels: the perception of environmental crisis and the strategies adopted to cope with it. After sketching the socio-economic configuration of the pastoral and peasant communities in the Ktaoua region and giving an overview of official data on the crisis, I turn to current discourses about it, in order to examine, firstly, if such perception is unique for the local actors and the external forces (state, development agencies, researchers), and secondly, if it is shared by all the components of the rural community itself. After setting forth the differing perceptions of the crisis among various actors, I describe some strategies used to cope with environmental stress. In the final section I try to reflect on the bases upon which a generally good level of 'resistance' to crisis is built up, thanks to the integrated organisation of nomads and sedentists in Tiraf.

The Ait Unzâr Nomads and Tiraf Village: History and the Present

Social Structures in Southeastern Morocco

In an area with an annual precipitation of less than 100 mm, the Dra Valley consists of a chain of six oases stretching from the mountains south of Ouarzazate to the northern fringes of the Sahara (see map 5.1). The rhythm of the agricultural and pastoral cycles here is determined mainly by the snow melts from the High Atlas and rainfall that cause the river Dra to flood. While geophysical configuration and climatic features impose basic constraints on natural resource exploitation, the relation of humans with these resources can be grasped only within the complex history of a multitude of social components. The autochthonous population, known as *Draoua*,[2] consists of sedentary, primarily subsistent farmers inhabiting the fortified villages (*qsâr*) and cultivating mainly date palms. A second component is represented by communities of nomad origin, who migrated with the spread of Islam in North Africa. Among the latter, even those who abandoned a nomadic life are still considered as having a higher status than the Draoua farmers: the pastoral connotations offer the background to a certain specificity of their present economic and political structures. As a third

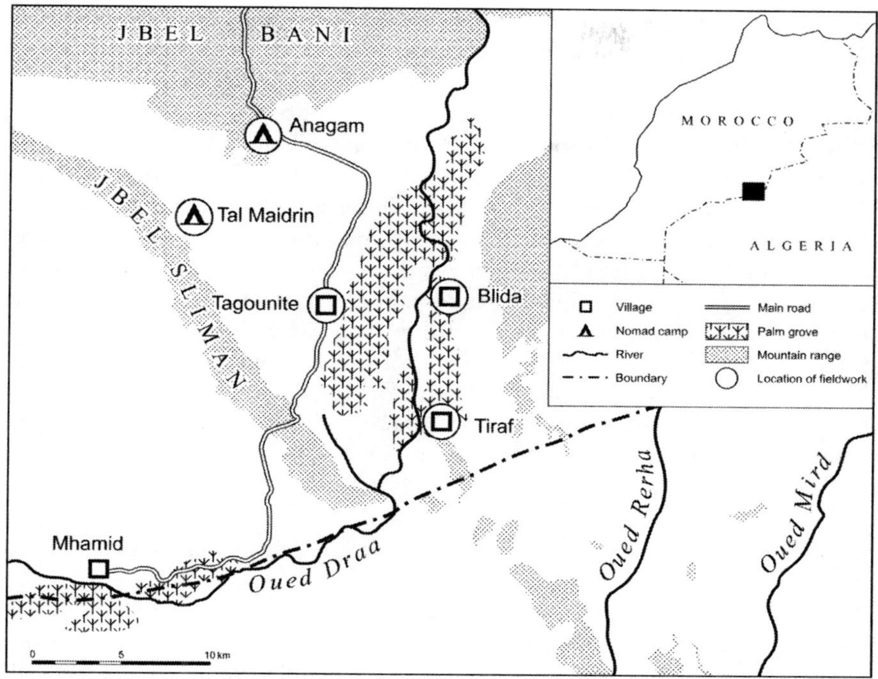

Map 5.1. The southern Draa Valley and the area of investigation

component there are communities of high social status that is related to notions of descent and the concomitant attribution of religious prerogatives; these communities are defined as *Chorfa* (the Prophet Mohammad's descendants) or *Mrabtîn* (saintly lineages of varied origin). Finally, at the bottom of this social hierarchy, are the communities defined as *'abîd*, considered to be the descendant of slaves from Sub-Saharan Africa. Despite the abolition of slavery and of relations of subordination between groups, such hierarchy – that induced some scholars to argue for the existence of a 'caste-based' society (Jacques-Meunié 1958) – is still visible in the differential access to resources and in some other boundaries strongly rooted in local daily life.

Because of its location on the crossroads between Sub-Saharan Africa and Mediterranean Morocco, the Dra Valley has for long been a strategic region. Lying on the caravan route from Timbuktu, the area was crucial for military encounters, commercial exchange and melting populations. Ever since the sixteenth century, various Berber-speaking nomadic groups gathered to form the huge Ait 'Atta confederation, succeeded in fighting the Mâqîl Arabs, who had occupied the Dra since the twelfth century, and established their hegemony (Hart 1981, 1984). During the pre-colonial period the area was considered as *bilâd as-sîba*, 'the country of insubordination', as opposed to the *bilâd l-Makhzan*, the country under the control of the central state (Gellner 1969). The Ait 'Atta of the Dra, together with some Berber groups of the Atlas, were fiercest in their resistance to French colonisation (Dunn 1977): while in 1912 the Protectorate was established in most of the country, the 'pacification' of the Dra Valley was achieved only in 1932–3 (Spillmann 1936), and military encounters between French troops and nomads are documented until as late as 1936 (Léfébure 1986). The remoteness of the region continued to influence its configuration in post-colonial times, in spite of administrative reorganisation and efforts to modernise the infrastructure. The Dra Valley is one of the most rural areas in Morocco, with traditional agriculture and herding dominating, development indicators lower than for the rest of the country, and social relations strongly rooted in tradition. Despite some major economic changes in the last two decades and the creation in 1997 of a Zagora Province encompassing all Dra inhabitants previously included in Ouarzazate Province, the sociological framework of the Valley still appears strongly conditioned by its historical background.

Sharing the Village of Tiraf: The Ait Unzâr and the Shaqaf

Despite their relative specificity, the various communities mentioned above have always practised some form of socio-economic integration. While the mountain slopes and grazing lands remain the domain of nomads, in all *qsâr* of the oases all communities participate in the common management of daily life. In spite of a roughly homogeneous regional frame, social articulation in every village depends strictly on its specific local history. The village of Tiraf lies on the west bank of Wadi Dra in the extreme southeastern part of the Ktaoua oasis. It is almost 10 km east of Tagounite, the administrative urban centre of the region, and 20 km west of the contested Algerian border. The presence of the nomadic Ait Unzâr as one of the two social components of Tiraf is intimately linked to the opening of the village its towards the eastern and southern Saharan grazing lands and its marginal location.

According to oral tradition, Abdallah Shaqaf, the eponymous ancestor of the Arabic speaking Draoua, founded Tiraf at the end of the eighteenth century. After a first destruction of their village by attacking nomadic groups, people of the *qsâr* approached the powerful Berber tribes for aid. Different sections of the Ait 'Atta confederation now took charge of protecting the Shaqaf of Tiraf, until the arrival in the mid-nineteenth century (Niclausse 1954) of one of their sections, the Ait Unzâr, who remained the exclusive protector of the village until French colonisation.[3] Today such exclusive relations are still manifest in various forms and the Ait Unzâr consider Tiraf as their 'capital'. Pacts of protection, generally defined as *ra'ya*, were widespread in the valley, mostly in the southern oases of Ktaoua and Mhamid. Under constant threat from aggressive nomadic pastoral communities passing along the Transaharan route or struggling for local hegemony, the sedentary populations often had no option but to take recourse to such pacts, which for nomads entailed the duty of military protection in exchange for the transfer of a portion (normally one quarter, called *rba*) of the houses, fields and water rights of the village. Such an alliance implied a subordinate status for the protected clients; most of them also became share-croppers (*khammâs*), receiving a fifth of the yield in exchange for their agricultural labour for the nomad landowners who were themselves mostly engaged in pastoral activities.

The Ait Unzâr, whose name means 'the ones of the rain', are part of one *khôms* (five primary divisions of the Ait 'Atta) composed of Ait Isfoul and Ait Alouane; the latter are divided in turn into four tribes: Ait Bou Msaoud, Aitî, Ait Ghanîma et Ait Unzâr. They are one of the most 'Saharan' groups within the Ait 'Atta confederation. Mainly camel herders, they practise horizontal nomadism, owing to the unpredictability of rain in this extremely arid area. Unlike most of their fellow tribesmen, among whom goat and sheep herding and a more regular vertical transhumance predominate, the Ait Unzâr do not have pasture rights in the mountains. Their traditional territory, stretching from the Hammâda in the south to the Algerian grazing lands in the east, where they live in contact with other non-Berber Saharan groups (such as the nomadic 'Arîb pastoralists), has experienced remarkable transformation. During colonisation, the French tried to fix tribal borders, thus replacing a more fluid definition of frontiers between groups sharing access to resources. During the last decades the proximity of the contested border with Algeria (1963) and the war in Western Sahara (1975) imposed further territorial restrictions (Casciarri, forthcoming). One of the last communities living mainly from nomadic herding, the Ait Unzâr now move in the area between Foum Zguid, Mhamid and Wadi Mird, but the village of Tiraf is for them all a common 'head-quarters': some families are settled there in a fairly definitive manner, most of them own cultivated fields and irrigation rights, and every Ait Unzâr is politically represented, according to his lineage section, at the level of local tribal institutions.

The present population composition of Tiraf reflects the history of the village. The demographically and politically dominant Draoua group, the Shaqaf, is divided into two lineages, Lmedani and Lhaddi, considered to be the descendants of the two sons of the founder, Abdallah. Four minor Draoua groups (Sammoud, Bigyouar, Sbiti, Fagrouti), coming from different places of the same region almost a century ago (first as farmers without land), joined the original sedentary group. All Draoua families today are Arabic speaking. The nomadic component is represented by a minority of the ancient protectors, the Ait Unzâr who, though maintaining a mixed economy, chose to partially sedentarise,[4] and by a Chorfa family of a saintly Idrisi lineage associated with the Ait Unzâr and established since early times in Tiraf. Both Ait Unzâr and Chorfa are Berber speaking. Finally, unlike in most villages of this region, in Tiraf there are no families of *'abîd*, the descendants of slaves.[5]

The management of resources and social relations is strictly linked to the history and population movements mentioned above. One can still observe the effects of the ancient attribution of one-fourth of the Draoua's fields to the nomad protectors upon the tenancy framework, thanks also to the local trend preventing land alienation through sale to foreigners[6] and minimising the fragmentation of holdings through endogamous marriage and dispossession of female heirs. Some forms of work not mediated by wage but with payment in kind and structured by the nomad-sedentary relation, still persist – for example, the Draoua sharecroppers for the Ait Unzâr (the *khammâs*-landownership is transmitted from one generation to the next), the Ait Unzâr *ra'yân*, guardians of the palms groves during the date harvests, or again the *'elim* guardian of the canal (*saqyia*). The most significant illustration of close cooperation between the Draoua and Ait Unzâr lies perhaps in the division of the rarest resource: water. For the inhabitants of Tiraf the traditional irrigation system remains almost the sole source of cultivation. While in other parts of the valley the spread of motor-pumps lessened the importance of ancient modes of irrigation (Ait Hamza 2002), Tiraf has not been affected by such 'technological revolution', both because of the higher salinity of groundwater and the scarcity of cash necessary for the purchase and maintenance of motor-pumps.[7] Cultivation takes place exclusively with water from the *saqyia* – the main canal with branches going to the individual plots – which gets filled by natural floods, but mainly through the discharge from the Mansour Ad-Dhabi dam in Ouarzazate. Water distribution in the Tiraf *saqyia* is based upon a detailed plan, whose basic criteria continue to be the ethnic parameters between groups (Ait Unzâr and Draoua) and genealogical considerations within each group (i.e., further internal division following lineage articulation).

The institutional framework functioning in Tiraf also confirms the centrality of nomad-sedentary interaction in the management of socio-economic life. Apart from the centralised system of local government, with the appointment of local representatives to each administrative unit in a pyramidal national system, in some villages of the valley traditional institutions still retain certain powers. The *qabîla*, a term that I shall gloss as 'tribe', is composed of representatives of different genealogical units, chosen by their respective community to represent them in an assembly which meets periodically and has real decision-making authority. The historical symbiosis between nomads and sedentists is expressed by the 'bipolar' form of tribal assemblies in Tiraf (see Figure 5.1). The Draoua *qabîla* comprises three thirds (*thuluth*): two thirds are issued from the sons of the ancestor Abdallah Shaqaf and one third corresponds to other Draoua of various origin. The Ait Unzâr *taqbilt* (Berbère version of the Arabic word *qabîla*) is formed from four fourths (*rbû*), corresponding to the four primary lineages of the tribe, called *ikhs*, 'the bone'. The two tribes act jointly in organising the basic concerns of collective life: sharing water rights, managing drinking water, deciding on collective labour, controlling the date harvest, communicating with state agencies, mediating conflicts – in other words, all decisions, including those impinging on some aspects of moral and cultural behaviour, that concern both of the local communities. The persisting unity of the pastoral and agricultural

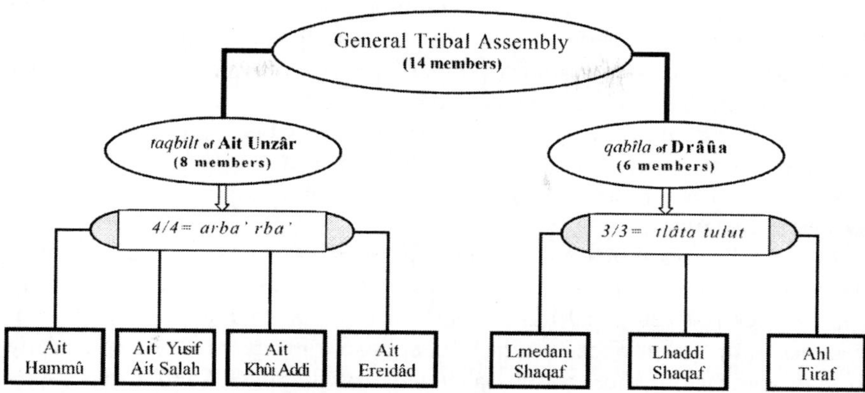

Figure 5.1. The bipolar tribal system in Tiraf

components and the strength of the tribal structure has its symbolic representation in the existence of a unique overall authority, Shaykh Hammân, who is at the same time *shaykh* of all Ait Unzâr nomads and of the village of Tiraf.[8]

The Ecological and Economic Crisis

The Recent Crisis in 'Useless Morocco': A Global Insight

In colonial times the Dra Valley was the object of a dual interest: political, because of the endemic insubordination of its populations; ethnographic, thanks to its 'archaic' institutions that had 'disappeared' elsewhere (De la Chapelle 1929; Jacques-Meunié 1947). In the last two decades the region has once again caught the attention of the scientific and state agencies. A rich bibliography documents the multitude of case studies on numerous topics carried out in the six oases[9]. Differing slightly in approach and aim, one assumption is common to them all: a severe crisis has struck the region and two basic factors, drought and desertification, are the main causes of the problem.

Indeed, the effects of the crisis are visible in changing environmental conditions: the decreasing precipitation, the increasing salinity of groundwater and the risk of its depletion, the encroachment of desert upon arable land, the spreading of the lethal palm parasite *bayoud*. At the production level, too, there are clear indicators of decline both in agriculture and herding. The social manifestations of crisis accompany such natural phenomena: the rural exodus, the sedentarisation of nomads, the migration fluxes, the uncertainty of subsistence strategies, the weakening of solidarity and family ties. The Mansour Ed-Dabhi dam, finished in 1972, which was thought of as a starting point for the development of the valley, did not bring the expected advantages. After a first euphoric phase of exaltation for the policy of *grande hydraulique*, mainly praising the rationalisation of traditional irrigation systems (Anafid 1990), the distribution of dammed irrigation water was threatened by a growing deficit up to the dramatic levels of the mid 1990s.[10] As a consequence, agricultural production is declining and unable to maintain its role as basic subsistence source for local populations.

A few changes, such as improvements of roads and transportation, electrification and tourism, do not really seem sufficient for balancing these negative trends. Even social indicators, such as access to education or medical treatment, after improvement in the initial post-colonial phase, declined recently to levels approaching those of Sub-Saharan Africa (Ramonet 2000). Crisis is now global, but listening to the official discourse one could think that by merely eliminating the water deficit, whose natural causes are stressed, the problems besetting people's lives in Wadi Dra would be solved.

Such a presumption is largely responsible for the recent multiplication of development projects in the Dra region. Through its agencies, the Moroccan state and its institutions tried to mitigate local problems and give a direction to processes of change. Its basic interventions focused mainly on the resource water by digging wells on nomad grazing lands, building drinking-water reservoirs in the villages, modernising the *saqyia* network, and stabilising dunes. Simultaneously, efforts were made to modernise agriculture by introducing tractors and chemical fertilisers, and herding through vaccination campaigns, selection and cross-breeding, while also supporting existing networks for the sale of the produce. At the institutional level, the most innovative step has probably been the devolution of responsibility in local water management to the associative groups, by formalising the existence of an AUEA (*Association d'Usagers d'Eaux Agricoles*) in every village between the 1980s and the 1990s (Anafid 1991). In addition, various international cooperation projects, NGOs, aid and development organisations – mainly European and North American – are also active. Most of these started their work after the state did, in the 1980s and increasingly during the 1990s. Their analysis of the crisis in Wadi Dra, according centrality to the water deficit, does not basically diverge from that of the state, but their interventions often enlarge the ecological question to a wider social dimension and stimulate the application of methods praising the so-called 'participatory approach'. Micro-credit, female handcraft production, natural reserve creation, eco-tourism, alphabetisation, popularisation of concepts in resource management and preservation form part of their activities.

A general review of common development intervention and response to crisis shows two basic features, without major distinction between state and non-state actors. First, there is a frequent statement of the great difficulty of efficient intervention that sometimes leads to the failure of a project,[11] a difficulty often ascribed to 'conservatism', resilience and the traditional attachment of people to past structures and behaviour. Second, there is a remarkable absence of balance in the geographical distribution of interventions. Even though this may seem paradoxical, the part of the valley most affected by crisis (the oases of Ktaoua and Mhamid) is the most neglected by these projects. As if the old colonial discourse that saw the Jebel Bani mountains as the real borderline with the Sahara – i.e., the geographical limit of possible modernisation and civilisation (Azam 1946) – were still continuing today, these Saharan extremities of the Dra Valley risk being further marginalised because less attention is paid to them as 'developable' areas. Thus, both state and NGOs implicitly yielded to the paradoxical and cynical logic according to which development has to be promoted where it is more profitable, rather than more needed.

The Signs of Crisis at the Local Level

Tiraf and the Ait Unzâr benefited from the general amelioration of living standards in the period after independence. Fieldwork data confirmed in this case the official documentation, and the comparison between older and younger generations is enlightening. As for most countries of the Third World, after the decolonisation phase, various domains experienced such growing trends. Vaccination campaigns and the spread of basic medical treatment determined the decline in mortality, especially of children and pregnant women.[12] Even if the age of first marriage continues to be lower than in urban areas, it is higher than before, and the frequency of childbirth is slightly less than it was earlier. Between the 1960s and the 1970s, Tiraf, like most *douâr*, was equipped with a primary school and basic education has been spreading, even if noticeable differences remain according to group and gender – nomad children and girls being more unschooled.[13] State interventions and technological innovations have facilitated the hardest task of previous generations: the daily quest for water with lower energy requirements, more efficient ways of storing water, the installation of collective taps, better quality and greater availability of domestic water. The development of roads and motorised transport favours the circulation of people and commodities. Some wider macro-economic factors and socio-cultural processes determine higher mobility, and though labour migration is temporary and limited to a few family members, in post-independence decades it is able to supplement traditional productive activities with some integrative cash incomes. In the wider context, at the level of social hierarchical relations, the subordinate status historically attributed to Draoua and *'abîd* groups (compared to nomad and religious elements) has progressively lost its economic and political connotations, thanks to processes of social ascent and emancipation, though undoubtedly persisting in identity reference and mainly in marriage practice.[14]

Nonetheless, Tiraf and the local nomad communities still occupy a marginal position in this Saharan southern part of the Dra Valley, which is a region with alarming socio-economic indicators when compared to the general national trends. Though between independence and the late 1970s, on the whole the local population enjoyed improved living standards, at the end of the 1970s, and increasingly during the 1980s, the periods of drought began to be longer and more intense. However, in the first twenty years, there was always a phase of recovery, so both local authorities and nomad and sedentary populations continued to see drought as a cyclic phenomenon. Finally, in the mid-1990s drought became acutely endemic in the region, and its effects started to look irreversible, with sedentarisation of nomads, massive and unplanned urbanisation, depopulation of rural spaces, and threats to means of subsistence. Data set out in table 5.1 concerning the two main productive activities, agriculture and herding, illustrate this trend, thereby confirming the impression both of the outside observer and local actors, that agriculture is much more drastically affected by the crisis than herding.

Every year the entire amount of discharge from the Mansour Ad-Dhabi dam, the main source of irrigation water since the 1970s, is planned for the period 1 September to 31 August. This is known locally as an 'irrigation campaign' (*campagne d'irrigation*). Over the years, with the worrying rainfall deficit, the discharge from the dam has diminished continuously and by 2002–3 the renewal of both groundwater and rangeland vegetation was endangered. In Tiraf, the salinity of groundwater reached dramatic levels: well water could be used only for ritual ablutions in the mosque or for some other washing, and even animals refused to drink it.

Table 5.1. The effects of drought on herding and agriculture respectively in the study area (1991–2003)

Production of Ktaoua Region and Tiraf Village		**1991/ 1992**	**1994/ 1995**	**1997/ 1998**	**2000/ 2001**	**2001/ 2002**	**2002/ 2003**
Herding (no. of heads)	**Cattle**	702	252	470	508	289	154
	Sheep	14,078	12,956	15,403	11,600	11,142	10,172
	Goats	28,157	23,096	23,882	15,698	14,779	14,176
	Camels	2,392	1,898	2,481	2,115	1,973	2,005
Agriculture (in tons)	**Dates**	6,700	8,000	6,200	1,600	1,200	630
		(240)*	(272)*	(210)*	(55)*	(40)*	(10)*
* Figures for Tiraf are given in brackets	**Cereals**	13,800	18,200	15,000	6,000	2,600	600
		(380)*	(470)*	(380)*	(220)*	(140)*	(25)*

Official data of the ORMVAO, Tagounite CMV, sources: Yusif Slimani (herding) and Mohamed Boudiaf (agriculture)

In the same period other factors contributed to further worsen the crisis of production. Emigration became increasingly difficult: at the transnational, international level, harsh new European legislation made it almost impossible; at the national level, employment opportunities in Moroccan towns got worse. The changes in consumption patterns (favoured by the arrival of television and advertising) brought an increasing dependency on commodities, a phenomenon that always becomes much more critical in times of meagre surplus of family production which must be sold to purchase items not locally produced. In a kind of vicious cycle, the development indicators again started to sink (cf. Casciarri 2002a for similar observations among Ahamda nomads of Sudan). At the moment of our first arrival in the field in October 2000, the crisis in the Dra Valley was in this severe and critical phase.

Local Discourses about Drought and Crisis

The All-Explaining Jfâf

One general observation emerges from oral testimonies collected during the fieldwork: the presence of the drought *leitmotiv* in almost every account, regardless of topics, periods and informants. The most commonly used term for drought, in the primary sense of 'lack of water', is undoubtedly *jfâf*, as in the standard and classical Arabic. Though other terms existence in *Tachelhit*, the Berber language spoken by the Ait Unzâr, they too use this Arabic term even when speaking in Berber.[15] In this critical period, the constant point of reference was the lack of water and, running parallel to this, local discourse was uniform in its evocation of periods of well-being as those strictly defined by the abundance of water.

There is undoubtedly basic agreement among all social actors about the centrality accorded to drought as the core of the crisis. But it is interesting to underline similarities and differences between various speakers about the same concern; in fact the perception of the all-explaining *jfâf* became more complex and articulated the deeper we examined the testimonies. The main variation was between nomads and farmers: the lack of water for the former does not have quite the same implications it does for the latter. All nomads complained mainly about the lack of grazing grasses (*rbî'a* in Arabic, *tuga* in *Tachelhit*). This standard Arabic term denotes the spring season, but in Morocco we find a metonymic identification with the most precious gift that spring offers to nomads: the growth after rainfall of a rich variety of plants that are nutritious for herds. The temporal connotation of *rbî'a* as a mere season is not a static one: one could say that in certain years there was no *rbî'a*, proving that the reference is less to the astronomic season than to its ecological and socio-economic characterisation.[16] For extensive herding availability of *rbî'a* on pastures is a major factor: animals may endure its lack by eating *sedr* – a global term for every pasture's perennial plants – but the herds which do not eat *rbî'a* are thin, produce less milk and are less likely to conceive; this in turn makes their use and exchange values very low. Moreover, as a minimal consumption of fresh grazing is always necessary, the nomad is dependant both on sedentary cultivation and cash revenues to obtain lucern or other fodder from the market. From the technical point of view, when *rbî'a* is insufficient, the work of herding becomes a heavy task, since during the day the shepherd has to move with herds far and long to find some feed for them. *Rbî'a* was always mentioned by the nomads as the main factor in and for their movement. In the current crisis, the rareness of *rbî'a* has led to a wider dispersion of groups: good pastures have diminished and are often even more scattered than before, and this has forced nomads to collectively rent lorries in order to move. A selection then occurs between those who can afford such expenses and those who are pushed to sedentarise and increasingly sell their animals to ensure sheer survival. The water whose scarcity is regretted by Ait Unzâr nomads is clearly the 'sky water', the rain as generator of good pasture, much more than groundwater, easily available and of very good quality in their territory.

The situation is quite different in the sedentary context. Here the lack is twofold: on the one hand, groundwater, on the other hand, water from the dam. As already mentioned, the salinity of groundwater is very high and is constantly increasing in Tiraf and surrounding areas. The villagers cannot rely for their domestic water requirements on the existing wells: they use multiple sources, showing attitudes of high adaptation to variability related to season and other factors.[17] They often complain about the insufficiency in the discharge from the Ouarzazate dam over the last ten years, that has resulted in the progressive decline of agricultural production to a level that allows no household food security. As mentioned earlier, the water from the traditional irrigation system cannot be replaced by pumped groundwater for reasons of salinity.

Thus, while the nomad Ait Unzâr mainly complain about the lack of rainwater and the concomitant lack of rangeland vegetation, for the settled farmers in Tiraf the problem is more the lack of irrigation water, coupled with the poor quality of groundwater. Both nomads and farmers agree in according a central place to drought – conceived as lack of water – in their explanations of the cause of their present crisis. Indeed *jfâf* has become a sort of scapegoat mentioned to explain or justify *every* kind of deficiency in *every* domain. This is clear if we consider a repertory of frequently occurring sentences: 'We do not have dates and wheat because of *jfaf*'; 'Our animals are thin and the herds decimated because of *jfâf*'; 'We have bad health and we drink bad water because of *jfâf*'; 'We are "travelling" [*musafrîn*, meaning temporary migration] because of *jfâf*'; 'We can not send children to school because of *jfâf*'; 'We do not marry because of *jfâf*'; and so on. Finally, drought is present in the foundation accounts of local communities. The story of the Ait Unzâr begins at the time of a great drought followed by a period of good rains and recovery.[18] The lives of local historical personalities, mainly saints, is also often linked to events concerning the discovery of a good well or some power that such ancient people had regarding the most important resource, water.

There is a marked centrality of the drought theme in the ritual domain too. Visits to the shrines of saints and the payment of *zyâra* in exchange for amulets or other services have always been widespread among the local population. In the last three years, however, I witnessed a continuous rise in such visits, and supplication to get rid of drought became a common theme among pilgrims. Additionally, some ancient rituals, focusing on demanding water and mainly practised by women, have been 'reactivated' after a long period of silence. Thus for example *Taghounja*, carried out by young unmarried girls in order to ask for rainfall, and probably representing one of the earliest elements of pre-Islamic background in the Dra valley (Jacques-Meunié 1973). *Taghounja* is a wood spoon symbolising the fiancée, dressed as a bride and taken in procession around the *qsar*, in a festive choreography, by the young girls of the village calling on her for blessing and the arrival of the Dra flood. The Ait Unzâr nomads have an analogous ritual, with slight variations: the central figure is called *Amghara* Barka,[19] who is also a piece of wood disguised as a bride, around whom young nomads girls gather playing drums, dancing and singing as in a proper marriage ceremony, asking for rains after a final slaughter. An ancient tradition of the Berber nomads of the region, the rite was celebrated by the Ait Unzâr quite recently in autumn 2002. While young girls celebrate *Taghounja* and its nomad version of *Amghara Barka*, adult women have other ritual spaces where devotion is mixed with the imploring of supernatural forces to intervene in ecological crises.

The women of *qsar* Tiraf celebrate the so-called *harîra*. Though the rite is often performed in proximity to other Muslim festivities (Ramadan, *'aid lkebir*, *'ashûr*), it has no fixed time. After some days of discussion, women may decide to appeal for a *hârîra* whenever they think it is needed, and they take place mostly during the drastic phases of drought. *Harîra*, the typical Moroccan soup, entails the preparation of a collective meal that takes place in four different places of the *qsar* and through the cooperation of all women, who after cooking, offer and exchange the food, thus establishing a circulation between these four groups. In a second phase, the food is also brought to the men, but the latter are not allowed to participate directly in the celebrations. The *harîra* takes place in open space, and represents a rare occasion when women, married and unmarried, are allowed to go out together and be absent from home until nightfall. In Tiraf the last *harîra* I attended was celebrated in autumn 2001, just before the beginning of the month of Ramadan, and women clearly said that the aim of this *harîra* was to ask for the end of drought.

Among the Ait Unzâr nomads, women suggested and organised a *ma'arouf* in September 2003, near the shrine of the saint Si Lmedani, in the open space surrounding Tiraf. This religious ceremony in honour of a saint had been 'suspended' since the end of the 1970s. Now, the central prayer associated with the sacrifice made in the name of the saint was for good rainfall. Men are usually contemptuous or even slightly critical of this female ritual universe, the alleged contradiction with Islamic principles being one of the main causes of such underestimation. For us it is interesting to observe that the almost obsessive quest for water and the magical or religious attempts to avert drought are a significant and persisting feature of the cognitive dimension of drought perception, both among nomads and sedentists.

Is Jfâf Merely a Natural Phenomenon?

Given the priority in discourse ascribed to the problem of *jfâf* and its identification with lack of water as the basis of the crisis it is possible to identify a perception that is almost homogeneous with the discourse of external agencies (the state, NGOs, scholars). They all appear to agree on a kind of 'naturalisation' of the crisis. Nonetheless, it is necessary to go beyond this primary analogy in order to ask whether the nomads and farmers are entirely convinced of such a natural explanation of the crisis or if they come up with other, non-natural factors.

Indeed, local perceptions reflect the complex interaction of various elements in the process through which the crisis has been engendered and maintains itself. Though these perceptions are basically common to both nomads and farmers, once again there are some differences between these two groups. Even though they say that their migration cycles depend upon the presence of *rbî'a*, most Ait Unzâr also insist on a crucial historical aspect: the delimitation of their pastoral territory following the creation of new international borders. Like the other Saharan groups of this region, the Ait Unzâr used to move within a huge home-range, pushing far south and east from the Dra Valley to the area between the Lower Doura Basin, the Hammâda, Foum Zguid and the region of Tata (see map). Until the first decades of the twentieth century it was not rare for them to push even beyond these areas and enter into what is today Mauritania and Algeria. The irregular precipitations in the Sahara conditioned the forms of resource appropriation: the access both to wells and pastures was normally open to various nomad groups, rather than for the exclusive use of a single tribe as is the case among the northern Ait 'Atta. Thanks to the vast dimensions of pastoral space and to the non-exclusivity of rights of access upon it,[20] increased mobility enabling access to other grazing lands was a common option to cope with a lack of resources in that part of their territory that was affected by drought. This strategy – common among nomad groups, especially in pre-colonial times (Bonte 1975) – began to be undermined by French colonial action, whose aim was to 'tribalise' pastoral territories, in order to ensure more efficient control on Saharan nomads by means of an official and exclusive attribution of pastures and water points (Casciarri, forthcoming). The older strategy ceased altogether in the post-colonial period, with the closure of the borders with Algeria and after the war in Western Sahara, with the new definition of southern territories as highly strategic regions.[21] If these factors accelerated general trends towards nomad sedentarisation, for some groups such as the Ait Unzâr who remained mainly nomadic, this became a major problem. It is then a political process – the reduction and redefinition of nomad territory – that made drought (understood as lack of water and grazing) a real factor of crisis.

In the discourse of farmers in Tiraf also, lack of water is not the sole factor linked by the people to the present crisis of agricultural production. The building of the Mansour Ad-Dhabi dam, completed in 1972, collecting in Ouarzazate the water flowing into Wadi Dra, had the advantage of rationalising the natural water resources of the region. At the same time, farmers became more dependent, because the organisation of their agricultural activities started being constrained by a 'new subject': the State and national water policies. Mostly during the last phase of ecological stress, the priority given to urban requirements, industry and tourism, constituted a further factor of deprivation of water formerly devoted to agriculture. People remember that until the mid-1970s, despite phases of severe drought, it was not rare for there to be water in the *saqyia* for a large part of the year. Even in the more arid Ktaoua, this enabled not only a fairly continuous irrigation of the palm trees (dates are the primary product that is sold), but also an annual harvest of barley, which is mainly used as food.

At the beginning of my research I attributed such accounts to a kind of idealisation of the past by elderly farmers; but some historical and ethnographic reports from the period prior to the construction of the dam appear to confirm these recollections. At the end of the nineteenth century De Foucauld (1888), describing the Dra region as he experienced it during a long journey undertaken in 1883–4, writes of the continuous though irregular flow of flood waters even in the southern part of the Dra. Water came down to the Hammâda, in the Sahara, where various flood-irrigated fields, called *madeir*, were cultivated by nomad groups. A century later Jacques-Meunié (1973) notes that six times between the 1960s and the 1970s the flood waters of Wadi Dra stretched up to the Atlantic Ocean, that is, 600 km south of the oasis of Mhamid! It seems clear that the construction of the dam has played a major role in the receding of these flood waters: it is perhaps also contributing to the rapid increase in the salinity of groundwater that was noted as the primary 'collateral effect' mainly in the lower part of the valley (Outhabit 1992). In the extreme south of Ktaoua oasis, Tiraf farmers twice suffered the consequences of this engineering masterpiece supposed to bring general progress to the valley: first, through the overall decrease of water available in their *saqyia* (much more dependent than in the north upon natural floods); second, thanks to the high salinity of groundwater, that prevents them from relying on wells for drinking water and using motor-pumps as alternatives for irrigation. When talking about the dramatic situation of agriculture, Tiraf farmers mention the relation in such a process between the natural factor (the diminishing rainfall) and the man made negative effects increasingly visible after the dam's construction.

Beyond the image of drought as unavoidable natural calamity, Ait Unzâr nomads focus upon the problems created by changes imposed on their pastoral space, while Tiraf farmers do likewise about central management and national water policies after the dam's construction. Both groups establish a link between this 'breaking point', starting slowly in the mid-1970s and increasing up to the 1990s, and changes in socio-economic relations on a wider scale. The clearest example concerns the transformation of migration dynamics. Since colonial times the latter provided the most efficient 'emergency exit' in drought phases, but in recent years, just when the drought situation became dramatic, the conditions of access to migration – especially the most attractive international one – varied considerably.

In addition to the problems facing migrants and referred to earlier, recently the process of commoditisation and the transformation of consumption patterns, have contributed towards greater dependency on the market, and this proves fatal in a context of crisis. Ecological crises are not new phenomena. Oral accounts and written documentation show that throughout their history these populations underwent various periods of drought.[22] But people say that even if ancient *jfâf* were ecologically as severe as the present one, there was always recovery, because the options to cope with drought were wider. Local knowledge often reports the sentence *saba' shina wa saba' zina*, 'seven bad [years] and seven good [years]', indicating the widespread perception of a cyclical pattern of drought. The exactitude of such seven-year cycles is not confirmed by meteorological data, but what is certain is that pastoral and agricultural communities, confronted since earlier times with a harsh ecological environment, possessed in the past a certain autonomy and a large gamut of solutions for coping with crisis. It is probable that this autonomy has been seriously affected during the last years of capitalist development within an international political context, contributing towards making the 'natural misfortune' of water scarcity greater and irreversible.

Local Strategies and Transforming Contexts

Farmers and Nomads Coping with Crisis

With some variations, Tiraf farmers and Ait Unzâr nomads share an overall perception of drought and its causes. The concrete strategies for coping with crisis show greater differences, the basic option for farmers being labour migration (and secondly children's education) and for the nomads military service and a higher diversification of domestic units.

Between the 1960s and the 1970s a set of factors – the demands of national and international markets, the emancipation from ancient forms of social subordination, the transformation of life ways, the development of communication and transport – provoked a fair part of the rural Moroccan population to migrate. Since then, labour emigration has become a major element of development in the Dra Valley. Sometimes this led people to completely abandon villages and settlement in urban areas, but it also led to a certain degree of 'return migration', with ex-emigrants engaged in local development for improving material conditions, thanks to the new incomes. As far as the Draoua of Tiraf are concerned, we remark two main aspects. First, long-distance emigration is a traditional resource already practised since the 1930s. Second, migration is mainly internal and temporary, and except a few men who emigrated recently to the Gulf countries, there are no cases here of transnational migration. Most households living in Tiraf today have at least one member of the original family who migrated during the colonisation. The frequent destination was Algeria – then a French colony – where these farmers worked in different sectors, such as those of road construction, industry and building.[23] The household strategy was to send one adult son, usually the eldest one, as a migrant worker, keeping the others in the village for work in the family fields. Even when migration actually lasted several years, it was mainly perceived as a temporary situation, and indeed, most of these migrants came back to the village to take charge again of their traditional activities.

Oral accounts underlined the overlapping of drought periods in the valley with phases of intense migration.[24] More than the desire for emancipation from a traditional way of life or for radical change, migration was seen here as a contingency, allowing farmers to remain farmers. For the Draoua of Tiraf these notions did not basically change in the period after independence. After Algerian independence and the end of colonisation, emigration was oriented more towards the big Moroccan towns, where urban development demanded increasing labour, mainly in the building and industrial sectors.[25] The migration figures in Tiraf for autumn 2003 showed the near exclusivity of sedentary Draoua as migrants. Among the 53 households of Tiraf, 32 (60 percent) have migrants; of the 521 individuals, 57 (11 percent) are migrants. Of these emigrants 93 percent remain in Morocco (64 percent of them in Casablanca) and only 7 percent go to Arab countries. Most of them (93 percent) do not have regular contracts, while 75 percent migrate for short periods (less than six months); 96.5 percent of all belong to the socio-ethnic group of the Draoua. Thus, even if for Draoua migration remains the preferred option to cope with crisis, the trends of the national and international markets (the worsening of labour conditions and the unreliability of migration abroad) weaken its capacity to help recover from the ecological crisis and determined the unpredictability of migration patterns.[26]

A secondary option towards mitigating the effects of unstable agricultural production and incomes has been the education of children. When primary schools were established in the *douâr*, most Draoua understood the importance of this new element, and schooling was often perceived as a long-term investment.[27] But if schooling as such is still appreciated here, and also seen as a means of upward social mobility, people do not trust it any longer as an option for coping with crisis. This is because of the deterioration of the Moroccan education system, especially in the rural context, the disengagement of the state from the sphere of education in the neo-liberal phase, and the increasing costs that are too high for most households in critical times (Casciarri 2002b). Nonetheless, the fact that compared to their nomad neighbours, a fair proportion of mainly male adults have enjoyed at least primary education, constitutes an element of pride and distinction in Draoua discourse.

For the Ait Unzâr nomads options to cope with crisis have been quite different. Numerically speaking, employment in the military is undoubtedly the preferred strategy. Hence, if all Draoua farmer families have at least one migrant member, almost all Ait Unzâr families have at least one man who is or has been a soldier.[28] The regional context determines this difference. Already known as rebellious at the time of French pacification, nomads were co-opted into the colonial service early on as civil or military personnel.[29] But it is mainly since the post-colonial phase that the military issue has became a prioritised option, for through its location this Saharan area is highly strategic both as a frontier with Algeria and because of the development of the war in the Sahara after 1975. For the Ait Unzâr army employment often did not involve abandoning pastoralism; their strategy has been to entrust one son, often the eldest, with the family herds, while the younger ones join the army, sometimes the father himself drawing a military pension. Military employment is perceived as particularly advantageous: it circumvents the harsh conditions of subordinated work; important information about rainfall and pasture conditions can be collected, since military posts are often located on grazing lands; and on the whole it is a job that is culturally perceived as continuing with the warlike tradition of fathers and grandfathers. Among nomads labour migration is of no significance as a source of income; when practised, it is, however, transnational – the three Ait Unzâr men who migrated to France in the 1960s are the only migrants to Europe from Tiraf. Today, a few young nomads are trying hard to penetrate the fortress of Europe through some form of illegal migration.

Finally a recent and increasing source of income is tourism. The Dra Valley is the destination of a tourism nourished by the Western myth of desert and adventure, and developed mainly in the last few years as a consequence of new Moroccan policies and of the difficult access to Algeria since the civil war in 1992. Some nomads are employed as camel guides or as 'living examples' of the Bedouin stereotype during the tours of caravan tourism. Compared to other groups, the Ait Unzâr have begun participating in this sector only recently and with much resistance. This is due to the awareness that incomes are very low – the nomad being the last link in a chain which is controlled by urban managers, Moroccan or European who retain most of the profit – but mainly because the tourism sector is considered to be highly precarious and unpredictable.

Drought and Marriage: Diverging Strategies in Times of Crisis

One last aspect of the reaction to crisis among farmers and nomads in Tiraf concerns marriage strategies, marriage being seen as a duty of good Muslims and central to social and biological reproduction. The Ait Unzâr and the Draoua do not marry one another; they share concepts of status endogamy, and tend in practice to marry close kin. However, the last decade of crisis has witnessed a change in discourse and practice in this sphere among each of these two groups, albeit in different ways.

In the Draoua discourse marriage is frequently connected with drought, both women and men, considering *jfâf* as the main reason for people *not* being able to marry any more. Notably they attribute to drought the lack of production and dwindling incomes, two basic elements needed for marriage transaction. Indeed, the payment of bridewealth and the organisation of festivities constitute very high expenses. The bridegroom's family needs a surplus in production (cereals, dates, livestock) both for ensuring the wedding feasts and buying other items not locally produced. When production, and hence surplus, does not suffice, other sources of cash income have to be accessed. Moreover, a certain assimilation of urban behaviour – increased by emigration and television – has created an inflation in bridewealth, whose minimum amount is currently 2500 DH (at the time of fieldwork 10 Moroccan Dirham = 1 €), keeping up with the general rise in prices.[30] Among the Draoua, wedding ceremonies – often presented as a major element of differentiation with Berbers and Arabs nomads – last up to one week and involve a highly complex ceremonial articulation that is very costly. The genealogical proximity of partners does not entail a decrease either in bridewealth or in festivities, as in other contexts of the Arab and Muslim world (Bonte 1994). While everyone complains that young people can not marry any more because of drought, the strong symbolic elements (implying ethnic and status differentiation) attached to marriage make it unacceptable to arrange 'cheaper' marriages; for example, by not extending the invitation to neighbouring villages, by reducing the duration of the ceremonies, by lowering the amount given in bridewealth. In fact, the consequence of such reductions would be the loss of family honour. The analysis of actual marriages in Tiraf goes beyond the purview of this paper, but it suffices to say that it shows that practice is entirely coherent with the discourse.[31]

The situation is entirely different among the Ait Unzâr, where no marked differences can be observed between earlier marriages and recent ones. Undoubtedly upsetting many aspects of life, among them drought does not, however, constitute a breaking-point in this domain. The most striking feature of Ait Unzâr marriage is the facility with which the marriage link is created and dissolved for both men and women of different ages. Age at marriage is generally low – around 18 to 20 years for men and 16 to 18 years for women – an aspect that is as condemned by Draoua, as is polygamy, another practice more common among nomads than among farmers. But an examination of genealogical evidence and present practice shows that divorce is also very common and remarriage often takes place shortly thereafter. As a result, household units often consist of husbands and wives who have been married more than once and of children related to one another as paternal or maternal half-siblings. No particular reprobation seems to be attached to female divorce – another point of difference with the Draoua – and even women with children from a first union easily and quickly remarry. Also the bridewealth demanded and given for a divorcee is usually the same as that given for a virgin, a trend found among Berber groups elsewhere too (Léfebure 1981). Wedding ceremonies last two or three days and normally take place in the camp of the bridegroom's parents. Even if formally every Ait Unzâr could consider himself as invited, participation is reduced because of territorial dispersion and difficulty of movement. Here, too, it has become normal to offer some 'modern' items as gifts from the market, but livestock remain a basic component both in marriage transactions and sacrificial rites.

The most striking difference with the sedentary communities is in the amount of bridewealth, which is generally very low (between 200 and 500 DH) among the Ait Unzâr, and is less affected by general inflation.[32] Their discourse on this subject is very pragmatic: they consider it normal and right that marriage remains accessible to all, including the poorest, especially in hard times such as the present. They say that this 'low-price policy' concerning marriage is shared by all the Ait 'Atta, through a kind of supra-tribal regulation endorsed at the level of the largest unit. Thus, this huge confederation of Southern Berbers, which has lost its political and military unity, appears to retain a function in the control of bridewealth, aiming at maintaining a low rate, more autonomous from global trends of commoditisation and inflation, and to fix it uniformly for unions between two Ait 'Atta partners, even when they belong to different tribal units. Thus the Ait Unzâr continue, even in periods of drought, to marry and divorce as frequently as before, and considering the high expenses incurred by the Draoua in getting married as foolish; for the latter, the fact that the Ait Unzâr, and generally nomad Berbers, marry their daughters for so little and so easily is an indication of their inferiority, and even of lack of honour.

Maintaining Strong Inter-Ethnic Links in Tiraf: Some Provisional Conclusions

The divergence of options used by Tiraf farmers and Ait Unzâr nomads to cope with crisis is not surprising, since socially, economically and culturally the two groups are relatively autonomous, though they share a common space. Apart from the centrality of drought, varying, group-specific perceptions of the factors involved in the crisis partly explain this difference. But one additional question arises from such an analysis of social organisation and resource management. During the course of fieldwork I became interested in understanding *how* and *why* such a multilevel diversity and strong autonomy within each of the two communities does not lead to open conflict and to the individualisation of socio-economic interests and behaviour. With broadening knowledge of this region, I observed that the people of Tiraf seemed to better adapt to crisis, or at least to be affected less dramatically than some of their neighbours. One possible factor which sets off the people of the Tiraf-Ait Unzâr complex as a whole from the rest of the region, is a kind of living solidarity and a persistence of complementary organisation at numerous levels of nomad-sedentary interaction. The variety of options, change and the impact of 'modernity', even a major all-embracing crisis, do not appear to lead to a final weakening of social ties, or to harsh conflict between the two groups whose historical relations structured the organisational web of an agro-pastoral setting. Such a joint management in the only part of southern Dra where the nomadic component is still important and really visible, seems to contradict the prejudiced assumption, rooted in pre-colonial times, reinforced by colonial ideology and living on in post-colonial society of the inevitable violence and inequality inherent in nomad-sedentary relations. Indeed, the inner cohesion of the Draoua and Ait Unzâr groups was in some way reinforced by the polar opposition between the two and the persisting strong identity and autonomy of 'we' versus 'they'.

A brief comparison with the rest of the Valley, especially with other *douâr* of the same region in Ktaoua – including the closest ones of Qsar Kebir and Blida – will illustrate the aspects that distinguish Tiraf from the general trend. Overall, the crucial phase of socio-economic change after independence impacted Dra Valley societies significantly between the 1960s and the 1970s. Economic growth led to the progressive dissolution of traditional forms of subsistence, mainly by remodelling agriculture and through the sedentarisation of nomads. In our case, however, the Ait Unzâr remained the only predominantly nomadic group in the Ktaoua region, and traditional date-cultivation continued to be the main source of subsistence for Tiraf farmers. Urbanisation and emigration generally led to an abandoning of oasis space, or to its transformation as a secondary habitat. In Tiraf, although many houses in the old *qsar* have recently been vacated, the traditional habitat maintains its coherence, not only architecturally, but also as physical and social space. Emigration is normally not conceived of as a definitive move. Elsewhere, usually, the income from wage labour enhanced forms of social differentiation, even within the same social or ethnic group, accelerated the individualisation of access to resources, and diminished the importance given to earlier forms of non-wage labour. But in Tiraf, emigrants are not manifestly a group 'apart', nor are they marked by a strikingly different status; the open access to primary resources continues to be managed mostly through solidarity, and collective criteria as well as traditional forms or labour with payment in kind subsist. In other *douâr* such transformations brought about a weakening of traditional institutions of political organisation, or their nominal existence paralleled by the stronger presence of a modern centralised system on a territorial base.

In Tiraf the assembly of the two *qabîla* of Ait Unzâr and Draoua is still managed according to the twofold criteria (ethnic divide between nomads and sedentists and further genealogical articulation), and exhibits vitality through rulings about the management of the main aspects of collective life – resource access, regulation of water rights system, relations between the two communities, matters of 'moral order' – autonomously from state institutions. Lastly, the historical relations that resulted from the military protection pacts between nomads and sedentists – an element that was dismantled elsewhere because of its implications for status hierarchy and subordination – is still functioning and respected in Tiraf, and its relevance is underlined both by the Ait Unzâr and the Draoua. As late as in 1999 the Draoua *qabîla* gathered to decide the number of nomad guardians to be entrusted with the control of the date harvest in the oasis, while the Ait Unzâr *qabîla* gathered to choose one representative for each of its four lineages to take on this responsibility.[33] The nearly 150 year-old foundation of this relationship and its relevance at various economic, political and social levels is frequently evoked to justify present forms of joint management: 'We gave them the quarter (*rba'*)', say Draoua; 'They gave us the quarter', echo Ait Unzâr.

The ethnic and lineage organisation of the Tiraf *saqyia* is linked to the ancient division of water as a resource and is still respected in the turns allotted for irrigation, but it should be stressed that this is also valid for more recent and modern water resources: the collective water point supplying Tiraf since the beginning of the 1990s, serves seven taps – four for the subdivisions of the Ait Unzâr *qabîla*, three for those the Draoua *qabîla*. This material inscription of social structure upon water distribution patterns becomes even more interesting when we learn that in the surrounding villages the same equipment was distributed following territorial divisions or even in terms of individualised households.

Finally, Ait Unzâr and Draoua act in coordinated patterns, while restating their tribal autonomy and coherence, on matters concerning the management of conflict upon collective land. In a conflict in the mid-1990s about some fields whose ownership was contested by the inhabitants of the neighbouring Qsar Kebir, the Ait Unzâr and the Draoua of Tiraf jointly struggled to stake their claim. When they succeeded, they divided the territory according to the *ra'ya* pact (i.e. 75 percent to Draoua and 25 percent to the nomads), before further distributed these parts among their respective lineage sections.

It is not my intention here to argue for the presence of a sort of 'archaism' as the basis for the persisting force of traditional forms of management grounded in nomad-sedentary relations. Nor do I intend to argue that such relations, originally those of domination, expresses themselves simply through a sort of harmony between the groups: the absolute closure between the Ait Unzâr and Draoua through endogamy in itself indicates that status considerations are jealously maintained. I wish simply to stress that, in spite of the attempts by both colonial and postcolonial regimes to get rid of tribal and traditional relations perceived as an impediment to 'modernisation', such relations are surviving well, efficiently applied in local management, and well integrated with structures of so-called modernity.

My analysis of the phenomenon of drought in the southern Dra Valley based primarily on the data presented in this paper strongly suggests that in order to understand the interaction between human beings and their natural environment, we must consider it in its broader historical and contemporary socio-economic and political framework. The relationship between natural and social elements is always a dialectical one, and this is true even in the Saharan region, where extreme climate and ecological constraints appear to be more imperative. It is undoubtedly easier and reassuring, especially for the agencies supposed to be working out development options and activities in the local context, to attribute the dramatic effects of crisis to an unmerciful nature, rather than to political decisions and complex human factors. If those who are officially responsible for defining the general frame of reference for resource management and economic development would take such factors into consideration, further questions may well emerge. For example, that of verifying whether traditional principles and behaviour – the concept of 'tradition' being understood, not as a sign of archaism but in a dynamic sense, as a set of well-rooted practices beyond the logic of purely individual interest and the market economy – could act as more adapted tools to cope with crises situations, especially when the crisis is not only a natural one. The organisation of Tiraf and the Ait Unzâr and their reactions to drought are well worth developing and testing through a broader and deeper comparison, to see if the preliminary observations and results presented here support such a general hypothesis. The question may be a crucial one for the multitude of local communities all over the world, whose material and social reproduction is today at risk because of the disruptive and rapid effects of globalisation.

Notes

1. Fieldwork was conducted over thirteen months between October 2000 and April 2004, as part of IMPETUS, an interdisciplinary research project of the Universities of Cologne and Bonn, that was funded by the Federal German Ministry of Education (BMBF, under grant no. 01LW0301A) and the Ministry of Science and Research (MWF, under grant no. 223-21200200) of the state of North Rhine-Westfalia. My acknowledgements are due mainly to Michael J. Casmir, who was the scientific director of my research. I am grateful for the help received from local institutions and authorities: notably the personnel of Ormvao and CMV in Ouarzazate, Zagora and Tagounite, the Qaid of Tagounite and the *shayikh* of Tiraf. I was introduced into the area by Prof. Mohamed Ait Hamza, our main Moroccan partner, to whom I express my gratitude. My warmest thanks are reserved for the nomad Ait Unzâr, the people of Tiraf and Tagounite, who all received me with kindness and accompanied me as friends and informants throughout my research.
2. The same group is sometimes defined as *haratyîn* (sing. *hartâni*), a word whose uncertain origin may indicate a semi-slave origin. Today the term is usually replaced by the more

neutral *Draoua* (sing. *draoui*). Even though the latter has geographical connotations, it is not really used for every inhabitant of the Dra Valley, because of the hierarchical implications still present in the perceptions of the local populations.

3. In order to weaken the political power of nomad tribes in the colonial period the French tried unsuccessfully to nullify the *ra'ya* pacts. After their formal abolition in 1936, they were however, forced to immediately reactivate the system, following the demands of the client communities (Niclausse 1954), and to admit its importance for the socio-economic and political organisation of local communities. The dynamics of the post-colonial period made the *ra'ya* progressively lose its weight, but in some places like Tiraf the system is still working, although in the absence of official institutional recognition.
4. Except the family of the Ait Unzâr *shayikh*, which is also settled in Tiraf for political reasons, these groups converted their seasonal presence in the village into a more stable settlement during the recent crisis, between the 1980s and 1990s). Nonetheless, they are still considered as *ruhhâla*, 'nomads': part of the family (often one or two adult sons) continue to move with herds on the pastoral territory and the settlement of the others is never seen as permanent, as is confirmed by some cases of 'renomadisation'.
5. Until 1984 Tiraf also had a community of *Mrabtîn*, the people of Si Lmedani, nomad and 'saintly warrior' of the pre-colonial and colonial periods, whose shrine is on the slopes of the Jbel Meggâg, near Tiraf. Twenty years ago the descendants of Si Lmedani, to whom some Ait Unzâr and Tiraf's Draoua are still affiliated, settled in the town of Tagounite and abandoned nomadism.
6. When Draoua and nomads talk about 'foreigners', (*barranyîn*, literally 'the ones of the outside'), they both imply every individual who belongs neither to the original group of Tiraf farmers nor to the Ait Unzâr. Though ethnically different and late comers, the Ait Unzâr have in this context lost their label as foreigners, thanks to the exclusive and ancient relations they enjoy with the *qsar* dwellers.
7. The salinity of Tiraf wells (by measurement of conductivity in µS) is between 10 µS and 14 µS. This is considerably higher than that measured in the nearby sites of Ktaoua oasis (Blida 7 µS, Tagounite 5-6 µS). To appreciate the very high level of salinity, it should be mentioned that normal drinking water is between roughly 0,5 µS and 2,5 µS and that even animals stop drinking water at almost 8-9 µS.
8. A local figure of traditional power, the position of *shaykh* was maintained during the colonial period, though the French controlled and oriented their nomination. In the post-colonial administrative system, the central authority appointed the *shaykh* after consultation wth local people. His jurisdiction comprises various *douâr*, every one having an appointed *muqaddem*. In this 'modern' and national version the *shaykh* loses the specificity of a lineage or tribal chief and his jurisdiction becomes territorial, but in the case of the Ait Unzâr the position of *shaykh* of Tiraf village coincides with the chief of the *qabîla* Ait Unzâr chosen by tribesmen on tribal and lineage (not localised) criteria.
9. An example of such recent interest can be found in the selective social sciences bibliography available on the Impetus Project website (Casciarri *et al.* 2004). 10.

Local experts consider six annual discharges as the minimum needed for a satisfying agricultural cycle. If we look at the irrigation activities over the last ten years, we find the average of 6–7 between 1993 and 1999 decreasing to reach the historical minimum of 2 discharges in 2002–3. Moreover, most discharges during the period 1999–2002 were less than the 40 million m^3 required for agriculture that was just sufficient to recover the groundwater level and fill up drinking-water reservoirs (Ahmed Besbes, ORMVAO - Zagora, pers. comm.).

11. The experience of the German Technical Cooperation agency (GTZ) in Zagora is significant. Looking at the multitude of projects launched during the last ten years and at the disappointment expressed in most final reports, some questions arise about the functioning of cooperation agencies in the Third World. Methodological and technical problems are often one source of such failure: for example, the priority given to budget evaluation for deciding (normally short) periods of field work, together with some methods of rapid data collection (RRA, MARP, etc.) that have unfortunately been largely used in the last decades have failed to yield a proper picture of social dynamics as a base for development intervention.
12. Genealogies for the first half of the twentieth century showed that in average households only 4–5 children reached adulthood and one or both parents frequently died. Today a woman in her forties frequently has 8–10 living children.
13. Almost all women over 35 years old today are illiterate; among men the numbers are less only because of Islamic schools. But today most men and women in their twenties have attended at least the first years of primary school. There are also rare cases of young people between 20 and 30 having studied up to university.
14. Today most nomads or former nomads have a lower economic status than most Draoua. But the persistence of a clear identity and status boundary between such groups remains, and is clearly expressed in marriage strategies: in a sample of 225 marriages, there were only two cases of inter-status marriage between a Draoua and a nomad, none being found between Draoua and any religious group.
15. In the same semantic domain, other expressions are frequently used. *Tamara* is one pregnant word used both by Arab and Berber speakers to indicate the global stress in drought periods, the difficulty of assuring one's life in harsh times. The verb *'aya*, meaning in standard Arabic 'to be unable' or 'to be tired', is a common euphemism for saying 'to become poor, to be reduced to minimal survival levels' and its use is also linked to descriptions of drought periods. Berber speakers often use the expression *ichka luqt*, 'times are hard', meaning the harshness of life entailing various elements, but basically linked to drought matters. Our Berber informants indicated the Tachelhit term *shidda* as close to the Arabic *jfâf*, and defined as 'the times when there is nothing to eat for either man or animal'.
16. A similar observation was made among other nomads, such as the Ahâmda of Central Sudan, who live in an arid region with rains concentrated in summertime, and who use the term the term *kharîf* indicating simultaneously the autumn season (as in standard Arabic) and the rangeland grasses emerging after rainfall (Casciarri 1997).
17. Between 2001 and 2003 I measured water consumption – for domestic use and for the drinking purposes of 1 to 4 heads of livestock living near the house – on four occasions for a period of one week in different seasons (November 2001, April 2002, March 2003, October 2003). I recorded the quantities of water fetched and consumed, distinguished according to different water sources and uses, by a sample of 5 households whose sizes varied from 4 to 20 members The results showed that Tiraf people use six sources (wells, *saqyia* canal, *matfia* covered reservoir, mobile reservoirs, *laouina* basin dug on mountains, collective taps) for four different uses (drinking, cooking, animals, washing), according to various criteria: water quality (salinity and cleanliness), access facility (property rights, proximity, labour and energy involved), seasonality, and cost considerations Total daily consumption (the average for an individual) varies from 8 to 15 l which is quite low compared to urban areas in the region, where, for example, 60 l per head was measured in Ouarzazate (Schluetter, pers. comm.).

18. Oral traditions have two versions of such foundation. In the first, a woman remains alone (without men, children and herds) because of drought and afterwards she regenerates the whole tribe thanks to heavy rains sent by God. In the second one, a wadi flood destroys men and herds which, exhausted by a long drought, offended God; here again the only survivor, a pregnant woman, reproduces the whole tribe.
19. In Tachelhit, *amghara* literally means 'great', but the term is also used to indicate the mother-in-law or an old respected woman – the masculine form *amghar* often designating a lineage or village leader, like the Arab *shayikh*. The second term, *barka*, is a feminine proper name linked to the root *BRK* ('to bless'). As the central person in the rite should be a young unmarried woman, the term *amghara* is more likely to be understood as referring to 'greatness' in the power of giving water, more than in the sense of age.
20. The lack of exclusive appropriation did not mean the absence of conflict between nomadic groups. Even temporary appropriation or access was always a subject of negotiation in a context of variable relations of strength and shifting alliances among these pastoral communities. On the contrary, the status of 'protectors' in the oasis space and the possession of fields determined exclusive property rights for nomads as well as for sedentary communities.
21. The existence of 'bad borderlines' since the 1960s (the *guerre des sables* with Algeria in 1963) and increasingly in the mid-1970s (the Green March in 1975 and the subsequent war in western Sahara) is what Ait Unzâr complain about most frequently, when discussing the present crisis of the pastoral way of life.
22. Such dramatic periods are used in local temporal definition. Most frequently evoked are *'amm ar-rûz*, 'the year of rice' (mid-1930s), when the French used to pay Dra workers with rice, and *'amm l-harîra*, 'the year of soup' (1945), when the colonial administration distributed soup to the population to limit the famine.
23. The population of southern Morocco was in high demanded. On the one hand, Draoua were known as 'hard workers' – which also means more easy to exploit – on the other hand, France was confronted with the resistance of Algerians who often did not accept to work for the colonial master.
24. Such a coincidence is also stressed in official French colonial documents. At the *Bureau d'Affaires Indigènes* of Tagounite, the monthly reports for 1933, shortly after the pacification of the south, note the seasonal exodus of manpower towards the towns in the north or on the Atlantic coast (Archives militaries de Vincennes, SHAT), following bad harvest seasons.
25. The rare cases of entire families who emigrated during the 1970s, did not bring about a definitive break with the village. Once their income improved between the 1980s and the 1990s, these families resettled in Tiraf, where they had left behind houses and fields in the care of some relatives.
26. The dynamics of such short-term, almost seasonal migration, under precarious conditions and low wages – most migrants work without an official contract and as daily wagers – is intimately linked with agricultural production: if the date harvest is likely to be a bad one, the village empties of adult men, but the latter are ready to return if a telephone call announces a future dam discharge in their region.
27. Even though the difficulties increase with the level of education (*collège* and *lycée* are often far away from village and transport is not available), in Tiraf there are two cases of young men who studied at University. One is now a teacher and the other, a clerk. Two other young men are studying at the Faculty of Agadir. Women are still almost completely excluded from higher education.

28. According to data collected in autumn 2003, 20 percent of Ait Unzâr households have at least one member in the army. Military employment can take different form, according to precise job and salary: as members of the *Forces Armés Royales*, whose functions are linked more to law and order, or 'ordinary' soldier in the Sahara, which is better paid. Military personnel have special rights to early retirement (at 45–50 years), which is a very attractive perspective for nomads who normally returned fully to pastoral activities after retirement.
29. The employment of Moroccan troops by the French Army was important during the Second World War, in the war with Algeria and sometimes after the war on metropolitan French territory.
30. Genealogical data together with oral accounts indicate a steady inflation of bridewealth over time. Starting at almost 100 DH in the 1950s, it rose to 500–1,000 DH between the 1960s and 1970s, reaching 2,000 DH between the 1980s and 1990s, and 2,500–4,000 DH in the last years (note that the current monthly minimal wage [SMIG] is around 2,500 DH). The amount is enormous when compared with the cost of living and the low level of available cash incomes.
31. During the last three years (2000–2003) the Draoua of Tiraf celebrated only four marriages – very few compared to former trends. It is not fortuitous that such marriages involved families with higher incomes, thanks to the importance of migrant revenues.
32. If we compare, as we did for Draoua, the marriages of different generations, we obtain the following figures: 10–50 DH in the 1960s, 150 DH between the 1970s and 1980s without significant inflation, and a standard bridewealth of between 200 and 500 DH up to now. Among their nomad neighbours, the 'Arîb, marriage is as expensive as among the Draoua and other sedentary communities, which means that low bridewealth amounts are not characteristic of all nomadic communities here.
33. Draoua and Ait Unzâr explained that the lack of such contract in the years 2000 to 2003 was merely due to the insufficiency of date production, both declaring that when agriculture recovers, the Ait Unzâr will again be called for this kind of work. At the same time, for Tiraf people, the Ait Unzâr are the only nomads allowed to approach the oasis space to gather fallen dates as *kharrâfa*.

References

Ait Hamza, M. 2002. *Mobilité socio-spatiale et développement local au Sud de l'Atlas marocain (Dadès-Todgha).* Passau: L.I.S. Verlag.

ANAFID (Association Nationale des Améliorations Foncières, de l'Irrigation et du Drainage) 1990. *Gestion des grands périmètres irrigués au Maroc I. Distribution de l'eau d'irrigation.* Rabat: ANAFID.

——— 1991. *Gestion des grands périmètres irrigués au Maroc II. Associations d'irrigants.* Rabat: ANAFID.

Azam, Capt. R. 1946. 'Sédentaires et nomades dans le Sud marocain: le coude du Dra', unpubl. paper. Paris: CHEAM (Centre d'Hautes Etudes d'Administration Musulmane) no. 1009.

Bonte, Pierre 1975. 'Pasteurs et nomades: l'exemple de la Mauritanie', in *Sécheresse et famines du Sahel*, ed. J. Copans, 62–86. Paris: Maspero.

———, ed. 1994. *Épouser au plus proche. Inceste, prohibitions et stratégies matrimoniales autour de la Méditerranée.* Paris: Éditions de l'EHESS.

Casciarri, Barbara 1997. 'Les pasteurs Ahâmda du Soudan central. Usages de la parenté arabe dans l'histoire d'une recomposition territoriale, politique et identitaire', unpubl. Ph.D. thesis. Paris: EHESS.

——— 2002a. 'Local Trends and Perceptions of Processes of Commoditisation in Central Sudan: the Responses of the Ahâmda Pastoral System to State Pressures and Capitalist Dynamics', *Nomadic Peoples* 6(2): 32–50.

——— 2002b. 'Gli accordi di Barcellona e la ristrutturazione della scuola pubblica in Marocco', unpubl. conference paper held at COBAS/CESP (Comitati di Base / Centro di Studi sulla Scuola Pubblica), *Scuola e globalizzazione*, Rome.

——— 2003. 'Rare Resources and Environmental Crises: Notes on Water Management among the Aït Unzâr Pastoralists in South-Eastern Morocco', *Nomadic Peoples* 7(1): 177–86.

——— forthcoming. 'Coping with Shrinking Spaces: The Ait Unzâr Pastoralists of Southern Morocco', in *Nomadic Societies in the Middle East and North Africa: Entering the 21st Century, Handbook of Oriental Studies*, ed. D. Chatty. Leiden: Brill.

———, S. El-Berr, Rym Etschmann and Claudia Liebelt. 2004. '*A Social Sciences Bibliography of Wadi Draa, Rural Morocco and the Maghreb in Relation to Water Resource Management*'. Cologne: University of Cologne. www.impetus-unikoeln.de.

De Foucauld, C. 1888. *Reconnaissance au Maroc 1883–1884*. Paris: Société d'éditions géographiques, maritimes et coloniales.

De la Chapelle, F. 1929. 'Une cité de l'Oued Dra sous le protectorat des nomades', *Hespèris* IX: 29–42.

Dunn, R.E. 1977. *Resistance in the Desert. Moroccan Responses to French Imperialism 1881–1912*. London: Croom Helm.

Gellner, Ernest 1969. *Saints of the Atlas*. London: Weidenfeld and Nicolson.

Hart, D.M. 1981. *Dadda 'Atta and its Forty Grandsons. The Socio-Political Organization of the Ait 'Atta of Southern Morocco*. Cambridge: Middle East and North African Studies.

——— 1984. *The Ait 'Atta of Southern Morocco. Daily Life and Recent History*. Cambridge: Middle East and North African Studies.

Jacques- Meunié, D. 1947. 'Les oasis de Lektaoua et des Mehamid. Institutions traditionnelles des Draoua', *Hespèris* XXXIV(1–2): 365–80.

——— 1958. 'Hiérarchie sociale au Maroc pré-saharien', *Hespèris* XLV(3–4): 137–50.

——— 1973. 'La Vallée du Dra au milieu du XX siècle', in *Maghreb et Sahara. Études géographiques offertes à Jean Despois*, ed. Xavier de Planhol 163–92. Paris: Sociètè de Géographie.

Léfébure, Claude 1981. 'Le choix du conjoint dans une communauté berbérophone du Maroc pré-saharien', in *Production pouvoir et parenté dans le monde méditerranéen de Sumur à nos jours*, eds. C.H. Bréteau et al., 281–92. Paris: Éditions Paul Geuthner.

——— 1986. Ait Kebbache, impasse sud-est. L'involution d'une tribu marocaine exclue du Sahara, *Revue de l'Occident Musulman et de la Méditerranée* 41–2: 69–76.

Niclausse, Capt. M. 1954. Rapports entre nomades et sédentaires dans le coude du Draa: la Raia, unpubl. paper. Paris: CHEAM no. 2306.

Outabhit, H. 1992. 'Effets sur l'environnement induits par l'édification du braage Mansour Ed-Dahbi en vue de l'irrigation du périmètre du Draa Moyen', *Environnement et développement*. Rabat: Imprimérie Royale.

Ramonet, I. 2000. 'Un Maroc indécis', *Le Monde Diplomatique* VII.

Spillmann, Capt. 1936. *Les Ait Atta et la pacification du Haut Dra*. Rabat: Éditions Felix Moncho.

6

Local Environmental Crises and Global Sea-Level Rise: The Case of Coastal Zones in Senegal[1]

Anita Engels

Introduction

By 2100 Global climate change might, it is thought, lead to a global rise of 15–95 cm in the sea-level, 'as a result of thermal expansion of the oceans and melting of glaciers and ice-sheets' (IPCC 1995: 5). This scenario is particularly threatening because of the importance of coastal zones which have attracted human settlements throughout human history, as they provide access to marine natural resources, trade opportunities, beaches and scenic views. The attraction of these regions has resulted in more than half of the world's population living within 60 km of the coastline (Clayton and O'Riordan 1995: 154). Much scientific effort has been invested in assessing the vulnerability of coastal populations to a future rise in sea-level (IPCC 1998a), in addition to other potential negative effects of climate change, such as more extreme rainfall or storm events.[2] In the long run, these efforts aim at providing coastal zone management plans on a worldwide scale (IPCC 1998a: 68). Conventional wisdom holds that it is more promising to join forces globally to assess and combat global environmental changes than to do so exclusively at a national level. This is especially true for developing countries, some of which may be severely affected by sea-level rise, while research and technologies to adapt to these changes are not readily available (Leatherman and Nicholls 1995). Research on climate change and sea-level rise has thus been coordinated at a global level to generate problem definitions, risk assessments, and management strategies that will be applicable all over the world, especially in those developing countries most in need of coordinated action.

Most of this globally coordinated research takes into consideration that, first, global sea-level has already risen by 10–25 cm over the past 100 years (IPCC 1995: 5). Additionally, even without any further sea-level rise, coastal zones are environmentally dynamic regions with high rates of geological change in short time periods, and constantly shifting coastlines (UN FCCC 1999: 9). Thus, living in such regions entails a particularly high level of uncertainty. Floods, coastal erosion and similar environmental problems are experienced in many locations throughout the world. Valuable insights can be gained by examining how coastal populations live in these dynamic and frequently changing environments. Analysing *local* perceptions and *local* management strategies might be helpful in developing appropriate coastal zone management plans for *global* environmental changes in the future. This paper focuses on questions of how environmental changes enter people's lives as problems or even crises, how they are dealt with, and how people plan to deal with them in the future. These questions will be discussed in the context of an investigation of coastal zones of West African Senegal.

This paper consists of two main parts. The first discusses local perceptions and management strategies with regard to coastal zones in Senegal, summarising the results of fieldwork in 1996 and 1997 (for more details, see Engels 2003). It will show that local perceptions are diverse and sometimes even conflicting, and that this diversity is a product of a social differentiation (e.g., along lines of ethnicity, age and gender) which cannot be resolved by technical means alone. The second part compares these perceptions with problem definitions generated by globally coordinated research on climate change and related sea-level rise. Here I argue that a global perspective on the earth's coastal zones diminishes the local diversity of perceptions and strategies by implicitly and explicitly prioritising certain definitions and strategies over others. I also suggest that the global perspective on climate change may have a systematic tendency to do so, an inevitable product of the attempt at worldwide standardisation. Finally, the paper draws some conclusions as to how studies of global environmental management and future sea-level rise can benefit from local analysis.

The data were collected over a five-month period in Senegal in 1996 and 1997. They come from three different sources, the most important being interviews with groups and individuals living in these regions and actively involved in efforts to improve the situation. Most of these interviews, predominantly in Wolof, Lebou, and Serer, were conducted with the help of translators. The second source was a collection of written documents produced by the actors involved – for example, planning documents or reports produced by the relevant government administration, and reports and papers written by NGOs. Thirdly, the support of Senegalese scientists working on marine and coastal questions was extremely helpful for understanding the ecological and technical aspects of the changing environment.[3]

Local Environmental Crises in Coastal Zones of Senegal

A quick glance at Senegal's geography suggests that problems of coastal zones might rank high on the country's agenda. In addition to about 500 km of ocean coast, two large estuaries (of the rivers Saloum and Casamance) and the delta of the river Senegal can also be categorised as low-lying extended coastal zones (Dennis et al. 1995). Coastal zones are inhabited by more than half the nation's population, and are central to Senegal's economy. For example, fish and seafood account for an important part of the economy, both for export and for domestic consumption. Extended sand beaches have attracted important investments in tourism. Three major cities (Dakar, Saint-Louis and Rufisque) and countless smaller communities have been built in coastal areas. Problems of coastal erosion and temporary floods are well known in many parts of Senegal, and it is therefore not surprising that the country's vulnerability to future sea-level rise has long been a topic of discussion.

The following examples (Rufisque, Djiffer and a group of villages in the estuary of the Saloum) are chosen to demonstrate that diverging and sometimes conflicting perceptions and strategies can be found, even within the same location (see map 6.1).

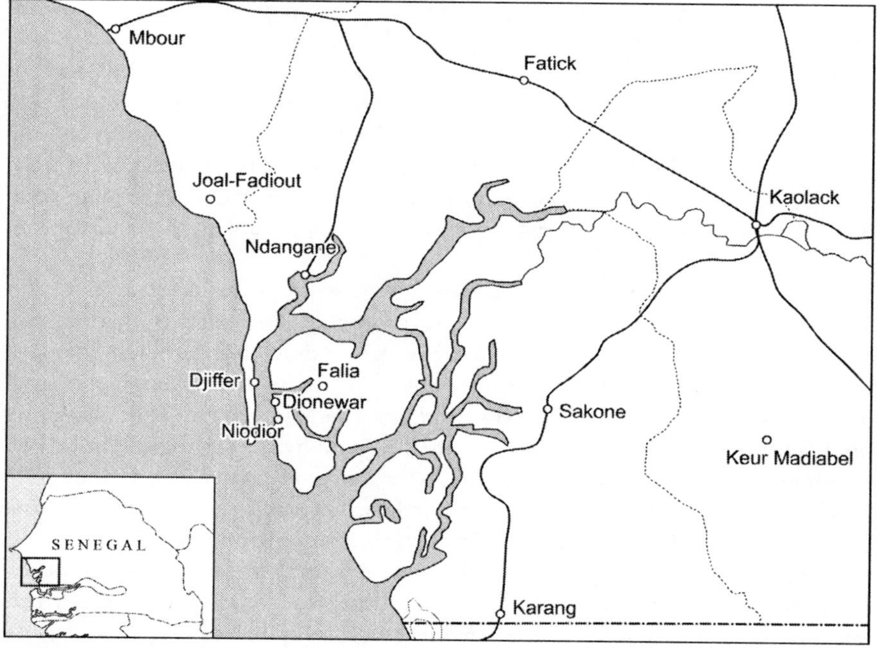

Map 6.1. Senegal and the area of investigation

Rufisque

I begin with the following observations based on interviews with inhabitants of Diokoul, market vendors and day-labourers at the wharf of Rufisque, the Directeur du Cabinet de la Mairie, the Chef du Développement Communautaire and the Assistant du Service des Travaux Publiques in Rufisque, the head of a local NGO (APDEM), and project workers of the Dakar-based ENDA TM-Equipe RUP (Rélais pour le développement urbain participé); see also APDEM 1996 and Gaye and Diallo 1994.

The city of Rufisque is situated 25 km south of Dakar, on the Atlantic coast. With nearly 200,000 inhabitants,[4] it is one of the largest cities in Senegal. It is home to important industrial businesses, such as a large cement factory, and is also a hub of trade for fish and other seafood. Since the main road that channels traffic to the eastern and southern regions of Senegal passes through Rufisque, the city plays an important role in the nation's infrastructure. Rufisque's development transformed the ecological features of this part of the coast significantly. To allow for larger human settlements, the area had to be drained, and natural seawater branches were replaced by a system of artificial channels guiding rainwater into the ocean. The extraction of sand and minerals along the beaches within city limits has also contributed to the transformation of the area.[5] An extended period of drought in the Sahelian region led to a decrease in vegetation, and, together with a slight local sea-level rise, has further led to changes in this coastal zone. Coastal erosion and severe floods have become frequent and well-known problems. According to the Senegalese geologist Niang-Diop (1995: 125), the average rate of annual ocean advance was 1.3 m between 1937 and 1980, and an increased 2.8 m per year between 1972 and 1976. Many houses have been destroyed, while others have been severely endangered by seawater undermining their foundations. In addition, two cemeteries will have to be removed in the near future. If the current rate of erosion continues or increases, parts of the main road that connects Dakar with the eastern and southern portions of the country will also be threatened.

The city and its population have reacted to these problems in several different ways. A multitude of political and technical solutions have been tried, with mixed results. Sand and mineral extraction is formally forbidden, but continues illegally. Plans for a huge dyke were developed by a team of Dutch engineers and researchers as early as the 1970s, but were not funded. The city administration reacted by implementing resettlement schemes,[6] and by attempting technological solutions. In Diokoul, one of the city districts most severely hit by erosion and flooding, problem perceptions and preferred strategies of the city administration differed notably from communities living in this particular district.

The main concerns of the city administration were to prevent land-loss within city limits, to protect existing buildings from being flooded, and to guarantee the safety of the main highway. Its preferred technical solution was to cut the city off from direct exposure to the sea by building large dykes to fix the position of the coastline for decades to come. Between 1983 and 1990 the first dyke was built parallel to the beach to protect houses and other structures from flooding. Planners hoped the dyke would protect the city for at least a decade, until it would be replaced by a larger and stronger structure; but by 1993 the area had flooded once again, and parts of the dyke gradually began to sink.

Soon after the dyke was built, a concrete wharf was added to it. This was supposed to facilitate the trading of fish and seafood, and was thus built with generous extra space for lorries to be loaded with fish destined for the city of Dakar. The wharf also made the collection of fees and taxes relatively easy for the city administration. In 1997, the idea was discussed of building a new, larger dyke along the outer coastline, strong enough to carry a newly built highway on top of it, thus simultaneously reducing the amount of traffic going through the city centre. Although the administration tried to establish contacts with donor agencies,[7] they concluded that this idea would be too costly to be realised in the near future.

Many of these technical attempts at fixing the coastline to protect the city as a whole were implemented in Dioukoul, a city district which directly borders the beach and is severely hit by coastal erosion. Unlike other districts of Rufisque, Diokoul is of relatively homogeneous ethnic composition. About 70 percent of the population consider themselves to be Lebou, a community which has a long tradition of living as fishermen in this particular region, and which is known for its strong sense of cultural identity (Mercier and Balandier 1953: 211, 213).[8] The fishermen either fish directly from the beach or from rocks near the shore, or travel out in open wooden boats (*pirogues*) to fish offshore. They use the beach to land their boats, to sell fish, and to repair their equipment. Women process the fish on the shore by drying and curing them on small wooden screens in the sun. Many Lebou houses are also built very near the beach, so that they, too, are affected by the advancing sea. In 1983, the NGO *ENDA Tiers Monde* began building a system of small groins in Diokoul to avoid further land loss. Groins are built perpendicularly to the beach, and they are designed to disrupt the water currents to allow for enrichment of the beach with sand and sediments. Ideally, not only is land loss prevented, but additional land is gained. The NGO was supported by technical staff of the University of Lausanne, and the project was organised as a community-based self-help activity (several interviews; see also Gaye and Diallo 1994). This structure was never completed and the remains eroded fast. Nevertheless, it is remembered as a community-based effort to fight the threatening consequences of the changing environment in a way that did not conflict with the local uses of the beach.

In contrast to this self-help project, many Lebou disapproved of most of the large technical solutions that were executed by the city administration in the following years, and they opposed the dyke construction in their quarter because they needed access to the beach to continue their daily economic practices. Those earning their living as fishermen also opposed the construction of the concrete wharf, claiming that landing their wooden boats at the concrete wall would be too dangerous. The preferred coping strategy of those Lebou living close to the beach in Dioukoul would be to retreat partially and let the ocean take over. This would mean resettlement to safer areas in order to secure open access to the beach and water, but interviewees claimed that they had not been included in any resettlement schemes.

The opposing perceptions of the nature of the problem and the appropriateness of solutions (fixation vs. partial retreat) depend on varying uses which come along with differing conceptions of the coast among different groups. For the administration, urban land is mainly a space for housing, industry and transport. The constructions found in this space are expensive and deemed worthy of protection. The overall objective of the city administration is therefore to fix the position of the coast. In contrast, many Lebou living in Dioukoul have a very different concept of the coast. For them, the beach is an intricate economic sphere, where natural resources are traded and processed at the same time. The particular ways in which fishing and trade is performed are seen by the Lebou I spoke to as part of their ethnic identity, and to continue with these practices is thus of vital importance for their cultural continuation. The wharf built and established by the city administration is also made for economic use of the coastal zone. However, whereas many Lebou use the sand beach for artisanal fishery and processing fish and seafood, the concrete wharf is expressly designed to enhance industrial processing and export trade. Any future coastal zone management plan for this area would have to include some kind of solution for these conflicting management strategies. By 1997, the Lebou had started to organise in NGOs and community groups in order to be better able to defend their use of the coast.

Estuary of the Saloum

The estuary of the Saloum river, about 150 km south of Dakar, is a large area made up of interconnected channels and islands. Mangrove trees grow well in this region, and it is thus a nursing ground for many species of birds, fish and shellfish. In recent years, a major ecological change has affected the area. The large estuary carrying warm water to the ocean had long been protected from the cold seawater currents by the sand-spit of Sangomar (Flèche de Sangomar). This sand-spit functioned as a shield stretching from north to south which, at its southern end, left an opening for the estuary. After a heavy storm in February 1987, the most fragile part of the sand-spit was flooded and breached. Breaches had been reported before, but in that year, for the first time, the breach did not close again. Instead, it rapidly widened, and by 1992 it had reached a length of 3 km, and had deepened considerably as well (Bâ et al. 1993).[9] Two different examples will now be presented to illustrate how the local population has reacted to these changes. One is the village of Djiffer, located at the southern edge of the eroding sand-spit;

the other is a group of villages situated on islands within the estuary. This area is inhabited by about seventy villages and smaller settlements, with a total population of about 200,000 (UICN 1996). The data presented below are taken from interviews with inhabitants of Djiffer, scientists of the University of Dakar and members of the Dakar-based NGO ENDA TM-Programme Energie.

Djiffer

The village of Djiffer faces the threat of being literally wiped away by the sea. The sand-spit has experienced a rate of erosion of 20 m per year along its ocean side, and a dramatic rate of 600–750 m per year at its southern edge (Bâ et al. 1993: 126). For a variety of reasons, the village has long attracted migrants from other parts of the country. Some hoped for jobs provided by a fish processing plant, others came because the village provides easy access to rich fish reserves inside the estuary, and also because of opportunities to earn money by smuggling goods to the Gambia. About half the population permanently resides in the village, while the other half moves in and out. Most of the migrants stay for a few months and live in small huts which they rent from locals. Migrant women find Djiffer to be particularly attractive, too, as they process and sell fish on the broad strip of sand beach along the river side. 'At the beach you can always make some money' was a very common claim made by the women working there. The presence of these migrants guarantees income to the local population as well, supporting the successful establishment of many small restaurants, shops and bars.

The former wealth of this village has declined in recent years, because coastal erosion led to the loss or removal of many important structures. A major fish processing plant which first opened in 1956 had to be closed in 1996, due to incursions of sand and sea. Other village structures, including a school and several administrative posts, were completely destroyed. A *campement touristique*[10] had to be rebuilt further north, at the better protected landward side of the strip. The population was well aware that their habitat is severely endangered and extremely fragile.

For many years the villagers' reaction to the dramatic environmental changes was gradual retreat. This entailed the rebuilding of replacement structures further north, for which the village received some government support. The village elders, mostly Serer, felt that retreat was the only option left; this perception was also in accordance with their religious convictions. Their understanding of Muslim faith led to a strong feeling of being left at God's mercy, regardless of the strategies that one would choose. Religious sacrifices of animals were therefore perceived as a strategy equally important to any technical protective measure. The other group of people living in this village, the migrants, did not attempt to fight the erosion, either. They preferred to exploit the opportunities offered by this location for as long as possible without having to invest in long-term protection, although they lived particularly close to the eroding fringes and were thus even more prone to the loss of housing and equipment than others.

The first people to take an active stance against the dramatic rate of erosion were the owners of the *campement touristique*, for the obvious reason that their investment was directly threatened. They organised the building of groins composed of sandbags. Without support from the local population and in the absence of better technology, this effort stood little chance of success. But very slowly, a number of the younger inhabitants of the village developed a growing concern for the future of their village, and wanted to protect the land from erosion rather than to retreat. They began to support the protective measures and openly questioned the until then preferred policy of the elders. A third source of support then emerged: for the first time the village of Djiffer became represented in the regional political administration. The *conseil rural* had its seat in Palmarin, an equally small village just a few kilometres north, on the same fragile sand-spit as Djiffer. This newly elected council came to the realisation that what had happened to Djiffer would sooner or later also happen to Palmarin, so it decided to promote a joint strategy.

It is unclear whether measures designed to protect against this degree of coastal erosion have any chance of success, but it is nevertheless interesting to see that three different possible courses of action were debated. These included, first, the rather unplanned retreat of the local population; second, the conscious risk-taking by the migrant population based on short-term economic interest; and third, the coastal fix as a strategy that emerged only recently. It is also worth noting the timescales involved. Although the destruction was so dramatic that it could not have been overlooked, it was still almost a decade after the breach before a protective strategy (coastal fix) had been developed that differed from passive reaction, the character and the appropriateness of which is still debated. In interviews, Senegalese scientists argued that human settlements on such fragile land were wrong from the very beginning, and that the resettlement of the whole population would be the only viable solution in the long run.

Niodior, Dionewar and Falia

The villages of Niodior, Dionewar and Falia, which are mostly populated by the ethnic group of Serer,[11] are situated on islands in the Saloum estuary. The following information is drawn from interviews with inhabitants of the three villages, members of the local forest administration and with the local agent of the Service d'Expansion Rural. Niodior is the largest of the three villages (4,600 individuals), followed by Dionewar and Falia with 3,500 and 500 persons respectively. The villages are accessible by boat. A daily *pirogue* operates as a ferry between the mainland and Niodior, providing the fastest passage to Dakar. Many privately owned *pirogues* also operate, many of which have outboard motors. The inhabitants of the three villages make their living by catching fish and collecting oysters and cockles; by growing millet, vegetables, and fruits; and to a lesser extent by breeding livestock (see Riss 1989 for other examples of agriculture in the Sine-Saloum). Niodior and Dionewar have been quite wealthy in the past. A 1962 report reveals that the area had a unique abundance of natural resources and a highly skilled population. It highlighted the richness of the Saloum's diversity of fish and shellfish species, especially cockles and oysters, but also shrimps (Service de l'Océanographie et des Pêches Maritime 1962: 2, 8).

However, the breaking of the Flèche de Sangomar in 1987 also had significant ecological impacts on the Saloum estuary. Much more sea water entered the estuary and, consequently, the following changes in the local environment were observed (Bâ et al. 1993; Diouf et al. 1993; UICN 1996):

- growing mean water and soil salinity
- changes in direction and speed of dominant currents[12]
- in some areas, land losses due to accelerated coastal erosion
- growing sedimentation and sand deposition in other areas
- declining mangrove populations
- declining reserves of fish, cockles and oysters

In 1997 the villagers' perception of their situation was dominated by declining income, diminishing stocks of fish, oysters and cockles, and by a number of practical problems caused by environmental changes stemming from the breach. In contrast to the examples of Rufisque and Djiffer, where conflicts over the appropriate solutions prevailed, a unified strategy of conservation could be observed in these three villages inside the estuary. Retreat, or even abandoning the villages to resettle on the mainland or on safer islands, was not seen as a possible solution.

The first important consequence of the breach can be best described as a problem of mobility. There is, first of all, the difficulty of access to the villages of Niodior and Dionewar. Some of the sand which erodes on the ocean side of the sand-spit enters the estuary and accumulates in the access channels to the villages. Large *pirogues* have difficulty travelling between the villages, and, by 1997, passage at low tide had already become impossible. In both Niodior and in Dionewar, people started digging passages through the low-water region and marking them carefully with sticks. This was a very time-consuming activity and could not be done as often as was necessary. The villagers' capacity to participate in traffic and commerce was thus seriously restricted, as were the already limited possibilities for action in cases of emergency. In addition to the restricted access of the *pirogues*, other problems of mobility in the villages became obvious. After the gap had opened, floods occurred more often and for longer time spans. This affected intra-village mobility as well as traffic between Niodior and Dionewar:

for example, a flood in 1992 reportedly destroyed a bridge between Niodior and Dionewar. This precarious link between the two villages is crucial for many children from Dionewar who attend secondary school in Niodior.

The possibility of direct and indirect land loss represents another important consequence of the breach. This was a danger to which the villages were directly exposed, since they were built in close proximity to the coastline. Houses, mosques, town squares and streets were threatened by coastal erosion, which had accelerated since 1987. Moreover, the breach presented problems beyond those of direct land loss. Villagers of both Dionewar and Niodior reported that the growing intrusion of salt water destroyed the soil of once-fertile areas. Also, increasing salinity reduced the availability of drinking-water.

One of the most important socio-economic consequences of the environmental changes was caused by a decline in several natural resources. The most striking examples were fish, oysters, cockles and the wood of mangroves lost due to a rising water salinity, which were all used both for consumption and trade. These changes had severe economic impacts on most of the villagers as their income declined. They had to compensate for the loss of income by travelling further out than before to find sufficient fish and oysters, and by spending more work hours to collect the same amount of cockles. The cockles collected in this region ('bloody cockle', or *pagne* in Wolof) suffered from a growing accumulation of sand in the mud, such that they could no longer grow in abundance. The strategy of travelling further out to sea posed technical problems and was seen as a dangerous solution because of the potential for mortal accidents[13].

This link between growing scarcity of natural resources and declining income reveals another important aspect of local environmental crises which might lead to differences in problem perceptions and strategies. The use of natural resources is subject to a relatively clear-cut division of labour along gender lines. Whereas fish are caught by men, the collection of oysters and cockles are female activities. As in many African rural areas, the use of resources and the generation, redistribution and investment of income take place in relatively distinct male and female economic spheres (Droy 1990; Lachenmann 1998; van Santen 1992). This suggests that there might be different economic impacts for men and women, depending on which resources are declining, and on the possibilities of using alternative resources, employing new technologies or diversifying into other fields of income generation. Such differential impacts were observed in the example of some women of Falia. Before the breach, these women reached their area of harvest by small *pirogues* which they were able to steer by themselves. They had small boats of short range, with a sail and paddles instead of outboard motors. Due to the changing conditions, they had to gather shellfish at locations far away from their village, and therefore had to rent the larger motor-driven boats owned and steered by men at high cost. In this case, the women faced, to a certain degree, the loss of a realm of independent economic activity, accompanied by a redistribution of income along gender lines.

In contrast to the situation in Djiffer, these villages developed very consistent strategies to combat land loss, protect their houses and maintain their access to mobility. They proposed a number of joint community efforts for protection, such as planting palm trees and more salt-resistant plants to fix the coastline, and constructing small dams by using local materials (sand and shells). They also developed a special way of building their houses by blocking the entrance with high steps, preventing intrusion of water during flooding. Differences with regard to specific strategies occurred both between the villages and between groups of women and groups of men within the same village. Yet, a strategy of conservation, however implemented locally, was perceived as more appropriate and preferable to a strategy of retreat or resettlement in a new and less endangered environment.

In spite of attempts at applying this whole range of conservation strategies, it was apparent that the local technologies of protection were too weak to cope with changes of this dramatic speed and scale. Accordingly, village officials expressed the urgent hope of receiving external aid.

Problems of the coastal zone are diverse, not only because of the diversity of ecological features of the coast itself, but also because of the forms of social differentiation of its population, for example by ethnic group, age and gender. A great variety of land-use patterns exists (housing, transportation, industrial or artisanal production, trade, agriculture, tourism), and different strategies emerge from them. Differences may stem from the ethnic composition of the population, from different forms of administrative planning and political representation, and also from the gender-related division of labour. In some cases, conflicting strategies emerge from this social differentiation: for example, retreat versus fixation, or long-term protection versus short-term exploitation. In the second part of this paper, I shall shift focus from the local to the global level, and examine global problem definitions and management strategies. Finally, I shall examine how these definitions and strategies match with the social diversity observed at the local level.

Global Sea-Level Rise: Impacts, Adaptation and Coastal Zone Management Plans

Local environmental crises, as depicted thus far, pose severe restrictions on the well-being of the local populations in question. The scientific scenarios of global climate change regularly warn that problems like these are likely to increase in number and intensity in the future. 'Accelerated sea-level rise is one of the more certain consequences of global warming' (Leatherman and Nicholls 1995: 1). For over a decade, international negotiations have aimed at reducing global emissions of CO_2 and other trace gases in order to prevent global warming, or at least to mitigate its effects. The negotiations have resulted in the Framework Convention on Climate Change (1992) and the Kyoto Protocol (1997), and they continue through the annual party conferences. This would not have been possible without an elaborate scientific assessment of global climate change. Within the organisational framework of the Inter-governmental Panel on Climate Change (IPCC), research about climate change itself, about its economic and social impacts, is coordinated on a worldwide scale[14]. However, this research not only provides knowledge about causes and consequences of global climate change; it also generates a global view on appropriate environmental management strategies. A whole range of possible mitigation and adaptation strategies is discussed in this context, and many of them refer to sea-level rise. It is therefore interesting to compare this global view with the perceptions observed at the local level.

Impacts of Global Sea-Level Rise: The Case of Senegal

By 1997, several scientific assessments of Senegal's vulnerability to future sea-level rise had been undertaken. Among these, one study provides a particularly useful example for comparison, because it was conducted as part of a larger programme that used the general framework provided by the IPCC to assess impacts of sea-level rise in ten different developing countries. It also produced some of the figures about potential costs of sea-level rise that were later included in the national policy document on climate change that Senegal submitted to the Secretariat of the Framework Convention on Climate Change in 1997 (République du Sénégal 1997). The study was funded by the U.S. Environmental Protection Agency, and it was undertaken in a cooperative effort between the University of Dakar and the University of Maryland in 1991. The results were published in 1995 in the *Journal of Coastal Research* (Leatherman and Nicholls 1995; Dennis et al. 1995). The study aimed to quantify potential impacts of sea-level rise on a national scale. To this end it identified land at risk, values at risk and population at risk; it also aimed to quantify the potential costs of different adaptation scenarios. Four different scenarios of future sea-level rise were used in the study (0.2 m, 0.5 m, 1 m and 2 m by 2100), but its focus was on the 1 m scenario.[15]

The results show that 3 percent of the total land area of Senegal would be at risk with a 1m sea-level rise (Dennis et al. 1995: 252). In particular, the three low-lying areas of indirect coast (the estuary of the Saloum, the estuary of the Casamance and the Senegal delta) would be inundated. However, the value at risk is concentrated on a rather limited part of the coast, mostly the direct coastline of sandy beach. Due to insufficient data, and for the sake of simplification and clarity, value was defined only by the market value (in 1990 U.S. dollars) of buildings that would be lost because of land loss. Neither agricultural land nor other (for example, infrastructural) values were included. Other negative impacts, like the probable disappearance of mangroves, were discussed qualitatively, but did not appear in the quantitative results. In a 1 m scenario, the value at risk was estimated to be 499-707 million U.S. dollars, which amounted to 12–17 percent of Senegal's GNP in 1990 (Dennis et al. 1995: 254). This value was highly concentrated in the sandy coast south of Dakar. The loss of buildings used for tourism accounted for 20–30 percent of this value at risk.

The population at risk for a 1m sea-level rise was estimated to be 1.4–2.3 percent of the total population (Dennis et al. 1995: 254). Due to weaknesses in the available data, the population of the Senegal delta and the two estuaries were excluded in this estimation. In summary, the study predicts that a 1 m rise in sea-level would affect large areas of Senegal's coastal zones, but the values at risk, as well as the populations at risk, were concentrated in a very limited area. Even though the authors stated that their estimates should be considered minimal values, the impact of sea-level rise would be substantial, to a large extent because hotels and tourist resorts would be lost.

In addition to the impacts, different protection scenarios were discussed in this study. The 'No Protection' scenario would mean that areas and values at risk would be lost. The 'Important Areas Protection' scenario estimated the potential costs of protecting values at risk. The 'Total Protection' scenario calculated the potential costs of protecting all areas at risk, regardless of their respective value. For a 1m rise, the costs for 'Important Areas Protection' were estimated at 255–845 million U.S. dollars. Only 70 km of the open coastline required protection under this scenario, and in most parts the costs were attributed to beach nourishment. The costs of the 'Total Protection' scenario would amount to 973–2,156 million U.S. dollars, mostly due to costs incurred for additional sea-walls. Thus a substantial increase in the costs for protection would result in only a very limited additional benefit. Although the authors point out that these estimates are 'unsuitable for cost-benefit analysis' (Dennis et al. 1995: 251), they nevertheless introduce this simple quantitative rationale to suggest that, 'if sea-level rise does occur, it appears that the most appropriate response would more closely resemble Important Areas Protection than Total Protection' (Dennis et al. 1995: 257).

The comparison between global and local views shows that in both perspectives, the impacts of coastal erosion and inundation in coastal zones appear to be substantial. However, there are striking differences between this global view on sea-level rise in Senegal and the local perceptions and strategies that have been discussed before. Due to the methodology chosen in the study, only fixation of the coastline (beach nourishment and sea-walls) is considered as an adaptation scenario. Partial retreat would only be categorised as part of the non-strategy of 'No Protection'. Due to its concentration on land loss, the study does not include problems of mobility or loss of income caused by declining natural resources as impacts of sea-level rise. Thus, the study includes economic losses for industry and tourism (through the loss of expensive buildings), but it omits any economic losses of rural populations, such as those in the estuary of the Saloum – not to mention the potentially differential impacts of sea-level rise along gender lines. Likewise, certain uses of the coastal zone are implicitly prioritised over others. Industry and tourism are highly valued, whereas agriculture, artisanal fishery and rural life in general are not taken into consideration. The estuary of the Saloum therefore appears as an area of risk, but not as an area of value. Neither the village of Djiffer nor the group of villages inside the estuary figure prominently in the estimated costs of sea-level rise. Accordingly, the study provides a strong rationale for protecting existing beaches through beach nourishment to support tourism, but it does not do so for supporting artisanal fishery of the Lebou. Similarly, the study provides a strong rationale for protecting the city of Rufisque from further coastal erosion by building seawalls, but it does not do so to protect the villages in the estuary of the Saloum. Whereas the analysis at the local level shows that the villagers had carefully developed coastal protection and adaptation strategies for which they hoped to receive external support, the study concludes that 'Future development in these areas is best avoided' (Dennis et al. 1995: 258).

This simple comparison highlights a striking mismatch between global and local views on environmental problems in coastal zones, and of resulting environmental management strategies. However, this is only one example, and generalisations should be drawn from it with care. It is quite clear that the results of a similar study might have turned out to be rather different. For example, adaptation scenarios different from protection as fixation are discussed elsewhere (Niang-Diop 1994; IPCC 1992). The authors themselves make it clear throughout the paper that their study is restricted in many aspects, and they clearly qualify the results. Thus, the limitations of data and methodologies can *in principle* be overcome. However, as will be argued in the following section, the inherent orientation of the IPCC towards worldwide standardisation implies a systematic constraint that limits its ability to cope with local social diversity.

Global Science and the Logic of Universal Comparability

The IPCC was established in 1988, when it was widely considered important to make national governments all over the world realise that future climate change posed a genuine threat necessitating international action. To facilitate international negotiations, two things were simultaneously required: individual national assessments and cross-national (universal) comparability of the assessments. The global carbon cycle was disaggregated into nationalised CO_2 budgets, thus defining to what extent individual states were actively causing future climate change. As Subak (1996: 52) observes, 'Beginning in the late 1980s, as national governments began to recognize the importance of global warming as a policy problem, the need for comprehensive inventories with reference to political borders became apparent'. This was followed by national assessments of potential impacts of climate change, and also by assessments of national policy options. These assessments held a danger that each country would use different methodologies. However, universal comparability was required in order to be effective for international policy negotiations. The IPCC subsequently developed worldwide standardisation of methodologies leading to the establishment of IPCC guidelines for national greenhouse gas inventories (IPCC 1995a; 1995b; 1995c). The approach of standardisation was also adopted for impact and vulnerability assessments:

> Climate impact assessment must address an inherently global phenomenon affecting all nations, so it is desirable that assessments are conducted in a transparent manner, with comparable assumptions and internally consistent procedures. Comparability among assessments is of great importance in appraising the range of appropriate response actions at the international, national and regional levels ... These are persuasive arguments for adopting a standardized approach to climate impact assessment. (Parry and Carter 1998: 4)

Standardisation of impact and vulnerability assessments with regard to coastal zones is documented in IPCC (1991; 1992; 1994). If worldwide comparability is the driving force behind the assessments, this may be to the detriment of detailed representations of local particularities. Thus, the standardisation of methodologies limits the assessments' sensitivity towards local diversity. Simplifications can be expected, resulting in a homogenisation of diverse and conflicting problem definitions. This can be seen in the Senegal study that concentrates on problems of direct land loss while ignoring problems of mobility or of indirect land loss due to growing salinity. This simplification is acknowledged to be a major limitation of the study by the authors, who justify this methodological choice by referring to the IPCC Common Methodology (Dennis et al. 1995: 244).

With regard to developing countries like Senegal, the standardisation of methodologies leads to additional difficulties. Developing countries often lack the expertise to accomplish scientific assessments without external support. Special programmes, workshops and training packages were developed to enable scientists from developing countries to use and apply the standard methodologies of the IPCC (Price 1996; Engels 2003). Likewise, developing countries often lack data necessary for carrying out assessments; moreover, the reliability of available data is weak. Rough estimates, oversimplifications and default data often substitute for the more detailed and precise analyses which are possible in many developed countries. The study of the impacts of sea-level rise in Senegal provides a fairly typical example. Because of these additional problems, endemic to developing countries, the probability that standardised methods and predefined data requirements lead to flaws and simplifications is even higher. The standardised methodologies also call for the quantification and monetary valuation of many aspects of the assessments. Monetary valuations are a very useful tool in negotiations. As in the case of the analysis of the impacts of a 1 m sea-level rise in Senegal, it is impressive to see estimates of potential costs amounting to 12–17 percent of the country's GNP. But insofar as the logic of monetary valuation systematically shifts the focus of debate from marginal rural areas to industrialised urban areas, this technique produces a highly selective picture of both problems and adaptation strategies. The IPCC promoted the standardisation of scientific methodologies in order to guarantee worldwide comparability of national assessments. Standardisation in this sense has a vital function, as it facilitates decision-making at the international level and helps to generate a global view of the problem of climate change and its impacts. On the other hand, the sweeping standardisation of methodologies systematically produces simplifications, generating a highly selective view of local problems and potential adaptation strategies. The overall rationale of these assessments is the perceived need to provide a tenable representation of the global problem, rather than the best possible representation of local details and particularities. It can thus be concluded that local coastal zone management plans should not be derived, in any straightforward manner, from the globally co-ordinated scientific study of accelerated sea-level rise.

Summary and Discussion

With the threat of future sea-level rise in mind, what lessons for coastal environmental management can be learned from this comparison of local environmental crises and global problem definitions? Efforts to improve the world's capacity to respond to changes in coastal environments might be guided by two complementary strategies (for a more general discussion of similar questions see Breit et al. 2003).

One strategy would be an attempt to increase the sensitivity of the globally coordinated science of climate change to local social diversity. The study of impacts of accelerated sea-level rise in Senegal (Dennis et al. 1995) was an early attempt to carry out this kind of global assessment in the context of developing countries, and was subject to time constraints and limited funding. Since then, many efforts have been undertaken by the scientific community to overcome some of the inherent difficulties of the assessments; see, for example, the impressive number of workshops and resulting papers on the improvement of national greenhouse gas inventories (IPCC 1998b, 1998c, 1999). It is acknowledged, for example, that the needs for adaptation measures will be extremely variable, and that the appropriateness of any given technology is highly dependent on local conditions, especially in terms of differences between developed and developing countries (UN FCCC 1999); see also Klein et al. (1999), who argue in favour of broadening the approach, from a rather technical and implementation-centred one to a more process-oriented approach that also takes into account the need for public participation. These ongoing efforts aim at a better representation of local problems in the global picture, which is a useful step towards improving the quality of global environmental assessment. However, I have argued here that there might be inherent limits to this perspective, as long as standardisation and universal comparability remain the ultimate driving forces.

For this reason, the local analysis presented here strongly suggests a complementary strategy which is two-fold. The first part of this strategy is a *decentralisation of research efforts* in order to develop coastal zone management strategies. Environmental changes linked to sea-level rise will be experienced and responded to at the local level, even though some of the causal factors for changes are global in character. Decentralisation of research would therefore imply the promotion of scientific and technical capacity building at the local level, improvements of availability and reliability of data on the particular local context, and finally the acceptance of a multitude of approaches not necessarily consistent with the pattern of universal comparability. There have been programmes of capacity building and data improvement in the past, but they have aimed at enabling scientists from Senegal and other developing countries to carry out national assessments for the international community. A decentralised orientation of capacity building and data improvement would instead concentrate on the abilities of scientists and technicians to more fully understand particular local conditions, specific local changes that have been experienced, and strategies that have been adopted. It may be the case that anthropological data on local practices of resource use in coastal zones of Senegal are as strongly needed as topographical data on the coastal zones (which have been generated in order to model the impacts of accelerated sea-level rise in Senegal). In general, it can be expected that data requirements for local environmental management are of a kind qualitatively different from those for standardised assessment methodologies.

The second part of the strategy is a call for greater *democratisation and political participation.* Analysis at the local level has shown that the core of the problem is political and not technical. Decisions about what kinds of land use should be prioritised precede questions of what technologies are best able, and available, to do so. For example, whether the Lebou will be guaranteed the right to continue the use of the beach for artisanal fishery, and whether funds will be made available to secure the beach for this purpose, are choices that cannot be based on technical or technological arguments alone. The same holds true for questions of how to allocate public funding and technologies to protect the 200,000 inhabitants of Rufisque, as compared to the 200,000 inhabitants of the estuary of the Saloum. Above all, the decision of whether or not to develop a region is of a highly local and political nature. Institutional support for democratic planning procedures at the local level, and the promotion of public participation in environmental management questions may, therefore, be of vital importance for improving the world's capacity to respond to global environmental changes.

Notes

1. This article presents parts of the author's dissertation (Engels 2003). The fieldwork in Senegal was funded by the Ministry for School and Education, Science and Research of Northrhine-Westfalia (Germany). Without the generous support of Youba Sokona and others of ENDA TM-Programme Energie, the project would not have been possible. The Deutsche Forschungsgemeinschaft funded the project that provided the institutional framework for the dissertation. The paper greatly benefited from comments on an earlier version by Don Kennedy, Amy Luers, Ron Mitchell, Isabelle Niang-Diop and Nikolas Wada.
2. Some models suggest these changes, but: 'Knowledge is currently insufficient to say whether there will be any changes in the occurrence or geographical distribution of severe storms, e.g., tropical cyclones' (IPCC 1995d: 23).
3. I would like to thank Isabelle Niang-Diop, Khadim Guéye and El Hadj Salif Diop (all three at the University Cheikh Anta Diop, Dakar) for the valuable insights they shared with me.
4. Information provided by the Directeur du Cabinet de la Mairie in an interview in February 1997. The census of 1988 counted 115,000 inhabitants.
5. Niang-Diop (1995: 78) calculated that more than 47,000 tons of sand were extracted annually between 1927 and 1933.
6. Many of the displaced inhabitants complained about the poor conditions of their new homes.
7. Recently introduced laws of decentralisation have enabled the city administration to establish autonomous contacts with donor agencies. Formerly, all the official contacts had to be established and acknowledged by a central ministry in Dakar.
8. The Lebou have inhabited the Cap-Vert peninsula since the sixteenth century (Sylla 1992). In 1998, the EcoArts Festival was created 'to awaken public awareness of the importance of preserving the coastal environment and to protect the social, cultural and artistic values of the populations of Yoff and the other Lebou villages indigenous to the Cap-Vert peninsula' (http://www.siup.sn/festival/perspect.htm).
9. After only one decade, the breach is now reported to be 4 km long. See a UNESCO report at http://www.unesco.org/csi/region/vison/htm. The breach is also under close scientific scrutiny by Senegalese scientists, both at the University of Dakar and at other research institutes, using satellite data and remote sensing techniques. There is also an ongoing project assessing the socio-ecological changes in this area that is funded by UNESCO and other organisations.
10. A *campement touristique* is a tourist resort made of a group of small huts that imitate Senegalese villages.
11. Many Serer live in the Sine-Saloum, but most of them have specialised in agriculture and the cultivation of peanuts rather than in fishing (Reverdy 1967; Gastellu 1981; Lombard 1993).
12. Before, the current velocity did not exceed 1.5 m/s, while in 1992, a velocity of 5–6 m/s was measured in one of the channels (Bâ et al. 1993: 130).
13. Indeed, in 1999, a severe storm caused a number of casualties among Senegalese fishermen.
14. The IPCC was established by the World Meteorological Organisation and the United Nations Environment Programme in 1988. It has produced assessment reports that have become standard works of reference that are widely used by decision-makers. For an overview see the IPCC's homepage, http://www.ipcc.ch/.

15. The 0.2 m scenario implied no acceleration of sea-level rise, as this rise can be expected to happen even without global climate change. At the other extreme, the 2 m scenario is now considered as unlikely (Nicholls et al. 1995: 37).

References

APDEM 1996. 'Association pour la promotion de la pèche et la défense de l'environnement maritime' – APDEM/Sénégal, Statuts. Rufisque.

Bâ, M. et al. 1993. 'Evolution de l'embouchure du Saloum de 1958 à 1992', in *Gestion des ressources côtières et littorales du Sénégal. Actes de l'atelier de Gorée*, eds. A.T. Diaw et al., 27–9 July 1992: 121–31. Gland: UICN.

Breit, H., A. Engels, T. Moss and M. Troja 2003. *How Institutions Change. Perspectives on Social Learning in Global and Local Environmental Contexts.* Opladen: Leske+Budrich.

Clayton, K. and T. O'Riordan. 1995. 'Coastal Processes and Management', in *Environmental Science for Environmental Management*, ed. T. O'Riordan, 151–64. Harlow: Longman.

Dennis, K.C., I. Niang-Diop and R.J. Nicholls 1995. 'Sea-Level Rise and Senegal: Potential Impacts and Consequences', *Journal of Coastal Research*, Special Issue 14: 243–61.

Diouf, P.S. et al. 1993. 'La pèche dans les estuaires du Sénégal', in *Gestion des ressources côtières et littorales du Sénégal. Actes de l'atelier de Gorée*, eds. A.T. Diaw et al., 311–22. Gland: UICN.

Droy, I. 1990. *Femmes et développement rural.* Paris: Karthala.

Engels, A. 2003. *Die geteilte Umwelt. Ungleichheit, Konflikt und ökologische Selbstgefährdung in der Weltgesellschaft.* Weilerswist: Velbrück Wissenschaft.

Gastellu, J.-M. 1981. *L'égalitarisme économique des Serer du Sénégal.* Paris: ORSTOM.

Gaye, M. and F. Diallo 1994. *Programme d'assainissement Diokoul et quartiers environnants. Rufisque-Sénégal. Etude de cas.* Dakar: ENDA TM-RUP/HIC.

IPCC 1991. *The Seven Steps to the Vulnerability Assessment of Coastal Areas to Sea-Level Rise – a Common Methodology.* IPCC Response Strategies Working Group, 20 September 1991, Revision no. 1.

——— 1992. *Global Climate Change and the Rising Challenge of the Sea. Report of the Coastal Zone Management Subgroup.* Rijkswaterstaat, The Netherlands: IPCC Working Group III.

——— 1994. *Preparing to Meet the Coastal Challenges of the 21st Century. Conference Report, 1–5 November 1993.* Noordwijk, The Netherlands: World Coast Conference.

——— 1995a. *IPCC Guidelines for National Greenhouse Gas Inventories*, vol. 1: *Greenhouse Gas Inventory Reporting Instructions.* London: IPCC WG I Technical Support Unit.

——— 1995b. *IPCC Guidelines for National Greenhouse Gas Inventories*, vol. 2: *Greenhouse Gas Inventory Workbook.* London: IPCC WG I Technical Support Unit.

——— 1995c. *IPCC Guidelines for National Greenhouse Gas Inventories*, vol. 3: *Greenhouse Gas Inventory Reference Manual.* London: IPCC WG I Technical Support Unit.

——— 1995d. *Second Assessment, Climate Change 1995.* Geneva: IPCC.

——— 1998a. *The Regional Impacts of Climate Change. An Assessment of Vulnerability, A Special Report of IPCC Working Group II*, ed. R.T. Watson, M.C. Zinyowera and R.H. Moss. Cambridge: Cambridge University Press.

——— 1998b. *Programme on National Greenhouse Gas Inventories. Managing Uncertainty in National Greenhouse Gas Inventories.* Meeting Report, 13–15 October 1998. Paris: IPCC,OECD and IEA.

——— 1998c. *Programme on National Greenhouse Gas Inventories. Expert Group Meeting on National Feedback on the Revised 1996 IPCC Guidelines for National Greenhouse Gas Inventories.* Meeting Report, 15–16 September 1998. Havana: IPCC, OECD and IEA.

——— 1999. *Programme for National Greenhouse Gas Inventories. Good Practices in Inventory Preparation for Industrial Processes and the New Gases.* Draft Meeting Report, 26–8 January 1999. Washington DC: IPCC, OECD and IEA.

Klein, R.J.T., R.J. Nicholls and N. Mimura 1999. 'Coastal Adaptation to Climate Change: Can the IPCC Technical Guidelines be Applied?', *Mitigation and Adaptation Strategies for Global Change* 4(3–4): 239–52.

Lachenmann, G. 1998. 'Strukturanpassung aus Frauensicht: Entwicklungskonzepte und Transformationsprozesse', in *Globalisierung aus Frauensicht. Bilanzen und Visionen*, eds. R. Klingebiel and S. Randeria, 294–329. Bonn: Dietz.

Leatherman, S.P. and R.J. Nicholls 1995. 'Accelerated Sea-Level Rise and Developing Countries: An Overview', *Journal of Coastal Research*, Special Issue 14: 1–14.

Lombard, J. 1993. *Riz des villes, mil des champs. En pays Serer – Sénégal.* Bordeaux: Centre d'Etudes de Géographie Tropicale, CNRS, Domaine Universitaire de Bordeaux.

Mercier, P. and G. Balandier 1953. 'Les pecheurs Lebou du Sénégal, particularisme et evolution', *Etudes Senegalaises* 3, Saint-Louis: Centre IFAN.

Niang-Diop, I. 1994. 'Les problèmes environnementaux de la côte du Sénégal', *Ecodécision*, January: 40–43.

——— 1995. *L'erosion côtière sur la Petite Côte du Sénégal à partir de l'exemple de Rufisque. Passé – présent – futur.* Ph.D. thesis, University of Angers.

Nicholls, R.J., S.P. Leatherman, K.C. Dennis and C.R. Volonté 1995. 'Impacts and Responses to Sea-Level Rise: Qualitative and Quantitative Assessments', *Journal of Coastal Research*, Special Issue 14: 26–43.

Parry, M. and T. Carter 1998. *Climate Impact and Adaptation Assessment. A Guide to the IPCC Approach.* London: Earthscan.

Price, M.F. 1996. 'The Reality of Implementing an International Convention. National Greenhouse Gas Inventories in Developing Countries', *Global Environmental Change* 6(3): 193–203.

République du Sénégal 1997. *Communication initiale du Sénégal à la Convention-Cadre des Nations-Unies sur les Changements Climatiques.*

Reverdy, J.-C. 1967. *Une société rurale au Sénégal. Les structures foncières, familiales et villageoises des Serer.* Aix-en-Provence: Centre Africain des Sciences Humaines Appliquées.

Riss, M.-D. 1989. *Femmes africaines en milieu rural. Les Sénégalaises du Sine Saloum.* Paris: Editions L'Harmattan.

Service de l'Océanographie et des Pêches Maritimes. 1962. 'Rapport pour la conférence économique du 12 Mai 1962, no. I84/PM/IR 3', in *Région du Sine-Saloum. Conférence Economique Regionale. 12 Mai 1962.*

Subak, S. 1996. 'The Science and Politics of National Greenhouse Gas Inventories', in *Politics of Climate Change: A European Perspective*, eds. T. O'Riordan and J. Jäger, 51–64. London and New York: Routledge.

Sylla, A. 1992. *Le peuple Lebou de la presqu'ile du Cap-Vert.* Dakar: Les Nouvelles Editions Africaines du Sénégal.

UICN. 1996. 'Inventaire, suivi et évaluation du site Ramsar du delta du Saloum (Sénégal – Afrique de l'ouest)'. Dakar.

UN FCCC 1999. *Coastal Adaptation Technologies.* Technical Paper. FCCC/TP/1999/1.

van Santen, J. 1992. 'Der Autonomieansatz in der niederländischen Entwicklungsdiskussion – Veränderungen in der Frauenökonomie bei den Mafa (Nord Kamerun) im Zuge der Islamisierung', *Peripherie* 12(47/48): 172–90.

7

Meshing a Tight Net: A Cultural Response to the Threat of Open Access Fishing Grounds

Andrea Bender

Introduction: Direct vs. Indirect Regulations of Common Pool Resources

The 1968 paper by Garrett Hardin on the 'Tragedy of the Commons' triggered a vivid discussion on how the depletion of renewable, yet limited, common pool resources can be prevented. Since then, a whole string of case studies has been carried out in order to specify regulatory measures for successful management. Differing from Hardin, these came to the conclusion that even jointly used resources are *not necessarily* doomed to be ruined. On the contrary, if communities of resource users craft institutions that regulate and monitor the exploitation of the respective resource, sustainability can be achieved (e.g. Casimir and Rao 1998; Feeny et al. 1990; McCay and Acheson 1987; Ostrom 1992).

A classic example of a 'commons dilemma' is the exploitation of living marine resources (Berkes 1985, 1994; Gordon 1954; McEvoy 1986; Scott 1955). In many parts of the world access to these is open, and fish stocks are meanwhile heavily over-exploited. In other regions, however, systems of managing such resources – either directly or indirectly – have been established. Some of these, particularly in the Pacific, are very sophisticated and have been efficient over long periods of time (Campbell et al. 1989; Dyer and McGoodwin 1994; Hviding 1996; Johannes 1981; Ruddle and Johannes 1990; South et al. 1994). Such successful regimes are grounded in a set of rights and rules which create incentives for cooperation (Pomeroy 1994). Stimulated by the work of Elinor Ostrom (1992, 1994; Ostrom et al. 1994), several efficiency criteria for such regimes have been identified, among them clearly defined boundaries and access restrictions, commitment to a responding value system, mutual monitoring and graded sanctions (Feeny 1994; Pinkerton 1994).

Since problem awareness and consensus on viable measures are considered essential prerequisites for management, most studies have focused on tenure systems that *directly* regulate the access to the resource and the degree of its exploitation (e.g., Christy 1982; Cordell and McKean 1992; McCay and Acheson 1987; Ruddle and Akimichi 1984; Ruddle et al. 1992). Other institutions, however, may also function as a regulatory mechanism, at least *indirectly.* Particularly those concerned with the protection of certain species for religious reasons or with the distribution of the yields may set incentives to reduce resource exploitation as well (Klee 1980). The less evident the working of such institutions, the more efficient they may be (for examples see Johannes 1978; Rappaport 1968). On the other hand, the less evident their functioning, the more easily they can disappear without substitution. If a user group is not aware of the regulative function of an institution, it may lose its flexibility to react to changing conditions and even disappear without a trace (Bender 2001c; Hviding and Baines 1994; Johannes and MacFarlane 1991; Ruddle 1994).

The goal of this chapter is to examine the efficiency of such an indirectly working cultural institution as an adaptive response to the uncertainty of economic success, as well as to the risk of overexploitation. Assuming that solidarity networks in the form of food-sharing institutions help to stabilise the intensity of resource exploitation, the comparison of two Tongan villages – one having a tightly meshed social net, the other a rather fragmented one – should reveal corresponding differences in resource extraction as well. Of particular interest will be the extent of the respective solidarity network and its interaction with other aspects of the social structure on one hand, with strategies of exploitation on the other.

The chapter starts with an overview of the relevant theoretical approaches to the problem drawn from different disciplines, followed by a short description of the cultural context and the island villages where the research took place. Then the interactions between the institution of food-sharing and the strategies of exploitation will be highlighted. Special attention will be paid to the issue that indirect regulations such as food-sharing may be threatened by rapid changes and then bring about practical problems which will be discussed in the last part.

Theoretical Background: Solidarity Networks as Sharing Institutions

Three types of institutions are usually differentiated in anthropology with regard to the distribution of yields from resource extraction: reciprocal, redistributive and market exchange (Harris 1987). For our purpose, however, it seems more appropriate to categorise them on the basis of which incentives for exploitation they set, although undoubtedly they do overlap to some degree.

(1) Institutions distributing the yields *within the user group* will be referred to as 'sharing institutions'. Among these, solidarity networks (e.g., in the form of kin-relationships or remittances) are of special interest as one of the most widespread and firmly established institutions in Pacific cultures. Given that the group itself or its demands do not grow dramatically, sharing institutions will not exert pressure on the degree of exploitation, since the amount of fish needed within the community is limited. Relying on this institution may even reduce efforts in resource exploitation, thus stabilising the ecological situation, as will be shown in due course.

(2) The other group of institutions causing the yields to flow *out of the local user group* will be called 'extracting institutions'. Tributes to an estate holder, for instance, governmental taxes or market transfers belong in this category. Since they enhance the distribution of locally used and needed resources beyond the community (for other purposes than consumption), higher – and principally even unlimited – amounts need to be harvested. This increase in demand consequently exerts pressure on the resource.

Both institutions need to be scrutinised within the context of the social structure of the user group. Sharing institutions may be enacted between persons of equal rank or within a kin group, whereas tributes (as an example of extracting institutions) have to be paid to higher ranking persons. In this chapter, extracting institutions will be taken into consideration in the context of marketing opportunities and paying tributes. The focus, however, will be on sharing institutions which create a solidarity network that shelters users from individual shortfalls. In Tonga, the most important institution in this category is that of food-sharing (see also Evans 2001).

The insurance character of such solidarity networks has been extensively analysed in studies in both economics and anthropology (e.g. Blewett 1995; Coate and Ravallion 1993; Fafchamps 1992; Gould 1982; Platteau 1991; Thomas and Worrall 1994). They showed that in order to ensure its efficiency, wealthy members – and thus potential contributors of required goods – are essential and need to be well known. Accumulation of goods itself is therefore usually not negatively sanctioned though *secret* accumulation is stigmatised as greedy. The complementary danger of improper efforts (greed) is 'moral hazard', a lack of adequate effort to avoid the insured case of shortfall.

Apart from these 'effort imbalances', solidarity networks are prone to the risk of social differentiation. Economic success of single members within the network may lead either to a structural asymmetry or to the formation of coalitions. In the first case, single persons attain a central position within the net, while they accumulate wealth and regular clients; people at the periphery of such nets of influence or interest are thereby rendered less secure. The latter case will inevitably take place if a sub-group can improve its own welfare by forming a coalition on its own. By reducing the mutual insurance arrangements of the members of their sub-group, however, they also weaken the rest of the system, particularly the situation of its needy members (Fafchamps 1992). To preclude all these risks – effort imbalances as well as a withdrawal from the system – solidarity networks depend heavily on high commitment to shared values and on norms of cooperation firmly embedded in cultural institutions (Anderson 1994; Bataille-Benguigui 1988; Carew-Reid 1990; Ruddle 1994).

Summarising the above, we find that these considerations strongly support the hypothesis that solidarity networks considerably influence the intensity of resource exploitation (cf. Bender et al. 2002). In an attempt to ensure the right to subsistence, they grant all members access to the vital resources. Whereas most literature on common-pool resources rarely takes such insurance systems into account, the following analysis of the regulatory function of the Tongan food-sharing institution will focus on them. The hypotheses are derived from the above arguments: tightly meshed networks should stabilise cooperation and enhance sustainable resource use while the regulatory function of fragmented networks should be weakened. Particularly in cases where better-off members set up a subgroup (coalition), increasing commercialisation and exploitation will also be enhanced because their efforts are no longer restrained by extensive sharing.

Research Design

In order to test the assumed interdependence between solidarity networks and strategies of resource use, the Polynesian Kingdom of Tonga was selected. In Tonga, marine resources play a significant role in the daily life of the islanders, and access to them is free. At the same time, however, the cultural value of cooperation *(fetokoni'aki)* and the tradition of sharing food and particularly fish are still strong and respected today. Accordingly, two widely disparate expectations may arise:

- Given the importance of fish for cash income and the open access to it, resource depletion seems to be the unavoidable consequence.

- However, thanks to the strong institution of food-sharing and values enhancing cooperation, a sustainable resource use may result as well.

In fact, both developments can be observed in the island group of Ha'apai – with examples of mainly subsistence-based fishermen in one island village (Lofanga) and more commercialised fishing in a neighbouring village ('Uiha). These villages thus provided ideal conditions for a comparative analysis.

The research conducted there during a period of fifteen months in total (between 1997 and 1999) involved participant observation, intensive conversations with key informants and half-structured interviews with fishermen from both villages. Among the main points of interest have been the documentation of their respective resource use strategies, details of their social net and potential conflicts within and between the communities. In addition, a census of both villages was taken and the ecological situation estimated on the basis of interviews with specialists and members of the local Ha'apai Conservation Area Project, the Ministry of Fisheries and several consultants.

The Setting: The Context of Fishing in Lofanga and 'Uiha

The Polynesian Kingdom of Tonga (map 7.1) is situated in the Pacific Ocean, south of the Equator and west of the International Date Line. Roughly a third of the whole population, meanwhile, lives in the capital, Nuku'alofa, on the main island Tongatapu. About 200 km to the north, the fifty-one islands of the Ha'apai-Group are widely scattered along the Tonga Ridge; most of these are coral islands not high above sea level, with fertile soils but little fresh water, apart from rain. Only a third of the Ha'apai islands are inhabited by – in the late 1990s – approximately 8,000 people.

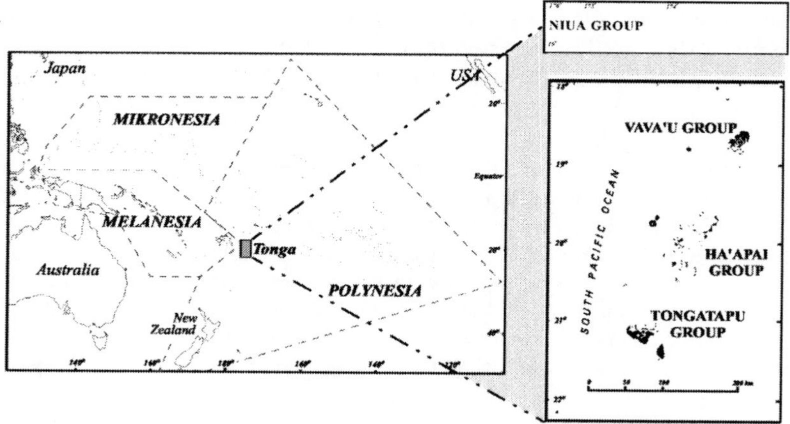

Map 7.1. The Polynesian Kingdom of Tonga in the southwestern Pacific Ocean.

Cultural Context: Between Fatongia and Fetokoni'aki

Since the first settlement of Austronesian seafarers on the Tongan islands some 3,500 years ago, their inhabitants have based their subsistence on planting as well as marine resources. Particularly in the outer islands of Ha'apai, this subsistence pattern still prevails. On their bush allotments for planting *('api 'uta),* the men cultivate tubers such as taro, yam, manioc and sweet potatoes in combination with bananas, coconut palms, mango, and breadfruit trees. Cash crops (i.e., squash, peanuts, pineapples, water melons, or vanilla) are only grown on a small scale. Although the vegetable food is supplemented by small-scale livestock, above all chicken and pigs for special occasions, the main source of protein is seafood. The coral reefs and lagoons surrounding the islands are rich in fish, shellfish, crabs and lobsters; octopus is a favourite dish for many islanders as well, and pelagic fish are caught by trolling on travels from island to island (Halapua 1982).

Most economic activities are gender-specific. Women and children engage in reef gleaning, while fishing is basically restricted to the male population. Due to a shortage of land, commercial fishing is one of the most promising (and for many men the only) option of cash income. Most Tongan households are forced to earn money for a number of reasons: to buy certain types of food and other daily goods, to pay school fees, to contribute money in the quarterly and annual fund-raising of their respective churches or to support their conferences.

In northern Ha'apai, most families belong to one of the various Methodist churches (e.g., Free Wesleyan Church, Church of Tonga Hou'eiki, Free Church of Tonga, or Tokai Kolo), to the Catholics, or to the Mormons. Their annual fund-raising takes place at different times of the year: the *kātoanga 'ofa* of the Catholics and the *misinale* of both Churches of Tonga in August, the contributions of Tokai Kolo in October, and the *misinale* of the Free Wesleyan Church in November. During these annual fund-raising campaigns people are 'asked' – and of course feel obliged – to contribute huge amounts of money. Ranging absolutely between T$ 400 and 600 (approximately US$ 300 to 450) per family, they exceed by far the monthly salary of a school teacher (who is the only person earning money at all on a regular basis). As one of my key informants described it:

> Every three months, we have the quarterly collection. We come together, bring some food there and pay. Once a year, the *misinale* takes place. Last week, for example, we had the *misinale* of my church [Free Church of Tonga]. We were supposed to collect about 7,000 Tongan dollars. Within my church, we are only eight families, and we were supposed to collect about 7,000, all last week. My father gave 500, and I added 300, so my family was close to 800. There is still another church donation, when we have a conference. Every three years, the church conference takes place in Ha'apai, that's when we have to spend a lot of money on it, supplying food and gifts.

The only church with a differing, namely *relative,* system are the Mormons. They ask their members only to pay the tithe of their cash income. This fund-raising system and the highly regarded school education they provide is increasingly attracting adherents.

Apart from these seasonal requirements, a fisherman's social net also has a regularly strong impact on his strategies. Many economic decisions in a Tongan household are influenced or even determined by higher ranking relatives. According to the *fahu*-system, sisters are higher in rank than their brothers, and older ones higher than younger ones. Whereas a man is always the head of his nuclear family, his (or his father's) sister and her family are superior to him. This higher rank gives them the right to demand services and material support. Similar obligations *(fatongia)* exist towards the *hou'eiki* and *matāpule* (the chiefs and their representatives or 'talking chiefs'), some of whom still strictly demand these, and nowadays even towards church ministers who hold comparable high positions. Such obligations often require huge amounts of seafood and especially of prestigious seafood like turtle, lobster or giant clams, most of which are now considered by the Ministry of Fisheries to be threatened.

While *rank* is ascribed with birth and defined in relation to one's relatives, *status* can be acquired in various ways, particularly through an advantageous manipulation of social relationships and reputation, through prestigious activities and through economic success combined with generosity. Although all kinds of aspiration to status are competitive, only strictly formalised modes of rivalry are accepted (Marcus 1978). Aggressive interactions and even negative emotions, particularly anger *('ita)* and envy *(meheka),* are sanctioned by the code of cultural values and norms that is grounded in the central concept of *'ofa*. *'Ofa* glosses as 'concern, kindness, care, help, generosity, and love' (Morton 1996: 80) and characterises the ideal emotional relationship between people. Thereby, it enhances cooperation and is indispensably linked to sharing – having *'ofa* is the essential prerequisite for sharing, and sharing is the best way to show it (Kavaliku 1977: 64). The act of sharing is thus more important than the goods themselves, and no expectation of immediate return is connected to it, except in certain clearly defined situations such as funerals. Apart from these, no rules exist for whom to give to or in which order. But not to share at all (according to one's ability, of course) provokes social disapproval and gossip.

These principles are most pronounced in the context of food-sharing, particularly that of sharing fish, referred to as *fetokoni'aki* (Evans 2001; Halapua 1982; Morton 1996). Literally meaning 'cooperation' or 'helping each other', *fetokoni'aki* is the value behind the institution. Whereas in urban centres market concepts are slowly superseding traditional concepts of sharing, on most of the outer islands in Ha'apai it is still considered shameful to sell fish to one's neighbours. The degree to which commercial strategies are socially acceptable depends on the *'inasi,* the part of the catch that is considered necessary for individual needs (Halapua 1982; Perminow 1993). This estimate may vary between villages and depends on the range of the sharing institution (as will be addressed in more detail below). Therefore, despite the small corner shops in some villages, the bulk of products for sale (such as cash-crops, fish, or woven mats) have to be exported to the district centre Pangai or to the capital Nuku'alofa.

Summarising the incentives for resource exploitation set by cultural context, both types of institutions can be identified. Extracting institutions are the *fatongia* and all those opportunities that call for money: fish has to be given away during feasts, to higher-ranking relatives and to the chiefs, and it has to be sold for church fund-raising *(misinale)* and for paying school-fees. These requirements thus increase the pressure on the natural resources. At the same time, sharing institutions are at work as well in the form of *fetokoni'aki*: People accordingly share fish with relatives and neighbours, and with old, sick or otherwise needy members of their village. Even foreigners just accidentally passing by are offered fish.

Interacting with these institutions is the socially defined competition for status that may enhance sharing or extracting, depending on the village context. In the latter case, social competition may eventually lead to competition in resource exploitation, and hence to overexploitation.

Institutional Context: Between Open Access and the 'Fisheries Regulations'

Since the enactment of the constitution in 1875 and the Land Acts of 1882 and 1927, all Tongans have free access to all marine resources in Tongan waters. According to the commons theory, this legal situation lays the foundation for an increasing potential for conflict between the users over their limited resources. And meanwhile, various reports of the Ministry of Fisheries indicate a growth in competition for fishing grounds between villages and suggest an increasing potential for resource-based conflicts (e.g., Gillett 1994; TFSR 1998).

Most fishermen interviewed in Ha'apai, however, seem to accept this kind of access regulation, and some even consider it a valuable achievement of Tongan culture:

> You already know what I will say: I do not believe that it [the fishing grounds] should belong to anybody. I think that God has given all these pieces of sea to anybody. And he allowed anybody free access to them. (Subsistence fisherman from Lofanga/Hihifo, 66 years old)
>
> [I am not angry] because it is the law of the first King of Tonga [George Tāufa'āhau Tupou I], back in the last century. It is a good thing, making all the people free, all the Tongan men living here. If we stay in 'Uiha and like to go fishing in Niua or in Vava'u [island groups north of Ha'apai], we will just go there. Nobody can stop me from going to any place in Tonga. (Commercial fisherman from 'Uiha, 42 years old)

These are no exceptions: while close to two thirds of eighty-two interviewed fishermen (63 percent) perceive their traditional fishing grounds as a kind of 'territory', only a proportion of these (35 percent) express the wish to exclude fishermen from neighbouring villages, and even fewer (22 percent) show anger about the current situation. When asked whether he thinks that 'their' fishing grounds should belong exclusively to the people of his village, the town officer of 'Uiha answered:

> No, because we do not have the law. If we had the law I might believe that this place is only for 'Uiha fishermen. But we do not have such a law. All the men in Ha'apai can go there ... I am not angry about it because we don't have such a law. If we had the law, I would be supposed to be angry because then, they were against the law.

An attempt was made by the Ministry of Fisheries in 1994 to compensate for this conceived lack of management with the 'Fisheries Regulations'. These regulations prescribe minimum sizes and closed seasons for various species, such as mullet (*Mugilidae*), turtle (particularly *Dermochelys coriacea*), lobster (*Panulirus sp., Parribacus sp.*), sea cucumber (*Holothuroidea*), and several molluscs such as the winged pearl oyster (*Pteria penquin*), triton (*Charonia tritonis*) or giant clam (*Tridacna sp.*). Additionally they prohibit such destructive fishing techniques as dynamiting or poisoning, and restrict highly efficient techniques as fish fences or scuba diving. Apart from compliance with these regulations, no signs of conservation measures could be found in the villages. Whether some of the traditional taboos were aiming to protect the most prestigious species is not clear (see e.g. Pulu 1981), however, since the time of Christianisation those taboos have fallen into decay.

Even the Fisheries Regulations themselves are not fully known among villagers. According to the fishermen and their town officers, they try at least to comply to the regulations they know, except that sometimes they accidentally violate the minimum sizes for lobsters. If they speak of illegal techniques, such as using poison or nets with undersized meshes, they accuse foreign fishermen of violation. Fulfilling the traditional *fatongia,* however, has a higher priority than the regulations – having no lobster to offer during a *misinale* or church conference is worse than having caught the wrong lobster. And many answers given in interviews indicate that a majority of fishermen do not consider such regulations necessary at all (Bender, 2001b); they are convinced, rather, that there has always been fish and always will be fish:

> There are plenty of fish out there. And you know why? God made them. We believe in God. He gives us enough to eat. He makes the fish, he makes lots of them. He gives it to us – let's eat it! (Subsistence fisherman from Pangai, 45 years old)

Monitoring of compliance with the regulations is difficult and enforcement weak due to the personal and financial limitations of the Ministry of Fisheries. This is why changes of access to the fishing grounds and the introduction of community-based resource management are now taken into consideration within the Ministry of Fisheries (Petelo, Matoto and Gillett 1995).

The Villages in Comparison: Lofanga and 'Uiha

Lofanga and 'Uiha, the two island villages that were studied during the fieldwork, belong to the northern part of the Ha'apai-Group. They are very similar to each other with regard to (a basic) infrastructure, population density (declining by about 20 percent during the last ten years) and most cultural aspects. The men work as fishermen and in their bush gardens, women engage in household activities, reef gleaning, mat weaving and other handicrafts. Differences between the villages are mainly restricted to their political structure, which is connected to the extracting institution of *fatongia,* and to the intensity and organisation of fishing (as will be detailed out in the next section).

The first island, Lofanga, with an area of about 1.4 km^2 is the estate of Crown Prince Tupouto'a and inhabited by 250 persons living in forty-four households. Forty-one men working part time as fishermen and in their bush gardens were interviewed. One earned a salary as teacher at the local primary school, and nearly all of them were heads of their respective households. Most of these fishermen belong to the Wesleyan Church (71 percent), some to the Free Church of Tonga (17 percent) and a few to the Mormon Church (12 percent). The estate holder Tupouto'a, then still Minister of Foreign Affairs and Defence, was living far away in the capital and did not interfere with his people's affairs and economic decisions. During the period of the field-research, the elected town-officer was absent as well for fund-raising in New Zealand. The only higher ranking persons were an *'eiki* (chief) and a *matāpule* (talking chief), both of whom, however, were comparable to the commoners on economic grounds.

In 'Uiha, one of two villages on the neighbouring island of the same name, approximately 515 people live in ninety-five households on the 3.2 km^2 estate of the Honourable Malupō. Again, forty-one men were interviewed, most of whom worked part time as fishermen and in their bush gardens; only a few were said to neglect the planting altogether. Nearly all of them were also heads of their households. One man earned a salary as town officer, two others as local ministers of their respective church. Among these, the Wesleyan Church is the biggest (with 32 percent); the second biggest group is that of the Mormons (20 percent); the remaining fishermen are fairly equally spread between other Methodist and Catholic churches (10 – 15 percent each). Although Malupō also resides in Nuku'alofa, he occasionally visits his village on 'Uiha, where about a dozen local *matāpule* represent him during the rest of the year. One of these talking chiefs is also town officer and was very active in organising communal activities in 1998. The *matāpule* among the interviewed fishermen did not differ considerably with regard to economic aspects from the commoners.

Catching and Sharing Fish: Indirect Regulations of Resource Exploitation

For most inhabitants of the outer islands of Ha'apai, fishing is essential. It is indispensable for their subsistence, enables them to fulfill their social obligations, and is in many cases their main source of cash income. Most prominent among the social obligations are the *fatongia,* tributes of highly esteemed seafood to higher ranking relatives and chiefs, and the annual fund-raising that forces people to sell fish. Contrary to this extracting institutions, the *fetokoni'aki* requires (indiscriminately) sharing food, particularly fish. The comparison of fishing strategies and food-sharing in Lofanga and 'Uiha will elucidate the interactions between them and help analyse their respective consequences.

Strategies of Exploitation in Both Villages: Subsistence versus Surplus

Principally, Lofanga and 'Uiha have many conditions in common. Fishermen from both villages have similar equipment and the same alternatives (or rather lack of alternatives) for income generation (apart from commercial fishing). The men from 'Uiha have similar access to land for planting as those in Lofanga. Thus, both could satisfy their needs with subsistence farming and fishing. With respect to the extracting institutions of yields distribution, families from both villages are seasonally required to obtain cash in order to fulfil similar *fatongia* which are meanwhile considered by some as a burden *(kavenga):*

> We have too many *kavenga,* and we have them very often. First of all, we have a noble who likes all of us in the village to help him. In addition, there is the government. Then comes the church fund-raising, and after fulfilling their obligations, we have to pay the school fees for the children. (Commercial fisherman from 'Uiha, 42 years old)

Apart from a few exceptions, fish cannot be sold locally, though, as a fisherman from Lofanga explains:

> Myself, I get embarrassed selling in Lofanga. I want to go to Pangai, and just sell it there; but in Lofanga – there are my relatives, all the people of the island are my family and relatives. I [would] feel shamed. (Subsistence fisherman from Lofanga, 65 years old)

Basically, the fishermen from both villages have the same opportunity to market fish, namely to the district centre Pangai or to the capital Nuku'alofa (see Kronen and Bender, in press), though they do not practice it to the same extent. On the contrary, a significantly higher number of fishermen in 'Uiha than in Lofanga have adopted rather commercial strategies. For the purpose of further analysis, fishermen will be categorised as more subsistence oriented versus rather commercial, mainly on the basis of three features: on the relation of the total amount of fish caught to the amount needed for consumption, on their time spent on fishing (in days per week) and on emic criteria, i.e., their categorisation by other fishermen as 'big fisher' (all figures on which this calculation is based were provided by the fishermen themselves):

- If the ratio of *total catch* to *amount for consumption* is lower than 2, *fishing days per week* less than 3, and if the person is *not* termed a 'big fisher' by other fishermen, then he will be categorised as subsistence fisherman ***(s)***.
- If the ratio of *total catch* to *amount for consumption* is higher than 10, *fishing days per week* more than 4, and if the person is termed a 'big fisher' by at least two other fishermen, then he will be categorised as commercial fisherman ***(c)***.
- Persons ranging in-between *(total catch / amount for consumption* 2–10, *fishing days per week* 3–4) are categorised as occasional or semi-commercial fishermen ***(sc)***.

According to this categorisation, only six of the forty-one fishermen interviewed in Lofanga can be considered as commercially oriented; they spend considerably more time on and in the water than their neighbours, they aim at larger catches and sell quite regularly on a weekly base. On the other hand, nine men stated to

Table 7.1. Example of a person's categorisation as subsistence fisher (Lofanga).

The person	***Ikaleka*** [name is changed]	
• age	41 years	
• church denomination	Free Wesleyan Church	
education	6 years General Primary School + 4 years College	
His household		
• members in household	10 persons: mother and sister, brother (also subsistence fisher) with wife and five children	
• amount of bush allotments	3 (with 1.2 ha altogether)	
• income	selling vanilla, copra and fish, sometimes remittances from relatives living overseas	
Fishing		
• techniques	*taumata'u* (hand-lining) and *uku* (diving)	
• total catch	enough for the family (i.e., 10 kg/week)	
• amount for consumption	10 kg/week	
• fishing days per week	once a week (more often only if a feast is coming; returns when it is enough for the family)	
• attribution as 'big fisher'	by nobody	
Categorisation	total catch / amount for consumption:	1 (= s)
	fishing days per week:	1 (= s)
	attribution a 'big fisher':	0 (= s)

be content with catching what they need for consumption in their households (for an example see table 7.1), while the majority of twenty-six fishermen intensify their efforts occasionally, particularly when church offerings or school fees are due. All of them work independently and come together for joint operations on a spontaneous basis. The most popular techniques here are handlining *(taumata'u)*, fishing with a net *(kupenga)*, diving *(uku)*, and octopus-luring *(makafeke)*.

In 'Uiha, about half of the fishermen interviewed also fish rather on a subsistence basis or sell fish occasionally. They are similar to those in Lofanga with regard to organisation and preferred techniques. The other half, however, are commercial fishermen (e,g., see table 7.2) who spend most of their time fishing,

Table 7.2. Example of a person's categorisation as commercial fisher ('Uiha).

The person	***Vakalahi*** [name is changed]
• age	28 years
• church denomination	Mormon
• education	6 years General Primary School + 5 years College
His household	
• members in household	6 persons: sister, wife and three children
• amount of bush allotments	4 (with 1.62 ha altogether) belongig to his father
• income	selling fish, bananas and woven mats, remittances from relatives living overseas
Fishing	
• techniques	*uku* (diving)
• total catch	135 kg/week (60 kg fish, 30 kg shellfish, 45 kg lobster)
• amount for consumption	25 kg/week
• fishing days per week	daily (Monday to Friday, sometimes even Saturday; returns on Wednesday or Friday, depending on the boat captain)
• attribution as 'big fisher'	by 2 other fishermen
Categorisation	total catch / amount for consumption: 5.4 (= c)
	fishing days per week: 5 (= c)
	attribution as 'big fisher': 2 (= c)

particularly diving *(uku)*. Instead of just a few hours twice or three times a week, they go out fishing for nearly the whole week. To be able to sell an amount of fish many times higher than the others, they have organised fairly stable 'fishing clubs'. Here, they gather around middlemen who provide them with technical support and some of the equipment they need, such as boats and ice. In return, the club members sell their catch to the middlemen who offer to market the yields.

Consequently, from working longer and harder, 'Uiha fishermen meanwhile exploit their resources to a higher degree than their neighbours and expand their activities into the traditional fishing grounds of Lofanga (Map 7.2). The degree of competition in 'Uiha, and above all between single fishing clubs, has grown as well, and is much higher now than it is in Lofanga (for more details see Bender 2001a).

But why do Lofangan fishermen not take up the strategies of their economically successful neighbours? Focusing on social aspects of village life brings out major differences between the two villages in the position of commercial fishermen within the community structure and their different responses to the institution of food-sharing.

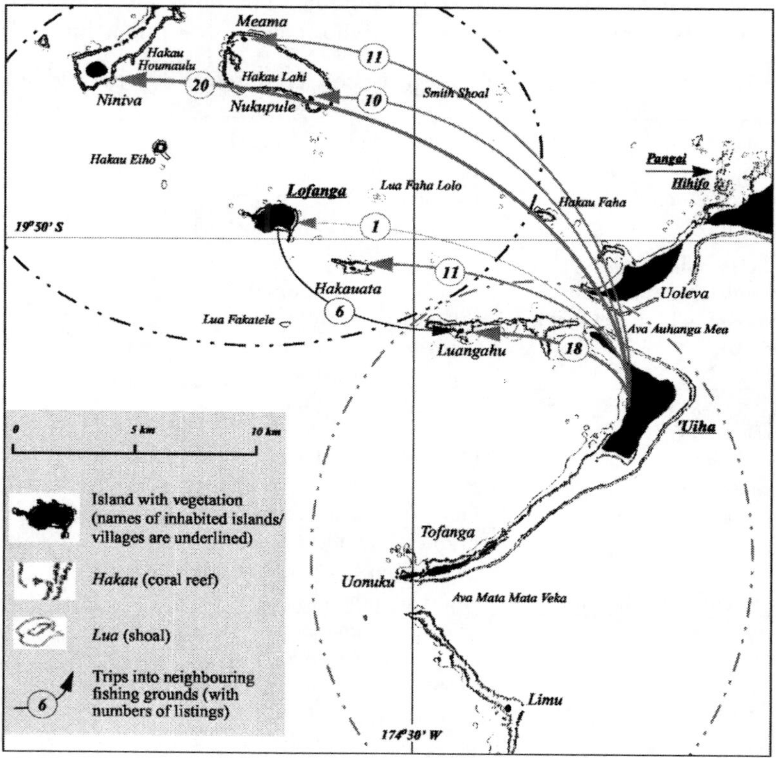

Map 7.2. Potential for territorial conflicts in the traditional fishing grounds of Lofanga and 'Uiha. Arrows in respective colours (black for Lofanga, grey for 'Uiha) mark trips into neighbouring fishing grounds.

Successful Fishermen in Lofanga and 'Uiha: Knots versus Holes in the Social Net

In Lofanga, fishing can still be characterised as rather traditional. The six men identified as commercial fishermen hold special positions within the community

– as chief, as members of the Mormon church or as newcomers – whereas other high ranking persons are absent.

In 'Uiha, on the contrary, the hierarchical structure within the village seems to be more pronounced. The town officer and the estate holder are present and encourage the inhabitants to enhance their efforts for the *fatongia.* Fishing has acquired features of a full-time profession beyond subsistence that everybody can take up, and that has even attracted people from other parts of the kingdom to come to the island. One third of the fishermen living in 'Uiha, most of them 'average' members of their community, are engaged in commercial diving for fish (*uku*). They are organised in fishing clubs with a steadier structure than the rather spontaneous teams in Lofanga. Attempts to establish similar fishing-clubs in Lofanga were only short-lived. Two men, both rather young and not particularly highly respected, started a business like the one in 'Uiha, in July and August 1998. From the beginning, they attracted only a few people who occasionally went out with them and sold them fish irregularly. Nobody rejected the idea explicitly, but after a while the enterprise quietly vanished. One of the middlemen argued that he had given up due to a lack of time, while the other has reduced the fishing-club business to the more customary fishing, together with others, while sharing the expenses. The statements of other fishermen, however, indicate low acceptance of fishing-clubs and a reluctance to participate in commercial fishing altogether.

At the same time, competition between fishermen in Lofanga has a strong social character: They try to improve their status in relation to their fellow fishermen rather than to attain economic advantage – catching a bit more than one's neighbour is thus an often declared goal, not the marketing of a bigger catch. In 'Uiha, on the contrary, the men not only fish longer and more intensively, but to an extent where they even neglect their farming and partly their social obligations, particularly concerning food-sharing. Here, the social character of competition has gradually changed into economic competition.

All these differences between Lofanga and 'Uiha are closely linked to the respective range of the food-sharing institution. While in Lofanga, the informal insurance system set up by this institution is still strong and complied with by nearly all members of the village community, this does not apply in 'Uiha to the same extent. All the more successful (as well as more conspicuous) fishermen in Lofanga share out of their catch considerably more often than average. Their relatives receive portions of the yields as well as neighbours, ministers and particularly old or otherwise weak people. The successful fishermen in 'Uiha share significantly less than those in Lofanga: just half of them (twelve out of twenty-one) were mentioned by the interviewed fishermen as givers of fish, and actually only two gave fish to people outside their immediate personal net, that is, to people other than close relatives or club fellows. Only occasionally would a person in 'Uiha ask a commercial fisherman for fish as a gift if he was not somehow obliged to him anyway. Instead, people would rather pay for fish they receive from them. The 'responsibility' to provide others with fish has partly been taken over by the semi-commercial fishermen: twice as many of those were asked by their village members in 'Uiha (64 percent) than in Lofanga (39 percent).

What economics (e.g. Fafchamps 1992; see above) identified as one of the biggest threats to an informal insurance system – the establishing of coalitions – has thus already happened in 'Uiha. The economically successful commercial fishermen have partly retreated from the solidarity network, forming a coalition of their own in the form of their fishing clubs. With their partial retreat, however, the commercial fishermen render the general insurance system much weaker. As a consequence, the rest of the village members are less secure, particularly if they cannot enhance their own efforts.

Sharing Food as a Regulatiory Mechanism

These results highlight three consequences of stable solidarity networks on the security of subsistence within a local user-group, two of which have already been discussed in the literature (e.g. Fafchamps 1992; Gould 1982; Platteau 1991; Spittler 1989; Thomas and Worrall 1994); the third was addressed only recently (Bender 2001a, 2007; Bender et al. 2002):

(1) Sharing contributes to *social* stability because it is based on cultural values of mutual concern and respect and helps strengthen cooperative behaviour.

(2) Apart from this, the redistribution of essential resources enhances *economic* stability as well since goods are shared – though not evenly – to an extent that secures subsistence for everybody.

(3) And finally, the sharing institution supports *ecological* stability through restraining incentives for efforts and gain-maximising strategies, thus fostering a more sustainable resource use.

An indicator for the restraining effect of the insurance system (*fetokoni'aki*) on resource exploitation is the higher degree of a moral hazard (lack of effort) in Lofanga compared to 'Uiha: among the forty-one interviewed fishermen in each village, seventeen men were listed by their colleagues in Lofanga as being lazy and relying on others too much, but only eight men in 'Uiha. More Lofangans thus seem to trust on the *fetokoni'aki* enough to be sure that they will get fish even if they do not make a significant effort to avoid shortfalls. This correspondence between insurance stability and intensity of resource exploitation corroborates the hypothesis that a stable insurance system will reduce incentives for commercial strategies and thus overexploitation along two dimensions. Since people always have to share out a considerable portion of their catch they may not feel motivated, and since they can get by anyway they do not have to make extensive efforts, either (cf. Bender et al. 2002).

Although very efficient, this indirect regulation of resource exploitation through the *fetokoni'aki* nevertheless comprises a specific risk. Management rules have to be flexible in order to be adaptive. Users must be aware of their regulatory function should it be necessary to compensate for declining institutions. Otherwise, alternatives might not be available in time, as in the 'Uihan case where the *fetokoni'aki* is weakening. Other risks such as population growth or technological innovations are less important in this case. Although the *fetokoni'aki* would cease to be efficient if its members increased in number, since then the exploitation would also have to be increased, this is obviously not happening in Ha'apai. Instead, the number of inhabitants is declining, and the people leaving even stabilise the situation through remittances that take pressure off local resources. In addition, there is every reason to believe that in tight networks, particularly in the Pacific, better technologies are not used to increase production, but to decrease the efforts (e.g. van der Grijp 1993; Halapua 1982). An increasing commercialisation, however, appears to weaken the insurance stability and change the traditionally social competition towards an economic one (cf. Bender 2007).

The question of why both villages have developed so differently cannot be answered with certitude, since the process started about thirty years ago. However, it can be assumed that while in Lofanga the sharing institution (in form of the *fetokoni'aki*) outweighed the extracting institution (in form of the *fatongia*), this relation became inverted in 'Uiha. The fulfilling of *fatongia* or *kavenga,* as one informant explained, is the main source of pride and prestige for a community. And for a long period of time, the people of 'Uiha seem to have had considerably more *kavenga* than those from Lofanga. The late estate holder of 'Uiha, Honourable Malupō, is said to have been an ambitious man. His position close to the Tongan king was connected to considerable requirements for support which he extended on his people. Typical occasions for such *fatongia* are, for instance, the king's birthday or a noble's funeral:

> This is the highest *kavenga* for the noble, to prepare for the King's birthday, every year. Because the King is the leader of the nobles. So, that's why every year we are supposed to have something to take to the celebration of the King's birthday … If another noble dies, or if a new noble is coming, we are supposed to prepare as well – to go there. An example: If the noble in Pangai died, the noble of 'Uiha would go out to the funeral of the noble in Pangai. So, we were supposed to talk to the people to collect everything, then we would go to the funeral of the noble in Pangai. (Town officer from 'Uiha, August 1998)

Since the 'Uiha people were thus forced to produce fish as well as crops or mats for contributing and giving away, the extracting institutions were outweighing the sharing institutions. In such a context, the establishment of fishing clubs was welcomed as an opportunity to enhance production and was driven further by social competition between fishermen for better results. With these changes came along the decline of the *fetokoni'aki*, the sharing institution.

Summary and Conclusion: Implications for Community-Based Management

The central place in the fishermen's daily life, as has been shown above, is held by their social net with its different functions of providing and requiring services and goods, as a factor influencing decisions, as an arena for status rivalry and as an instrument for monitoring and control of the compliance to cultural norms. Related to this are two types of institutions, the extracting institution *fatongia* and the sharing institution *fetokoni'aki*. By granting the means of livelihood to everybody through food-sharing, the *fetokoni'aki* constitutes an informal insurance system that enhances cooperation and responds to the uncertainty of economic success. The *fatongia*, on the contrary, enhances social competition for status and exerts economic pressure on the people – to such a degree that it is meanwhile perceived by many as a burden (*kavenga*) – as well as ecological pressure on the natural resources.

The comparison of the villages of Lofanga and 'Uiha clearly show differences in the proportion of both types of institution. In Lofanga, the *fetokoni'aki* is outweighing the *fatongia* while in 'Uiha the situation is reversed. These differences are reflected in differences in the social structure and the respective strategies of exploitation. The tightly meshed social net in Lofanga corresponds to higher trust in insurance security and to lower exploitation. The successful and commercially oriented fishermen hold conspicuous positions within the village and are integrated in the net as main givers of fish. In contrast, the social net in 'Uiha is rather fragmented after the partial retreat of the commercial club fishermen from the insurance system. These share fish to a considerably lesser extent and nearly exclusively with close relatives or club fellows. In the process, they exploit their fish stocks to a higher degree than the fishermen of Lofanga and have expanded their activities to the fishing grounds of neighbouring villages.

These results support the main hypothesis that food-sharing institutions maintain the security of subsistence within the user-group through enhancing social and economic stability. Additionally, they help to stabilise resource exploitation. In reducing incentives to over-harvest, the sharing institution has even proved to be more influential than any direct attempt to regulate fishing. However, it is threatened by changes in the social structure of the villages. As the example of 'Uiha demonstrates, a decline in the sharing institution may result in increasing resource exploitation as well – probably to an extent where the stocks become threatened. The severest problem with indirect regulations such as the food-sharing institution is that people may not be aware of their ecological function, and that alternatives for regulation may not be conceived as necessary (cf. Bender 2001c; Nerb et al., this volume).

The newly proposed implementation of community-based management in Tonga therefore holds risks as well as opportunities. While community-based management is perfectly compatible with the principle of sharing vital resources, this is also valid for sharing fishing grounds, thus impeding the idea of an exclusion of foreign fishermen. Furthermore, resource management has no strong tradition and will not simply 'happen' just because it becomes community-based (Bender 2007). For many fishermen, management means 'to manage how to catch the big fish'. And finally, without lowered *fatongia,* the people will even *have to* carry on selling fish and procuring money in order to fulfil their *kavenga.*

Acknowledgments

A former version of this chapter was presented at the VIII Biennial Conference of the International Association for the Study of Common Property (IASCP) in Bloomington, June 2000. The work on which it is based was funded by the German Research Foundation (DFG) through an interdisciplinary project (Er 267/1-x) within the Priority Programme *Global Environmental Change – Social and Behavioural Dimensions.* Additional support was provided by the Freiburg Institute of Paleoscientific Studies. I am grateful to the fishermen in Ha'apai, to Sione Faka'osi, Mick Hortle and their respective families who made this study possible, to 'Ofa Fakahau, Sitiveni Halapua, Patricia Kailola, and Randy Thaman for helpful comments, and to my colleagues Sieghard Beller, Renate Eisentraut, Andreas M. Ernst, Wolfram Kägi, Ernst Mohr, Stefan Seitz and Hans Spada for encouraging discussions along the way. Josef Nerb and Katja Lay helped to improve the manuscript with critical comments.

References

Anderson, Eugene N. 1994. 'Fish as Gods and Kin', in *Folk Management in the World's Fisheries,* eds. C.L. Dyer and J.R. McGoodwin, 139–60. Niwot: University Press of Colorado.

Bataille-Benguigui, Marie-Claire 1988. 'The Fish of Tonga: Prey or Social Partners?', *Journal of the Polynesian Society* 97(2): 185–98.

Bender, Andrea 2001a. *Fischer im Netz: Strategien der Ressourcennutzung und Konfliktbewältigung in Ha'apai, Tonga* (*Fisher in the Net: Strategies of Resource Use and Conflict Management in Ha'apai, Tonga*). Herbolzheim: Centaurus.

——— 2001b. '"God Will Send Us the Fish" – Perception and Evaluation of an Environmental Risk in Ha'apai, Tonga', *Research in Social Problems and Public Policy* 9: 165–90.

——— 2001c. 'Die "Tabu-Falle": Über die Ambivalenz religiös motivierter Verhaltensregeln zum Artenschutz' ('The "Taboo Trap": Considerations on the Ambivalence of Religiously Motivated Behavioural Guidelines for Species Protection'), in *Studien in memoriam Wilhelm Schüle,* eds. D. Büchner and F.I.P.S., 27–39. Rahden: Verlag Marie Leidorf.

——— 2007. 'Changes in Social Orientation: Threats to a Cultural Institution in Marine Resource Exploitation in Tonga', *Human Organization* 66(1): 11–21.

———,Wolfram Kägi and Ernst Mohr 2002. 'Informal Insurance and Sustainable Management of Common Pool Marine Resources in Ha'apai, Tonga', *Economic Development and Cultural Change* 50(2): 427–39.

Berkes, Fikret 1985. 'Fishermen and the Tragedy of the Commons', *Environmental Conservation* 12(3): 199–206.

——— 1994. 'Property Rights and Coastal Fisheries', in *Community Management and Common Property of Coastal Fisheries in Asia and the Pacific: Concepts, Methods and Experiences*, ed. R.S. Pomeroy, 51–62. Manila: ICLARM (International Center for Living Aquatic Resource Management) Conference Proceedings 45.

Blewett, Robert A. 1995. 'Property Rights as a Cause of the Tragedy of the Commons: Institutional Change and the Pastoral Maasai of Kenya', *Eastern Economic Journal* 21(4): 477–90.

Campbell, Harry F., Ken M. Menz and Geoffrey Waugh, eds. 1989. *Economics of Fishery Management in the Pacific Islands Region.* Canberra: The Australian Center for International Agricultural Research.

Carew-Reid, Jeremy 1990. 'Conservation and Protected Areas on South-Pacific Islands: The Importance of Tradition', *Environmental Conservation* 17(1): 29–38.

Casimir, Michael J. and Aparna Rao 1998. 'Sustainable Herd Management and the Tragedy of No Mans Land: An Analysis of West Himalayan Pastures Using Remote Sensing Techniques', *Human Ecology* 26(1): 113–34.

Christy, Francis T. Jr. 1982. *Territorial Use Rights in Marine Fisheries: Definitions and Conditions.* Rome: FAO Fisheries Technical Paper 227.

Coate, Stephen and Martin Ravallion 1993. 'Reciprocity Without Commitment: Characterization and Performance of Informal Insurance Arrangements', *Journal of Development Economics* 40: 1–24.

Cordell, John C. and Margaret A. McKean 1992. 'Sea Tenure in Bahia, Brazil', in *Making the Commons Work*, ed. D.W. Bromley, 183–205. San Francisco: Institute of Contemporary Studies Press.

Dyer, Christopher L. and James R. McGoodwin, eds. 1994. *Folk Management in the World's Fisheries: Lessons for Modern Fisheries Management.* Niwot: University Press of Colorado.

Evans, Mike 2001. *Persistence of the Gift: Tongan Tradition in Transnational Context.* Waterloo: Wilfrid Laurier University Press.

Fafchamps, Marcel 1992. 'Solidarity Networks in Preindustrial Societies: Rational Peasants With a Moral Economy', *Economic Development and Cultural Change* 41: 147–74.

Feeny, David 1994. 'Frameworks for Understanding Resource Management on the Commons', in *Community Management and Common Property of Coastal Fisheries in Asia and the Pacific*, ed. R. Pomeroy, 20–33. Manila: ICLARM (International Center for Living Aquatic Resource Management) Conference Proceedings 45.

———, Fikret Berkes; Bonnie J. McCay and James M. Acheson 1990. 'The Tragedy of the Commons: Twenty-Two Years Later', *Human Ecology* 18(1): 1–19.

Gillett, Robert D. 1994. *A Compilation of Various Reports by the FAO Fisheries Adviser to Tonga*, April 1993 to March 1994, Rome: FAO.

Gordon, H. Scott 1954. 'The Economic Theory of a Common Property Resource: The Fishery', *Journal of Political Economy* 62: 124–42.

Gould, Richard A. 1982. 'To Have and Have Not: The Ecology of Sharing Among Hunter-Gatherers', in *Resource Managers: North American and Australian Hunter-Gatherers*, eds. N. Williams and E. Hunn, 69–91. Boulder, CO: Westview Press.

Grijp, Paul van der 1993. *Islanders of the South: Production, Kinship and Ideology in the Polynesian Kingdom of Tonga.* Leiden: KITLV Press.

Halapua, Sitiveni 1982. *Fishermen of Tonga: Their Means of Survival.* Suva: Institute of Pacific Studies, USP.

Hardin, Garrett R. 1968. 'The Tragedy of the Commons', *Science* 162: 1243–48.

Harris, Marvin 1987. *Cultural Anthropology.* New York: Harper and Row.

Hviding, Edvard 1996. *Guardians of Marovo Lagoon: Practice, Place and Politics in Maritime Melanesia.* Honolulu: University of Hawaii Press.

——— and Graham B.K. Baines 1994. 'Community-Based Fisheries Management: Tradition and the Challenges of Development in Marovo, Solomon Islands', *Development and Change* 25: 13–39.

Johannes, Robert E. 1978. 'Traditional Marine Conservation Methods in Oceania and Their Demise', *Annual Review of Ecology and Systematics* 9: 349–64.

——— 1981. *Words of the Lagoon: Fishing and Marine Lore in the Palau district of Micronesia.* Berkeley: University of California Press.

——— and J.W. MacFarlane 1991. *Traditional Fishing in the Torres Strait Islands.* Canberra: Australian Department of Primary Industries and Energy.

Kavaliku, S. Langi 1977. 'Ofa! The Treasure of Tonga', *Pacific Perspective* 6(2): 47–67.

Klee, Gary A. 1980. 'Oceania', in *World Systems of Traditional Resource Management,* ed. G.A. Klee. London: Arnold.

Kronen, Mecki and Andrea Bender, in press. 'Assessing Marine Resource Exploitation in Lofanga, Tonga: One Case Study – Two Approaches', *Human Ecology* 35 (2).

McCay, Bonnie J. and James M. Acheson, eds. 1987. *The Question of the Commons.* Tucson: University of Arizona Press.

McEvoy, Arthur F. 1986. *The Fisherman's Problem: Ecology and Law in the California Fisheries, 1850–1980.* Cambridge: Cambridge University Press.

Marcus, George E. 1978. 'Status Rivalry in a Polynesian Steady-State Society', *Ethos* 6(4): 242–69.

Morton, Helen 1996. *Becoming Tongan: An Ethnography of Childhood.* Honolulu: University of Hawai Press.

Ostrom, Elinor 1992. *Crafting Institutions for Self-Governing Irrigation Systems.* San Francisco: Contemporary Studies Press.

——— 1994. 'Institutional Analysis, Design Principles and Threats to Sustainable Community Governance and Management of Commons', in *Community Management and Common Property of Coastal Fisheries in Asia and the Pacific,* ed. R. Pomeroy, 34–50. Manila: ICLARM (International Center for Living Aquatic Resource Management) Conference Proceedings 45.

———, Roy Gardner and James Walker 1994. *Rules, Games, and Common-Pool Resources.* Ann Arbor: University of Michigan Press.

Perminow, Arne A. 1993. 'Between the Forest and the Big Lagoon: The Microeconomy of Kotu Island in the Kingdom of Tonga', *Pacific Viewpoint* 34(2): 179–92.

Petelo, Anitimoni; Sione Matoto and Robert Gillett 1995. 'The Case for Community-Based Fisheries Management in Tonga', paper presented at the SPC/FFA Inshore Fisheries Management Workshop, Noumea, June 1995.

Pinkerton, Evelyn W. 1994. 'Summary and Conclusions', in *Folk Management in the Worlds Fisheries,* eds. C.L. Dyer and J.R. McGoodwin, 317–37. Niwot: University Press of Colorado.

Platteau, Jean-Philippe 1991. 'Traditional Systems of Social Security and Hunger Insurance: Past Achievements and Modern Challenges', in *Social Security in Developing Countries*, eds. E. Ahmad, J. Drèze, J. Hills and A. Sen, 112–70. Oxford: Clarendon.

Pomeroy, Robert S. 1994. 'Introduction', in *Community Management and Common Property of Coastal Fisheries in Asia and the Pacific: Concepts, Methods and Experiences*, ed. R. Pomeroy, 1–11. Manila: ICLARM (International Center for Living Aquatic Resource Management) Conference Proceedings 45.

Pulu, Tupou L. 1981. *Ko e f?ngota faka-Tonga* (*Tongan Fishing*). Anchorage: National Bilingual Materials Development Center, University of Alaska.

Rappaport, Roy A. 1968. *Pigs for the Ancestors.* New Haven: Yale University Press.

Ruddle, Kenneth 1994. 'Changing the Focus of Coastal Fisheries Management', in *Community Management and Common Property of Coastal Fisheries in Asia and the Pacific*, ed. R.S. Pomeroy, 63–86. Manila: ICLARM (International Center for Living Aquatic Resource Management) Conference Proceedings 45.

——— and Tomoya Akimichi, eds. 1984. *Maritime Institutions in the Western Pacific.* Osaka: National Museum of Ethnology, Senri Ethnological Studies 17.

———, Edvard Hviding and Robert E. Johannes 1992. 'Marine Resources Management in the Context of Customary Tenure', *Marine Resource Economics* 7: 249–73.

Ruddle, Kenneth and Robert E. Johannes, eds. 1990. *Traditional Marine Resource Management in the Pacific Basin: An Anthology.* Jakarta: UNESCO Regional Office for Science and Technology for Southeast Asia.

Scott, A. 1955. 'The Fishery: The Objective of Sole Ownership', *Journal of Political Economy* 63: 116–24.

South, G. Robin, Denis Goulet, Seremaia Tuqiri and Marguerite Church, eds. 1994. *Traditional Marine Tenure and Sustainable Management of Marine Resources in Asia and the Pacific.* Fiji: International Ocean Institute.

Spittler, Gerd 1989. *Dürren, Krieg und Hungerkrisen bei den Kel Ewey, 1900–1985.* Stuttgart: Steiner Verlag.

TFSR (Tonga Fisheries Sector Review) 1998. *Tonga Fisheries Sector Review*, vol. 1: *Main Report of the Consultants.* Bangkok: Food and Agriculture Organization of the United Nations, and Australian Agency for International Development.

Thomas, Jonathan P. and Tim Worrall 1994. *Informal Insurance Arrangements in Village Economies.* University of Warwick: Department of Economics.

Part II

Knowledge, Meaning and Discourse

8

Dangers, Experience and Luck: Living with Uncertainty in the Andes

Barbara Göbel

Introduction

Studies on risk in economic anthropology have concentrated on the question of how rural communities of the non-Western world ensure their subsistence in highly unpredictable environments. Two different approaches to the phenomenon of risk have been used: decision theory and moral economy. The models from decision theory, which in part are influenced by evolutionary ecology and cultural ecology, emphasise the adaptive advantages of individual strategies that take security aspects into account (see for example Barlett 1980; Browman 1987a; 1987b; Cashdan 1990; de Garine and Harrison 1988; Halstead and O'Shea 1989; Ortiz 1980). These strategies are often called 'minimax strategies', because securing the minimum required for subsistence plays a central role in their logic. In view of the uncertain conditions in which peasants have to live, it makes much more sense for them to aim at a minimisation of losses, rather than at a maximisation of production. The moral economy approach also stresses the importance of the 'safety-first principle' for peasant economies. But, contrary to decision theory, it focuses from a holistic standpoint on social institutions, such as reciprocity or redistribution, and their colonial and post-colonial erosion (e.g., Scott 1977; Watts 1988). The contribution of both approaches is that they have attracted attention to the complex problems connected with stochastically fluctuating ecological and socio-economic conditions and have elucidated structural features that buffer the impacts of the risks. Notwithstanding these achievements, risk studies in economic anthropology reveal an important shortcoming. They take neither indigenous conceptualisations of risk nor cultural meanings of coping strategies into account. And in spite of focusing on environmental risks, these studies do not consider local conceptualisations of nature. In my opinion, only such an extension of risk analysis would allow us to better understand how risk logics are produced and operate at the level of situated experience (see also Lupton 1999; Whyte 1999).

Coping with environmental risks is a matter of central importance in the lives of Andean pastoralists. Daily conversations in Huancar are centred around this topic. It also structures many activities in the pastoral context, and the identification, explanation and handling of environmental risks is subject to extensive cultural elaboration. This contradicts the picture of a harmonious and well-balanced relationship between humans and nature which is drawn in many studies of the indigenous Andean populations (e.g., Arnold and Yapita 1998; Bastien 1978; Gose 1994; Isbell 1985; Masuda et al. 1985; Urton 1981). On the contrary, for the inhabitants of the part of the Andes studied here, tensions, ruptures and instabilities are not exceptions in their relationship with the environment. Rather, they are the norm, which is not desired, but which has nevertheless to be accepted.

One central idea of the pastoralists in Huancar is that people have to move with their animals in an environment impregnated with dangers. They refer to the risks emanating from the environment as *peligros* (dangers) or *problemas* (problems)[1], which they define as unpredictable events which cannot be controlled at all or only partially, since it is not possible to foresee either the exact time of the disaster, nor its exact nature, nor yet its full extent[2]. They perceive these environmental risks as concrete phenomena, and not as abstract events, nor do they bring forth a vague existential angst. They not only refer to the shape of risks, but also to their tangible economic consequences. A risky event has a negative effect, which for the pastoralists becomes materially visible in the form of a concrete damage (*daño*): the herd animal suddenly loses weight, fat or wool, it starts to behave in an abnormal, unstable manner (e.g., it is either too passive or too active), it falls ill or dies. Related to this 'specificity' and 'visibility' of risks, the pastoralists emphasise that risks have an influence on decision-making processes. This means that risks are always consciously linked to actions; they trigger actions, as they have to be taken into account when deciding on what to do. In this connection, the handling of environmental risks in the Andean highlands is not perceived as an exceptional challenge, but as a matter of daily concern and effort[3].

Pastoralists in Huancar say that differences between households regarding the impacts of these environmental dangers depend mainly on two factors. First, whether a risky event concretely hits an household or not. If this is the case, then the basic productive and reproductive constitution of the household's herd matters; in other words, the impact of the risky event will vary depending on the ground on which it falls. In the local perception both factors – whether a household 'attracts' a risky event or not and the impact this will have - are decisively influenced by the degree of experience accumulated within a household and by its degree of luck (*suerte*). In order to explain what this means, the socio-economic structure of Huancar, indigenous conceptions of economic production and well-being, as well as the relations between humans and animals must be briefly introduced.

The Setting: The District of Huancar

Environmental Conditions

The District of Huancar is located in the *Puna de Atacama*, which is one of the most arid sectors of the Andean highlands (Troll 1968). The area is characterised by the prevalence of salt lakes, volcanoes and a scattered grass and shrub vegetation. Water resources are very scarce, for the one small river which traverses the district from south to north is polluted with salt and arsenic (see map 8.1).

The potential rainy season in this area extends only from December to March (see fig. 8.3). Average annual rainfall does not exceed 170.5 mm (mean for the years 1973 to 1997, standard deviation 92.43 mm), with a minimum of 23 mm and a maximum of 368 mm during the time span considered (Bianchi and Yánez 1992; Buitrago, pers. comm.). Precipitation can fluctuate enormously from one

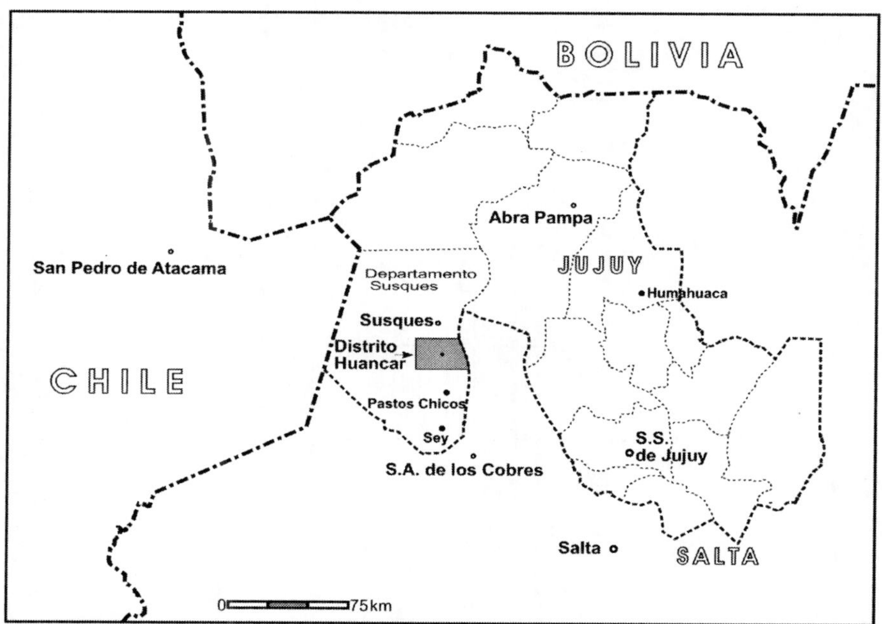

Map 8.1. Localisation of the district of Huancar in northwestern Argentina

year to the next[4]. In addition, rainfall is locally scattered; it can rain in one grazing area and not at all in a neighbouring one. Another peculiarity of this high mountainous region is the maximum daily temperatures, which can reach 40 °C. Frequent frost, hail and snowfall, as well as strong, dusty winds and lightning, are also characteristic climatic traits of the region (fig. 8.1).

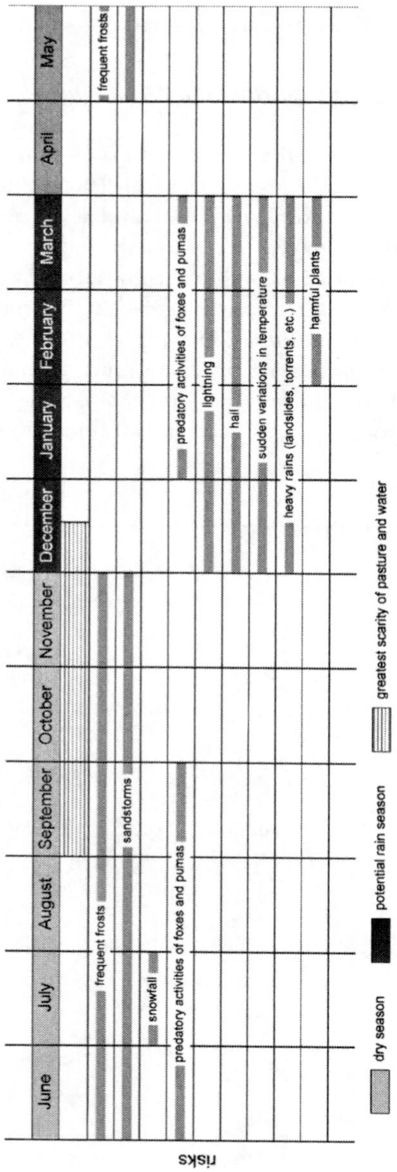

Figure 8.1. Risks of the annual production cycle

Social Structure

In Huancar the household – *familia* – is regarded as the basic unit of economic production, distribution and consumption, and the central arena of social reproduction. An average household consists of seven persons (spectrum one to nineteen persons). Half of these households include three generations: father and/or mother, their children and the daughters' children (figs. 8.2, 8.3). This is related to the fact that more than half the women with children (under 14 years) do not live with a permanent partner, but remain with their children in their natal families (fig. 8.3). As a result, there are many households with no adult men between 14 and 60 years, but only boys and/or old men (fig. 8.3). Between 1993 and 1999 this was the case for 31 percent of the households, which had women as heads of household (fig. 8.3). Matrifocal households without adult men, or only old men, do not necessarily have a lower social status, nor are they in a worse position economically (Göbel 1998b)[5]. Various arrangements exist through which they can hire male labour, and cooperative networks between households are of great relevance for such work arrangements.

The social network of a household includes mainly ritual kinsmen[6] as well as more distant relatives who live further away. Close relatives (e.g., siblings) whose homesteads are in the immediate neighbourhood (map 8.2)[7] are included much less in such arrangements, because, it is said, they often develop harmful feelings of envy. Since they live so close by, they are likely to be much better informed about the activities of the household and its economic success. From the pastoralists' perspective it therefore seems advisable to set social distance against spatial proximity.

The Pastoral Economy

For the majority of the people in Huancar animal husbandry is of great economic importance. Herds are composed of llamas, sheep and goats. The totality of these animals are called *hacienda*. The average herd size is 136 animals (median of herd census 1986–1999), but there is some considerable variation between households here. While four households have 300 or more animals (households 43, 42, 17, 16), the flocks of two other families consist of only about fifty animals (households 26, 9), which is considered to be the minimum for the subsistence of two persons (map 8.2). Beyond that, the herd size of each household can fluctuate enormously from one year to the next.

All herd animals are owned individually, and hence to each animal a human person is ascribed, this 'owner' being called *dueño* or *dueña*. His or her 'ownership' is however restricted: the final decision on whether an animal is sheared, castrated or slaughtered is not taken by him or her, but by the household chief herdswoman, who is regarded socially as responsible for the whole herd and has

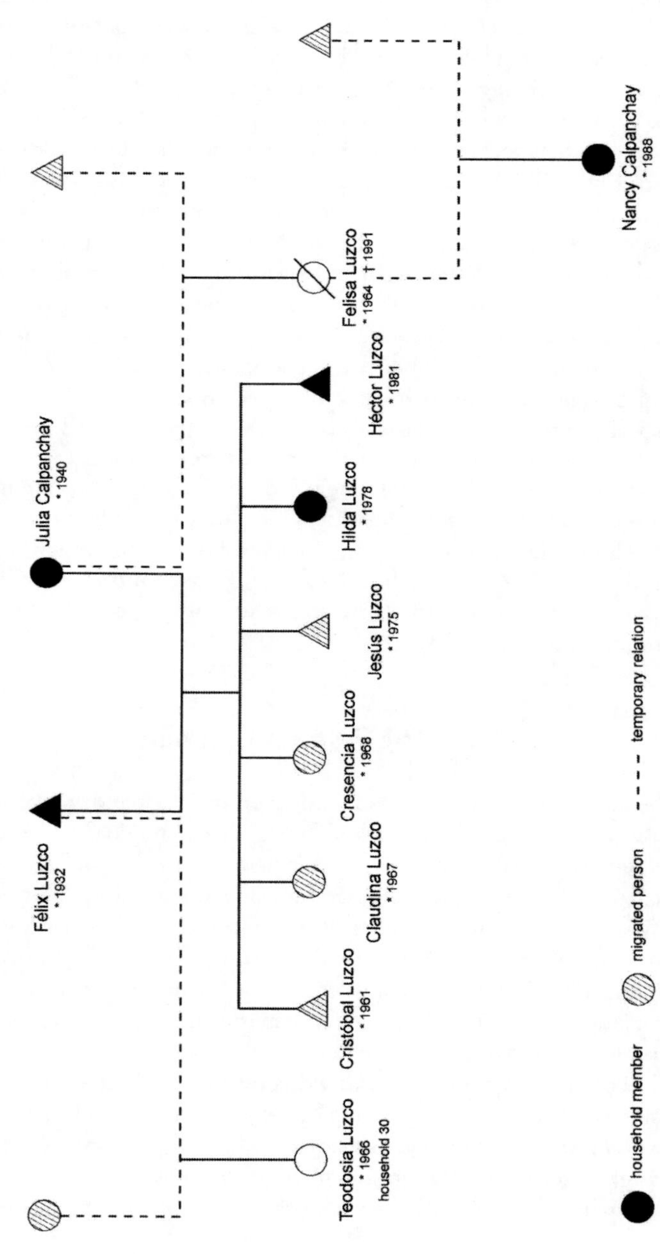

Figure 8.2. Composition of a patrifocal household (household 36)

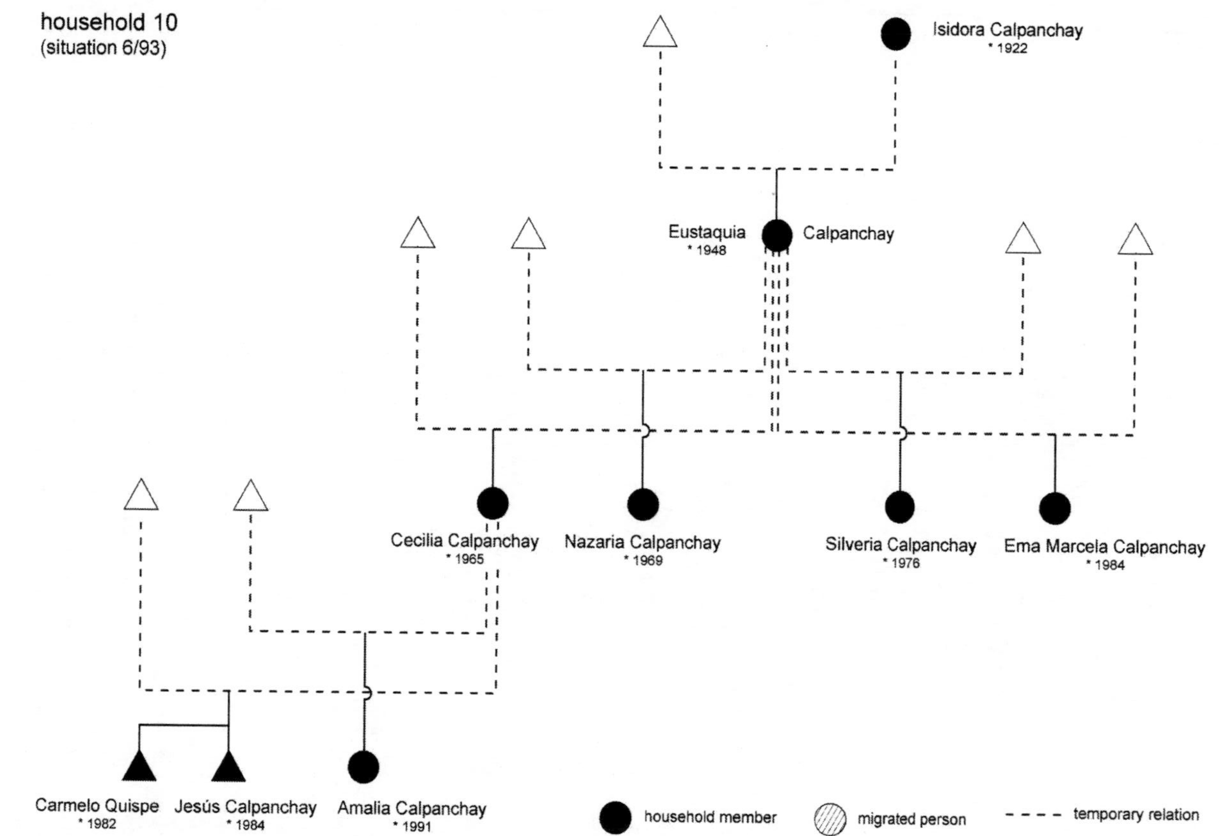

Figure 8.3. Composition of a matrifocal household (household 10)

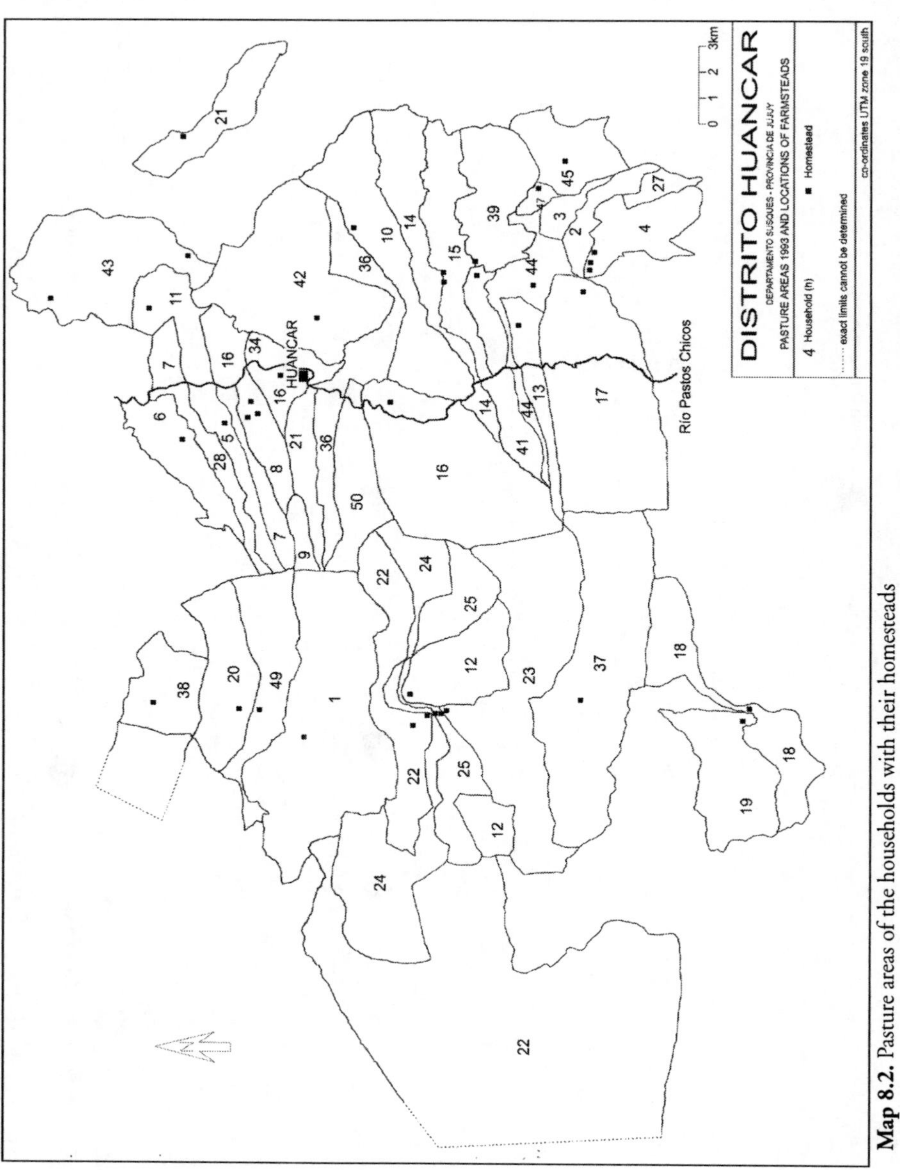

Map 8.2. Pasture areas of the households with their homesteads

the final say in all decisions. In the case of a patrifocal household, the chief herdswoman is the wife of the male household head; in the case of a matrifocal household it is the woman who is its effective head (cf. figs 8.2 and 8.3). The chief herdswoman is addressed by other households as *dueña*, or owner of the herd. One of her major tasks is the daily management of livestock. She is assisted by the household's older and younger women and by the children, mainly the girls. Younger and middle-aged men are absent for most of the year, as they travel with trade caravans to agricultural regions, or seek temporary work in mines or plantations in the lowlands (see also Göbel 1998a, 1998b).

Unlike more fertile regions of the Andes, where concentrations of grazing land occur in the form of high mountain moors (*vegas* or *bofedales*), Huancar has no communal pastures or waterholes (cf. Brush and Guillet 1985: 26; Browman 1974; Orlove 1981; West 1983: 94 for Andean communal property). Each household in Huancar holds exclusive rights to the use of a particular grazing area, in which are located the central homestead of the household, its waterholes, and the various herding stations. On average each household has five herding stations, the number of stations ranging from 0 (household 47) to 11 (household 22; cf. map 8.2 and for more details Göbel 2003). Most herding stations consist only of a circular windbreak made from stones or bushes. The degree of mobility of the herders and herd animals is relatively great as compared to other pastoral systems in the Andes (cf. Flores Ochoa 1968; Orlove 1981; Palacios Ríos 1981; West 1983). About every three to four weeks the whole family moves with the llamas, sheep and goats to a new pasture area, travelling from one herding station to the next or returning to the main compound. Pasture areas have an average size of 1,649 ha, the smallest one being 115 ha (household 47) and the largest one more than 10,766 ha (household 22; cf. map 8.2). Due to the bad pasture conditions and the lack of water, the average stocking rate is low[8]. As the pastoralists emphasise, the dimensions of the grazing area are not the only factors of relevance for a household's herd size. The quantity and quality of pastures and waterholes and the availability of labour also matters. But the most decisive factors are, in their opinion, the experience of the chief herdswoman and the degree of luck accumulated within the household.

Human–Animal Relations

The relations between the people and their herd animals are very close. Llamas, sheep and goats are not set outside the human sphere, but are considered as members of the household alongside the people and as part of its social network. As the inhabitants of Huancar – male or female – put it, not adult men but llamas, sheep and goats are the vital constituent of a pastoral household. They often say: 'It is not necessary to have a husband, it is essential to have llamas, sheep or goats.' One reason for the central position of herd animals in the household is the fact that the people live with them very closely. Between people and herd animals there is intimate cohabitation, in a spatial and temporal sense. The herdswomen in particular spend more time with their llamas, sheep and goats than with non-household members, partly due to the great distances between homesteads, and partly to the frequent moves to new pasture grounds.

They watch over the animals all day long and sleep at the herding station in the open air, next to the enclosures for the sheep and goats and the sleeping-place of the llamas. During most of the year there is very little social contact between households: the herdswomen meet members of other households only on special occasions, such as religious feasts or school meetings.

In addition, the embedding of the herd animals in the human sphere is connected with their ontological status. The inhabitants of Huancar assume that llamas, sheep and goats have human characteristics and abilities. They have a soul (*alma*), intelligence (*mentalidad*), feelings (*sentimientos*) and memory (*memoria*). Just like humans, every animal has its own individuality, which is expressed in the particular features of its appearance and character and summed up in the name it is given in the first month of life. It has firm roots in the place where it has grown up, and identifies itself with the animals and people with whom it has been socialised. Knowledge about the animals' genealogical relations is shared by all human members of the household. The chief herdswoman especially knows every animal from its birth, with its particularities and its life history. But even children aged 6 or 7 can recite the genealogy of each llama, each sheep and each goat in their household's herd. They know which animal is its mother, which are its nearest relatives besides its own siblings, and how many offspring it has.

The dense and complex relationship between humans and herd animals is characterised by patterns of interpersonal sociality. It contains clear parallels to the way a mother should normally behave towards her child, or to the care and concern which children are expected to show towards their younger siblings. Frequently heard comments are: 'You have to look after a herd animal, think of it, like it, not get irritable and loud with it, talk to it calmly, keep it under control but allow it some freedom.' Since the animals, like small children, cannot talk properly, people must try to understand intuitively what they are saying in order to be able to give them what they need. By continuously feeding and raising them, just as people continuously feed their children, the herdswoman makes the herd animals into fellow social beings (Ellen 1999: 63). Thus, they are socialised into a particular household in very similar ways to children.

The anthropomorphisation of herd animals also involves the exchange of vital forces between people and animals and the transmission of momentary physical and emotional conditions. These notions of proximity and consubstantialisation between people and herd animals do not imply that the latter have no economic value. On the contrary, the inhabitants of Huancar frequently stress that they keep llamas, sheep and goats not just for pleasure (*de ganas*), but because they want to use their meat, fat, blood, milk, wool and hides. It is the duty of the animals to provide humans with these products, just as it is the duty of the women to look after the animals, and that of the men to exchange the animal products for maize, beans, or potatoes. The indigenous conception is based on the conviction that from a certain age, every member of the household, whether human or non-human, has to fulfil specific economic functions in order to ensure the survival of the household.

Well-Being and Economic Production

Like the other members of the household, herd animals cannot fulfill their economic function in a satisfactory way if they are not happy or comfortable. One of the greatest preoccupations of the chief herdswoman is therefore to care properly for her llamas, sheep and goats, so that they will feel comfortable and be able to provide the other members of the household with meat, fat, blood, milk, wool and hides. Not only their daily activities, but also a large part of the people's conversations revolve around topics connected with the animals' welfare. Well-being is expressed with the words *estar tranquilo*, meaning a well-balanced mental and physical state in animals and humans. The ideal state of equilibrium is achieved not only when basic needs such as hunger, thirst, and warmth are satisfied, or when no pain is felt; it is also a state without extreme emotions, such as grief, fear or excessive joy, or of physical movement, such as hasty, hurried movements, sudden cessation of movement, or complete immobility.

Threats to Well-Being

It is no easy task to make the animals feel comfortable and to maintain this state of equilibrium for as long as possible, for herd animals are continuously exposed to dangers which could upset the balance and threaten their health and even their life. Well-being is thus an ideal state which can be strived for, but which can only be maintained for a limited length of time.

But what are the risks which disturb the well-being of the animals and therefore also that of humans? On the one hand, the inhabitants in Huancar list a number of climatic uncertainties: the lack of rainfall in one year or in a sequence of years (drought) but also cloud-bursting rainfalls with landslides, extreme fluctuations in daily temperature, frost, sudden hail and snow, strong dust-laden winds and lightning. In dry years, when pasture conditions get worse, some plants that are considered to be poisonous or pathogenic (*malpasto*) become another risk. Other unpredictable events which can make an animal weak or ill, or even kill it, are attacks by pumas or foxes (for a description of damage caused by pumas and foxes and its complex interpretations by Andean pastoralists, see Göbel 1999). Pastoralists know from experience in which months which climatic events or predator attacks are likely to occur most frequently (e.g., snow in July, lightning and rain between December and March; cf. fig. 8.1). But neither the exact time nor the severity of the event can be predicted beforehand.

The factors mentioned above are also named as threats to animal production in scientific studies of risk management in the Andes (e.g. Browman 1987a, 1987b), and are grouped together under the general heading 'ecological risks'. But what these studies do not mention is that the pastoralists or agropastoralists do not necessarily categorise them thus. The authors also do not include in their scientific analysis that the pastoralists or agropastoralists take into account a far greater range of risks immanent in their environment, and that they fit them into a network of causal relations in a culturally specific way.

The people in Huancar say that an animal can also fall ill or die because it has been cursed (*maldecio*) or bewitched (*hechizo*) by a close relative of the household: the brother-in-law, sister-in-law, brother or sister of the chief herdswoman may have laid a curse or a charm on the herd, because he or she is envious of the economic success of the members of the household. As already mentioned, relations between close relatives who live near each other are very tense. These curses and charms take effect through the immediate environment in which a herd animal moves; they 'infect' the environment, whereby herd animals, particularly weak ones, can fall ill. Unlike more visible risks, such as lightning, hail, or drought, curses and charms are only identifiable indirectly, namely after a loss has occurred. A further threat to the animals is *susto*, fright. *Susto* is the separation of the soul (*ánimo*) from the body, which may cause illness or even death in an animal. But what triggers *susto*? An animal may take fright if it passes too near a 'dangerous place' (*lugar peligroso*), or if it stays there too long. Such 'dangerous places' are, for example, springs, hollows in the ground containing white or glittering minerals, or sand dunes, which, as open or moving surfaces, are considered to be openings of *pachamama*, Mother Earth. At these openings she can swallow up an animal's soul. The local expression for this process is 'to be swallowed by the earth' ('*ser tragado por la tierra*') or 'to be caught by the earth' ('*ser agarrado por la tierra*'). The loss of the soul destroys the unity of the herd animal or human, and immediately affects certain organs and the animal or human falls ill, or even dies.

Mother Earth (*pachamama*) plays an active role in the pastoral economy, and is of central importance in the handling of risks. This is so because the pastoralists of Huancar relate to their environment through *pachamama*. Like other Andean pastoralists and peasants, they too conceptualise *pachamama* in myriad, sometimes ambivalent ways (see also Mariscotti de Görlitz 1978). She is conceived of as both an abstract entity that maintains the life cycle, through its power to create, support and destroy life, as well as in concrete forms. The pastoralists think that *pachamama* possesses human qualities and dispositions. Like human beings, she has identifiable needs (e.g., hunger, thirst), intentions (e.g., to protect her animals), emotions (e.g., anger, sadness, happiness) and memory. The pastoralists see no contradiction between these human characteristics of *pachamama* and the belief that she is localisable in different material components of the environment, such as springs, hollows in the ground or sand dunes. The reason for this is that they perceive basic components of nature as anthropomorphised Others with an agency of their own. At *pachamama*'s openings humans can enter into close contact with her. There, she is very sensitive to the actions of humans or livestock. which is why the openings can turn into very dangerous places. If, for example, household members have behave in an inappropriate way or if they have violated taboos, humans and animals will feel *pachamama*'s anger in a particularly clear manner at her openings. In the same way she can express any other bad mood, hunger or thirst here. In order to calm all these emotions, needs and wants she tries to catch the soul of an animal or a human person; as a reaction to the loss of their soul, they will catch fright and get *susto*.

The Impacts of Damage

The Economic Impacts

Due to the risky conditions in which the people have to live with their herds, there are great fluctuations in the health of the animals, their fertility and productivity.[9] On average, between 30 and 50 percent of young animals die before they are a year old. In an extremely dry year this proportion may rise to 80 percent or more. Although the mortality of adult animals is not as high as that of newborn or young animals, it is also perceived as a severe threat to a pastoral household. It implies the loss of considerably more meat, wool and labour investments than the loss of a newborn or young animal. A comparison of herd sizes in 1992, a year with normal climatic conditions, with those of 1996, an extremely dry year, shows average losses of 38 percent in the whole herd.[10] In 1992, meat, fat and wool production was extremely low and the families were unable to produce cheese from sheep or goat's milk, which is an important addition to their diet in the southern summer.

Because of such potential danger of animal losses the people cannot reliably predict what quantities of meat, wool, hides, milk and cheese they will be able to dispose of. These production uncertainties not only affect decision-making with regard to herd management (e.g., frequency of movement with animals, fodder and labour requirements), but also decisions concerning consumption patterns and the reliance on other sources of income. Such uncertainties also have a severe impact on economic exchange. In view of these imponderables long-term economic planning is impossible.

Emotional Impacts of Damage and the Extension of Damage

Besides these economic consequences, the illness or death of a herd animal also has great emotional impacts on the human members of the household. Many human diseases are related to the emotional shock, sadness or despair unleashed by such negative events. The disrupting effects of these risks is further enhanced, it is felt, by the fact that damage can be transferred between human and non-human members of the household. For example, a curse which was originally directed against a person can be deflected, and may attack an animal instead of the person or vice versa. The very close relations between herdswomen and the animals they tend include intensive exchanges of mood, vital essence and physical constitution. *Susto* (fright), weakness or sadness can be transmitted from a person to an animal, and vice versa, the direction of transfer usually being from the stronger one to the weaker. In particular, sadness (*tristeza*) is dangerous and infectious, for it renders the body and soul of people and animals out of equilibrium, thus making them more vulnerable to illness, and even death. If, for example, a person or an animal passes a 'dangerous place' while in a sad mood, there is a greater probability that their soul will be caught or swallowed up by *pachamama* than if they were well-balanced (*tranquilo*). And when one animal or person suffers a fright, this is more likely to be transmitted to sad animals or persons than to animals or persons who are happy.

Handling Uncertainty

Huancar pastoralists emphasise that the risks to which they and their animals are exposed cannot be controlled, or at best only partially. Since a risk cannot be directly averted, it is especially important to be as well prepared as possible for potential loss or damage. They regard three factors as being fundamental for optimal conditions of reproduction and growth of the animals in face of the impending risks: first, the experience of the herdswoman who mainly looks after the herd; second, the accumulation of 'luck potential' within the household; and, third, taking care of these luck potential.

The Relevance of Experience

The experience (*experiencia*) of a herdswoman is regarded as particularly important for the welfare of a herd animal and thus also for its productivity. Her experience is said to consist of three closely connected elements: the knowledge (*saber como criar hacienda*) passed on to her by older members of the family, especially her grandmother, mother and elder sister; the knowledge which she gains through practice over the course of time; and her commitment in caring for the animals, which means concentrating on the work and circumspection in dealing with them, and her emotional ability to communicate with the animals and develop sufficient sensitivity to be able to correctly interpret indications of their condition and their needs. However, this commitment is only possible if the herdswoman reinforces her relationship with the animals through positive emotions, and by taking pleasure in her work: 'You have to put your heart in it and have a ear for it and you have to like it.'

In addition to this a basic commitment, momentary commitment is also important. Due to the possibility of direct transmission of the herdswoman's physical and mental state to a herd animal, it is important that she should try to be emotionally stable and in a well-balanced state of health when tending the animals. She should try not to worry unnecessarily, and not get upset about problems or losses suffered, and should also avoid mentioning in conversation potential sources of danger for the herd animals, which might otherwise become restless.

But, given the nature and magnitude of potential risks, letting animals be cared for by an experienced herdswoman is not enough to create the necessary conditions for herd growth. A second important area is the management of luck potential.

The 'Andean' Concept of Luck

The 'Andean' concept of luck, *suerte*, has not yet been treated systematically in the literature, although there are many indications that it is different from 'Spanish' ideas of *suerte*[11]. The term occurs in rural areas of the Andes exclusively in connection with resources whose growth fluctuates extremely and is therefore considered uncontrollable. These resources include agricultural crops, herd animals and minerals which are conceptualised as living veins. *Suerte* refers to economic success in dealing with these resources; in the context of animal husbandry in Huancar, it is equivalent to *multiplico*, multiplication. Multiplication in its turn, refers to an adequate production of meat, fat, wool and milk, but in particular also to reproductive success. This means the fertility of an uncastrated male animal, and in the case of a female animal, the number of young which survive the first year of life and thus attain an age after which they are of economic use.

A basic notion among the inhabitants of Huancar is that an animal inherits a good constitution and a positive reproduction potential not only from its animal-parents, but rather, that these depend decisively on the owner of the animal (*dueño*), who transmits them to the animal along with character traits such as greed, restlessness and gentleness. *Suerte* is thus a potential which is exchanged between humans and animals, especially at the moment when a particular animal is assigned to a human person, when it passes from this person to the animal's body. It is not necessary for the human and the animal to see or touch each other on this occasion: it suffices that the animal be mentioned by named to the owner as his property and that the human person is also designated by named to the animal as its owner. A common statement is: 'The animal comes to know who is his owner through thought. Through the act of naming the owner, the *suerte* reaches the animal, the *suerte* arrives. The physical presence of the owner is not crucial, but it is important that his *suerte* is there'. From this moment onwards the owner's *suerte* potential is embodied in this animal, and is materially present in its whole body. It is especially concentrated and therefore visible in the *onda*, a piece of fat on the small intestine and in the nerves on the ribs. It is further concentrated in the coat of llama sires, rams and billy goats. In particular, llamas with multicoloured spots (*llamas overas*) concentrate *suerte*, because their fleece resembles the many hues of the mountains where *pachamama* lives. Here one can observe the close link between *suerte*, in terms of production and procreation and the effect of Mother Earth as a life-creating agency.

But not all human persons are able to transfer a good physical constitution and a good reproductive capacity to the animals ascribed to them, for *suerte* potential is not distributed equally among humans. This is so because the potential for *suerte* in humans is an innate ability, which a person either has or has not. Unlike experience, *suerte* cannot be acquired. Some have, for example, a skilful hand for economic success with llamas, and others do not. In other words, it is assumed that llamas assigned to the first group of people are highly likely to be productive and to bear young which survive the first year, while this is unlikely for the second group: the mother animals are likely to be in poor health and to suffer abortions, or their offspring will die. Thus a direct connection is established between the attribution of an animal to a person and the effect of the abilities of this person on the animal.

The Accumulation of Luck Potential within a Household

Since some persons have *suerte* and others do not, it is obviously important for the chief herdswoman and her family to put as many herd animals as possible into the possession of persons with *suerte*, for only in this way can she face impending risks from a good starting position – a large basic stock of productive and reproductive potentials. She has less influence on the subsequent development of the herd, but at least she has begun the game with a good hand. However, in order to be able to do this the chief herdswoman needs to know which members of the family or of the social network have *suerte* with which animal species. A central point in the understanding of *suerte* is that it must be socially known before it can be activated. So what mechanisms exist in Huancar to get to know the *suerte* potential of any person?

The members of a household receive animals at a number of rituals which mark different stages of life and in which ritual-kinship relationships (*compadrazgo*-ties; see note 6 below) are established: birth; baptism; coming through of the first tooth; first haircut at the age of 3 or 4 (*ruti*); confirmation at the age of 14, when children enter adulthood; and marriage. Generally, animals aged between 1 and 2 are given to the ritual's protagonist by his recently designated godfather (*padrino*) or godmother (*madrina*), his parents, siblings or members of the household's wider social network. These life-stage rituals are connected with ideas about a child's or an adult's growth. For example, a child is given animals when its first tooth comes through, so that these animals may multiply like its teeth. These metaphors of physical growth reflect the logic of *suerte*. Just as the teeth come through without any direct intervention on the part of the person, the animals of a carrier of *suerte* potential will multiply without her/him having to do anything directly. The transfer of animals in this way is described as testing whether *suerte* is present ('*probar la suerte*' or '*ver la suerte*'), and it is justified with the argument that the chief herdswoman wants to see whether the animal given to the child is productive, i.e., puts on a lot of meat and fat and develops a good fleece, or whether a mother animal produces young within one to two years which survive the first year. For example, on the occasion of its first haircut, a child is given a female llama. Transferred animals are always more than one year old and thus have already demonstrated their potential for survival. If this llama has a good basic constitution and produces offspring which survive the first year, they know that the child has *suerte* with llamas. From now on llamas will be frequently transferred to him. If the child is not lucky the first time, its *suerte* is tested with llamas once or twice more. If it still has no luck, this child is never given a llama again. After the llamas, his luck is tested in a similar manner on subsequent occasions with goats and sheep.

As already mentioned, the newly designated owner (*dueño*) of the animal does not acquire any exclusive rights to the use of the animal. The chief herdswoman makes all final decisions affecting the animal, such as whether it should be castrated, slaughtered or shorn. Thus the transfer of an animal is mainly a symbolic transfer of property, with the aim of fixing a person's *suerte* potential on this animal. The whole household takes advantage of the *suerte* potential, which the animal has received from its human owner. In this connection it seems appropriate to speak of *suerte* as symbolic capital in the sense used by Bourdieu (1977), of the household which can be converted by the chief herdswoman into economic capital when required. All household members benefit from this economic capital, since they all eat the animal's meat or the corn, exchanged for the textiles produced from the animal's wool. Only in the rare cases when one of the children or grandchildren owning animals marries does the animal's owner (*dueño*) get full power of disposal over his animals, so that he can integrate them into the newly founded household.

When making strategic use of other people's *suerte* potential, the chief herdswoman responsible for the herd does not limit herself to her husband or children and grandchildren living in the household. She also transfers animals to family members who have migrated from the area. Here, too, the central idea is that their *suerte* must first be tested before it can be exploited. In general, the recipients of animals are the chief herdswoman's emigrant children or grandchildren. She never transfers animals to the spouses of her children, because no blood relations link them (see fig. 8.4), and an important prerequisite for the transmission of *suerte* from a person to an animal is that this person has blood relations with the human members of the household in which this animal will live. In many households the symbolic transfer of animals to migrants account for 40 percent or more of the entire herd.[12] 'I live from the *suerte* of my children who have moved away', said one chief herdswoman, after telling me that she had distributed all her animals symbolically among her emigrant children, because she

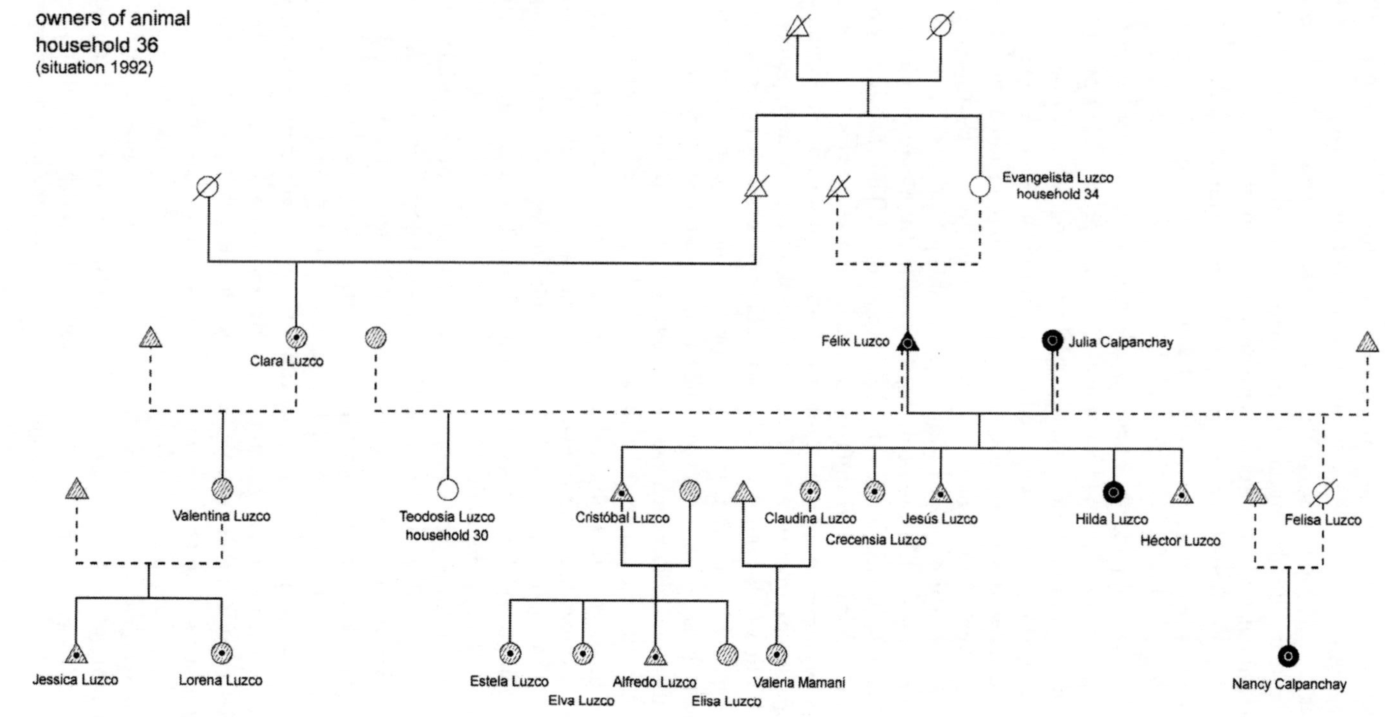

Figure 8.4. Ownership of animals (household 36)

herself has no *suerte*, either with llamas, sheep or goats. The preference for the transfer of animals to migrants is justified by the claim that their *suerte* is more stable. As they live far away and have no direct contact with the animals, the probability of their doing anything which could harm the well-being of the animals and thus also their productivity and procreation (*multiplico*) is very slight. They cannot arouse the anger of *pachamama*. For the migrants, on the other hand, symbolic ownership of animals is a way of maintaining and strengthening relations with their place of origin, or that of their parents. Such bonds legitimate their participation at rituals and at feasts. If they come on a visit, they are given some meat and wool as compensation for the use of their animals by the chief herdswoman and her household.

Another mechanism for using other people's *suerte* potential consists in giving one's animals to another household for herding for a limited period of time. The most common form of agreement is the *al partir* arrangement, whereby half the young animals born within one year are given to the herdswoman who has tended the herd during this time, the other half being given to the original family who handed the herd over. This means that the herd increase is distributed evenly between the two parties to the agreement. Such agreements are generally made with persons within the social network of the household, where mutual obligations are regulated through kinship or *compadrazgo* ties. These people are not only more willing to take on the extra animals, but it can also be assumed that they will look after them with greater dedication.

When does a chief herdswoman decide to enter into an *al partir* arrangement? One important reason for doing so is the steady decline of the reproductive rate of her herd. Such a decline is often explained by the absence or disappearance of luck within the household. If, for example, the number of a household's llamas diminishes continuously because the household's human members have little or no luck, the chief herdswoman will prefer to hand the llamas over for a limited period of time to another household whose members have *suerte*. The reason given is that it is convenient for her to use the luck of another household till the llama herd has recovered. She expects that the 'foreign luck' will have a positive influence on the birth rate and well-being of the newborn animals. Although the chief herdswoman has to pay the counterpart of the arrangement with half the offspring born during the agreed time span, she gets the other half. In her opinion, even this small profit is better than having no young animals at all. A herdswoman from a household with luck is interested in taking over a foreign herd, because this allows her to increase the number of her animals. To enter into an *al partir* arrangement requires, however, that the herdswoman can fall back on sufficient labour within the household for an adequate control of both the outside and the household herds.

Taking Care of Luck

The chief herdswoman will strive to obtain as great a concentration of *suerte* potential within the household as she can. But she and all other household members are fully aware that although this creates good conditions for the productivity and procreation of the animals, it by no means ensures economic success. Because of all the dangers, the fact that a person has *suerte* with llamas does not necessarily mean that the offspring of this llama will survive.[13] The *suerte* potential accumulated within a household are not static, but always in flux. *Suerte* can grow, but it can also shrink or even disappear, for there are many factors which can harm it. One reason for its decline is improper human behaviour. For instance, arbitrary use of resources (*usar de ganas*), not guided by the premise of necessity, can unleash the anger of *pachamama*. If a household member kills a wild or domestic animal, or uses a plant simply for pleasure rather than because of a concrete need, Mother Earth will take *suerte* potential away from the household. Breaching of prohibitions and violating taboos can also have a harmful effect on *suerte*. For example, no herd animals should be slaughtered, shorn or castrated on Tuesdays and Fridays, on the 7th, 17 or 27th of a month or 'when the moon changes',[14] because all these are dangerous days for *suerte*. Herd animals may not be counted and herd sizes should not be mentioned in conversation, for this would reveal the desire for a bigger herd. Indeed, such a strong desire for herd growth can have exactly the opposite effect. In addition to the negative effects of improper behaviour, for which many further examples could be given, the environment in which humans and animals have to live is also full of risks which pose a threat to *suerte*.

The chief herdwoman's strategic accumulation of *suerte* potential must therefore be accompanied by considerable efforts on the part of all human household members to maintain *suerte*: 'It is not enough just to have *suerte*, you also have to take good care of it', people in Huancar emphasise. At the centre of the daily efforts to protect *suerte* are measures to obtain the goodwill of *pachamama* towards the human and animal household and the herd. There is a whole range of behaviour norms and ritual activities which are regarded as contributing to a well-balanced relationship with Mother Earth. These are intended to remove tensions, imbalances or breaks in the tightly woven network of interactions between humans and *pachamama*. A vital element in obtaining Mother Earth's goodwill is the logic of reciprocity, which means that a person may only take something (such as natural resources) if he/she also gives something in return (such as a drink offering).

Endangering Luck: Slaughtering a Herd Animal

The slaughtering of a llama, sheep or goat is a good example from daily life which clearly illustrates the required behaviour and the great variety of norms, taboos and ritual actions that are involved in maintaining *suerte*. The killing of an animal is a particularly critical situation. For one thing, it brings with it the danger that with the transformation of the animal's status and the disintegration of its body, the *suerte* which the animal embodied during its life will be dissolved or destroyed, with negative effects on the *suerte* of the other animals. In addition, slaughtering clearly reveals the people's desire to consume a member of the household, whom they have known since its birth and with whom they have lived in close contact. The act of killing therefore involves not only a new definition of the people's relationship with the animal, but also leads to tensions between them and the rest of the herd, and with Mother Earth. The other herd animals could take fright on realising that, potentially, the same fate awaits them. And Mother Earth feels herself challenged in her position as a life-creating agency, and this may lead her to punish the people. All these tensions endanger the *suerte* of the herd animals and their production and reproduction abilities. With each slaughtering, there is the danger of triggering a chain reaction, which would considerably disturb the well-being of the household's remaining animals and thus also harm the humans. The efforts of the chief herdswoman and her family are therefore concentrated on removing the tensions between them and the herd animals and with Mother Earth, and to ensure as far as possible that *suerte* remains in the household.

It is important to arrange the context of the slaughter as harmoniously as possible, so that the well-being of the animals is not unnecessarily affected, and the negative effects of the act of killing are kept within limits. Since emotional and physical states can be transmitted between humans and animals, a good physical condition, a positive attitude and a well-balanced mood are of great importance. For example, a herdswoman who wants to slaughter an animal should not enter the animal's enclosure if she is hungry. She should first chew many coca leaves and drink plenty of alcohol, in order to be in a good mood and in full possession of her physical strength. This ensures that the animal to be slaughtered will not feel hungry and that the rest of the herd will also feel happy. If the herdswoman were hungry and depressed when she entered the corral, she would immediately transmit her sadness to the animals and they would lose weight. However, while the herdswoman is within the enclosure she should not eat anything, for otherwise she might eat up the *suerte* of the herd, and the animals would starve for lack of pasture.

The animal to be slaughtered must be treated respectfully, and it is important to avoid hasty movements, loud voices or the use of unnecessary violence. An animal should die as quickly as possible, but in peace, without being frightened, without suffering and without having to defend itself too much. If this is not the case, the well-being of the whole herd is in danger and the *suerte* potential of the animals could disappear. An animal must never be killed inside the enclosure, because this can have negative effects on the rest of the herd. The enclosure is a place where the animals are deeply rooted; it is their house and their home. Every household therefore has a small slaughtering ground, about 30 m outside the corral. It can be identified from the dried contents of the intestines, which are always pressed out over the same bush, and from the white stones under the bush which cover the sacrificial hole. Here the animal is laid on the ground with its head toward the east, where the sun rises, and close to a bush. The eyes of the animal are covered with coca leaves so that it can no longer see its animal-relatives and animal-friends, or the people with whom it has lived. Thus communication between the animal and the members of its social network is interrupted. This makes the parting easier for the animal and reduces the chances of the other animals left in the enclosure taking fright. It also means that the herdswoman does not have to look into the animal's eyes when she slaughters it. Before killing the animal by cutting its throat, alcohol and coca leaves for *pachamama* are placed in a sacrificial hole (*juiri*) right next to the animal, and she and the rest of the herd are asked for understanding and forgiveness. A considerable amount of the blood of the slaughtered animal also flows into this hole as an offering. The blood, the alcohol and the coca leaves are regarded as food for Mother Earth, as payment (*pago*) for the use of the animal. With these offerings the people try to obtain the goodwill of *pachamama* toward humans and herd animals, and to remove possible tensions. In a more general sense, feeding Mother Earth is a way of maintaining the cycle of life: life is destroyed by killing an animal, but at the same time the offerings help to ensure that new life can be created, for in Andean cosmology, life and death are insolubly joined together (Allen 1988; Bastien 1978; Gose 1994).

Through a number of further acts the herdswoman tries to establish continuities between the slaughtered animal on the one hand, and the human and animal household members as well as *pachamama* on the other. As the following examples show, the herdswoman tries to keep the body parts of the slaughtered animal together and to symbolically reconstitute some of its substances. The objective of these acts is to prevent *suerte* from falling apart, or from disappearing from the herd. Thus, the blood of the slaughtered animal may not be scattered, as otherwise the *suerte* will be scattered. When the herdswoman takes the carcass of the animal apart, she must swallow the *onda*, the piece of fat which contains the *suerte* of the animal in concentrated form, while it is still warm, so that the *suerte* does not disappear and is transferred back to the herd through her. The content of the intestines must be pressed out over the bush at the slaughtering ground, and not thrown into the river, so that the *suerte* does not float away. When the skin is removed, it is important to ensure that no hole is cut or scraped into it, because otherwise the *suerte* would be damaged and would diminish. On the day the animal is slaughtered, its bones must not be broken in order to eat the marrow, for the *suerte* is still too warm and could be harmed: 'the *suerte* might be broken', as people say. If the bones are broken by a guest, he must give the household a live animal: 'he has to replace the animal that he has damaged, that he has eaten.' Only on the day after the slaughter, when the *suerte* has grown cold, may the bones be broken. However, the animal bones must always be collected at a particular place in the compound or herding station; they may not be given to the dogs or left lying around on the ground, as otherwise the *suerte* would be scattered. When processing the body of a slaughtered animal, no wool or fibres from the animal may be thrown on the ground, scattered or burned. Any pieces of wool lying around must be collected and buried in a small hole in the ground, at some distance from the river. All this is to prevent the *suerte* from leaving the herd and correspondingly also the household.

As people in Huancar underline, not all the individuals involved in the slaughter of an animal – or in other economic activities with herd animals – work with the same intensity for the maintenance of the *suerte* potential of the herd. Efforts for caring for *suerte* potential not only vary from person to person, but also from household to household. On the one hand, there is a basic corpus of measures to be taken and a basic stock of requirements to be met which are considered to be absolutely necessary for stabilising the *suerte* potential within the herd. But on the other hand it is publicly known that some households or some members of a household put a great deal more of effort into caring for the *suerte* than others do, by carrying out more extensive practices, fulfilling a wider range of requirements, observing prescribed behaviour more carefully, or making more generous sacrifices. For example, nobody in Huancar would think of slaughtering an animal without turning its head toward the east, making sacrifices to *pachamama* in the form of alcohol, coca leaves and the animal's blood, and respectfully removing their hat while doing this. However, some herdswomen also scatter drops of alcohol and blood towards the north, south, east and west, pronounce the name of the main homestead, the herding stations, pastures and waterholes, and of other 'dangerous places', and say prayers, not only to *pachamama* but also to the saints of the slaughtered animal (St Anthony for llamas, St John for sheep, St Bartholomew for goats). Other households would do this only on the occasion of a ritual slaughtering.

Living with Uncertainty in the Andes: Some Concluding Remarks

The preceding descriptions of the pastoralists' efforts towards creating optimal conditions for pastoral production elucidates three characteristic traits of risk handling in Huancar. One is a logic of diversification which spreads responsibilities within the household, in case of productive and reproductive failures. Another particularity is the relevance of social networks for creating optimal conditions for pastoral production, in spite of the difficult conditions. These networks consist of human as well as non-human persons. The third characteristic trait is the inter-wovenness of cultural patterns of significance and strategic moments in the handling of risks.

Diversification and the Handling of Risk

The pastoralists combine in their struggle with risky environmental conditions individual efforts with the recognition of innate human potentials. They rely as much on animal-tending skills, which can be learned or carried out by any person, as on productive and reproductive potentials that are innate only to certain individuals. What can be influenced individually is experience (*experiencia*). Knowledge of herd management is passed on from one generation of herdswomen to the next, and can also be acquired through practice. The degree of commitment which the herdswoman shows in her behaviour toward the animals is also considered as being individually controllable. It is a customary requirement for a herdswoman to strive to develop her sensitivity to the needs of the animals, and to take care to be as physically and emotionally well-balanced as possible; yet the extent to which she actually complies with these requirements is her own personal decision. Another factor which is in the realm of individual influence is the extent of work (e.g., the intensity of ritual actions) one wants to invest in the maintenance of *suerte* potential within the household. What is not individually controllable is whether a person has *suerte* with one type of animal or not. *Suerte* is an innate potential, which cannot be acquired through practical experience of tending of animals, nor by means of ritual actions – although the latter are of great importance in stabilising *suerte* potential. Unlike knowledge about herd management, *suerte* potential cannot be transferred from one person to another; its transfer and conversion into visible fertility is limited to the animal assigned to a person. For this transfer to be effective, it is only necessary for both parties to be informed of the new ownership arrangement by the chief herdswoman. She plays the active role in the transfer of *suerte*, and also in maintaining *suerte*. The chief herdswoman tries to assign as many animals in her herd as possible to persons with *suerte*, whether these are relatives or members of the household's social network, in order to accumulate as much *suerte* potential as possible in her household.

This combination of actively creating a good starting position for herd growth through personal effort, where the chief herdswoman is the driving force, and by using the innate, uninfluenceable fertility potential of persons who do not necessarily have to be involved in herding, results in a wide scattering of responsibilities. If one takes into account the close relationships between herders and herd animals, which include the transmissibility of emotional and physical states, then such a scattering of responsibilities certainly makes sense. For it mainly serves to protect the chief herdswoman – the one most affected by daily uncertainties and latent threats – from excessive psychological pressure. Negative feelings such as worry, fear, doubt, or sadness cannot be completely eliminated, but they can be averted if economic failure can be attributed not just to one's own errors, but also to other factors such as the uninfluenceable absence of *suerte*[15]. This also helps to avoid the risk of the chief herdswoman losing her state of emotional and physical equilibrium and of her instability spreading like wildfire, with all the potentially negative consequences this may have for the animals.

Social Networks and the Handling of Risk

The activation of social networks is of central importance for every households' risk management. In particular, the chief herdswoman falls back upon on social relations with human and non-human individuals. In her daily struggle to cope with impending risks, the chief herdswoman is at the centre of a complex mesh of interactions involving a number of other actors, and skilfully tries to coordinate their interplay. In the core area of this network of interactions are not only those persons and herd animals who live with the chief herdswoman in the same household, but also Mother Earth (*pachamama*), who – as already mentioned – is conceptualised as a materially localisable entity with individual needs, will and emotions. She enables and maintains life, but she can also destroy it, for instance, if her needs are not adequately satisfied by humans, or if she is disturbed by the people and animals of a household. A more peripheral position in the mesh of interactions is occupied by actors who either do not tend the herd animals at all or only for limited periods. These are members of the family who have migrated and members of households with whom cooperation is practised. The latter may be either close relations who do not live in the immediate neighbourhood, or persons who are quasi-relatives because of ritual kinship ties (*compadrazgo* ties). Outside this mesh of interactions – at least as far as successful handling of risks to the herd is concerned – are first close relatives who live in the direct neighbourhood and who are therefore seen as posing a threat, and second, all households with which there are no cooperation relations. Thus we see that the decisive criterion for identifying those actors from whom a positive contribution to risk management can be expected, is not the fact of belonging to the human or non-human sphere, but the extent of their effectiveness with regard to the production of meat, fat, wool and milk.

Webs of Significance and Strategic Appropriations

In the pastoralists' efforts to create good conditions for the production and procreation of their llamas, sheep and goats, despite all imponderables, cultural patterns of significance and strategic moments are inseparably interwoven. The above discussion showed that the special features of economic trade under risky conditions cannot be adequately described and explained without referring to the world-view of the herders, their basic notions concerning human-animal relations, or their conceptualisation of the environment. For example, only after considering the ontological status of the herd animals is it possible to understand how the physical and mental state of the chief herdswomen can have such dangerous effects on the well-being of the llamas, sheep and goats; and accordingly, that any preparation against possible risks and attempts to limit loss or damage cannot be concentrated on the animals only, but must also include to a decisive degree the herdswoman as a person. The concept of *suerte*, which is closely linked to ideas of Mother Earth (*pachamama*), to conceptualisations of persons, animals and their bodies, and to notions of fertility and the exchange and transformation of vital forces and substances, is also of central importance for understanding the way risks are handled.

This culturally bound perception of risk does not imply that the actors would not express their own individual interests through their actions. We have seen this particularly in the strategic measures taken by the chief herdswoman with regard to *suerte* potential. She skillfully tries to activate the members of her network in order to accumulate as much *suerte* potential as possible in her household. She expresses this aim openly in words, i.e., she makes no attempt to conceal her ambition. Any analysis of risk management which ignored this clearly formulated calculation would therefore be too one-sided. It must take into account that people are actively engaged in trying to cope with uncertainty, that they try to hedge against uncertainty through action.

Notes

1. In their everyday discourses they do not differentiate very strictly between these two terms. However, the term *peligro* is used more frequently in the context of sudden events that are quite locally restricted, such as a stroke; the term *problemas* often appears in connection with events such as droughts, which have a more processual character and a more generalised spatial impact. While, for example, a stroke effects one or only a vey few animals, a drought which develops overa longer period of time affects the whole herd.
2. This understanding of *problemas* and *peligros* comprises core elements of common scientific definitions of 'risk' (see for example Fischhoff et al. 1981; Kasperson and Kasperson 1987; Renn 1998; Yates and Stone 1992).
3. For all these reasons I prefer the term 'risk' to Luhmann's (1991) concept of 'danger', in order to describe the pastoralists' perception of environmental threats.
4. If we take a year with 170.5 mm of precipitation to be a standard year, 24 percent of the years between 1973 and 1997 had been extremely dry (less than 78 mm), 28 percent dry (78–170.5 mm), 32 percent humid (170.5–263 mm), 8 percent very humid (263–355.5 mm), and 8 percent extremely humid (more than 355.5 mm). Not only this variation, but also the analysis of consecutive years, make clear how greatly the amount of precipitation can fluctuate from year to year (e.g., 1977: 165 mm; 1978: 63 mm; 1979: 366 mm; 1980: 23 mm; 1981: 184 mm; 1982: 49 mm; 1983: 65 mm; 1984: 368 mm).

5. Thus, three of the largest herds in Huancar are from matrifocal households (households 1, 37 and 10).
6. Ritual-kinship or *compadrazgo* is a social institution which is widespread in Spain and Latin America and through which persons, who are related neither by blood or marriage receive a status similar to that of consanginous or affinal kin (see Bloch and Guggenheim 1981; Gudeman 1975). *Compadrazgo* ties are in the Andes of great social, economic and religious importance, because they comprise lifelong obligations of reciprocal assistance (e.g., Allen 1988; Bolton and Mayer 1977; Bourque 1995a, 1995b; Isbell 1985; Urton 1981). They are created during different life-cycle rituals (baptism, coming through of the first tooth, first haircut or *ruti*, confirmation marriage). On each of these occasions fictive kinship relationships are established between the godchild (godson – *ahijado* or goddaughter – *ahijada*) and the newly elected godparents (godfather – *padrino* and godmother – *madrina*), as well as between the parents of the godchild and the godchild's godparents. The latter address each other as *compadre* (if the godfather or the godchild's father is addressed) or *comadre* (if godmother or the godchild's mother is addressed). Godparents should never be close biological kin. Therefore distant relatives or non-kin are selected as godparents.
7. The following close relatives have their homesteads in the immediate neighbourhood (cf. map 2): households 2, 3, 4 in Agua Cavada, households 7, 8, 9 in Aguada; households 14 and 15 in Cuevas; households 18 and 19 in Focos; households 23, 24, 25 in Hornos de Zule; households 34, 36, 50 in Huancar; households 39 and 41 in Minas.
8. The average stocking rate is one TLU (Tropical Livestock Unit) per 67.29 ha. This corresponds to 6.729 ha per sheep/goat or 20.187 ha per llama. But stocking rates vary considerably from one household to the other. The range is from 9.24 ha to 293.35 ha per TLU (0.924 ha to 29.355 ha per sheep/goat or 2.772 ha to 88.005 ha per llama).
9. A herdswoman with a herd of about 300 animals illustrated this as follows: 'In a normal year from 80 ewes we get 50 lambs. Of these lambs only 25 to 30 survive the first year of life.' She mentioned the same numbers for 70 female goats. With regard to llamas she said: 'In an average year 50 llama mares will produce 25 foals. But from these foals only 12 to 15 *tequis*, llama-foals, will survive.'
10. To consider only the losses, in 1996 the households had on average 40 percent fewer llamas than in 1992, 56 percent fewer sheep and 45 percent less goats.
11. For example, unlike the colloquial Spanish of the cities, *suerte* is not used in many rural areas of the Andes in connection with social relations or health or in referring to a person's destiny, in the sense of a positive course of life.
12. A good example is the herd of household 36 for which Julia C. is responsible (cf. fig. 1). In 1992, 36.5 percent of the household's llamas, sheep and goats were owned by migrants and 63.5 percent by members of the household. In 1996, 40 percent of the animals were owned by migrants and 60 percent by household members; in 1999 the relation was 40.5 percent to 59.5 percent. The distribution of animal ownership in 1992 was as follows:

    Animals of household members (no. 99): chief herdswoman Julia C. (Ego) = 19, husband Félix L. = 34, daughter Hilda L. = 10, son Héctor L. = 19, granddaughter Nancy C. = 17. Animals of migrants (no. 57): son Cristóbal L. = 16, granddaughter Estela L. = 11, granddaughter Elva L. = 4, grandson Alfredo L. = 2, daughter Claudina L. = 17, granddaughter Valeria L. = 1, daughter Cresencia L. = 2, son Jesús L. = 4.

    The breakdown of animal ownership confirms the norm not to hand over animals to migrated affines (see also fig. 8.4).

13. In my opinion it is therefore appropriate to speak of *suerte* potential.
14. With this the day is meant, when the full moons starts to shrink and 'crosses' – as people say – from full moon to new moon.
15. I cannot present here a detailed description of typical features of the discussion of causes after loss or damage has occurred, or of related notions of causal chains and time dimensions and the possible effects of loss or damage (see Göbel 1999). But I want to underline that these aspects should be included if a full understanding of cultural risk management is to be achieved.

References

Allen, Catherine J. 1988. *The Hold Life Has. Coca and Cultural Identity in an Andean Community*. Washington: Smithsonian Institution Press.

Arnold, Denise and Juan de Dios Yapita 1998. *Río de vellón, río de canto. Cantar a los animales. Una poética andina de la creación.* La Paz: ILCA, Hisbol.

Barlett, Peggy, ed. 1980. *Agricultural Decision Making. Anthropological Contributions to Rural Development.* New York: Academic Press.

Bastien, Joseph W. 1978. *Mountain of the Condor. Metaphor and Ritual in an Andean Ayllu.* St. Paul: West Publishing.

Bianchi, A. and C.E. Yánez 1992. *Precipitaciones en el Noroeste argentino.* Salta: INTA.

Bloch, Maurice and Stephen Guggenheim 1981. 'Compadrazgo, Baptism and the Symbolism of a Second Birth', *Man* 16: 376–86.

Bolton, Richard and Enrique Mayer 1977. *Andean Kinship and Marriage.* Washington: AAA.

Bourdieu, Pierre 1977. *Outline of a Theory of Praxis.* Cambridge: Cambridge University Press.

Bourque, Nicole 1995a. 'Developing People And Plants: Life-Cycle and Agricultural Festivals in the Andes', *Ethnology* 34: 75–87.

——— 1995b. 'Savages and Angels: The Spiritual, Social And Physical Development of Individuals And Households in Andean Life-Cycle Festivals', *Ethnos* 60: 99–114.

Browman, David 1974. 'Pastoral Nomadism in the Andes', *Current Anthropology* 15: 188–96.

——— 1987a. 'Agro–Pastoral Risk Management in the Central Andes', *Research in Economic Anthropology* 8: 171–200.

———, ed. 1987b. *Arid Land Use Strategies and Risk Management in the Andes.* Boulder: Westview Press.

Brush, Stephen and David Guillet 1985. 'Small-Scale Agro-Pastoral Production in the Central Andes', *Mountain Research and Development* 5: 19–30.

Cashdan, Elizabeth, ed. 1990. *Risk and Uncertainty in Tribal and Peasant Economies.* Boulder: Westview Press.

De Garine, Igor, and George A. Harrison, eds. 1988. *Coping with Uncertainty in Food Supply* Oxford: Clarendon Press.

Ellen, Roy 1999. 'Categories of Animality and Canine Abuse. Exploring Contradictions in Nuaulu Social Relationships with Dogs', *Anthropos* 94: 57–68.

Fischhoff, Baruch, Sarah Lichtenstein, Paul Slovic, S. Derby and Ralph. L. Keeney 1981. *Acceptable Risk.* New York: Cambridge University Press.

Flores Ochoa, Jorge A. 1968. *Los Pastores de Paratía.* Lima: Instituto Indigenista Interamericano.

Göbel, Barbara 1998a. 'Räume geschlechtlicher Differenz und ökonomisches Handeln (Andenhochland Nordwest-Argentiniens)', in *Differenz und Geschlecht. Neue Ansätze in der Ethnologischen Forschungsperspektive*, eds. Brigitta Hauser-Schäublin and Birgitt Röttger-Rössler, 136–62. Berlin: Reimer.

——— 1998b. 'Risk, Uncertainty and Economic Exchange in a Pastoral Community of the Andean Highlands (NW-Argentine)', in *Kinship, Networks And Exchange*, eds. Thomas Schweizer, And Douglas White, 158–77. Cambridge: Cambridge University Press.

——— 1999. 'Why Herd Animals Die: Environmental Perception and Cultural Risk Management in the Andes', in *Coping With Changing Environments: Social Dimensions of Endangered Ecosystems in the Developing World*, eds. Beate Lohnert and Helmut Geist, 205–29. Aldershot: Ashgate.

——— 2003. 'Identidades Sociales Y Medio Ambiente: La Multiplicidad de los Significados del Espacio en la Puna De Atacama', *Cuadernos del Instituto Nacional de Antropología*, 19: 267–96. Buenos Aires.

Gose, Peter 1994. *Deathly Waters and Hungry Mountains. Agrarian Ritual And Class Formation in an Andean Town.* Toronto: University of Toronto Press.

Gudeman, Stephen 1975. 'Spiritual Relationships and Selecting a Godparent', *Man* 10: 221–37.

Halstead, P. and J. Oshea, eds. 1989. *Bad Year Economics: Cultural Responses to Risk and Uncertainty.* Cambridge: Cambridge University Press.

Isbell, Jean 1985. *To Defend Ourselves. Ecology and Ritual in an Andean Village.* Illinois: Waveland Press.

Kasperson, Roger E. and Jeanne X. Kasperson 1987. *Nuclear Risk Analysis in Comparative Perspective.* Winchester: Allen and Unwin.

Luhmann, Niklas 1991. Soziologie des Risikos. Berlin: De Gruyter.

Lupton, Deborah 1999. 'Introduction: Risk and Sociocultural Theory', in *Risk and Sociocultural Theory: New Directions and Perspectives*, ed. Lupton, Deborah, 1–11.Cambridge: Cambridge University Press.

Mariscotti de Görlitz, Anna María 1978. *Pachamama Santa Tierra. Contribución al Estudio de la Religión Autóctona en los Andes Centrales Meridionales.* (Indiana Supplement 8). Berlin: Gebr. Mann.

Masuda, Shozo, Izumi Shimada and Craig Morris, eds. 1985. *Andean Ecology and Civilization. An Interdisciplinary Perspective on Andean Ecological Complementary.* Tokyo: University of Tokyo Press.

Orlove, Benjamin 1981. 'Native Andean Pastoralists: Traditional Adaptations and Recent Changes', in *Contemporary Nomadic and Pastoral Peoples: Africa and Latin America* (Studies in Third World Societies 17), ed. Philip Salzman, 95–136. Williamsburg/Virginia: Department of Anthropology.

Ortiz, Sutti 1980. 'Forecast, Decision, and the Farmers Response to Uncertain Environments', in *Agricultural Decision Making. Anthropological Contribution to Rural Development*, ed. P. Barlett, 177–202. New York: Academic Press.

Palacios Ríos, Félix 1981. 'Tecnología del Pastoreo', in *La Tecnología en el Mundo Andino*, eds. Henri Lechtman and Ana María Soldi, 217–232. México: UNAM.

Renn, Ortwin 1998. 'Three Decades of Risk Research: Accomplishments and New Challenges', *Journal of Risk Research* 1: 49–71.

Scott, James 1977. *The Moral Economy of the Peasant. Rebellion and Subsistence in Southeast Asia*, New Haven: Yale University Press.

Troll, C. 1968. 'The Cordilleras of the Tropical Americas . Aspects of Climatic Phytogeographical and Agrarian Ecology', in *Geo-Ecology of Mountainous Regions of the Tropical Americas*, ed. C. Troll, 15–56. Bonn: Dümmlers.

Urton, Gary 1981. *At the Crossroads of the Earth and the Sky. An Andean Cosmology.* Austin: University of Texas Press.

Watts, Michael 1988. 'Coping With the Market: Uncertainty and Food Security Among Hausa Peasants', in *Coping With Uncertainty in Food Supply*, eds. I. de Garine and G. Harrison, 260–89. Oxford: Oxford University Press.

West, Terry 1983. 'Family Herds – Individual Owners. Livestock Ritual and Inheritance Among the Aymara of Bolivia', in *The Keeping of Animals: Adaptation and Social Relations in Livestock Producing Communities*, eds. Riva Berleant-Schiller and Eugenia Shanklin 93–106. Totowa/NJ: Allanheld and Osmun.

Whyte, Susan R. 1999. *Questioning Misfortune. The Pragmatics of Uncertainty in Eastern Ugand.* Cambridge: Cambridge University Press.

Yates, Frank J. and Eric R. Stone 1992. 'The Risk Construct', in *Risk-Taking Behavior*, ed. Frank Yates, 1–25. Toronto: John Wiley.

9

Transforming Livelihoods: Meanings and Concepts of Drought, Coping and Risk Management in Botswana

Fred Krüger and Andrea Grotzke

Aspects of Environmental Risk and Social Change in Botswana

According to meteorological statistics, and in terms of the long-term mean of rainfall, one out of three years in Botswana is a drought year (fig. 9.1). Particularly devastating are several droughts in succession (e.g., 1981/82–1986/87), or droughts that are accompanied by extremely high temperatures and extend over larger parts of the southern African sub-continent (e.g., the 1991/92 'drought of the century'). But even apart from the mere lack of sufficient precipitation, the high spatial variation of rainfall may cause severe problems for some areas even in years with overall precipitation above average. Drought can thus be seen as the major natural hazard for rural livelihoods in Botswana. From this perspective, environmental risk is a function of the probability of the drought hazard striking and the outcome of the hazard event in terms of loss of lives and/or assets. Surprisingly enough, for the last twenty years this environmental risk has been low in Botswana, despite the extremely high probability of a meteorological drought. Contrary to many Sahelian or even other southern African states, in the last decades there have been no losses of human lives directly related to drought events. This is mainly due to reasonably efficient autonomous coping strategies of drought-affected households, but also to very effective government drought relief schemes which have drawn much attention for their extraordinary success (Holm and Morgan 1985; Hay 1988; Teklu 1994;

Krüger 1997, 1999). On the other hand, a number of shortcomings of these programmes have lately been revealed. There seems to be a growing gap between what is officially intended by the drought-relief measures, and what their actual outcome is in the target areas and their true impact on the target groups. As will be shown in this paper, this has a lot to do with transforming connotations of risk and a general process of modernisation and urbanisation, all contributing to changing vulnerability patterns in rural areas.

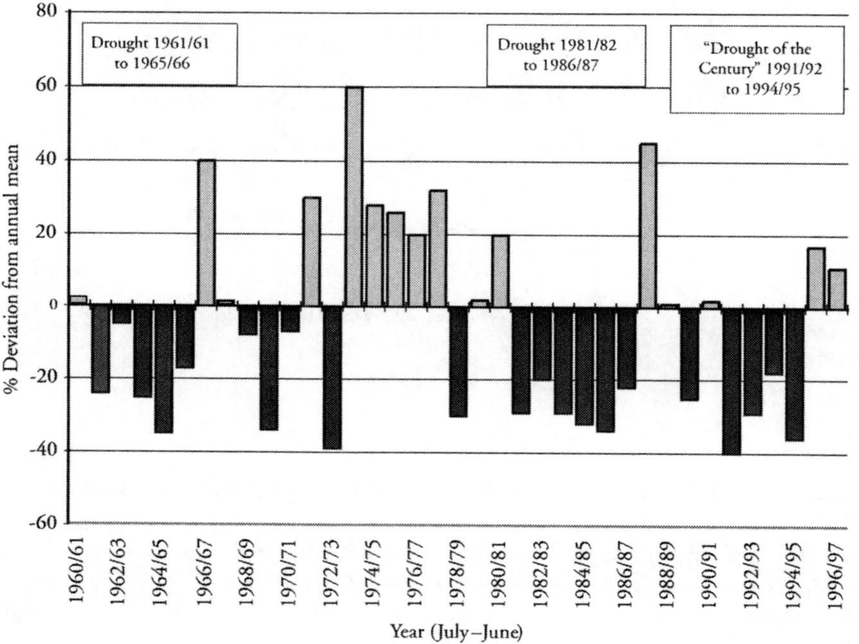

Source: Author's calculations based on data from Dept. of Meteorological Services, Gaborone

Figure 9.1. Mean annual rainfall in Botswana 1960–1997

We argue here, and shall try to explain in more detail below, that these transition processes are related to two major aspects of social change: (a) transformations in adaptation and coping measures of (potentially) drought-affected rural households, and (b) changing notions of risk in both rural communities and state institutions. Both factors are leading to a growing dependency of rural households on external support and relief schemes. It can be assumed that these social changes are associated with various other processes, which can currently be observed in Botswana: a rapid modernisation in terms of technological advancement, urbanisation and AIDS. The latter will probably cause the most drastic transformation of society in decades. Accurate data indicate that approximately 30 percent of the population is HIV-positive (AIDS/STD-Unit 1999; cf. also MacDonald 1996; for a more detailed analysis see Krüger 2002), and AIDS and diseases such as TB are responsible for a rapid increase in mortality and a decrease in life expectancy to an extent that has never before been experienced in Botswana. Mortality among members of the economically active age groups is particularly high, adding to the human tragedy, apart from hindering social reconstruction since the skilled workforce is literally thinned out. A process less severe but also of great importance to social change is urbanisation. 'Traditional' rural ways of living are slowly altered, and 'urban', modern perceptions and lifestyles are becoming more relevant. Obviously, urbanisation involves the fast growth of cities (the annual growth rate of Botswana's capital Gaborone is *c.* 6 to 8 percent p.a.), but what matters more than these merely quantitative changes is a growing difference between what is considered a typical 'rural' and a typical 'urban' quality of life. The Human Poverty Index (HPI-1) as published by the UNDP gives a rough but clear idea of urban-rural disparities in Botswana (fig. 9.2). People living in rural areas have less access to clean drinking water, mortality rates among children are higher, income opportunities are scarce, etc. Urbanisation in Botswana means that while living conditions improve in rural areas, they improve faster in the cities, and rural-urban disparities are getting worse.

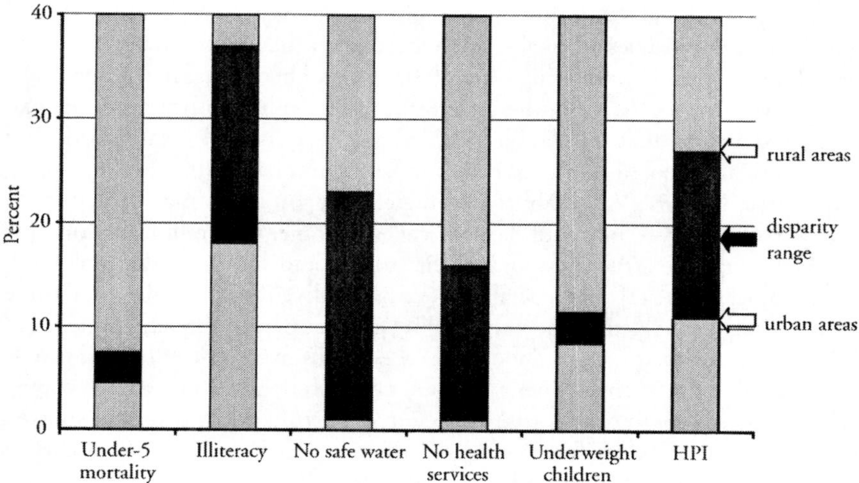

HPI = Human Poverty Index

Source: UNDP Human Development Report 1999 and Government of Botswana; altered

Figure 9.2. Urban-rural disparities in human poverty in Botswana 1996

AIDS and urbanisation and the problems associated with these processes are, however, relatively new developments. In rural areas, there are other factors influencing and influenced by social change, which have persisted in Botswana for decades. People have always had to adapt to environmental conditions, which pose a threat to rural livelihoods, namely poor soils and very unreliable rainfall. These environmental challenges contribute to the rural-urban disparities mentioned above, because rural spheres of life where livelihoods based on arable land or livestock herding are strongly shaped by adaptation measures that are aimed at successfully coping with drought.

A Short Note on the Theoretical Framework

When looking at threatened livelihoods it is useful to fall back upon two conceptional frameworks which have become of increasing importance in social sciences development research: (a) geographical models of social vulnerability and livelihood (in-) security, and (b) concepts of risk sociology.

The vulnerability approach, and with it the sustainable livelihoods framework (cf. Chambers 1989; Watts and Bohle 1993; Krüger 1997, 2003; Carney et al. 1999; Derichs and Rauch 2000) are actor-oriented, but also include institutional aspects. They draw on elements of marginalisation and poverty research, hazard geography, political economy and political ecology. The livelihood and vulnerability approaches are analytical models rather than theories, but they have helped a great deal in improving research design and better understanding social insecurity patterns. As Chambers (1989) argues, vulnerability is more than poverty. It means that vulnerable people have very limited means to defend themselves, are exposed to risk, shocks and stress, and have difficulties in coping with these factors. Vulnerability is dependent on the (mal-)functioning interrelations between man and the physical environment, on political, economic and social baseline structures, and on life events and trends in the biological, psychological, mental and social context. The livelihood model sees these interrelations embedded in the vulnerability context of a society and argues that difficulties in safeguarding livelihoods derive either from insufficient access people have to vital assets (such as financial capital or natural resources), or from coping strategies which communities try to apply in order to tackle threats and stresses, but which prove to be malfunctioning or inadequate. In short, any instabilities or disruptions in the availability and accessibility of vital assets may cause an increase of vulnerability which, on its part, may lead to a breakdown of adaptation and coping measures and to severe livelihood crises. In the case of Botswana, social vulnerability in rural areas is mainly dependent on human-environment connections (lack or high space and time variation of rainfall, poor soils, and inadequate capabilities to adapt to these factors) and economic entitlements (lack of financial resources to buy food if harvests fail or cattle starve).

Thus, vulnerability and livelihood concepts stress structural and functional aspects of society. They are action-oriented in the sense that coping strategies and the mobilisation of assets are closely looked at. However, while conditions of risk are dealt with in the context of action in everyday life, no satisfactory explanations for the underlying reasons for these actions are provided (Krüger and Macamo 2003). Risk, as has been stated above, may be seen as a function of the probability of a hazard event and a community's vulnerability to the impact of that hazard (Blaikie et al. 1994; FEWS 2003). But it may also be argued that risk is a social construct – as a way in which a given society comes to terms with insecurity. Societies can only successfully deal with dangers (e.g., a drought event) if they manage to adequately translate this danger into risk (see, for example, Douglas 1992; Luhmann 1991 or, for a compact outline of these concepts, Krüger and Macamo 2003). This process of translation is, in fact, a means to introduce calculability and accountability into everyday life. Calculability is a result of communicative and action processes in which those affected by hazards translate them into something which can be handled: into risks. If a danger is not sufficiently 'deciphered' into risk, vulnerability to crises and conflicts increases. A successful translation process would be based on the timely detection of a (potentially) hazardous event, on finding the best solution for avoiding, adapting to or coping with that event, and on well-timed and extensive implementation of that solution. In this process, a lot can go wrong: people may not notice the danger in the first place, or they may misinterpret it as being less harmful than it really is, or their capacity in finding adequate solutions may be insufficient (e.g., because they lack experience in dealing with such threats), or they are still suffering from the impact of a preceding event and thus have reduced coping capabilities, or established local adaptation measures are disrupted due to external interventions aiming at the mitigation of the hazard impact, and so on. The larger the insecurity of the affected community in dealing with a hazardous event, the higher the risk of severe livelihood disruptions. In Botswana, the translation of drought from danger to risk has hitherto been more or less successful because solution-finding capacities in both local communities and the government have been strong.

But as will be shown below, notions of risk among both drought-affected people and the state are beginning to shift, and a more severe impact of drought on rural communities may result in this transition. By combining the concept of risk with major elements of the livelihood approach, which focuses on coping strategies, we shall now consider in detail the changing patterns of vulnerability in rural areas in Botswana.

Drought-Induced Vulnerability: Changing Perceptions of Risk and Coping in Rural Areas

Baseline of the Study and Key Questions

In the following parts of this paper we shall first take a look at issues of risk and vulnerability in eastern and southern rural Botswana in general. Our line of argument will then be supported by the results of small empirical fieldwork that we carried out in 1996 and 1999.

In the wake of earlier research on vulnerability patterns in Botswana (Krüger 1994, 1997) it became obvious that the impact of state drought relief schemes on the livelihoods of rural communities had – apart from some studies on increased food security – not been analysed in depth for the past decade. It seemed that the relative success of the relief programmes rendered any analysis of their compatibility with local risk interpretations and coping capacities unnecessary. After communicating with drought relief officers and numerous villagers across Botswana, we had the impression that there were first signs of a gap between the intentions of public support schemes and the expectations of rural households having to deal with drought. The key question of our study, which commenced in 1996 and was completed in 1999, was whether the concepts of drought in Botswana involve a perception of *risk* which in turn comprises notions of instability, uncertainty or threat, or whether drought is rather seen as a component of life to which one has to adapt, without necessarily having a concept of 'preparedness' or 'prevention' in the Western (i.e., European) sense in mind. And, does the meaning of drought change in the wake of the social transformation processes outlined above? If so, does this have an impact on livelihood security in drought-affected areas? Obviously, livelihoods depend largely on efficient drought 'management', be this adaptation, coping, or other forms of dealing with unreliable and marginal rainfall conditions and any socio-economic disruptions involved. In turn, 'management' depends on the ways drought is perceived and valued. With government drought relief programmes well established in Botswana, it is worthwhile to analyse drought perception from two different angles: how is drought seen by the state, i.e., government institutions, and what are the drought perceptions of rural households potentially or actually affected by drought events? How, if at all, do both the state and local communities translate the danger of drought into accountable risk?

The State's Perception of Drought

In general, drought must not merely be seen as a natural incident involving lack of rainfall and subsequent critical decline in agricultural plant or animal production (cf. Krüger 1999). Apart from this meteorological definition, drought events include disruptions of relations within and between the physical environment and the social and economic spheres. Botswana's semi-humid ecosystem, with temporally and regionally unreliable rainfall distribution, is highly susceptible to drought, and so are the country's social and economic systems, from the institutional level of the national economy to the local household or individual level of people in drought-affected regions. In a step-by-step process since the early 1970s, the Botswana government tried to conceptualise drought and establish measures for effective drought-relief. A number of local physical surveys and various studies on the social aspects of drought helped to outline a basic framework for the implementation and later constant modification of official drought-relief schemes (cf. Teklu 1994; Krüger 1997, 1999, 2002). This led to a perception of drought which was clearly economically biased. In short, drought was seen as a severe disturbance of the economic system of food supply and food demand, and until the late 1980s, the obvious answer to drought events and famine risk was to bolster food production in order to support the supply side of the system. However, the target of the 'National Food Strategy' (NFS) to reach a food self-suffiency in Botswana proved impossible to meet. Domestic food-grain production was too limited due to poor rainfall and soil conditions. For the last ten years, therefore, the main focus of drought-relief has been shifted from the supply-and-demand side of food security to a far more diversified scheme comprising a large number of different drought-relief and recovery components. A clear distinction is now made between general availability of food and specific access to food – a new official perception of the threat of drought and vulnerability which draws on Amartya Sen's concept of declining food entitlements. Sen (1981) had argued that famine occurs not necessarily because of a lack in food production and supply, but because people lose access to food, in other words they lose the ability to produce it, purchase it or barter for it. Consequently, at the household level, a drought event is perceived as a major reason for deteriorating income-generating opportunities and the decline in the value of productive assets (namely land and cattle). Thus, in government opinion, the negative effects of drought can only be mitigated by transferring income to households which have to face drought-induced destitution, by preserving their productive assets, and, in general, by sustaining their livelihoods through a variety of different relief measures.

The major objective of state drought relief is not to provide food (although there is a food distribution scheme included in the relief programmes), but to combat destitution by trying to alleviate the erosion of entitlements. Public cash-for-work schemes form an important element of drought relief. These Labour-Based Relief Programmes do not usually target specific groups, but serve as a blanket cover for most rural households who are drought-stricken or have little or no assets. Through these temporary employment measures the government wishes to ensure that markets remain operational even under drought conditions, and attempts to intercept financial losses and the decline of household purchasing power. The public labour-based programmes involve road works, the construction of houses and dams, etc., and participants receive a small salary intended to compensate poor harvests, drought-induced losses of cattle, etc. The workforce employed by these programmes is largely female, as it is mainly the women who usually work in the fields and, in times of rainfall deficiency, are ready to participate in the scheme as there is little to do in the fields because of the drought. Measures to protect productive rural assets include various tillage and grain subsidies for small-scale farmers and vaccination of cattle. The feeding programme, which is another component of government drought relief, usually targets the most vulnerable groups, i.e., children and the inhabitants of remote areas.

Earlier, most of the relief components used to be temporary and were only implemented in times of drought. The intention of the government was to assist rural households in their otherwise autonomous and self-reliant efforts to cope, and not to provide an all-embracing support which would probably curtail all self-help motivations. An official proclamation of a 'drought year' by the President, based on regional estimations of rainfall, cattle and crop condition, health status of the rural population, etc., provides the basis for all relief measures. In the past, the relief and recovery programmes proved very successful and always helped prevent famine. Although questionable in parts, and revealing a number of shortcomings (cf. Krüger 1999; Mazonde 2000), these programmes, in general, are still working well and have helped greatly to support rural livelihood systems. Our empirical fieldwork and expert interviews have brought to light various recent subtle changes in these public relief schemes, which may in the long run threaten the effectiveness of the programmes as well as the sustainability of rural livelihoods. These changes seem to coincide with social transformations and have a lot to do with the way risks are handled, i.e., the way a drought threat or hazard is translated into an event with calculable outcomes. These changes may be categorised into three domains: first, state institutions drifting away from the concept of declining entitlements to a much broader justification of drought relief; second, the impact of public relief measures on rural households and village communities apparently extending beyond what was originally intended by the programmes; and third, agricultural activities and self-reliant, autonomous adaptation and coping strategies of households threatened by drought tending to be more and more neglected. There now follow a few examples illustrating these changes.

1. In an interview with officers of the Ministry of Finance and Development Planning in Gaborone it became quite clear that supporting entitlements is no longer the only major objective of government drought relief. 'Drought is all about votes!' was the impression given during the interview. Obviously, implementation of relief schemes also serves to woo voters. The ruling Botswana Democratic Party, although still firmly in power, sees itself confronted by an opposition which is gaining influence, and thus drought-relief measures are used to prove government efficiency and social

responsibility. Indeed, single components of the programmes which were originally designed along narrow lines of actual demand are now being broadened to serve as a social welfare cover for most rural groups. Some measures are no longer limited to times of drought but extended over the whole year. 1999 was officially proclaimed a 'drought year', and it would have been even if it had rained enough – 1999 was an election year, and by having it declared a 'drought year' the President could justify all relief measures being continued. The government's strong intention to achieve food security through efforts to sustain economic entitlements, and to cautiously avoid any collision of drought-relief measures with well-functioning autonomous coping strategies which might lead to an erosion of these strategies, is now shifting towards a new perception of drought management as a general social welfare programme.

2. Even if one of their objectives is to secure votes, these welfare measures do of course support rural livelihoods; but, unfortunately, they have a negative social impact, too. Rural households are beginning to *rely* on these programmes for their living, and may indeed lose their ability to fall back upon traditional adaptation and coping strategies. Reliance on public drought relief was what state institutions used to avoid at all costs, but by extending public help and introducing general social welfare, rural households are in fact becoming more dependent on public assistance.

3. As will be shown below, there is a growing tendency for rural households to neglect preparation of household and agricultural activities in anticipation of the rainy season, which may or may not bring sufficient rainfall. In some cases, households have even begun to view active farming as obsolete for subsistence because of the public assistance they receive. 'Either it must rain, or the government must intervene', was a statement heard during one of the expert interviews. Thus, a perception of drought which may have been described as one of 'risk' is transforming into a view of drought as what could be called 'a sign for the government to step in', and this transformation may well lead to 'weaker' adaptation measures which are less efficient to defend drought-induced entitlement declines. The problem is that the relief programmes in their extended form as blanket cover are very costly.[1] Today, with sufficient revenues from diamond exports and a safe financial margin in the state's budget, the year-long continuation of relief measures is still affordable. However, Botswana's economy relies heavily on the diamond industry, and if revenues decline the state will not be able to maintain the blanket cover. This would badly effect a population which has become dependent on external support, which has lost its ability to buffer or quickly react to drought-induced income deterioration, and which has forgotten what it once knew about finding the best solution to cope.

Rural Communities and Drought

While the state apparatus needs a clear approach to drought and risk in order to design adequate relief and recovery programmes, people directly affected may not have a structured step-by-step concept to reduce household vulnerability. Still, they have, over decades, developed numerous adaptation measures. Household activities, especially those related to agricultural production or food storage, have been customised to alleviate the risk of famine. Apart from human *activities* there is also the social *value system* which reflects the immanent importance of rainfall, or rather lack of it. For example, a formal Setswana greeting used in ceremonies, welcome addresses and almost all political statements is *Pula*, meaning 'Let there be rain!'. Even Botswana's currency was named Pula to emphasise the importance of rain and its close connection to financial wealth.

The unpredictability of drought events requires a constant variation and adaptation of household strategies. Drought is not necessarily seen as a single hazard factor involving threat and insecurity to which one has to react directly and spontaneously, but rather as a precondition into which one has to embed one's livelihood activities on a long-term basis (for a more detailed description of traditional drought responses see, e.g., Hitchcock 1979). The overall objective of household activities is to spread risks – once a drought event sets in, its probable impact can be calculated and the danger of losses be kept low. Traditionally, many spatial and temporal activity patterns have been adjusted to mitigate the negative effects of drought. If we take a look at land use patterns, for example, we find that in Botswana fields are widely scattered around the villages, and often 5 km or more away from the main settlement and hundreds of metres apart from each other. As the spatial distribution of rainfall varies a lot, and some small areas might receive sufficient rain from thunder showers, areas just a few kilometres away may not get a single drop of rain in a whole season. By dispersing the plots there is a better chance that at least some fields receive enough rain for a harvest. This drought-related land use pattern is recognisable in fig. 3, which depicts a scene from the village of Letlhakeng, but is typical for the whole of southeastern and eastern Botswana where rain-fed agriculture is practised. Scattering fields is a method of risk mitigation introduced not only in Botswana, but in many other regions with unreliable rainfall (for Peru, e.g., Goland 1993; for the Karakoram, McDonald 1998).

But the dispersion of plots for arable farming has never been done at a single person's or household's discretion. Plots are distributed by demand, but under BaTswana traditional law (which is slowly being replaced by other rules; see below) it is the village or tribal chief who is in charge of plot allocation. For the sake of the village or tribal group, the chief will always distribute the plots with the interests of other community members in mind; he is the representative of a collective interest to scatter fields in a way that best serves the entire community – and which is, as such, the best collective adaptation measure to drought. Traditional risk acting, here, is collective acting. But we now have indications that this collective dealing with drought is beginning to dissolve into a more individualised solution seeking.

Over the past two decades, there has been a notable change in coping measures (Krüger 1999). This change comes along with transforming social structures and modernisation. Farmers used to view drought as a problem concerning the family, the village ward or the tribe. As the example of plot allocation shows, drought was looked upon as a *group problem* which was to be solved by consensus within the group. Villages, for example, are divided into several quarters (wards) along family clusters or larger lineage groupings (see fig. 4). Each ward, and the village as a whole, has a *kgotla*, which is an enclosed location for participatory decision-making and/or public legitimisation of decisions. Families of ward representatives, headmen and chiefs negotiate all matters concerning the community, including collective directions of how to deal with drought-related issues; for more extensive descriptions of the Kgotla system and the chief's responsibilities see Schapera and Comaroff (1991), Somolekae (1998) and Molutsi (1998). Kgotla directives are now more and more complemented or even replaced either by interventions through state institutions and public drought relief measures or individual, intra-household or personal decisions. Today, given the rapidly modernising Botswana society with its wider range of coping opportunities, but also a larger importance of individual values and rights, drought is often perceived as an *individual problem*, with strategies taken up by individuals as outcomes of individually satisfying mediation (cf. Mazonde 2000). This is clearly indicated by the fact that necessary adaptation strategies and desirable options are now negotiated – if at all – between members of a family or household rather than between members of, for example, the village or tribal community.[2] Often, these negotiations represent a conflict between the pursuit of a family member's personal aims and wishes on the one hand and the well-being of the household as a social entity on the other. For example, there are many cases today where families can no longer fall back upon household labour which would be potentially available for assistance in food production – for example, helping out with weeding or field ploughing. Instead, younger family members often opt for salaried employment rather than assisting their parents in subsistence crop production.[3] Among many rural youth, drought is still perceived as a decline in purchasing power and wealth (a perception they shared with government institutions), but to cope with this decline new, more individualised actions can be observed.

The Village of Letlhakeng

In order to investigate the true socio-economic consequences of public drought relief for vulnerable rural households, and to find out more about changing attitudes and meanings concerning risk and coping, we carried out a survey in the village of Letlhakeng. This village was chosen because the frequency of drought

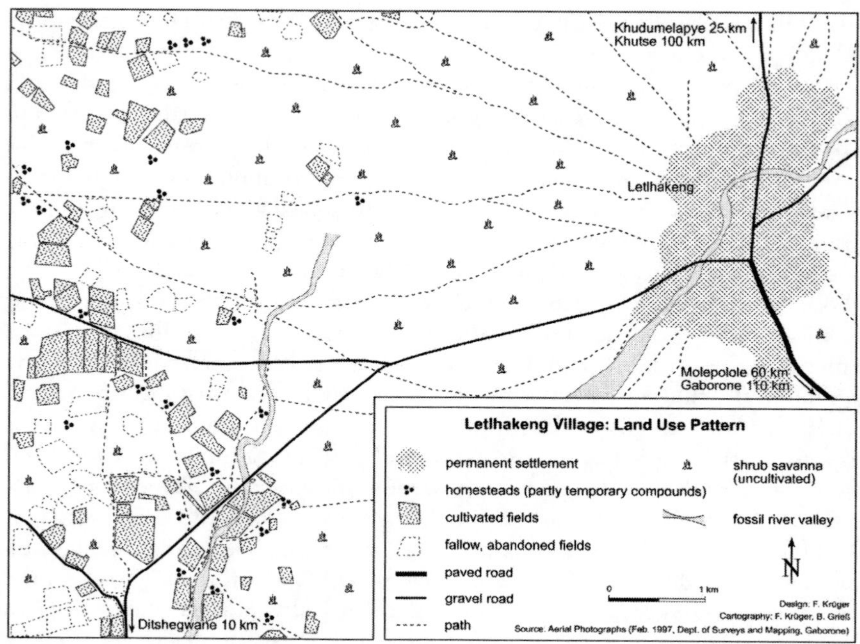

Map 9.1. Letlhakeng village: land use pattern

events here accords more or less with the national average; its social structure comprising both BaKgalagadi and BaTswana ethnic groups is not homogenous, and thus the scope of drought-related activities could be expected to be broad; it is still a rural settlement but, as in many other villages in Botswana, traces of modernisation and urbanisation have recently become clearly noticeable; some field research had been carried out here earlier, on which one could fall back for comparison (Helle-Valle 1997; Mazonde 2000); and, last but not least, Letlhakeng is situated on the edge of the Kalahari but is still relatively easily accessible, and this seemed important to us, given the very limited time available for our appraisal into account.

Research Methods

Our brief field research in Letlhakeng was carried out in April and May 1999. It is important to note that we did *not* aim at achieving representative results for a larger population, but rather intended to either support or falsify the results of expert interviews we had carried out in the first phase of our project, our observations from an earlier research trip on vulnerability patterns (cf. Krüger 1997) as well as statements on drought concepts by other authors cited in this

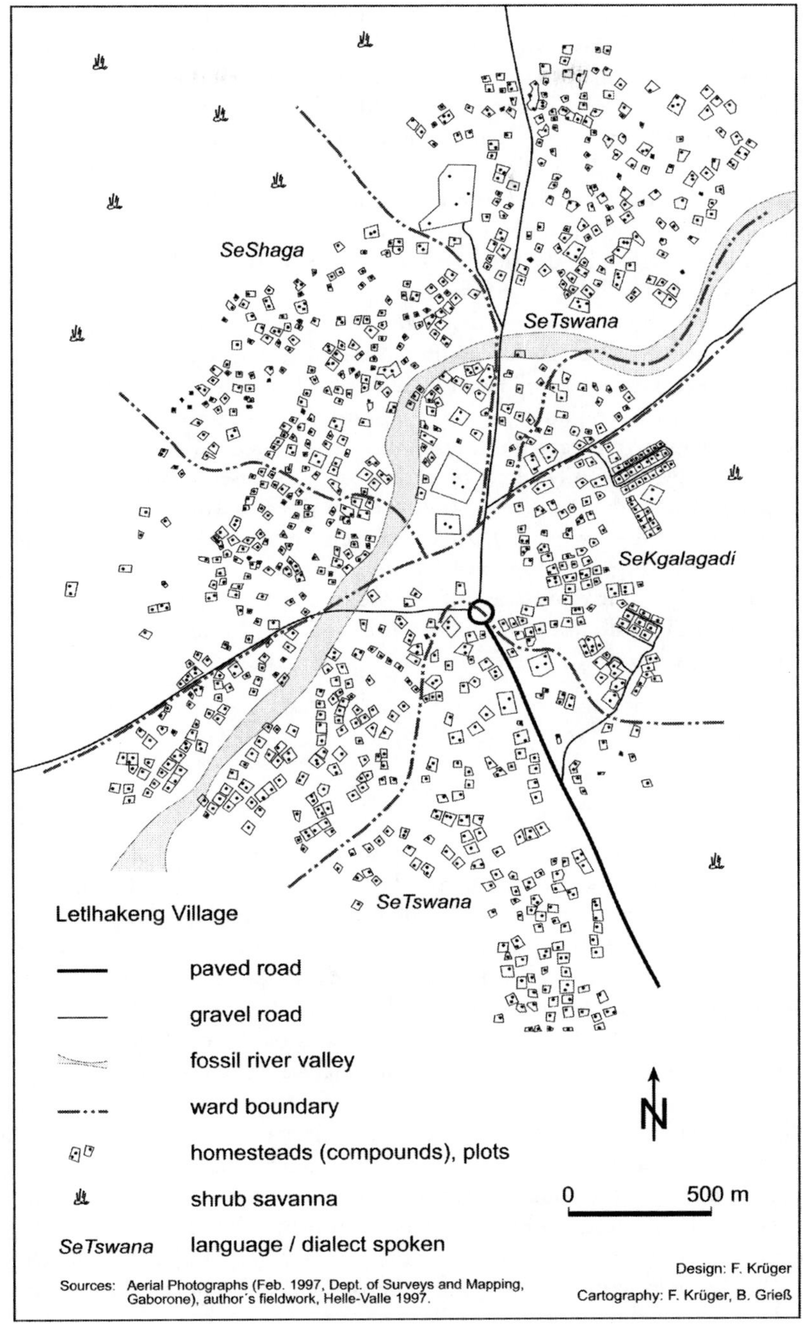

Map 9.2. Letlhakeng village

paper. The fieldwork in Letlhakeng consisted of twenty-seven in-depth and semi-structured household interviews that included the following topics: household composition, all aspects of income generation for livelihood security, perception of drought and strategies to cope with it, and decision-making processes. Each interview lasted from approximately forty-five minutes to two hours, and was carried out with the help of field assistants who had to translate from SeTswana into English. Unfortunately some older informants only spoke SeKgalagadi, which had first to be translated into SeTswana by younger household members and then into English by the field assistants. Usually the head of household and several other household members were present during the interview. The interviews were transcribed, translated and discussed and their contents verified as well as possible by our BaTswana field assistants, who were senior geography students at the University of Botswana. A set of detailed aerial photographs, which were made available by the Department of Surveys and Mapping, Gaborone, helped to locate the households interviewed. We tried to cover the whole village by randomly selecting at least three households per ward. Apart from the household interviews, several employees of the administration of Kweneng West sub-district in Letlhakeng were interviewed in order to better understand the organisation and implementation of the Drought Relief Programmes. Of course, we are fully aware of the limitations of this research design; the findings do not claim to be representative in a quantitative sense, but they clearly enable the identification of certain tendencies of risk action and coping patterns.

The Village

Letlhakeng is located in the Kweneng West sub-district, 100 km west of Gaborone and 60 km west of the district capital, Molepolole. The Kweneng West sub-district administration has its headquarters in the village. Other basic central functions include a health clinic, primary and junior secondary schools, a library, a petrol station, and a small number of shops, most of them general stores. Letlhakeng is equipped with electricity and water facilities. A paved road connects it to Molepolole and the rest of the eastern parts of the country. This enables travellers to cover the distance between the village and Gaborone in about one-and-a half hours. From Letlhakeng, unpaved four-by-four-roads lead to some smaller settlements. Three fossil river valleys meet in Letlhakeng. An older interviewee remembered having had permanent surface water up to the 1960s, but this dried up in the course of two longer drought spells (cf. fig. 1). The soil consists mostly of greyish-white and reddish-brown sands and the most fertile areas around Letlhakeng are found near the fossil valleys. This is also where most of the fields are located, and only a few households cultivate sorghum or maize directly at their compounds in the village itself.

The village population has grown considerably in the past decades. In 1981 the population census registered 2,616 inhabitants, whereas in 1991 4,378 people lived here (CSO 1991). Letlhakeng is organised in six wards, which result from different periods of immigration (fig. 9.4). The people of Moiphisi ward were probably the first to arrive around 1830. Molehele ward was not built until the 1940s (Helle-Valle 1997: 80). The mother tongue of the inhabitants of the wards Mokwele, Tshosa and Moiphisi is SeTswana, while that of Molehele and Modimo is SeKgalagadi,[4] which is, indeed, spoken by the majority here. People in Shageng ward speak SeShaga, which is regarded as a dialect of SeKgalagadi. In earlier times life was largely organised within the boundaries of each ward, but nowadays these boundaries appear to be breaking up. Marriages, for example, took place only between members of either the three SeKgalagadi-speaking or the three SeTswana-speaking wards; today, this practice has become insignificant. It is now also possible to move from one ward to another, although one's 'own' ward is always preferred and the name of one's ward is regarded as one's 'address'.

Sources of Income

In order to adapt to drought-affected environments, local communities tend to engage in a broad range of different activities to safeguard their livelihoods. In terms of the livelihood model, persons try to secure or mobilise as many assets as possible, and as best as they can. From the perspective of the risk approach, the spreading of livelihood activities is one way of translating danger into calculated risk and reducing the probability of a devastating outcome of a drought event. The inhabitants of Letlhakeng, too, have different strategies to secure a living. It is striking how many different monetary and non-monetary income sources exist – on average, each household interviewed has about five different sources of income.[5]

Formal employment opportunities are very scarce. Administrative jobs are mostly taken by 'strangers' coming from other parts of the country and transferred to Letlhakeng after finishing their education or training in Gaborone or in a foreign country. But a wide array of strategies to earn a living exists in the informal sector. Half the households are still regularly or irregularly involved in arable farming, which is mostly based not on commercial but on subsistence production. If the peasants bring in a good harvest, part of it is sometimes sold to neighbours. Sorghum, maize, beans and watermelons are the main crops. Nearly every household interviewed had been engaged in agriculture in the past. If they had given up cultivation this was due to, for example, lack of rain, problems with cattle destroying the unfenced fields, or no money to plough. Thirteen households own livestock (cattle, goats, chicken or donkeys). However, this number has to be differentiated: only three of the questioned households claimed they possessed cattle and some 'chicken owners' were proud of having one or two chickens. Most of the households did actually own cattle in the past, but the animals died or got lost and could not be replaced.

Eleven households indicated that they received some kind of support from relatives or neighbours. Such help can range from regular transfers in the form of money to sporadic help from neighbours in the form of participating in daily meals. One household, for example, is supported by its eldest son who works as a teacher in Gaborone and regularly sends his parents money. A form of mutual support was mentioned by an old woman: a group of four female relatives have organised themselves in a small credit system. All are above sixty years of age, so each of them receives a government pension of 110 Pula per month. Each of these women pays a monthly rate of 50 Pula into a joint 'bank', and every month one of the women gets all the money collected and can thus cover her additional expenses. Members of eighteen households are in search of irregular income generating activities which are thought to meet their spontaneous needs for cash. An older woman, for instance, sells tobacco every now and then and whenever she wants to buy some meat. Another younger woman goes to a bar where she asks men for drinks. A soft drink costs two Pula. After she has had a drink bought, she sells it back to the bar owner. She told us that in this manner she can earn about 20 to 25 Pula in one evening; she uses this money to buy cosmetics and other items she could not normally afford. Other spontaneous income generating opportunities are the sale of firewood or helping people to clean their compound or build a hut. These examples show the large variety of spontaneous activities and the great wealth of ideas in the effort to secure unsustained livelihoods. More regular activities are brewing beer or working at the cattle post or on the fields of other villagers. Working at cattle posts which do not belong to one's household is called *mafisa* and is an old tradition in Tswana society. Usually, men take care of the cattle of another family and during their stay at the cattle post these herdsmen can use the milk and other dairy products; at the end of the year they may receive a calf. This gives the workers the opportunity to gradually build up their own herds. It is, however, becoming more and more common to pay wages in cash rather than in cattle. Another traditional system that can be considered as the agricultural equivalent of *mafisa* is *majako*, which consists of working on the fields of other people and is done mainly by women and children. The women live on the 'lands' during the ploughing season and take care of the fields, but usually they are not paid directly. The owner patrols his fields regularly and brings some maize meal and sugar for his labourers. If the harvest is good, the women involved in *mafisa* get their share in the form of one bag of sorghum or beans. Apart from income-generating possibilities in Letlhakeng itself, some households have at least one member who works outside the village, for example, as a maid in Gaborone, in the mines of South Africa[6] or as a government employee. The state programmes mentioned in the first section of this paper are also a major source of income for most of the households. Twenty-four of the twenty-seven households asked take part in at least one such programme, including the Drought Relief Programme and non drought-related welfare schemes.

The Meanings of Drought

For a large part of the population of Letlhakeng livelihood security is still closely linked to rainfall conditions. Many families still rely directly on arable farming or livestock raising. But for those who are more indirectly involved and paid in cash or kind in the *mafisa* and/or *majako* systems, the weather, too, is important, because their labour, and thus their income, is related to sufficient rainfall. One interviewee explicitly asked us to consider that she can work for other families only if harvest expectations are good and the landowning families can therefore afford to employ other people. This shows that, in the opinion of a larger part of the village population, rain is extremely important. Though drought is not merely a matter of sufficient rainfall, and affects all aspects of rural livelihoods, for most of the persons questioned drought is synonymous with no rain: livestock dies, there is no food, people cannot harvest anything. Drought means hunger and can be deadly, whereas rain means life.

However, other views were also expressed. The following statements came from people who neither cultivate nor have any livestock. For them, rain is less important; nevertheless, they all had a specific idea of drought. For one woman, for example, drought means that she does not have any food at all, no matter if it rains or not. In another household, people felt they never had a time without drought because they never had enough money. Another interviewee stated that drought means hunger and can be deadly; she would not suffer drought if she had a job, no matter what sort of job. For an older woman drought is connected with risk because she has no money to repair her hut; she feared that she might not wake up one morning because she had been buried under the ruins of her house. Two mothers expressed their fears that their children would become thieves and therefore prisoners because they had nothing to eat in times of drought. Drought, in all these cases, stands for 'lack', 'wants' or 'needs'. It is an expression for a livelihood situation which is marginal or not sustainable, and involves highly individualistic concepts of danger, risk, and coping. Meanings of drought can shift through changing living conditions. A woman said that it had been very important to receive rain during the time she was still cultivating her family's fields. Drought then had meant 'no rain'. Today drought was ever present. Drought now meant death because she had nothing to eat. Apart from that, she used drought, at the time of the interview, as a metaphor for 'no place to live' because she had no hut of her own. 'El Niño' is much talked about in Botswana today, and the term is also known in Letlhakeng. It was very important for one woman to mention El Niño, because she had heard about this climatological phenomenon in the radio. She interpreted El Niño as 'too much sun' and the reason why it did not rain enough.

Coping with Drought – Past and Present

These varying statements demonstrate that 'drought' has a very broad range of different meanings for people. We can identify three different sets: (1) For most peasants, drought is still closely connected to rainfall conditions which play a central role in food security and welfare. This understanding, then, implies that lack of rainfall is perceived as a threat to which one has to react by adjusting one's livelihood activities in order to either cope with or, better, avoid disastrous impacts. From past experience, the efficiency and outcomes of different coping measures are known, and local communities will, as best as they can in the context of vulnerability, again try to choose the most adequate strategies. (2) Other views of drought include far-reaching abstractions, as could be shown with the 'El Niño' interpretation. Here, personal involvement is minimised, because El Niño is a 'distant' concept communicated through the media and dislocated from the individual livelihood setting. Knowledge about the true nature and impact of El Niño is rudimentary at best, and therefore opting for the best solution is almost impossible for individuals. In short, one may be able to cope with drought, but not with El Niño. (3) Finally, drought is used as a symbol or metaphor for insecure livelihoods in general. It is not a single danger or threat, but a more or less unspecific description of the state of one's living conditions. Those persons who had specifically linked drought to lack of rainfall and subsequent coping measures often hinted at changes in the nature of their livelihood strategies over the past years. The situations during spells of drought 'in the past' and 'today' were evaluated differently. Some stated that the situation had been better in the past because the parents had successfully engaged in arable farming and owned livestock – mainly cattle – which had made it relatively easy for the family to ride droughts out. Cattle could be sold or slaughtered for food. Some said that it had rained more in the past, harvests had thus been better, and so the family had been able to store seeds and food for harder times. However, others stated that the situation today was better. For most of these villagers, this was due to the existence of state support schemes.

Most people agreed that the elements of coping measures had changed tremendously over the past decades. Some, for instance, mentioned the collection of wild fruits and roots containing water and hunting as coping strategies of the past. These strategies were no longer in use. A young man pointed out that the collection of roots belonged to the past because there had been too many changes and new influences and, apart from that, even if he knew these roots and fruits he would not collect them because it would destroy the ecosystem. An older man told us that in the past people had been organised in groups or collectives where they had worked together[7]. Today, these collectives did not exist anymore, so people were, in his opinion, not able to collect fruits. He also said that hunting was not possible any more because it was now illegal. A mother stated that her daughters did not know the roots and fruits and therefore could not collect them. She was too weak to do it by herself, and saw no reason to teach her children how to identify edible plants. Some persons also stated that social nets had been stronger, and during times of crises people had supported each other within the families. With family ties loosening, this safety net was beginning to dissolve.

Current drought coping strategies involve the intensification of everyday income strategies such as trying to work for other families. But most of the people interviewed stated that this was not very successful. Many commented on the increasing importance of cash. While food shortages in the past generally had been a matter of lacking supply, today food is readily available in the the village shops, but it has to be *bought*, and therefore cash is needed. Someone explained that he had agreed upon a small credit with one of the shopkeepers and had to pay his bills only once a month. He was working as a night watchman and thus had a regular income which made this extra time to pay possible. In his view, this was the best strategy to cope with drought throughout the month. However, most of the informants expressed their opinion that it was the government's duty to help during times of crises. 'Without government assistance', one interviewee said, 'we would be going to die'. Or: 'once this programme is going to be stopped we are going to suffer'; and: 'the government is of great help, I can see that it helps other people'. Some persons stated that their only strategy during drought lay in dependence on the government. Clearly, public drought-relief schemes nowadays form a central part of securing livelihoods in Letlhakeng. Only one interviewee was of the view that people should not wait until everything was done by the state, but try as best as they could to help themselves. But most of the villagers actually demanded government assistance and pointed out the importance, and necessity, of distribution of seeds and food aid. While stating quite clearly that they expected the government to step in in times of drought, some villagers also criticised the procedures of government support. They felt excluded from the programmes because they saw their neighbours participating in the food or cash-for-work scheme and did not understand why they themselves could not take part. They accused government officials of discrimination and thus limiting access to the programmes. Participation in the public relief measures is based on self-registration of families or individuals in need – a system which also received critical comments because it implies that potential participants always have to know when the programmes are activated and when and where to register. This information is not always easily accessible for those who live in remote areas or have no radio or other reliable news sources. So, despite the fact that the public support schemes now form a vital part of drought relief, many villagers and employees of the sub-district administration were of critical of the programmes. They agreed that the threat of famine was eliminated, but that the public support measures did little to sustainably improve their living conditions. Indeed, a major shortcoming of the programmes lies in the fact that they do not motivate participants to engage in self-initiated activities to improve livelihoods. The nature of the support schemes was seen by most interviewees, not so much as one of 'drought relief' but more as one of 'general welfare'.

The Importance of Governmental Assistance Schemes

Some facts about the actual relief measures in Letlhakeng will now underline the importance of the public support schemes. It must be emphasised that there are two 'lines' of governmental support: the Drought Relief Programme, such as the Labour-based Relief Programme, food rations, distributions of free seeds, vaccination of cattle, etc. (see above and cf. Krüger 1997), and government schemes which are independent of drought – such as a monthly pension scheme of 110 Pula for everybody above 60 years of age, the daily or weekly food rations for malnourished children, tuberculosis patients, pregnant women and breastfeeding mothers, the monthly rations for permanent destitutes, etc. People seem to depend very much on both lines. Apart from this, the boundaries between these two categories of programmes seem to blur if one considers that drought years are also declared during years where the national drought indicators do not call for their announcement. Also, at the end of a drought year the distribution of food, for example, is only slowly phased out in order to help people to gradually mobilise their own autonomous coping strategies. As one employee of the subdistrict administration put it: 'We cannot just stop giving them food.'

For the households interviewed the food scheme seemed to be the most important part of the programmes. The so-called destitutes receive a monthly food ration. People in need are divided into permanent destitutes (group A) and drought-induced destitutes (group B – the people who are, for instance, hit by a harvest failure). In May 1999 – a drought year had been announced from June 1998 to June 1999 – the Social Welfare Officer counted 498 permanent and 509 temporary destitutes in Letlhakeng which is about one fifth of the village population. The destitutes get a food ration which is worth 90.30 Pula distributed by the shops in the village. Households which are registered in group A normally receive one ration per eight household members, group B destitutes get one ration per four household members. In the opinion of the Senior Community Development Officer the number of destitutes had increased rapidly in recent years because the extended family system was beginning to break apart. Some household members stated that they depended entirely on these food rations. Some elder people pointed out that younger family members were beginning to rely on their parents' or grandparents' pensions schemes, which was just enough to survive. The Labour-based Relief Programme was important especially for women. From September 1998 to February 1999, ninety-six women and thirty men took part in the programme. Under professional supervision, they constructed an office building for the Village Development Committee, a storing room and a bus-stop shelter. The demand for work had been higher than the supply. As mentioned above, some women had tried to register, without success; others had already registered but were not called for work.

Conclusion: Transforming Meanings, Changing Livelihoods, New Vulnerability Patterns

We have shown in this paper that the rural population in Botswana is far from forming one homogeneous group, and that there are huge variations in drought perception and interpretation. Those engaged in agricultural activities have a clear understanding of the links between drought hazards and adaptation measures. The danger of a drought event is directly translated into risk by engaging in various different coping strategies. Conceiving 'drought' as 'lack of rainfall' determines their everyday life and defines many spatial and temporal household activities in order to prevent or mitigate losses, should the hazard strike. Drought, here, is not an unpredictable danger, but rather an essential, and calculable, part of their livelihood patterns. By deciphering the hazard into a risk, it is embedded into everyday life and induces routines to handle it. Those whose livelihoods are not directly associated with agriculture use the term drought to express lack of employment or money, and as such understand it in a much broader sense.

In order to reach all communities, and not only those directly hit by drought through harvest or cattle losses, the Botswana government tries to stabilise threatened livelihoods by introducing long-term national welfare schemes. As shown in the paper, it became obvious that this involves a shift in the State's perception of drought relief, from the 'classic' entitlement approach, which is widely acknowledged as a multi-layer concept to understand and reduce famine risk, to a broader conception, unfortunately including strategies to gain votes. The new welfare measures are relatively effective but also very costly, and they have an unintended side-effect of contributing to the transformation and probably the deterioration of autonomous coping strategies in rural areas. There is no doubt that, by sub-Saharan African standards at least, the public welfare schemes in Botswana are unique, and that they are extraordinarily helpful in improving the income situation of rural households. Vulnerability of rural households is, indeed, reduced. However, the government had always tried to emphasise self-reliance of drought-affected people, and had tried to promote risk awareness and preparedness at the community and household levels, beyond the scope of public support and interventions. This line of action cannot be maintained any longer, because the population today expects the government to intervene, and, in general, sees no reason for being denied public assistance. It remains uncertain whether the new government schemes will really lead to a more sustainable mitigation of household insecurity in the long run. Households tend to rely more and more on national relief, but should this relief have to be denied, for example, due to lack of financial resources, traditionally functioning coping measures are no longer within easy reach.

We must keep in mind, though, that the impact of risk conceptions on vulnerability is not dependent only on drought-related issues. As has been shown at the beginning of this paper, AIDS and urbanisation have become major factors of influence in Botswana's society, and both are, in very different ways, expressions of modernisation. They play a huge part in altering vulnerability patterns, which had, for decades, been closely related to drought-related entitlement declines, and they play a role in uncoupling perceptions, decisions and activities from the rural living context. In the wake of urbanisation, for example, agricultural activities become less important and environmental perceptions get more and more disconnected from the 'real' physical environment. We have seen that, triggered by media reports, 'El Niño' has become a phrase to describe drought, but it is an interpretation of little value in the 'true' everyday adaptation routine in rural Botswana, a livelihood routine which today is based a great deal more on public assistance than in the past.

Notes

1. It is almost impossible to get reliable figures for the overall costs of drought-relief schemes in Botswana. An internal government paper (MFDP 1992) estimates the total expenses for wages and infrastructural improvements for the labour-based programme alone (from June 1992 to June 1993) at 37.18 million Pula, equivalent to 14.9 million Euro.
2. Our own conversations with several local chiefs, in the course of several research projects in Botswana since 1991, indicate that, indeed, Kgotla meetings became rarer, or are attended by fewer people, and drought-related issues involving collective decisions are now seldom brought forward. The authority of the Kgotla, in general, is diminishing.
3. A decline in household labour force available for farm work, etc., is now also brought about by the impact of the HIV/AIDS pandemic. Its impact on food security has up to now not been assessed extensively in Botswana.
4. The SeKgalagadi-speaking BaKgalagadi are not to be seen as a homogeneous ethnic group or tribe. The people who are called BaKgalagadi have three things in common: (1) they all originate from South Africa; (2) they have split off from larger social groups in the past; and (3) they have, due to their small size, been forced out of relatively fertile areas in the east (see Helle-Valle 1997: 82). This, of course, says little about ethnicity. Helle-Valle counted 78 percent SeKgalagadi- and 15 percent SeTswana-speaking members of the village community; 7 percent belonged to other groups (op. cit.).
5. Helle-Valle (1997: 119) found that, on average, a household in Letlhakeng engages in 4.1 types of different economic activities. He excluded, however, remittances from other households and earnings through social security measures
6. Working in mines used to be a very important source of monetary income in Letlhakeng. Even in 1990 members of 26 percent of all households were still engaged in mining in South Africa (Helle-Valle 1997: 107).
7. He probably referred to the age regiments (*mephato*) which were organised through the initiation rites. In times of crises these age regiments had to work and fight together (see Schapera and Comaroff 1991).

References

AIDS/STD-Unit (Ministry of Health) 1999. *AIDS Statistics.* Gaborone. (Updated via Internet: http://www.info.bw/~aidstd.unit/).

Blaikie, P., T. Cannon, I. Davis and B. Wisner 1994. *At Risk.* London and New York: Routledge.

Carney, D. et al. 1999. *Livelihoods Approaches Compared.* London: DFID.

Chambers, R. 1989. 'Editorial Introduction: Vulnerability, Coping and Policy', *IDS Bulletin* 20(2): 1–7.

CSO (Central Statistics Office) 1991. Stats Brief, no. 91/4, Gaborone.

Derichs, A. and T. Rauch 2000. 'LRE und der "Sustainable Rural Livelihoods" Ansatz', *Entwicklungsethnologie* 9(2): 60–78.

Douglas, M. 1992. 'Risk and Danger', in *Risk and Blame. Essay in Cultural Theory,* ed. M. Douglas, 38–54. London and New York: Routledge.

Edge, W.A. and M.H. Lekorwe, eds. 1998. *Botswana – Politics and Society.* Pretoria: Schaik.

FEWS (Famine Early Warning System) 2003. http://www.fews.net/livelihoods/framework/ (access: 20.01.2003).

Goland, C. 1993. 'Field Scattering as Agricultural Risk Management. A Case Study from Cuyo Cuyo, Department of Puno, Peru', *Mountain Research and Development* 13: 317–33.

Hay, R. 1988. 'Famine Incomes and Development: Has Botswana Anything to Teach Africa?', *World Development* 16(9): 1113–25.

Helle-Valle, J. 1997. *Change and Diversity in a Kgalagadi Village, Botswana.* Dissertations and Theses no. 1/97, Oslo: Centre for Development and the Environment.

Hitchcock, R. 1979. 'The Traditional Response to Drought in Botswana', in *The Botswana Society,* ed. M. Hinchey, 91–7. Symposium on Drought in Botswana. Gaborone.

Holm J. and R. Morgan 1985. 'Coping with Drought in Botswana: An African Success', *The Journal of Modern African Studies* 23(3): 463–82.

Krüger, F. 1994. 'Urbanization and Vulnerable Urban Groups in Gaborone/Botswana', *GeoJournal* 34(4): 287–93.

——— 1997. *Urbanisierung und Verwundbarkeit in Botswana, Sozio-ökonomische Prozesse in Asien und Afrika* 1, Pfaffenweiler: Centaurus.

——— 1999. 'Drought Hazards and Treatened Livelihoods – Environmental Perceptions in Botswana', in *Coping with Changing Environments,* eds. B. Lohnert und H. Geist, 175–90. Aldershot: Ashgate.

——— 2002. 'From Winner to Loser? Botswana's Society under the Impact of Aids', *Petermanns Geographische Mitteilungen* 146(3): 50–9.

——— 2003. 'Handlungsorientierte Entwicklungsforschung: Trends, Perspektiven, Defizite', *Petermanns Geographische Mitteilungen* 147(1): 6–15.

——— and E. Macamo 2003. 'Existenzsicherung unter Risikobedingungen – Sozialwissenschaftliche Analyseansätze zum Umgang mit Krisen, Konflikten und Katastrophen', *Geographica Helvetica* 57(2): 47–55.

Luhmann, N. 1991. *Soziologie des Risikos.* Berlin: de Gruyter.

MacDonald, D.S. 1996. 'Notes on the Socio-Economic and Cultural Factors Influencing the Transmissions of HIV in Botswana', *Social Science Medicine* 42(9): 1325–33.

McDonald, K.I. 1998. 'Rationality, Representation, and Risk Mediation Characteristics of a Karakorum Mountain Farming System', *Human Ecology* 26(2): 287–321.

Mazonde, I. 2000. 'Social Transformation and Food Security in the Household: The Experience of Rural Botswana', in *Botswana – Alltagswelten im Umbruch*, eds. F. Krüger, G. Rakelmann and P. Schierholz, 53–73. Münster, Hamburg, London: LIT Verlag.

MFDP (Ministry of Finance and Development Planning) 1992. 'Aide Memoire – The Drought Situation in Botswana and the Government Response' (unpublished).

Mgadla, P.T. 1998. 'The Kgosi in a Traditional Tswana Setting', in *Botswana – Politics and Society*, eds. W.A. Edge and M.H. Lekorwe, 3–10. Pretoria: Schaik.

Molutsi, P.P. 1998. 'Elections and Electoral Experience in Botswana', in *Botswana – Politics and Society*, eds. W.A. Edge and M.H. Lekorwe, 363–77. Pretoria: Schaik.

Schapera, I. and J. Camoroff 1991. *The Tswana*, rev. edn. London: Kegan Paul International Ltd.

Sen, A. 1981. *Poverty and Famines. An Essay on Entitlements and Deprivation.* Oxford: Clarendon.

Somolekae, G.M. and M.H. Lekorwe 1998. 'The Chieftaincy System and Politics in Botswana, 1966–95', in *Botswana – Politics and Society*, eds. W.A. Edge and M.H. Lekorwe, 186–98. Pretoria: Schaik.

Teklu, T. 1994. 'The Prevention and Migration of Famine: Policy Lessons from Botswana and Sudan', *Disasters* 18(1): 35–47.

Watts, M. and H.-G. Bohle 1993. 'The Space of Vulnerability: The Causal Structure of Hunger and famine', *Progress in Human Geography* 17(1): 43–67.

10

CULTURAL POLITICS OF NATURAL DISASTERS: DISCOURSES ON VOLCANIC ERUPTIONS IN INDONESIA

Judith Schlehe

Research on Natural Disasters in the Social Sciences

In Western thought, nature is conceptualised as environment, 'out there', excluding the 'inner nature' of man. But the term 'natural disaster' should not distract from human factors being responsible for, or having an influence on, natural events. Even when the primary causes are not 'man-made', as is the case for example with earthquakes and volcanic eruptions, the effects on human beings make the designation 'disastrous' unquestionable. Hence, human involvement cannot be denied, 'because "natural" disasters always occur from a combination of nature and society.' (Geipel 1992, translation mine). Many disasters are a complex mix of natural hazards and human action. In this context it must also be remembered that in the twentieth century, not nature but political power and violence have engendered the highest numbers of victims.

The dominant view of contemporary natural hazards is still determined by geophysical and geotechnical perspectives and the aims of managerial capability (Hewitt 1983: 7; cf. also Chester 1993: 238f.). But in more complex, recent approaches a disaster has also been defined as 'Disaster = Hazard x Vulnerability' (Shook 1997: 79), indicating that the vulnerability of a society or an environment determines the degree to which an event becomes a disaster.[1] In most studies, vulnerability is indicated by factors such as population density, stability of houses, possibilities for evacuation, etc., but, interestingly enough, neither the interpretations of the affected people nor the symbolic meanings embedded in their lives and world-views are included. There are, however, at least some approaches which criticise conventional disaster work for treating symptoms, rather than causes by not recognising that vulnerability is deeply rooted in political relations, international economic systems and development policies (Blaikie et al. 1994: 233). Special emphasis is laid in these approaches on the relationship between underdevelopment and hazard impact in the Third World, since it is in the poorest countries that natural disasters claim most lives.

In a report prepared for the 'International Decade of Natural Disaster Reduction' (IDNDR) declared by the United Nations for the 1990s, it is stated that 'for the relief of disasters it is of fundamental importance that … the social conditions in the affected countries are included' (Plate et al. 1993: 21). But whatever the physical reality and the social and political conditions, disasters must also be seen in terms of how they are perceived and estimated by those who are directly involved. To date, scientific disaster research has not made many efforts to study and compare the cross-cultural experiences, perspectives and perceptions of the affected and threatened peoples (Alexander 1993: 573), nor to investigate the existing body of knowledge on ways of dealing with natural forces. This does not mean that there are no perception approaches in hazard research which investigate the influence of perceptions on the activities of the affected populations. But older studies tend to be deterministic, based on a purely reactive conception of man (Tzschaschel 1986: 50), whereas more recent scholarship (Smith 2001: 70)[2] focuses mainly on the individual. These studies hardly connect subjective influences derived from personal perceptions with social and cultural contexts. This is also the case in psychological stress research that investigates the special coping-strategies with which people react to threatening events in their environments. These strategies are not seen as meaningful adaptations of behaviour within a particular context, but rather as inadequate denial and negation of hazards (Ketterer and Spada 1993). Such studies in disaster-psychology and -sociology are mostly restricted to concrete ways of dealing with calamities, thus paying little attention to the broader social, political and religious contexts in which affected individuals act. More recently, several anthropological studies have been published that trace myths and legends back to natural phenomena.[3] This is for the most part historical reconstruction. In contrast, the detailed description of the ways of coping with the eruption of Mount Pinatubo (Philippines) in 1991 by Seitz (1998, 2004) focuses primarily on the practical ways in which a group dealt with the eruption in accordance with traditional economic and social structures.[4] Furthermore, Seitz provides a critical review of the aid and resettlement programmes (see also Seitz, this volume). The cultural and social construction of catastrophe in anthropological perspective and the varieties of cultural response are described and analysed for various regions and times by Oliver-Smith and Hoffman (Oliver-Smith and Hoffman 1999; Hoffman and Oliver-Smith 2002).

In a similar way the present article[5] seeks to examine the emic background and the symbolic basis of human perceptions of nature and natural disasters in a certain historical situation. Starting from a few general remarks on the concepts of nature, I shall concentrate on the connections between volcanoes and politics in Java. Before entering into the details of Javanese interpretations of Mt Merapi's eruptions in the 1990s, I shall give a few examples from Indonesian history concerning volcanic eruptions in the nineteenth and twentieth centuries. My aim is to show the cultural appropriation and political significance of volcanoes by demonstrating the creativity of the affected peoples in explaining eruptions.

Conceptualisations of Nature

The processes of appropriating nature are diverse in different cultures, since reality is perceived, structured and negotiated in multiple, changeable contexts. It has been widely asserted in recent studies that nature is not an objective given, but a cultural construct which is historically mediated and permanently changing (e.g. Luig 1995: 6), varying historically and ethnographically according to different levels of discourse. Thus, the qualities of our environment have much to do with human consciousness and, most importantly, there is no opposition between nature and culture. Nature provides metaphors for culture, and humans can experience nature only and when mediated by cultural categories. Yet, a scientific deconstruction of nature does not necessarily prevent us from a critical perspective on how nature is made meaningful through cognition and active processes of practical engagement (Ellen 1996: 3), often by means of rituals.[6]

Due to a structural analogy of nature and societies, seen as mutually constitutive, natural disasters in Africa and Asia are more often than not explained simply by natural causes, but are traced back to the incorrect conduct of human beings. Although by no means uniform, nature is constructed as parallel to human society; it is anthropomorphised, and close associations are drawn between cosmos, morality and social conduct (Frömming and Schlehe 2005; Luig 1995: 9). Accordingly, in Javanese world-view, too, the individual, society, nature and the cosmos are inseparably connected and are ideally in a state of harmonious balance (Magnis-Suseno 1981). Some authors even claim to find a timeless essence of Javanese human's benign relationship to nature or an intrinsic sense of harmony with, or reverence for, the magical properties of the natural world (cf. Day 1994: 180, 198). But generalised statements of this kind are often merely a projection of Western ecological thinking concerning Asian philosophies, which are then associated with a positive correspondence and balance with nature and an harmonious image of an inseparable, holistic unity of man and environment. This is a romanticised counter-image of the European culture's relationship to nature, seen as based on dominance and exploitation (Pedersen 1995). But, as will be exemplified in this chapter, in Java nature provides a source for the construction of manifold meanings and experiences, as well as for the interpretation and manipulation of social relations in the political and social spheres. Specific manners of emotional attachment to the land as well as aesthetic perceptions are rooted in political, social and also economic practices, and these are determined by age, class and gender. As these constructions are variable – in Indonesia as well as elsewhere – they cannot be reduced to a modern ecological and conservationist representation of nature which is always directed towards unity, harmony and empowerment, as a 'global ideology of nature' suggests (cf. Bruun and Kalland 1995: 269).

If we try to reconstruct the specific Javanese way of conceptualising nature, we shall certainly recognise some ambivalence. People experience powerful, awe-inspiring and destructive forces in nature, as well as life-giving qualities. In general, the 'dangerous' sites in nature are not perceived in a purely negative way; they are considered spiritually endowed and sacred (*keramat*). They also enable one to acquire special powers and blessings. Especially volcanoes are foci of magical power and supernatural forces. In former times people climbed mountains and volcanoes (in central Java: Merapi, Turgo, Lawu, Merbabu) and went to the south coast in order to forge magical weapons. Old Javanese poets describe themselves as wandering through settings of seashore and mountain in search of poetic inspiration and mystical experience (Day 1994: 185). Nowadays many people still go there for ascetic practises and meditation or to receive spiritual potency, inspiration, esoteric knowledge and objects with magical powers, or to achieve mystical means of becoming wealthy. But in this context we can observe a shift of focus to another sort of empowered terrain: there is a new tendency, especially among younger people, to prefer for spiritual pursuits a human-made, constructed topography of monuments, for example, graves and mausoleums (Pemberton 1994: 276).

The Political Significance of Nature in Java

The rulers of the ancient southeast Asian kingdoms constructed their legitimisation through mystical connections with nature. What is depicted in representations of the natural world in the temple and literary art of early Java (ninth to fifteenth centuries) is the king's landscape rather than a purely 'natural' one. These representations imply the king's implicit, ordering presence within the natural world which they claimed to be inherently their own (Day 1994: 194–202). In this context it is noticeable that the 'lords of the mountains' referred to the Indic concept of a world mountain. In the image of the cosmic Mt Meru in Hindu-Buddhist mythology we find an analogy between macro- and micro perspectives. It is symbolic both of the world/terrestrial order, and of the spiritual/cosmic order, and it mediates between the two. The axis of the world goes in both directions: human souls can ascend and divine blessing can descend.

Thus, there is no static image of the mountain. It is regarded as dynamic, symbolising the metamorphosis of the lower, material, worldly, to the higher, immaterial, spiritual realm and in the social sphere, from ruled to ruler (Wright 1994: 44). On the summits we find the seats of the gods, spirits and ancestors which determine human affairs in an active way.

Candidates for the throne in Java (often usurpers) had to climb mountains and meditate in caves and rivers in order to obtain the legitimisation of the invisible transcendental powers. Indigenous written sources, the court chronicles of the kingdom of Mataram in Central Java, for instance, refer to the connections of the founder of the kingdom, Panembahan Senopati (AD 1575–1601), to the spirits of the Merapi volcano on the one hand and to the spirit-queen of the South Sea, Ratu Kidul, on the other (Babad Tanah Jawi, ed. Sudibjo 1980: 103–6). Senopati, a Muslim, legitimised his conquest by reference to these indigenous, non-Islamic figures. Before he seized power, he sent his uncle and advisor to the Merapi, while he himself made the pilgrimage to the south coast where his legitimacy was affirmed by the Queen of the Sea, Ratu Kidul. Since that time the rulers of Mataram have been mystically connected to this spirit queen by bonds of love and marriage (Schlehe 1998). The Sultan's palace (*kraton*) is situated half-way between sea and volcano, and the Sultans are legitimated and protected by both spirit kingdoms. Following Ratu Kidul's promise to support Senopati and all his successors, the kingdom (since 1755 divided into the Sultanates of Surakarta/Solo and Jogjakarta) has always been protected against Merapi's eruptions. Kyai Sapujagad, the giant spirit-ruler in the kingdom of the crater, a former servant of Senopati, has to take care that the lava never flows in the southern direction, to the *kraton* of Jogjakarta. Therefore, to this day the population of Jogja feels safe and protected from the eruptions of the Merapi volcano. In return, both the spirits of the mountains and those from the sea receive garments and food as offerings from Senopati and his successors in the yearly *Labuhan* sacrificial ceremony.

Thus, in Java the mandate for political authority is connected with the role of the rulers as divine mediators with the whole living universe. But once there are calamities, the ruler loses his power. In this context it is important to note that ideas about spirits not only legitimise political power, but can also 'delegitimise' it. A Balinese priest, Mangku Made Wiryo, interviewed in 1996, said: 'The process of nature (*alam*) will take care of justice for mankind in the future. It will become obvious who is greedy and these people will be judged by nature. Greedy is the one who turns the power and strength of the rich against the poor. That's called greedy. This one will be judged by nature. Because mankind doesn't have the strength to judge him.' This is in accordance with the ancient Javanese expectation that as a final apocalyptic event, and also during the last stage of a kingdom, calamities and chaos will occur in nature. Out of the debris of this catastrophe will arise a revitalised cosmos and the possibility of a profoundly different era. Hence despotic systems of power are destroyed by natural disasters, diseases and so forth. Such ideas can be traced back to the very popular prophecies of Joyoboyo,[7] who forecast that Java would be ruled by foreigners, finally achieving independence: first there would be suffering, but in the end, about five hundred years after the demise of the Majapahit Kingdom, it would return to its old dimensions in a Golden Age. Poverty, repression and social unrest, as well as crop failures, epidemics and eruptions of Merapi, are all regarded as apocalyptic events that occur in the 'age of curse'. But the coming of Ratu Adil (just king/renewer of the world/messiah), will herald a happy era.

By the end of the 1990s I often heard in Java that Ratu Adil can also be a woman. In the coming era the female element will substitute the male one. In this way the initial popularity of Megawati Sukarnoputri, who was elected vice president in 1999 and president in 2001, was embedded in mystical connections between politics and nature. According to these mystical principles, turmoil and change in the present cosmos are understood as necessities: what exists has to be destroyed for a new world to be created.

Explanations of Volcanic Eruptions in Indonesia: Examples from History

The Indonesian scientist Lapian collected several historical examples in order to illustrate the considerable influence that natural disasters have had on local history in different parts of Indonesia. The eruption of the volcano Tambora (2,860 m) in Sumbawa in 1815 was the largest natural disaster in Indonesia and in the whole history of mankind: 80 times more energy was set free than in the Krakatau eruption of 1883; 11,000 people died immediately, 37,800 starved and died from diseases following the eruption, 3,600 fled the island on which only five years later there was a harvest again. Caused by the ash rainfalls on the neighbouring islands, there was a spread of famine and epidemics, and even in Europe the climate changed dramatically in the following years. Bernice de Jong Boers (1995: 58) concludes that altogether the eruption caused at least 117,000 human deaths. Local sources on Sumbawa, as recorded by Lapian (1992), say the events were caused by an old man who had been wronged – according to one version this was one Haji Mustafa; according to another, a certain Tuan Said Idrus, an Arab trader from Bengkulu. It is said that he had been killed on a mountain following the orders of the Raja of Tambora. Therefore his murderers were pursued by a fire until the whole kingdom was in flames (Lapian 1992: 218). What I was told by a man from Sumbawa is that people there had been rich but decadent before the eruption. They caused it by cheating an *ulama*, a Muslim scholar and religious teacher, who had come to teach them about good and bad, purity and impurity. He was invited to eat rice and meat together and they made a joke out of cheating him by giving him dog's meat.

Probably not knowing about the Tambora, the German novelist Arno Schmidt (1975) characterised the eruption of Krakatau in a fictive dialogue as follows:

> At 10.02 a.m., on 27 August 1883, the biggest event, the disaster with the vastest dimensions of which written history knows occurred – the only identified global event that effected the whole world. – Still the biggest, in spite of all nuclear tests (Schmidt 1975: 46).

During the eruption of the Krakatau (822 m high, after the eruption a hole of 250 m) in 1883 the whole island exploded or collapsed – views on this still differ – with the force of 10,000 bombs of the Hiroshima type, causing tidal waves whose impact could be felt as far as Europe. The biggest wave was 40 m high, and caused the death of at least 36,000 people, mostly from Banten (West Java) and Lampung (South Sumatra). Clouds of ash enveloped the earth and caused dust and ash to rain down up to 6,000 km away. The following local explanations exist for the eruption of the Krakatau:

a) Religious, Islamic interpretations:

- It was a punishment from Allah because Islamic law had been violated.
- The faithful saw it as an admonition from Allah to combat the unfaithful.

b) Political interpretations:

- In Lampung people drew a connection to the war in Aceh (North Sumatra). The eruption was interpreted as punishment for the Dutch who at the time had occupied the big mosque of Kutaraja.
- The eruption was seen as supporting resistance against the Dutch, who left the area because Lampung became economically uninteresting for them after all their plantations were devastated. There are several eye-witness reports of the eruption, but these are all written by foreigners, by members of the crews of warships or merchant ships, by colonial officers, soldiers or missionaries. For instance, Simkin and Fiske (1983) quote eighty-seven such reports, but from only one can we draw indirect conclusions regarding the perceptions of the local people. A Dutchman, who was successful in escaping from Anyer, reports that many European men and even more women who had run away from the tsunami to the mountains, died on the roadside, because none of the locals helped them, nobody gave them any food. On the contrary they were chased away, and according to this Dutchman the locals blamed the foreigners for the disaster (Simkin and Fiske 1983: 74).
- As a reaction to the eruption the local centre of the colonial government moved from Anyer to Cilegon. In 1888 social unrest and rebellions against the colonial government with far-reaching effects followed. These rebellions were caused, among others, by the poverty of the farmers after the eruption.

c) Interpretations in accordance with the local *adat* (traditional system of values and rules):

- In Banten, a *Bupati* (leader of the local government) had broken the taboo against celebrating circumcision and marriage at the same time. This is seen as the reason why all his guests were killed by a tsunami (Lapian 1992: 219–25).

It is obvious that several explanations existed simultaneously but unfortunately, due to a lack of sources, we cannot reconstruct when and in which context a particular explanation was used.

I have no information on local interpretations of the rise of Anak Krakatau (the Child of Krakatau; 270 m), that arose from the sea in the Sunda Strait caused by several eruptions following the year 1927. It is still one of the most dangerous volcanoes in Indonesia. We know only that panic broke out among the inhabitants of the coastal regions of West Java and South Sumatra. In contrast, a minor eruption in 1972 was taken calmly and as a routine matter (Blong 1984: 154). But that Anak Krakatau is seen in a mystical way can be concluded from the local fishermen's habit of sacrificing goats there on special days (Thornton 1996: 280). An anthropological investigation of the local perceptions of this very active volcano is needed.[8] Other volcanic eruptions make the symbolic connection to religion and politics even more obvious. For instance, the eruption of Mount Agung (3,142 m) on Bali in 1963 was not only directly associated with certain rituals missing during a ceremony which takes place at the Besakih temple[9] every hundred years (*Eka Dasa Rudra*). This 1963 eruption is also depicted in highly dramatic accounts in a narrative strategy that obviously imitates the famous *puputan* in 1908 – the ritual suicide of Balinese noblemen facing the supremacy of the Dutch colonisers. It is said that in 1963 some ceremonially dressed priests faced the deadly lava, showing their acceptance of the gods' judgement (McNeely and Wachtel 1991: 23f.). At the same time the eruption of Mt Agung was interpreted as an indication of the political events in 1965 that resulted in the fall of President Sukarno and the death at the hands of government troops of some 500,000 people, following a failed coup by the Indonesian Communist Party. In the same way the eruption of Mt Galunggung in West Java in 1982 (Chester 1993: 291) was seen by Javanese mystics as a sign that the divine source of power of President Suharto was fading away (Blong 1984: 178). Another interesting example is the contested symbolic meaning of the Kelimutu (Keli Mutu 1,613 m) on Flores as described by Frömming (2001, 2005). Its proximity to East Timor led to it being adopted as a symbol of the Movement for Independence there. Simultaneously, and in a quite contrary manner, the government adopted it as a symbol of the Indonesian Nation State.[10] But most important in this respect is Mt Merapi, due to its location in the centre of the Mataram kingdom, not only geographically, but even more in the Javanese worldview.

Mt Merapi

The committee responsible for volcanoes in the 'International Decade for Natural Disaster Reduction' selected fifteen highly dangerous volcanoes world-wide. One of these 'decade high risk volcanoes' is Mt Merapi (2,911 m) situated at the frontier of the Daerah Istimewa Yogyakarta (Special Province of Yogyakarta) and the province Jawa Tengah (Central Java). It is said to be one of the most active of Indonesia's more than 130 active volcanoes, and its recent and historical activity is characterised by glowing avalanches resulting from the collapse of an andesitic lava dome. Most dangerous are the hot clouds, '*awan panas*' (pyroclastic ash and rockflow), poisonous gases and volcanic material which are washed down by rain (Pichler 1985: 79). The worst-case scenario would be if an inner blockade prevented lava and gas from escaping. This would cause a gigantic explosion, like the earlier one at Krakatau. There is an average of 7.5 years between bigger eruptions at Merapi, which have had many victims and destroyed many villages.[11] Usually the lava flows to the west or southwest, following the river valleys. The number of victims is so large because of the high population density. At least 50,000 people live on Merapi's southwestern slopes, and there are villages up to nearly 1,700 m and as close as 5 km to the crater. People here make their living mainly from raising cattle, cultivating vegetables and collecting wood and grass. When a big lava dome collapsed and caused an eruption on 22 November 1994, the stream of lava and the hot cloud turned south for the first time, in the direction of Jogjakarta. It did not reach the city but there were sixty-nine victims, most of them from the village of Turgo. In addition, 5,500 people were evacuated and housed in shelters. The activity continued with minor eruptions of hot ash-clouds, again travelling to the south. There was another big eruption on 17 January 1997, with a cloud of ash and sand that grew vertically up to 4,000 m. It was said that it 'looked like a giant'. For a time, 18,000 people had to be evacuated (*Kompas* 18/1/97). This was good propaganda for the government just before the elections, yet many people refused to leave their villages.

In the village of Kinahrejao the *juru kunci*[12], Mbah Marijan, a man of high reputation as spiritual expert and gatekeeper (I shall refer to him later, as he is the leader of the *Labuhan* ceremony), went, together with fifty men, to the mosque when the volcano started to erupt, in order to pray. They did not leave the village (*Republika* 18/1/97). One hundred families from Kinahrejo and Turgo remained in their houses, and most of the trucks which were supposed to pick them up had to return empty. The people living on the slopes of Merapi regard Kinahrejo as a 'key village', in the sense that nothing would happen to the other villages as long as Kinahrejo was not destroyed (*Kompas* 19/1/97). When I visited old Mbah Marijan in March 1997, I realised that his memory had become weak. Nevertheless, he was very often visited by journalists and invited for lectures to Jogjakarta, and in 2006 he still led the *Labuhan* ceremony. How can it be that an old man in a remote village holds such a key position? What does he stand for?

In the following I wish to explain how the eruptions of Mt Merapi in the 1990s with their peculiar direction towards the south, to Jogjakarta, were interpreted by the inhabitants. I shall also refer to the representations in the media and the reaction of the government.[13] The feeling of safety of the citizens of Jogjakarta and the persistence with which the people living in the volcano's vicinity remain there, can only be understood if we combine pragmatic views with culture-specific and religious interpretations and their relevance to practice. At the same time, I shall try and show that the reactions to an event in nature can reflect much more than just the local perception of nature and risk.

Perspectives of the Residents Living on the Slopes of Mt Merapi

The villagers inhabiting the southern slopes of Mt Merapi, the most famous being the villages of Turgo and Kinahrejo,[14] regard the volcano as sacred (*keramat*), manifesting the powers of non-human beings. The myth of its origin explains that Java was lopsided until the Merapi and other mountains were created (Schlehe 1996: 394).Within the crater, the villagers say, there is a spirit kingdom (*kerajaan makhluk halus*), inhabited by rulers, soldiers and servants, living in a palace (*kraton*) which looks like that of the Sultan of Jogjakarta. The servants are said to be the spirits of good deceased persons. There is also a population consisting of spirits, working as farmers and herders, having vehicles and streets (Triyoga 1991: 45f.). Asked how the villagers, as Muslims, combine these beliefs with Islam, they say that they see no contradiction, as spirit realms are subject to the rule of God (*Tuhan, Allah*). But they do not mix or syncretise the belief systems; rather, they hold them up as parallels.

With their inner eyes (*mata batin*), some people can perceive the rivers carrying life-giving water to human beings and plants flowing from Mt Merapi to the south coast as 'streets' of the spirits. And it is regarded as most important that a connecting street like this is not blocked by anything. Elderly people claim that before the world became so noisy from motors, radios and other modern items, they often heard certain spirits, *lampor*, on the rivers or in the air above the rivers which connect the spirit kingdoms of the mountain with the spirit kingdom of the sea.[15] This was seen as a sign that the spirits visited one another.

In the village of Kinahrejo, people believe that after death humans work the same way in the kingdom of the Merapi as they did when they were still alive. If somebody disappears in the mountains and the corpse is not found, this means that Eyang[16] Merapi had need for workers. The spirits of the volcano and the ancestor spirits maintain close relationships with humans. They can warn certain people before there is a volcanic eruption. Usually they do this in dreams or inspirations. Other warning signs are sounds from the crater, lightning above the mountain and wild animals that approach the villages to let the residents know that the Merapi is going to erupt. The relationships between the spirits that belong to different kingdoms are often conceptualised as sexual. They marry one another[17] and work together in supporting each Sultan. If Mt Merapi erupts, some people say that the lava flow is an ejaculation of the mountain spirits.

In my eyes, it gives people some subjective sense of security to believe that only those persons become victims of the volcano who have done something wrong to Eyang Merapi, or who have committed sins or forgotten the ancestors or the *adat* (the traditional normative system). People feel that they are not just at the mercy of something incomprehensible, but that they can do a lot to influence or at least explain their fate and to counteract threats from the volcano. Thus there is a certain attribution of events in nature to human responsibility and a creative cultural integration of the experiences of threats and hazards. This I see neither as fatalism or repression, nor as a form of 'control', as many of the approaches used in natural disaster research would perhaps suggest (Hidajat 2001: 43f.), but as the cultural creation of a vivid interrelation between the forces of nature and human agents. Life after death, social life in the village, and the environment are connected. This includes both the natural environment and the nearby town. In the same context we can see the smaller rituals and offerings (*sesajen*) of the villagers and the *Labuhan* ceremony of Jogjakarta's Sultan's Palace (*kraton*) as an integral and integrating part of life at the volcano.

The Labuhan Ceremony

The annual *Labuhan* sacrificial ceremony is a revitalisation of the relationship between the *kraton*, the villages, the mountains and the sea (Bigeon 1982; Schlehe 1998). The ceremony is held on the south coast, at Mt Lawu and Mt Merapi simultaneously. The offerings are meant to protect the ruler, the court and the kingdom and are supposed to guarantee a harmonious relationship with the world of the spirits. Most importantly, the ceremony dedicated to Mt Merapi acts as a reminder of mythological promise referred to above that Mataram will always be protected against Merapi's eruptions because the ruler of the volcano realm will never send the lava towards the *kraton*. The ceremony from Jogjakarta[18] starts at the *kraton*, where the offerings are ritually prepared and stored for days at certain places. They consist of textiles for garments, perfume, incense, money and every eight years, a horse saddle. On the first morning of the ceremony a group of court officials (*abdi dalem*) goes with the offerings by car to the house of the *juru kunci* in the village Kinahrejo. The *juru kunci*, Mbah Marijan, is the leader of the ceremony, legitimised by the *kraton*. In his house the women of the village prepare the food for a ceremonial meal (*selamatan*) for humans and spirits which takes place late at night. Participants are the *abdi dalem*, the *juru kunci* and his helpers, representatives of the local government and many male and female guests. Early next morning the procession starts the ascent up the mountain with the offerings. Already, months beforehand, the *juru kunci* and his helpers have prepared the path. Yellow umbrellas are held up, a horse carries the saddle and the women of the village carry the heavy baskets full of food. The procession stops twice, at the entrance gates to the *kraton* Merapi, to pray. Usually the main ceremony then takes place just below the tree-line.[19] The offerings are given by spreading them out while incense is burned and people pray. The *juru kunci* and his assistants distribute some food among all participants. One of the very central figures in the *Labuhan* Merapi is a woman, whose task is to accompany the ceremony with her prayers. Hence, although on the official level the ceremony is dominated by men, male and female roles are complementary in the spiritual tasks.

Government Measures and the Residents' Resistance

According to Soehardi, a lecturer in Anthropology at the Gadjah Mada University of Jogjakarta, there are two things that threaten the people who live at Mt Merapi: volcanic eruptions and transmigration (Soehardi 1995). In former times the ancestors of the villagers lived in lower regions. But they had to flee from the forced agricultural labour and taxes levied by the Dutch. They laid out fields in the high rain forest, but already during the colonial period, the government developed programmes to prevent the villagers from collecting wood and grass and clearing fields. Inhabitants of the surrounding cities of Jogjakarta, Surakarta and Magelang believed that they were threatened by soil erosion and flooding (Handojo 1985: 48) and they feared for their water supply. Therefore the Dutch declared the forest a protected area in 1912.

To combat volcanic hazards, the Merapi Volcano Observatory with five observatory posts was founded in Jogjakarta in 1953. With highly precise technological instruments, Indonesian and foreign scientists try to establish a warning system, but reliable forecasts are still impossible to make. Furthermore, it is difficult to warn the villagers because the communication system is weak. A related measure was the establishment of hazard zones.[20] But there are still many people who live there, even in the forbidden zone;[21] they fear the resettlement (*transmigrasi*) programmes of the government more than the volcano. *Transmigrasi* is not only for people living in dangerous areas, but in general to decrease the population density in the overcrowded islands of Indonesia, and to advance development in 'underdeveloped' regions.[22]

The main areas designated for resettlement are Sumatra, Kalimantan, South Sulawesi and West Papua (Irian Jaya). Most of the new villages are situated in primary rain forest, and settlements frequently fail due to different soil conditions, the lack of government infrastructure and because settlers are disappointed by their new surroundings (Handojo 1985: 52). But in the light of the events in recent years we know that a main problem is that the indigenous population in the resettlement areas often envies and hates the newcomers, and interaction leads to extremely violent conflicts. From the perspective of the

Javanese, there were warning voices already sounding before open conflicts broke out. The government *transmigrasi* programmes were accused of considering only the material and physical wellbeing of the people, thereby neglecting the spiritual dimension. Javanese do not like to move their homes; people are not used to mobility, and hardly ever leave the vicinities of their villages. According to Soehardi, this has to do with the key concept of *rukun*, meaning social harmony and the position of an individual person in his or her social, material and spiritual surroundings.[23] After a shift a person has to adapt to a new physical and metaphysical world (Soehardi 1995: 5). Women especially suffer heavily when they lose their social and family networks which they need, for example, for help with the children.

After an eruption in 1961 that took five lives, 4,517 people were forced to migrate to Sumatra. Many of them returned soon afterwards, because of disease, heat and the otherwise difficult natural conditions in Sumatra. The Indonesian anthropologist Laksono (1988: 196) found that in the area he studied the risks of living in foreign surroundings (Sumatra) were statistically higher than the risk of being killed by the volcano. In fact, the volcano is not just a threat. It makes the land enormously fertile due to the minerals and the volcanic ash that it produces. There is enough water in the area, the lava stones can be used, and the farmers own much more land than other farmers in Java do. Therefore the villagers, strengthened by their beliefs in spirits and rituals, resist the government's resettlement policy.

The above-mentioned *juru kunci* Mbah Marijan has become a popular hero because of his refusal to leave his village Kinahrejo. He is quoted by the local press on every possible occasion, and many people trust him more than they do the volcanologists. He is against all resettlement and claims that it is his duty to remain in the place of his birth where his ancestors lived before him. He feels responsible for the *Labuhan* ceremony and for the welfare of the inhabitants, not only of his village, but of Jogja and Mataram as well. He surrenders only to the orders of the *kraton* and of Merapi. The residents of Kinahrejo think in the same way and have not, Mbah Marijan insists, been influenced by him, as is often said. 'Remember, if it is our destiny, we will die anywhere. The people of Kinahrejo feel that it was their destiny to be born to be a fortress to protect the welfare of the *kraton* and the people of Mataram' (Mbah Marijan in *Bernas* 24/12/94 and 9/1/95). The *Labuhan* ceremony may not and cannot be performed in another place, otherwise something terrible would happen. Kinahrejo as part of this world and as part of the *kraton* Merapi, has a mediating function. It was not fatalism that made so many people admire Mbah Marijan, but rather his active role in ritual and the frankness with which he proclaimed his convictions publicly during the regime of the New Order. These convictions are based on both his spiritual and practical experiences. His belief that Kinahrejo was safe was supported by the fact that the construction of new buildings for tourism in the region still continued. This meant that the government also considered the area to be safe. The government's argument that the area around Kinahrejo must be reforested due to its importance to Jogja's water supply was rendered obsolete by the construction of an enormous golf course there, which involved the clearing and substitution of innumerable trees by grass. And grass does not retain water as trees do, but must be watered itself.

After the eruption in 1994 people were reluctant to resettle to Sumatra as the government suggested, but according to official figures, finally 282 families agreed. Nevertheless, when asked in an investigation in 1998, all respondents still living on the slopes of Merapi said that they were not willing to take part in a *transmigrasi*-programme (Hidajat 2001: 32, 46). It seems obvious, then, that people have good reasons to be suspicious about resettlement measures because they realise that these are not necessarily beneficial for them. However, it seems dangerous for them to generalise their negative experiences with the government and extend them to all government related measure, so that even the volcanologist's emergency warnings are not taken seriously any more.

What Did the Spirits Want to Warn Against?

There are several Indonesian publications which focus on the perceptions and beliefs of the villagers living on the slopes of Mt Merapi (Handojo 1985; Laksono 1988; Triyoga 1991). In addition, the citizens of Jogjakarta are also exposed to a potential threat, and for them Mt Merapi is of immense mystical significance. I thus intended to include their interpretations of the new direction of the eruption in my investigations. In my field research soon after the eruption in 1994 I mainly focused on mystical explanations which are based on cultural traditions, reinterpreting these in manifold ways. Important opinion-forming fora in this context are local and national newspapers and magazines, which very often report on mythological traditions or on the views of mystic specialists. In articles, conversations and interviews I could detect the following perspectives.

According to cultural concepts and following the experiences of the local population, there are normally warning signs. Thus, for example, after the eruption in November 1994 several people said that they had heard supernatural warning voices, and in one church Holy Mary appeared (*Buana Minggu*, 4/12/94). In general, however, people wondered why there was such an unusual lack of warning signs. The dreams or other signs usually alerting the wise old people had not occurred. For instance, there was no supernatural music in the crater and the wild animals did not descend from the mountain (*Kedaulatan Rakyat*, 26/11/94; *Minggu Pagi*, 1/12/94; *Bernas*, 1/12/94), and hence the question arose of whether people did not follow the traditional signs or whether these were indeed absent. A related question was whether the eruption should be seen as a natural disaster or as a man-made event, caused by human faults or errors (*Kedaulatan Rakyat*, 3/12/94).

Heddy Shri Ahimsa Putra, a lecturer in Anthropology at Gadjah Mada University, Jogjakarta, explained that there were hints from nature, like tigers, monkeys and rabbits coming to the villages. Furthermore, the cattle were anxious, there were warning sounds emanating from the crater, and certain people did have warning dreams and visions. But they did not take these seriously and did not inform their fellows. According to him, this was caused by modern infrastructure – asphalt roads and electricity made villagers less sensible to signs from nature; they live like citizens, without connections to nature through spiritual practices. Furthermore, because of increasing spatial mobility, the dreams reached the 'wrong' people: migrants to Turgo, originating from Imogiri and other villages, who were unable to interpret the signs properly (Ahimsa Putra 1995).

A very important aspect was that the day of the eruption, 22 November 1994, was a Tuesday *Kliwon*. According to the Javanese calendar this is a day of great mystical significance. On Tuesday and Friday *Kliwon* (every thirty-five days) the spirits are very active, they go out and demand food from humans in the form of offerings. Many Javanese interpreted the fact that the eruption had occurred on such a day as a proof of its supernatural meaning. This caused a lot of philosophical speculation about the connection between events in nature and human conduct. The central questions were: what should people be reminded of by the eruption, what were they being warned of, and towards whom were the spirits' admonition directed?

(1) Mythological Explanations

Only very few people told me that the eruption in 1994 was just destiny (*takdir*). For the majority of the inhabitants of Jogjakarta, far more widespread than any fatalistic explanation was the statement that their protective myth had been reconfirmed. Although the eruption had taken a southward direction towards the city, the city itself was not harmed. Jogja, its *kraton* and its Sultan are protected in a special, supernatural way. Therefore, the inhabitants do not feel threatened by the Merapi even though they can see its white cloud of steam from many places in town almost every morning when the weather is clear. In accordance with the mystical principle that says that out of the debris of disaster a revitalised cosmos will arise, and with it the possibility of a profoundly different era, a former spiritual advisor of the *kraton*[24] explained the eruption in terms of a time cycle: every seven hundred years a new era begins, the old one ending with a disaster (interview Ki Juru Permono, 1995).

Similarly, people assume that the natural cycle of eruptions is necessary as they render the soil especially fertile. According to Romo Sindhunata, a catholic priest, the local knowledge of this natural cycle is preserved in the mythological connection between volcanic activity, sexual union of the spirits and the soil's fertility (interview Romo Sindhunatha, 1995). When the male spirits of the mountain and the female ones of the sea marry each other[25] they need humans to help in their marriage ceremonies. Thus an eruption takes human lives, because the *kraton* Merapi needs servants (*abdi dalem*) (cf. also *Bernas* 1/12/94; *Kompas* 6/12/94).

(2) Responsibility of the Villagers

In 1994 there was a need for an explanation as to why the village of Turgo was hit so hard that time. Not only did the eruption turn south, but also, people had been convinced that Mt Merapi would never dare to direct its lava towards Mt Turgo. The latter is supposed to be older than the Merapi and is regarded as its 'aunt' (Handojo 1985: 82). Furthermore, the local population feels protected from Merapi by Seh Maolana Jumadil Qubra, a Muslim saint whose grave, located on the peak of Mt Turgo, is considered as a shrine.

It was now said that the villagers were to be blamed for the eruption, because they had not given the right offerings to Merapi's spirits (*Kedaulatan Rakyat*, 24/11/94). Some people thought that the eruption was a protest by Seh Jumadil Qubra against the villager's general moral decay (*Bernas*, 1/12/94), and against the indecent requests by the pilgrims, who visit his shrine (*Kedaulatan Rakyat*, 23/11/94). For the pilgrims' requests for blessings often go hand in hand with quite materialist desires, including those for success in business and career, for winning lottery numbers, etc. Incorrect moral conduct (for example, prostitution), also at other sacred sites, was often also seen as an explanation for this eruption.

(3) Responsibility of All People

Some newspaper articles suggested that the reason behind the disaster could be the disturbance of the ecosystem through increasing pollution. But in most cases it remains unclear whether such an explanation should be understood in an ecological or in a moral sense (*Kedaulatan Rakyat*, 3/12/94; *Minggu Pagi*, 1/12/94). A matter of debate was, for example, a golf course of 60 ha which at that time was still under construction, and was located south of Kinahrejo, in a mystically significant area that had been designated by the government as ecologically protected. Romo Sindhunata, who thinks that in Indonesia criticism is more effective when it is connected to mysticism, told me: 'When I criticise the golf course directly by saying that it destroys the system of the river Opak, which is a road, then, suddenly, everybody will think about it … and an old myth is revitalised' (interview, 1995). Like him, many people said that not only the golf course, but a lot of new buildings, including the ones of Gadjah Mada University, disturb the connection between the *kraton* Merapi and the *kraton* Kidul, thereby provoking the spirits' protest (interviews, Mbah Marijan 1995; Romo Sindhu 1995; Pak Gondo 1995).

Or again, as the mystical organisation *Sapta Darma* suggested, everyone had been admonished: Mt Merapi had sent a reminder from God (*peringatan Tuhan*) that people should not value external, wordly things and needs (*kebutuhan wadag*) above spiritual aspects. God had sent a sign that people should surrender to him (*laku sujudnya*) (interview Ibu Sri Pawenang, 1991; cf. also *Kedaulatan*

Rakyat, 5/12/94; *Sarinah* 26/12/94), and by emphasis on the interior state (*batin*) that accompanies the outer ritual form (*lahir*). As another respondent put it, 'We never learn, we never want to straighten ourselves up. We don't use our healthy intellect, but act emotionally. That's why we are cursed (*dilaknati*)'. In the same sense Sultan Hamenku Buwono X said that the eruption should be interpreted as a warning to all people to think about what is right and what is wrong in life.

(4) Responsibility of Political Leaders

Because the spirits of the volcano and the sea had promised to protect the rulers of the kingdom of Mataram, many people blamed, directly or indirectly, those in power for the volcanic eruption: first and foremost the Sultan of Jogjakarta, but also the ruling elite in Jakarta. As discussed above, natural disasters and the moral decay of the people can be explained by the failure of a ruler to gather supernatural, cosmic power in himself. If he is regarded as lacking in spiritual power, he may lose his political power as well.

Sultan Hamengku Buwono IX of Jogjakarta, who died in 1988, was held in the highest esteem by the majority of the population. He was respected both as a politician and as a person with extraordinary spiritual power. In 1989 his son, Hamengku Buwono X, was enthroned as the Sultan but without political power; the role of governor going to Paku Alam VIII. Hamengku Buwono X differs from his father in many respects. Some sections of the population criticised him and his wife (his only one, a fact that annoys some people) for their disinterest in spiritual things and for their modern orientation and lifestyle. Possibly, this made the spirits angry and triggered their sending an admonition (interview, Pak Arwan, 1994). This opinion was not published in newspapers but was often expressed in conversations, though some informants insisted that the tape recorder be turned off when we discussed this topic. Because the new Sultan and his *kraton* did not respond to the eruption by performing additional, special rituals, other people held their own sacrificial ceremonies. One of these was a son of Pakualam VIII, at that time governor of the Special Region of Jogjakarta. During his ceremony Ratu Kidul is said to have appeared (interview, Bpk Gondokusumo, 1995). In this context a certain rivalry between the courts of the Sultan and the Pakualaman must be mentioned. Some people in Jogja associated the courts' different reactions to Mt Merapi's eruption with the question of who would succeed the aged Pakualam as governor. It was said that the Sultan wished to succeed Pakualam, but the eruption was seen by some people as a sign of his lack of spiritual legitimacy. Nonetheless, in 1998 he did become governor and due to his attitude during the political unrest at the end of the 1990s, his popularity rose considerably.

In general, some say, those who hold power should be reminded that there is no justice in the Republic yet. The saint Jumadil Qubra mentioned above was 'quoted' in this context too: through a medium (a woman whom he entered in possession) he reminded the population of its hope for independence during the era of colonisation. Yet now, after the forced retreat of the Dutch, Indonesians are the ones who are grasping for the power which was formerly in the hands of foreigners (*Kedaulatan Rakyat* 23/11/95; cf. Ahimsa Putra 1995: 20).

Early in 1995, two months after the eruption, a seminar was organised at the University of Jogjakarta in which volcanologists, anthropologists and so-called paranormals (spiritual specialists) came together to discuss the reactions of the affected people. During this seminar a paranormal expert (*tokoh paranormal*) from Jogjakarta, Pak Permadi, suggested that the holistic view of the connection between volcano, sea and human people is not superstition, as both scientists and orthodox Muslims would suggest, but that this connection between micro- and macrocosmos can be explained as follows: 'If people are not content with the way they are treated by those in power but are unable to defend themselves, then their rage will be absorbed by nature in the form of energy. And when nature is furious this will cause a disaster like a volcanic eruption; because nature does not fear human rulers' (Permadi 1995: 4). Permadi perceived the eruption of Mt Merapi in 1994 as a sign that god (*Tuhan*) will bring the *jaman edan* (crazy, wild, cursed time) to an end. Therefore he expected more natural disasters, epidemics, famines resulting for example in a high rise in prices which would cause social unrest. Permadi prophesised that Semar or Sabdopalon[26] would appear and remind humankind that god will soon put an end to the time in which greed rules Java and the whole kingdom. The same will happen in the whole world. The severe crisis which will hit, weaken and destroy the big nations (America, Japan) will push Indonesia into the position of the leading power in the world because it is already prepared for the future.[27]

Conclusion: Volcanoes as Fields of Discourse

In Indonesia anthropomorphisation and the social appropriation of nature reveals a plurality of meanings, not just in a socio-economic sense but in the political, moral and religious sphere as well. Therefore, symbolically mediated interpretations of nature and morality related to religious ideas and practices, as well as empirical knowledge, habits, economic interests, and socio-political conditions together form the basis for human attitudes towards threats from nature. Hence, interpretations of natural disasters are forever negotiated and contested. In Java they are always associated with spiritual meaning. In an actual crisis situation, mystical traditions are revived and reinterpreted. The question arises as to what message the people are meant to receive from the event's occurrence. The eruption of Mt Tambora was connected with the spread of Islam. The explosion of the Krakatau was, besides the religious and moral explanations, seen as indicative of the retreat of the Dutch colonial regime. The eruptions of the Merapi in the 1990s which turned to the south were seen as a warning. Warning of what? Anthropological field research revealed that on the one hand, traditional Javanese views of natural events became evident on the basis of their interpretations of the eruption in 1994. On the other hand, these interpretations were mixed with actual values and problems in a fairly explosive manner. People can interpret and use these beliefs in many ways.

The many-sided discourse about nature reflects Java's social dynamics. One tendency is apparent: natural forces are no longer regarded as simply playing the role of a moral instance and harmoniously supporting and legitimising the status quo. Rather, natural events and revitalised beliefs in spirits may well be directed against those in power. Events in nature and beliefs in spirits become means of political criticism; they represent the place of rebellion, which can require a transformation of the moral instance. But there is no straight, absolute answer to the question of what the spirits were warning against. Certain sections of the population and certain individuals associated their own beliefs with the event. Thus, the cultural and mystical interpretations of the volcanic eruption can be viewed as reflections of issues that are considered relevant in Javanese society at a specific point of time, with all its variety and contradictions.

A remarkable outcome of this research is that the residents living in the vicinity of Merapi are neither the helpless victims of the volcano nor of the government. Individuals confronted with natural threats can draw cognitive coping strategies as well as subjective security from their belief in spirits. Human agency is interrelated with agency attributed to entities in nature.[28] Therefore, my example does not support a modern-traditional division of the world's societies as we find, for instance, in the work of for example Ulrich Beck or Anthony Giddens. According to them, traditional cultures have used the ideas of fate, luck or the will of the gods and spirits to explain hazards. The concept of risk is, for them, connected with modernity, future-orientation, human decisions and individual actors (Giddens 1999). But the example presented here indicates that 'the will of the gods and spirits' could at all times be combined with complex adjustments to social processes and moral issues, thereby acting out human decisions and also expressing the interests of individual actors who package their ideas in peculiar mythological versions of events.

Nevertheless, we should not forget that the people who are directly threatened and at times affected are not those who have power in the country, they are the people living on the slopes of the volcanoes. And it is alarming that the negative experiences with the government's transmigration measures, combined with general criticism of the government mediated by the 'voices of spirits', prevent people from taking the volcanologists' warnings seriously and leads them to ignore evacuation orders by government institutions. This is, however, not exceptional: other studies show as well that a considerable numbers of deaths in disasters take place because people are not willing to be evacuated (Ketterer and Spada 1993: 79). An anthropological contribution to the interdisciplinary project of disaster research can be to make the attitudes of the local population and of particular key persons more widely understood. Studies of risk perception and coping strategies should take the broader contexts of social, political and religious circumstances into account. In addition, since the scope or range of what people can do to affect their situation is broader than we might think, these studies should also investigate the activities and limits of individuals and their subjective experiences. This means that it is not only necessary to inform the public in threatened areas extensively,[29] and that we should not just gather data about people at risk but also engage in dialogue with them. Otherwise even the most sophisticated surveillance and forecast techniques will be of very little use.

Epilogue

After the first submission of this article in 2001, Indonesia was hit by several severe disasters. In 2006 Mt Merapi erupted causing two fatalities. At around the same time, an earthquake near Jogjakarta claimed approximately 6,000 victims and left more than 1 million people homeless. Many people connected the two events, and the above mentioned *juru kunci* Mbah Marijan became a kind of a local hero in this area and beyond. By comparing the cultural interpretations in 2006 and in the1990s, similarities but also new tendencies can be identified. Fieldwork reveals that the explanations for the disasters are nowadays more related to negotiations between what people perceive as tradition and modernity. In general, there seems to be a trend towards cultural polarization. Javanese victims associate the disasters with tensions caused by contradictions between traditional values, local identity and syncretic worldviews on the one hand and modernisation, globalisation and orthodox Islam on the other hand. These two poles are personified in Mbah Marijan and the Sultan, and sometimes even in the former president Suharto and the current president Susilo Bambang Yudhoyono. This example shows that interpretations of natural disasters can also reflect discontent with the process of *reformasi* and democratisation (cf. Schlehe 2006).

Notes

1. Some authors also include resilience, which means the ability to recover and regenerate. At any rate, there is still no fully acceptable definition of vulnerability available (cf. Smith 2001: 25).
2. There is, for instance, research on adjustments to reduce 'cognitive dissonance' that arises when two conflicting beliefs are held simultaneously, as when a person perceives the environment to be hazardous, but continues to live in it. This is labelled as 'dissonant perception'. Other models of risk perception would be 'determinate perception' and 'probabilistic perception'. The former means that people seek to place extreme events in some pattern, as for example repetitive cycles; the latter means that people accept that disasters will occur, but combine this with a need to transfer the responsibility to a higher authority, for example to God (Smith 2001: 70–1).

3. For instance, Melanesian and Polynesian myths have been interpreted as descriptions of volcanic eruptions which occurred thousands of years ago (Taylor 1995; cf. also Blong 1975).
4. The Aeta developed survival strategies, in which the social and economic behaviour typical for foraging societies, such as flexibility in the utilisation of resources and spatial mobility, facilitated the adjustment.
5. I would like to thank Michael J. Casimir for his helpful comments on this paper.
6. The modern Western notion of nature is less than 200 years old. In antique and medieval Europe the cosmos was seen as a living organism in which all objects were interrelated. Nature was regarded as a system of signs that referred to and provided insights into the wisdom, providence and omnipotence of God the Creator. However, seen from the mechanistic perspective of the modern age Western world, nature is seen as a useful but dead object, subordinated by man, lacking any divine aspect. Therefore the historian of science Carolyn Merchant writes about the 'death of nature', whereas the anthropologist Thomas Bargatzky describes in the same context 'the invention of nature' (1994), meaning that the idea of nature in sharp contrast to culture and to the divine sphere is a modern Western invention. But, according to sociologist Ulrich Beck, the notion of the present 'world risk society' can be characterised by the loss of clear distinction between nature and culture, as we are living in a constructed artificial world of civilisation (Beck 2000: 221).
7. The oldest of these texts is from about 1750, but it is based on older prototypes. The name Joyoboyo (Yayabaya) is derived from a king of Kediri (*c.* 1135–57).
8. To date, except volcanologists, mainly biologists are interested in the slow revival of a tropical forest ecosystem. Without human intervention during one century a new ecosystem developed with 400 plants, 50 butterflies, 40 birds and many more species (Thornton 1996: 286).
9. Besakih, mother temple of Bali and spiritual and religious centre of the universe for all Hindu Indonesians, is situated on the slopes of Mt Agung, which is a central point of reference for the Balinese.
10. The Kelimutu has three crater lakes of different colours which change frequently. These changes are invested with symbolic meanings. For instance, a change in colour of one of the lakes from green to red-brown in 1975 was seen in the context of the blood-bath created by the Indonesian government during the violent annexation of East Timor. A change in colour of another lake from light-brown to black in 1998 was connected with the conflicts, riots and upheavals in Indonesia during that year (Frömming 2000).
11. The geographer and sailor Karl Helbig (1903–91), who was a pioneer in research on Indonesia, described very vividly an eruption of Mt Merapi in his book *Ferne Tropen-Insel Java* (1946) in a chapter entitled 'Weh uns, der Feurige'.
12. A *juru kunci* is a guardian of a sacred place.
13. This paper is based on five weeks of field research from December 1994 to January 1995, supported by the Deutsche Forschungsgemeinschaft, and visits in 1997 and 1999. Besides the data collected during these stays in the Merapi area, in Jogjakarta and in Parangtritis, I use interviews from a fourteen-month field research in the same region between 1989 and 1991.
14. For perceptions of villagers in other regions at Merapi see Triyoga 1991, Hidajat 2001.
15. *Lampor* are related to storms, heavy rainfalls and floods. Occasionally they get coconuts and palm sugar as offerings at the Opak River (Jumeiri et al. 1983/84: 96–102).

16. In this context people address the volcano with the familiar title *Eyang*, which means grandfather in a respectful sense.
17. The traditional explanation when people drown in the rivers of south central Java is that the spirits need helpers for their marriage ceremonies.
18. After the kingdom of Mataram was divided in 1755 into Solo and Jogjakarta, both *kratons* were meant to hold the ceremony. But the *Labuhan* of the *kraton* Solo at Merapi is not performed regularly any more. The Jogja side does so and in 1995 I took part in it. Despite the recent eruption, *Labuhan* was held in a routine way.
19. In case of increased volcanic activities the ceremony is held at the second post, situated at the height of 1.500 m.
20. There is an off-limits zone of *c.* 186 km^2 around the crater, in which no one is permitted to live; a type I hazard zone of *c.* 100 km^2 around the crater where settlements are allowed and where people in case of large eruptions are evacuated; and a type II hazard zone of *c.* 99 km^2 along the rivers to a distance as far as 40 km from the crater, where settlements are allowed, although they are threatened by lahars, especially during the rainy season.
21. Acording to Soehardi (1995), 15,000 people live permanently in the forbidden zone.
22. After the fall of President Suharto resettlement programmes continued, but to a lesser extent, and not in crisis regions.
23. *Rukun* is the principle of harmony and avoidance of conflict which includes the control of emotions (Magnis-Suseno 1981: 37–53).
24. Ki Juru Pernomo traces his ancestors to Ki Juru Mertani, the former advisor of Panembahan Senopati, who went to Mt Merapi while Senopati was on his pilgrimage to the south coast; both intended to obtain the blessings of the respective spiritual rulers.
25. Often, the spirits' sexual union is conceived of as a marriage (*hajat*) of Kyai Sapujagad and Ratu Kidul.
26. This reminds me of the version in which Semar was incarnated in the form of Sabdopalon, a minister in the last court of Majapahit. Sabdopalon announced a 500 year period during which Java would be dominated by external forces. At the end of the cycle he would return, ushering in a new golden age (Stange 1989: 121).
27. In a similar sense John Pemberton cites an experienced ascetic from Solo who stated as early as 1984: 'If Mt Merapi explodes, the Jakarta group will just float away' (Pemberton 1994: 309). Interestingly, this man made offerings to Mt Merapi with the explicit intention of making it erupt. 'I send up a sack of flower petals as my offerings, but Soeharto's group goes up there with an entire flower market, so the mountain remains quiet. Spirits like lots of offerings. ... the spirits can be suckered too. After all, they're Javanese, aren't they?' (op. cit. p. 310).
28. We can only speculate on whether Javanese people who explain natural events by the spirits' influences in general feel more competent than people who rely on geophysical explanations, which they usually do not really understand. In any case, we should avoid devaluing them, as is sometimes the case in the 'scientific' approaches.
29. See the IDNDR catalogue of measures for the decade volcanoes (cf. Schmincke et al. 1993: 354).

References

Ahimsa Putra and Heddy Shri 1995. 'Tanda-Tanda dan Bencana Merapi. Persepsi dan Interpretasi'. Seminar: Korban Bencana dan Solidaritas Sosial: Interpretasi Antropologi atas Bencana Merapi. Jurusan Antropologi, Universitas Gadah Mada, Yogyakarta 31. January 1995, unpublished manuscript.

Alexander, David 1993. *Natural Disasters*. London: UCL Press.

Bargazky, Thomas, ed. 1994. *The Invention of Nature*. Frankfurt am Main: Lang.

Beck, Ulrich 2000. 'Risk Society Revisited: Theory, Politics and Research Programmes', in *The Risk Society and Beyond. Critical Issues for Social Theory*, eds. Barbara Adam, Ulrich Beck and Joost van Loon, 211–29. London: Sage.

Bigeon, Cécile 1982. 'Labuhan. Rite Royal du Kraton de Yogyakarta, Célébré sur la Plage Parangtritis', *Archipel* 24: 117–26.

Blaikie, Piers, Terry Cannon, Ian Davis and Ben Wisner 1994. *At Risk. Natural Hazards, People's Vulnerability, and Disasters*. London: Routledge.

Blong, R.J. 1975. 'The Krakatoa Myth and the New Guinea Highlands', *Journal of the Polynesian Society* 84: 213–17.

——— 1984. *Volcanic Hazards. A Sourcebook on the Effects of Eruptions*. Sydney: Academic Press.

Bruun, Ole and Arne Kalland 1995. *Asian Perceptions of Nature. A Critical Approach*, eds. Bruun, Ole and Arne Kalland, Richmond: Curzon Press.

Chester, David 1993. *Volcanoes and Society*. London: Edward Arnold.

Day, Tony 1994. '"Landscape" in Early Java', in *Recovering the Orient. Artists, Scholars, Appropriations*, eds. Andrew Gerstle and Anthony Milner, 175–203. Chur: Harwood Academic Publishers.

Ellen, Roy 1996. 'Introduction', in *Redefining Nature. Ecology, Culture and Domestication* eds. Roy Ellen and Katsuyoshi Fukui, 1–36. Oxford: Berg.

Frömming, Urte Undine 2001. 'Volcanoes: Symbolic Places of Resistance', in *Violence in Indonesia*, eds. Ingrid Wessel and Georgia Wimhöfer, 270–81. Hamburg: Abera.

Frömming, Urte Undine 2005. *Naturkatastrophen. Kulturelle Deutung und Verarbeitung*. Frankfurt am Main: Campus.

Geipel, Robert 1992. *Naturrisiken: Katastrophenbewältigung im sozialen Umfeld*. Darmstadt: Wissenschaftliche Buchgesellschaft.

Giddens, Anthony 1999. *Runaway World*. London: BBC. [http://news.bbc.co.uk/hi/english/static/events/reith_99]

Handojo, Adi Pranowo 1985. *Manusia dan Hutan. Proses Perubahan Ekologi di Lereng Gunung Merapi*. Yogyakarta: Gadjah Mada University Press.

Helbig, Karl 1946. *Ferne Tropen-Insel Java. Ein Buch vom Schicksal fremder Menschen und Tiere*. Stuttgart: Gundert Verlag.

Hewitt, Kenneth 1983. 'The Idea of Calamity in a Technocratic Age', in *Interpretations of Calamity – From the Viewpoint of Human Ecology*, ed. Kenneth Hewitt. Boston: Allen and Unwin.

Hidajat, Ria 2001. 'Risikowahrnehmung und Katastrophenvorbeugung am Merapi in Indonesien', in *Deutsches Kommitee für Katastophenfürsorge* (German Committee for Diasaster Reduction), Bonn.

Hoffman, Susanna and Anthony Oliver-Smith, eds. 2002. *Catastrophe and Culture. The Anthropology of Disaster*. Santa Fe: School of American Research Press.

Jong Boers, Bernice de 1995. 'Mount Tambora in 1815: a Volcanic Eruption in Indonesia and its Aftermath', *Indonesia* 60: 36–59.

Jumeiri, Siti Rumidjah, Soelarto et al. 1983/84. *Upacara Tradisional dalam Kaitannya dengan Peristiwa Alam dan Kepercayaan Daerah Istimewa Yogyakarta.* Yogyakarta: Dep. Pendidikan dan Kebudayaan.

Kaehlig, Carl-Bernd, Andrew Wight and Chris Smith 1996. *Volcanoes of Indonesia. Creators and Destroyers.* Singapore: Times Editions.

Ketterer, Werner and Hans Spada 1993. 'Der Mensch als Betroffener und Verursacher von Naturkatastrophen: Der Beitrag umweltpsychologischer Forschung', in *Naturkatastrophen und Katastrophenvorbeugung: Bericht des Wissenschaftlichen Beirats der DFG für das Deutsch Komitee für die "International Decade for Natural Disaster Reduction" (IDNDR) / Deutsche Forschungsgemeinschaft*, eds. Erich Plate, Lars Clausen et al., 73–107 Weinheim: VCH.

Laksono, Paschalis M.1988. 'Perceptions of Volcanic Hazards: Villagers versus Government Officials in Central Java', in *The Real and Imagined Role of Culture in Development*, ed. Michael Dove, 183–200. Honolulu: University of Hawaii Press.

Lapian, A.B. 1992. 'Bencana Alam dan Penulisan Sejarah (Krakatau 1883 dan Cilegon 1888)', in *Dari Babad dan Hikayat sampai Sejarah Kritis*, eds. T. Ibrahim Alfian et. al. Yogyakarta: Gadjah Mada University Press.

Luig, Ute 1995. *Naturaneignung als symbolischer Prozeß in afrikanischen Gesellschaften.* Berlin: Arbeitshefte aus dem Forschungsschwerpunkt Moderner Orient 10.

McNeely, Jeffrey and Paul Spencer Wachtel 1991. *Soul of the Tiger. Searching for Nature's Answers in Southeast Asia.* Singapore: Oxford University Press.

Magnis-Suseno, Franz von 1981. *Javanische Weisheit und Ethik. Studien zu einer östlichen Moral.* Munich: Oldenbourg.

Oliver-Smith, Anthony and Susanna M. Hoffman 1999. *The Angry Earth. Disaster in Anthropological Perspective.* New York: Routledge.

Pedersen, Poul 1995. 'Nature, Religion and Cultural Identity: The Religious Environmentalist Paradigm', in *Asian Perceptions of Nature. A Critical Approach*, eds. Ole Bruun and A. Kalland, 258–76. Richmond: Curzon Press.

Pemberton, John 1994. *On the Subject of 'Java'.* Ithaca and London: Cornell University Press.

Permadi 1995. 'Gunung Merapi. Tinjauan dari Sisi Spiritual/Paranormal'. Seminar: Korban Bencana dan Solidaritas Sosial: Interpretasi Antropologi atas Bencana Merapi. Jurusan Antropologi, Universitas Gadah Mada, Yogyakarta 31. January.1995, unpublished manuscript.

Pichler, Hans 1985. 'Risikofaktor Vulkan', *Geographische Rundschau* 37: 72–81.

Plate, Erich, Wolfgang Kron and Sabine Seiert 1993. 'Beitrag der deutschen Wissenschaft zur "International Decade for Natural Disaster Reduction (IDNDR)"', in *Naturkatastrophen und Katastrophenvorbeugung*, eds. Erich Plate, Lars Clausen et al., 1–71. Weinheim: VCH.

Schlehe, Judith 1996. 'Reinterpretations of Mystical Traditions: Explanations of a Volcanic Eruption in Java', *Anthropos* 91: 391–409.

——— 1998. *Die Meereskönigin des Südens, Ratu Kidul. Geisterpolitik im javanischen Alltag.* Berlin: Reimer.

——— 2006. 'Nach dem Erdbeben auf Java: Kulturelle Polarisierungen, soziale Solidarität und Abgrenzung', *Internationales Asienforum*, 37(3–4): 213–37.

——— and Undine Frömming 2005. 'Volcanoes and Religion', in *The Encyclopedia of Religion and Nature*, eds. Taylor, Bron and Jeffrey Kaplan, 1707–9. London: Continuum International.

Schmidt, Arno 1975. *Krakatau. Erzählungen.* Stuttgart: Reclam (Orig. 1958).

Schmincke, Hans-Ulrich 1994. 'Vulkaneruptionen, Vulkangefahren, Vulkankatastrophen', *Geographische Rundschau* 7–8: 440–8.

——— et al. 1993. 'Vulkanismus', in *Naturkatastrophen und Katastrophenvorbeugung: Bericht des Wissenschaftlichen Beirats der DFG für das Deutsche Komitee für die 'International Decade for Natural Disaster Reduction' (IDNDR) / Deutsche Forschungsgemeinschaft*, eds. Erich Plate, Lars Clausen et al., 352–407. Weinheim: VCH.

Scholz, Ulrich 1997. 'Transmigrasi – ein Desaster? Probleme und Chancen des indonesischen Umsiedlungsprogramms', *Geographische Rundschau* 44, 33–39.

Seitz, Stefan 1998. 'Coping Strategies in an Ethnic Minority Group: The Aeta of Mount Pinatubo', *Disasters* 22(1): 76–90.

Seitz, Stefan 2004. *The Atea at the Mt Pinatubo, Philippines: A Minority Group Coping with Disaster.* Translated by Michael Bletzer. Quezon City, Philippines: New Day Publishers.

Shook, Gary 1997. 'An Assessment of Disaster Risk and its Management in Thailand', *Disasters* 21(1): 77–88.

Simkin, Tom and Richard Fiske 1983. *Krakatau 1883.* Washington DC: Smithsonian Institution Press.

Smith, Keith 2001. *Environmental Hazards. Assessing Risk and Reducing Disaster.*3rd. ed. London, New York: Routledge.

Soehardi 1995. 'Merapi Berbahaya, Beda Persepsi'. Seminar: Korban Bencana dan Solidaritas Sosial: Interpretasi Antropologi atas Bencana Merapi. Jurusan Antropologi, Universitas Gadah Mada, Yogyakarta 31. January 1995, unpublished manuscript.

Stange, Paul 1989. 'Interpreting Javanist Millenial Imagery', in *Creating Indonesian cultures*, ed. Paul Alexander, 113–134. Sydney: Oceania Publishing.

Sudibjo, Z.H., ed. 1980. *Babad Tanah Jawi.* Jakarta: Dep. Pendidikan dan Kebudayaan. Proyek Penerbitan Buku Sastra Indonesia dan Daerah.

Taylor, Paul W. 1995. 'Myths, Legends and Volcanic Activity: An Example from Northern Tonga', *Journal of the Polynesian Society* 104(3): 323–46.

Thornton, Ian 1996. *Krakatau. The Destruction and Reassembly of an Island Ecosystem.* Cambridge, MA and London: Harvard University Press.

Triyoga, Lucas Sasongko 1991. *Manusia Jawa dan Gunung Merapi. Persepsi dan Sistem Kepercayaannya.* Yogyakarta: Gadjah Mada University Press.

Tzschaschel, Sabine 1986. *Geographische Forschung auf der Individualebene. Darstellung und Kritik der Mikrogeographie.* Kallmünz/Regensburg: Lassleben.

Wright, Astri 1994. *Soul, Spirit and Mountain. Preoccupations of Contemporary Indonesian Painters.* Oxford: Oxford University Press.

Newspaper Articles

Bernas: 23/11/94; 1/12/94; 23/12/94; 24/12/94; 3/1/95; 4/1/95; 9/1/95, 19/1/97.

Buana Minggu 4/12/94.

Gatra: 10/12/94.

Kedaulatan Rakyat: 23/11/94; 24/11/94; 26/11/94; 3/12/94; 5/12/94; 10/12/94; 4/1/95; 16/1/95.

Kompas: 28/11/94; 5/12/94; 6/12/94; 11/2/95; 18/1/97; 19/1/97; 20/1/97; 24/1/97.

Minggu Pagi: 1/12/94; 15/1/95.

Pos Kota: 24/11/94.

Sarinah: 26/12/94.

11

Knowing the Sea in the 'Time of Progress': Environmental Change, Parallel Knowledges and the Uses of Metaphor in Kerala (South India)

Götz Hoeppe

Introduction

This text considers how knowledge change is expressed in speech, focusing on the members of a community of fisherfolk who have experienced several decades of dramatic social, economic and environmental change. It draws on fourteen months of fieldwork in Chamakkala, a coastal village in the South Indian state of Kerala. The village's fishermen, mostly Hindus, commonly subsume recent developments and changes, whether in the sea, in fishing, in the village, or in the world at large as pertaining to the 'time of progress'. Referred to as *purōgamiccu kālaṃ*[1] (literally 'progressed time') in Kerala's Malayalam language, this period is commonly opposed to the previous 'old times' (*paḻaya kālaṅṅaḷ*). Conspicuous consumption (cars, houses), new links to the outside world, electrification, new piped water supply systems and toilets, welfare plans of the government Fisheries Department, reservation quotas in government employment,[2] the labour migration of men to countries of the Arabian Gulf and the influx of their remittances into the local economy, are as much part of the 'time of progress' as the introduction of new fisheries' technology, the emergence of competition in fishery and the older generation's perception of the dwindling moral conduct of younger fishermen. In addition, marine resources are believed to be declining due to overfishing. This is only one of a number of changes that are thought to be inflicted by humans upon the environment. Furthermore, foreign knowledges about a variety of issues have arrived and old viewpoints are being challenged by the young.

During fieldwork I asked myself how, in the process of all these developments, the 'local' knowledge[3] of Chamakkala's fishermen had been confronted by external, possibly 'global', knowledges. Perhaps the situation in Chamakkala resembled that in other parts of the 'developing world', where local cultures have been confronted by external influences. A number of ethnographic studies have been devoted to local responses to such external influences, and have revealed the manifold and creative ways in which various forms of symbolic expression have emerged and are amalgamated locally (e.g., Piot 1999; Tsing 2005). However, few studies have considered how the conceptualisation of the environment and people's 'local environmental knowledge' is affected by such influences (cf. Appadurai 1989; Gold and Gujar 2002).

In the course of my fieldwork in Chamakkala I realised that the fishermen's knowledge is, and has been, a composite of ecological, technological, biological and sociological knowledges. Writing about agricultural knowledge, Arjun Appadurai (1989: 174) noted that such categories

> only weakly convey the structure of agricultural knowledge in a place like India, where these domains are not so separated and where knowledge of water, animals, soil, persons, deities, crops, markets, and manure form part of an interacting whole.

If the fishermen's knowledge is of a similar composite character, a most dramatic scenario of knowledge-change seems unlikely: the complete replacement of 'local' knowledge by 'global' knowledge, the latter supposedly 'scientific', with no relation between them. Faced with 'foreign' technology in a comprehensive way may, however, affect many aspects of the locals' knowledge, including their 'epistemological style', i. e., the way in which things are known and in which this knowledge is organised, but it will nevertheless do so in a complex way. Indeed, ethnographic fieldwork has shown that such situations are never simple. For example, in a study of the knowledge-change of the people of Whalsay, a fishing community in Scotland, Anthony Cohen (1993) distinguishes three possibilities in a situation where 'local' knowledge faces 'foreign' knowledge: locals may either 'capitulate' and discard their 'traditional' knowledge, or make 'syncretic accomodations' between local and 'foreign' environmental knowledge, or again, they may subvert extraneous knowledge altogether (op. cit. p. 32). Self-consciously, the Whalsay islanders chose the latter two possibilities. They were aware of their choice and able to apply their own specific 'local interpretive prism' (op. cit. 35) to the extraneous knowledge with which they were confronted.

Notably, Cohen emphasises the important role which inequalities in power relations have in the spread of 'foreign' knowledges.

In this text I am interested in Appadurai's 'interacting whole' of agricultural knowledge as well as in what Cohen called (local) 'syncretic accomodations' between environmental knowledges pertaining to contradicting ontologies. Ethnographers have identified a variety of such accomodations, most being apparently less dramatic than the rupture implied by a complete abandonment of 'traditional' or 'indigenous' knowledge (Ellen et al. 2000). One example is the adoption of shifting units of measurement, which may conceal, at first sight, the use of an entirely different, incommensurable style of thought (Appadurai 1989). Another example is the relabelling of terms in what is perceived as being a 'modern' fashion, while structurally retaining previously established conceptualisations (e.g., the replacement of local terms with their suspected English-language equivalents; see below). Yet another example is 'cleansing' local knowledge of 'fallacies' – a process that is enabled through the increased availability of foreign knowledge via new media, such as newspapers, radio and television. In Chamakkala, most fishermen are literate and a number of them are avid readers of Malayalam newspapers such as *Mathrubhumi, Deshabhimani* and *Malayala Manorama.* Many people listen to the state radio regularly, not the least for the weather forecast. Few fishermen watch TV regularly, but especially younger people often see movies in the two local cinemas. Newspapers and the radio are of much importance in introducing foreign knowledges and political debates into the local world. Refurbishing 'old' knowledges with 'new' ones in this manner is not a new way of dealing with incongruent knowledges, as the historian Paul Veyne (1988) reminds one in his study of the belief of the ancient Greeks' in their myths. When considering such processes of 'cleansing', one may wonder if, rather than (or: in addition to) separating 'true' statements from 'wrong' ones, different ontologies are distinguished. I shall pay particular attention to this idea.

Ethnographers have noticed many of their informants' lack of concern in dealing, simultaneously, with knowledges relating to contradicting ontologies – henceforth I shall call these 'parallel knowledges'. An example from South India is a study by Mark Nichter (1980) on the way in which people make use of medical 'multiple therapy systems'. Drawing on fieldwork data gathered in Karnataka, Nichter was surprised by the readiness with which patients were willing to switch from one medical practitioner to another, irrespective of the ontological status of the medicine systems on which their therapies were based, including cosmopolitan, homeopathic, Ayurvedic and local traditions. In this series, cosmopolitan medicine was perceived as having an ambivalent 'power', particularly so when contrasted to local medicine. The former was said to act rapidly and efficiently, though being of a vasicillating and unstable nature. In contrast, local medicines were perceived of as acting more smoothly but also more slowly and, perhaps, less efficiently (Nichter 1980: 228). The association of foreign medicines and foreign knowledges with power has been noted in different contexts (e.g. Osella and Osella 2000; Tsing 1993: 30, 257; Tsing 2005).

The processes of accommodating old knowledges with new ones have in common that they emphasise a certain persistence of tradition in facing the 'new' and the 'foreign'. I am wary that this expresses some ethnographers' desire to see 'traditional' or 'local' knowledge conserved in the face of the persistently ever-encroaching 'global'. While being aware of this possibility, I do wish to shed some light on the role of metaphor and other forms of figurative speech in the persistence of 'local' or 'traditional' knowledge. In language, knowledge may be expressed in different ways. In a general sense, one may distinguish between statements and 'truths' which are understood (and expressed) literally and those that are understood (and expressed) figuratively or, specifically, metaphorically. Among others, Brenda Beck (1978: 88) and Mary Hesse (1980: 116) have noted that the border between figurative and literal speech may change over time, while Reinhart Koselleck (1989) pointed to the inertia of speech in episodes of rapid knowledge change. For an ethnographer, paying attention to metaphors and figurative language more generally offers the possibility of pursuing a 'conceptual archaeology' (Gentner et al. 2001: 210) that may yield clues about changing conceptualisations. In my case, what is more, parallel knowledges may co-exist in the fishermen's mind, one (or some) being perceived literally, the other(s) figuratively. One may then wonder if interactions between 'the literal' and 'the figurative' are articulated in the fishermen's speech.

In this chapter, I shall consider the material of my fieldwork in regard to the ways in which the fishermen's 'local' knowledge is affected by external knowledges (whose internal structure I shall not be concerned with here; but see Turnbull 2000 for the internal heterogeneity of scientific knowledge). Kerala provides an intriguing framework for such a study. For many years, it has been a 'favourite anomaly' of development economists (Wallich 1995: 19). While the average per capita income is low, life-expectancy is high, literacy exceeds 90 percent and the public health system is well-developed (Parayil 2000: 1f.). These are the characteristics of the 'Kerala model of development', which is often ascribed to Kerala's unique demography (60 percent Hindus, 20 percent each Muslims and Christians; cf. Tarabout 1997: 246) and its recent history which includes, for example, the first elected communist government worldwide (in 1956; cf. Jeffrey 1992; Parayil 2000) and a high level of political mobilisation. Despite undeniable successes, the 'Kerala model' has its weak sides, and the fisheries reveal some of these. Statistical data show that the fishing folk, for a long time marginalised at the fringes of a predominantly agricultural society, lags behind in terms of land holdings, health status, child mortality and literacy. It has remained an 'outlier' of the 'Kerala model' of development (Kurien 2000). In addition, as mentioned above, the development of the fisheries has resulted in a worrisome over-exploitation of the state's marine resources.

In this text I proceed as follows. In the next section, I present a brief overview of the local ethnographic context. The third section summarises how the fishermen of Chamakkala conceptualise their relation to the marine environment. In the subsequent section, I contrast the changes in the marine environment that have been perceived and debated in public discourse at the state level and, locally, on the beach. In the following section, I present cases from my fieldwork which exemplify some ways in which local knowledge has responded to foreign knowledges and public discourse – and discuss how this is reflected in the fishermen's spoken language. I end this text with brief conclusions.

Throughout this paper, I restrict myself to the study of knowledge as it has been related to or inferred by me in the conversations which I and Sureshkumar Muttichoor (henceforth: Suresh), my co-worker in the field, conducted with the fishermen. This may be criticised with the claim that much of a people's knowledge, especially when pertaining to a practical activity such as fishing, may rest in the performance itself (Richards 1993) and is neither stored nor expressible in a linguistic fashion (Bloch 1998). While I am sympathetic to these views, I have argued elsewhere (Hoeppe 2007: 14–16) that reasonable inferences about how these men conceive the marine environment can be made from language, especially when considering metaphors and other forms of figurative speech.

Local Context

My fieldwork location Chamakkala is the seaside ward of a *panchayat* (local administrative unit) in central Kerala's Thrissur District (see map 11.1). As is typical for the region, the village is non-nucleated and spread out, houses usually being surrounded by garden land. The population density markedly increases towards the beach (2,290 persons per km^2), where families often live in thatched huts or in small houses on public land. Most families with active fishermen live here. In early 2000, I carried out a survey of 326 households near the beach. Of a population of 1,903 persons in these households, 54 percent were Muslim, 33 percent Araya, 8 percent Izhava and 5 percent Vettuva. In contrast to this overall composition of the local population, most fishermen are Arayas. Araya, Izhava and Vettuva are ('caste-less') *avarna* Hindu castes. Further inland in the village live the members of other *avarna* and some *savarna* Hindu castes (including Brahmins and Nayars) and Roman Catholic Christians.

Work migration to the Arabian Gulf has had a significant impact on the village, but has affected the various local communities to a different extent. On average, there is one male Gulf migrant per Muslim household, while only in every third Araya household there is a migrant. In very few cases are male migrants accompanied by their wives. The remittances brought or sent to the village have considerably influenced the local economy, including fishing. Migration to the Arabian Gulf has been a challenge for many young men who want to leave the low-status, low- and irregular-income work of fishing. On their return to the village as residents, economically successful migrants do not usually return to fishery, but start small businesses in the eastern, inland part of the

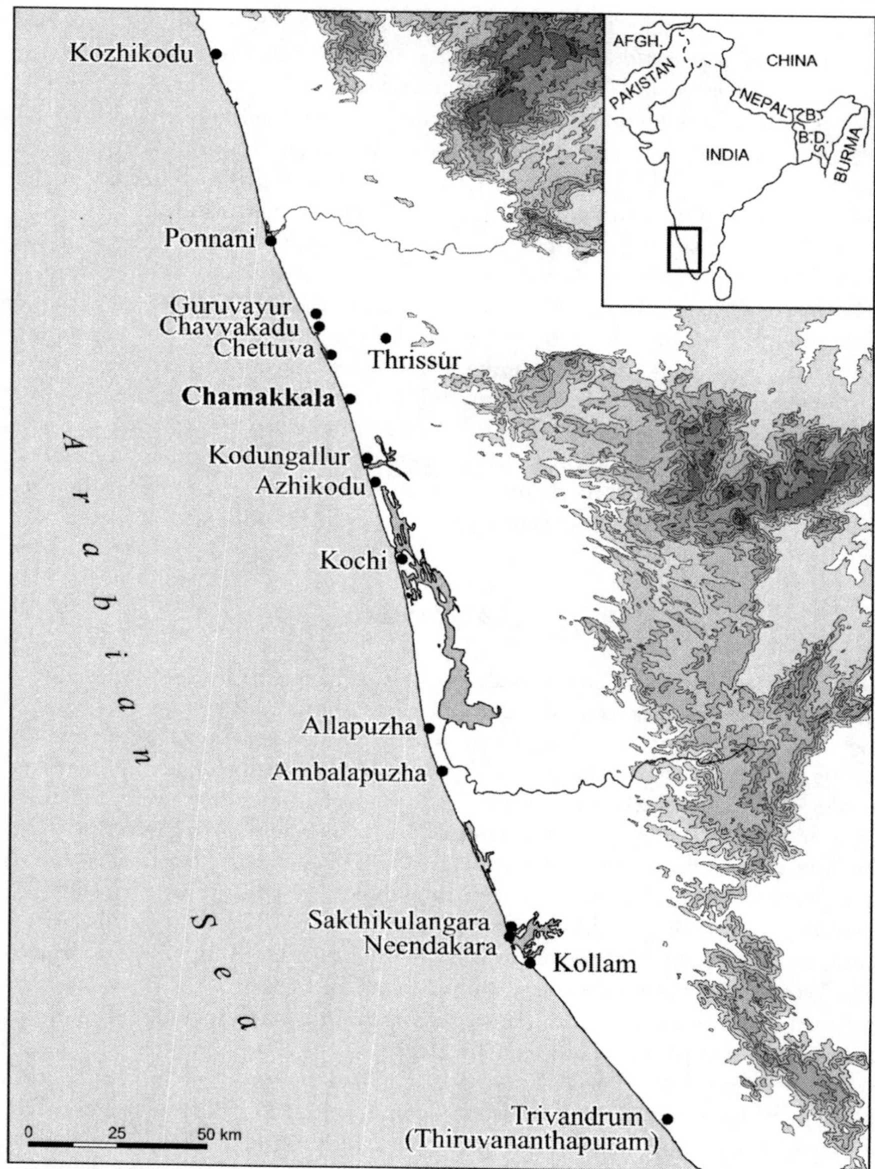

Map 11.1. The South-Indian state of Kerala and the area of investigation

village. Another important, recent development has been the liberalisation of the Indian economy since 1991, resulting in the widespread and legal availability of foreign consumer goods in the village.

In early 2000, there were 110 Araya, 8 Muslim and one Vettuva fishermen in Chamakkala and 42 Muslim, 6 Araya and one Vettuva fish vendors, who sell the fish catch locally, equipped either with a bicycle and plastic box or with a *kottayankāvu̥*, a pole carried over the shoulder with a basket at each end. Fishing and fish-trading are carried out exclusively by men; women are occasionally engaged in salting and drying fish, both of little economic significance since ice was introduced to preserve fish in the 1970s.

Until the mid-1980s, the *vañci* used to be the dominant boat type in this coastal strip: a dugout canoe for five fishermen, usually equipped with gillnets of different mesh size for the catch of *cāla* (Indian oil sardines, *Sardinella longiceps*), *ayila* (Indian mackerel, *Rastrelliger kanagurta*) and, during the monsoon, *cemmīn* (prawns, *Penaeus spp.*). In the mid-1980s, a new boat design was introduced in Chamakkala: the *taññu vaḷḷaṃ*. This boat, often simply called *vaḷḷaṃ*, is a large (15–20 m long) plank-built canoe which is driven by up to three outboard motors of 40 hp each. On fishing trips it is accompanied by a carrier *vaḷḷaṃ*, also equipped with outboard motors, which brings the catch to the shore. Ring seine-nets are the typical gear used with the *vaḷḷaṃ*-s, an encircling kind of net. Today there are four *vaḷḷaṃ* teams in Chamakkala, three of them operating year-round, one only seasonally during the southwest monsoon. A *vaḷḷaṃ* team comprises between twenty and fifty members, some of them jointly owning the equipment as shareholders. The unprecedented investments needed for the introduction of the *vaḷḷaṃ*-s were made possible in part through loans granted via the state-owned cooperative Matsyafed, and through remittances from labour in the Arabian Gulf. Besides the *vaḷḷaṃ*-s there are seven small *vañci*-s in Chamakkala: non-motorised two-men dugouts, operating in the shore with gill nets. In 2000, fish caught by Chamakkala *vaḷḷaṃ*-s was sold locally only in part. Catches of prawns were usually exported via the harbour in Kochi, a business in which local traders are only the first in a series of middlemen. Thanks to the introduction of ice, catches of sardines and mackerel are sold to places in India's inland as far away as Bangalore (Karnataka).

In the literature about the fisheries of Kerala, the introduction of the *vaḷḷaṃ*- has often been described as a reaction to the remarkable increase in the number of trawlers since the 1960s, a development which has been claimed to be a result of the promotion of prawn fishery by the Indo-Norwegian Pilot Project conducted since 1953 in southern Kerala (Kurien 1985). In this sense, the technological developments utilised by Kerala's artisanal fishermen – who previously lacked competition and had exclusive access to the state's marine resources – is understood as a response to the rapid increase in the number of trawling boats which are mostly owned by capitalists who lack any historical ties to Kerala's fishing folk. These owners include politicians (including Baby John, the leader of a small leftist party) and movie actors.

Knowing the Sea by Relating to It

Chamakkala fishermen commonly refer to the ocean as the 'west' (*paṭiññāṟu*), but rarely use the Malayalam word for 'sea' (*kaṭal*). Fishing is the '(manual) work of the west' (*paṭiññāttu pani*). Most fishermen agree that the sea is female in character. In general comments, reflections and lamentations, older men refer to the sea as 'mother' (*amma*) or 'sea mother' (*kaṭalamma*). Notably, this is a category of kinship which entails notions of care and protection of the mother for her children. Even though there are no temples consecrated to *kaṭalamma*, she is often identified with the Goddess (*devi*) of the Hindu pantheon.

Besides this explicit notion of the sea's female nature, the fishermen's speech contains many references to its 'bodiliness' and 'subjectivity'. The former is manifested by what one may call a 'physiology of heat'. The terms that are used by the fishermen to refer to the constitution of the sea are identical to those used in referring to the female human body. A state of heat (*cūṭu*), agitation (*kṣōbhaṃ*) and anger (*kōpaṃ*) is opposed to a state of coldness (*tanuppu*) and calmness (*śāntaṃ*). As in the female body, the 'heat'[4] of the sea is imagined as varying according to a regular pattern. This latter is illustrated by a myth in which the seasonal cycle of the 'heat' of the sea is considered as an expression for the (female) sea's desire for intercourse with the (male) river water from the Western Ghat mountains; this includes large rivers such as the Bharatapuzha as well as a number of small streams. The sea wants to come to the mountains to 'cool' its desire. In debating their union, sea and mountains realise that this would imply the people along Kerala's coastal strip to drown – an immoral implication, since they have made the promise to humans that this would not happen (provided that humans themselves behaved morally). In the end, the sea's desire is cooled by the 'mountain water' (*mala veḷḷaṃ*): water which has poured down in the Western Ghats during the southwest monsoon (June to August), and which subsequently enters the sea through the rivers. When the mountain water enters the sea, the latter is expected to be rough for a few days, but subsequently its 'heat' is supposed to be 'cooled'. As a consequence, fish, thought to prefer cool environments, may enter the near-coastal inshore waters. The currents in the sea (*nīru, oḻukku*) are said to be affected by the mountain water as well, and a counter-current from west to east is supposed to carry along small fish.

Another example of the sea's 'bodiliness' is provided by the verbs which describe it either as (passively) 'lying down' (*kiṭakkuka*) or (actively) 'standing up' (*iṟaṅṅuka*). In case of the latter the sea in the west is supposed to be situated higher than the beach. Being in contradiction with the commonsensical experience of water flowing down, the notion of the standing of the sea has been considered as an example for the morally constituted power of the sea to protect the people who live in the coastal area. This protective attitude of the sea is commonly ascribed to its innate truthfulness (*satyaṃ*), a quality composed of notions of benevolence, protectiveness and provision. It is the *satyaṃulla mutal kaṭal*, the 'from the beginning truthful sea.'

As we have seen, the fishermen refer to the sea as mother, yet unlike the hunter-gatherer societies considered by Bird-David (1990), where the conceptualisation of the environment as parents makes their members the mere recipients of an unidirectional 'flow' of benevolence (a 'giving environment'), Chamakkala fishermen emphasise that the moral, protective behaviour of the ocean presupposes them to reciprocate it and act in accordance with well-defined rules of morality and purity. As such, one may speak of a morally sanctioned, reciprocal relationship between the fishermen and the sea. Thus, the sea's 'subjectivity' and 'agency' are emphasised.

While both success in fishing and accidents may be interpreted in the light of these relationships, the fishermen know well that neither the ocean nor the fish are predictable in an absolute sense. Thus, irregularities of wind, rain or currents in the sea are often considered as a '*vikṛti* of "nature" (*prakṛti*)'. The word *vikṛti* may be translated as 'change, abnormality, vicious attitude or mischief' (Warrier et al. 1999: 972) and is commonly used in contexts of affectionate familiarity between human persons (see Hoeppe 2007: Chapters 4 and 5 for a more extensive interpretation).

The behaviour of sea and fish cannot be predicted. An old man explains: 'If what has to happen does not happen then it is the mischief (*vikṛti*) of "nature" (*prakṛti*)'. The mischievousness of the sea, its irregularities and the impossibility of making predictions about its future behaviour remind the fishermen of the limitations of knowledge. Not only do the fishermen consider their own knowledge, but also that of government institutions, to be limited.

Divergent Views of Environmental Change

In public discourse, recent changes in Kerala's marine environment began with the intervention by the 'Indo-Norwegian Project' from 1953 into the 1960s (Kurien 1985; Kurien and Thankappan Achari 1988; Hoeppe 2007). This development project opened the way for the export of local catches, especially prawns, to foreign markets. Previously, prawns had little commercial significance. The 'pink gold rush' of an export-oriented prawn fishery began, and was characterised by immense profits for the traders involved. Already then, most of the traders did not belong to the fishing community. Subsequently, there was a drive towards introducing large numbers of trawling boats. Most of these were owned by financially potent people lacking a background in fishing. Feeling the economic competition and noticing the overexploitation of marine resources, organisations of South Kerala's Christian fisherfolk responded with violent protest and were initially backed by the Catholic Church. These protests, which commenced in the mid-1970s and continue today, involved Hindu and Muslim fisherfolk to a much lesser degree. When I inquired about reasons for this absence of protest, Chamakkala fishermen argued not only with the considerable distance to Thiruvananthapuram, Kerala's state capital, but also with the claim that the trawler's impact on local fishing was felt here less than in South Kerala.[5] Supported financially by Matsyafed, a state-owned apex organisation of fishermen cooperatives, the artisanal fisherfolk soon responded with the motorisation of their craft and the introduction of more efficient gear. Thirdly, the then ruling communist state government reacted to the fishermen's demands by introducing, in 1980, the Kerala Marine Fisheries Regulation Act (KMFRA), which formally reserved fishing in the near-coastal waters to artisanal fishermen. After examinations of the overfishing issue by government-appointed committees and a heated public debate in Kerala, a seasonal ban on trawling has been implemented year by year since 1988. Its purpose is to secure the livelihood of the artisanal fisherfolk and conserve Kerala's much-exploited prawn resources. Discussions about whether or not this ban is insufficient or exaggerated have been going on ever since. With the liberalisation of the Indian economy in 1991, foreign industrial fishing vessels have been permitted to operate for joint ventures in India's exclusive economic zone (EEZ, extending about 370 kilometres into the sea). The effect of these ships is critically observed and protests of the fisherfolk aimed at withdrawing the licenses of these ships have been going on since the mid-1990s. Technologically, the adoption of new craft and gear has led to the efficiency of 'artisanal' fisheries approaching that of the trawlers.

The decline in the stock of prawns is the only change in Kerala's marine environment that figures in the public debate on the trawling ban. The fishermen of Chamakkala view the changes in the marine environment differently. While generally acknowledging the destructive effect of the trawlers, most of them agree that in recent decades the marine environment has been affected more profoundly than simply by overfishing through trawlers. The seasonal regularity of the ocean, which is considered to be profoundly disturbed in recent decades, is perceived as being the primary result of human impact on the marine environment. This is commonly ascribed to the building of dams in the mountains east of the coast (the Western Ghats), which are preventing the monsoon rain water from the mountains (the *mala veḷḷaṃ*, literally 'mountain water') from entering the sea. This is said to have affected not only the punctuality (*kṛtyaṃ*) of the onset of the monsoon, but also the currents and the arrival of certain fish species in the near-shore waters. In addition, a new regularity in the motion of fish has been caused by the introduction of the ban on trawling, and is ascribed to the periods when the noise of engines disturbs the fish. I shall return to this point later.

There is a general consensus among Chamakkala fishermen that the variety of fish species caught and the size of the catches have also declined. Smaller fish, especially those of the 'monsoon catch' (*varśapeytụ*, the fish usually caught during the southwest monsoon, June to August), and white sardines (*cūṭa*), are perceived to have become rare. Others, like shark and rays, are thought either to have become rare, or to have migrated to the outer sea (*puṟaṃ kaṭal*), far away from the coast. Unlike these species, the catches of Indian oil sardines (*cāla*) and, less so, mackerel (*ayila*) have been previously known to fluctuate considerably. What is perceived to be a recent phenomenon, though, is the alleged migration of sardines to the Bay of Bengal. As I shall elaborate in the next section, many of these changes are related to the operation of trawlers and other motorised boats. Much less certain than these changes are a number of 'global' influences which the fishermen sometimes debate on the beach, yet whose effect on the local marine environment remains uncertain. Examples include the melting of Antarctic ice-shelves and the pollution of the ocean as an effect of the Gulf War of 1991.

Modes of Knowledge Change in Chamakkala

I shall now describe some examples of knowledge change from Chamakkala and the ways in which it is expressed in speech. In doing so, I shall try to disentangle several modes – that is, specific ways in which an old concept is transformed – which I perceived to be relevant for knowledge change during the last decades, or alternatively between members of the three generations of fishermen who were alive during my fieldwork. I do not claim to provide an exhaustive list of all possibilities. While I believe that some modes can be established empirically, I wish to emphasise that much environmental knowledge varies significantly between individuals, including those belonging to the same generation.

(1) New Standards of Measurement

Measurement is context-tied and its changes, including the introduction of new units, may indicate shifts in the meaning of measuring itself (Appadurai 1989: 178). Daniel (1996: Chapter 3) draws attention to the violence imposed by new units and practices of measurement being introduced by the colonial government in Sri Lanka's tea production.

Shifts in units of measurement have occurred in the fisheries of Chamakkala as well. Western units of time, space and mass have entered the local world. All these coexist with local units: the Malayalam calendar is used parallel to the Western calendar, positions in the sea are expressed in terms of the *bhagaṃ* unit (water depth in arm spans) as well as in 'kilometres from the coastline' and the local *kottụ* ('basket'; corresponding to the English unit *maund*, i.e., about 37 kg) is still more common than the 'kilogram'.

There is a preference to use the Malayalam calendar for the timing of religious activities, while the Western calendar is used for most commercial purposes and bureaucracy, including government regulations. Typical for regional time reckoning in India, the Malayalam calendar counts the years starting with the beginning of a former local dynasty, the *kollaṃ* era, which began in the year 825 of the Julian calendar. In Chamakkala, each year begins with the month *ciṅṅaṃ* ('lion') in mid-August, like the eleven other months corresponding to a sign of the zodiac (but these are shifted in respect to the Gregorian calendar; see Tarabout 1986: 68–77). The expected date of the roughening of the sea at the beginning of the southwest monsoon, as well as the *pankukaśų* distribution (the annual distribution of money saved in a joint account, as it used to be practised by *vañci* teams), are typically referred to in the Malayalam calendar (as the fifteenth day of the *iṭavaṃ* month; about June, 1). In contrast, the dates of the trawling ban(s) are always linked to the Western calendar. As such, a regularity of the environment, which was previously expressed by a local unit of timekeeping, is lost, but a government-regulated seasonality, which is linked to a global unit of timekeeping, has been introduced, further underlining the alienness of the impact on the sea of trawlers and their regulation by the government. It hints at an intervention of the personalistic conceptualisation of the sea (Hoeppe 2007: 8, 123–5, 147–51).

As is typical for central and northern Kerala, in Chamakkala the sea bottom is sandy and descends towards the west with a shallow slope. This slope is considered to be more or less constant up to the westernmost places reachable with the boats. Knowing thus the depth of the water at a given locality gives an idea about this place's distance from the beach. The depth (*tārca*) at a given place is expressed in *bhagaṃ*.

The shift from *bhagaṃ* to kilometre as a measure for the distance from the beach invites a speculation about the conceptualisation of marine space. Since previously the depth of the sea and the distance from the beach were denoted by the same unit, one could surmise that the sea's spatial structure was largely cognised as a scale of depth. The recent introduction of denoting distances in kilometres may have added another dimension and made a more precise description of this space possible.

(II) *Cleansing the Myth, First Example: The Encounter of the Sea and the Mountains*

As already mentioned, many fishermen in Chamakkala agree that the seasonal regularity of the sea has been disturbed profoundly in recent decades. Since the 1950s, a number of dams have been built in the Western Ghats, storing water for irrigation and the generation of electricity. Their construction is widely thought to have disrupted the earlier seasonal regularity, and this is believed to impede local fisheries in three different ways. Firstly, in the language of the myth of the intercourse of the female sea with the male mountains (see above), the near-shore sea remains 'hot' instead of being 'cooled'. After all, the intercourse of the waters is needed for the sea to cool down. Uncooled, the near-shore sea remains unattractive for the fish which are believed to prefer cold environments.[6] Secondly, the surmised counter-current carrying along the small fish is absent. Thirdly, the mud carried along with the mountain water, which some claim to be nutritious and as such attractive for the fish, is now lacking.

As one may have expected, it appears from this brief summary of some local perceptions that a significant fraction of the surmised environmental change is interpreted in the framework of previously established conceptualisations. The myth of the intercourse of the sea with the mountains, still known only to a few old men at the time of my fieldwork, has lost much of its explanatory power for younger and even middle-aged fishermen. Many of them claim not even to have heard of it. Nevertheless, the conceptualisation itself has been retained in explaining environmental change. For example, the thought that fish prefer cold and quiet environments is maintained and interpreted in light of the lack of the cooling mountain water and the arrival of the noise of the trawlers. The old conceptualisation has been separated from its moral context. One may say, then, that the old conceptualisation has been cleansed of its moral content. The myth, particularly its moral aspect – the duty of the sea and the mountains to protect the population of Kerala from being drowned – has given way to a rationalisation that is based on a set of explicit processes: the motion of fish and its dependance on the heat and noise levels in the sea. While the myth implied the mutuality of humans and the environment, no such social relationship is apparent in the functionalist explanation that restricts itself to variation in these two parameters and their relevance to the migration of fish. Younger and middle-aged fishermen may retain the notion of *kaṭalamma*, the sea mother, in speech; yet when they explain how they perceive processes in the sea and the environment, such as the seasonal cycle, they neither refer to her nor to the other 'subjective', anthropomorphic aspects of the sea mentioned above.

An example in which the functionalist conceptualisation is relevant is the fishermen's judgement of how the trawling boats affect local fisheries. While often understood to be generally harmful, the skipper of a Chamakkala *vaḷḷaṃ*, explains:

> Trawling is not always a *dōśaṃ* [fault, problem]. It is not a *dōśaṃ* when it is done in the *puṟaṃ kaṭal* [outer sea]. If they are doing the fishing [*vali*] there, the fishes come to the coast (literally, 'are stepping down to the east', *mīn kiḻakkōṭṭu iraṅṅuka*). They [the trawlers] may not come to within twenty kilometres [from the coast], if they are coming further than that to the east then we [the artisanal fishermen] will not get anything, that can be a *dōśaṃ*.

The reasoning of this and other fishermen is that, by scaring the fish towards the shore, the trawler's noise substitutes the effect which the variation of heat previously had on the migration of fish. In this sense, the trawlers refurbish a seasonal regularity in the sea which has been disturbed by human's constructing dams in the mountains. Nevertheless, local fishermen agree that near the coast the effect of trawlers is profoundly negative.

(III) *Cleansing the Myth, Second Example: The Fate of the Lotus Sea*

In a nutshell, Chamakkala fishermen classify marine space according to its distance from the coastline: the near-shore waters (up to about 2 km into the sea) are called *arāyi* or *paṭi*, the region between two and eight kilometres from the shore is called *iṭamaddyaṃ* ('space in between'). Beyond that, there is the *puṟaṃ kaṭal*, the 'outer sea'. However, when older fishermen talk about seasonal processes in the sea, they speak about another, even more distant region: the Lotus Sea (*tāmaru kaṭal*).

Descriptions of the Lotus Sea are fairly uniform. It is said to be a distant part of the ocean, far in the west, which is covered with lotus petals in the hot season (*vēnal pakal*). Sunrays cannot traverse this cover. When the heat of the seawater rises at the beginning of the hot season, the shade below the lotus flowers is the only cool region in the sea. This makes it an attractive destination for the fish. Several fish species (especially *ayila*, mackerel) are supposed to spawn in the Lotus Sea. They form groups (*kūṭṭaṃ or pelappu*), in which they descend towards the coast at the beginning of the southwest monsoon (*kālavarśaṃ*). At this time, the rough sea may cause the stems of the lotus flowers to break and the Lotus Sea to dissolve until the end of the monsoon.

While the *puṟaṃ kaṭal* is visible daily and known to the fishermen from direct experience, knowledge about the Lotus Sea is inferential and reflects assumptions about the behaviour of the fish, which is often talked about in terms of human behaviour. Common analogies are derived from the local village context. For example, many small freshwater ponds (*kuḷaṅṅaḷ*, singular *kuḷaṃ)* in the village are covered with lotus petals and fish are seen to be hiding under these petals. Nevertheless, the smell and taste of those fish which are said to have migrated to the Lotus Sea are considered as the strongest argument for its existence. Not only fishermen are of this opinion; I have also heard this from older villagers inland who have no personal relation to fishing. The smell and taste of lotus is assumed to have been assimilated by the fish during their sojourn in the Lotus Sea.

The processes of formation and dissolution of the Lotus Sea are commonly linked to its regular character (according to a rule, *niyamaṃ*) or, more often, to the 'scriptures' (*śāstraṅṅaḷ*, singular *śāstraṃ*). When I tried to pursue this point further and asked which scripture (*śāstraṃ*) was meant, the answers were always evasive. Kumaran (80), a retired fisherman and middleman, gave a typical reply: 'it is said that there are seven seas. This is the Arabian Sea (*aṟabi kaṭal*), the Lotus Sea (*tāmaru kaṭal*) is behind it.' Kumaran was not the only person to mention the Lotus Sea as one of the seven seas.

Descriptions of lotuses, including those in lakes or rivers, are an exceedingly popular theme in Indic mythology. The idea of seven circular ring-seas surrounding the Earth, intermitted by ring-continents, is shared by Puranic and later Buddhist and Jaina cosmologies (Kirfel 1968: 112–27, 186, 242–53). But only in Jaina cosmology is there is something like a Lotus sea, the *pushkaroda* ocean, 'named thus since, because of the sun and moon, it shines like lotus' (translated from the German after Kirfel 1968: 252f.). But this ocean is vastly different from the fishermen's conceptualisation. It is the third of the seven ring seas, filled with a nectar-like fluid and lying far behind two other ring seas and two ring continents. It remains doubtful if these traditions are related in any meaningful way to the Lotus Sea as it is conceived by the fishermen in Chamakkala.

To qualify accounts of the Lotus Sea with reference to a rule or a written source, as Kumaran does, may seem to lend them authority. It might be an attempt to give credibility to a claim, which one cannot judge through one's own experience. On the contrary, it may also express personal scepticism towards an old and possibly outdated concept. This latter viewpoint is expressed by Chandran, formerly a fisherman and now a middleman in his mid-60s:

> The Lotus Sea is known as the Seventh Sea, but there is no clear evidence [*rēkha*]. So many people say that the Lotus Sea is there. But one cannot support [the claim] that it is there officially [*itụ audhyōdika māyiṭṭụ uṇṭō eṇụ samarṯikkaḷ paṟṟilla*].

Like Kumaran, Chandran mentions the concept of the seven seas, but in doing so he articulates his own critical position. Doubt about the existence of the Lotus Sea is therefore present even in the older generation. In contrast, Krishnankutti, a retired fisherman in his 70s, is convinced of its existence and claims that some people have seen it. In talking with Suresh, my co-worker in the field, and me, he never felt the need to refer to any scripture to prove his point. His age-mate Gangadharan, disagrees: 'We have seen the end of the sea (*ā kaṭalinṟe aṭṭaṃ oke kaṇdetti*). Now we know that there is no Lotus Sea'. Having lived in South India all his life, Gangadharan cannot have seen the 'end of the sea' himself. But many younger men have: as migrants to the Arabian Gulf they have taken an aeroplane to reach the other side of the Arabian Sea. Some of them have watched the sea attentively through the aeroplane window, but none had seen a sea covered with lotus petals. Ramanathan, who worked in Saudia Arabia before returning to fishing, does not, however, feel that this observation disproves the existence of the Lotus Sea. He says:

> Sometimes the *ayila* [mackerel] of the *tulaṃ* month has got this smell, doesn't it? In *ciṅṅaṃ*, *kanni* and *tulaṃ* [mid-August to mid-November] we catch this fish in the west. Then we move to the place where *ayila* is living. Previously we did not go beyond ten *bhagaṃ*, that means ten kilometres ... When we did not have any other fish then we would move there to put the net. The fishes from that area have a special smell (*pratyēkata vāsana*) of lotus (*tāmarụ*), so it was called the Lotus Sea. Other than that there is no other sea there.'

With the background of his own experiences, Ramanathan 'rationalises' the concept of the Lotus Sea. He does not disapprove of the idea, but reduces its conceptualisation to a version that is consistent with empirical observation, i.e., the smell of lotus in the fish. In short, one may say that he has cleansed the myth of the Lotus Sea. Unlike in the case of the myth mentioned earlier, here this cleansing does not imply the separation of ontological domains which co-existed formerly. This does not come as a surprise, for even in the old men's reminiscences, ideas of morality were not relevant in conceptualising this most distant part of the sea.

(IV) From Literality to Figurativeness: The Rising of the Sea

When Chamakkala fishermen refer to the westward and eastward motions of fish and boats in the sea, they commonly use the verbs *kayaṟuka* (to rise, increase, mount) and *iṟaṅṅuka* (to descend, decrease) respectively. The same verbs are used in an everyday context when describing motion into or out of a confined, and usually elevated, space, e.g., a room (*muṟi*).[7] Examples are: *muṟiyil kayaṟuka* ('to enter a room') and *muṟiyil ninnu̦ iṟaṅṅuka* ('to leave a room'). Is the use of these verbs solely a matter of convention, or does it literally imply, in the fishermen's imagination, that the sea rises toward the west? Kumaran (not the person mentioned above), in his early 70s, gives this answer:

Götz: The fish will go up and up. What does it mean? [*mīn kayaṟi kayaṟi pōkkuṃ eṇāl eṅṅāṇu̦?*].

Kumaran: That they move away from the coast, that is all (*atāyatu̦ karayil ninnu̦ pōkkuṇu̦ eṇu̦ mātraṃ*).

Götz: Is the sea going up towards the west? [*kaṭalu̦ paṭiññāṭṭu̦ pōkkuṃ tōṟuṃ poṅṅiyānu̦ varunatu̦?*].

Kumaran: That is our thought [*uddēśaṃ*]. Of course, you may ask: how can water move up towards one end? But if we move five *bhagaṃ* [into the sea] then we can see the mountains in the east, except for the small ones. When we reach to ten *bhagaṃ* then we can see all the mountains.

Like all the older, many of the middle-aged, and some of the younger people I talked with, Kumaran asserts that the sea is rising (*pongal*) above land level towards the west. Even though he agrees that this claim runs counter to everyday experience, he feels it to be vindicated by the empirical observation of the mountains being visible from the sea. Others support this claim by arguing that it would always be more difficult to row a certain distance towards the west than to return towards the east, thereby utilising the analogy of the physical effort needed to climb a mountain and a similar effect to mount (*kayaṟuka*) the sea. Even though the rise of the sea is considered by many to be proven by empirical observation, it is nevertheless considered a remarkable fact. Vasu, a fisherman in his late 60s, explains:

> The sea is standing (*nilkkuttatụ*) above us. This is a great wonder (*atiśayaṃ*). The sea is higher up than we are! Water at this height can flow towards us, shouldn't it? If you pour water into a vessel then it will rest in its bottom. But the sea is up high and we are below that in the plain land. Because of this the seawater can flow here. This [the standing of the sea] is by the might of God (*daivattinṟe kaḻivụ*). We are saying that this is due to the might of God.

Note that Vasu refers to the sea as actively standing (*nilkkuka*) in contrast with the passive lying down (*kiṭakkuka*), which is also used in talking about the position of the sea. Like Kumaran, Vasu contends that the rising of the sea contradicts common sense, since water does usually flow down. In attributing this rise to the might of God (*daivattinṟe kaḻivụ*) he asserts that God cares for the people who live along the coastal strip. In both cases people on the coast are consciously protected, either by the sea itself or by God (*daivaṃ*). Notably, the Malayalam term *daivaṃ* is used by Hindus, Muslims and Christians alike. This world is inherently unstable, since continuous blessing is required. The sea's active and conscious protection of humans is often traced to its *satyaṃ* (truthfulness). Moral misconduct may obscure the blessing of God or the sea's *satyaṃ* and may result in a flood. Several older fishermen assured me that a large flood that had just affected the Indian state of Orissa (October 1999) must have been due to the improper moral conduct of the people living there.

Not all of Chamakkala's fishermen, however, share the view that the ocean is rising above land level towards the west. Venu (40) and Vijayan (43), both shareholders on a *vaḷḷaṃ*, strongly disagree:

Götz: When the fish have moved to the west you are saying: 'gone up up' [*kayaṟi kayaṟi pōyi*].

Vijayan: Yes. We shall say 'gone up' [*kayaṟi pōyi*].

Götz: Some people say that the sea is standing [*nilkkunattụ*] above the land.

Vijayan: That is not true. We have to consider what the people from here are saying and what the science is saying [*nātiluḷḷa ālkāṟanmar parayunatuṃ śāstriyamāyittuḷḷatuṃ*]. If we are climbing up some stairs then we can surely say that the height of this land is increasing. That is scientific [*atụ śāstriyamāttānụ*] ...

Venu: We are not able to talk about that. It is difficult to say that the sea is higher than the earth. We cannot say so.

Vijayan: Water is flowing down. If this [land] here is below the sea, then the water must be flowing here.

Götz: Some people say that the sea is not flowing here because of its truthfulness [*satyaṃ*].

Vijayan: [Laughs.] Ha, ha. [More seriously] That is true in one way. But what if we are thinking in another way?

Vijayan does not deny the rising outright, but argues against it by referring to the authority of a scientific viewpoint. The word *śāstraṃ*, which he uses, has its own ambivalences, since it does not always refer to modern science, as Vijayan certainly implies here, but also to scriptural sources of the Brahmanical tradition. Like all fishermen, Vijayan and Venu use the verb *kayaṟuka* in describing the movement of fish towards the west. However, in regarding the sea as flat, their use of *kayaṟuka* is metaphorical. The older fishermen had used this verb literally, i.e. they understood the sea to rise towards the west. In a situation of a changing worldview, brought about by schooling, media and travel, what a metaphor is to some may not be one to others. The most critical opinion about the rising of the sea could perhaps be expected from those fishermen who had been working in the Arabian Gulf as migrant workers. Ramanathan, introduced above, is one of the few men who returned to fishing after working as a labourer in Saudi Arabia. He says:

> In the west [*paṭiññāṟu*] [the sea] is high and in the east [*kiḻakku*] it is low. It is standing [*nilkkukayāṇu*] like this. The Arabian Sea [*aṟabi kaṭal*] has no right [*avakāśaṃ*] to pursue anything over here [i.e. flow over here]. But then, in the Gulf it is different. There it is going down towards the west, but here it is going up towards the west.

It seems that Ramanathan's view of the structure of the sea has indeed been affected by his stay in the Persian Gulf, not in terms of doubting the rise of the sea, but by adding that in the Gulf the sea is going down in the west. He makes the old view consistent with his new experiences. In saying that the sea has no (traditional) right (*avakāśaṃ*) to move towards the east, Ramanathan hints at a contract or agreement that seems to exist there between the sea and the people. This is most likely a reference to the myth of the intercourse of the sea with water from the mountains which I mentioned earlier. Thus, the moral notion of 'truthfulness' (*satyaṃ*) appears to be maintained in local discourse, but it is not 'allowed' to interfere with rationalistic concepts of impersonal forces according to which water flows down. The split of the (perceived) ontological domains of physical reality and morality is realised here by moving from a literal to a figurative understanding of marine space.

(v) Re-labelling Old Conceptualisations: What do Fish Eat?

Old fishermen sometimes emphasise that rainwater may mix with the salt water of the sea. They believe that this mixing results in the formation of *tari* (small fragment, seed), thought to be the food of prawns (*cemmīn*). While usually staying near the bottom of the ocean, they rise to the surface to eat it. Phalgunan, in his late 40s, who has spent eighteen years working on fishing ships in the Persian Gulf, gives an account which differs slightly from this widespread view:

> At the time of rain this saltwater and freshwater will mix. From it the substance called plankton is formed. It happens in the middle depth of the sea [*kaṭalinṟe iṭattaṭṭu*]. But then it moves to the wide bottom [of the sea] [*aṭipparappu*]. When the heat of the sun is receding, when it is raining for three or four months, this substance [*sādanaṃ*] will settle down (...). I mean the substance called plankton. This plankton is produced in the rainy season [*varśakālaṃ*]. The plankton is produced when the waters are joining [*kuṭiyōjikkumbol*]. It stays in the top of the sea [*kaṭalinṟe mukal*]. The *cemmīn* is coming up in order to eat it. In the months *dhanu* and *makaraṃ* [mid-December to mid-February] the plankton is moving down, then *cemmīn* should be caught from the bottom. Now it comes from the pelagic. Therefore, it [*cemmīn*] eats the food [*bhakśanaṃ*] from that place. We [humans] are also moving to the places where food [*bhakśanaṃ*] is available.

Phalgunan's account is almost identical with the statements of older people, except for his introduction of three English terms: 'mix', 'plankton' and 'pelagic'. He uses the noun 'plankton' as a synonym of *tari*, the adjective 'pelagic' side-by-side with its synonym *kaṭalinṟe mukal*, and the verb 'to mix' next to its Malayalam equivalent *kuṭiyōjikkumbol*. He has poured the old wine of 'local knowledge' into the new bottle of (global) 'science'. As mentioned in the introduction to this chapter, the apparent use of English terms and concepts is perhaps an allusion to the particular power implied by the knowledge associated with them. This is suggestive in Phalgunan's case, for he explicitly praises the benefits of the 'fisheries science', a superior way of knowing and, in the end, of making use of the sea. On the other hand, one must also note that English terms have become a customary part of many regional languages in India, including Malayalam.

(vi) New Metaphors: Talking about the cākara

The seasonal formation of a coastal mudbank has been observed in the eighteen years prior to my arrival in Chamakkala. Recognisable as a distinct patch of calm, turbid water, it stretches for about 3 km along the coast and for about 2 km into the sea. It is a calm area in the sea, surrounded by the rough monsoonal swells. Known from several places along the coast of Kerala, this phenomenon is called a *cākara* (from *cāku*, death, and *kara*, shore). Though usually translated into English as 'mud bank', a Malayalam-English dictionary translates *cākara* as 'occurrence of mud-banks and appearance of plenty of fish for a short period at some places along the Kerala coast during the monsoon', and adds the idiomatic meaning of *cākara* as a 'season of plenty, plentifulness' (Warrier et al. 1999: 369). This is no wonder, since locally the *cākara* is of great importance, as it is often the only place where the fishermen can enter the sea during the rough swells of the southwest monsoon – the season in which the largest catches are usually made. Occurrences of *cākara*-s are often linked (wrongly) to large catches of costly prawns, and allegedly high financial gain for the fishermen. *Cākara*-s may form at the beginning of the monsoon (typically in early June) and dissolve at its end (August/September). This formation and dissolution are known to be rather unsteady processes. During my fieldwork in Chamakkala, I was particularly curious about the fishermen's perceptions of these processes.

In their talk about the *cākara*, the fishermen commonly used metaphors which emphasise the mudbank's apparent 'agency'. For example, they commonly talked about its birth (*utbhavaṃ*) and about the place on the shore where it would reside (*tamasikkuka*). Later it was considered to be on the 'look-out for a comfortable place to lie down' (*kiṭakkānulla saukaryamānụ pulli nōkkunatụ*). The Malayalam pronoun *pulli*, often used when talking about the *cākara*, addresses a familiar male (third person singular) person. Some places were regarded as more convenient (*saukaryamulla*) for the *cākara*'s residence than others, but this year (2000) it seemed rather undecided throughout the season. A local Muslim sorcerer (*mantravādi*), whom the *cākara* had always obeyed (*kēlkkuka*), was called to the beach.[8] But the outcome of his rituals was judged with skepticism and it was claimed that other sorcerers were pulling (*valikkuka*) on it from different sides. While one *cākara* had initially formed in mid-2000, it seemed to have split into two parts. Some claimed that it had been cut (*kaśnikkuka* or *marikkuka*) by the use of *mantraṃ*-s, a general term for magical spells of Hindu and Muslim sorcerers. Some people must have behaved towards it with truthlessness (*asatyaṃ*). These examples show that the marine environment is talked about in terms of agency until today.

There is a consensus that the *cākara* has become less predictable than in the past. This is illustrated by occasional statements such as 'today the *cākara* moves with the *mantravādi*-s' and 'nowadays *cākara* is [behaves] like a politician [*cākara ippōḷatte rāśṭriyakāreppōle*]'. Both the works of sorcerers and the doings of politicians are unpredictable, unreliable and can be influenced with money. The introduction of these metaphors or analogies links the agency of humans to the changes which people observe in the sea. Expressed differently, a characteristic of sociality – the doings and consequences of 'truthless' behaviour which is considered characteristic of the present 'time of progress' – is identified both in the sea as well as in the doings of people. As such, the changes perceived in the marine environment mirror the social change perceived on the land.

Conclusions

Both in a state-wide public discourse as well as in the village Chamakkala, profound changes in the marine environment have been perceived and are debated. Yet there is considerable divergence in the understanding of what these changes are and what they mean. Initially I hoped to understand these differences by considering, at the village level, the interaction of surmised 'local' and 'global' environmental knowledges.

I realised soon that there has been no clear-cut replacement of 'local' knowledge by 'foreign' or 'global' knowledges. Similarly, in speech, the border between the figurative and the literal often remains blurred, keeps shifting and depends on individual speakers. Middle-aged men are more open-minded towards new, i.e., global, technology than older men. Their speech does not differ much formally, but it soon became clear to me that what older men meant literally was understood metaphorically by the middle-aged. Nevertheless, they continue using the same words – and understand their meaning, for the metaphors are part of the communicative process among men of different ages who participate in the work of fishing. But does the extraneous, 'global' knowledge, itself being understood literally, push local knowledge into the domain of the figurative? In several cases this seems to occur, for example, in regard to the notion of the rising of the sea. Other cases are more ambivalent, such as the notion of *kaṭalamma*, or more generally, the motherliness of the sea. Fishermen who do not hesitate to make statements about new technology or their own migration experience (two apparently global topics) do, in other contexts, talk quite naturally about the truthfulness of the sea and its rising toward the west as expressions of a personal, moral relatedness with the fishermen. This would seem like another hint of the persistence of the local, or of the strategic use of either concept (Hoeppe 2007: Chapter 7). That the domains of the literal and the figurative do not remain uncontested is illustrated by how the myth is cleansed and how the alleged rising of the sea as being precipitated by moral interaction has been criticised and denied lately. The selective use of figurative language makes it possible to speak (and reflect) about the two domains of 'truth' at the same time, even in the same sentence, given the consensus of speakers and hearers about the border between literal and figurative language. Can a 'literal global' and a 'figurative local' co-exist, is the question that remains.

Notes

1. In this text, important Malayalam words are written in italics and transliterated following the Library of Congress notation, a style largely adopted by e.g. Tarabout (1986). Place names and personal names are not transcribed. Unless otherwise noted I write the plurals of Malayalam words with the singular word, added by '-s.' I do so because of the complications of using the Malayalam plural construction.
2. Reservation quotas have been introduced by the Indian government in order to make it easier for the members of low status castes to achieve higher education and secure government employment. Since the 1970s, the Araya caste has been classified as OBC ('other backward castes') and thus, its members are eligible to certain reservations.
3. On the ambivalences and difficulties in the usage of the term 'local knowledge', see Ellen and Harris (2000).
4. I shall write 'heat' with quotation marks since it is not always understood thermometrically, but may be used metaphorically as well.
5. This is plausible, given that in southern Kerala mostly demersal fish species (i.e., those living near the sea bottom) are caught, while in Chamakkala fishing is mostly pelagic, i.e., aimed at near-surface species, such as Indian oil sardines and mackerel.
6. In Chamakkala, there is no general agreement to classify fish as food into 'hot' or 'cold' ones, as it is done with other food (cf. Daniel 1984: 184).
7. Houses in Kerala are usually built with an elevated floor, to prevent rainwater from entering.
8. For this particular discussion it is of little importance which sorcerers were Hindu and which Muslims.

References

Appadurai, Arjun 1989. 'Transformations in the Culture of Agriculture, in *Contemporary Indian Tradition: Voices on Culture, Nature, and the Challenge of Change*, ed. C. M. Borden, 173–89. Washington, DC: Smithsonian Institution Press.

Beck, Brenda E.F. 1978. 'The Metaphor as a Mediator between Semantic and Analogic Modes of Thought', *Current Anthropology*, 19: 83–88, 94–97.

Bird-David, Nurit 1990. 'The Giving Environment: Another Perspective on the Economic System of Hunter-Gatherers', *Current Anthropology*, 31: 183–96.

Bloch, Maurice 1998. *How We Think They Think: Anthropological Approaches to Cognition, Memory and Literacy.* Boulder: Westview Press.

Cohen, Anthony P. 1993. 'Segmentary Knowledge: A Whalsay Sketch', in *An Anthropological Critique of Development: The Growth of Ignorance*, ed. Mark Hobart, 31–42. London: Routledge.

Daniel, E. Valentine 1984. *Fluid Signs: Being a Person the Tamil Way.* Berkeley: University of California Press.

Daniel, E. Valentine 1996. *Charred Lullabies: Chapters in an Anthropography of Violence.* Princeton: Princeton University Press.

Ellen, Roy and Holly Harris 2000. 'Introduction', in *Indigenous Environmental Knowledge and its Transformations: Critical Anthropological Perspectives*, eds. Roy Ellen, Peter Parkes and Alan Bicker, 1–33. Amsterdam: Harwood Academic Publishers.

Ellen, Roy, Peter Parkes and Alan Bicker, eds. 2000. *Indigenous Environmental Knowledge and its Transformations: Critical Anthropological Perspectives*. Amsterdam: Harwood Academic Publishers.

Foucault, Michel 1980. *Power/Knowledge: Selected Interviews and Other Writings 1972–77*, New York: Pantheon Books.

Gentner, D., B. Bowdle, P. Wolff and C. Boronat 2001. 'Metaphor is Like Analogy', in *The Analogical Mind: Perspectives from Cognitive Science*, eds. D. Gentner, K.J. Holyoak and B.N. Kokinov, 199–253. Cambridge, MA: MIT Press.

George, M.J. 1988. *Study of Shrimp Trawling in the South West Coast of India, Particularly Kerala*. Trivandrum: Programme for Community Organisation.

Gold, Ann Grodzins and Bhoju Ram Gujar 2002. *In the Time of Trees and Sorrows: Nature, Power, and Memory in Rajasthan*. Durham: Duke University Press.

Gundert, Hermann 1995 [1872]. *A Malayalam and English Dictionary*. Kottayam: D.C. Books.

Hesse, Mary 1980. *Revolutions and Reconstructions in the Philosophy of Science*. Brighton: Harvester Press.

Hoeppe, Götz 2007. *Conversations on the Beach: Fishermen's Knowledge, Metaphor and Environmental Change in South India*. New York/Oxford: Berghahn Books.

Ingold, Tim 2000. *The Perception of the Environment: Essays on Livelihood, Dwelling and Skil*. London: Routledge.

Jeffrey, Robin 1992. *Politics, Women and Well-Being: How Kerala Became 'a Model'*. London: Macmillan.

Kirfel, Willibald 1968 [1920]. *Die Kosmologie der Inder nach den Quellen dargestellt*. Hildesheim: Georg Olms.

Koselleck, Reinhart 1989. 'Sprachwandel und Ereignisgeschichte', *Merkur. Deutsche Zeitschrift für Europäisches Denken* 43: 657–73.

Kurien, John 1985. 'Technical Assistance Projects and Socio-Economic Change: Norwegian Intervention in Kerala's Fisheries Development', *Economic and Political Weekly* 20: A70–A88.

——— 2000. 'The Kerala Model: Its Central Tendency and the "Outlier"', in *Kerala: The Development Experience: Reflections on Sustainability and Replicability*, ed. G. Parayil, 178–97. London: Zed Publications.

——— and T.R. Achari Thankappan 1988. 'Overfishing along Kerala Coast: Causes and Consequences', *Economic and Political Weekly* 25: 2011–18.

Nichter, Mark 1980. 'The Layperson's Perception of Medicine as Perspective into the Utilization of Multiple Therapy Systems in the Indian Context', *Social Science and Medicine* 14B: 225–33.

Osella, Filippo and Caroline Osella 2000. *Social Mobility in Kerala: Modernity and Identity in Conflict*. London: Pluto Press.

Parayil, Govindan 2000. 'Is Kerala's Development Experience a "Model"?', in *Kerala: The Development Experience: Reflections on Sustainability and Replicability*, ed. G. Parayil, London: Zed Publications, 1–15.

Piot, Charles 1999. *Remotely Global: Village Modernity in Western Africa*. Chicago: University of Chicago Press.

Richards, Paul 1993. 'Cultivation: Knowledge or Performance?', in *An Anthropological Critique of Development: The Growth of Ignorance*, ed. Mark Hobart, 61–78. London: Routledge.

Tarabout, Gilles 1986. *Sacrifier et donner a voir: Les temples de Kerala, Inde du Sud, étude anthropologique*. Paris: École Française d'Extreme Orient.

Tarabout, Gilles 1997. 'Une configuration Sociale régionale: le Kérala', *Historiens et Géographes* 356: 243–56.

Tsing, Anna Lowenhaupt 1993. *In the Realm of the Diamond Queen: Marginality in an Out-of-the-way Place.* Princeton: Princeton University Press.

Tsing, Anna Lowenhaupt 2005. *Friction: An Ethnography of Global Connection.* Princeton: Princeton University Press.

Turnbull, David 2000. *Masons, Tricksters and Cartographers: Comparative Studies in Scientific and Indigenous Knowledge.* London: Routledge.

Veyne, Paul 1988. *Did the Greeks Believe in their Myths? An Essay on the Constitutive Imagination.* Chicago: University of Chicago Press.

Wallich, Paul 1995. 'A Mystery Inside a Riddle Inside an Enigma', *Scientific American* 272: 19.

Warrier, M.I., E.P. Narayana Bhattathiri and K.R. Warrier 1999. *Malayalam-Imglish Nighantu* (Malayalam-English Dictionary). Kottayam: D.C. Books.

12

Mass Tourism and Ecological Problems in Seaside Resorts of Southern Thailand: Environmental Perceptions, Assessments and Behaviour Regarding the Problem of Waste

Karl Vorlaufer, Heike Becker-Baumann and Gabriela Schmitt

Introduction

On 26 December 2004 a seaquake whose epicentre lay close to Sumatra's west coast led to a disastrous tsunami which hit the Thai mainland and island coasts with an unprecedented fury. Some 8,000 people lost their lives or went missing; of these some 5,000 were foreign tourists. The waves did not affect the entire coastline and the localised coastal morphology largely influenced both the volume and the effects of the tsunami. Those coasts which were no longer protected by mangroves and coral reefs were especially exposed, as also those with beaches gradually sloping into the ocean. Such coasts are often preferred for developing tourist centres, and in the process of often uncontrolled development of such centres mangrove forests and beach vegetation (especially casuarina and coconut palms) have also been cut down, dunes levelled and built over. As a result, both tourist resorts and fishing villages built too close to the beach were destroyed by the waves. The entire tourist infrastructure on the island of Phi Phi Don as well as Khao Lak, some 150 km north of Phuket island, were entirely destroyed. The tourism industry in Thailand is, however, probably affected by the tsunami only in a limited fashion, partly because many potential tourists to the area will find alternatives on coasts and islands not affected by the tsunami, notably the island of Samui.

Tourism and Its Environmental Impacts

Mass tourism itself represents a special danger to ecological stability because it is often very closely related with other syndromes, such as

- the Favela Syndrome – i.e., environmental degradation through unregulated and rapid urbanisation and the emergence of huge shanty towns and slums adjacent to tourist centres;
- the Suburbia Syndrome – i.e., ecological damage caused by a planned but excessive expansion of urban residential areas and their infrastructures;
- the Garbage Dump Syndrome – i.e., environmental impact through high accumulation of solid and liquid waste and its partly regulated, but mostly unregulated dumping and removal.

A combination and cumulative reinforcement of these syndromes is caused by substantial demographic growth, above all due to considerable immigration in the course of increasing tourism, and the direct and indirect employment opportunities this creates (Vorlaufer 1996). In its annual appraisal the German federal government's scientific advisory committee on global environmental changes identified sixteen major syndromes of global change as causing and amplifying global environmental impact (WBGU 1998; see also Reusswig 1999). The mass tourism syndrome 'Development and Damage of Natural Space for Recreational Purposes' has generally been classified as part of the syndrome-group 'Use'. It describes the causes, connections and processual forms of environmental damage that can result from an excessive tourist use of sensitive ecological systems (e.g., of water and land resources). During recent decades the mass tourism syndrome has become relevant for an increasing number of developing countries whose ecologically fragile terrestrial and aquatic ecosystems have been closely incorporated into world tourism (Vorlaufer 1996).

Tourism in Southern Thailand: Locations, Scope and Environmental Problems

Thailand has long ranked among the world's most important tourist destinations. In 1999, 8.7 million foreign visitors were counted (1985: 2.4 million; 1990: 5.3 million; WTO 2000) and the relatively strong economic growth in Thailand in the last decades has also led to an increase in domestic tourism (Vorlaufer 2001). The people of Thailand in particular have the responsibility of ensuring ecological stability and thus also sustainable tourism. The economic boom of the last decades has transformed Thailand enormously. The fast-growing income of large parts of the population has generated new consumption patterns everywhere in the country, including tourist places. Plastic bags in particular are used in huge quantities and very often just thrown on the ground. Everywhere plastic is the most visible phenomenon of the inappropriate environmental behaviour of large sections of Thai society. Beginning around 1975, at first hesitantly and then more rapidly, wide coastal areas of southern Thailand have been transformed into favoured tourist destinations (Cohen 1996, 1982; Vorlaufer 1995, 2001). Within a few years formerly socio-economically marginalised parts of the mainland coast, but above all islands and island groups, have often been transformed by mass tourism. Former fishing and farming villages have grown to urban settlements with several thousand inhabitants, attracting many immigrants in a very short time (Vorlaufer 1997). The number of visitors per 1,000 inhabitants is often very high here. Given the largely unavailable or unsatisfactory technical and financial potential, as well as the shortage of manpower with adequate knowledge and skills, a sustainable protection of the environment is hardly possible. Because of the worsening ecological crisis and the increasing threat to an 'intact' environment which is the basis of tourism, the need for adequate environmental management – and above all a greater sensitisation of the tourists, but especially the local population and a corresponding modification of environmental behaviour – is urgent and acute (Becker-Baumann and Schmitt 2006). In our study[1] we look at the environmental impacts caused substantially (though not exclusively) by mass tourism, in particular the collection and inadequate removal or dumping of solid and liquid waste. Our main aim is to analyse the environmental perceptions, assessments and behaviour of the local population.

We concentrate on tourism locations in southern Thailand. These vary in size, in dynamics of development, to some degree also in their resources and carrying capacities and thus in their ability to absorb environmental impacts. Furthermore, the various locations attract visitors who differ in socio-economic and demographic respects (see map 12.1).

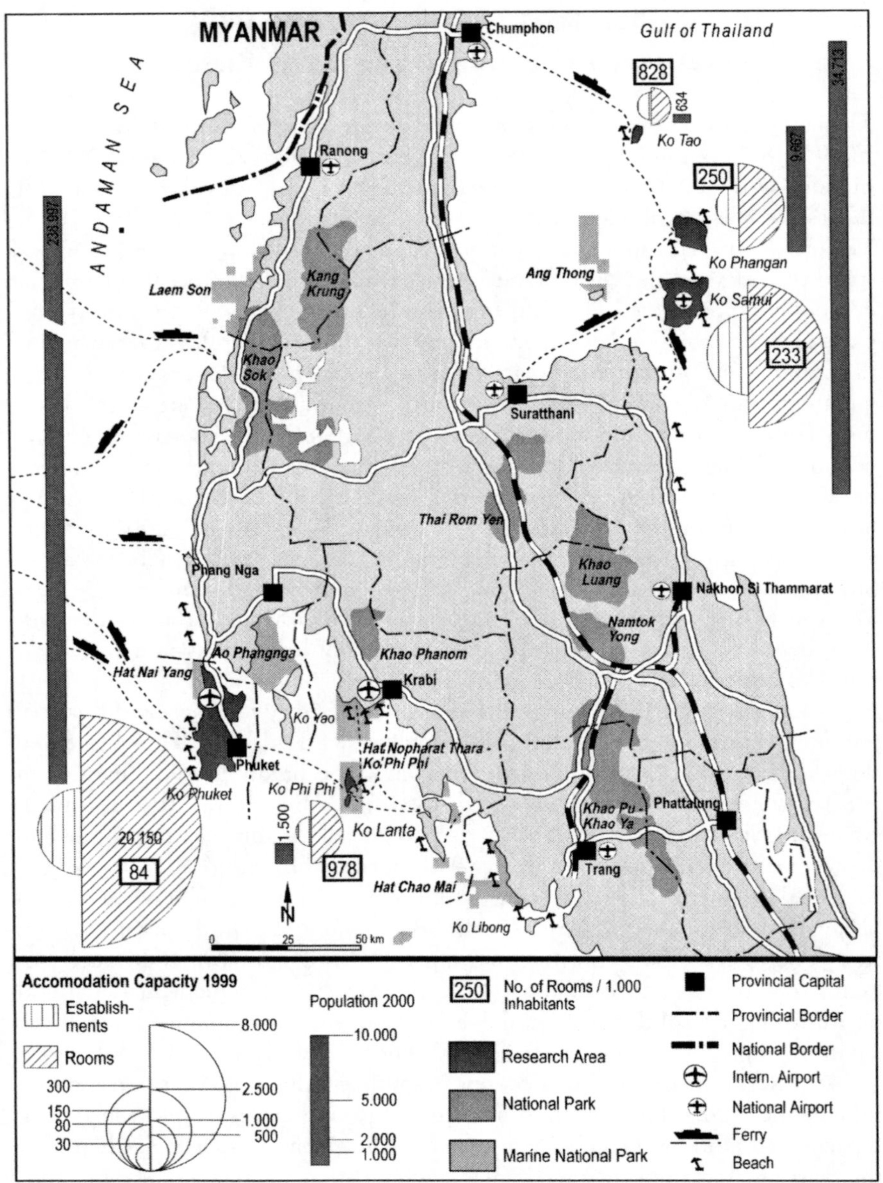

Map 12.1. Southern Thailand and the places of investigation

By far the most important tourist centre is Phuket Island: 543 km^2 in area and counting 239,000 inhabitants in 2000 (75,732 in 1960; 130,996 in 1980; 166,308 in 1990; source: NSO). Its 'capital' with the same name has numerous beaches and 'seaside resorts' which are located along the western coast. In 1975 Patong, the main tourist place in Phuket, was still a tiny fishing and farming village. With its 122 hotels and 6,277 guest rooms today it makes up 35 per cent of the total accommodation capacity on the island (TAT 2000). Furthermore, Patong has an over-proportional concentration of shops and entertainment facilities, with around 325 souvenir shops, 320 restaurants and 300 places of entertainment (own survey). Today, Patong counts about 11,500 inhabitants and about 16,600 persons are directly employed in tourism. As Phuket is equipped with a large, modern incineration plant and a relatively efficient waste disposal system since 1997, there seem to be less serious waste problems here than for example on Ko Phi Phi (Ko = island).

Phi Phi is 28 km^2 and has approximately 1,500 inhabitants. This island, which is very popular because of its spectacular tower carst, has 92 hotels and 1,617 guest rooms. Tourism development started timidly around 1985, but has become very dynamic since 1990. The small size of the island combined with an extremely high density of guest rooms and tourists limits its tourist carrying capacity. Terrestrial balancing areas for the absorption of, for instance, waste produced by tourism hardly exist. Backpackers and individual tourists account for the large majority of the island`s visitors, exceeding even the package-tour tourists and the guests of the few luxury hotels. Small bungalow accommodation, often of simple standard, is common for the hotel industry.

The second largest tourist centre of southern Thailand is the island of Samui, where tourism developed around 1980, at first slowly but soon thereafter fairly quickly. Today, Samui has about 37,168 inhabitants in addition to 265 hotels and 7,156 guest rooms (TAT 2000). Like Phuket, it has had an incineration plant since 1998. However, due to the large numbers of visitors and inhabitants, waste problems are not yet solved. Samui is dominated by relatively large hotels which are characteristic of package-tour tourism. Some beaches, however, also have backpackers and smaller bungalow accommodation.

In the early 1990s, after the most important beaches on Ko Samui had been transformed by mass tourism, the nearby island of Ko Phangan was discovered by backpackers, who still represent the large majority of the visitors there. In contrast to Samui and Phuket, small businesses often of simplest standards, dominate the hotel industry here. In contrast to larger hotels, this usually indicates the absence of adequate environmental behaviour, notably regarding refuse disposal. Since the public waste-disposal system is highly inadequate (in contrast to Phuket and Samui, no incineration plant), Ko Phangan is ecologically one of the most endangered mass-tourist destinations.

This is even more true of the island of Tao, which also became accessible to heavy tourism only in the early 1990s. Situated approximately 50 km from Ko Phangan and settled only about seventy years ago, it still belongs to the administrative region of Ko Phangan (Zimmermannn 1998). The island is only 21 km^2 in area and its rough mountain terrain allows for settlements only on level ground. There are currently about 700 registered and some 1,500 unregistered inhabitants, mostly immigrants. In 1983 there was only one bungalow accommodation with five guest rooms. In 1998, however, 32 establishments with 525 guest rooms existed. In 1995, 70,095 tourist arrivals were registered; at present 100,000 is closer to the reality. Given its area and its number of inhabitants, Ko Tao has a high visitor density. As on Ko Phi Phi, here too a part of the garbage (above all soft drink cans, glass and plastic bottles) is now being transported by ships to the mainland. But a much larger amount of waste is disposed of on a garbage dump in the interior of the island.

Hypotheses and Methodology

We begin with the hypothesis that the perceptions and assessments of direct and indirect environmental impacts caused by tourism, as well as the ecologically sensitive behaviour patterns of the local population, are influenced substantially either by the varying intensity of integration into the tourist sector or by the degree of direct economic dependency on this industry. From this statement we derive the central thesis that persons who are employed in the tourism sector indicate more sensitive environmental perceptions, more critical environmental assessments and more adequate environmental behaviour than others, because they discern the values of an ecologically 'intact' environment as the basis of tourism and therefore also of their own current subsistence. In this manner, persons employed in tourism can be regarded as 'agents' who set an example to the rest of the population, both in terms of positively changing environmental perceptions and assessments and of superior environmental behaviour.

In our survey different actors in the tourist industry, but also households who are not connected with tourism, were interviewed, mostly on the basis of standardised interviews. Almost 50 percent of the hotel owners and managers and in addition approximately thirty tourism and environment experts were interviewed on the basis of open conversations (see table 12.1).

Table 12.1. Types and numbers of those interviewed

Tourists	1,063
Households	879
Tourism Employees	1,013
Hotel Owners and Managers	100
Owners and Managers of other Touristic Enterprises	261
Tourism and Environment Experts	30

The empirical work was mainly conducted in cooperation with the Faculty of Hotel and Tourism Management of the Prince of Songkla University, Phuket. For the standardised interviews students from this University were engaged as interviewers. The tourist questionnaire was translated into five languages (German, English, Thai, Japanese and Italian); the household questionnaire and the questionnaire for the tourist enterprises were in Thai and the employees' questionnaire was in English and Thai. Through the cooperation with the Prince of Songkla University, Phuket, it proved possible to reduce constraints connected with cross-cultural and multilingual studies (Braukmeier 1992). This was necessary to ensure that terms and concepts of fundamental importance for our survey (e.g., environmental awareness) were translated or glossed, and explained correctly in order to maximise the validity of the data collected. The tourism employees were interviewed in the hotels, and all segments of hotel staff (gardener, chef, office staff, receptionist, etc.) were considered. The selective choice of the hotels was based on statistics regarding their size (number of rooms) and (semi-official) rating (e.g., from standard to five star). Thus small, medium-sized and large hotels of low to high standard were included. The household survey covered all types of households (of fishermen, farmers, service workers, industrial workers, etc.) scattered over the various islands (Phuket, Samui, Phi Phi, Tao and Phangan). These interviews were conducted in the homes of the interviewees using random sampling. The perceptions, assessments and behaviour patterns of the local population regarding environmental problems caused by tourism in general, and problems of solid and liquid waste in particular, were recorded using the surveys and then analysed in the framework of our hypotheses.

Three types of persons are differentiated according to the extent of their involvement in the tourism business:

Type I: Persons currently employed in tourism (data basis: 985 persons: 849 from the employees' survey; 136 from the household survey);

Type II: Persons formerly but not currently employed in tourism (data basis: 63 persons from the household questionnaire);

Type III: Persons neither formerly nor currently employed in tourism (data basis: 394 persons from the household questionnaire).

In order to obtain representative data, the number of interviewed tourists by nationality was fixed according to their respective share in all guest arrivals (official statistics) at the hotels one year before our survey. The percentage of tourists interviewed in any one tourist centre had to be equivalent to that centre's share of total hotel room capacity in the study area. At the tourist centres the tourists were interviewed on the streets and beaches, in restaurants, etc.

After the interviews we showed two photographs to each interviewee, requesting them to narrate what they perceived. We decided to show the photographs at the end of the interviews because we could then be relatively confident that they had become sensitive to environmental problems by then. Thus it was possible to minimise the number of answers irrelevant to our research questions.

Environmental Perceptions, Environmental Assessments and Environmental Behaviour

Perceptions of environmental problems presuppose a certain knowledge regarding threats to the natural basis of life. Assessments of the environment can follow the perceptions of the environment's endangered state. This assessment arises, for example, from the estimation of the extent to which an 'intact' environment is a prerequisite for the secure existence of both the individual and society. For our study it is particularly relevant that ecological stability in tourist regions be valued as the basis of attractiveness for tourism, and thus as a necessity for the tourist industry. The result of this perception and the accompanying assessment can be a behaviour pattern aimed at minimising ecological damage.

We assume that environmental awareness consists of the three following components: the ability to perceive environmental problems, assess them and derive an adequate behaviour.[2] In this paper we consider the following aspects and methods:

- analysis of photographs as an indicator of environmental perception;
- as indicators of environmental assessment standardised interviews were used to trace the general effects of tourism on the environment;
- standardised interviews were also used to trace individual waste disposal patterns as indicators of environmental behaviour.

Photo 12.1. Pattaya Beach

Photo 12.2. Waste in front of a tourist hut – Bophut Beach / Ko Samui

Environmental Perception Using Image Analysis[3] as Indicator

As already mentioned, two photographs were presented to the interviewees at the end of each interview, in order to record their patterns of environmental perception. In both pictures, environmental impacts of varying quality are depicted (photo 12.1 and photo 12.2). We selected the motifs with an 'Eurocentric eye', and in our view they clearly illustrate the problem of waste and other environmentally relevant phenomena connected with tourism. With the help of the medium of photography, the verbalisation of the observer gives us access to his or her perceptions. The interviewees were asked to describe the photos briefly and their comments were noted precisely. The locations of the pictures were not revealed to the interviewees; however, most of them obviously had an idea of where the photographs had been taken. The abundance of photographic information is mirrored in the variety of responses elicited. In order to take this variety into account, each individual response was coded into the three following groups:

1. grouping according to content, by considering only the objects actually named. This resulted in the assignment of the responses either to an 'overall view' or to one of the following seven elements 'buildings/ hotel', 'beach', 'jet ski/ motor sports', 'persons', 'garbage/ flotsam and jetsam', 'palms/ vegetation', 'tourism';
2. a further classification of the responses into (a) purely descriptive, (b) interpretative, or (c) emotional, indifferent;

3. categorised responses in group two were additionally classified as 'positive', 'negative' or 'neutral'.

Thus responses such as 'beautiful beach', 'overcrowded beach' or 'beach contamination caused by tourists' were subsumed under the element 'beach'. When pictorial elements were not explicitly pointed out, the remarks were classified as an 'overall view'.

The first general frequency analysis indicates two trends. First, the statements about both pictures indicate a clear weightage with regard to interpretative and emotional comments. We not only found an increase of responses which went beyond the spontaneously descriptive, but we also found descriptions in the sense of listing the pictorial elements. Second, interpretations of the interviewees concerning the 'overall view' or single pictorial elements had mainly negative connotations, such as 'profit-oriented service enclave' or 'destruction of the environment'. Purely emotional remarks like 'ugly' or 'infuriating' almost always referred to the 'overall view' or occasionally to the field of tourism.

Subsequently, the denotation of individual pictorial elements was examined according to the above mentioned trends (cf. fig.12.1 and photo 12.1; fig. 12.2 and photo 12.2). Here it can be seen that the distribution of the denotation of single elements is significantly different for the two pictures. While the description of photo12.2 includes the elements 'garbage' and 'tourism', photo 12.1 additionally elicited the frequent naming of the elements 'buildings/hotel', 'persons' and 'overall picture'.

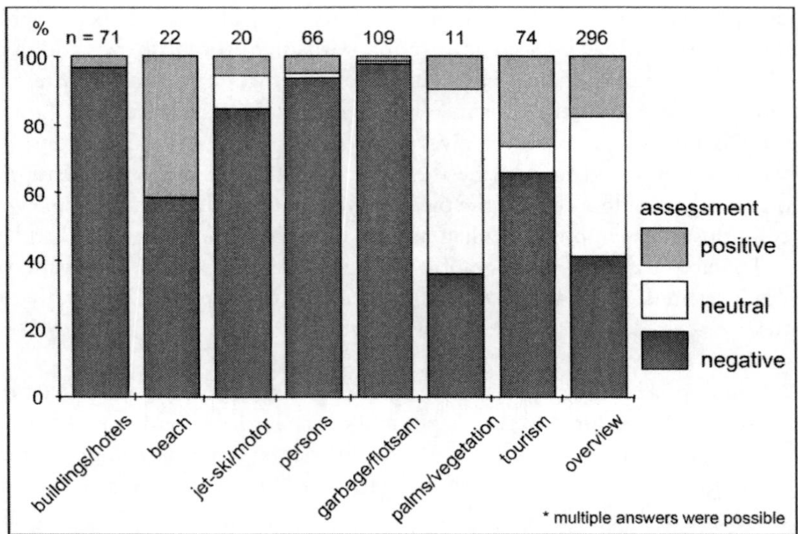

Figure 12.1. Number of denotations and assessments of pictorial elements in photo 12.1*

Source. Own survey, 2000

Photo 12.1 shows a more differentiated depiction of its pictorial elements than photo 12.2; accordingly, the responses are more diverse. A substantial distinction is, above all, the fact that persons can be seen in the first photo. As the information 'person' has generally high priority for the human observer, people are often noticed first and therefore mentioned first as well. Furthermore, it turns out that for photo 12.1 the major land development is noticed clearly as negative and is often associated with tourism. The number of negative comments on photo 12.1 can also be directly connected to the obviously widespread knowledge that this picture is of Pattaya, the largest seaside resort located in central Thailand. The negative reaction to the picture of this resort east of Bangkok is filled with images of mass tourism, and above all, sex tourism – images which have been widely communicated in Thailand and elicit corresponding negative associations.

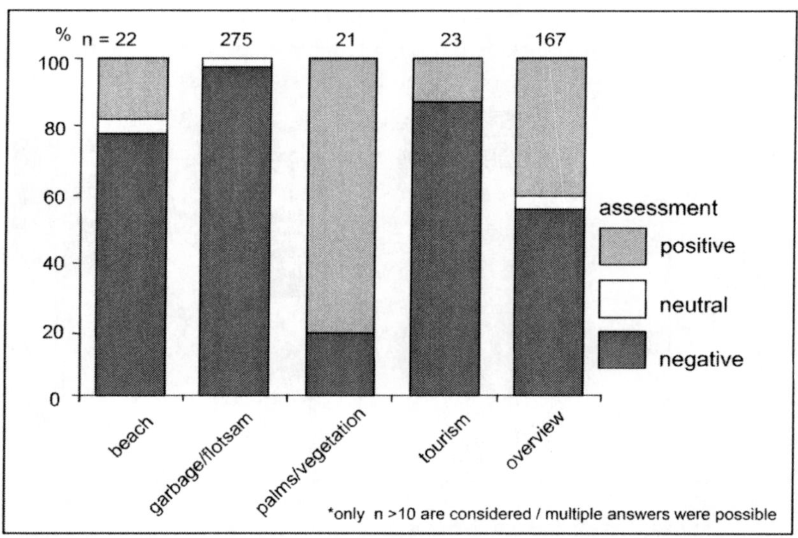

Figure 12.2. Number of denotations and assessments of pictorial elements in photo 12.2*

Source. Own survey, 2000

Photo 12.2 clearly focuses on the pictorial elements 'garbage/flotsam and jetsam' and 'tourism'. Remarkably, since neither people nor hotels are depicted in this photograph, tourism can only be recognised here by association. It must however be remembered that the pictures were shown to the interviewees after the standardised interviews. Contemplating them at a different time could have led to a considerable variation of associations.

Without exception, both pictorial elements elicited comments which quickly gave an explanation for a negative phenomenon, such as 'the garbage is caused by tourists'. The interpretations of the persons interviewed, which were categorised by the pictorial element 'tourism', generally related effects which can result from tourism. Thus, some people were occasionally held responsible, e.g., 'the tourists', or generalising comments were made, such as 'tourism destroys the environment'. A deserted beach was supposed to be 'natural' and therefore perceived positively, especially when in combination with lush palm vegetation. The simple, well-adapted built structures in photo 12.2 were positively perceived as well.

Figs 12.3 and 12.4 specify the denotations of selected elements in photos 12.1 and 12.2 respectively regarding how the personal involvement of the interviewees in the tourism industry (type I to type III) affects the perception of the pictorial elements, and especially their negative assessment. In each case the persons of type I (tourism employees) show a higher perception of negatively assessed elements than those of type III (persons who never worked in tourism) (fig.12.3).

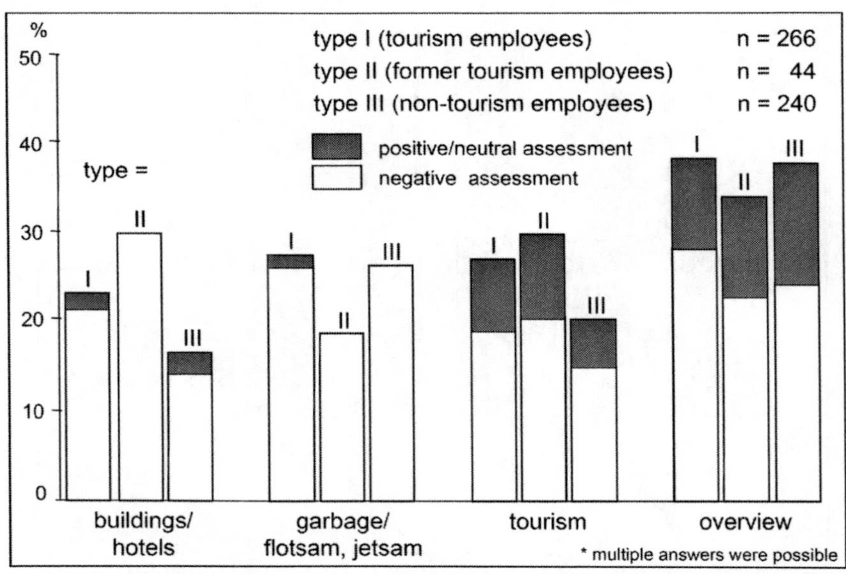

Figure 12.3. Assessment of selected pictorial elements in photo 12.1 by type of interviewee (accumulated in percent)*

Source. Own survey, 2000

Remarkably, the comments concerning the amount of waste were quite common, although no waste can be directly seen in photo 12.1.[4] Here, the knowledge of the effects of the scene depicted must clearly have influenced the statements, and accordingly, this had a greater effect in the group of tourism employees than in the group of type III interviewees. Likewise, the percentage of statements which referred to the tourist use of the depicted scenery was strongly pronounced. In this case as well, the remarks made by type I and II showed a more negatively associated perception. There were, however, also positive assessments of this element, but these were clearly made less often by type II interviewees. The multistorey building in this picture was also perceived negatively and presumably influenced the perception of the negatively connotated tourist use to a large degree.

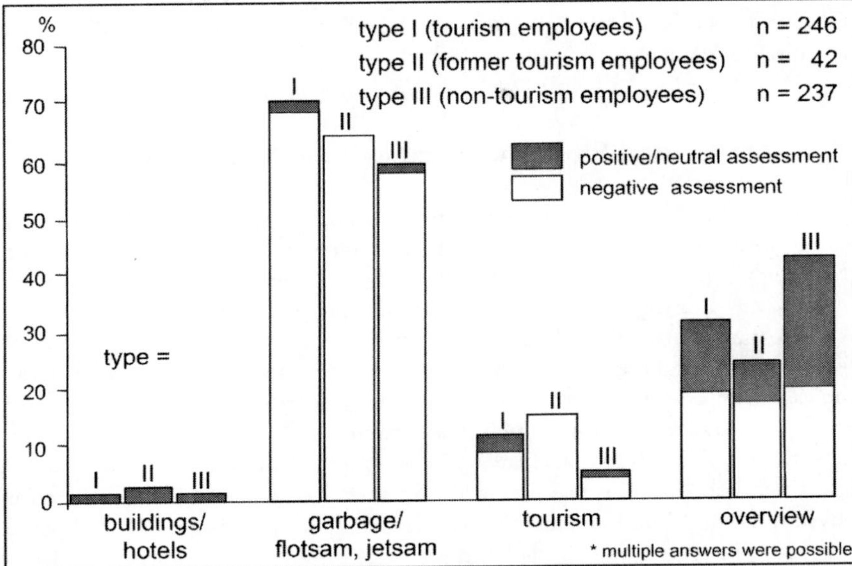

Figure 12.4. Assessment of selected pictorial elements in photo 12.2 by type of interviewee (accumulated in percent)*

Source. Own survey, 2000

The negative perceptions surrounding photo 12.2 referred predominantly to the garbage in the foreground of the picture (fig. 12.4). The 'overall view' was generally perceived rather positively by the interviewees, yet the assessments by the interviewees of type III were clearly more positive than those of the two other groups. However, the type I interviewees demonstrated a more sensitive perception of harmful environmental impacts here as well. 'Tourism' was more seldom and less negatively mentioned in this photo than in photo 12.1. Only the type I interviewees expressed themselves positively here.

The analysis of the responses of the interviewees demonstrates that tourism employees are more prone – compared to those who are not employed in the industry – to perceive both the advantages and disadvantages which result from tourist use. Their perceptions are influenced by their experience and knowledge of the interdependence between tourism and the environment. It is further interesting to note that they clearly differ depending on the context of the interview – at work or at home. In the group of type I interviewees, those who were questioned in the household survey were more critical in their perceptions.

This decisively indicates why the responses of type II interviewees (those formerly employed in the tourism industry) stand out from both the other groups in figs 12.3 and 12.4. It seems reasonable to assume that type II interviewees developed an awareness about the problem, but are no longer directly dependent on the industry and therefore have more room for interpretation and are thus able to perceive more critically and also to name the effects of tourism, especially in view of ecological damage.

The Central Problem: Poor Environmental Awareness

Our standardised interviews, but notably the in-depth interviews with local people who are engaged in environmental protection, show that a large share of the population has a poor awareness concerning environmental problems caused by tourism. During the last few years many people from outside the tourist centres, mainly from Bangkok, have been working towards improving this. A section of the local population which is profiting economically, particularly from the tourism boom, has little interest in supporting these efforts towards environmental protection which from their point of view are costly and superfluous. This influential local elite which profits from tourism is still publicly rejecting such 'interference' in local affairs and often prompting substantial physical threats. Simultaneously, however, a small but growing number of people who also profit from the tourism industry (e.g., hotels, restaurants, bars, discos, shops, etc.) are becoming more involved in environmental protection measures, because environmental problems have become so overwhelming and all encompassing. Tourists must not only smell the garbage, but also endure its sight. Additionally, some interviewees mentioned that particularly at the close of the main season and towards the end of the dry season, especially on the smaller islands of Tao and Phi Phi, portable water is often too rare, too salty or just plain smelly. Obviously, some of those involved in the tourism economy have begun to comprehend that as pollution continues to increase, the region's economic basis, an attractive recreational landscape, is at risk of being destroyed.

Our observations and in-depth interviews show that some of these people, often the European hotel managers, have an increased environmental awareness, not only because of their concern for the environment, but also because they hope for an improved image; especially since many tourist destinations in Thailand have begun to advertise their region under the label of 'eco-tourism'. Therefore, environment protection measures such as beach and road clean-ups are often supported by massive marketing campaigns. Meanwhile, apart from these cosmetic measures, the first initiatives have been formed to address the problems of pollution and to change awareness of the environment – for example, environmental education in schools. In Ko Samui, exemplary initial projects with the aim of environmental education and the creation of environmental awareness have been included in the Master Plan (2000). The finances made available for these projects – environmental education 110,000 Baht / 2,300 Euro, environmental protection measures 800,000 Baht / 20,000 Euro – are so modest, however, that no major effects can be expected (in comparison, 300 million Baht / 7.5 million Euro will be spent on road construction, TAT 1995). Nevertheless, environmental awareness has steadily increased during recent years, probably mainly because environmental problems can no longer be ignored.

To falsify one of our hypotheses in the interviews, Thais and tourists of different nationalities were asked to estimate one another's environmental awareness. The Thais were also asked to estimate the environmental awareness of the Thais in general.

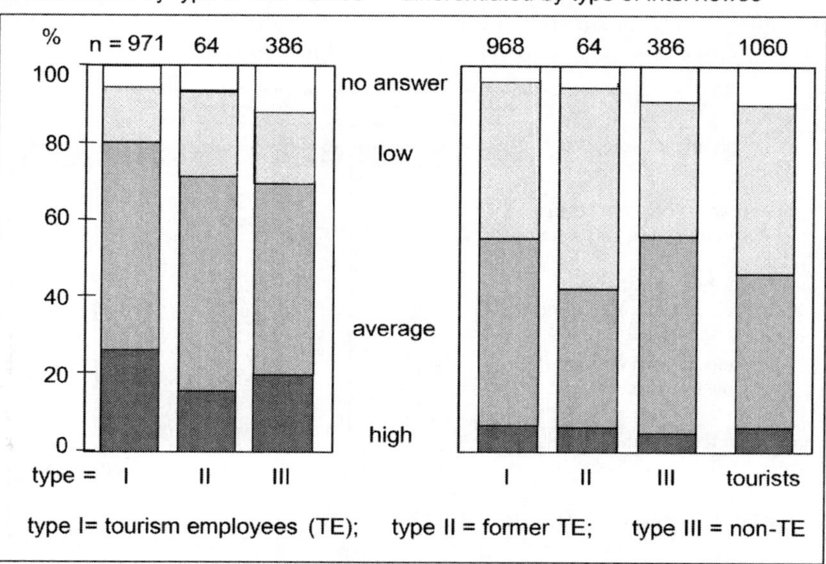

Figure 12.5. Estimation of environmental awareness of tourists and of Thais

Source. Own survey, 2000

The diagrams in fig. 12.5 show that a higher environmental awareness is attributed to the tourists than to the local population. The estimation of the tourists' environmental awareness was more positive in the answers of type I and type II than of type III interviewees. Tourism employees and former employees especially mentioned the tourists' concern about waste on the streets, and that tourists asked for special bins to sort their waste. The Thais questioned ranked the environmental awareness of Thais in general on a lower level, and the tourists also were more pessimistic in their evaluation of the awareness of the Thais. Here rubbish disposal is the main theme. The tourists in particular cannot accept that some Thais burn their plastic rubbish together with other rubbish in the streets or in their gardens. Many tourists, but also some locals, are critical of the fact that many Thais use about ten plastic bags per day just to transport their food back home from the night market.

Assessment of the Tourism Industry's Impacts on the Environment

Tourism employees largely depend on the tourism economy and are therefore interested in its growth. This emerges, for example, in the question about the positive effects of tourism. Of the employees (type I), 42 percent can confirm positive effects of tourism development, while only 28.2 percent of those who are not employed in tourism (type III) evaluate tourism development positively. Of the type II interviewees, 29.8 percent mentioned positive effects.

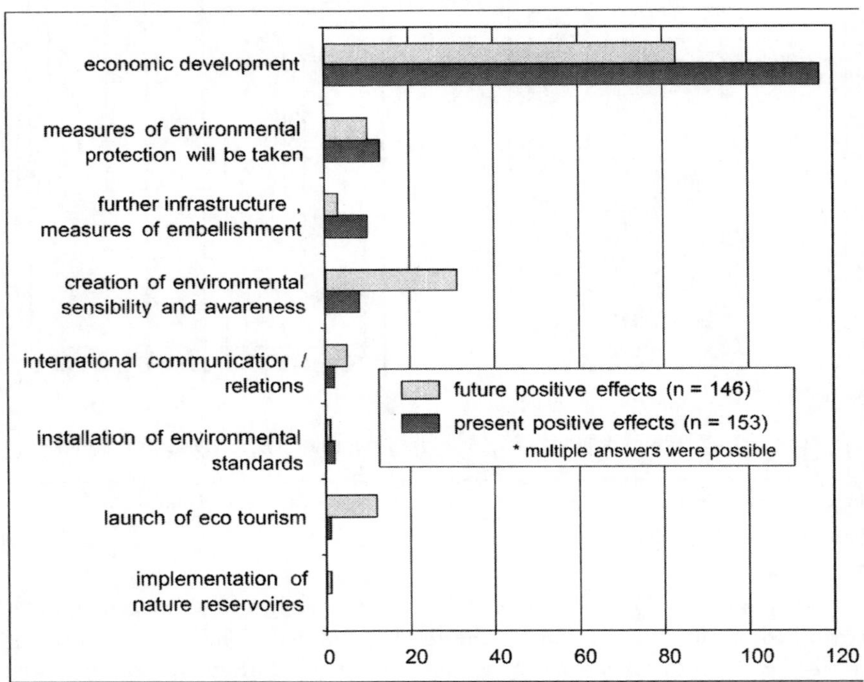

Figure 12.6. Number of denotations of present and future positive effects of tourism

Source. Own survey, 2000

A similar relation can be found in the question about the future positive effects of tourism: 47 percent of type I interviewees perceive opportunities, whereas only 35.4 percent of type III see opportunities through positive impulses of tourism – but even this represents an increase compared with the present situation. Economic development in general, an increase in employment opportunities, infrastructural development and better future prospects were mentioned by over 70 percent. A further 14.6 percent of the answers indicated that tourism is considered to contribute to the protection of the environment – among other reasons because of the implementation of protected areas/nature reserves, a more beautiful scenery, and environmental protection activities such as beach cleaning.

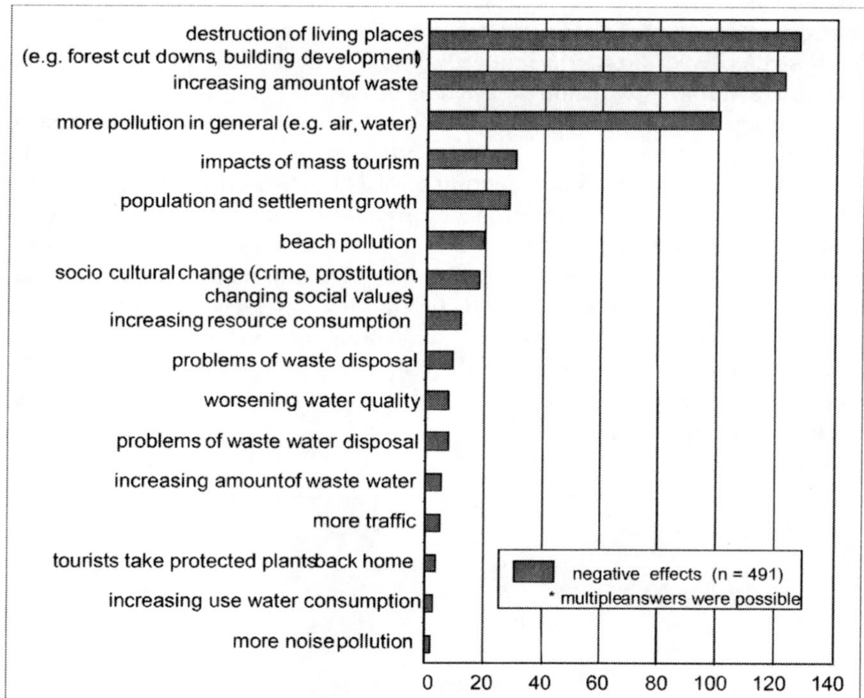

Figure 12.7. Number of denotations of negative effects of tourism*

Source. Own survey, 2000

Concerning the negative effects of tourism, the type I interviewees are again the more critical ones. On average, 59.4 percent of them think that tourism has negative consequences too, whereas only 48.9 percent of type III share their view. Generally the interviewees classify more negative effects than positive effects of tourism.

In addition to environmental pollution in general (19.22 percent) and the destruction of natural living spaces (22.05 percent), the problems of waste management (27.16 percent) were mentioned as having particularly negative effects. Use and waste-water problems were pointed out in fourteen cases. Noise pollution and traffic problems were specified three times only. Further negative effects were seen in the general impact of mass tourism, such as the too rapid and uncontrolled growth of population and of tourism facilities, etc., while the necessary infrastructural adjustments are missing (13.4 percent). 2.82 percent mentioned problems of social change such as the rise in crime, prostitution and changing social values.

An analysis of the negative effects mentioned shows clearly that the problems caused by tourism have been detected by the majority of the local population. Above all, it is the phenomenon of the Waste Dump Syndrome which is mentioned. More than 20 percent of the persons interviewed associate the continuous development of tourism centres and the extension of settlement areas by those employed directly or indirectly in the tourism industry (cf. Favela and Suburbia Syndrome) with the destruction of natural living spaces – forests cut down for land development, destruction of coral reefs, infrastructure development.

A few interviewees did not really respond to the question concerning the impact of tourism, and did not mention special positive or negative effects. They referred rather to the problems of incompetence of those persons or institutions in their opinion responsible. When they were asked about positive effects, 8.4 percent of the persons interviewed mentioned persons or institutions responsible, especially in the local population. In future these interviewees expect a lot of positive actions from the government. Concerning the negative effects, almost 12 percent attributed responsibility to the competent authorities and institutions. These effects were said to be caused mainly by tourists (30 denotations) but also by '(cash-)greedy' businessmen.

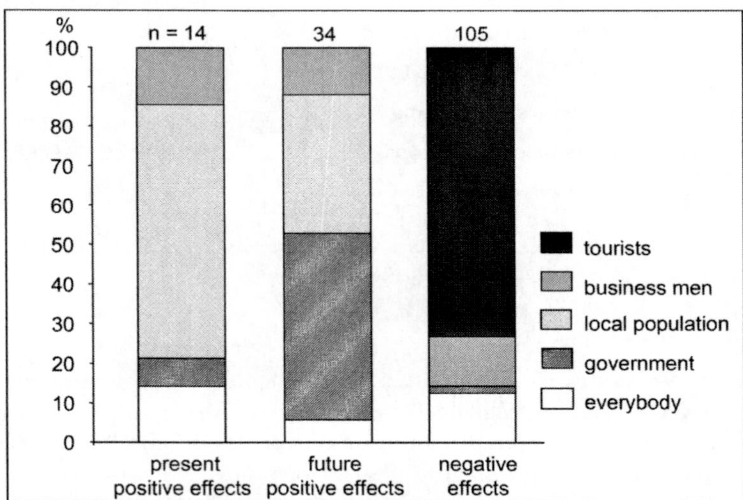

Figure 12.8. Responsibility allocations through the interviewees by type of interviewee as answer to the question of positive or negative effects of tourism on the environment

Source. Own survey, 2000

Environmental Behaviour: The Example of Waste Disposal

Communal Waste Disposal

Waste disposal as an indicator of environmental behaviour was examined by us more thoroughly.[5] As mentioned earlier, only Phuket and Ko Samui have incineration plants. Therefore, besides Bangkok, southern Thailand has two of the three incineration plants of the country. With the installation of these plants here, the increasing waste problem which accompanies the growth of tourism should be tackled. The exhaust fumes and the rest ash caused by these plants attain Asian standards, but do not meet the much more rigorous European standards.

Today Phuket's incineration plant has already reached its maximum daily capacity of 200 tonnes of waste; Samui's incineration plant is running at half its capacity with 70 tonnes of waste per day. Since 53.8 percent of the interviewees dispose of their waste inappropriately, we suggest that the plant in Samui would have reached its full capacity by now if the waste-removal services ran more regularly. Today the surplus heat at Samui is not used, although using it would not only improve the efficiency of the plant, but for bigger hotels this would be a more ecological way of obtaining hot water. Usually newer incineration plants also produce power, but this does not happen at Samui.

The communal waste economy differentiates between dry and wet garbage. Wet garbage is waste from the gardens and mostly that part of the kitchen waste which can not be used as pig-feed; everything else is dry garbage. The wet waste is generally put in garbage dumps and many big hotels have their own dumps. Both the controlled and the uncontrolled garbage dumps are defective (no foil sealing up the dump, etc.). In the long run this could lead to grave ecological problems such as pollution and contamination of the soil and of groundwater. The main part of the dry waste is sent to the incineration plants, and some is transported to controlled garbage dumps. In 1999 more than one third of the rubbish which was burned in Samui's incineration plant came from hotels (25 tonnes/day).

A variety of problems are involved in the organisation of waste removal services. Ko Samui has fourteen small vans at the moment, and a further ten will be bought in the next ten years; in Phuket twenty trucks are running at the moment. The lack of enough vehicles leads to remote locations being visited irregularly, if at all. Generally the rotation of waste removal takes too long. Usually the garbage vehicles drive along the main road once every day. On Samui the removal will take place twice a day now, but how this will be organised in terms of personnel is not clear. Employees of the waste-removal service have several possibilities of making some extra money. On the one hand it is very lucrative for them to sort out waste for recycling; on the other, some hotels pay them fairly high amounts of slush fundings (in addition to their communal waste collection fees) if they empty the hotel's waste containers more often.

Despite changing waste products (plastic, aluminium, etc.) caused by new local consumption patterns, waste-disposal methods are often traditional: burning and burying. This leads to great ecological burdens, since non-filtered dioxins are released when waste is burned and the groundwater can get contaminated if the waste is buried. Incinerating the waste seems then, to be more ecologically sound. A new alternative is recycling, and more than 50 percent of this is based on the waste from the big hotels. Almost 30 percent of it is collected by dealers in shops and a further 10 percent in restaurants and bars. Only a small number of private persons (*c.*10 percent) use this form of disposal at the moment, and only a few households sort out their waste.

Behaviour of Waste Disposal by Type of Interviewees

Only some of the local people are involved in waste separation and the willingness to do this job which brought in a monthly income of about 30 Baht (*c.* 0.75 Euro) per family was also limited. The analysis of the empirical data shows that there are distinctly more persons involved in waste separation among type I (approximately 10 percent) than among type III interviewees. The percentage of people engaged in waste separation also increased from type II to type I interviewees. Still, it is unlikely that the higher number of tourism employees who practise waste separation can be explained exclusively by their higher environmental sensitisation (see table 12.2). Many employees of larger international hotels which practise waste separation live in dormitories owned by these hotels and are provided with appropriate containers. Therefore, these individuals have better access to the necessary infrastructure. Furthermore, hotel employees are often educated by the management about environmental problems, and notably about waste disposal. For this sub-group of type I interviewees their waste-disposal behaviour was examined separately.

Table 12.2. Waste sorter among the interviewees (in percent)

	Dormitory*	**Type I**	**Type II**	**Type III**
YES	31.8	26.6	20.6	17.7
NO	67.4	71.8	79.4	82.3
no answer	0.8	1.6	–	–

* Hotel employees accommodated in the hotels' dormitories
Source: own survey, 2000

Since the interviewees of type II are more often involved in sorting waste than those of type III, the main hypothesis of the investigation is confirmed: persons who depend directly on tourism usually show a more positive environmental behaviour than the rest of the Thai population. We may assume this, in spite of the fact that the percentages between the persons of type II and type III differ only slightly.

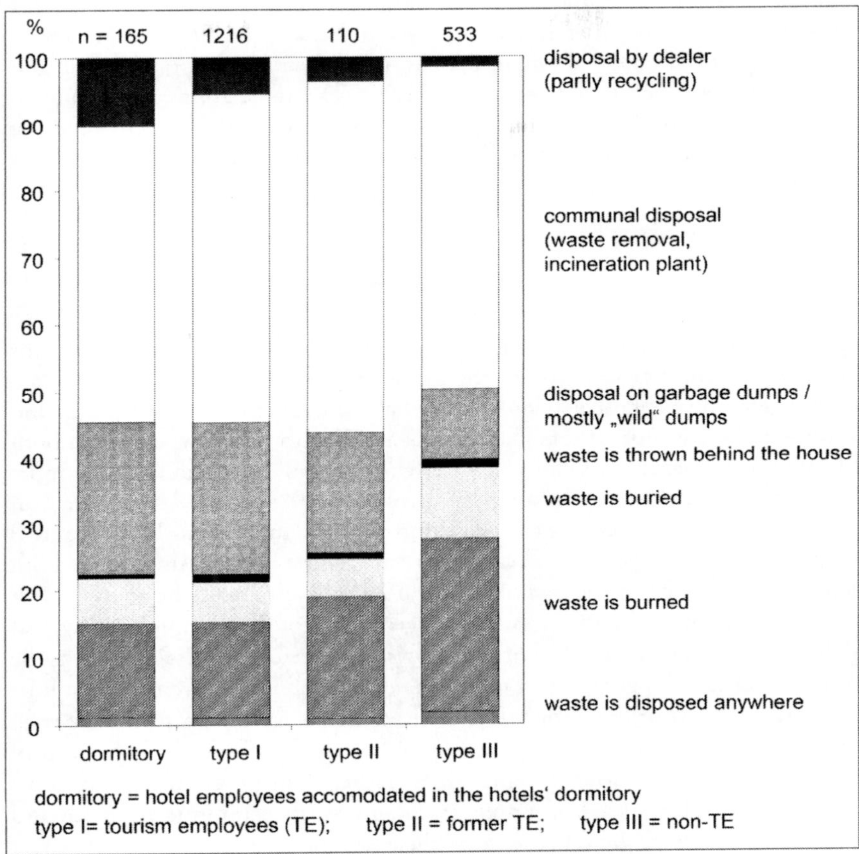

Figure 12.9. Ways of waste disposal by different types of interviewees

Source. Own survey, 2000

The analysis of the different ways of waste disposal shows that distinctly more members of households without former or present employment in tourism dispose off their waste in an inappropriate manner through burning, burying, throwing it behind the house or just anywhere (almost 15 percent more than type I). As already mentioned, these methods of disposal are especially inappropriate because of the resultant toxic emissions or the effects on the soil and groundwater. The disposal on dumps is not much better either, but it is less injurious. Firstly, especially on Phuket, some of the dumps belong to the communal disposal service and are therefore controlled officially with the rubbish being incinerated regularly.

The wild dumps which can be found all along the streets (and really big ones on Samui) are much more harmful, and especially so when used even by the communal staff. But as some of these are cleaned in connection with special events (e.g., Green Day), there is at least a possibility that this rubbish is later disposed off more appropriately. Second, close to some of the bigger 'wild' dumps small villages have emerged where people make their living from sorting out recyclable waste which they later sell to dealers. The most appropriate kinds of disposal are those by dealers (which is mostly connected with recycling) and the communal disposal system. The collection charge of 30 Baht/household service is affordable for most interviewees.[6]

Conclusion

The analysis of the empirical data confirmed our central hypothesis: that persons employed currently or formerly in the tourist economy have developed a more adequate environmental behaviour than inhabitants of the tourism centres who are not involved in this sector. The persons classified by us in type I and II both indicate greater sensitivity concerning environmental perceptions and a more critical assessment of environmental problems. We showed that tourism employees behave more ecologically appropriately not only when a better disposal infrastructure is in place, but also when such facilities are missing. Since both these persons as well as the rest of the local population credit the tourists with greater environmental awareness, we suggest that tourism employees try and model their behaviour on that of the tourists. Therefore tourists appear to be positive models and 'agents' of an increasing environmental awareness for at least a considerable part of the population. Positive effects for the protection or even rehabilitation of an 'intact' environment could thus flow from the behaviour of tourists. Furthermore, tourism employees, rather than other sub-populations, recognise the value of a healthy environment as an economic resource and therefore as a prerequisite for sustaining their own livelihoods.

The areas studied have been greatly impacted by tourism. Due to economic growth a large part of the local population has become relatively prosperous, and this has made Western consumer goods affordable. However, the adoption of Western consumption patterns is not promoted by tourism alone; widespread television and increasingly the internet are important media for creating new wants, which can be increasingly satisfied outside the tourism centres as well.

Undoubtedly tourism is partly responsible for environmental problems, and this was also articulated by the majority of Thais interviewed. Simultaneously, however, our results suggest that through the agency of tourism the increasing propagation of environmental awareness is facilitated.[7] Now as earlier, Thais employed in tourism can be considered as 'hinges' between tourists and the remaining population, so that environmental awareness generated through tourism can be adopted by those who do not directly depend on tourism and may even live outside the tourist centres. It is paradoxical that mass-tourism is both partly responsible for massive ecological damage but also serves as a substantial basis for preserving ecological stability and contributing to its restoration. One indicator for this is that in Thailand, besides Bangkok, only Phuket and Samui are provided with relatively efficient incineration plants and that here measures to deal with the waste problem were taken earlier than even in many large cities with a similarly dramatically rising amount of waste.

In order to protect the economic and financial significance of the tourist industry, the political authorities are increasingly obliged to replete the resource 'intact environment' in a sustainable way. However, in Thailand as in the West there is a discrepancy and contradiction between the detection of ecological damage and the modification of environmentally relevant individual behaviour. Tourism is widely judged to be the only cause of ecological damage, while inadequate individual environmental behaviour is either denied or ignored. The principle 'causers are always the others' obviously exists in Thai culture too and this is even more relevant when the measures required to protect the environment demand costs, burdens, a change in behaviour or even painful limitation of consumption by each household or enterprise. Furthermore, the tourist industry and 'actors' engaged in environmental policy at the local and national levels in Thailand have greatly contradictory economic interests and political aims. In particular, large, financially strong groups in the tourist economy, often closely connected with the national and local elites, aim to further develop tourism even if this involves excessive strain, if not the outright destruction of non-renewable resources. Only a minority, particularly the large hotels under international management, increasingly recognise that sustainable development through tourism can be realised only if the ecological and cultural dimensions of sustainability (cf. Vorlaufer 1999) are taken into account and that it is therefore imperative that individuals as well as different social groups pay more attention to ecological stability.

This imperative is more obvious still today, after the recent tsunami. Thanks to the partial destruction of the drainage and central sewage system in Patong, waste-water of some twelve thousand inhabitants is now flowing directly into the ocean. All open-water bodies and wells have been contaminated by the carcasses, corpses, debris and garbage which were swept inland up to 1 km by the flood waters, especially in Khao Lak. The clearance of debris was in many places highly problematic because of the lack of suitable waste deposit centres. In Phi Phi for example about 8,000 tons of debris had to be transported by ship, but several communities on the mainland and on the bigger islands such as Lanta refused to have the waste unloaded, for fear that the spirits of the dead would, together with the debris, bring them bad luck.

Increasingly now, unaffected resorts such as Samui will be exposed to greater mass tourism, and with this the pressure on the environment there will increase.

The concerned government institutions see an opportunity now to rebuild the so far unplanned and dense tourist resorts following ecological requirements. Mangroves, coral reefs and beach vegetation are to be better protected in order to regenerate. But it is to be feared that economic interests will once again triumph over environmental requirements in many places; it can only be hoped that the pressing problems of waste and garbage disposal will be considered in all earnestness.

Notes

1. We thank the German Research Foundation (Deutsche Forschungsgemeinschaft) for funding our project 'Consumption of resources, problems of waste disposal and endangerment of the environment through mass-tourism in coastal areas of Thailand' which was part of the SPP 'Mensch und globale Umweltveränderungen – sozial- und verhaltenswissenschaftliche Dimensionen'. For further information see http://www.psychologie/uni-freiburg.de/umwelt-spp.html.
2. Regarding the discussion about environmental awareness and research about it see Preisendörfer (1999).
3. For a controversial discussion of the meaningfulness of image analyses see Flick (1998), Flitner (1999) and Markwell (2000).
4. This might also be caused by the fact that the photographs were shown at the end of the interviews so that the interviewees could be influenced by the theme of the questionnaire.
5. A type-adequate analysis of the rubbish was conducted through observation in the households, hotels, etc. (and on the markets for consumption patterns).
6 Monthly household incomes of type I = 11,911 Baht; of type II = 17,101 Baht; of type III = 13,196 Baht.
7 This result corresponds with that of an earlier transnational study by Liu et al. (1987) in which they compared the environmental awareness of residents at tourist places in Hawaii, Wales and Turkey. The surveys revealed that residents living in areas with more mature tourist industry are more aware of both positive and negative environmental impacts.

References

Bangkok Post. www.bangkokpost.com

Becker-Baumann, H. and G. Schmitt 2006. 'Thailand auf dem Weg zu einem nachhaltigen Tourismus: Wunsch oder Wirklichkeit?' in *Nachhaltigkeit als regulative Idee in der geographischen Stadt- und Tourismusforschung,* ed. H. Schneider, 191–226. Hamburg: LIT-Verlag.

Braukmeier, E. 1992. 'Methodische Probleme empirischer Sozialforschung in der Dritten Welt', *Zeitschrift für Wirtschaftsgeographie* 38(1–2): 5–20.

Cohen, E. 1982. 'Marginal Paradises: Bungalow Tourism on the Islands of Southern Thailand', *Annals of Tourism Research* 9: 189–228.

——— 1996. 'Thai Tourism – Hill Tribes, Islands and Open-Ended Prostitution', *Contemporary Thailand* 4. Bangkok.

Flick, U. 1998. *Qualitative Forschung. Theorie, Methoden, Anwendung in Psychologie und Sozialwissenschaften.* Hamburg: Rowohlt.

Flitner, M. 1999. 'Im Bilderwald. Politische Ökologie und die Ordnungen des Blicks', *Zeitschrift für Wirtschaftsgeographie* 43(3–4): 169–83.

Krische, S. 2000. *Umweltprobleme im Urbanisierungsprozess der Entwicklungsländer. Ein geographischer Beitrag zur Alltagsökologie, Wahrnehmung von Umweltgefahren und den Handlungsmöglichkeiten von Migranten in den Sekundärstädten Baguio und Zamboanga City, Philippinen.* (Düsseldorfer Geographische Schriften 39). Düsseldorf: Geographisches Institut der Universität.

Kuckartz, U. 1998. *Umweltbewusstsein und Umweltverhalten.* (Konzept Nachhaltigkeit). Berlin. Springer.

Liu, J.C., P.J Sheldon and T. Var 1987. 'Resident Perception of the Environmental Impacts of Tourism', *Annals of Tourism Research* 14: 17–37.

Markwell, K.W. 2000. 'Photo-Documentation and Analyses as Research Strategies in Human Geography', *Australian Geographical Studies* 38(1): 91–98.

NSO (National Statistical Office). *Population and Housing Census.* 1960, 1970, 1980, 1990, 2000. Bangkok.

Preisendörfer, P. 1999. *Umwelteinstellungen und Umweltverhalten in Deutschland. Empirische Befunde und Analysen auf der Grundlage der Bevölkerungsumfragen 'Umweltbewußtsein in Deutschland 1991–1998'.* Opladen: Leske + Budrich.

Reusswig, F. 1999. 'Syndrome des Globalen Wandels als transdisziplinäres Konzept', *Zeitschrift für Wirtschaftsgeographie* 43: 184–201.

Sander, I. 2000. 'Umweltpolitik in Thailand. Chancen für eine ökologische Modernisierung', in *Thailand: Aktuelle Wandlungsprozesse in Politik, Wirtschaft, Umwelt und Gesellschaft*, eds. I. Sander and G. Reinecke. Hamburg: Institut für Asienkunde.

TAT (Tourism Authority of Thailand), ed. 1995. *The Revision of the Action Plan for Tourism Development of Ko Samui under its Carrying Capacity.* Bangkok.

———, ed. 2000. *Accomodation Lists for 1999 (Phuket, Suratthani).* Phuket, Suratthani.

———, ed. 2001. *Master Plan for National Tourism Industry* (2001–10). Bangkok.

Vorlaufer, K. 1995. 'Regionale Disparitäten, Tourismus und Regionalentwicklung in Thailand', *Petermanns Geographische Mitteilungen* 139: 353–81.

——— 1996. *Tourismus in Entwicklungsländern. Möglichkeiten und Grenzen einer nachhaltigen Entwicklung durch Fremdenverkehr.* Darmstadt: Wissenschaftliche Buchgesellschaft.

——— 1997. 'Tourism, Employment and Income in Secondary Cities and Tourist Centres in Kenya, Thailand and the Philippines', in *Employment and Housing. Central Aspects of Urbanization in Cross-Cultural Perspective*, eds. H. Schneider and K. Vorlaufer, 201–31. Aldershot: Avebury.

——— 1999. 'Bali – Massentourismus und nachhaltige Entwicklung: Die sozio-ökonomische Dimension', *Erkunde* 53: 273–301.

——— 2001. 'Tourismus – ein Instrument zum Abbau regionaler Disparitäten in Entwicklungsländern?', *Geographie und Schule* 133: 11–22.

——— 2002. 'Umweltgefährdungen durch Massentourismus in Küstenräumen Südthailands: Eine praxisorientierte Studie über Umweltwahrnehmung, -bewertung und -verhalten unterschiedlicher Akteure', *Umweltpsychologie* 6(1): 100–10.

——— 2005. 'Der Tsunami und seine Auswirkungen in Thailand, Teil 1 und 2', *Geographische Rundschau* 57(4): 14–17 and (6): 60–65.

——— and Becker-Baumann 2002. 'Umweltwahrnehmung und Bewertung von Umweltbelastungen durch Touristen in Fremdenverkehrszentren Südthailands unter besonderer Berücksichtigung der Abfallproblematik', *Umweltpsychologie* 6(2): 46–72.

——— and Becker-Baumann 2003. 'Massentourismus und Umweltbelastungen in Entwicklungsländern: Umweltbewertung und -verhalten der Thai-Bevölkerung in Tourismuszentren Südthailands; Bilanz und Ausblick', in *Geographie der Freizeit und des Tourismus,* eds. C. Becker, H. Hopfinger and A. Steinecke, 876–87. Munich: Oldenbourg.

WBGU (Wissenschaftlicher Beirat der Bundesregierung Globale Umweltveränderungen) 1998. *Welt im Wandel: Wege zu einem nachhaltigen Umgang mit Süßwasser. Jahresgutachten 1997.* Berlin, Heidelberg: Springer.

WTO (World Tourism Organization) 2000. *Yearbook of Tourism Statistics.* Madrid.

Zimmermann, A. 1998. 'Regionalentwicklung Ko Taos unter dem Einfluss des Tourismus'. Unpubl. Ph.D. thesis, University of Bern.

13

Local Experts – Expert Locals: A Comparative Perspective on Biodiversity and Environmental Knowledge Systems in Australia and Namibia

Thomas Widlok

Introduction: Why Compare?

Research conducted within the framework of multidisciplinary programmes such as the German Research Council (DFG) programme on the 'human dimensions of global environmental change'[1] is embedded in a tension between the aim to document the complexity of social and environmental processes that are instances of current global environmental problems and the aim to work out generalisable patterns which help understand present and future environmental issues in their diversity. These two conflicting aims sometimes appear to coincide with disciplinary boundaries such as that between model-building disciplines (above all cognitive psychology) and case-based disciplines (for instance ethnographic studies in anthropology). However, cooperation between projects has shown that this is not primarily a dualism of disciplines but a more general tension between research aims which can also produce new insights. In fact, it is not only projects in multidisciplinary programmes that have to deal with this tension; this is true for the social sciences more generally (Bowen and Petersen 1999: 1).

The project described in this chapter has tried to work productively with this tension in a format that is best described as an 'ethnographic comparison'.

Ethnographic comparisons are controlled 'small-n' comparisons based primarily on data collected through ethnographic field research using a variety of qualitative methods. The main problem, namely that of the incorporation of local expertise into systems of expert knowledge, is investigated in two settings which are socially and culturally distinct in very specific ways. While Australian Aboriginal society seems to have been highly differentiated with regard to access to, and the transmission of, knowledge, anthropologists working with Khoisan-speaking people in southern Africa have reported a high degree of flexibility and lack of concern with orthodoxy. A systematic comparison of these two cases, provided that the contrast holds, allows us to investigate whether knowledge transfers are easier from one structured system to another or from a rather unstructured arena into a structured system. Or, to put it differently, is it easier to share local knowledge that it is already fairly codified than local knowledge that is fairly uncodified? How does the way in which local knowledge is organised alter the expert systems that are created to incorporate it? The comparisons are therefore not regionally controlled but mark a wide spectrum as they bring together two distant regions – with very little direct mutual influence – and two largely distinct environmental issues, namely 'burning the bush' and 'controlling access to wild plants'. The assumption is that similar patterns can emerge in different regions of the world and with regard to different aspects of environmental use and change. The two cases of this 'critical comparison' may be usefully considered as instances of a more general process whereby an attempt is being made to incorporate 'ethnosystems' into something like an 'expert system' for environmental management. Rather than comparing static constellations, I attempt to compare trajectories, processes of interaction between 'local' and 'expert' agents (see Bowen and Petersen 1999: 4), who constitute one another as 'locals' and as 'experts' in the course of their interaction.

Case One: Accessing Wild Resources in the Namib Desert

Locals and Experts in the !Khuiseb Valley

The recent emphasis on the global dimension of environmental change suggests that only the joint effort of people in different geographical places and different social positions can prevent environmental damage. Shared knowledge may lead to the sufficiently concerted action that is required to manage environmental change and potentially destructive impact on the environment. However, this begs the question as to how people in different places and positions need to communicate and coordinate their action to achieve this aim. In my case study from Namibia I want to critically assess the interaction between 'experts' and 'locals'. This critique must begin with an assessment of who is 'an expert' and who is 'a local'. A superficial distinction can be made with regard to the management of the !Khuiseb flora by distinguishing on the one hand external experts, scientists trained in botany, paid by international bodies, publishing their results in international journals and on the other hand local people, mostly Khoisan-speaking Topnaar (also known by the autonym 'πAoni' and under the more general label 'Nama'), who know the environment they live in and live off through everyday activities and whose concerns are primarily their own prospects of living well in their environment. Upon closer inspection, the distinction is less sharp because some 'external experts' are temporary residents in the !Khuiseb valley which is home to the Desert Research Station at Gobabeb. Many 'local' residents, by contrast, spend most of their time in the coastal town of Walvis Bay where they earn money working in trade and industry and spend that money largely on imported industrial products. Many urban residents of the Topnaar ethnic group consider themselves 'locals' of the !Khuiseb valley, although they may not spend most of their time there. Apart from an emotional attachment to certain places in the region, being local to this area provides them with one of the few assets from which they hope to benefit. They hope to compensate a lack of money, property, status and influence (compared to other urban dwellers) by maintaining their status as 'locals'. The 'experts' at the Desert Research Station benefit from their presence in the !Khuiseb as it allows them to collect data and to build up expertise that is acknowledged outside the area. Despite the local attachment that some of the 'externals' have, they derive their livelihood and status from their expert status gained through university degrees and their work with non-local corporations. Recently the successful interaction between 'experts' and 'locals' has itself been the theme of development money spent on environmental education[2] in the area, which has confirmed the two role models of 'local' and 'expert', in this case filled by the Topnaar and by natural scientists respectively.

The situation in Namibia exemplifies some general trends in environmental management and development work. In the early stages of development work the roles of 'experts' and 'locals' were clearly distinguished in the dominant discourse which guided the development encounter. 'Experts' came from the so-called First World and assisted 'locals' who by definition were living in the so-called Third World. The mode of interaction was one of 'transfer', transferring goods such as machinery but also improved crops. More recently and more generally, the transfer was conceived of as being primarily a transfer of 'knowledge', above all the knowledge to produce and maintain some of the goods that were previously imported. This is not the place to review the growth of development ideas, but it should suffice to say that despite the changes in *what* is being transferred and despite the rhetoric of 'partnership', development discourse is still rightly characterised as a transfer from experts (those who initiate the transfer) towards locals (those who are at the receiving end of the transfer). The work of *translating* the imported knowledge into local concepts and practices is left to the 'locals', but is itself not part of the development encounter. It is useful to distinguish transfer, as from external experts to locals, from the translation of knowledge, as a process involving either experts or locals or both, in which the nature of the knowledge in question is necessarily altered (see Rottenburg 2000). In fact, development activities were rarely one-way transactions since the donors sought in return to receive construction or delivery contracts, cheap raw materials, political favours or simply a positive reputation from the 'locals' receiving the aid. More recently development agencies have emphasised that there is 'local' knowledge and expertise which needs to be recognised, maintained and if possible exported, as well. This is most markedly the case for local knowledge of the natural environment and local ways of protecting biodiversity.

The National Biodiversity Task Force

In Namibia, the National Biodiversity Task Force has been very important in defining what constitutes biodiversity knowledge. Under the auspices of the Ministry of Environment and Tourism, which also runs the Namib-Naukluft Park covering much of the !Khuiseb valley, numerous internal documents and publications (see references in Griffin and Barnard 1996) have been prepared, culminating in a voluminous biodiversity country report (Barnard 1998). Since the guiding principle of the UN declaration on biodiversity is that each nation of the world has sovereign rights to exploit its resources and the duty to care for its own biodiversity (see Glowka et al. 1994: 29), the state in Namibia – as elsewhere – makes use of this sovereign right by defining biodiversity as a national resource. The co-ordinator of the Namibian national biodiversity programme and the curator of the State Museum in Namibia emphasise the national interest in biodiversity research but not without underlining the role of biological specialists in this task:

> The more evolutionary options (genetic variation) at your disposal, the more likely your chances of surviving major events [Griffin and Barnard 1996: 122]. Namibia is fortunate in having a fair share of ... taxonomists and biogeographers, as all strategies and management plans are ultimately based on the specific knowledge provided by these specialist scientists. (op. cit. p. 123)

Here, biodiversity, at the level of the nation state, is effectively transformed into the national task of inventorying. The conversion of biodiversity into national tasks is facilitated by the fact that no matter how biodiversity is defined in the narrow scientific sense, whether primarily in terms of genetic variability within species or of functional relations between species, knowledge about biodiversity includes estimates of largely unknown resources and potentials in the context of national politics. Superficially, it may seem that variation among living organisms is easily recognised and defined – but in practice knowledge about biodiversity is an extrapolation of the number of species yet to be discovered, paired with assumptions about the potential enshrined in the expected number of species. In

Namibia knowledge of biodiversity consists largely of information extrapolated from national inventories. Scientific knowledge about the diversity of frogs in Namibia, for instance, has increased from two known species a hundred years ago to forty-five known species today with an estimated 'final diversity' of sixty species (Griffin and Barnard 1996: 123).[3] The overall discrepancy between known species and estimated biodiversity is probably much higher because frogs and other animals larger than insects and invertebrates make up less than nine percent of Namibia's biodiversity (see table 13.1).

Table 13.1. Namibia's Biodiversity as estimated by the National Biodiversity Task Force (see Griffin and Barnard 1996: 123)

Namibia's Biodiversity	
Category	**Percentage**
Insects	85.5
Arachnids (spiders)	5.6
Other vertebrates	5.5
Plants	1.8
Birds	0.34
Lower animals	0.5
Fish	0.3
Lower plants	0.3
Reptiles	0.13
Mammals	0.13
Frogs	0.03

State-employed scientists face contestants to the key positions for managing biodiversity at the national level. While state institutions sometimes claim the status of being local and that of being expert at the same time, this position is now contested by non-governmental organisations that have mushroomed since Namibian independence, particularly in the field of conservation and land management. The Desert Research Station in the !Khuiseb is now, after a long period of internal negotiation, no longer run by members of the Ministry of Environment and Tourism but by two NGOs, one dealing with the administration of the station itself and the other dealing with research projects at Gobabeb and elsewhere in the country. Further non-governmental players have emerged from what originally was a group of state employed researchers. In their function as environmental educators they have begun to occupy positions in the arena of national politics.[4] International corporations, by contrast, seem to be less involved than one might expect in a country like Namibia, which generally welcomes foreign investment. The national biodiversity report states that 'extensive collecting for the pharmaceutical industry, or bioprospecting, has not taken place legally in Namibia', but that there are '*local* suspicions that material collected for academic research or without permit has served other purposes' (Barnard 1998: 98, emphasis added). By elaborating on the issue here I do not wish to fuel such suspicions or to suggest that any of the particular researchers I mention was involved in illegal bioprospecting. Rather, I want to point at the more general dynamics involved in documenting and spreading 'local knowledge'.

Towards the Appropriation of Local Expertise on Biodiversity

After a long period of antagonism between conservationists and indigenous peoples' organisations concerning issues related to the conflict between 'parks and peoples', non-governmental conservation organisations have recently made efforts to embrace what they have operationalised as 'cultural diversity' (Maffi et al. 2000). They have called for the contribution of 'indigenous and traditional peoples' to the conservation of fragile ecosystems or of biological diversity more generally.[5] However, it would be misleading to conceive of this export of 'local expertise' as equivalent to the earlier transfer of 'expert development knowledge' to the local level. To begin with, the export is rarely initiated by the locals. Biodiversity, for instance, is a value that is defined at a level beyond the local setting. Local people, in particular indigenous hunting and gathering people – who are sometimes particularly hailed for their protection of local habitats (see Kemf 1993)[6] – are usually concerned about a few key resources and not about the highest possible diversity, say of useful plant species (see Widlok 1999: 87). In the case under consideration here, the local Topnaar have been at times regarded as 'a harvesting people' because their concern is with a single endemic plant, the *!nara* (*Acanthosicos horridus*, a cucurbit) and its products which they use for a livelihood (see Budack 1983). The biodiversity value of a species is established in reference to that of other species elsewhere and is therefore, by definition, not part of local knowledge but of the knowledge of those experts who try to initiate the *in situ* protection or expert prospecting of the potential that is seen in a given species or community of species. This is not only a result of biodiversity being a concept of the natural sciences which are dominated by 'external' experts. Although endemism is an important factor for establishing the biodiversity value of a species, more recent definitions of biodiversity emphasise that diachronically the potential for creating biodiversity is not enshrined within particular key species but is generated in the interaction between individual specimen that develop into different species in the course of interaction with other beings inhabiting their habitat.[7]

Ethnobotany and Property Rights

A few years before my fieldwork on land management in the !Khuiseb began, the Topnaar who are now considered the indigenous population of that area, were approached by a team of Belgian botanists who were funded by the European Commission. The Commission is also named as the copyright holder of the main publication resulting from this research – 'The Ethnobotany of the Topnaar' (Van den Eynden et al. 1992). The aim of this study was 'to find out how people have traditionally used plants … and to preserve valuable, traditional knowledge for both future generations and other communities' (Van Damme 1992: i). For that purpose the authors present a description of eighty-one plants which were or are still used for medicinal and other purposes by the Topnaar. While the main body of text consists of the botanical classification and description of these plants, local uses were recorded for each plant and (in annexes) translations in Afrikaans and Nama were provided. Ethnobotanical research of this kind has been carried out before for other ethnic groups in Namibia and it has been published in a similar format (see Rodin 1985 for a Kwanyama ethnobotany, Story 1958 for a !Kung ethnobotany). These ethnobotanical enterprises share the notion that a record of the 'intimate knowledge of the natural resources' had to be rescued before the local population suffers its 'inevitable' loss of 'intimate contact with nature and in the end its very identity' (Dyer 1958: 4). What is remarkable about the Topnaar ethnobotany is that, given its recent date, the researchers are aware that their work 'opens the debate about who actually owns this knowledge and who should use it' (Van Damme 1992: i). The botanists do not, however, enter this debate but rather bluntly state that 'it seems obvious and logical that all men should share and benefit from these plants' properties' (Van Damme 1992: i).[8] Under the threat of ecological and cultural changes, they expect an 'inevitable' loss of Topnaar ethnobotanical knowledge and consequently the loss of these plants 'from [*sic*] humanity forever' (Van Damme 1992: ii). The loss is feared particularly for locally restricted (endemic) plants and for locally restricted knowledge. Given that these plants 'have never before been recorded as being used by the Topnaar people' (Van Damme 1992: ii), compiling an ethnobotany of the Topnaar at this point in time seems to be able to claim to present *the* definitive ethnobotany of the Topnaar. This can be seen to run parallel to claims of some ethnographers to have authoritatively captured a 'disappearing culture'. There is no reason to doubt that the preservation of local knowledge also for the benefit of locals was part of the researchers' motivation (Van Damme 1992: ii), and the Topnaar who I had contact with appreciated the work done by the botanists and did not air any suspicion towards this research but doubt about its usefulness. In the words of the Topnaar chief: 'There are all these people, also from Gobabeb, who come and learn about the *!nara* ... They do it for their own future but what do we gain from this?'.[9] However, own their appreciation seems to have been generated by quite different interests than those maintained by the experts.

The external researchers in a sense successfully appropriated what was previously locally restricted knowledge about potential uses of biodiversity, and since this was in line with the national efforts towards an inventory, they had the support of the national authorities. But the Topnaar themselves also cooperated in this task. In the course of my field research I investigated why the Topnaar should so easily accept the opening of access to their traditional knowledge. The main benefit that Topnaar saw in the ethnobotanical work was that it provided them with documentation that underlines the connection between the Topnaar and their land. It could therefore be used to support pending land claims against the administration of the Namib-Naukluft Park of which the !Khuiseb forms a part. Being in the process of consolidating their ethnic identity and cultural heritage (see Widlok 1998a, 1998b), the Topnaar had an interest in a publication that would bring together the ethnobotanical knowledge that was dispersed among knowledgeable individuals and which could also be made available to members of the group who no longer live directly off the land (e.g., the urban professionals) but who could maintain their status as descendants of indigenous land-users (see Ingold 2000: 132 for a more general discussion of these issues). More importantly, valuable ethnobotanical knowledge is converted into valuable symbolic capital.

The knowledge which was previously needed to make use of plants could now be used to make claims for land rights and claims for ethnic identity, and by implication for being represented as an ethnically and territorially based group. This conversion of knowledge was not envisaged by the botanists when they elicited local knowledge about plants. It explains why the project may be considered to be successful by both the experts and the locals without necessarily achieving its aims in the more narrow sense, namely, to 'preserve valuable, traditional knowledge for both future generations and other communities' (Van Damme 1992: i). In this case it was the political side-benefit of receiving a book that demonstrates local attachment to the land that seems to be of greater importance than the actual ethnobotanical details contained in the book. As I have been told repeatedly by Topnaar, 'If you have been there [in the *!nara* fields] you have truly been to Topnaar country'. Similarly, the property regime that restricts access to the wild fruit plants of the !Khuiseb, in particular to the *!nara*, is transformed from a system that guarantees a livelihood to harvesters living in a harsh ecological environment to a primarily symbolic system generating exclusive rights to members of the Topnaar ethnic group in a harsh political environment. The *!nara* fields of the !Khuiseb now have a variety of use potentials ranging from tourism to the affirmation of the Topnaar as a traditional land owning group in Namibia.

The argument can be made (see Widlok 2001) that the greatest potential of biodiversity-related research is not at the level of ecosystems or species at but at the level of genetic diversity, that is removed from the level of information gathering about local botanical taxonomies or the local uses of natural products.

The example of Topnaar ethnobotany exemplifies the multifaceted relations between locals and experts in this situation. But there are other fields of expert interest in biodiversity which illustrate the problems of converting knowledge to which I will turn in the following section. I will sketch the statistical analysis of the distribution of invertebrates and the biochemical analysis of scorpion neurotoxins which also form part of the work carried out by external experts in the !Khuiseb and which arguably are of greater potential and importance to locals and experts alike.

Problems of Converting Local Knowledge into Ethnosystems

While the ethnobotanical research involves plants that are of practical value to the Topnaar, in particular the *!nara* melon which is of high nutritional, economic and cultural value for them, other biological research projects carried out in the region deal with insects and other invertebrates which are only of marginal interest to the Topnaar. However, the discrepancy between species that are of interest to specialist experts and those of interest to local people is not coincidental. More than 90 percent of Namibia's biodiversity is to be found among insects and spiders (Griffin and Barnard 1996: 123). Consequently, the country's most important ecological research centre is not in the Etosha National Park where elephants, lions and other African mammals live, but in the middle of the Namib desert, in the !Khuiseb valley, which is a good spot for studying insects.

On an international level it is the diversity of insects and invertebrates that gives Namibia as a nation its particular potential. On a global scale, the major portion of global genetic diversity is to be found at the level of micro-organisms including viruses and toxins which may not be considered to be independent organisms at all. Both insects and micro-organisms are creatures which 'simply lack phenomenal resolution for humans' and are therefore not easily distinguished as species from the perspective of locals (Atran 1990: 33). From an expert perspective, by contrast, these species are the critical potential and it is the function of biodiversity-related research at Gobabeb, the Desert Research Station in the Namib, to chart this potential.

Research Within and Outside the Namib-Naukluft Park

The most laborious long-term research project of the Desert Research Unit at Gobabeb is the regular stock-keeping of invertebrates and other small desert animals by recording the frequency of small insects, spiders, etc., in the three local desert habitats (dunes, gravel plains, riverbed). Almost daily one of the research assistants drives out into the desert where fields of dozens of numbered 'pit-traps' have been put up. These pit-traps are usually empty tins that have been put into the ground so that crawling insects can easily fall in as they move around but cannot get out again before they are released by a member of the station staff on his or her daily round. The research assistant takes a detailed record of the number of individual specimen found in the various traps at various points in time. If in doubt, the animals are taken to the research station where they can be identified on the basis of a large specimen collection. One of the objectives of this project is to establish the correlation between long-term climatic cycles and the occurrence and number of insects found in the various habitats.[10]

For a long time the entomologists of Gobabeb and local Topnaar herders lived side by side without worrying (about) each other. With Namibian independence and a growing discourse of local people's empowerment, however, the Topnaar claim a share in the amount of external funds available for living and working in the !Khuiseb. The disproportionate interest of white researchers in small animals still largely amuses many of the local Topnaar ('We were catching *xoxan* [creepy animals] for the researchers without knowing what they were good for'). This may change when local people start demanding that research funds go into the study of species that are economically relevant to them. For the time being, the local people do not mind this information being taken. They emphasise that it is not the establishment of a research station but that of a national park which they object to, because the latter interferes with their use of the environment as it restricts their movement, their livestock keeping, and their use of wild plants and animals. This was made clear by the Topnaar chief in a public speech in which he pointed out:

> The nature people [conservationists] came and burnt the [Topnaar] huts and then they came to say that they will tear down the school and build a new school in Gibeon [a resettlement site in southern Namibia] in order to force the πAoni to move. Then the Ministry [of Environment and Tourism] introduced wild animals, rhinos, so that they could chase off the πAoni. People came from the office of the administrator general [during South African administration before independence] with eight Land Rovers. They did not stop at Iduseb [where the πAoni chief stayed] but went to Gobabeb where they were shown a film about the nature of the Namib, the animals and the dunes. The people, the donkeys, the goats, they were not shown.

It is important to note that the Namib Naukluft Park which covers the !Khuiseb valley was established at the beginning of the century and expanded in following decades with criteria in mind which were quite different to the protection of genetic diversity. This is, of course, true for nature reserves in Namibia more generally (see Barnard 1998: 98). Current nature park regulations do not match the requirements for dealing with questions of biodiversity protection. During my field research a physicist from Europe with an interest in neurotoxins worked in and around Gobabeb where he planned to collect a few specimen of poisonous scorpions, 'milk' them in a South African or European laboratory and analyse the chemical structure of the toxin. Initially, the Namibian nature conservation authorities did not allow this. They insisted that animals should not be taken out of the Namib-Naukluft Park, which includes much of the !Khuiseb valley, especially as it was not guaranteed that they would return unharmed. As a consequence the researcher negotiated with local farmers living just outside the national park that he would buy some scorpions from them. This caused no problem since the farmers were more than happy to get rid of these highly poisonous animals.

Sovereign Rights and Land

The nature conservation prohibitions enforced in this case are a good example of state authorities trying to ensure their sovereign rights over natural resources. But they were in a sense anachronistic in that they failed to respond adequately to genetic biodiversity prospecting which was aimed at the toxin. The toxin which could be isolated from the scorpion contained the genetic resources that are of prime value for this kind of prospecting.[11]

The powerful toxin, not the scorpion as part of a protected environment, has considerable medicinal and pharmaceutical potential. To a physicist, 400 million years of successful survival of scorpions is an indicator of a high mutation rate in the gene coding for neurotoxins and this was the targeted information. Information about the chemical structure of scorpion toxins at this stage is of no value to the local people, and it could be argued that the information is not simply contained in the scorpion toxin anyway, but is produced externally. In fact the question of sharing the potential value related to biodiversity in general or in the substance of scorpion toxin in particular is a non-topic for the Topnaar, who have habitual residence rights in the !Khuiseb but who cannot claim ownership of the organisms with whom they share their land.

The situation is quite different with regard to the nation state which considers itself not only to be the owner of the land, including flora and fauna, covered by nature reserves, but that extends its claim of sovereignty to the biodiversity found on its territory more generally. Not surprisingly, therefore, state institutions take a particular interest in biodiversity issues. In the context of the issues discussed here it is striking that the state also redefines the positions of expert and local and in a sense occupies both spaces. With regard to the international biodiversity discourse, nation states guarding *in situ* protection take the position of locals, claiming a share of the benefits emerging from the *ex situ* manipulation of the raw materials of biodiversity that originate from their countries. Vis-à-vis individual and corporate actors within the country (including individual subsistence farmers or foragers as well as commercial companies and ethnic or regional communities), the state takes the position of the expert who establishes and guards the social benefits, who provides incentives and intervenes if deemed necessary. In calculating the costs and benefits of natural protection non-state actors are deemed 'private interests', while state benefits are 'social benefits' (Richardson 1998: 266). It is therefore central that both scientific experts as well as indigenous locals come to grips with the pivotal role of the state in matters concerning the sharing of knowledge in the field of biodiversity and elsewhere.

Returning to the ethnobotanical research among the Topnaar described above, it is noteworthy that the claim that Topnaar ethnobotanical knowledge would be 'valuable information for other communities living in an analogous ecological context' (Van den Eynden et al. 1992: 89) has not yet been substantiated. Instead, NGOs operating in the !Khuiseb and in the Richtersveld of South Africa were instrumental in bringing together representatives of two communities living not only in analogous ecological but also in analogous political contexts in Namibia and South Africa. The exchange that took place was primarily directed at issues concerning the co-management of national parks. That is to say the kind of information that is now primarily sought for and shared by these local communities relates not to details of ethnobotany, but rather to the negotiation of prevalent property relations.

The !nara Property Regime

In the Topnaar case the property regime that regulates access to the endemic *!nara* plant and its valuable fruit has undergone considerable change in recent decades (see Widlok 2001). Although this system of property relations differs from the better known traditional systems of communal pastoral land tenure in the area, it has suffered a similar decline, increasing the threat of overexploitation leading to decreasing biodiversity (see Barnard 1998: 271). The cultural diversity at stake here is therefore not one relating to details of cultural knowledge about plants, but rather one concerning the various layers of property regimes. Since the Namibian state, as modern states usually do, ultimately defines itself as a unit which has ownership and control over a certain territory, it cannot easily give up the state monopoly on defining the property regime(s) of the country. In the case of Namibia, land and its resources are either privately (individually, corporately) owned or they are state-owned with either state ministries (e.g., Environment and Tourism, Lands and Resettlement, Mining) or traditional authorities (e.g., the Ndonga king or Mbukushu chiefs) administrating access to the land. Residents in national parks (such as the Topnaar of the !Khuiseb) as well as hunter-gatherer groups with leaders who are not recognised as traditional authorities (such as the Hai//om of Mangetti; see Widlok 1999) are only tolerated as squatters on land that they do not have control over and may be subject to resettlement.

Ethnosystems and Expert Systems

There is, therefore, a striking discrepancy between the growing recognition of local people as 'experts' in their own right and the apparent failure to arrive at a successful reproduction, let alone a successful transfer/conversion, of local land-use practices under the changed conditions dictated by the nation state. The puzzle is resolved when looking more closely at the way in which 'experts' are prepared to consider the 'expertise' of locals, namely under the condition that local knowledge can be codified along the lines of an 'expert system'. Projects such as the ethnobotany of the Topnaar are expert systems in the broad sense since they aim to add cumulatively to solving the problem of how to survive under certain ecological conditions. Expert systems in the narrower sense are computer programmes for which formal rules are defined that are operative in a clearly demarcated domain. The two conditions of domain-specificity and rule formulation can be recognised in the ethnobotany approach. The domain 'use of flora in a distinct region' is clearly defined and the rules captured are those of naming and classifying plants as well as the procedures for preparing and applying products from these plants for specific dietary or medicinal purposes. Although it may be a matter of debate as to what the 'analogous contexts' are for which this particular expert system is supposed to work, the experts see sufficient similarities between more universally applicable expert systems and the somewhat more restricted local expert systems.

It has been suggested that local systems of expertise be called 'ethnosystems' (Slikkerveer and Dechering 1995). The term 'ethnosystems' conceptualises the specificity of these local systems through the image of a locally based ethnic group and therefore faces the same criticism as the underlying image of ethnic groups as homogenous, stable, and clearly bounded units. Furthermore, the assumption that there are critical similarities between expert systems and ethnosystems insofar as both are delimited by a domain and have formal rules, does not hold. As I have shown elsewhere (Widlok 2001), the relations regulating access to the fruits and plants of the *!nara* in fact eclipses many other social relations, including those of trading and harvesting arrangements, but also the involvement in other economic activities (for subsistence as well as wage labour), in relations with kin and non-kin, Topnaar and non-Topnaar. Upon close inspection, the rules governing the *!nara* property regime, that is, the institutional make-up of the regime, need to be considered in terms of different layers, i.e., norms, regulations, objectifications, relations and actors. Changes have affected these layers in different ways, causing contradictions within the system of ownership rules itself. For instance: a continuing high value placed on the *!nara* as the paradigmatic foodstuff of the Topnaar, invigorated by rediscovered *!nara* songs, goes hand in hand with the declining importance of the *!nara* as an economic source of income. The institutions that regulate access to useful plants, at least to the *!nara* as the pivotal plant of the Topnaar, form a complex property regime and not merely a domain of knowledge. One aspect of this property regime is that it has been an arena for conflicting conversions from 'local' into 'expert' and vice versa. In the remainder of this chapter I want to show that a similar argument can be made with regard to fire regimes in Australia, my second case study.

Case Two: Burning the Australian Bush

Locals and Experts in the Kimberley Region

My argument up to this point could be criticised for relying exclusively on evidence from a single society. Khoisan groups, including 'Bushmen' but also the Topnaar of Namibia, have been portrayed as being particularly tolerant towards heterodoxy (Barnard 1992),[12] they are renowned for their flexibility, adaptability and fluidity governing the organisation of knowledge as well as other aspects of life. The remainder of this paper deals with an ethnographic case study with regard to which the opposite has been claimed, that is, a strong emphasis on form and structure in the way in which knowledge and society are organised, namely the Australian Aborigines.

Australia and Namibia, as nation states, are different in many respects but I want to argue that in both instances state agencies take on similar functions as mediators between local and expert knowledge and that the differences in the formal structure of these states are negligible in this context. In Australia considerable ethnobotanical research has been carried out which is comparable to the work I have discussed above for Namibia. In the Kimberley, ethnobotanical research was carried out by professional botanists (see references in Beard 1979), but more recently also by Aborigines themselves. The first volume ever published by Magabala Books, the local Aboriginal publisher in the Kimberley region, is an ethnobotany of Dampierland (Mayi 1987). It seems that ethnobotany is the first field that is explored once local expertise in environmental matters is acknowledged.[13]

In Australia two further steps have been taken to convert such an initial interest in local expertise into an expert system. Firstly, ethnobotanical information is copyrighted. The copyright for the ethnobotany of Dampierland, for instance, is held corporately by the Mamabulanjin Aboriginal Corporation. Secondly, researchers set out not only to document Aboriginal 'encyclopaedic knowledge of Australian plants and animals' (Isaacs 1996: 13), but also to capture some of the more comprehensive procedures of land management. It seems that the greatest effort in this field has been made in linking the documentation of Aboriginal plant knowledge with management skills contained in Aboriginal bush fire regimes (see Latz 1996). It is with regard to the latter that an expert system in the narrow sense of the word has become useful. This operates as a decision-support system on desktop computers and makes use of satellite imagery and GIS technology (Craig 1999: 23). Such a computer-aided decision support system is a computer programme that helps to make decisions about when and where it is ecologically useful to carry out controlled bushfires. 'GEOKAK' (see table 2), for instance, is a programme developed by the CSIRO specifically for the Kakadu National Park and is designed to 'determine the vegetation effects if a fire were to burn in a given environmental unit' (Walker, Davis and Gill 1985: 156).

Table 13.2. Excerpt from sample consultation with a fire control expert system (GEOKAK, see Walker, Davis and Gill 1985)

1. What is the season?	Hot
2. What is the litter cover expressed as percentage?	40
3. What is the fire danger rating? If you don't know I will attempt to infer a value.	Unknown
4. What is the 3 pm humidity, as a percentage?	30
5. What is the maximum daytime temperature?	35
6. What is the wind strength?	Moderate
7. What is the amount of biomass available for burning?	Moderate
[...]	
10 What is the biomass of the grass?	Moderate

Result:
I was unable to come to any conclusion about the grassfire flame length
The litterfire flame length = 0
I was unable to come to any conclusion about the % kill of Gr. Pteridifolia arial shoots
I was unable to come to any conclusion about the % kill of Gr. Pteridifolia on plant seeds
I was unable to come to any conclusion about the % kill of Gr. Pteridifolia ground seeds

In parallel to the development that I have described above for Namibia, the Australian debate about bushfires has in recent years focused on biodiversity, more precisely on 'the dramatic impact of fire on biodiversity in lands like Australia' (Coombs 1995: vii). Fire has for a long time been of concern to Aborigines and European settlers alike, even though for quite different reasons. Currently the development of an environmental management system for the benefit of Australia's biodiversity seems to be the dominant issue. However, the relation between this prospective expert system and the local expertise of Aborigines in this matter is precarious and deserves further attention.

National Fire Research

In an attempt at redressing the colonial arrogance of considering only those to be 'experts' who had gained their expertise through European schooling and culture, it is now a commonplace to underline that locals, too, are experts in their own right. In fact, critics of European-based systems of thought and action go as far as to claim that locals are the true and only experts on many issues, particularly those involving environmental questions (Shepard 1998). This is based on the understanding that scientific expertise is in fact just another local system, hegemonically spread across the world (Shiva 1993). In contradistinction to the Namibian case, the indigenous people of Australia have from the start been involved in the biodiversity debate that took off in the 1990s.[14] Scientists in the country recognised that a 'communication failure' had occurred (Coombs 1995: vii; Lewis 1989), that the problem was not one of information gaps (Rose 1995:1) but of 'communication gaps', that is to say relevant information is there but there are problems in conveying and converting the information. The strategy advocated for making the necessary institutional changes is the free 'sharing' of information and that 'we learn from Aborigines, from local experience and from the knowledge that science can provide' (Coombs 1995: viif.). Note that in this instance, and elsewhere in the discussion, Aborigines are not considered to be tantamount to the group of 'locals' which also includes Australians of European descent who have gathered a lot of practical experiences with bushfires by working and living in the rural parts of the country. Thus, while the problems of communication are realised, the differentiation between expertise from local experience and of scientific knowledge seems fairly unproblematic. This may be true more generally for countries with a strong presence of 'Western' expertise co-occurring with that of one or several groups identified as 'the indigenous people' (see Béteille 1998). In the context of fire management in Australia the basic distinction is made between 'Aboriginal natural ecologists' and 'university-trained scientific ecologists' (Rose 1995: 1) and seems not to be contested. This has a parallel in southern Africa, where it is mostly outside advocates of indigenous peoples who emphasise the special position of Khoisan-speaking indigenous people as 'practical conservationists' who cannot be 'lumped with the rest of us civilised, materialistic, poaching humans' (Perrott 1992: 63). But the overdue recognition of the right of all people living in an environment to bring in their expertise is one thing, the recognition of how this collaboration is best achieved is yet another matter which remains largely unresolved in Australia.

The most striking fact about the contribution of Aboriginal people who were invited to contribute to symposia such as 'Country in Flames' (in 1994, see Rose 1995) is that they emphasise the local limitation of their knowledge. As one participant put it: 'non-Aboriginal people look at Aboriginal people and think that we all have the same philosophy. Marranunggu philosophy is quite different to Patrick [Green]'s philosophy over in the Kimberleys. Marranunggu philosophy is different to Joe[Yunupingu]'s philosophy over in East Arnhem' (Ford quoted in Rose 1995: 69).[15] Clearly, the Aboriginal people involved would not support the idea of an 'ethnosystem', insofar as they do not claim to speak for a whole ethnic group of Australian Aborigines – for instance, 'the Bunaba' in Green's case, but only for a 'family area' (Green quoted in Rose 1995: 63). At the same time the evidence they give supports the view that these are distinct systems with a considerable degree of closure. The shared Aboriginal way of expressing this closure is by pointing out that the country itself is different, that it contains the information required for constructing the local system but that the information can only be elicited by those who 'know the country'. Conversely harmful or indiscriminate burning is attributed to people, including Aboriginal people 'who did not know the country' (Bright quoted in Rose 1995: 62).[16]

Accidental and Purposeful Burning of Land

A distinction between accidental and purposeful burning is not only made by administrators and scientists, but also by Aborigines. This emerges from many informal interviews in which I asked Aboriginal people about who they thought had caused a fire that we had observed. Many fires near settlements were considered 'accidental', caused by children who 'light during the day when the wind blows towards house'. I was told repeatedly that 'no one with a clear mind' would burn under the conditions that sometimes occur (strong winds, for instance). Fires that were lit out of ignorance were considered accidental. Aborigines whom I interviewed often attributed young people with lighting such fires, for instance because they wanted an area to be free of grass that could hide sticks which might puncture the tyres of their cars. At the same time fires have been used to develop a network of vehicle tracks for a multitude of purposes (hunting, gathering, visiting one's country) and to regain access to land (see Nash 1990: 2). Therefore, the distinction between burning as purposeful behaviour or as a consequence of not listening properly to the elders who could teach when and how to set a purposeful fire is not always easily drawn. Bushfires are not necessarily welcomed across the board by Aborigines, partly because it is not only non-Aborigines but Aboriginal communities as well who occasionally suffer economic losses as fires destroy vehicles, graders, and other machinery and equipment used by Aborigines today. Furthermore, Aborigines complain that in the public sphere they are often blamed (and fined) for bushfires, rather than considered experts on bushfires. In fact, the typical attitude of non-expert non-Aboriginal people (mostly white people in the rural areas) living in northern Australia is to be critical of both, Aborigines and scientific experts alike. Non-Aboriginal managers of cattle-stations and others frequently blame Aborigines for causing fires simply because they go hungry and hope to catch a lizard or two by burning stretches of land (and destroying natural resources in the process), and for being as destructive with the environment 'just as they are with machinery, like children'. Non-Aboriginal bushfire experts are also criticised, for instance by station managers, for 'wasting public money', 'imposing white people's ideas about tall grass'. As I was told by a station manager, who thought that more cattle (that keep the grass short) was the most effective remedy against bush fires: 'If there are more bushfires now than in the past, it is because there is less cattle and more conservation areas where people are supposed to grow tall grass.'

Building Expert Systems for Fire Management

In the Australian situation, even less so than in the Namibian context, there is no facile alignment of 'experts' and 'locals' along the lines of being a local resident or being an Aboriginal. For that reason, too, it is problematic to treat 'science' as just another local culture because there are obvious differences in the ways in which 'locals' and 'scientists' perceive their expertise. While locals continue to emphasise the diversity of cultural domains and fields of expertise, even within Aboriginal Australia (see Rose 1995: 69), scientists may consider their efforts to be specialised (and diverse) but they still consider them as one enterprise based on cumulative efforts in a variety of contexts. The 'expert system' is the model for these scientific efforts. Attempts have been made to develop expert systems for indigenous knowledge in the form of computer programmes which define formal rules that are operative in a clearly demarcated domain (e.g., Babu et al. 1995). In Australia, expert systems of Aboriginal fire use have been created and used in the non-computerised form of 'mental-cultural calendars' (Lewis 1989: 946–7). While there are discussions about the applicability of a particular expert system in any specific context, this does not question the overall strategy of designing these expert systems in order to utilise them across individual situations. To make expert knowledge independent of its local origins is not only a side-effect of expert systems, but it lies at the heart of the enterprise, as illustrated by this quote from a manual allowing you to 'build your own expert system':

> Write a program which will solve problems (in general) and you have a system which will replace people. With the added advantages of not breaking down, forgetting, going wrong, wanting to be paid, and so on [Naylor 1986: 6].[17]

Or, put less polemically by scientific fire experts from Australia:

> An 'expert system' may be defined as a computer system which uses knowledge and inference procedures to solve problems that are difficult enough to require significant human expertise for their solution, and which performs at least as well as the human experts [Naminga and Davis 1985: 29].

Not every expert system may be computerised, but the expectation is always that expert systems, even though they are specialised, are accessible and applicable across people and situations – like computer programmes. Local systems of expertise, by contrast, are explicitly restricted to a specific context, in the case of environmental knowledge restricted to both a specific landscape and a specific group of people who have a tradition of living in this landscape. Consequently, there are contexts involving confrontation between an indigenous group and wider political and economic institutions. The anthropologists who see themselves in the role of mediators between experts and locals may look upon these local systems of expertise in terms of 'ethnosystems', local knowledge modelled on the image of a locally based ethnic group (see above). This model suggests that there are critical similarities between expert systems and local systems which allow a transfer of knowledge and expertise from one system to another. It may be argued that both systems are delimited by a domain, for example a geographical area like the 'Kimberley High Rainfall Zone' (Craig 1997) in parallel with the landscape inhabited by an ethnic group. And both may be said to involve formal rules, for example the detailed techniques of burning and the cultural rules regulating the life of the ethnic group (see Nash 1990). However, as I want to illustrate with regard to the case of Aboriginal fire use, these apparent parallels may not be sufficient for a simple transfer to take place.

Towards an Expert System for Fire Management

There is broad agreement now that fire, including Aboriginal fire use, had an outstanding effect on shaping the Australian landscape (see Latz 1996; Pyne 1991). Arguably the high combustibility of the eucalyptus tree makes fire a more powerful element of land management in Australia than it is in those parts of Africa which otherwise have similar climatic conditions. It is also a widely accepted fact that interfering with the existing fire regime through European colonisation of the continent has again had unintended long-term consequences leading to large-scale environmental change and environmental damage in terms of biodiversity loss and the threat to established plant and animal communities (see Lewis 1989; Rose 1995). This damage seems to be largely due to the prevailing fire regime which prohibited regular bushfires by Aborigines, leading to an accumulation of fuel over the years and across large areas resulting in irregular but devastating fires. There is, therefore, growing agreement that controlled burning has to be carried out in Australia. The role of expert systems in this context would be, simply speaking, that of an aid to making a decision as to 'whether, when and how to burn' (Craig 1999: 24) in a specific place at a specific time. Such a 'decision support system' aims at designing a desirable fire regime, that is, 'the temporal and spatial characteristics of fires' for a particular environment over a specified period (see Craig 1999: 6). It presupposes the collection of reliable data specifying the effects of the existing fire regime, namely the local fire history (when was this stretch of land last burned?), a database relating to the regeneration of the plants in the area (what are the effects of fire on plants in their various stages of the seasonal cycle?), and an update on climatic and other factors which determine the intensity of a fire (what are the prevailing winds etc. that will determine the development of the fire?). The sources for these kinds of information are remote sensing via satellites, biological databases and weather forecasts, but Aboriginal expertise is also sought after. A. Craig, a government specialist on fire management in the Kimberley region, writes that 'urgent efforts are required to document the traditional knowledge of local

Aboriginal people in relation to landscape fire' (1997: 161). He reiterates the now established view that 'contemporary land management can benefit from the documentation and interpretation of this traditional knowledge' (op. cit. p. 178; see also Lewis 1989). During field research in 1998 I worked towards such documentation of the traditional knowledge on bushfires in the Fitzroy Valley (Kimberley region, northwest Australia). The overall result shows that Aboriginal people in the region, even if their traditional country was at some distance from the Fitzroy river and their current residence, were very perceptive in recognising the state of land with regard to its fire history.

Aborigines around Fitzroy Crossing readily describe desert landscapes in terms of their fire history by naming the stages in grass regeneration. Walmajarri speakers, living south of the Fitzroy valley in pre-colonial times, but today probably the majority population in the region, would distinguish *nyunma* (recently burnt grass with fresh shoots of green), *waruwaru* (about a year after burning with substantial patches of sand still visible) and *parrawa* (regrown grass after a fire within the previous three years, hunting still possible), and *yurnara* (thick old grass making walking and hunting on foot difficult and ready for burning). Some informants identified another stage between *parrawa* and *yurnara*, named *nyirrinyan*, for the period with dense grass (see also Richards and Hudson n. d.: 208; Lowe and Pike 1994: 86). Illustrations provided by Lowe and Pike (1994) show that it is in fact not difficult to distinguish these stages in the abstract. On the ground, however, the situation is not always so straightforward because small fires leave islands of unburnt grass here and there, and regrowth differs depending on the soil and probably also depending on the very erratic rainfall. They also point out (op. cit. p. 85) that the classification is one that grew out of a classification of land with regard to its potential for hunting, communication and orientation, and not specifically with regard to its stages of growth. What they have pointed out with regard to the conceptual classification is also true with regard to fire management practices. The mosaic pattern of more and less burnt patches, which is now so highly valued by ecologists because it preserves the different species communities of a geographical area in its various stages, is a product of activities directed towards aims other than protecting habitats. For instance, *lirramunu*, the typical strategy for starting a fire for the purpose of communal hunting, creates controlled patches of burnt grass because fire is lit from different directions at the same time. The fire is particularly productive because it not only catches animals that cannot escape but also because animals that manage to flee from the fire run towards the hunters and can then be killed. However, a basic point about Aboriginal knowledge of fire is that 'fire is a tool with many human uses' (Nash 1990: 1).

Apart from hunting, there are other purposeful uses for fire including the signalling of habitation through producing smoke and the 'looking after' of sacred sites. Both may be considered fire management only insofar as they rely on a specific combination of burning and non-burning. Practicing a nomadic lifestyle, lighting patches of grass as Aborigines travelled, signalled presence to other

Aboriginal people, because fires and smoke were limited in their seasonal and spatial dimensions. Asking about the location of remote outstations, I occasionally received responses like: 'When you were at Christmas Creek and you looked to the south did you see the smoke of the Bushfires there? This is where our country is.' Fire as a signal becomes meaningless once, with more permanent and denser occupation of the land, fires truly become ubiquitous. Similarly, while high grass is often considered 'dirty' and not appropriate for land that should be looked after, Aborigines also recognise the destructive force of five and therefore emphasise that for the protection of particular sacred sites controlled burning is the right strategy (see Latz and Green quoted in Rose 1995: 68f.; Nash 1990: 1). Incidentally, controlled burning for the protection of either natural heritage sites (for instance, giant *boab* trees) or settlement sites (buildings, telecom installations, caravan parks, etc.) is the most frequent form of fire management currently exercised in the Kimberley, and elsewhere in Australia. The 'fire plans' designed for doing these protective burns are elaborate and give an indication of how complex any controlled burns would be that aim to manage larger stretches of land for the protection not merely of sites but of ecological zones in general.

Because of the multiplicity of purposes that were implicated in Aboriginal fire use it is impossible to 'mimic' Aboriginal occupancy in a larger region, even though 'ideal management for the whole of Northern Australia might be a return to traditional Aboriginal fire regimes' (Bowman 1995: 107). The aim of an expert system is to reduce complexity without reducing the expertise. However, for a system like the Aboriginal fire regime that is in fact built on a multiplicity of systems of hunting, communication and ritual activity rather than on a monolithic knowledge system that could easily be converted into the currency of computer-aided expert system for land conservation, the problems become obvious.

Problems of Converting Local Knowledge into Expert Systems

The very simple and crude form of the early attempts to construct a computer-aided expert system for fire use should not mislead us to assume that Aboriginal fire use and its effects on land cannot be simulated. The information needed for this purpose is largely available. However, this does not imply that converting the 'knowledge' that is partially communicated by Aborigines, but also partially contained in a diversity of Aboriginal practices and partially also in the country itself, puts us into the position to create the same effects on the land. As Bowman (1995: 106) has observed: 'Technological approaches to land management may not be able to mimic traditional Aboriginal burning practices. Setting fires from aircraft cannot simulate the effect of traditional Aboriginal people burning their country during the course of their annual round. The cost of paying people to burn landscapes on foot may be prohibitively expensive.'[18] Apart from information and communication gaps (see above) there are also gaps between the sharing of information and the shared use of information in practice. Information about fire practices may flow freely, but its conversion into practice may take place separately in more or less segregated segments of society. In Australia these gaps exist both among non-Aborigines and among Aborigines.

In order to get expert systems working there are prerequisites other than collecting, coordinating and systematising knowledge and information. Despite shared information on the problems of the existing fire regime, the political consensus on the direction for changing this fire regime does not come automatically. This includes questions like what aspects of flora and fauna need management, which species should be exterminated and which should be conserved in a particular place (see Bowman 1995: 107). Furthermore, the practical effect of any expert system depends on a political process whereby the relevant people (landowners, land managers) are motivated to support the land management strategy and receive the financial resources enabling them to put a plan into action (see Craig 1999: 24). Parallel to the natural ecology there is also 'the social ecology of postfire succession' (Pyne 1991: 413) which in Australia means that a major destructive fire will be followed by an elaborate enquiry and report, sometimes followed by legal reforms that are directed at improved bushfire suppression, increased funding for bushfire research for a few years before the new measures to mitigate bushfire effects gradually sease being put into practice until the 'status quo ante returns' (op. cit. p. 413). This last point illustrates that, although it is the nation state (or the government of individual states within a federation) which demand the creation of expert systems, the state is not a monolithic block, but rather competition between corporate bodies within the state plays a major role in the process. The same could be said about the policy of combating desertification in countries like Namibia. It is conceived of as a national task but just as with fire management in Australia, establishing an expert system involves the reallocation of state resources and therefore competition between interested parties within the state administration, and the state at large. In Namibia there is a 'social ecology of land appropriation succession', that is to say, cases in which land was reallocated to new users (and new uses) – be this through government resettlement, illegal fencing or violent dispossession, as occurred recently in Zimbabwe – have triggered activities of various government and non-governmental organisations that aim for land reform and changes in the access to the natural products of that land.

The Political Context of Land Management

It therefore needs emphasising that expert systems only work effectively when integrated properly in their political context. However, it is important to realise that this political dimension is not only limited to dealings between state institutions but for instance is also relevant to understanding the situation of Aborigines in this process. There is some evidence that communication between Aborigines and other Australians sometimes fails because Aborigines in these public contexts are mostly concerned with establishing their right as (original) landowners, and therefore their right to determine the premises for land management. Meanwhile, other Australians are mainly interested to elicit and incorporate technical Aboriginal knowledge in order to keep costs down and to make expert systems work (see Lewis 1989). This is in direct parallel to the Namibian case discussed above where Topnaar cooperated with Belgian scientists in compiling an ethnobotany but for quite different reasons. In Australia the situation is further complicated by the fact that the right to legitimately and appropriately burn the country was at least in some cases considered a privilege of local people in a very strong sense, namely relating to people with a genealogical link to a clan that was considered to be localised in its relation to specific sites. In this context the cultural knowledge of when and where to burn becomes the cultural property of a specific group of people. In the short term this may mean that calculating the costs of institutionalising burning practices may involve compensation demanded by Aboriginal corporations who want to convert their knowledge into material benefits. More generally, however, this puts into question the applicability of the expert system strategy. If certain types of knowledge only gain their value as a good in a specific domain, that of the household or clan, it may not be possible to simply convert goods into generalised benefits or values promised by expert systems. Recent advances made in the anthropological study of goods (see Gregory 1997) seem to also apply to the distinction between what constitutes a 'good' fire regime versus a 'bad' fire regime. The question certainly is no longer one of interference versus non-interference because Aboriginal fire regimes, too, did interfere with 'natural' processes. Furthermore, given the disruption caused by colonial dominance and suppression of traditional fire regimes, any non-interference at this stage is an active step towards supporting earlier interferences. Moreover, given that biodiversity is, strictly speaking, a process and not an inventory, fire regimes in Australia (or property regimes in Namibia) cannot be judged with reference to a 'neutral ground'. Rather, developing and reinventing a good fire regime will always implicate repercussions between actions taken and how they relate to the construction of 'goods' and what constitutes a good life more generally in the social groups that are involved.

Property Regimes and Fire Regimes and Their Relation to Environmental Change

Recent conservation efforts have shifted away from the protection of individual plant or animal species and the protection of parks without people towards the preservation or restoration of high biodiversity zones as specified in the WWF 'ecoregion-based conservation strategy' (see Maffi et al. 2000). These ecoregions are used by people, frequently 'indigenous people' with a long record of having used the region so that their management regimes are considered to contain valuable knowledge input for any future use of these regions. At the same time the claim is made both by ethnobotanists and by bushfire experts that the knowledge of local people can or at least should be transferred to other contexts or even to expert systems that can then be adapted to a number of contexts. In this contribution I have put this claim to the test and the two test cases suggest that a number of problems arise in such attempts at transferring knowledge. Local knowledge is sometimes misinterpreted as being domain-specific knowledge, in the sense that any expert system is designed for a specific domain, a clearly defined area in which it functions. Khoisan property arrangements and Aboriginal fire uses are specific but it is helpful to insist that they constitute specific regimes, that is, complex systems with numerous functions and implications, rather than simply domains. The notion of 'regime' not only captures the political dimension of the knowledge contained in it. It also hints at its complex internal make-up, highlighting that knowledge may be distributed unequally among the people and the objects involved. Furthermore, it hints at the fact that these regimes, which are now valued, have for a long time been repressed by other regimes, in particular the regime of European settlers. Competition between regimes is therefore to be expected and allowances have to be made for this fact in the process of converting knowledge which may be more like a process of interpretation and translation than a simple process of transfer as suggested by dominant development discourse.

Just as the lives of Khoisan-speaking people in southern Africa and the lives of Aboriginal people in Australia have been altered considerably by the presence of a dominant settler community, the non-European property regimes in southern Africa and Aboriginal fire regimes in Australia have been transformed in the process. They have not necessarily been assimilated to a scientific world-view, but they have been altered because in neither case do they constitute isolated philosophical schemes aloof from everyday life, but manifestations of distributed knowledge which inevitably change since the land itself and other media outside the human brains which carry parts of that knowledge have changed over time. In fact it is very likely that – maybe on a smaller scale – similar changes occurred before the impact of European settlers, simply because the environment was changed by humans. These changes had repercussions on the system of distributed knowledge as a whole and the human component within it in particular. Probably, Aborigines and Khoisan peoples have for a much longer period than we can document followed their various goal-oriented activities which have had unpredicted and unintended environmental effects. The knowledge systems that they have created in the process are not domain-specific in the narrow sense, because as we see them today they have been nurtured from activities in very different domains, and it seems that they have proven their usefulness and resilience exactly because they cut across different domains. Although this complicates the picture, it is also encouraging to the extent that it suggests that knowledge is not enshrined in 'a local culture', but that it can be accessed through different media that make up the regime as a whole. Bushfire scientists have learned to derive relevant information from the country itself (Bowman 1995: 108) and equally different Khoisan groups within southern Africa have developed their Khoisan cultural heritage in diverse ways (Widlok 1998b). While it is probably appropriate to talk about some cultural knowledge being 'lost forever' when situations change radically because cultural knowledge cannot be artificially stored and reinstalled in practice without transformation, it is also encouraging to realise that cultural knowledge is also continually created as it is transported across domains and translated across regimes.

Conclusion

This article has investigated the relationship between two types of expertise now commonly found in close proximity all over the world: the environmental knowledge of indigenous people – sometimes misleadingly called 'ethnosystems' - and the environmental programmes of internationally trained experts, which are often designed like computer programmes, known as 'expert systems'. Following widespread disillusion with modernisation projects, considerable hope is now vested in the successful cooperation between 'local expertise' and 'international expertise' when dealing with diverse local manifestations of global environmental change. However, the interaction and communication between indigenous people with expert knowledge and experts who work locally often breaks down. In this article I have tried to establish the reasons for these breakdowns in communication which prevent the emergence of cumulative expertise based on comparative ethnography carried out in Namibia and Australia.

In both settings there is regular contact between the two kinds of expertise, that is indigenous people and 'external' experts working side by side. In the !Khuiseb valley of Namibia 'traditional' ways of using wild resources, especially the endemic *!nara* plant, and of restricting access to these resources have been disrupted severely by dispossessing the local Topnaar of their land. More recently, the national biodiversity administrators as well as international researchers have tried to collect information from 'the locals'. The dominant perception, it seems, is that information is a scarce resource and the biodiversity discourse is a way of staking claims to controlling this information. In Australia, after decades of ignorance regarding indigenous Australian fire management, it has now become accepted wisdom that the indigenous people of Australia, too, have shaped the land and its future potential, primarily through their use of fire. Bushfires are a major factor of environmental change in Australia and in order to deal with this factor, experts now turn to the knowledge of indigenous Australians – so far with only very limited success. In both cases the cultural practices involved prove to be non-domain specific, that is to say the 'expert knowledge' is diffused into practices generated in a number of domains of social life. In Namibia ethnobotanical knowledge is a source for political claims in the field of land tenure and the recognition of ethnic identity. In Australia knowledge relating to bushfires is a by-product of hunting skills, a nomadic lifestyle and the localisation of the clan as a social group that defines what is a 'good' fire in this particular case. The Topnaar use of wild resources is a property regime, the fire use patterns of the Kimberley Aborigines is a fire regime. While the Aboriginal classification of regenerative stages of the landscape after a bushfire or the prescriptive rules about who should appropriately set fire to a particular stretch of land may be considered to be more formal than Khoisan classifications and rules about access to wild resources, the degree of formalisation seems to be negligible compared to the fundamental problems of converting any of these regimes into expert systems (of various kinds). Converting knowledge between regimes, I argue, needs to be distinguished from transferring knowledge between domains of expert systems. Recognising these incongruities between local systems of expertise and expert systems is a necessary first step towards institutionalising the successful communication and interaction that is lacking.

Notes

1. I gratefully acknowledge the support of the Deutsche Forschungsgemeinschaft (DFG) which funded my comparative research project in Namibia and Australia between 1995 and 2000. I am also grateful to the James Swan Fund of the Pitt Rivers Museum, Oxford, for providing supplementary funds for my research in Namibia. The DFG project was initiated and facilitated by Michael Casimir as the project holder to whom I am grateful for providing me with the autonomy to independently carry out my research and formulate my results. My colleagues at the Institut für Ethnologie at the University Cologne as well as numerous individuals in Namibia and Australia have helped me in the process of research but they are not responsible for the shortcomings that may remain.
2. The Namibian Ministry of Education conscripted an NGO project group called 'Enviroteach' to provide biodiversity-relevant material to selected schools across the country. Enviroteach is part of DRFN (the Desert Research Foundation of Namibia) and was until recently based at Gobabeb, the desert research station in the !Khuiseb valley. In the early 1990s the media producers and environmental educationalists constituted the main presence of external specialists in the !Khuiseb, outnumbering visiting academic researchers and their local assistants. Although the Enviroteach publications regularly used case material from the !Khuiseb environment, the local school was not involved in the project. The policy of the NGO, like that of the state authorities involved, was to

make biodiversity a national issue and to position itself as a mediator between 'locals' and 'experts'.

3. 'Final diversity' seems an odd concept in the context of ongoing evolution, but it is not for the operationalisation of diversity in a national inventory. Representatives of the national conservation institutions involved readily admit that their figures are 'by no means accurate' and add that the compilation of a complete national inventory is a task that they feel is not adequately valued (Griffin and Barnard 1996: 124–5).
4. Namibia which, prior to independence, had a strong group of NGOs opposing government policies of 'wildlife management' (see Widlok 1999: 33ff.) now has a host of NGOs which, like the environmental educationists of Enviroteach and NAPCOD (the 'Namibia's Programme to Combat Desertification'), basically support national programmes of biodiversity prospecting (see Barnard 1998; Tarr 1996: 207f.). But while there may be agreement about the value of biodiversity in the abstract, the political alliances in biodiversity prospecting can be shown to change over time.
5. Here are some quotes from relevant publications of IWGIA, the international workgroup for indigenous affairs, based in Scandinavia, not accidentally also the centre of donor agencies operating in Namibia: 'While the loss of biodiversity is now well-recognised, [...] cultural diversity is perhaps under even more serious threat ...' (McNeely 1997: 175). 'The local knowledge that people have about their resources and how they should be managed provides a critical resource for all of humanity' (op. cit. p. 185). Cultural diversity is defined in direct analogy to biodiversity, namely as 'the human intellectual "gene pool", the basic raw material for adapting to the local environment' (op. cit. p. 192). In a similar fashion, cultural variability, that is, the abstract potential for cultural innovation, is operationalised in terms of the existing *number* of cultures, above all 'the great variety of *indigenous* cultures in all parts of the world' (emphasis added). Biological and cultural diversity seem so strongly interrelated, that the concept 'biocultural diversity' has been introduced (op. cit. p. 185).
6. Indigenous peoples are presented, and occasionally present themselves, as 'the best conservers of the environment' who by following 'their own cultural premises' (Gray 1991: ii) and 'through the recognition of their rights to their territories' can protect biodiversity (op. cit. p. 55). It seems likely that in parallel to the claim that the preservation of biodiversity requires the help of a national team of biologists international cultural brokers who propagate cultural diversity consider their own lobbying as indispensable for the recognition of local expertise.
7. The international definitions of biodiversity, above all that of the UN convention on biodiversity, refer to it as 'variability *among* living organisms' (Glowka et al. 1994: 16, emphasis added) evading the specialised discussions about what counts as an organism (viruses, 'dormant' genetic material of dead organisms), how to count types of organism and what it means to establish variability *among*, not *of*, organisms. There is much indication that symbiosis and sociality involving different types of organism may be a major source of diversity, for instance, the relation between social insects such as termites and the micro-organisms that help them to overcome their carbon/nitrogen imbalance (Higashi and Abe 1997). Much biodiversity potential seems to lie between species, and not simply within them.
8. It is noteworthy that the ownership of specimen collected in the course of this research is not specified. It can be assumed that it lies with the University of Gent but that the National Herbarium of Namibia requested the researchers to submit a specimen of any plant collected. There seems to be a parallel here between ethnobotanical research and

some ethnomuseological research to the extent that in both cases the creation of collections (of specimen and ethnographica) initiated research, with institutions like botanical gardens and ethnology museums ultimately owning the objects as well as the copyright on their descriptions (see Rodin 1985).

9 Only recently research about the *!nara* has been conducted in direct consultation with Topnaar interests (see Henschel and Dausab in press).

10. The ants, beetles, spiders of the Namib do not necessarily fall under the biodiversity convention since they are neither threatened nor of particular cultural value. They may be considered 'indicator species' of importance for research. But they have only been made indicator species within the set-up of this particular study – simply by virtue of the fact that they are easy to catch and to count.

11. The physicist did not accept my suggestion that his activity, too, could be considered to be biodiversity prospecting which effectively circumvents national and local control without being illegal. He underlined that it was far from certain that his research would lead to any marketable product since he, too, was only taking a guess about the potential of one particular aspect of biodiversity. On the other hand, he admitted that the information gained would likely be used by European pharmaceutical companies, but that locals would eventually benefit from this specialised culture of science and industry, outweighing the fact that the local culture of the Topnaar had prevented the degradation of the environment and thereby protected the survival of the scorpions, and questioning the distinction between local and expert benefits in this context.

12. This is the established view which, however, seems to be at least partly influenced by an observer effect, generated by anthropologists who were looking for examples of 'formless' or 'informal' modes of organising cultural knowledge and social relations (Shapiro 1998).

13. At least it is striking that in Namibia, too, one of the first NGO experts who visited 'Bushmanland' before non-governmental development activities began to mushroom in the 1990s, was an agriculturalist who compiled an ethnobotanical report (and whom I accompanied during his field trip in 1987).

14. The exponential growth of the biodiversity discourse can be seen in the sharp increase in articles dealing with this topic in scientific journals between 1988 and 1994 (Harper and Hawksworth 1995: 6).

15. The same representative adds: 'Until Aboriginal people are able to get their skills in western education, to be able to communicate to you about our philosophies, it's really going to be difficult for non-Aboriginal people and Aboriginal people to understand what we talk about for our country' (Ford quoted in Rose 1995: 69). The 'we' in this context does not refer to 'the Aboriginal people' but very specifically to three individuals from the Mak Mak Marranunggu clan. She continues: 'They [Aborigines from other areas] might have some of the groundings that are the same but they are still different and this is what non-Aboriginal people need to understand' (Ford quoted in Rose 1995: 69).

16. Area specificity of knowledge is something that is readily acknowledged as relevant by non-Aboriginal specialists who would be the first to argue that there cannot be a single expert system for fire management which would work for all of Australia (see Craig 1997, 1998). Inviting Aborigines from different areas is therefore common to the extent that local residence sometimes is given precedence over local expertise. Patrick Green, whom I interviewed in his hometown, argued that he was invited to talk at the Symposiom 'Country in Flames' not because he was particularly knowledgeable about bush fires but because he was the only person available from the Kimberley. Clearly there is only partial overlap between the relevant geographical units identified by scientific fire managers and

the 'countries' that convey authoritative knowledge for various Aboriginal groups. However, it needs also to be noted that there are striking similarities in fire mangement across groups in Australia. Nash's account of the Warlpiri 'double hunting fire' *lirramirni* (1990: 1) matches that of the Walmajarri *lirramunu* as described below. Thus, Aboriginal insistence on the local restriction of knowledge underlines the fact that we are dealing with 'knowledge regimes' involving the legitimacy of access to knowledge and not simply with 'knowledge domains'.

17. In a similar vein the manual says 'every time a group of computer scientists talked to someone who was an expert in some field, they would listen to him for, maybe, a couple of hours. then they would start to long for the day when he could be replaced by a computer so that they could switch him off, and then forget to pay him' (Naylor 1986: 6). While this may have been written tongue in cheek the underlying assumption is that expertise can be copied from human experience to machines: 'All that people consist of is a collection of brain cells, wired together somehow, and all that computers consist of is a collection of memory cells, also wired together somehow' (Naylor 1986: 6).
18. Nash's work on the Walbiri suggests that travelling by car may in fact be a practicable compromise (1990: 1).

References

Atran, S. 1990. *Cognitive Foundations of Natural History. Towards an Anthropology of Science.* Cambridge: Cambridge University Press.

Babu, S.C., M. Warren, and B. Rajasekaran 1995. 'Expert Systems for Indigenous Knowledge in Crop Varietal Selection', in *The Cultural Dimension of Development. Indigenous Knowledge Systems*, eds. M. Warren, J. Slikkerveer, and D. Brokensha, 211–17. London: Intermediate Technology Publications.

Barnard, A. 1992. *Hunters and Herders of Southern Africa. A Comparative Ethnography of the Khoisan Peoples.* Cambridge: Cambridge University Press.

Barnard, P., ed. 1998. *Biological Diversity in Namibia: A Country Study.* Windhoek: Namibia National Biodiversity Task Force.

Beard, J.S. 1979. *The Vegetation of the Kimberley Area. Vegetation Survey of Western Australia.* Nedlands: University of Western Australia Press.

Béteille, A. 1998. 'The Idea of Indigenous People', *Current Anthropology* 39: 187–91.

Bowen, J. and R. Petersen 1999. 'Introduction: Critical Comparisons', in *Critical Comparisons in Politics and Culture*, eds. J. Bowen and R. Petersen, 1–20. Cambridge: Cambridge University Press.

Bowman, D. 1995. 'Why the Skillful use of Fire is Critical for the Management of Biodiversity in Northern Australia', in *Country in Flames. Proceedings of the 1994 Symposium on Biodiversity and Fire in North Australia*, ed. D. Rose, 103–10. *Biodiversity Series Paper*, vol. 3. Canberra: Biodiversity Unit. Australian National University.

Budack, K. 1983. 'A Harvesting People on the South Atlantic Coast', *Ethnologie. South African Journal of Ethnology* 6: 1–7.

Coombs, H. 1995. 'Foreword', in *Country in Flames. Proceedings of the 1994 Symposium on Biodiversity and Fire in North Australia*, ed. D. Rose, vii–viii *Biodiversity Series Paper*, Vol. 3. Canberra: Australian National University.

Craig, A. 1997. 'A Review of Information on the Effects of Fire in Relation to the Management of Rangelands in the Kimberley High-Rainfall Zone', *Tropical Grasslands* 31: 161–87.

——— 1999. 'Fire Management of Rangelands in the Kimberley Low-Rainfall Zone: a Review', *Rangeland Journal* 21: 39–70.

Dyer, R. 1958. 'Foreword', in *Some Plants Used by the Bushmen in Obtaining Food and Water*, ed. R. Story. Botanical Survey of South Africa Memoir, vol. 30, 4. Pretoria: Department of Agriculture. Division of Botany.

Glowka, L., F. Burhenne-Guilmin and H. Synge, eds. 1994. *A Guide to the Convention on Biological Diversity*, vol. 30. *Environmental Policy and Law Paper*. Gland: International Union for Conservation of Nature and Natural Resources.

Gray, A. 1991. *Between the Spice of Life and the Melting Pot: Biodiversity Conservation and its Impact on Indigenous Peoples. IWGIA Document* vol. 70. Copenhagen: International Work Group for Indigenous Affairs (IWGIA).

Gregory, C.A. 1997. *Savage Money. The Anthropology and Politics of Commodity Exchange*. Amsterdam: Harwood.

Griffin, M. and P. Barnard 1996. 'What is This Thing Called Biodiversity?', in *Namibia Environment* 1, ed. P. Tarr, 122–25. Windhoek: Ministry of Environment and Tourism.

Harper, J. and D. Hawksworth 1995. 'Preface', in *Biodiversity. Measurement and Estimation*, ed. D. Hawksworth, 5–12. London: Chapman & Hall.

Henschel, J. and R. Dausab, eds. in press. *Sustainable Management of !nara by the Topnaar Community of the Lower Kuiseb Valley: A Baseline Study of !nara Resource Management and its Potential for Development*. Windhoek: Desert Research Foundation of Namibia.

Higashi, M. and T. Abe 1997. 'Global Diversification of Termites Driven by the Evolution of Symbiosis and Sociality', in *Biodiversity: An Ecological Perspectiv*, eds. S. Levin and M. Higashi, 83–112. New York: Springer.

Ingold, T. 2000. *The Perception of the Environment. Essays on Livelihood, Dwelling and Skill*. London: Routledge.

Isaacs, J. 1996. *Bush Food. Aboriginal Food and Herbal Medicine*. Sydney: Lansdowne.

Kemf, E., ed. 1993. *The Law of the Mother – Protecting Indigenous Peoples and Protected Areas*. San Francisco: Sierra Club Books.

Latz, P. 1996. *Bushfire & Bushtucker. Aboriginal Plant Use in Central Australia*. Alice Springs: IAD Press.

Lewis, H. 1989. 'Ecological and Technological Knowledge of Fire: Aborigines Versus Park Rangers in Northern Australia', *American Anthropologist* 91: 940–61.

Lowe, P. and J. Pike. 1994. *Jilji. Life in the Great Sandy Desert*. Broome: Magabala Books.

Maffi, L., G. Oviedo and P. Larsen 2000. *Indigenous and Traditional Peoples of the World and Ecoregion-Based Conservation: An Integrated Approach to Conserving the World's Biological and Cultural Diversity*. WWF International – People and Conservation Unit. Terralingua: Partnerships for Linguistic and Biological Diversity.

Mayi, G. 1987. *Some Bush Fruits of Dampierland*. Broome: Magabala Books.

McNeely, J. 1997. 'Interaction Between Biological Diversity and Cultural Diversity', in *Indigenous Peoples, Environment and Development. Proceedings of the conference, Zurich, May 15–18, 1995*. vol. 85. *IWGIA Document*, eds. S. Büchi, C. Erni, L. Jurt, and C. Rüegg, 173–96. Copenhagen: International Work Group for Indigenous Affairs.

Naminga, P.M. and J.R. Davis 1985. 'An Overview of Expert Systems' in *Towards and Expert System for Fire Management at Kakadu National Park*, eds. J. Walker, J.R. Davis, and A.M. Gill, 29–43. Technical Memorandum 85/2. Canberra: CSIRO.

Nash, D., ed. 1990. 'Warlpiri Fire Management'. Paper presented at theTechnical Workshop on the Management of Spinifex Deserts for Nature Conservation. Wanneroo: WA Wildlife Research Centre.

Naylor, C. 1986. *Build Your Own Expert System.* Wilmslow: Sigma Press.

Perrott, J. 1992. *Bush for the Bushman.* Greenville: Beaver Pond.

Pyne, S. 1991. *Burning Bush. A Fire History of Australia.* New York: Henry Holt.

Richards, E. and J. Hudson. n.d. *Walmajarri-English Dictionary.* Darwin: Summer Institute of Linguistics.

Richardson, J. 1998. 'Economics of Biodiversity Conservation', in *Biological Diversity in Namibia: A Country Study,* ed. P. Barnard, 227–78. Windhoek: Namibia National Biodiversity Task Force.

Rodin, R. 1985. *The Ethnobotany of the Kwanyama Ovambos. Monographs in Systematic Botany,* vol. 9. Missouri: Missouri Botanical Garden.

Rose, D. 1995. *Country in Flames. Proceedings of the 1994 Symposium on Biodiversity and Fire in North Australia,* vol. 3. Canberra: Biodiversity Unit. Australian National University.

Rottenburg, R. 2000. 'Diffusion – Translation – Macht. Drei Aspekte der Entwicklungszusammenarbeit mit Afrika', *Africa 2000.* German African Studies Association 17th Biennial Conference, Leipzig.

Shapiro, W. 1998. 'Ideology, "History of Religions", and Hunter-Gatherer Studies', *Journal of the Royal Anthropological Institute* 4: 489–510.

Shepard, P. 1998. 'A Post-Historic Primitivism', in *Limited Wants, Unlimited Means. A Reader on Hunter-Gatherer Economics and the Environment,* ed. J. Gowdy, 281–325. Washington: Island Press.

Shiva, V. 1993. *Monocultures of the Mind. Perspectives on Biodiversity and Biotechnology.* London: Zed Books.

Slikkerveer, J. and W. Dechering 1995. 'LEAD: The Leiden Ethnosystems And Development Programme', in *The Cultural Dimension of Development. Indigenous Knowledge Systems,* eds. M. Warren, J. Slikkerveer, and D. Brokensha, 435–40. London: Intermediate Technology Publications.

Story, R. 1958. *Some Plants Used by the Bushmen in Obtaining Food and Water. Botanical Survey of South Africa Memoir,* vol. 30. Pretoria: Department of Agriculture. Division of Botany.

Tarr, P., ed. 1996. *Namibia Environment,* vol. 1. Windhoek: Ministry of Environment and Tourism.

Van Damme, P. 1992. 'Preface', in *The Ethnobotany of the Topnaar,* eds. V. Van den Eynden, P. Vernemmen and P. Van Damme, i–ii. Gent: University of Gent.

Van den Eynden, V., P. Vernemmen and P. Van Damme, eds. 1992. *The Ethnobotany of the Topnaar.* Gent: Universiteit Gent.

Walker, J., J.R. Davis and A.M. Gill, eds. 1985. *Towards and Expert System for Fire Management at Kakadu National Park.* Technical Memorandum 85/2. Canberra: CSIRO.

Widlok, T. 1998a. 'Digging a Grave for Culture. Cultural Heritage and Power Relations in a Namibian Khoisan Group', in *The Khoisan Identities and Cultural Heritage Conference,* ed. A. Bank, 256–62. Belville: Institute for Historical Research, University of the Western Cape.

——— 1998b. 'Unearthing Culture. Khoisan Funerals and Social Change', *Anthropos* 93: 115–26.

——— 1999. *Living on Mangetti. 'Bushman' Autonomy and Namibian Independence.* Oxford: Oxford University Press.

——— 2001. 'Relational Properties. Understanding Ownership in the Namib Desert and Beyond', *Zeitschrift für Ethnologie* 126: 237–68.

NOTES ON CONTRIBUTORS

Heike Becker-Baumann M.A. was employeed at the Department of Geography at the Heinrich-Heine-University Düsseldorf until September 2002. She assisted in a research project 'Consumption of Resources, Problems of Waste Disposal and Endangerment of the Environment through Mass-Tourism in Coastal Areas of Thailand' sponsored by the 'Deutsche Forschungsgemeinschaft' (German Research Community) and is now working on a dissertation about 'Industrial Tourism in the Ruhr Area. A Contribution to Sustainable Regional Development?'.

Andrea Bender is Assistant Professor in the Department of Psychology and a Research Fellow in Cognitive Psychology, University of Freiburg, Germany. She received her Ph.D. in Anthropology from the University of Freiburg in 2000. Her research interests include cognitive and linguistic anthropology, cognitive psychology and Oceania. She has concentrated on ecological concepts and behaviour, emotions, concepts of space and time, and ethnomathematics. She carried out field research in Tonga in 1997–99, in 2001 and in 2004/5.

Gisela Böhm is Professor of Psychometrics and Research Methods at the University of Bergen. She received her Ph.D. from the Technical University of Berlin in 1993. Her research centres on social cognition, decision making and risk perception and has focused on mental models, moral judgment and emotional reactions in subjective risk evaluation. She is also interested in research methods and data analysis. Before joining the University of Bergen Gisela Böhm held positions at the University of Bremen (Germany) and the University for Pedagogics, Ludwigsburg (Germany). She was visiting professor at the universities of Dortmund, Freiburg, Lüneburg and at Helmut-Schmidt University, Hamburg (all Germany). She is Chair of the Bergen Decision Lab.

Heiko Breit received his Diploma degree in sociology from the University of the Saarland (Saarbrücken) in 1986, where he also worked in the Psychological Institute until 1996. In 1996 he moved to the German Institute for International Educational Research in Frankfurt/Main where he works in the Culture and Education section. He finished his doctorate in 2002 at the University of the Saarland. His main research interests are qualitative analyses on cultural and moral issues, particularly the development of judgements on justice, responsibility and democracy.

Barbara Casciarri is Professor of Anthropology at the University of St Denis-Paris 8. She has done extensive fieldwork among the Arab nomadic pastoralists of central Sudan, focusing on their political organisation and kinship system. More recently she has been researching the management of water resources among Berber nomad groups and oasis farmers in southeastern Morocco. Currently, she is doing a restudy of the pastoralists in Sudan.

Michael J. Casimir is Professor of Ethnology at the Institute of Cultural and Social Anthropology, Cologne. He has conducted prolonged fieldwork on the ecology, economy, environmental management and nutritional and socialisation patterns among pastoral nomads in west Afghanistan and Kashmir. Together with Aparna Rao he was chairperson of the *Commission on Nomadic Peoples* of the *International Union of Ethnological and Anthropological Sciences* (1995–1998), and was until 2004 one of the editors of *Nomadic Peoples*, the official journal of the Commission. His major publications include *Flocks and Food. A Biocultural Approach to the Study of Pastoral Foodways* (Böhlan, 1991) and, together with Aparna Rao, *Mobility and Territoriality* (ed. Berg, 1992) and *Nomadism in South Asia* (ed. Oxford University Press, 2003).

Thomas Döring received his Diploma degree in psychology in 1994 and finished his doctorate in 2003. After completing his Diploma he worked at the University of the Saarland (Saarbrücken). In 1996 he moved to the German Institute for International Educational Research in Frankfurt/Main as a co-worker in the section Culture and Education. Since 2004 he has worked at the Adolf-Bender-Center in St. Wendel, Saarland, Germany. His main research interests are moral judgments, control beliefs, risk management and xenophobia.

Lutz H. Eckensberger is Professor of Psychology at the University of the Saarland (Saarbrücken). He received his Diploma degree in 1996 and finished his doctorate in 1979. He was Director of the German Institute for International Educational Research from 1998–2004 where he is currently head of the Culture and Education section. He also holds a Chair of Psychology at the Johann Wolfgang Goethe University in Frankfurt. In 1985–86 he was Fellow of the Centre for Advanced Studies in Berlin. Besides his focus on methodology, his main interest is moral development under a cultural and action theory perspective. He also works on the contextualization of morality, which implies the analysis of the relation between facts and norms, cognition and affect, control and risk taking, as well as self and solidarity with others. He has published over 90 articles in books and journals and edited 15 books.

Anita Engels received her doctoral degree in sociology from the University of Bielefeld in 1999. She spent a post-doc research fellowship at Stanford University where she started working on institutional aspects of an emerging global market for emissions trading. Currently she is Professor of Sociology at the Centre for Globalisation and Governance where she teaches courses on globalisation and social change. Her research interests are the emergence of 'green' markets, ecological modernisation, and exploring the links between globalisation theories and organisational theories. Her current research project is a cross-national comparison of company behaviour in the EU Emissions Trading Scheme.

Barbara Göbel has been the Director of the Ibero-American Institute, Berlin since June 2005. She also serves on the boards of diverse national and international organizations working on development and environment issues or on Latin America. She studied social anthropology, prehistory, economic and social history at the Universities of Munich and Göttingen (Germany); in 1990 she received a Ph.D. from the latter. She has been Lecturer at the Universities of Göttingen, Tübingen, Hohenhein, Bonn and Cologne (Germany) and Visiting Professor at several universities in Argentina, Bolivia and Chile. She also worked at the Laboratoire d' Anthropologie Sociale in Paris (France). Barbara Göbel has more than three and a half years ethnographic fieldwork experience in the Andes, mainly NW-Argentina., N-Chile and S-Bolivia where she worked on economic and environmental topics. Between 2002 and 2005 she was the Executive Director of the International Programme on Global Environmental Change (IHDP).

Andrea Grotzke studied economics and geography at the University of Freiburg, Germany. After extensive fieldwork in southern Africa, where she analysed small scale co-operative farming systems, she worked for several consulting agencies. Her work focuses on consultancy regarding the financing of sustainable energy projects, and on issues of renewable energy schemes.

Götz Hoeppe is a member of the research group on the sociology of knowledge and finance at the University of Constance and part-time Lecturer in Social Anthropology at Heidelberg University. He obtained his Ph.D. in social anthropology at the Freie Universität Berlin for a study of Hindu and Muslim fishermen's local knowledge and their perceptions of environmental change in a Kerala village (India). He has published *Conversations on the Beach: Fishermen's Knowledge, Metaphor and Environmental Change in South India* (Berghahn Books, 2007) and *Why the Sky is Blue: Discovering the Color of Life* (Princeton University Press, 2007).

Annette Huppert works at the German Institute for International Educational Research in Frankfurt/Main. She studied psychology with a focus on cultural and developmental psychology and psychoanalysis. She got her Diploma in 1998 at the University of the Saarland. Her main research interests are qualitative analysis on normative cultural standards, particularly moral development and the development of responsibility.

Fred W. Krüger is Professor of Geography and a member of the board of directors of the Institute of Geography at the University of Erlangen-Nuremberg, Germany. His research and teaching interests focus on Urban Studies and Development Geography. In the latter, he specialises on theoretical approaches and the empirical, actor-oriented analysis of poverty (especially in cities), vulnerability, coping, livelihood security, and concepts of risk. A regional focus lies on southern Africa. A major current research project deals with the impact of HIV/AIDS on human livelihoods in Botswana. Past research activities in the context of the 'developing world' involved urban planning issues, social vulnerability patterns, and drought management in southern Africa.

Josef Nerb is Professor of Educational Psychology at the Department of Education, University of Freiburg (Germany) from where he also had received his Ph.D. With a grant from the Alexander von Humboldt Foundation he did a post-doc study at the University of Waterloo, Canada.

Hans-Rüdiger Pfister is Professor of Business Psychology at the University of Lüneburg. He received his Ph.D. at the Technical University of Berlin in 1990. Prior to joining the University of Lüneburg in 2001, he worked as a senior researcher at the Fraunhofer Institute IPSI in Darmstadt and the Knowledge Media Research Centre in Tübingen. His research interests include behavioural decision making, the role of emotions in decision making, and risk perception, computer-supported collaborative learning and human-computer interaction. He was founder and is currently Deputy Head of the Institute of Experimental Industrial Psychology (LueneLab) at the University of Lüneburg.

Judith Schlehe has been Professor and Head of Department of the Institute for Social and CulturalAnthropology, University of Freiburg/Brsg since 2002. She studied cultural anthropology, sociology and psychology, received her Ph.D. at University of Freiburg in 1987. She was a Visiting Professor at University of Bremen (1995–98) and Mainz (2000). Her main fields of research are cultural globalisation and intercultural issues, gender, religion, tourism and the anthropology of disaster. She has published *Die Meereskönigin des Südens, Ratu Kidul. Geisterpolitik im javanischen Alltag*, (Berlin: Reimer, 1998) and recently 'Nach dem Erdbeben auf Java: Kulturelle Polarisierungen, soziale Solidarität und Abgrenzung' *Internationales Asienforum* 37(3–4) (2006).

Gabriela Schmitt worked for the ministry for intergeneration and familiy affairs, women and integration of the state of Northrhine-Westfalia until December 2006. She was employed at the Department of Geography at the Heinrich-Heine-University Düsseldorf and assisted in a research project about 'Consumption of Resources, Problems of Waste Disposal and Endangerment of the Environment through Mass-Tourism in Coastal Areas of Thailand' sponsored by the 'Deutsche Forschungsgemeinschaft' (German Research Community) until October 2001. Her main research areas are sustainable development, sustainable tourism, environmental education, global education/learning.

Stefan Seitz is professor of Ethnology at the University of Freiburg, Germany. He earned his Ph.D. in 1970 and finished his Habilitation in 1975. He has done anthropological fieldwork in Central and East Africa as well as in Insular Southeast Asia. His research has been with Pygmies in Rwanda and the Congo, with the Punan of Borneo, the Batak of Palawan, the Ayta at the Mt. Pinatubo in Zambales, Philippines, and the Mamanua in Mindanao, Philippines.

Hans Spada is Full Professor at the Department of Psychology, Research Group Cognition-Emotion-Communication, University of Freiburg. He studied psychology at the University of Vienna, earned his doctorate there, and qualified as a University Lecturer at the Universities of Vienna and Kiel. He was President of the Deutsche Gesellschaft für Psychologie, Chairman of the Ph.D.-Program Human and Machine Intelligence, and the European Science Foundation Program Learning in Humans and Machines. He is member of the Virtual Ph.D.-Program Knowledge Acquisition and Knowledge Exchange with the New Media. He is author/ editor/ co-editor of 10 books including: *Learning in Human and Machines: Towards an Interdisciplinary Learning Science*, (Pergamon 1996); *Environmental Risks*, (Cambridge University Press 2001); *Barriers and Biases in Computer-mediated Knowledge Communication – and How They May Be Overcome*, (Cambridge University Press 2005), and author/ co-author of about 100 papers. (http://www.psychologie.uni-freiburg.de/Members/spada/).

Karl Vorlaufer as Professor Emeritus was the holder of the Chair for Cultural Geography and Development Research at the Department of Geography at the Heinrich-Heine-University Düsseldorf until (2002). He is one of the editors of the journal *Zeitschrift für Wirtschaftsgeographie (Journal for Economic Geography)*, has conducted several research projects sponsored by the 'Deutsche Forschungsgemeinschaft' (German Research Community) and the 'Volkwagen-Stiftung' (VW-Foundation). He has published widely on the topics: tourism in developing countries, sustainable development, economy and population dynamics and urban geography. His regional specialisation comprises South-East and South Asia; and Africa south of the Sahara.

Thomas Widlok currently works at the Max Planck Institute for Psycholinguistics in Nijmegen and the Department of Anthropology, Durham University. He received his Ph.D. in Anthropology at the London School of Economics and Political Science. He is author of *Living on Mangetti* (Oxford University Press, 1999), co-editor of *Property and Equality* (Berghahn Books, 2005) and has published widely on the ethnography of hunter-gatherers in southern Africa and in Australia as well as on comparative anthropological issues.

INDEX